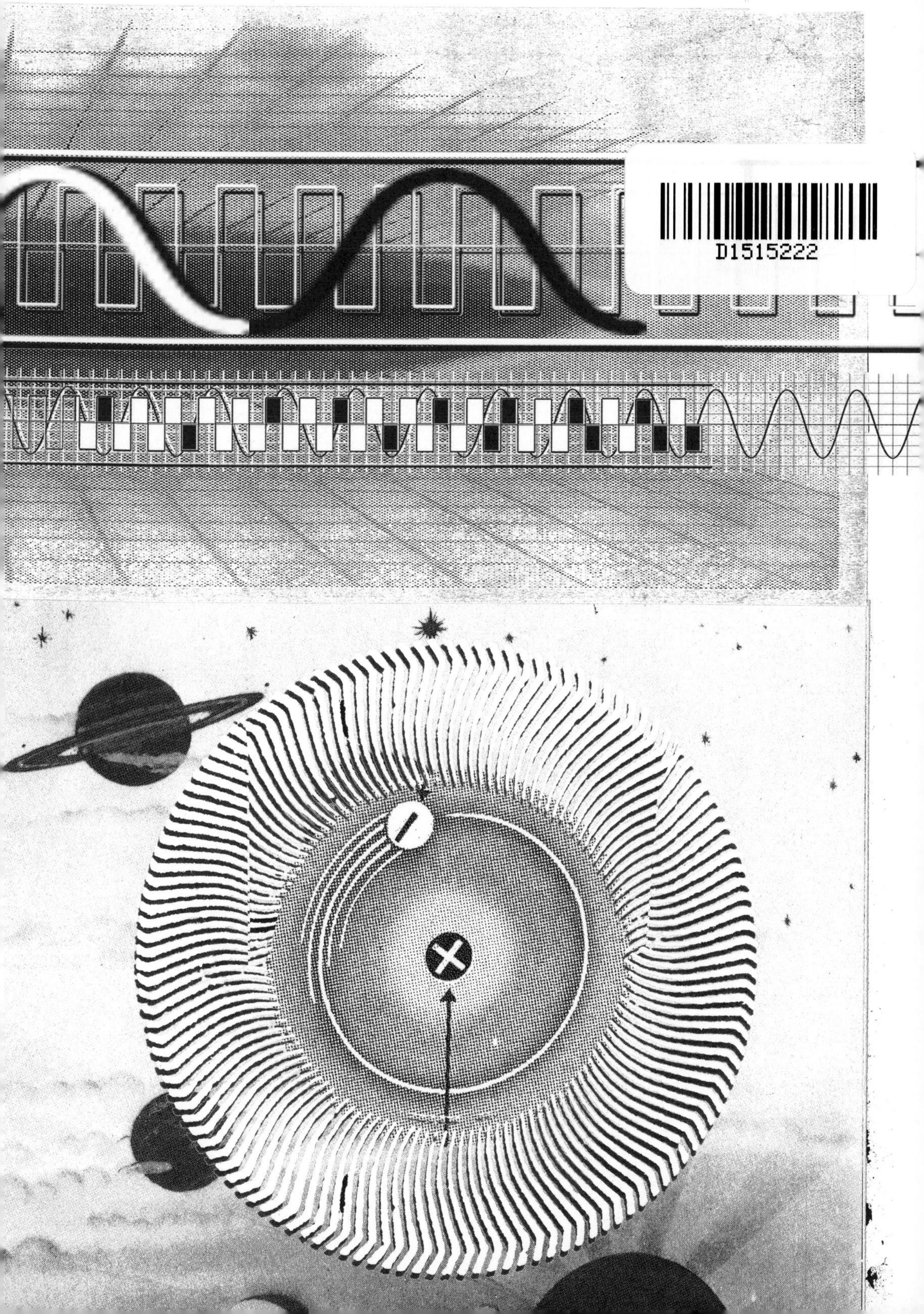

# WINTER'S COSMOS BY MICHAEL COMEAU

© 1972 LaSalle Extension University, A Correspondence Institution



Cut Along Dotted Line – Seal (Tape, Paste or Staple) and Mail Today.

46 19

Published by Koyama Press
koyamapress.com

First edition: May 2018

Koyama Press gratefully acknowledges the Canada Council for the Arts and the Ontario Arts Council program, for their support of our publishing

STARRING

AMY LAM
AS
Dr. TRACY ANABELLE NGUYEN

AND

JON McCURLEY
AS
CAPTAIN JONATHON GERALD HOFFSTAN

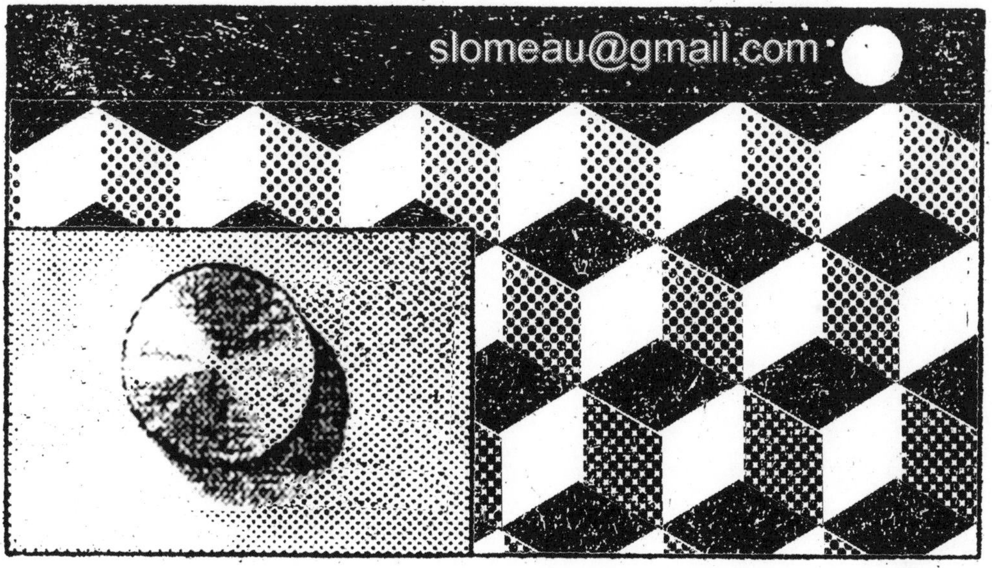
slomeau@gmail.com



ISBN: 978-1-927668-55-9

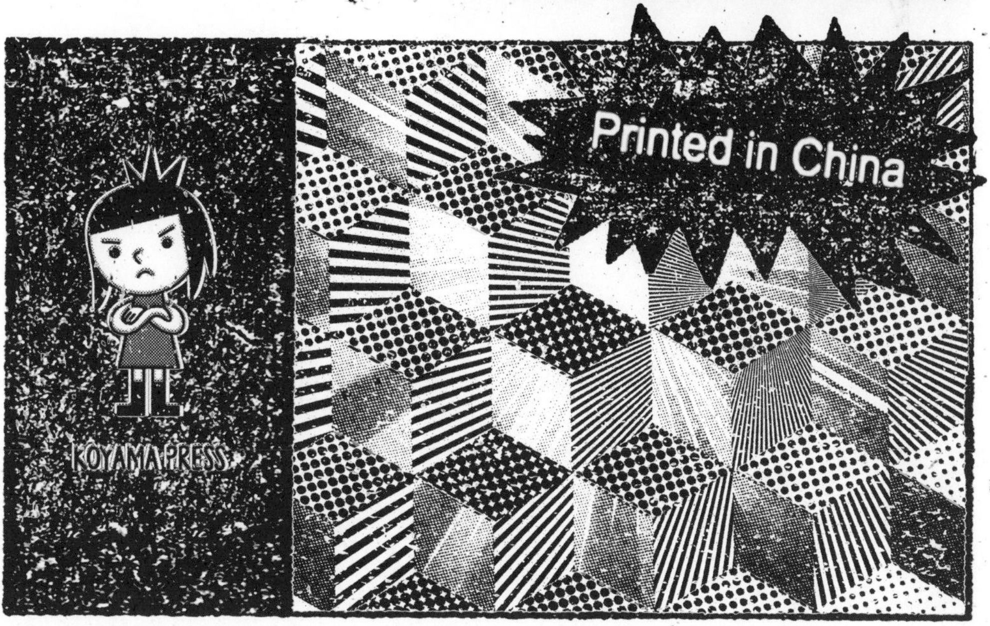
Printed in China
KOYAMA PRESS

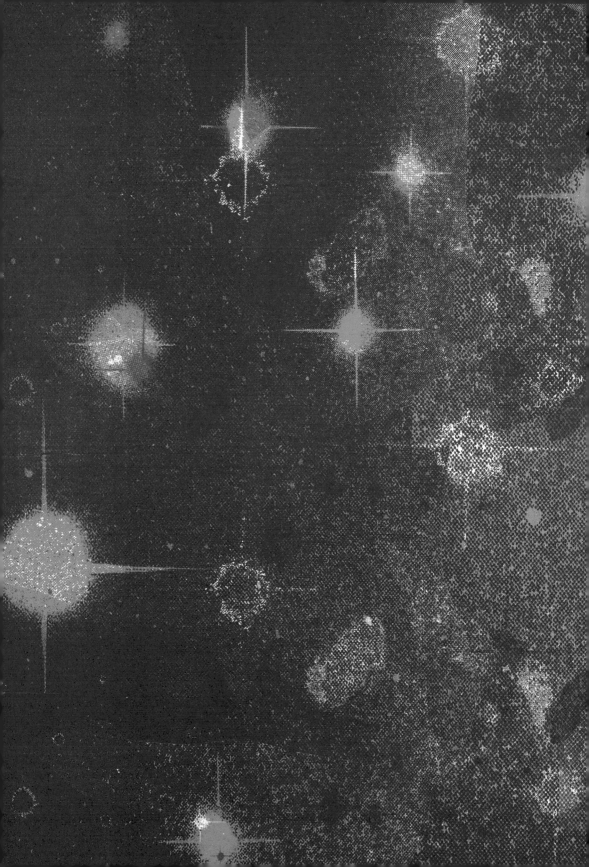

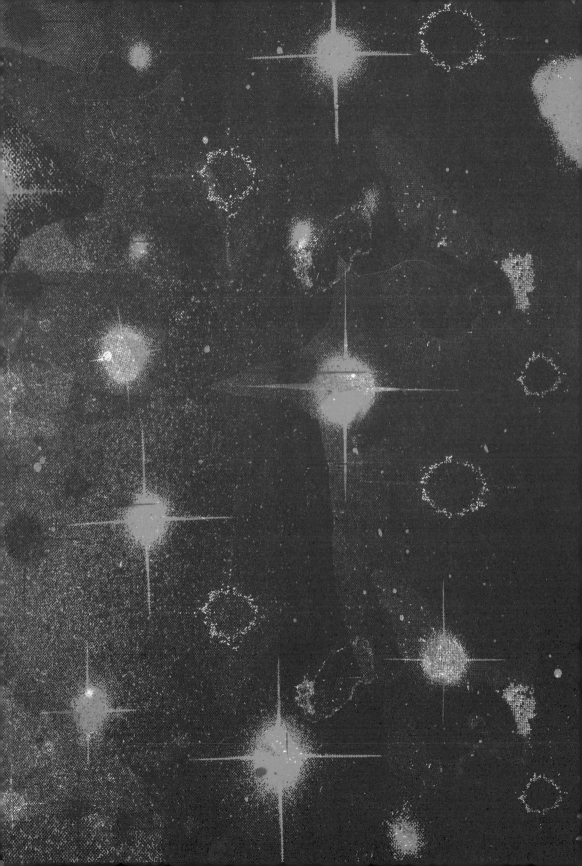

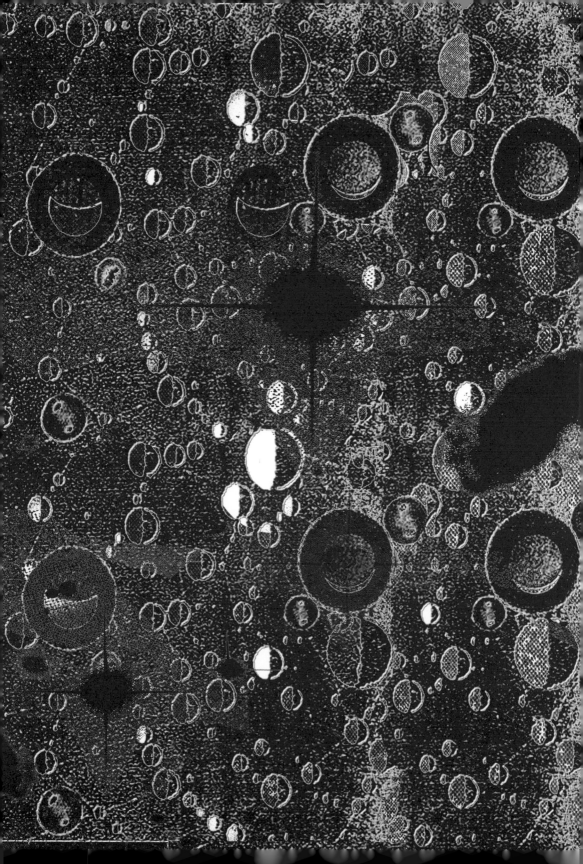

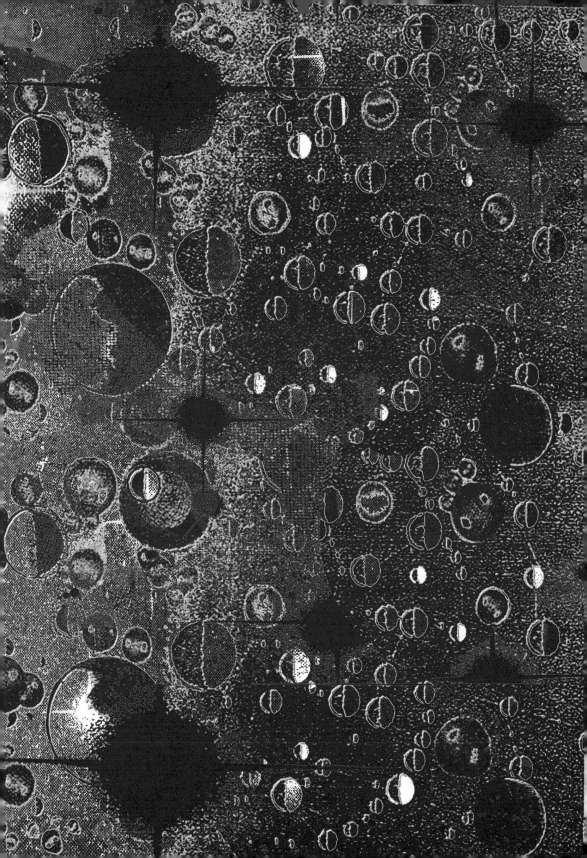

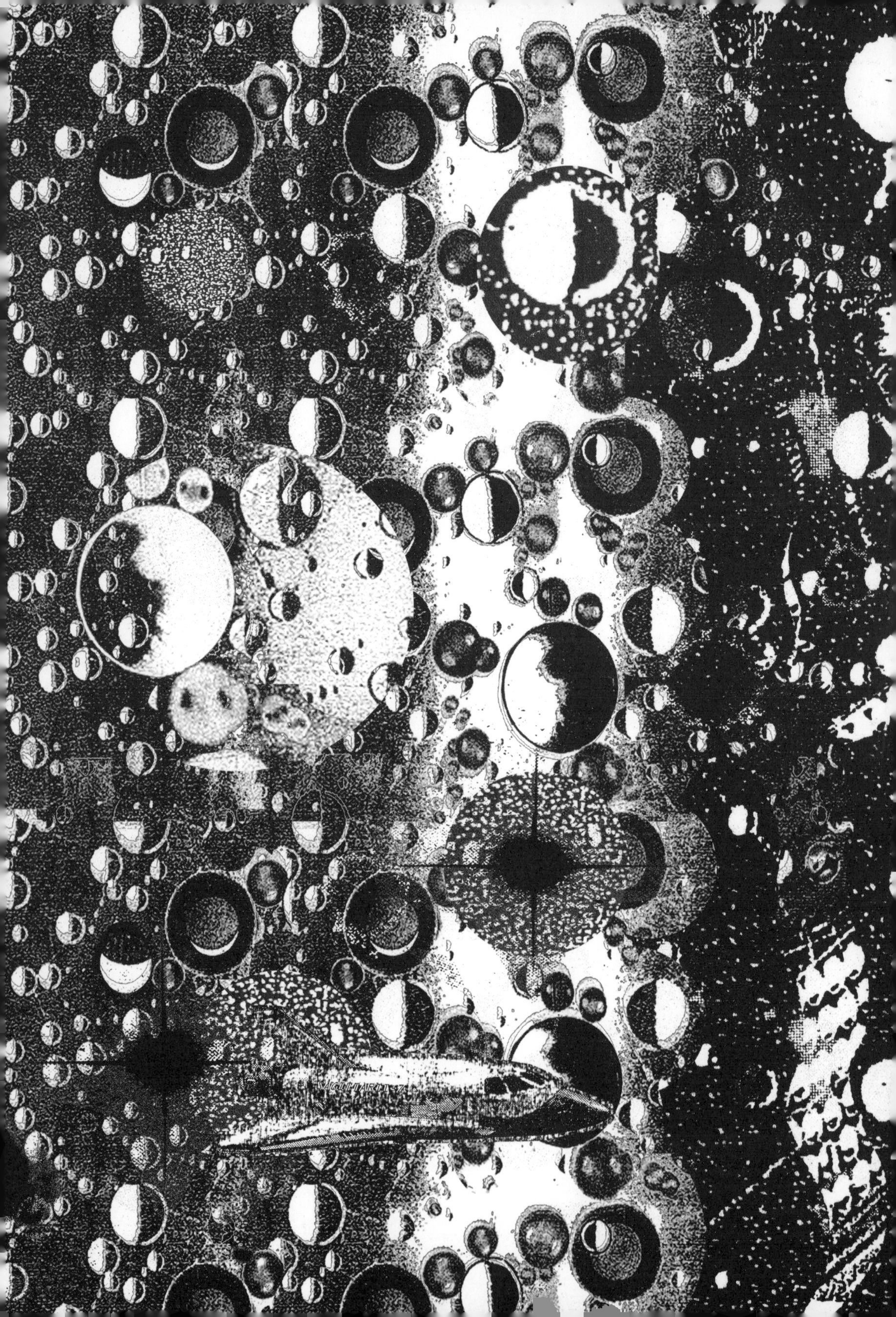
SAGITTARII-7

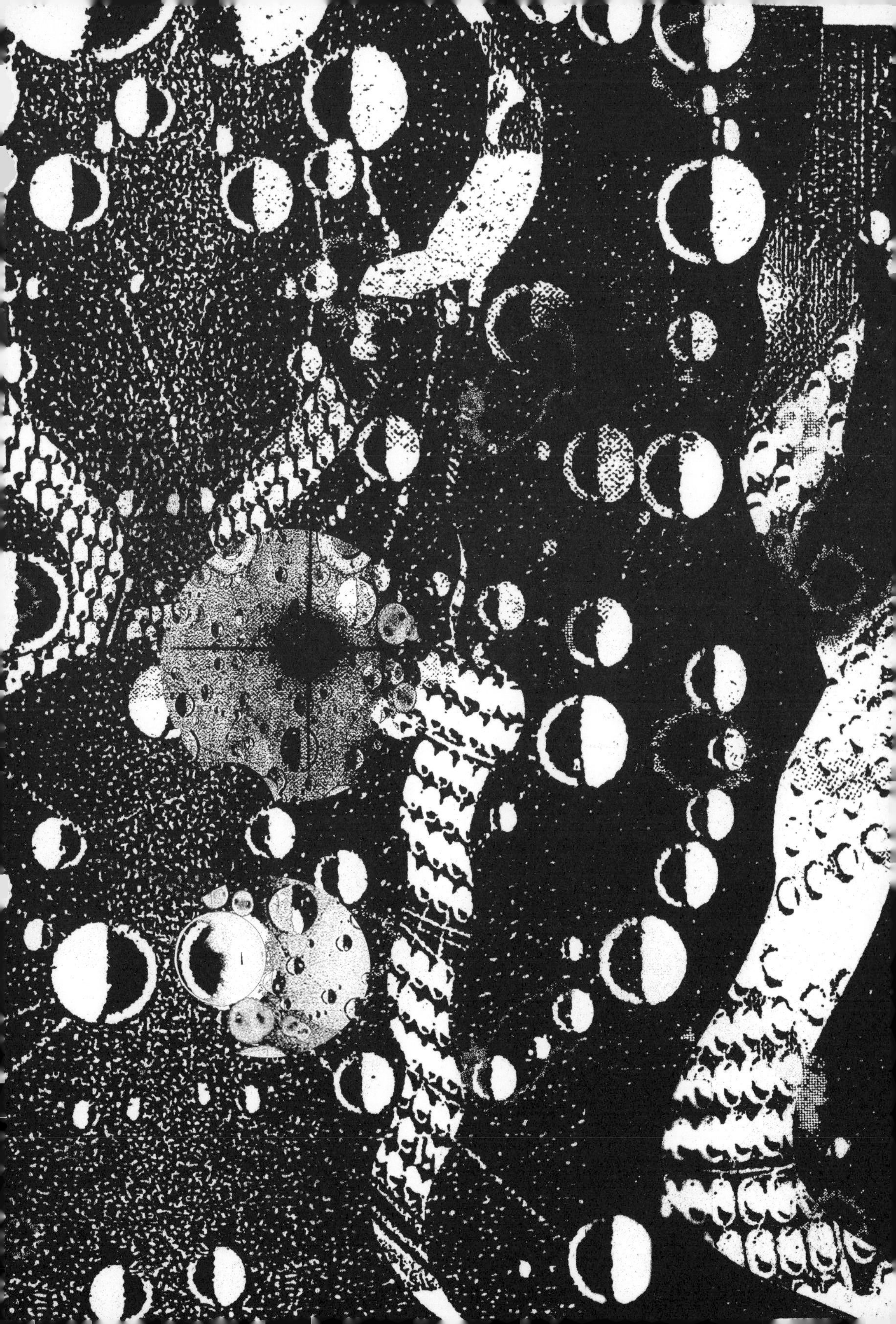

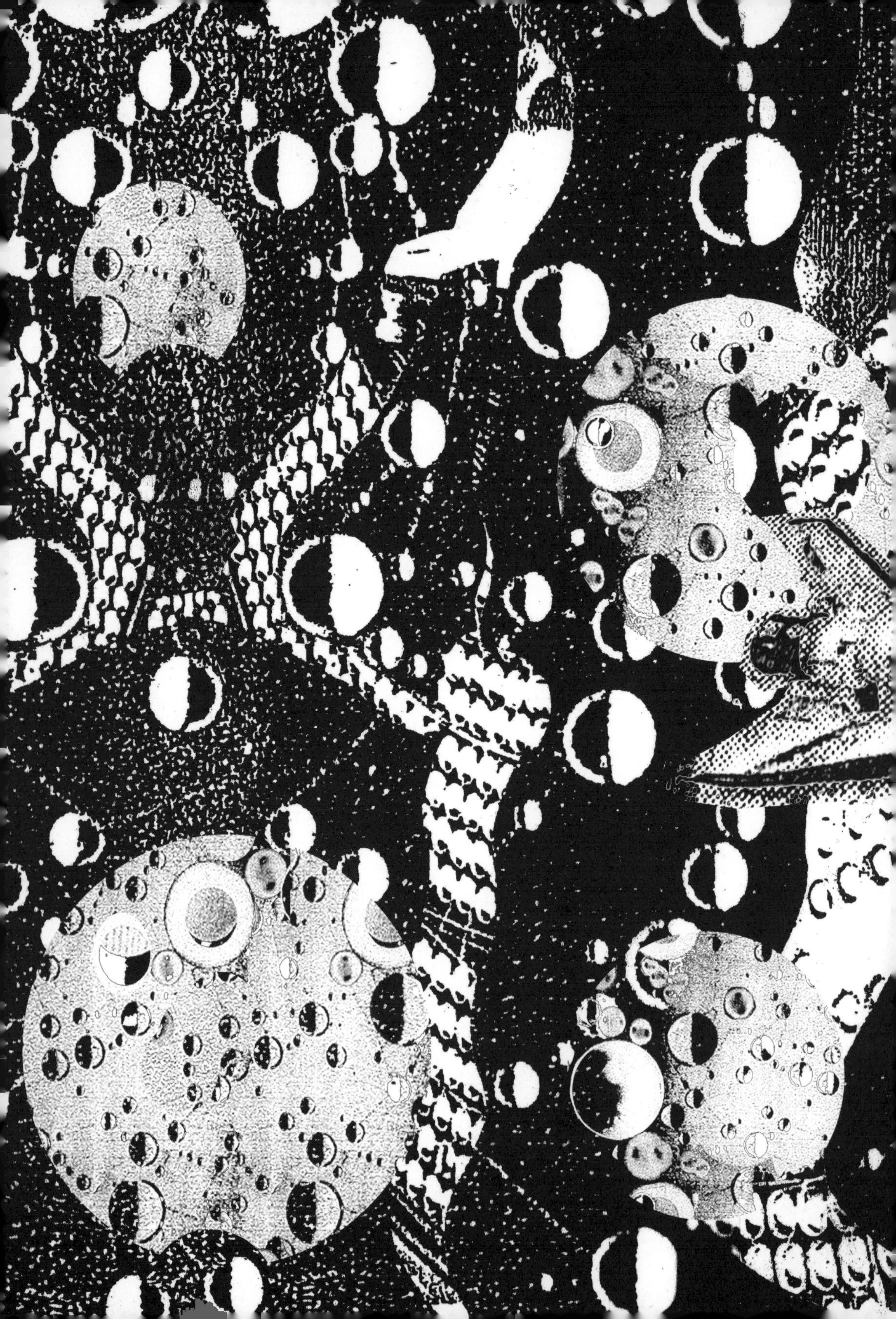

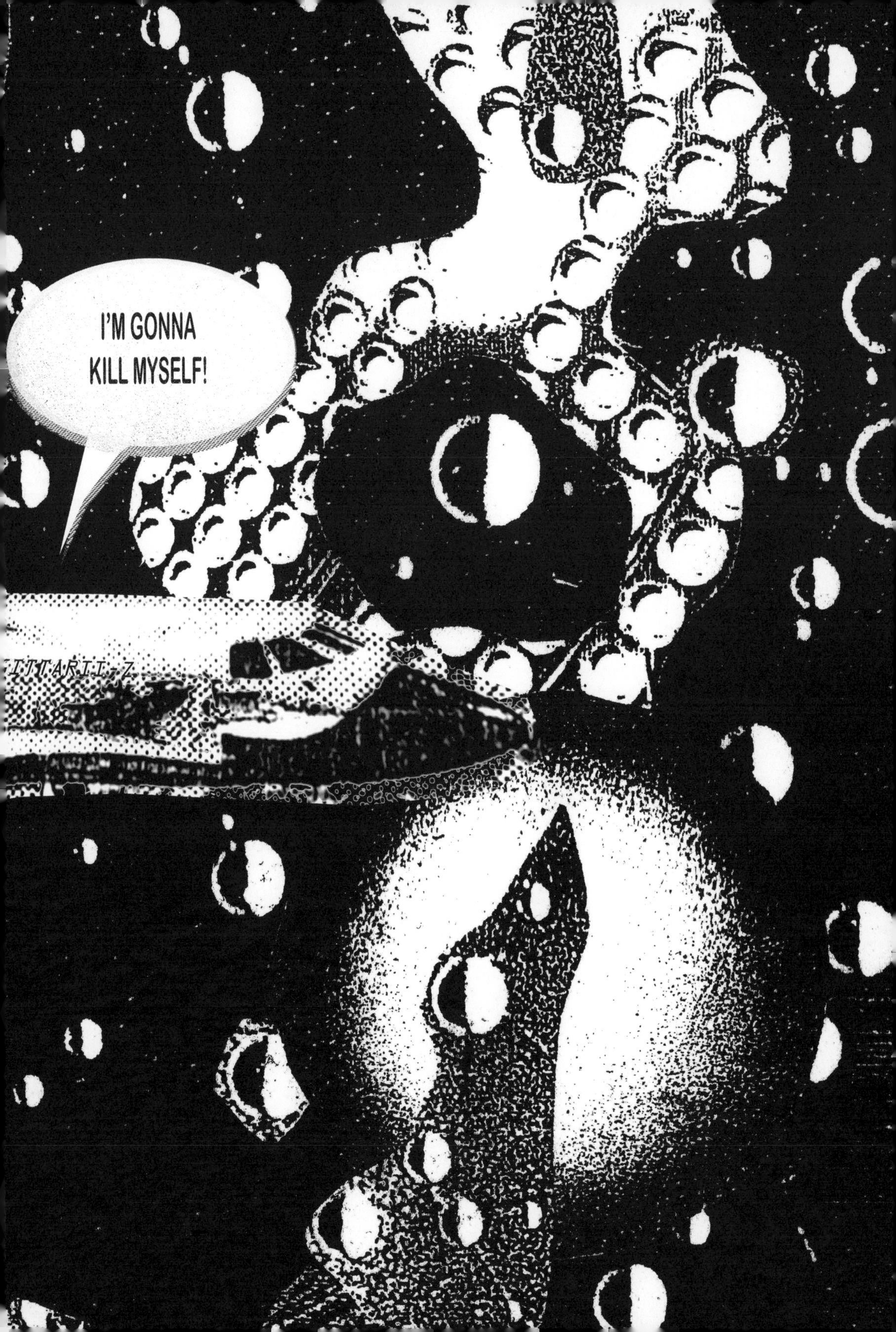
I'M GONNA KILL MYSELF!

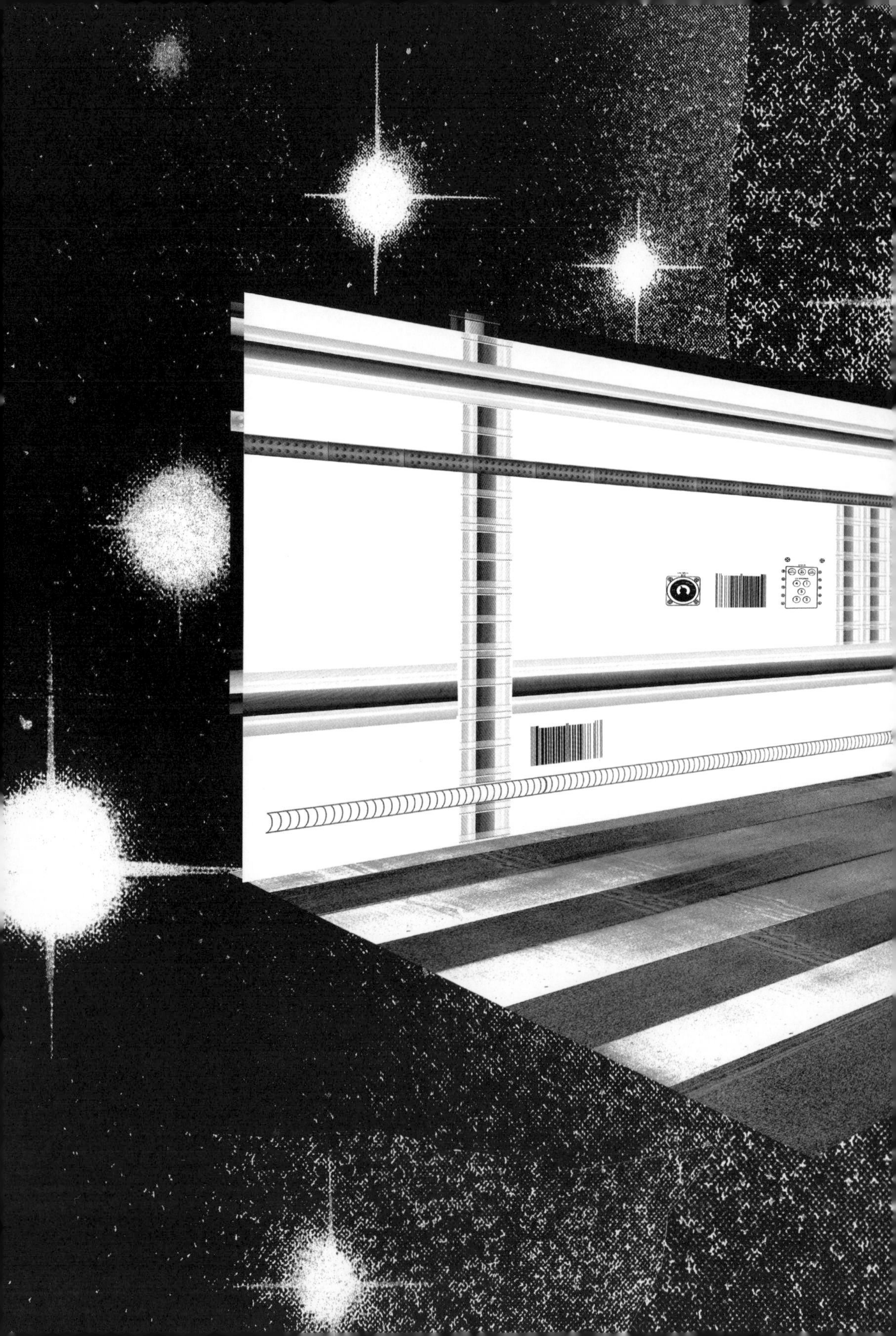

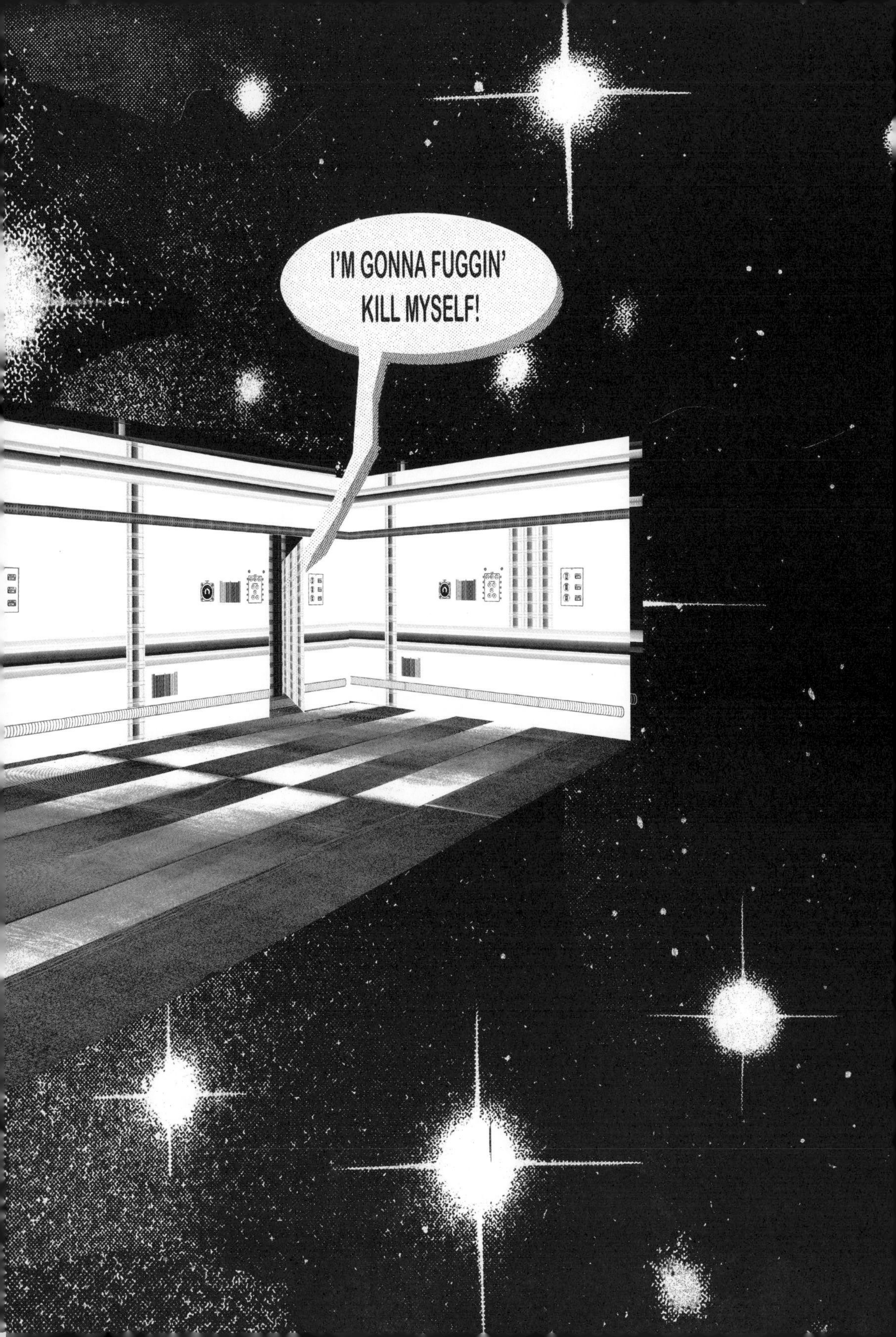
I'M GONNA FUGGIN' KILL MYSELF!

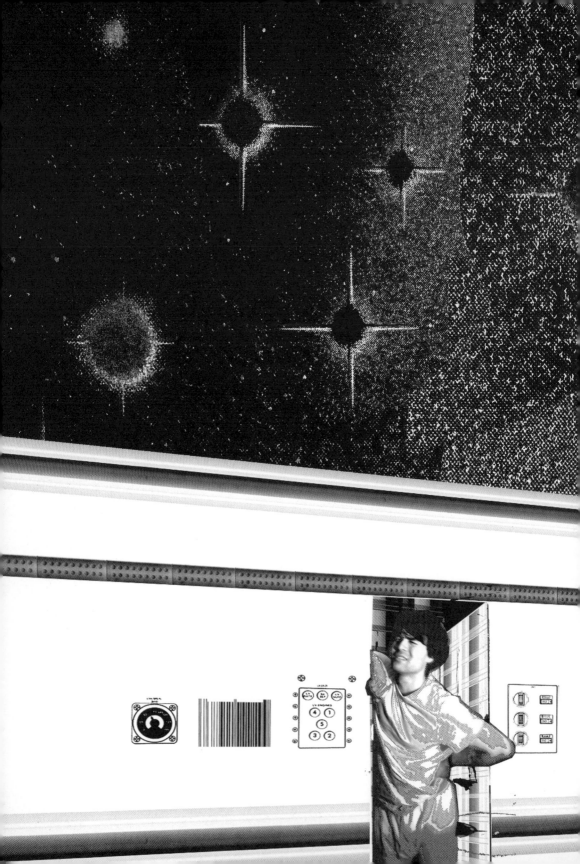

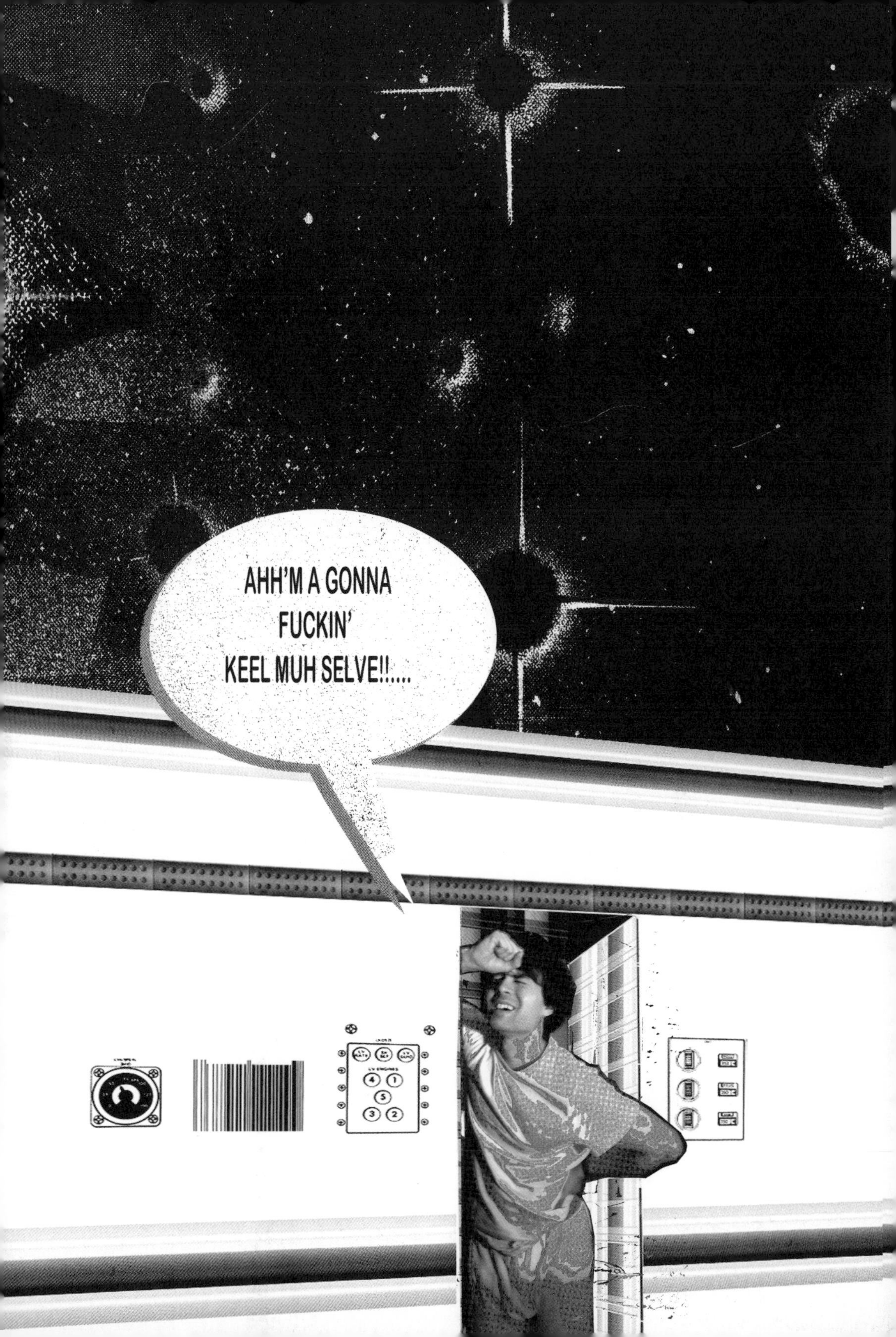
AHH'M A GONNA
FUCKIN'
KEEL MUH SELVE!!.....

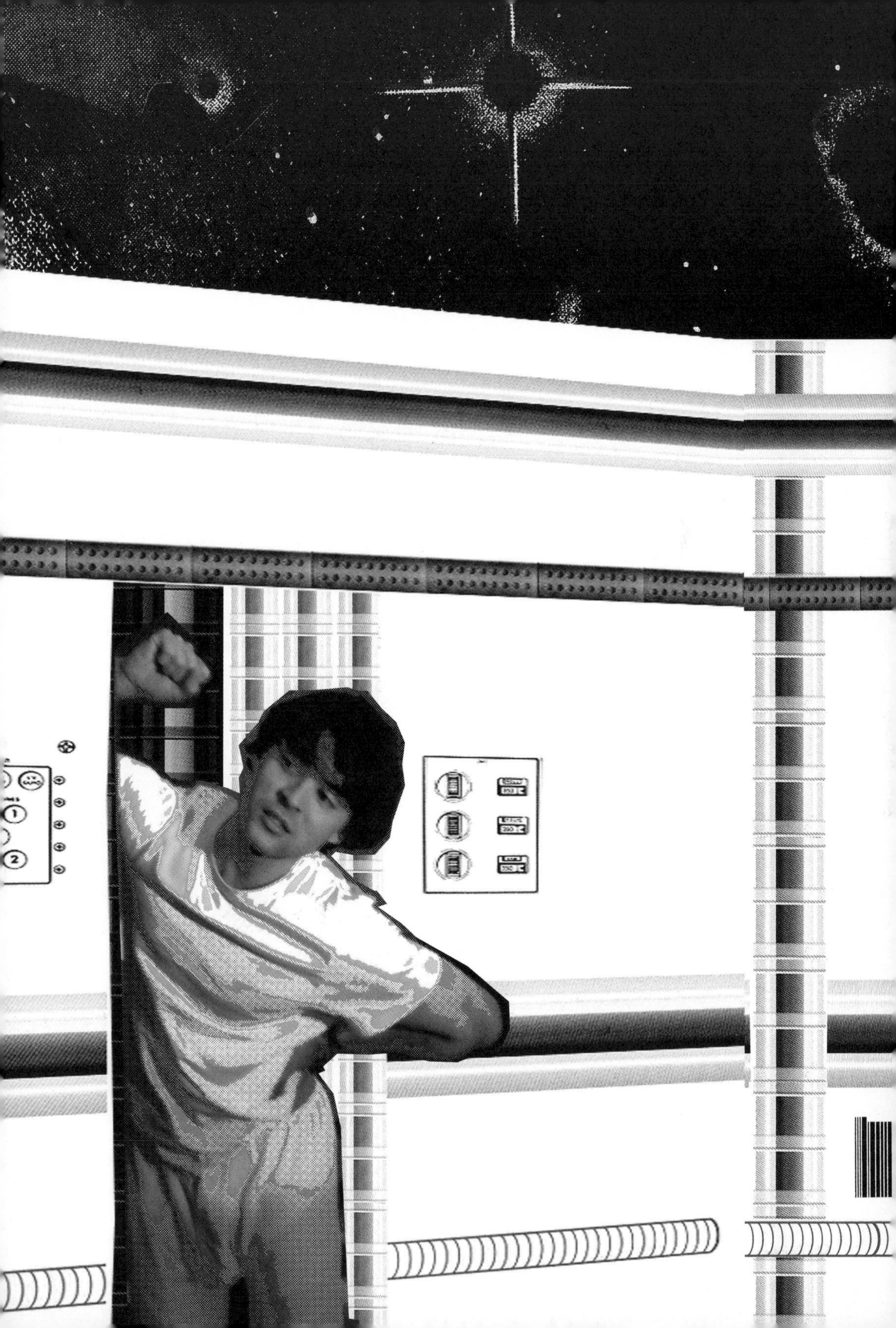

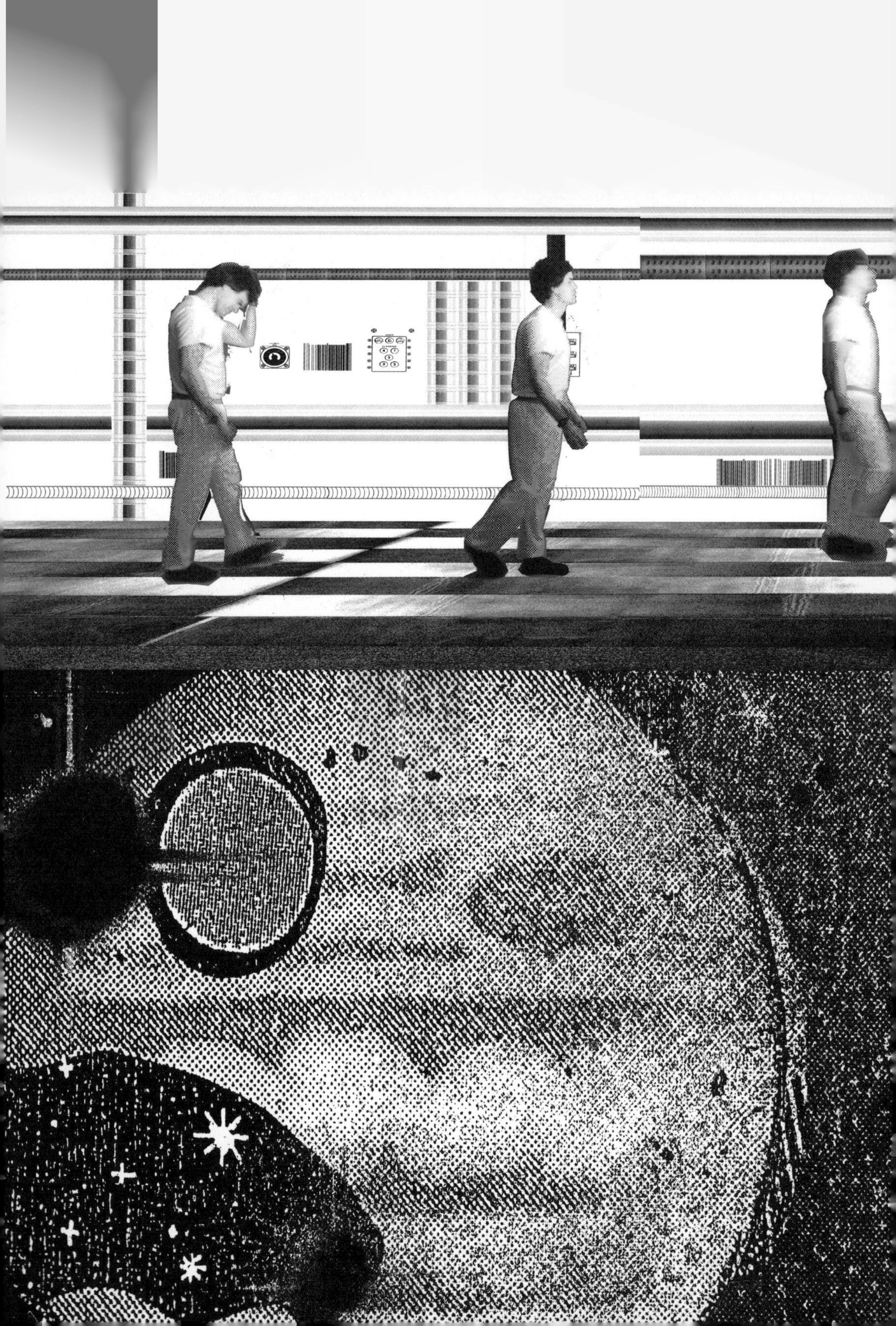

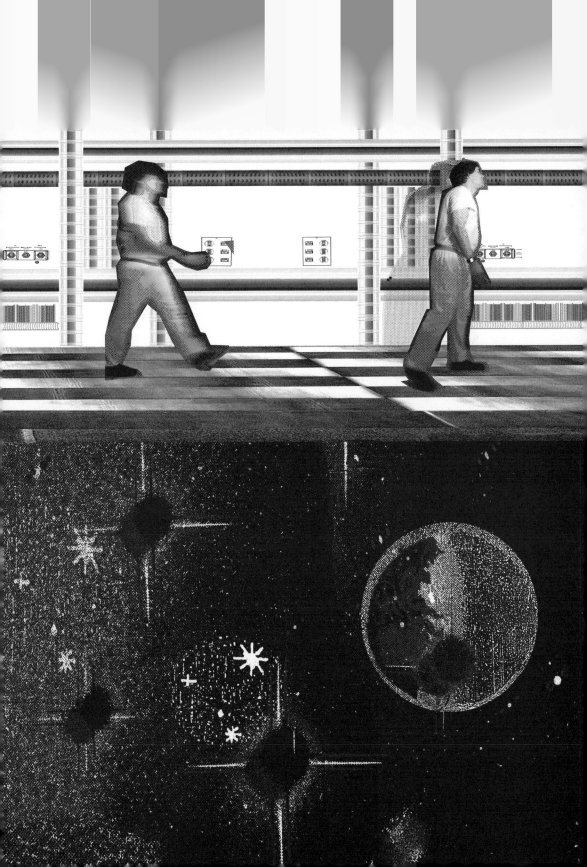

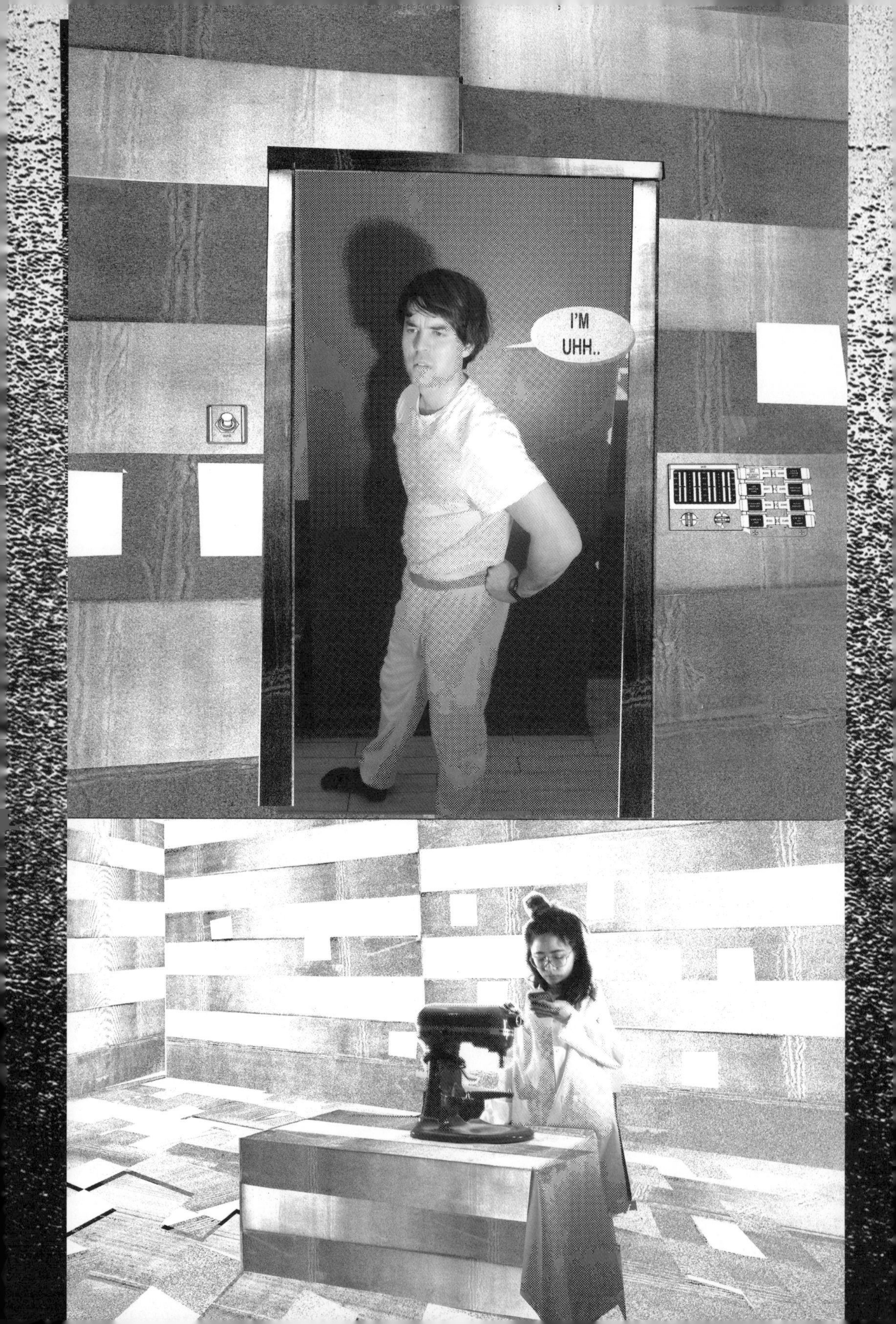
I'M UHH..

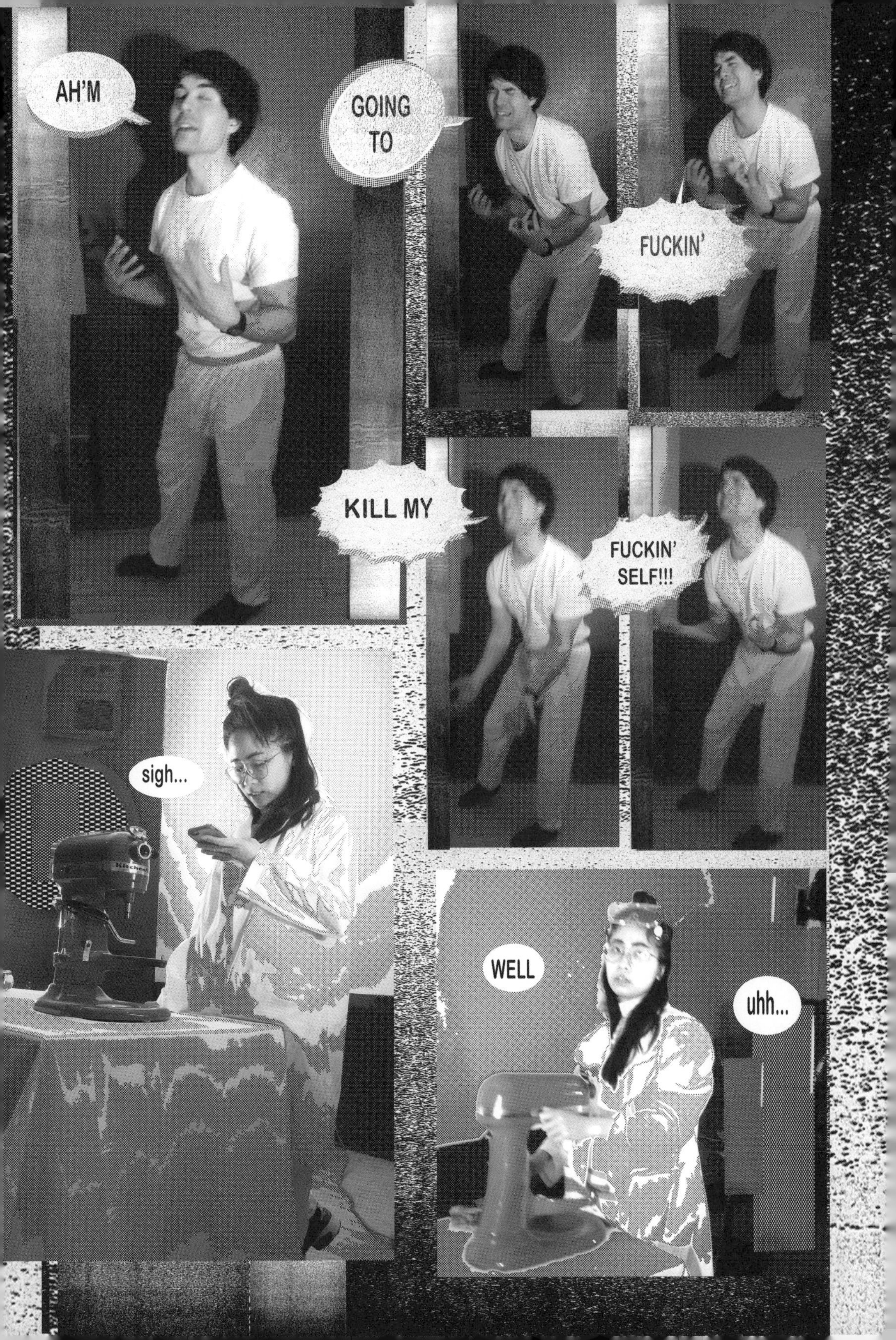
AH'M
GOING TO
FUCKIN'
KILL MY
FUCKIN' SELF!!!
sigh...
WELL
uhh...

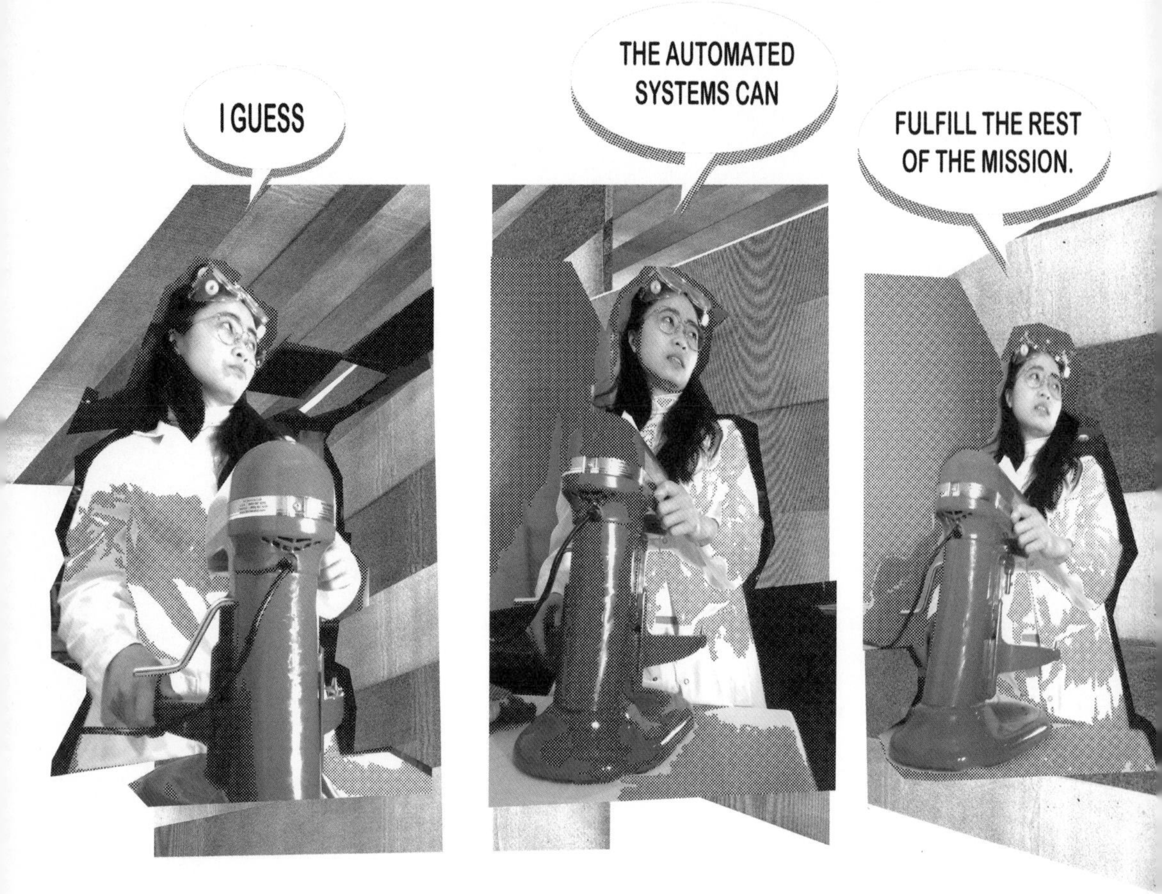
I GUESS
THE AUTOMATED SYSTEMS CAN
FULFILL THE REST OF THE MISSION.

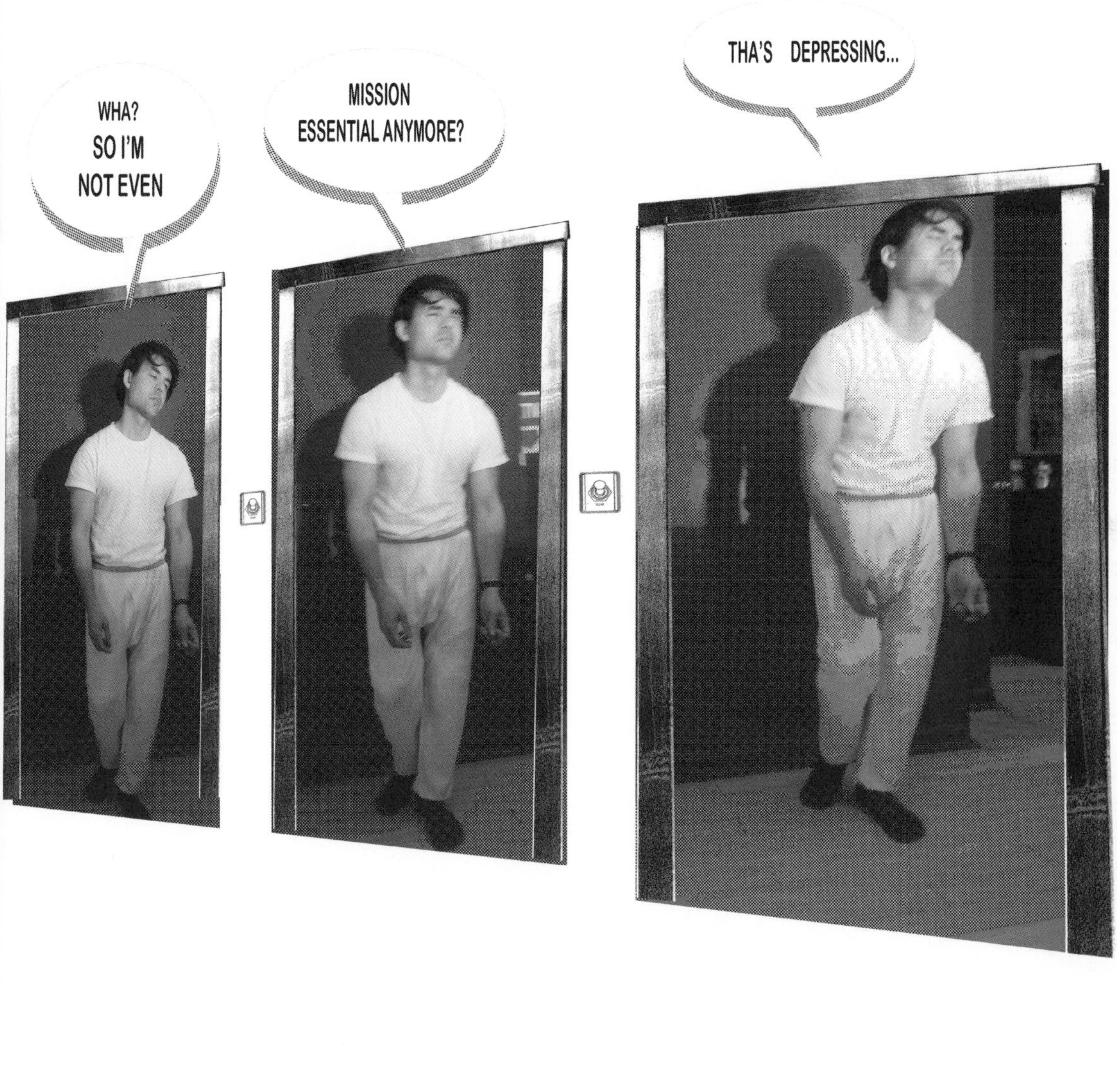
WHA? SO I'M NOT EVEN
MISSION ESSENTIAL ANYMORE?
THA'S DEPRESSING...

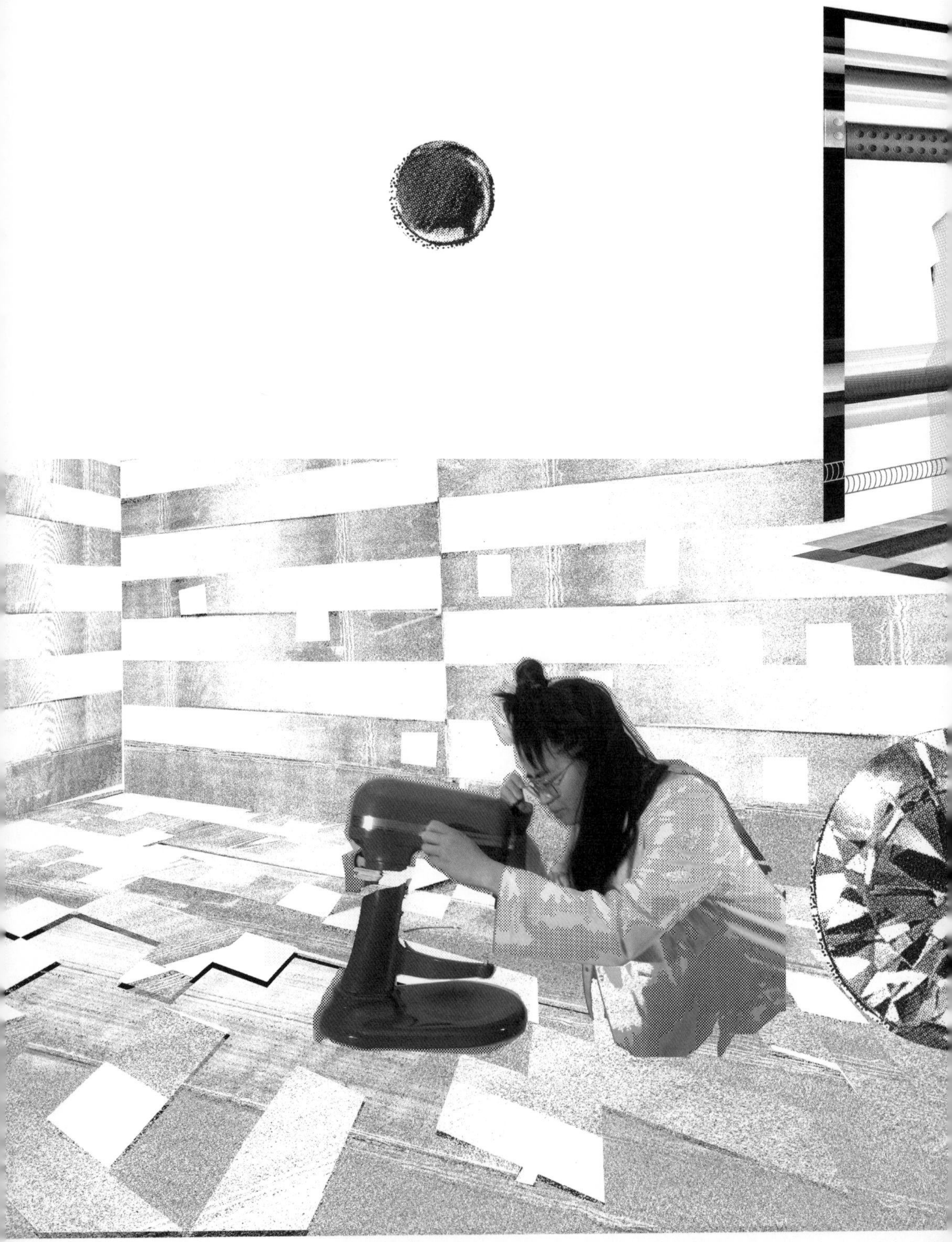

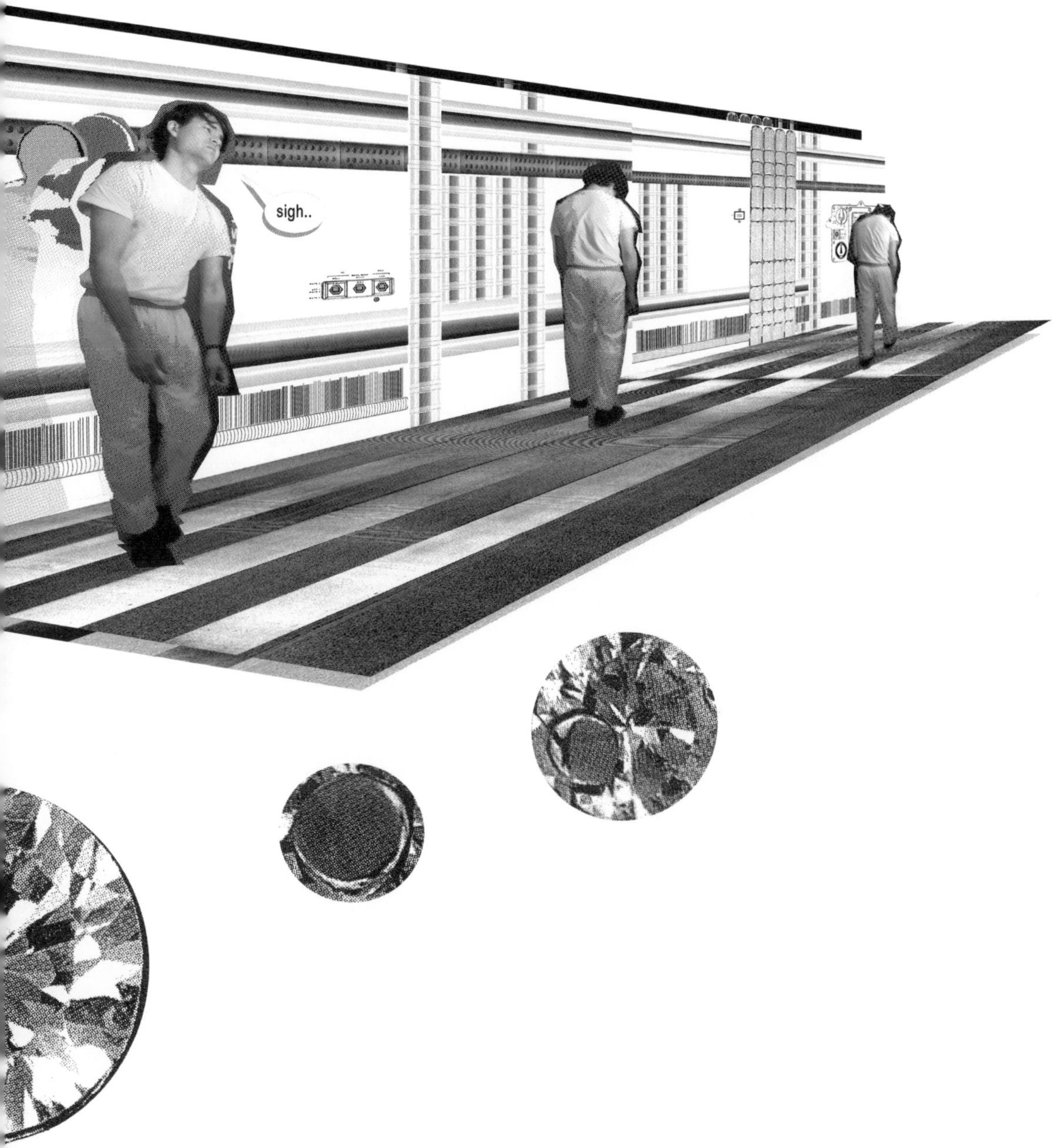
sigh..

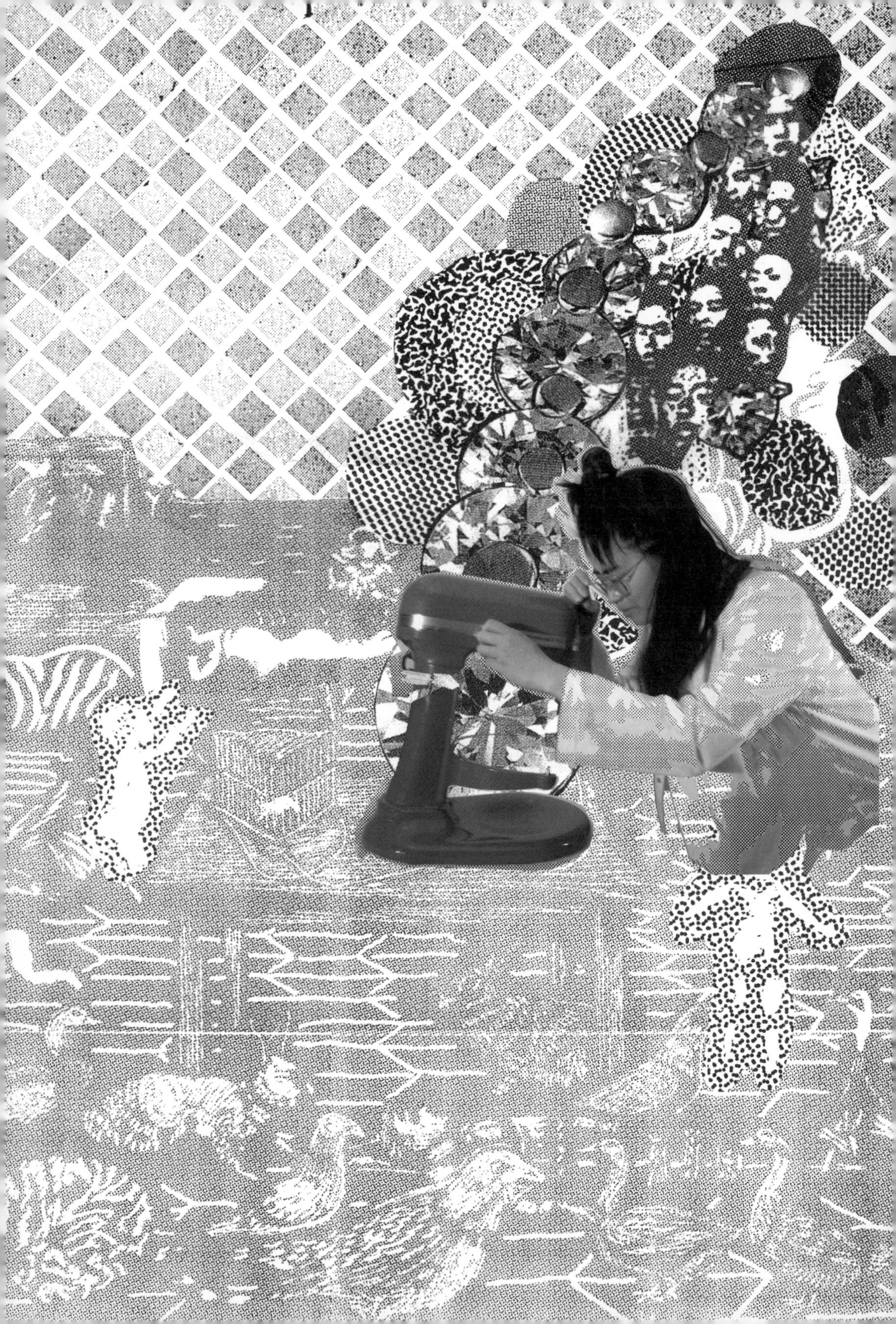

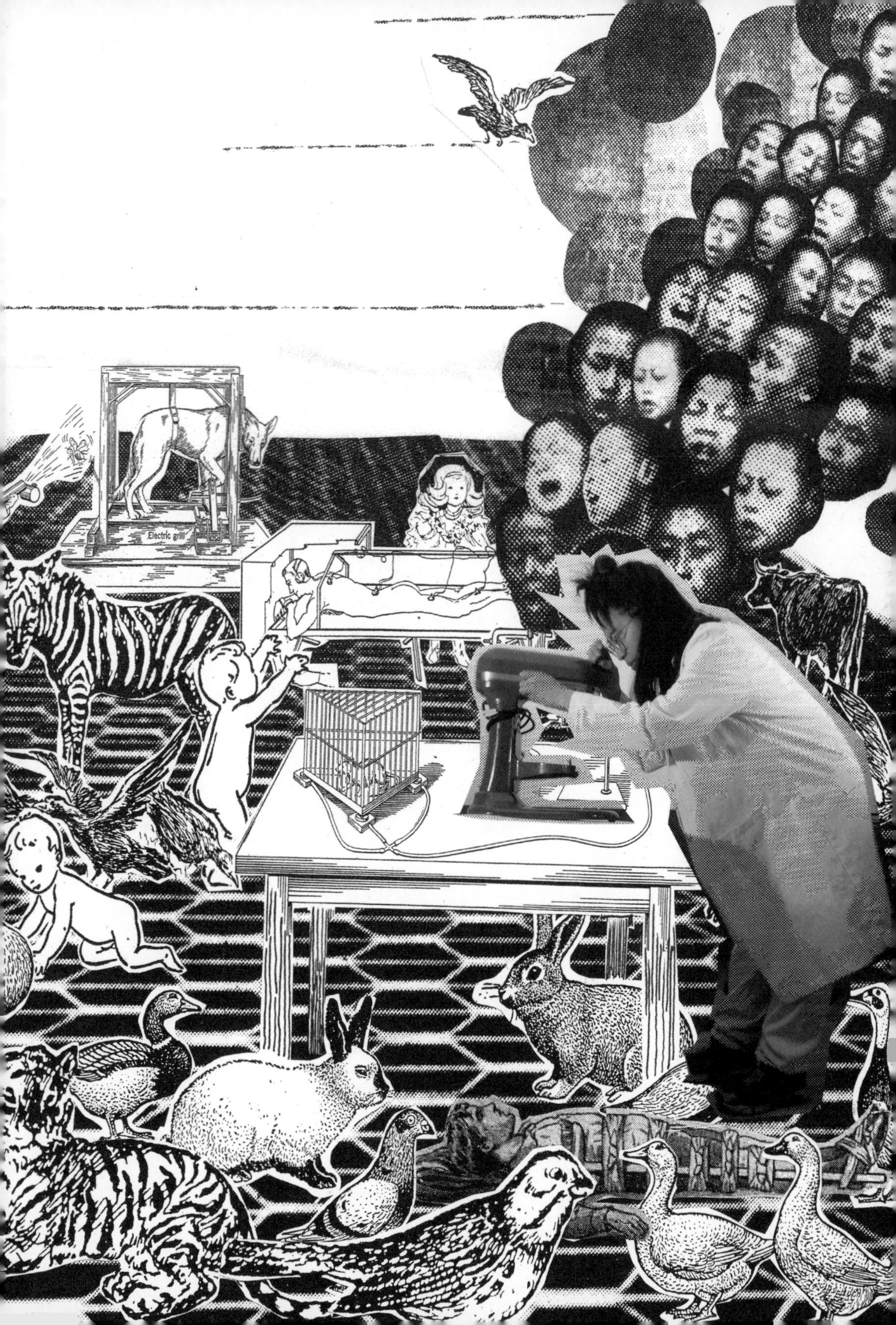
Electric grill

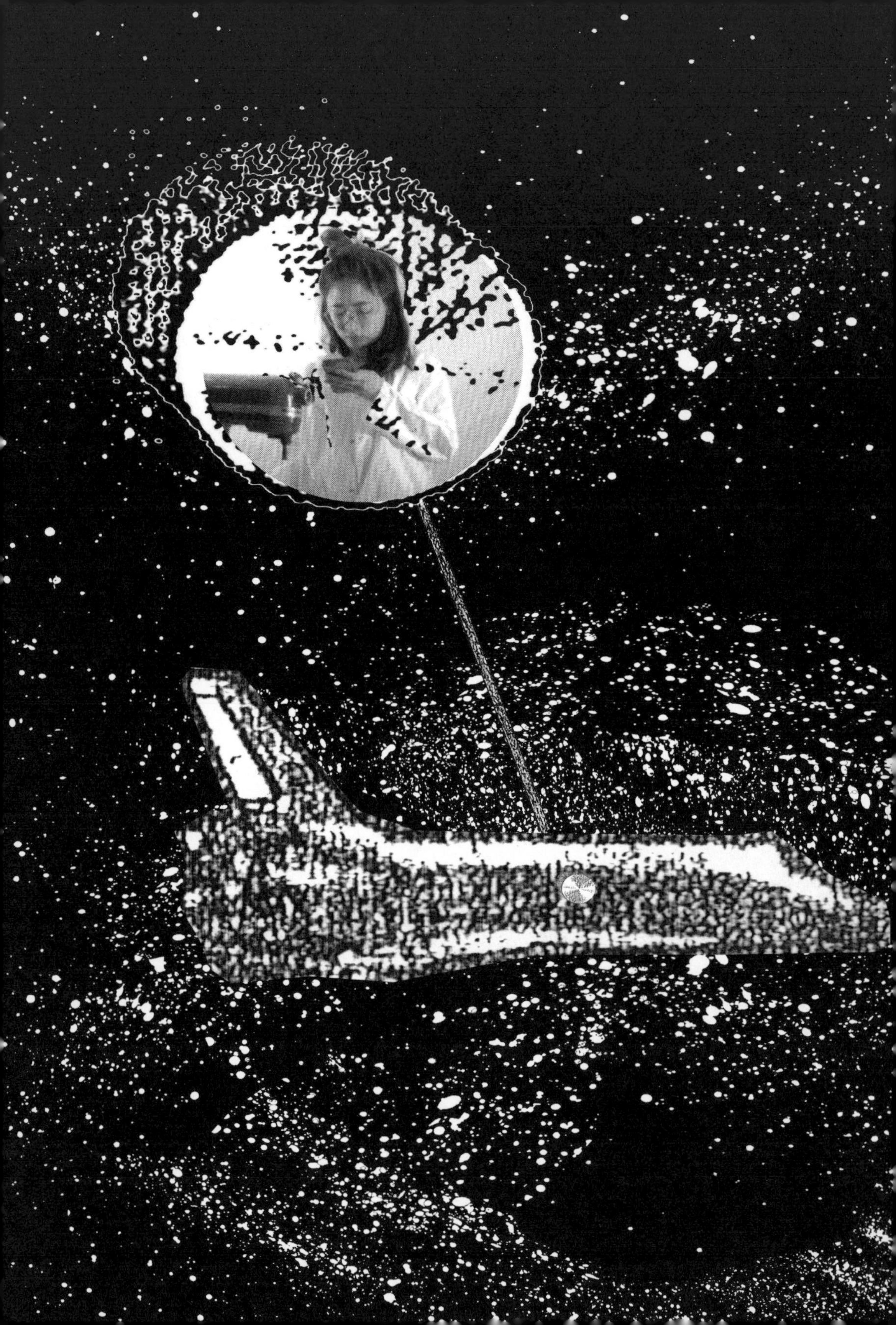

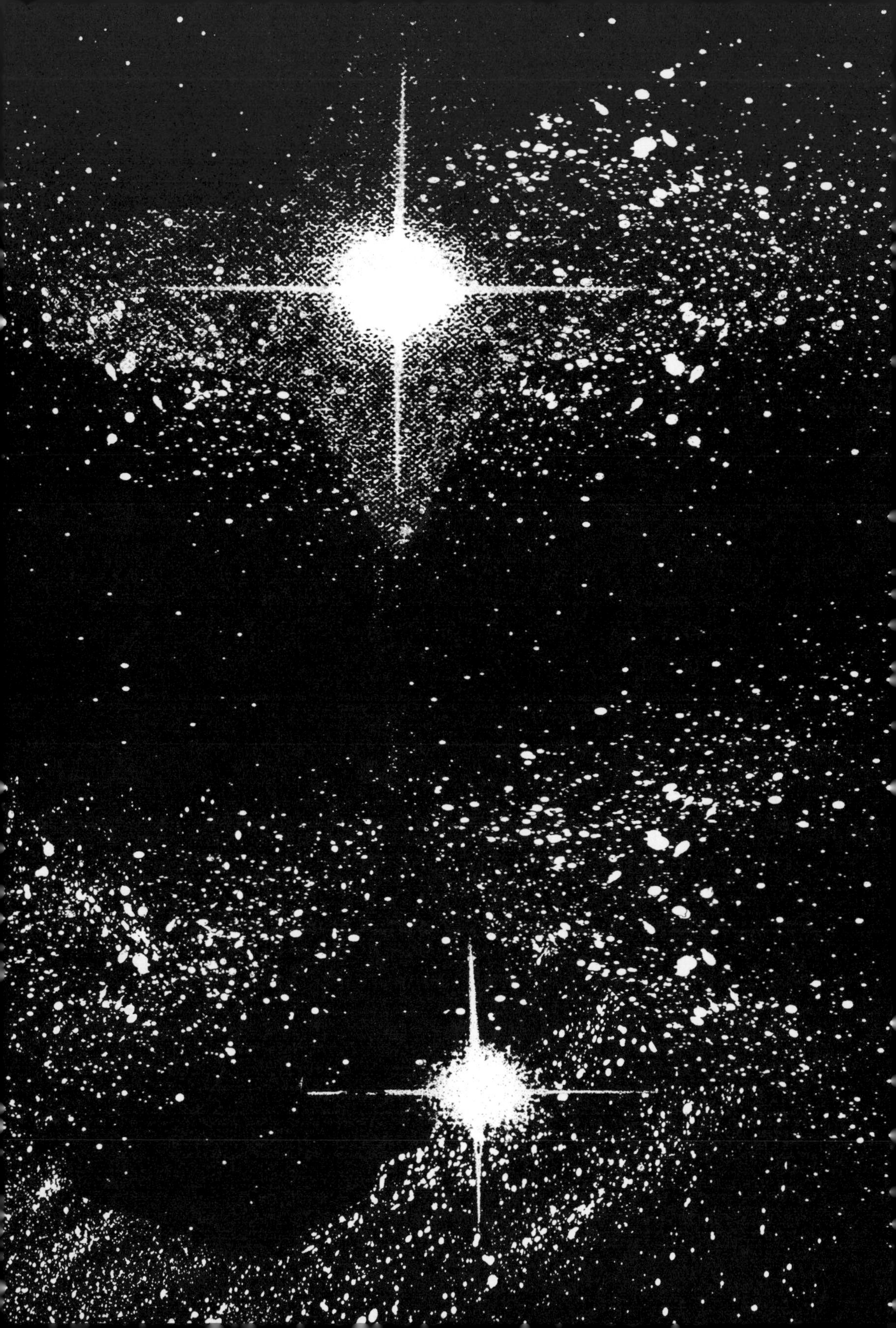

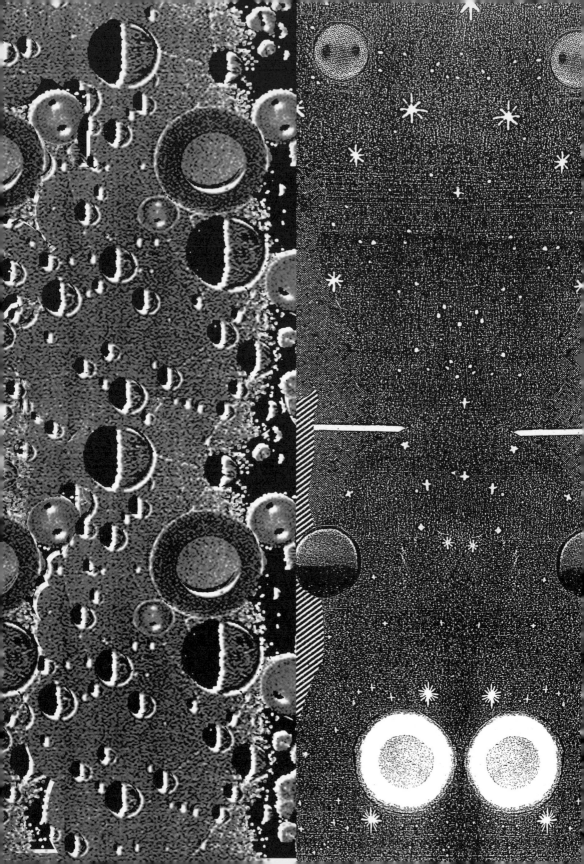

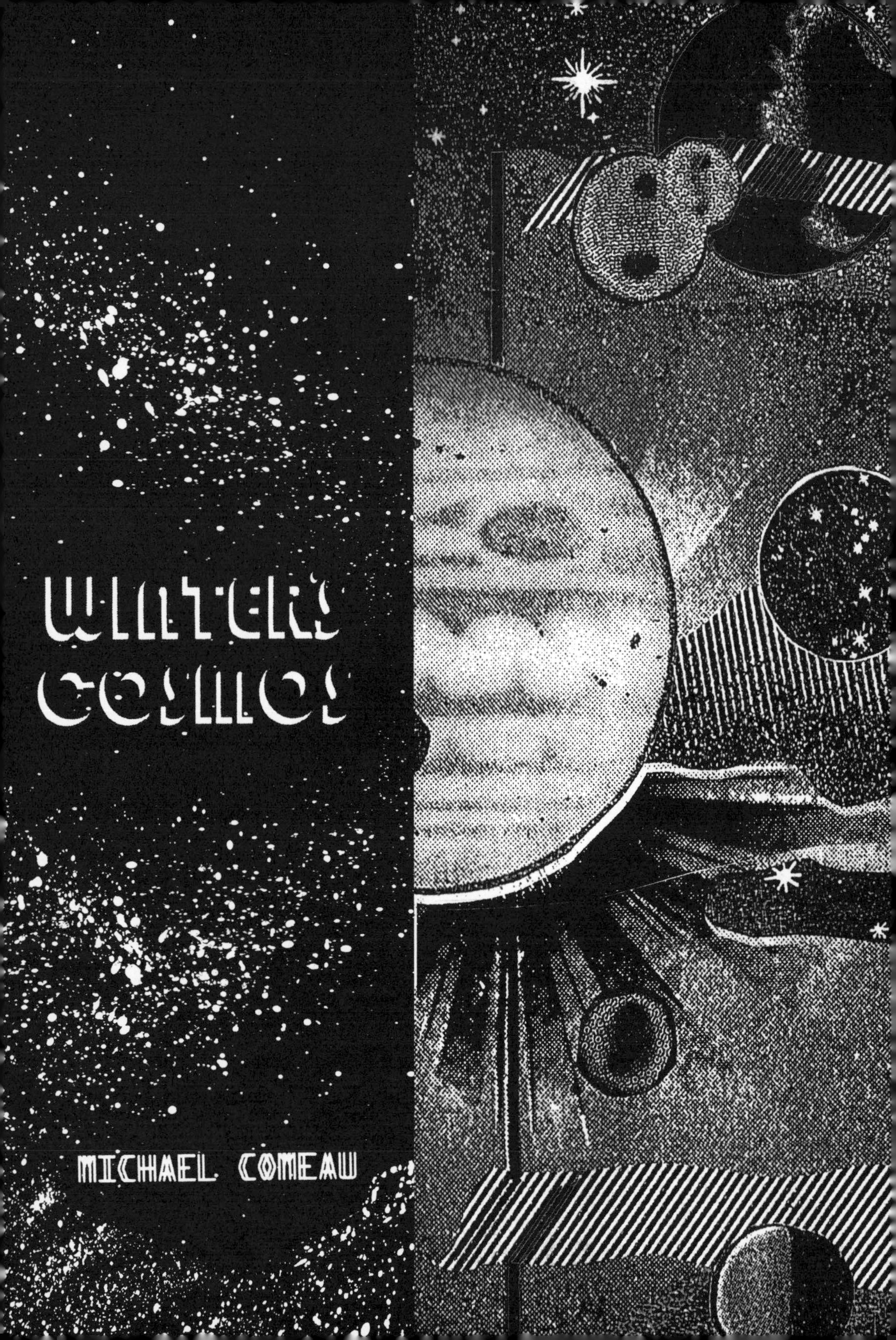
WINTER
COSMOS
MICHAEL COMEAU

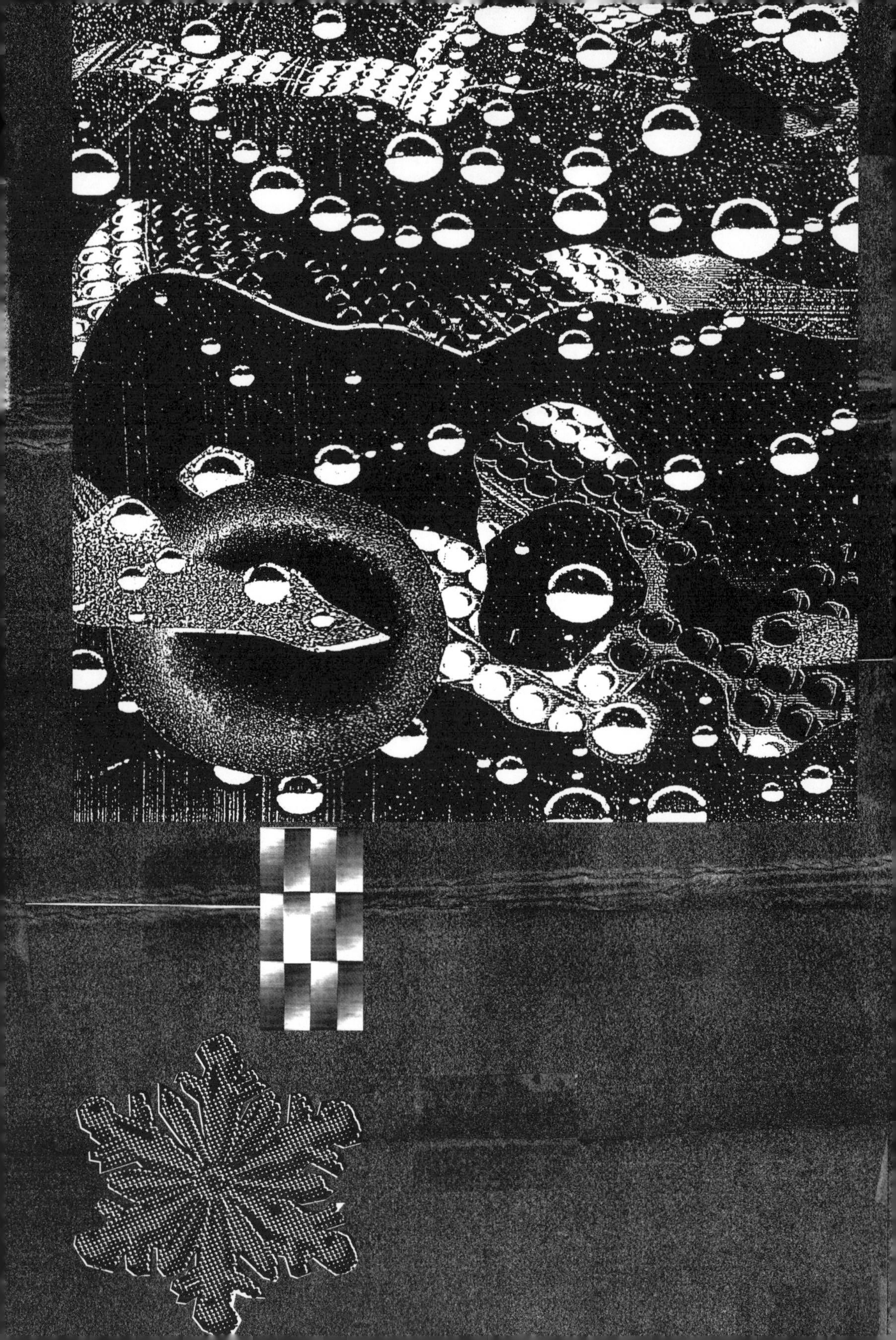

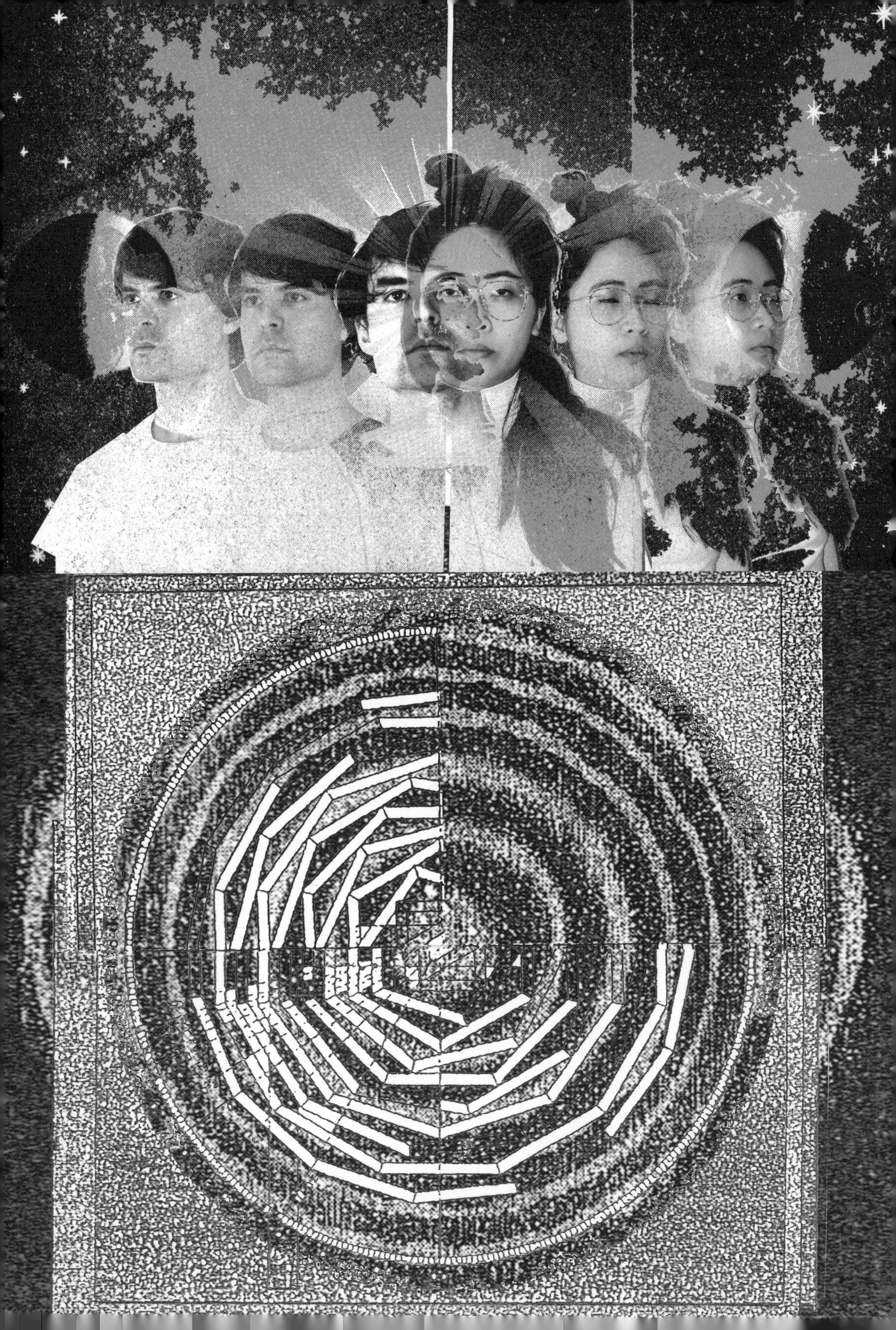

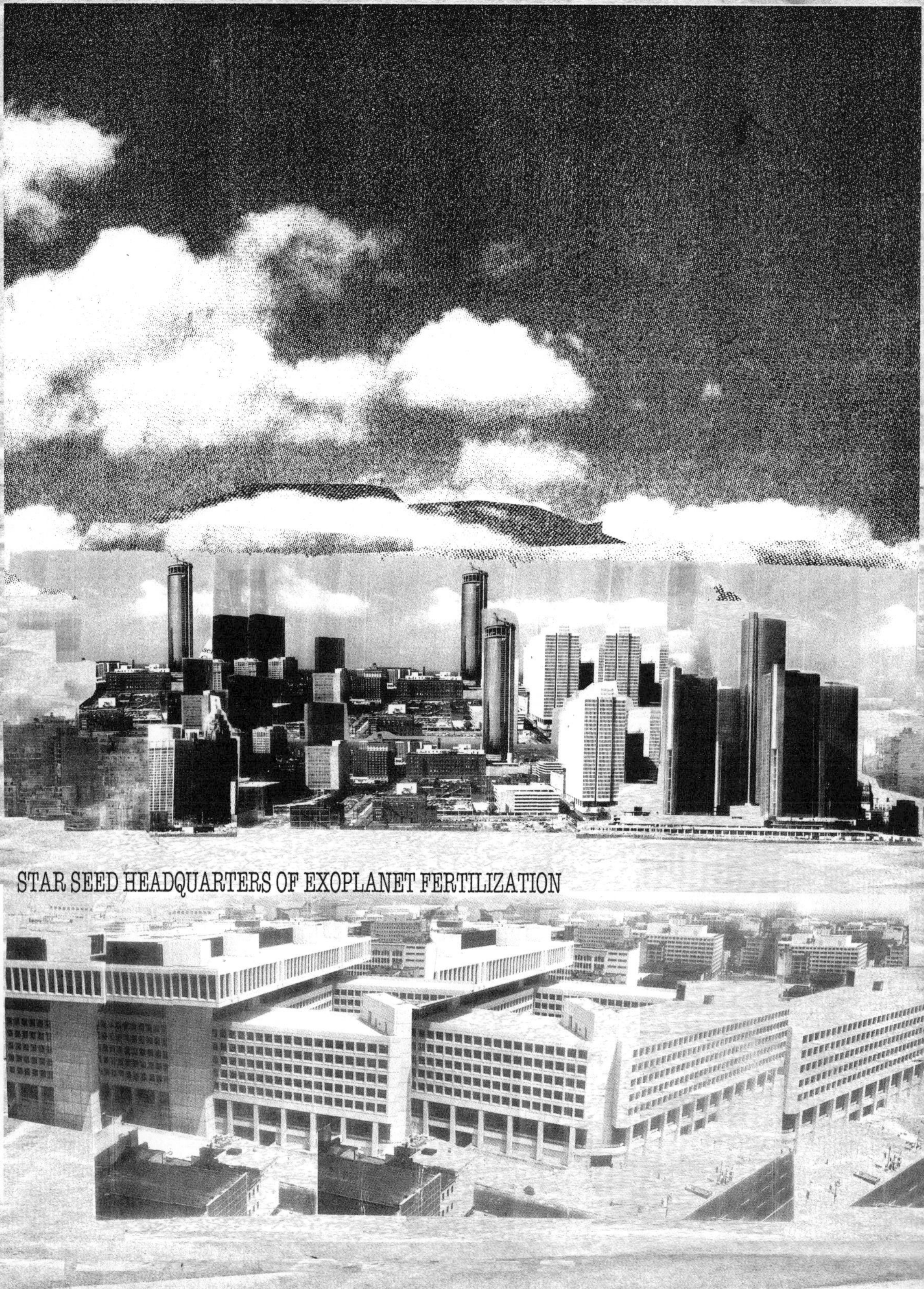
STAR SEED HEADQUARTERS OF EXOPLANET FERTILIZATION

# EVER WANT TO IMPREGNATE A PLANET?

noted futurist

THEON
DEKKEN

STAR
SEED

**75 POWER** TELESCOPE 25X-45X-75X $3.98

**NEW** 3 in one telescopes, 3 variable 25X 45X-75X magnification. Brass bound, 25 power for ultra bright images 45 & 75 power for long range. Guaranteed to bring distant stars, moons, objects, sports 75 times closer. Most powerful scope sold anywhere near this amazing low price. American made, 5 sections. Opens 36", closes 1 ft.; contains 4 ground & polished lenses. Can also be used as powerful compound microscope. Mass production enables us to offer telescope complete at $3.98 postpaid. Money back guarantee.

**CRITERION CO., Dept. BML-85, 331 Church St., Hartford, Conn.**

## EXPLORE SPACE!

**Telescope Kits Direct from Manufacturer**

Many 'Do-it-Yourself' projects for the amateur: build telescopes, projectors, microscopes. Mirrors and parts. Many other optical kits.

Esco-Hampton, P. O. Box 772, Sparta, New Jersey

## MAKE YOUR OWN TELESCOPE

Mirror Making Kits ..............$4.50 up
Aluminizing Mirrors ..6"—$3.50; 8"—$4.50
Quality Parts
Eyepieces • Cells • Prisms

PRECISION OPTICAL SUPPLY CO.
1001 E. 163rd St., N. Y. 59, N. Y.

FREE Catalog
Complete Instructions only 10c

**250 POWER ....**

Complete Telescope Lens Kit

only $3.49 postpaid

Conquer Space, Explore the Universe, Planets, Moon Craters, New Stars, etc. Complete Lens Kit consists of 80 inch focal length ground and polished objective lens, eyepiece lenses for 50 POWER, 100 POWER, 150 POWER, 200 POWER, 250 Power, and all necessary lens fittings. Easy to make from simple step by step instructions. (Tripod and mount not included.) Money back guarantee.

**BUSSE SALES CO., Hartford 1, Conn., Dept. ML-80**

Opportunities in TRAVEL
GIANT WALL MAP
SAMPLE LESSON
ALL 3 FREE

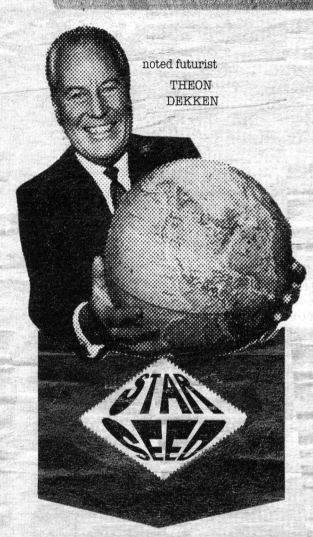

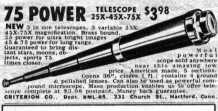

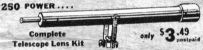

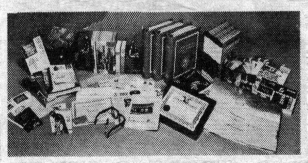

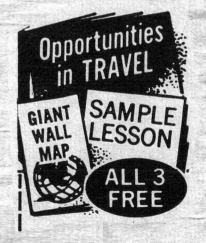

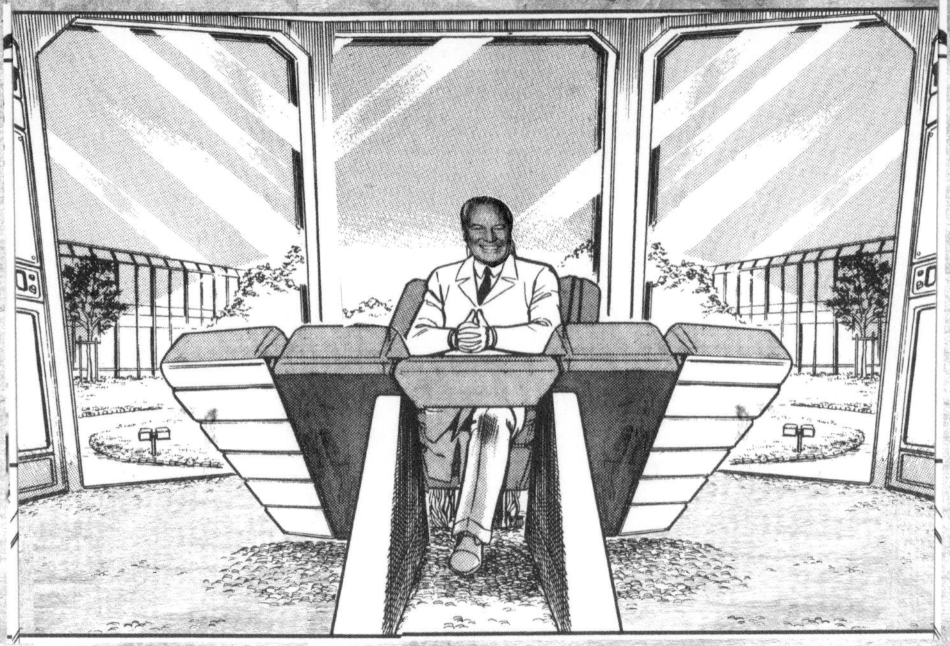

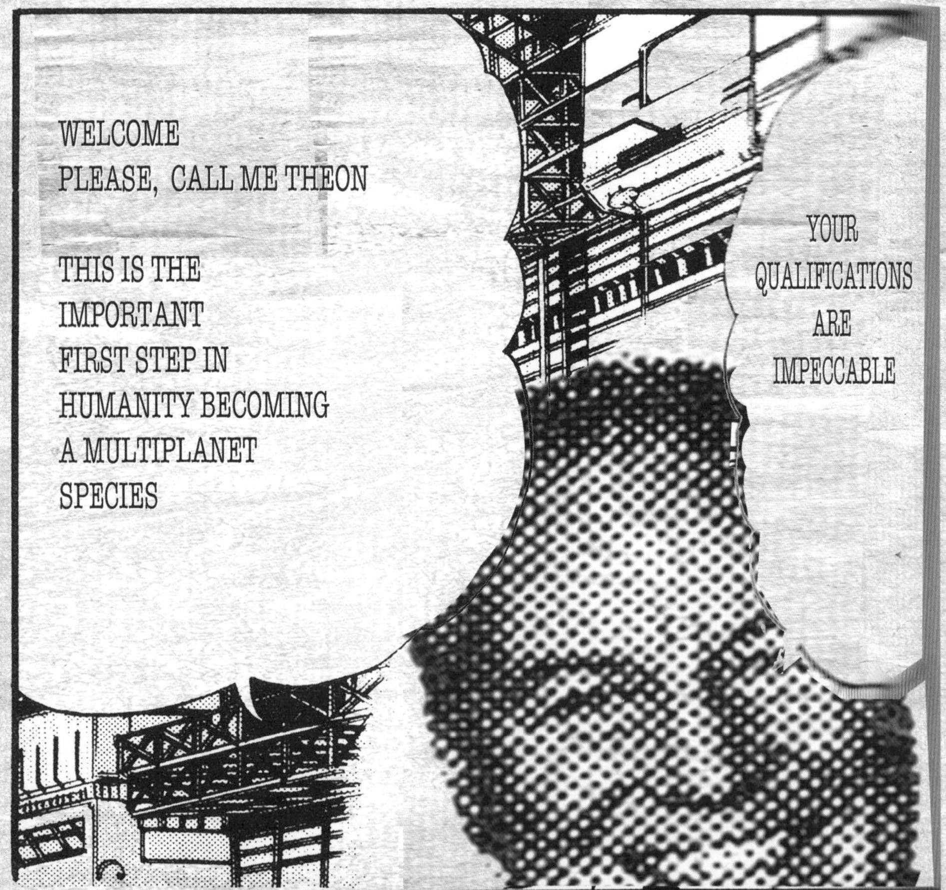
WELCOME
PLEASE, CALL ME THEON
THIS IS THE IMPORTANT FIRST STEP IN HUMANITY BECOMING A MULTIPLANET SPECIES
YOUR QUALIFICATIONS ARE IMPECCABLE

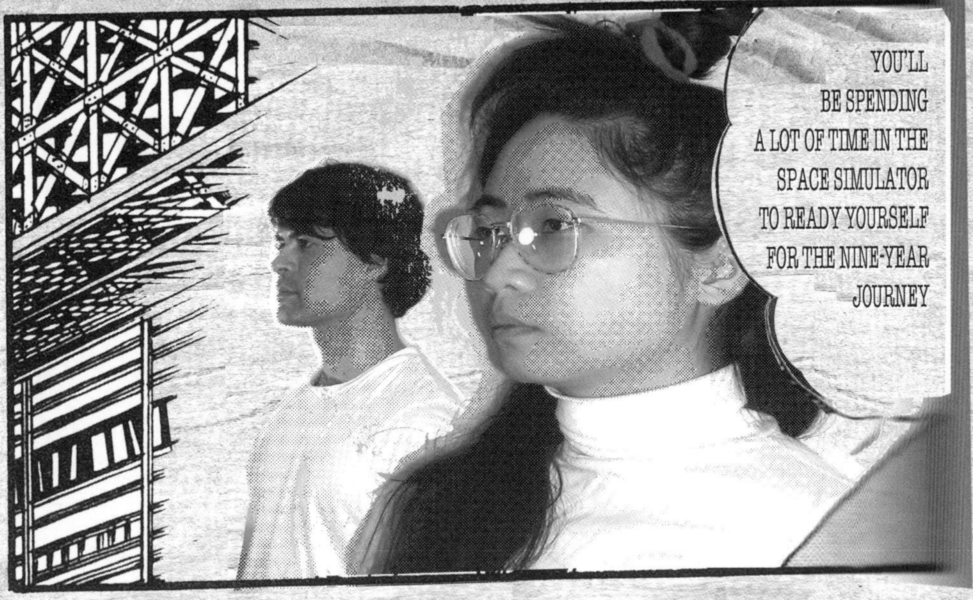
YOU'LL BE SPENDING A LOT OF TIME IN THE SPACE SIMULATOR TO READY YOURSELF FOR THE NINE-YEAR JOURNEY

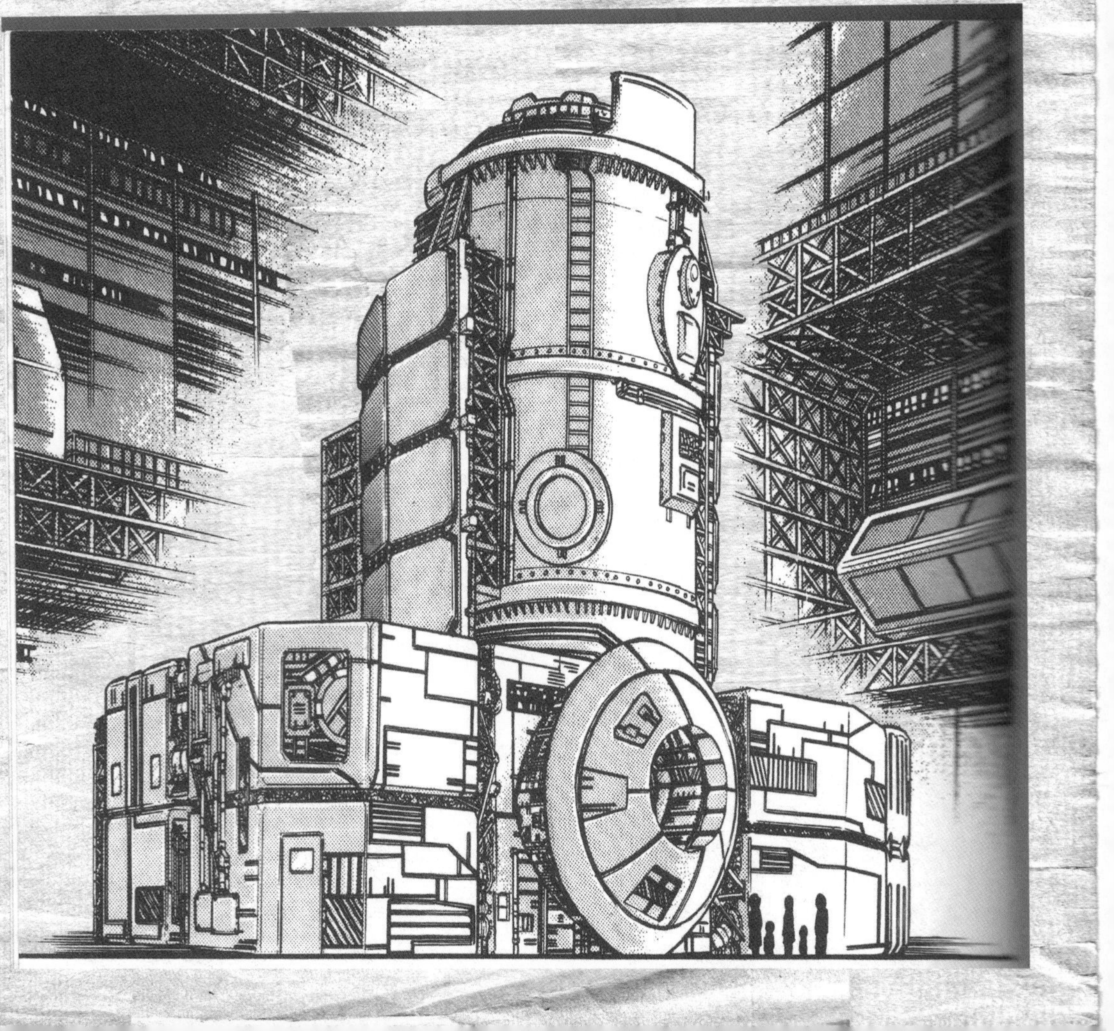

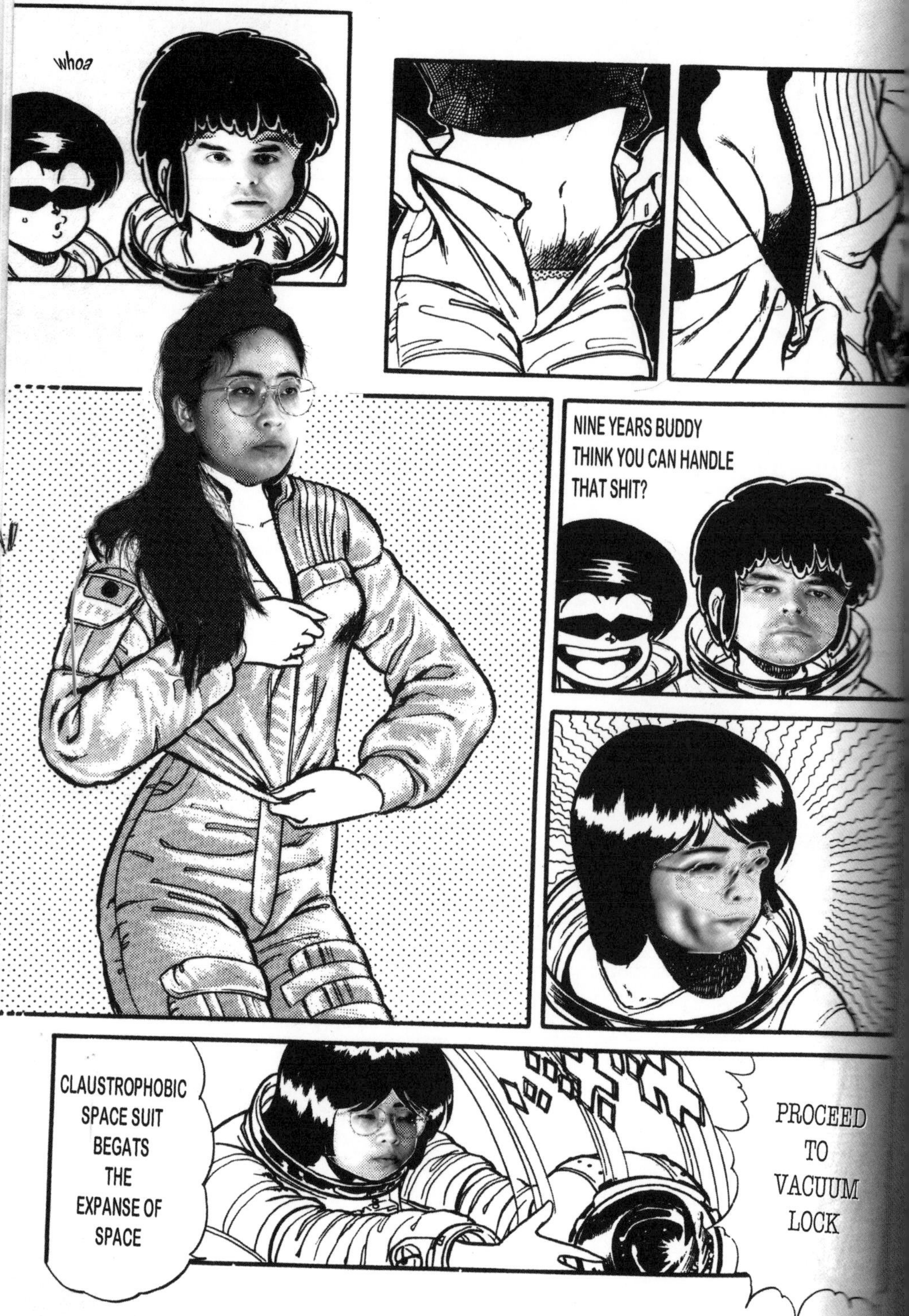
whoa
NINE YEARS BUDDY THINK YOU CAN HANDLE THAT SHIT?
CLAUSTROPHOBIC SPACE SUIT BEGATS THE EXPANSE OF SPACE
PROCEED TO VACUUM LOCK

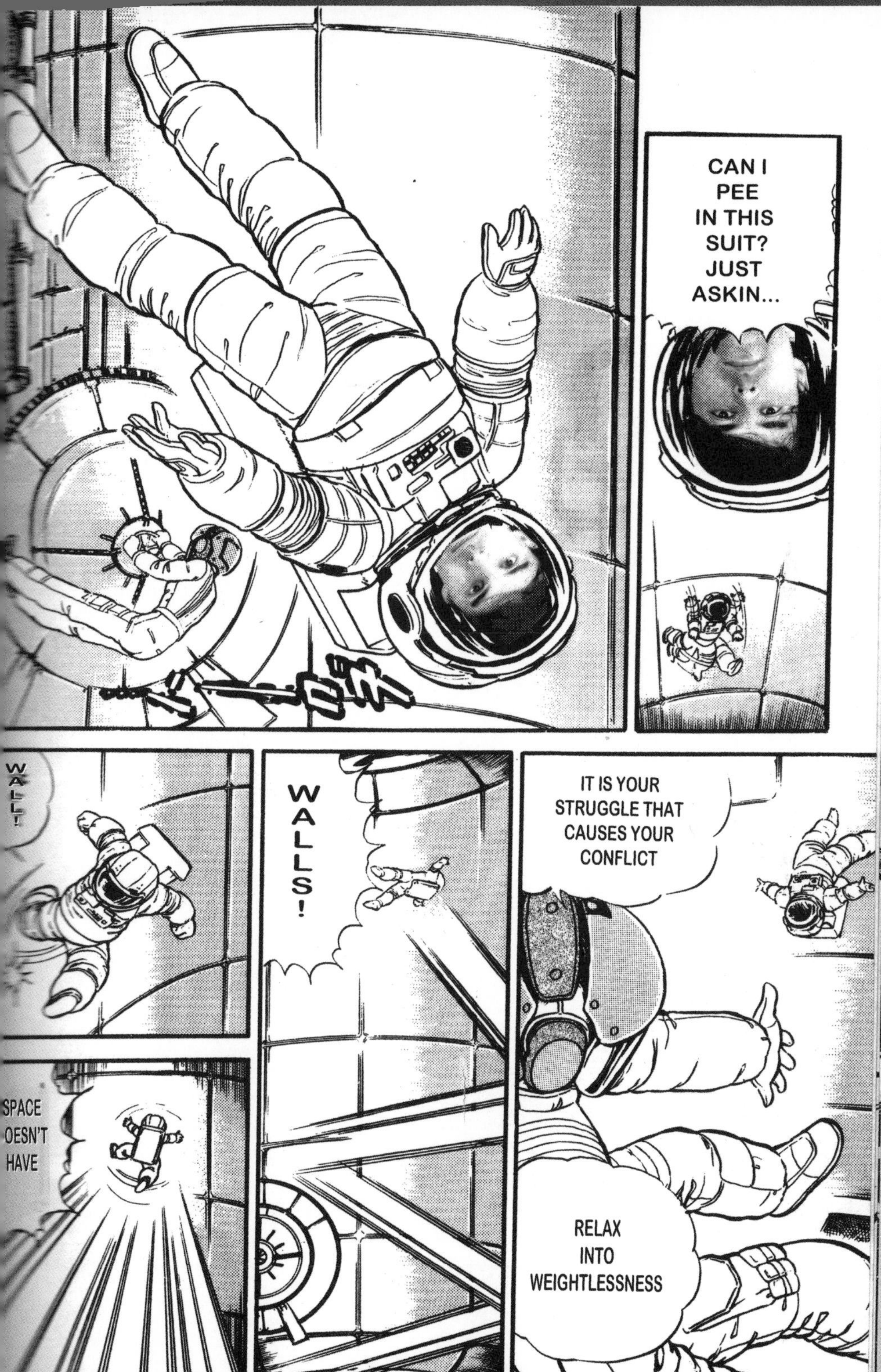
CAN I PEE IN THIS SUIT? JUST ASKIN...
IT IS YOUR STRUGGLE THAT CAUSES YOUR CONFLICT
RELAX INTO WEIGHTLESSNESS
WALLS!
WALL!
SPACE OESN'T HAVE

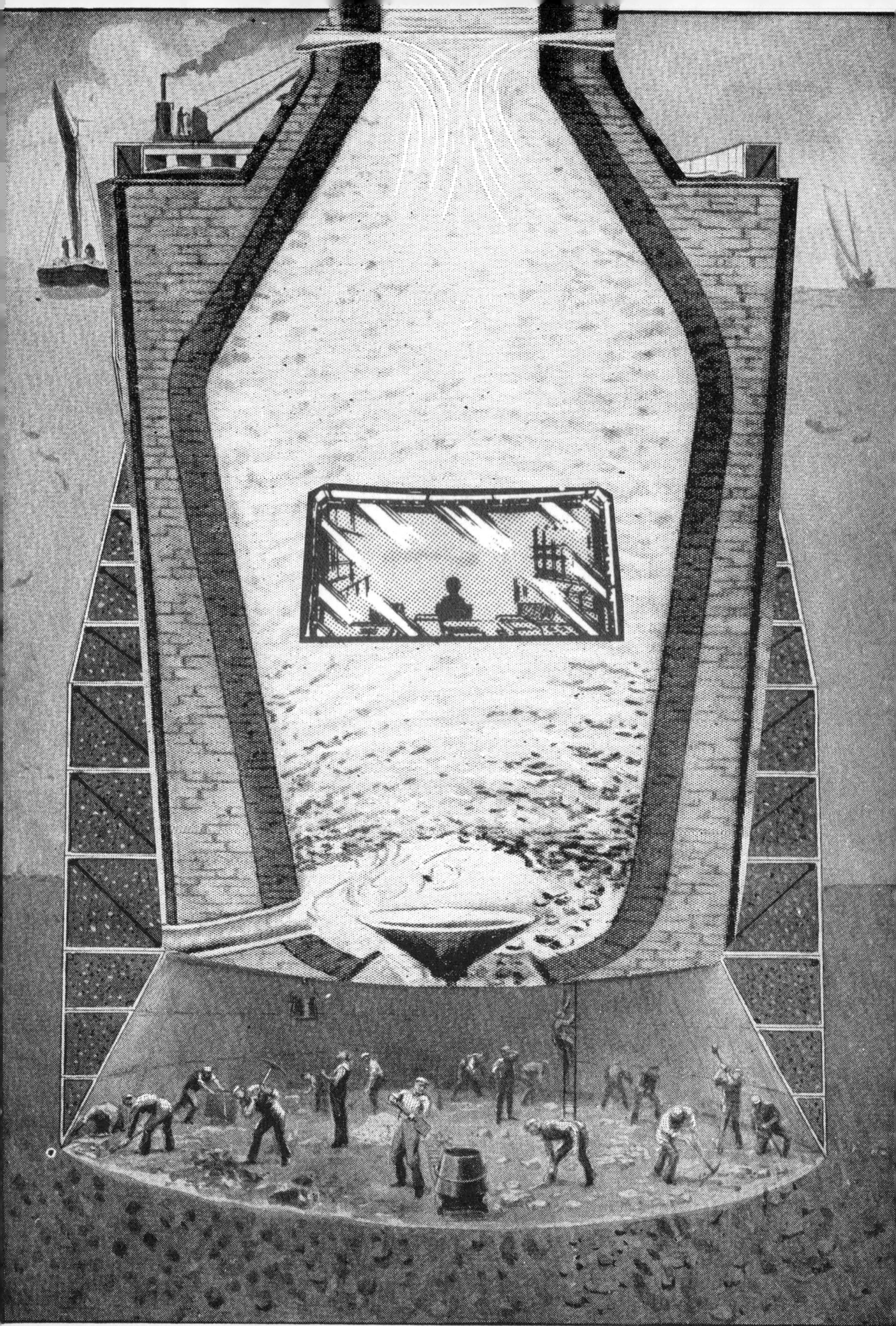

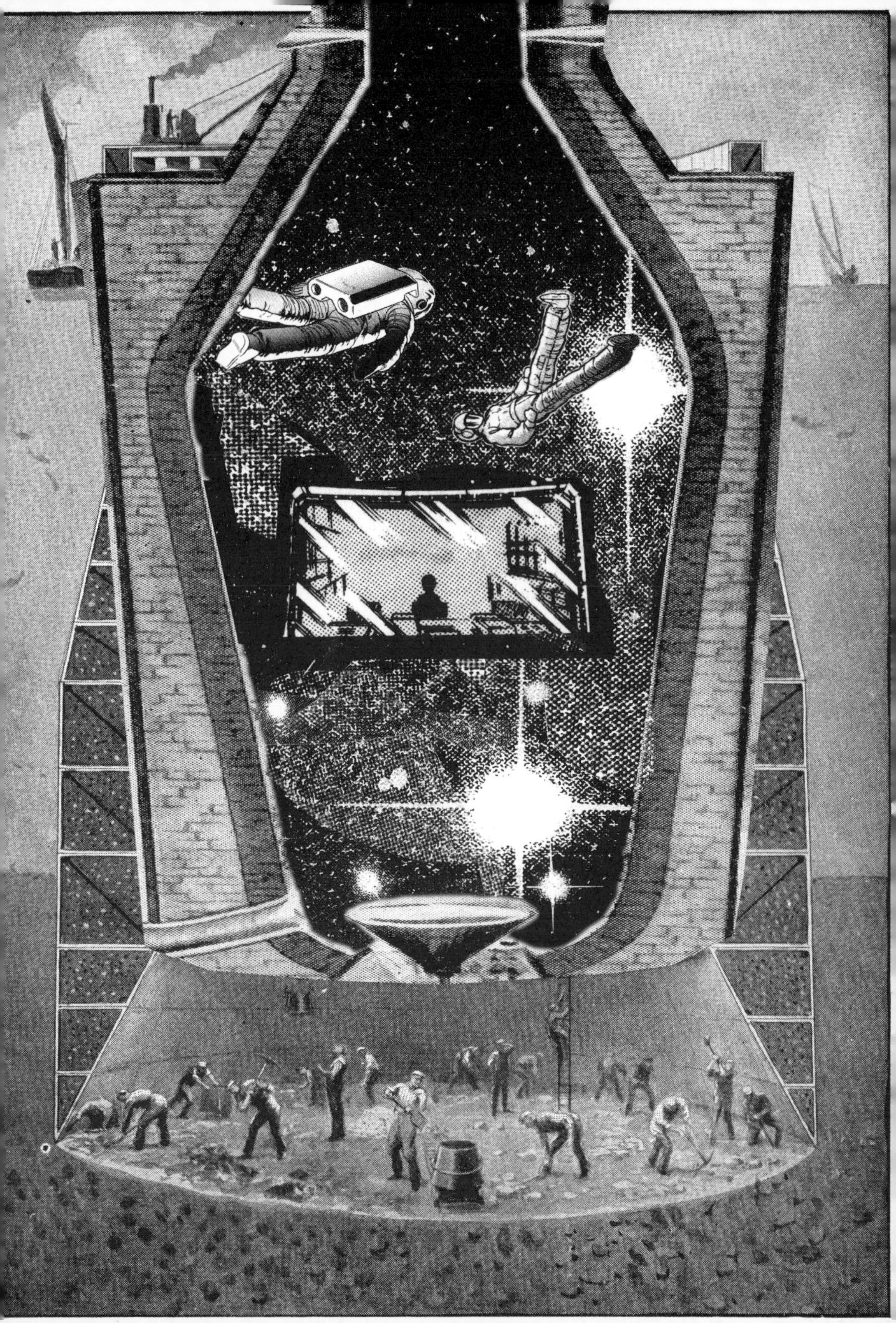

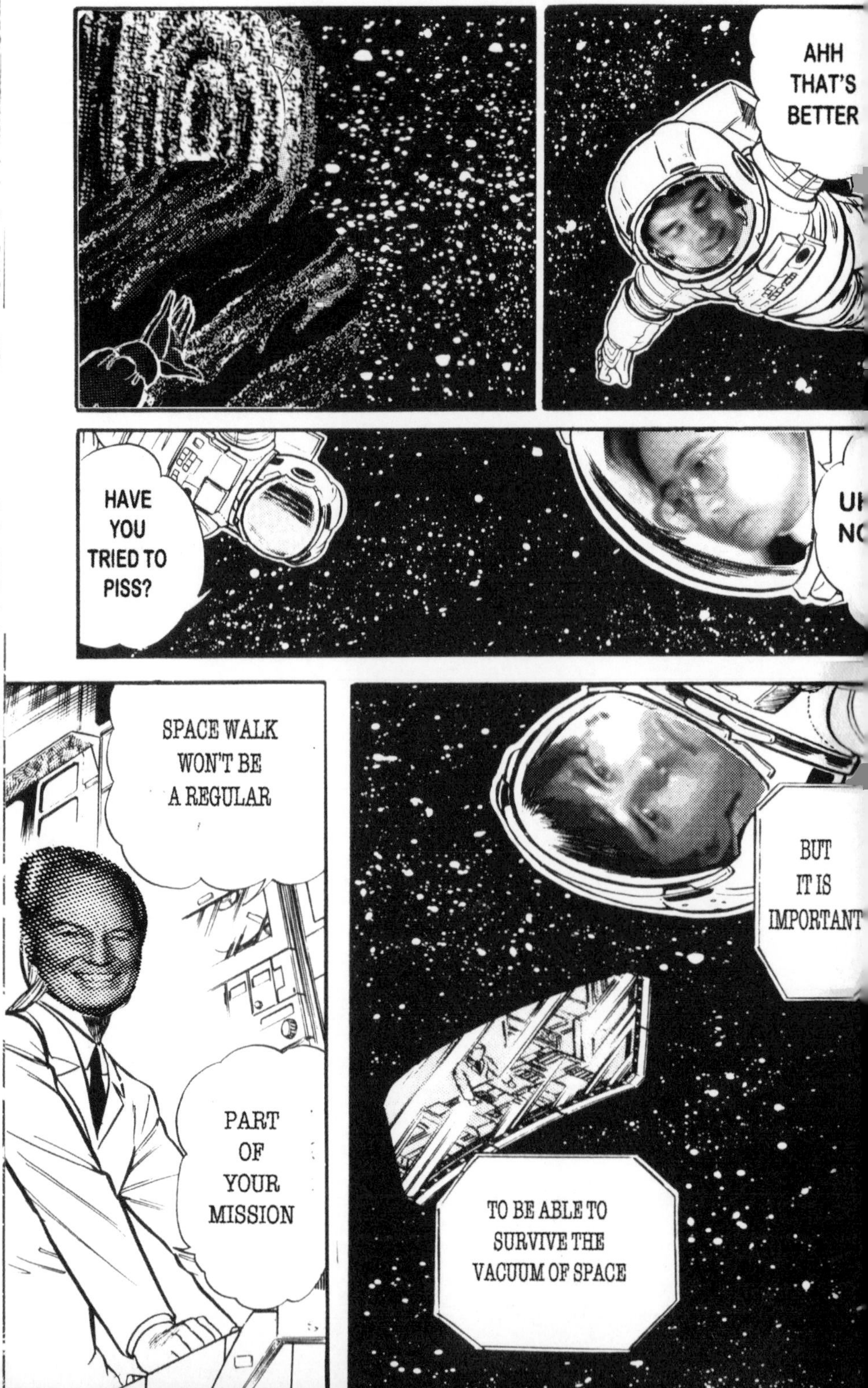
AHH THAT'S BETTER
HAVE YOU TRIED TO PISS?
SPACE WALK WON'T BE A REGULAR
PART OF YOUR MISSION
BUT IT IS IMPORTANT
TO BE ABLE TO SURVIVE THE VACUUM OF SPACE

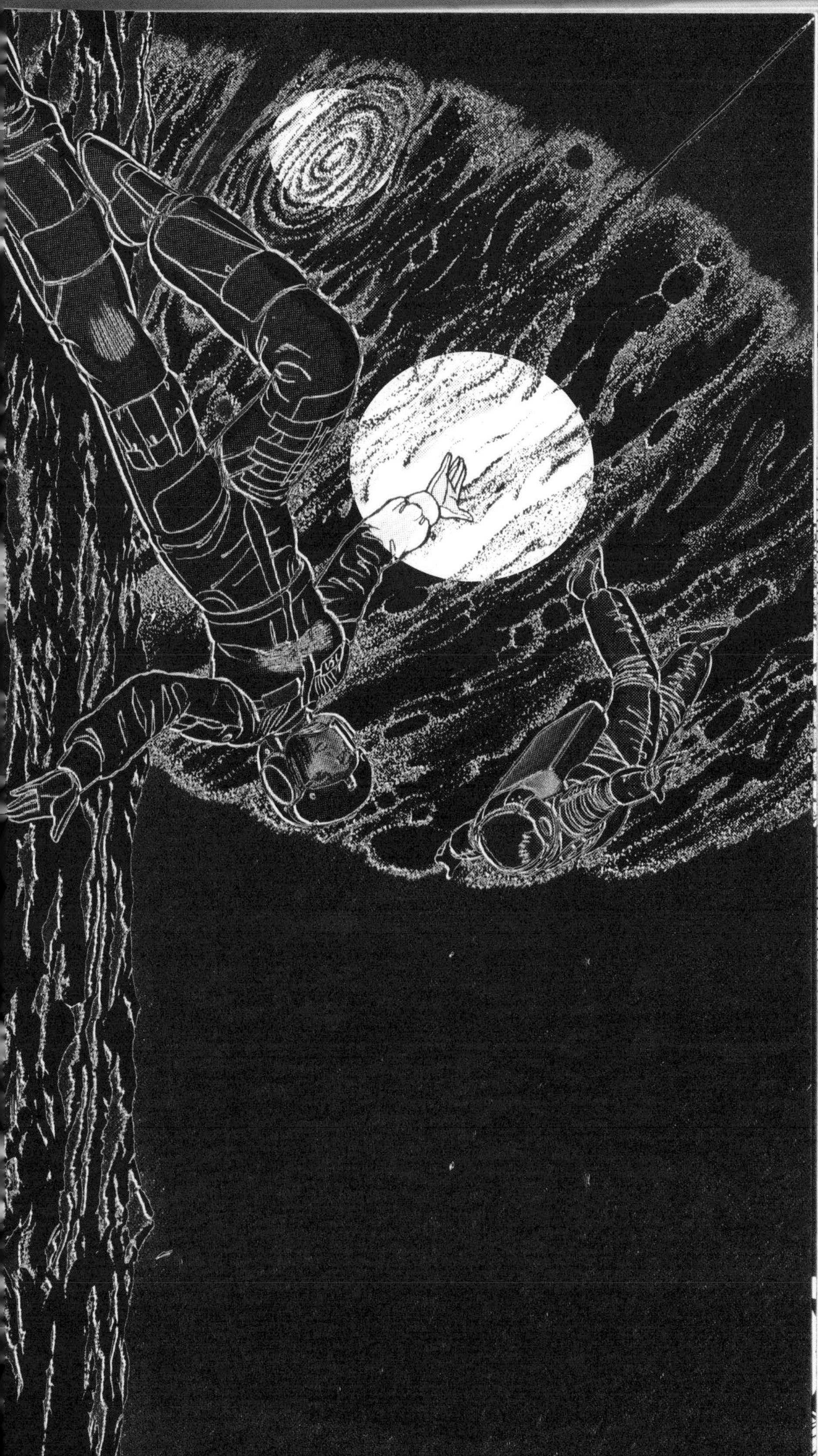

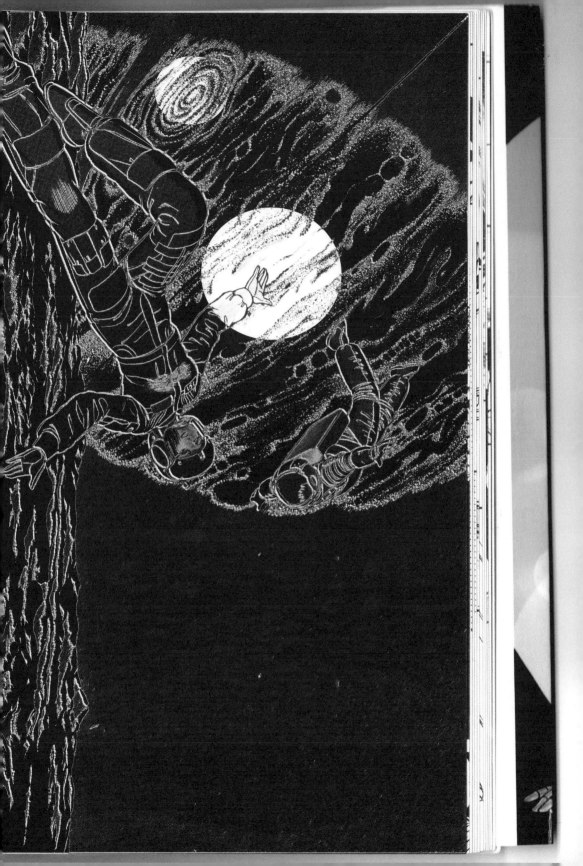

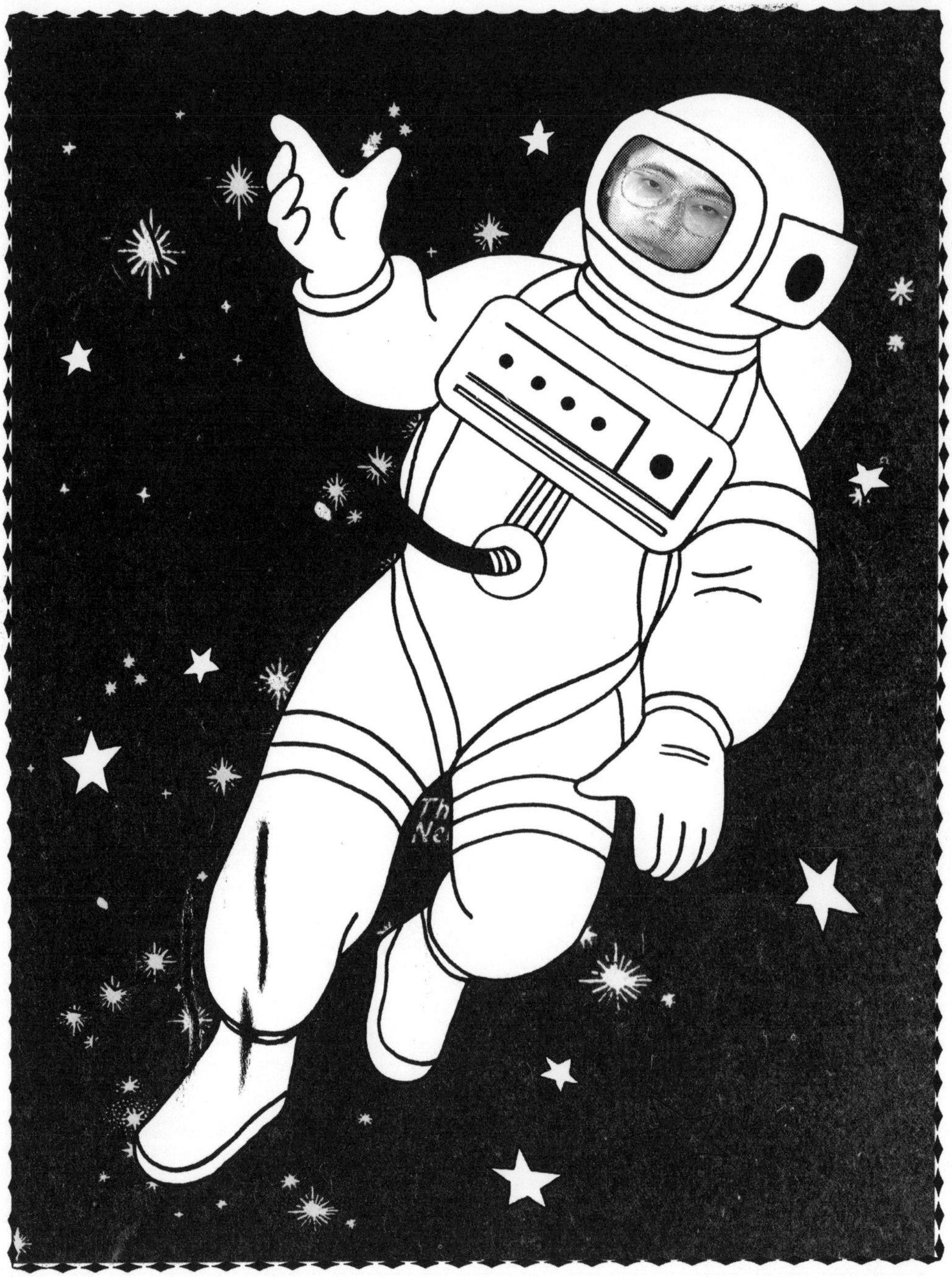

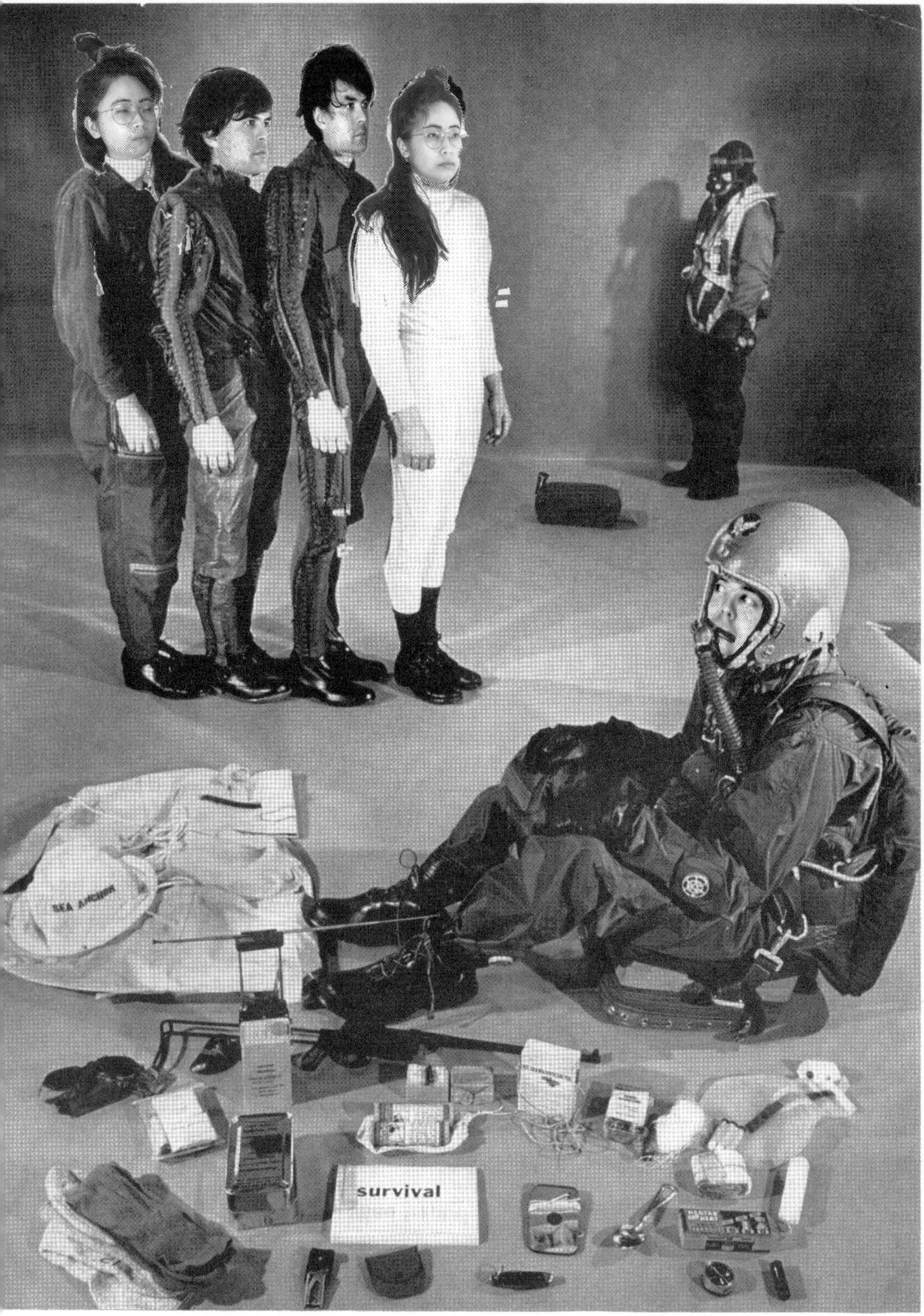
SEA ANCHOR
survival

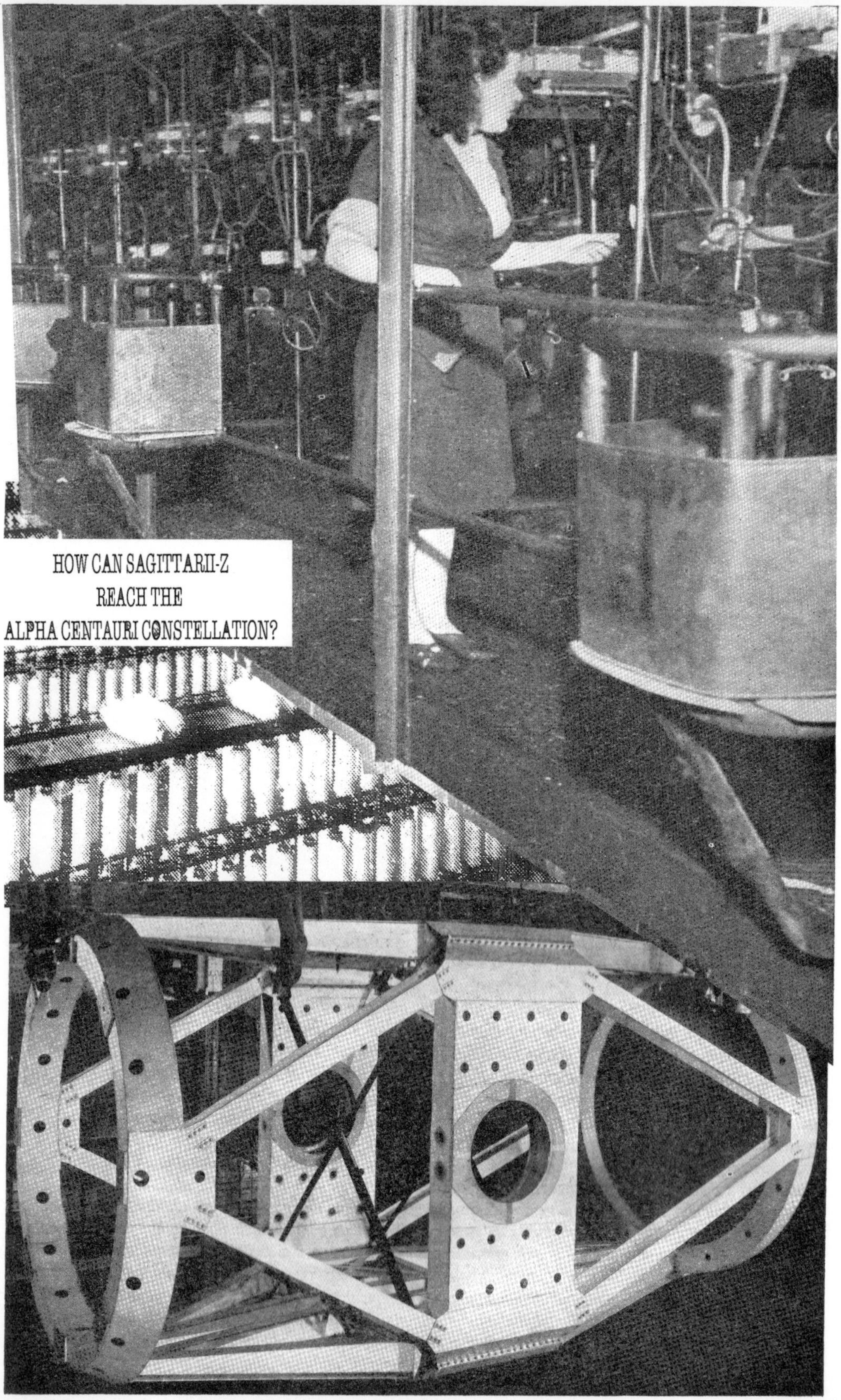
HOW CAN SAGITTARII-Z
REACH THE
ALPHA CENTAURI CONSTELLATION?

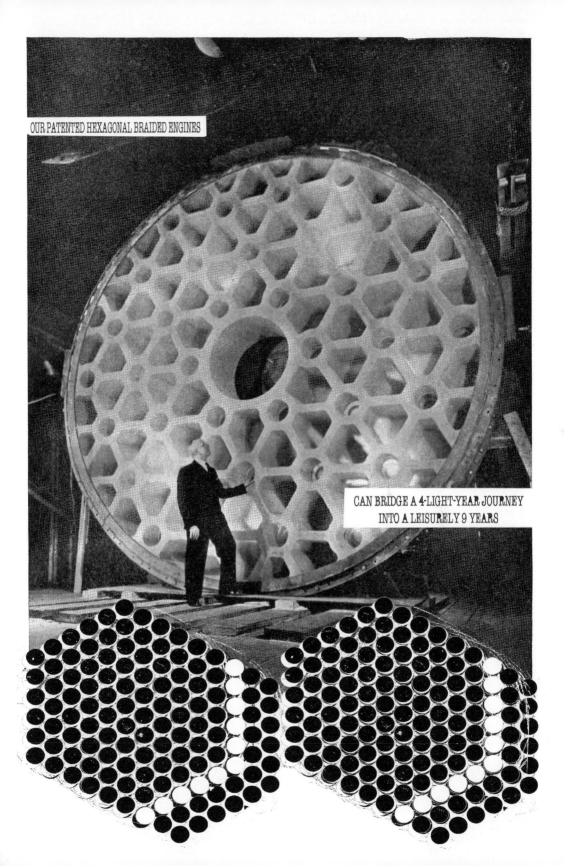

OUR PATENTED HEXAGONAL BRAIDED ENGINES

CAN BRIDGE A 4-LIGHT-YEAR JOURNEY
INTO A LEISURELY 9 YEARS

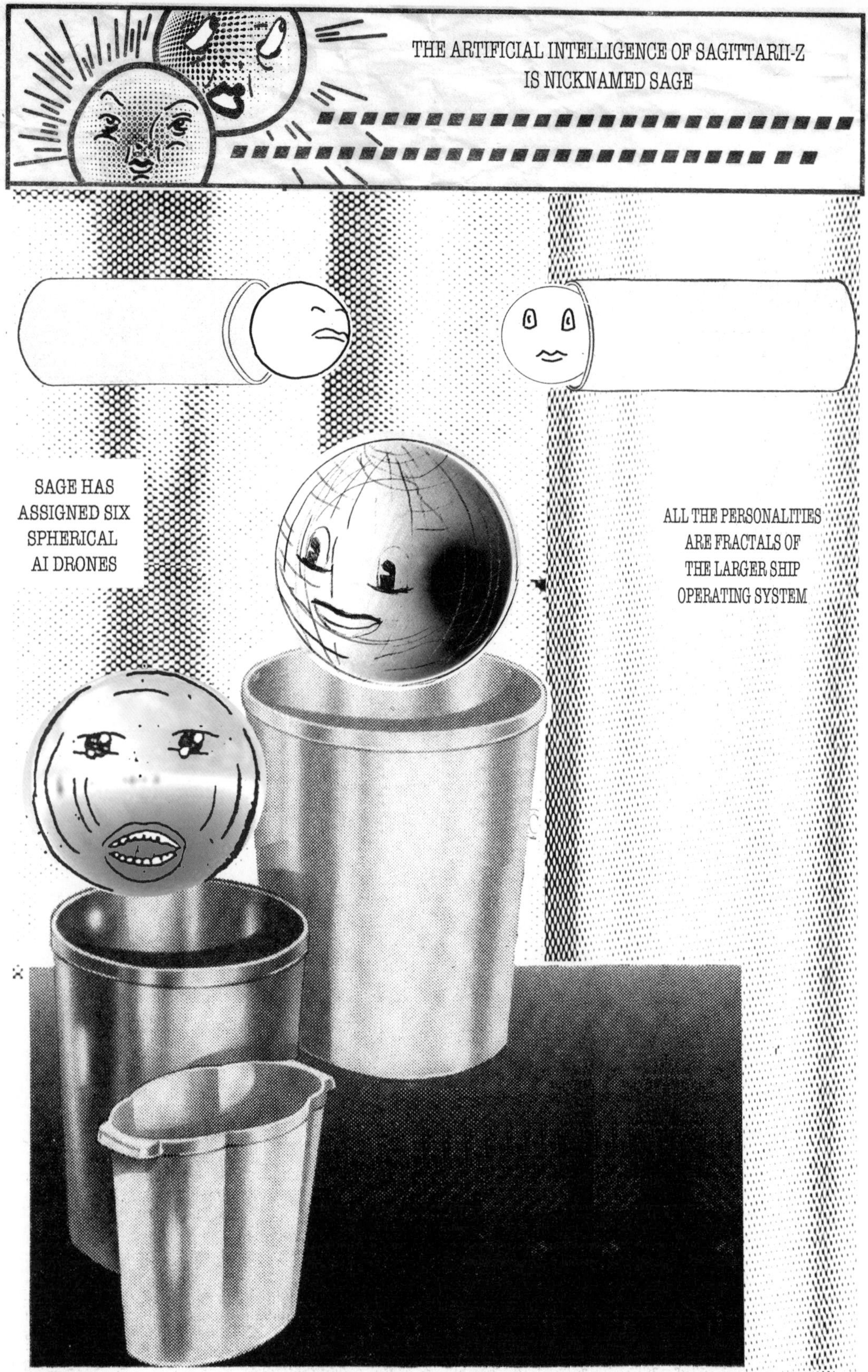
THE ARTIFICIAL INTELLIGENCE OF SAGITTARII-Z IS NICKNAMED SAGE
SAGE HAS ASSIGNED SIX SPHERICAL AI DRONES
ALL THE PERSONALITIES ARE FRACTALS OF THE LARGER SHIP OPERATING SYSTEM

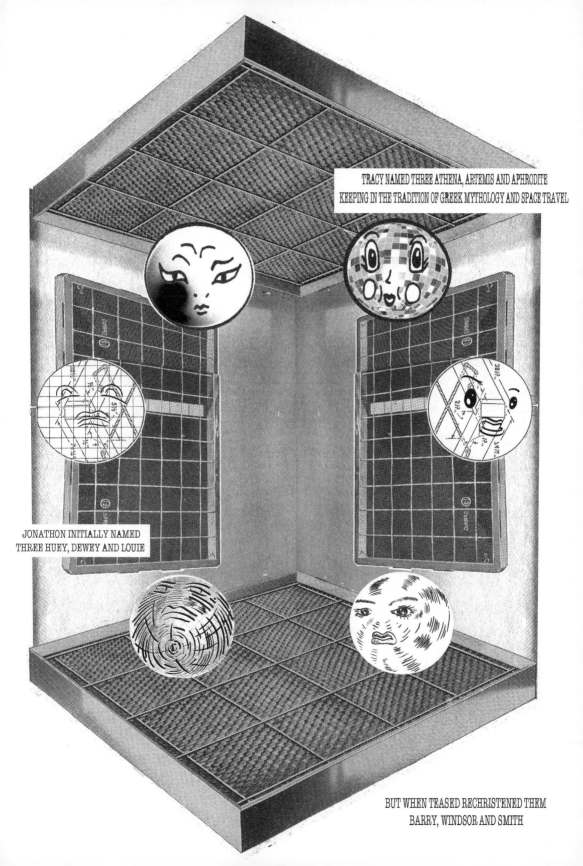

TRACY NAMED THREE ATHENA, ARTEMIS AND APHRODITE
KEEPING IN THE TRADITION OF GREEK MYTHOLOGY AND SPACE TRAVEL

JONATHON INITIALLY NAMED
THREE HUEY, DEWEY AND LOUIE

BUT WHEN TEASED RECHRISTENED THEM
BARRY, WINDSOR AND SMITH

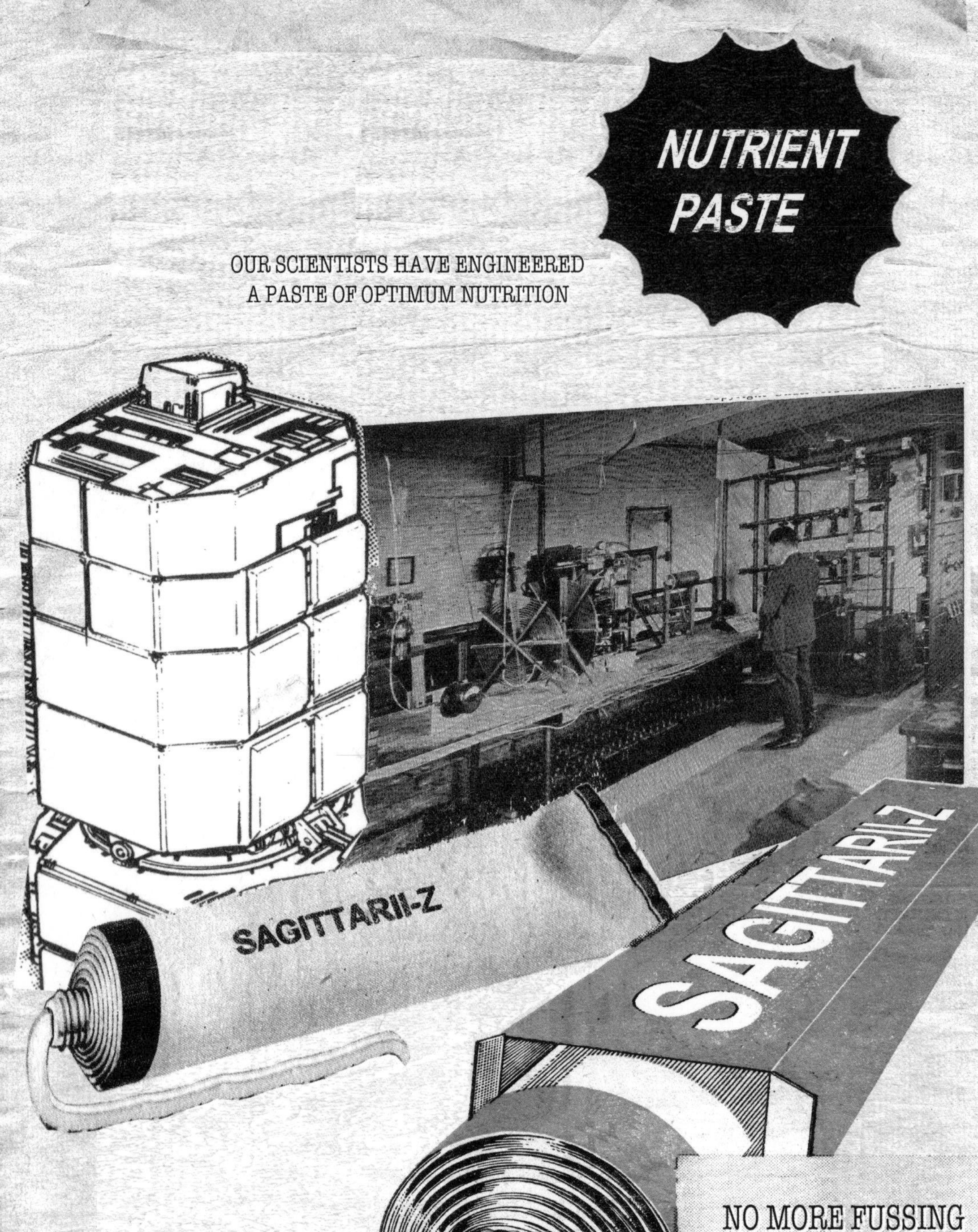
NUTRIENT PASTE
OUR SCIENTISTS HAVE ENGINEERED A PASTE OF OPTIMUM NUTRITION
SAGITTARII-Z
SAGITTARII-Z
NO MORE FUSSING IN THE KITCHEN

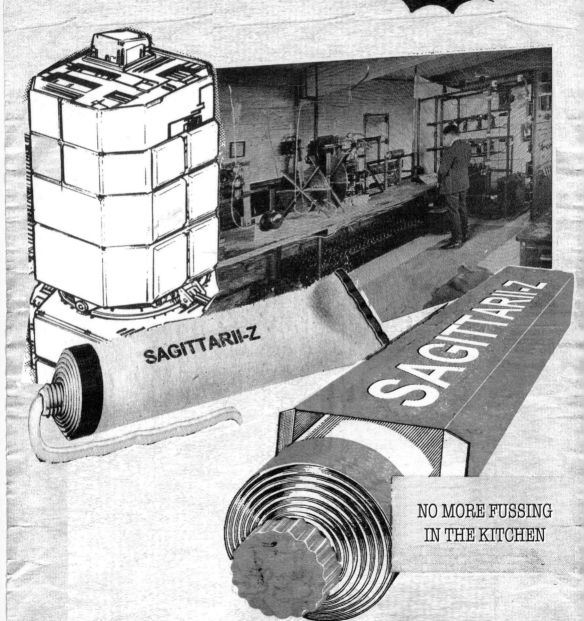

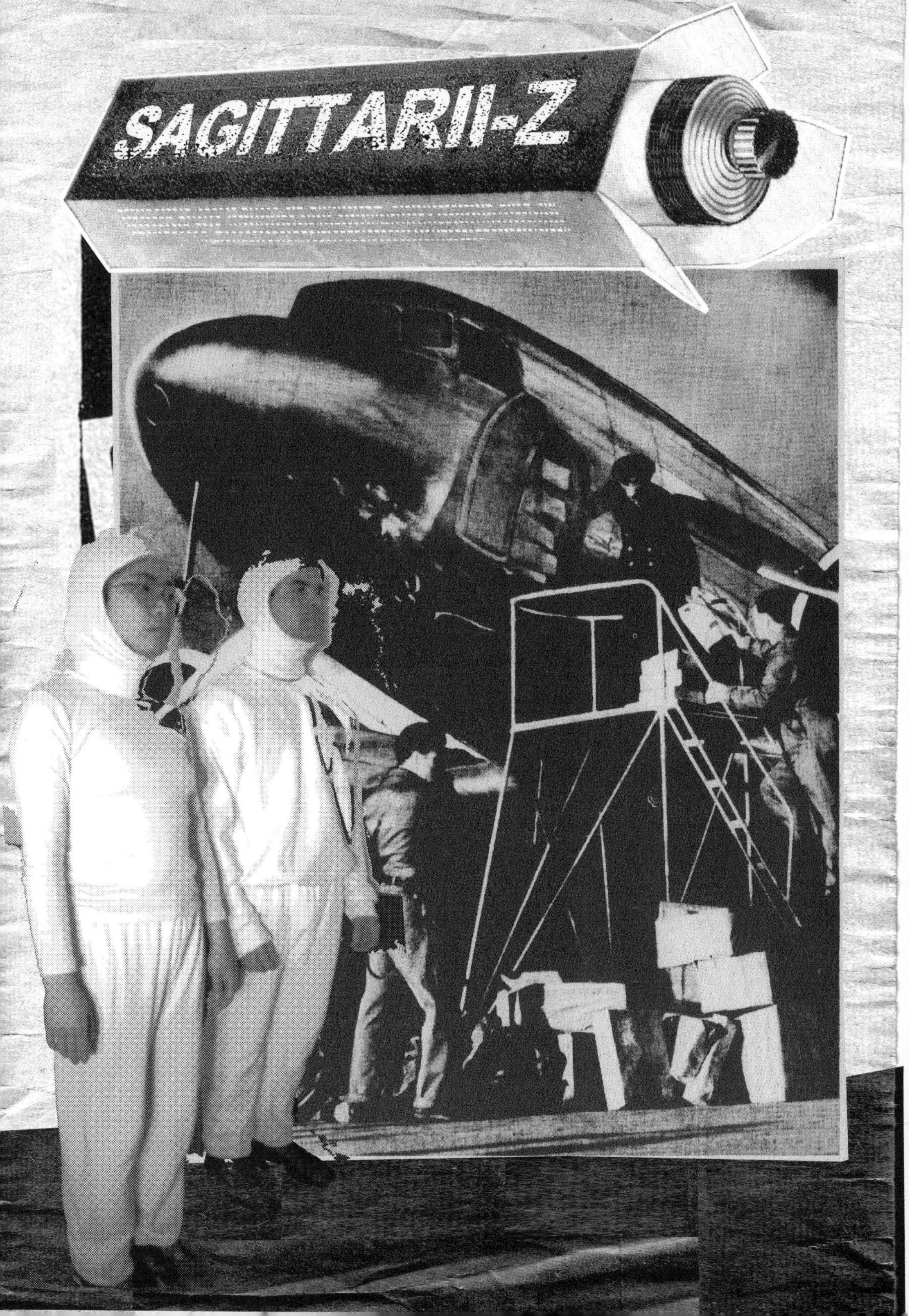
SAGITTARII-Z

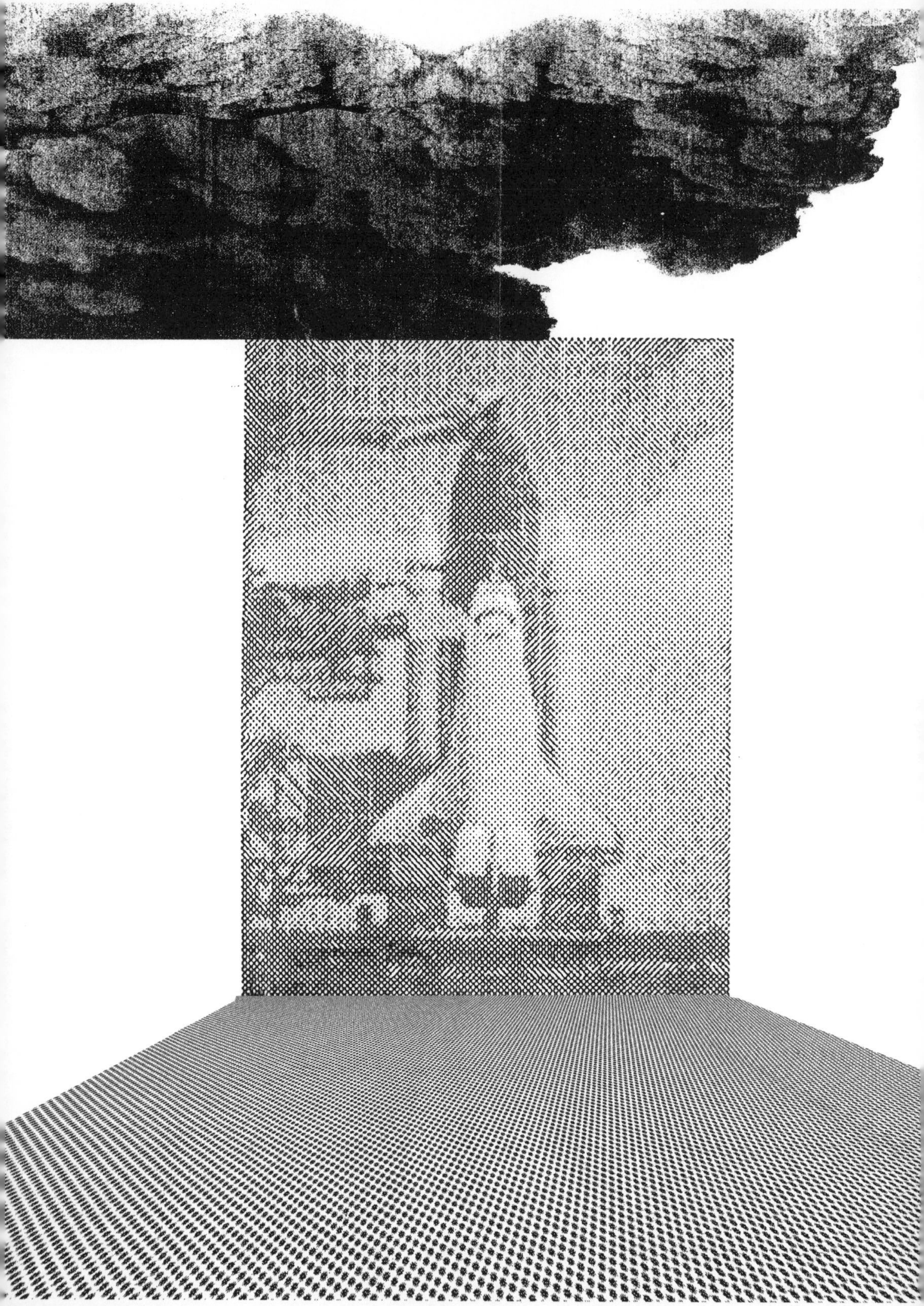

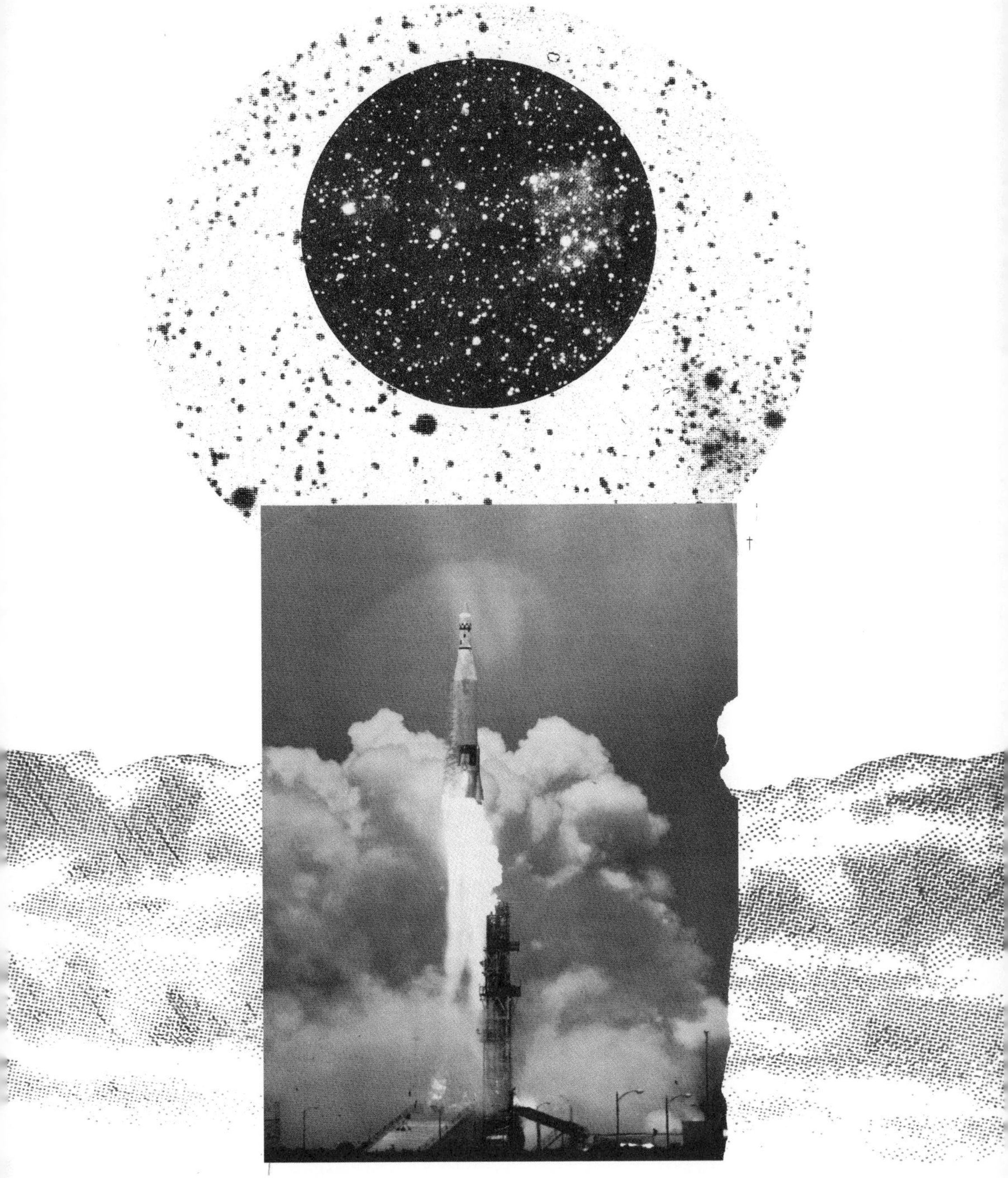

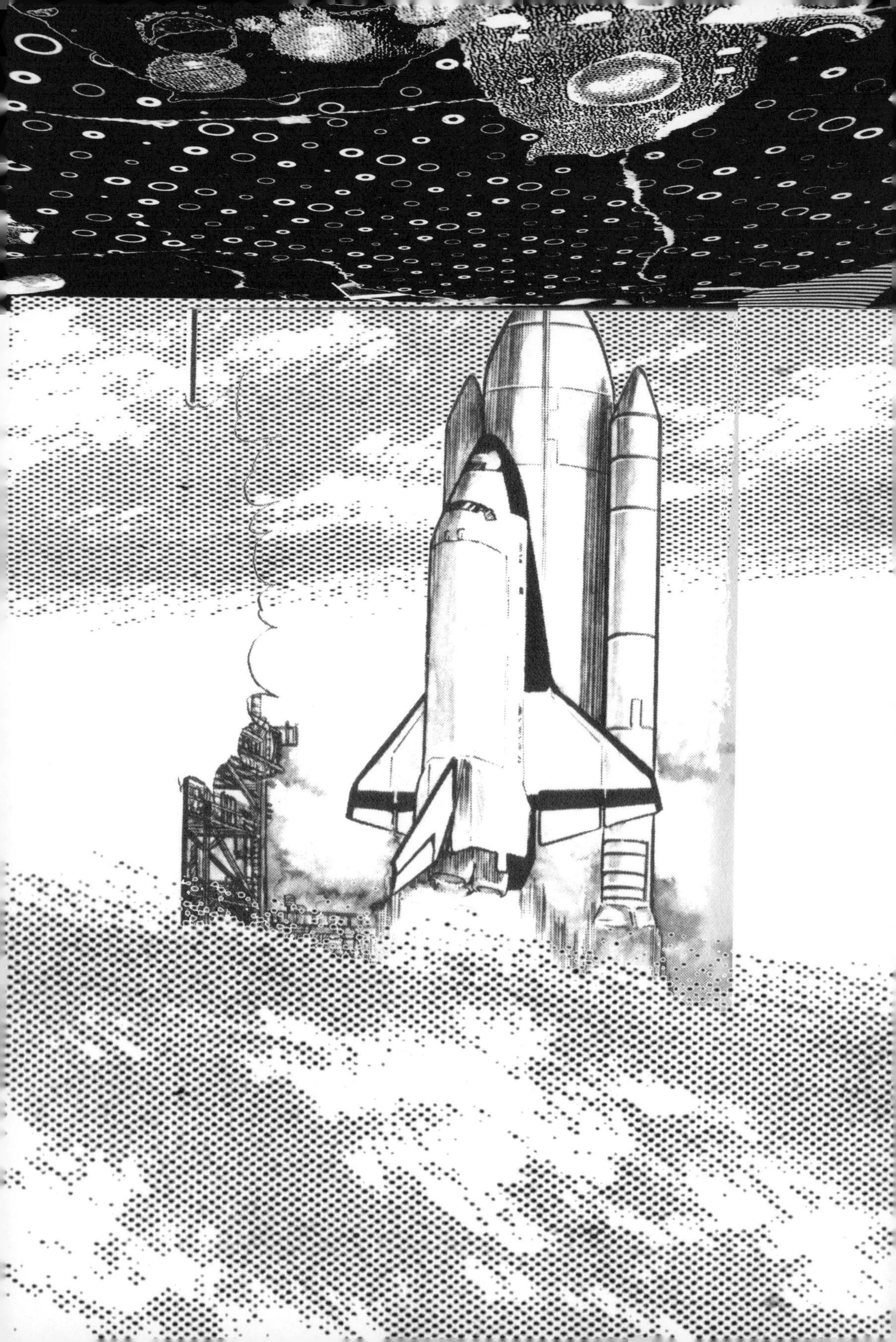

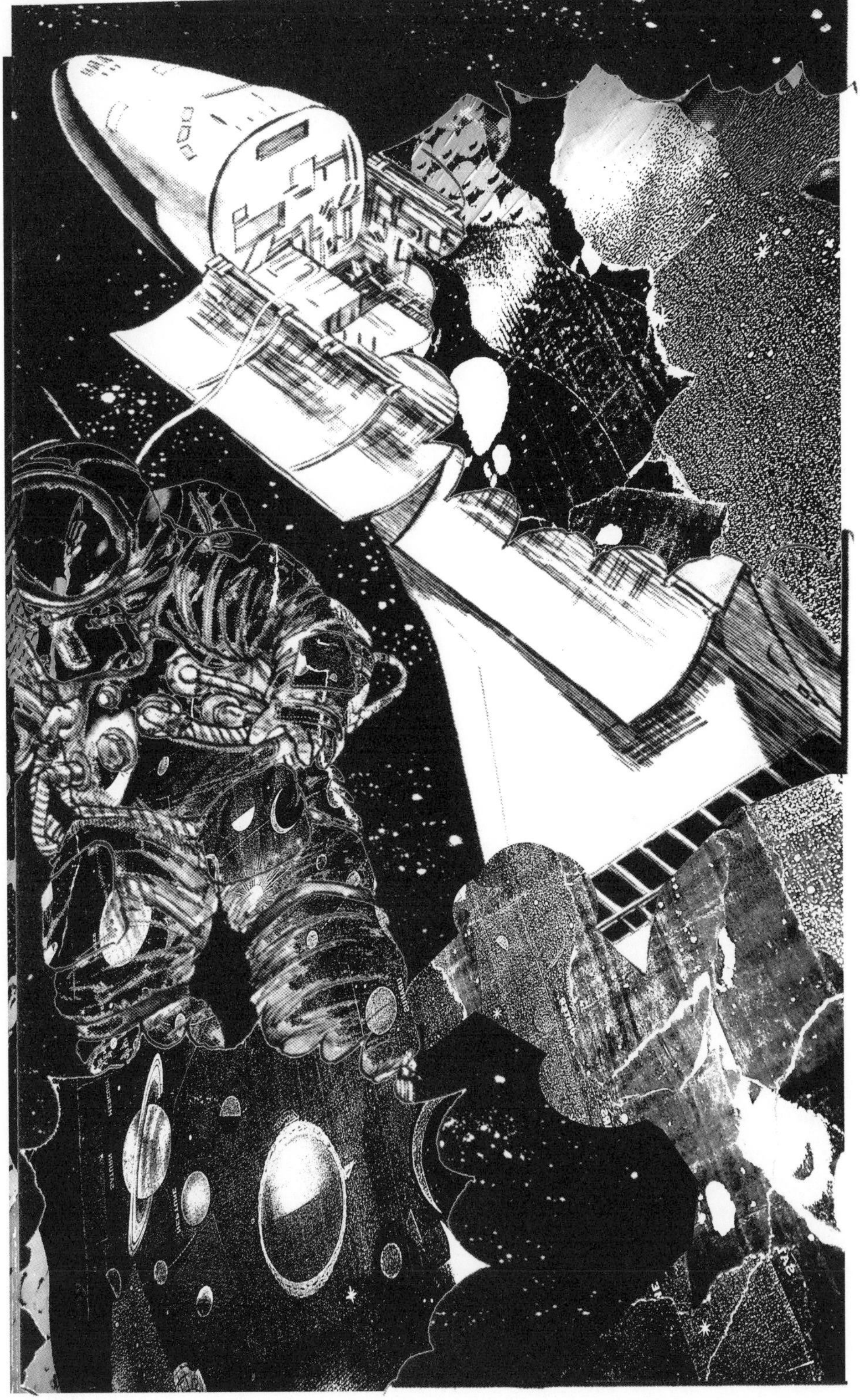

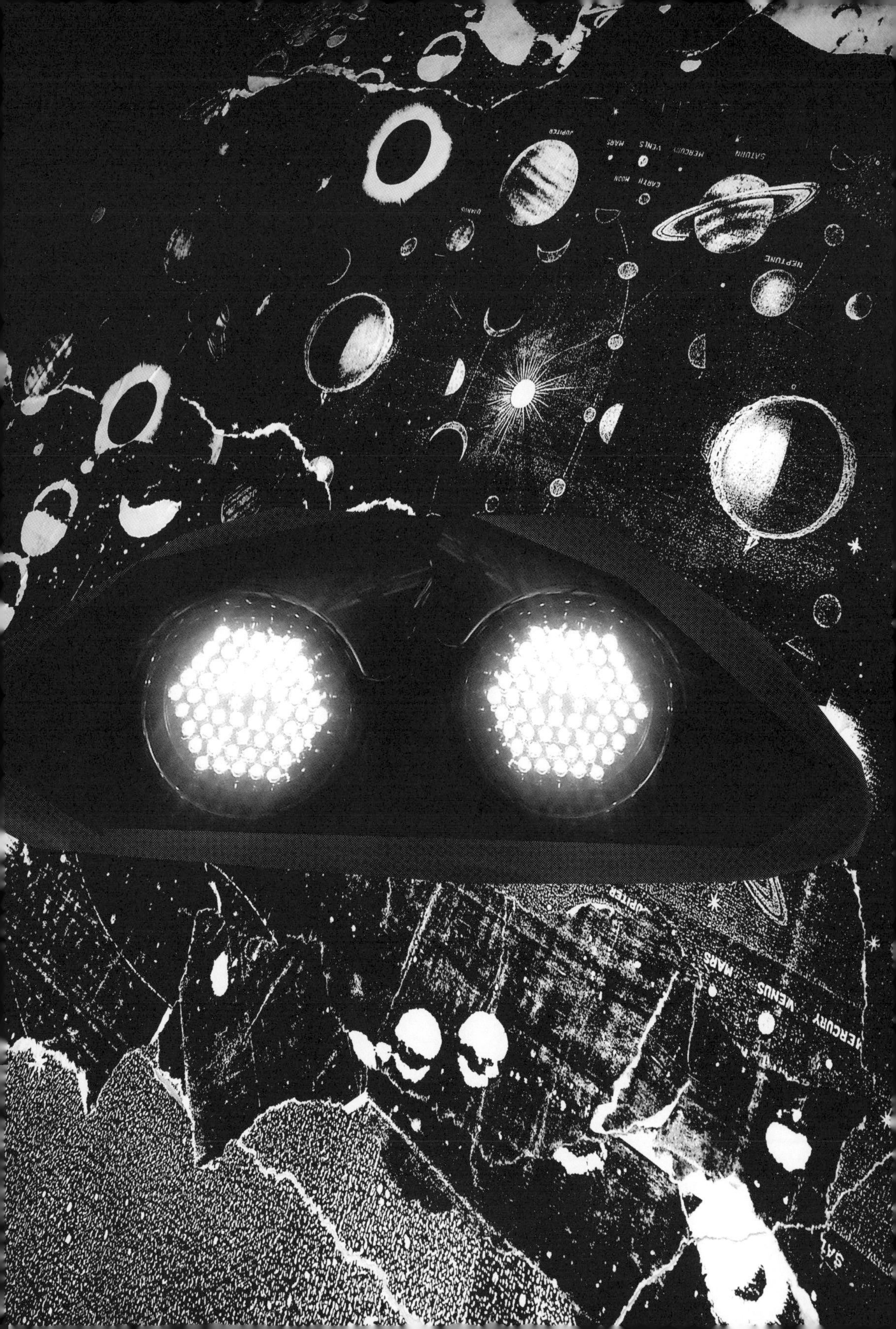

JUPITER
MARS
VENUS
MERCURY

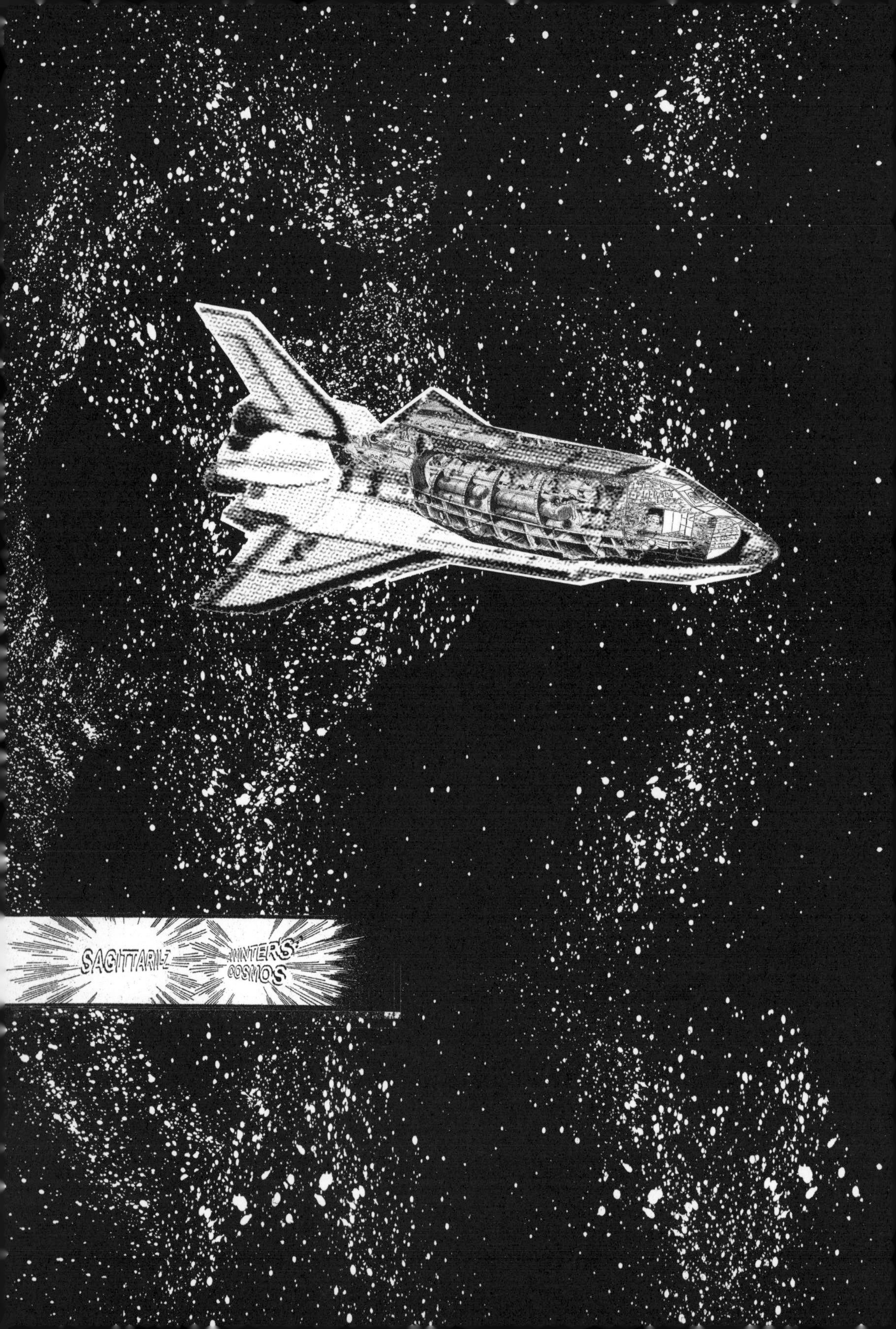
SAGITTARII-Z
WINTERS' COSMOS

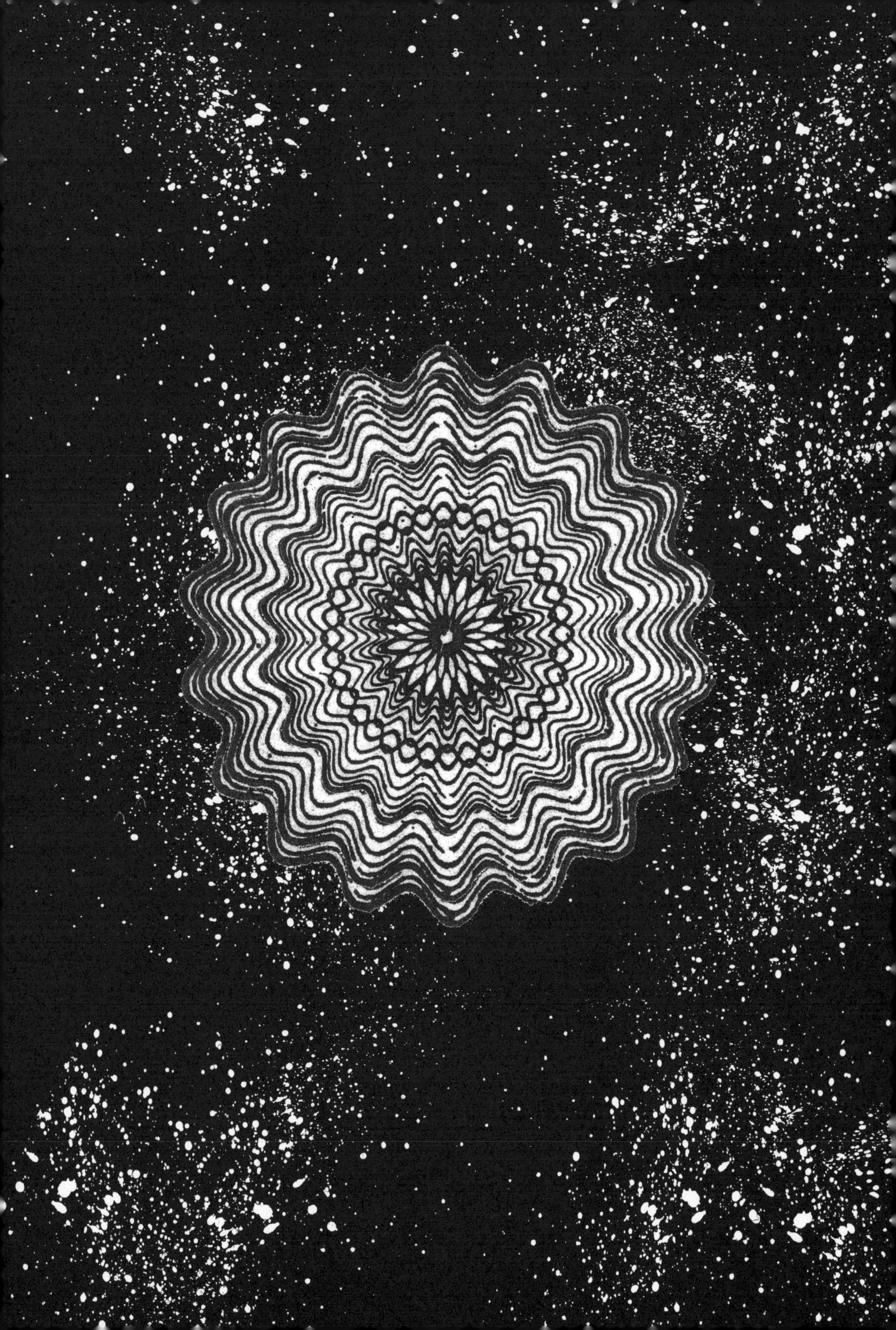

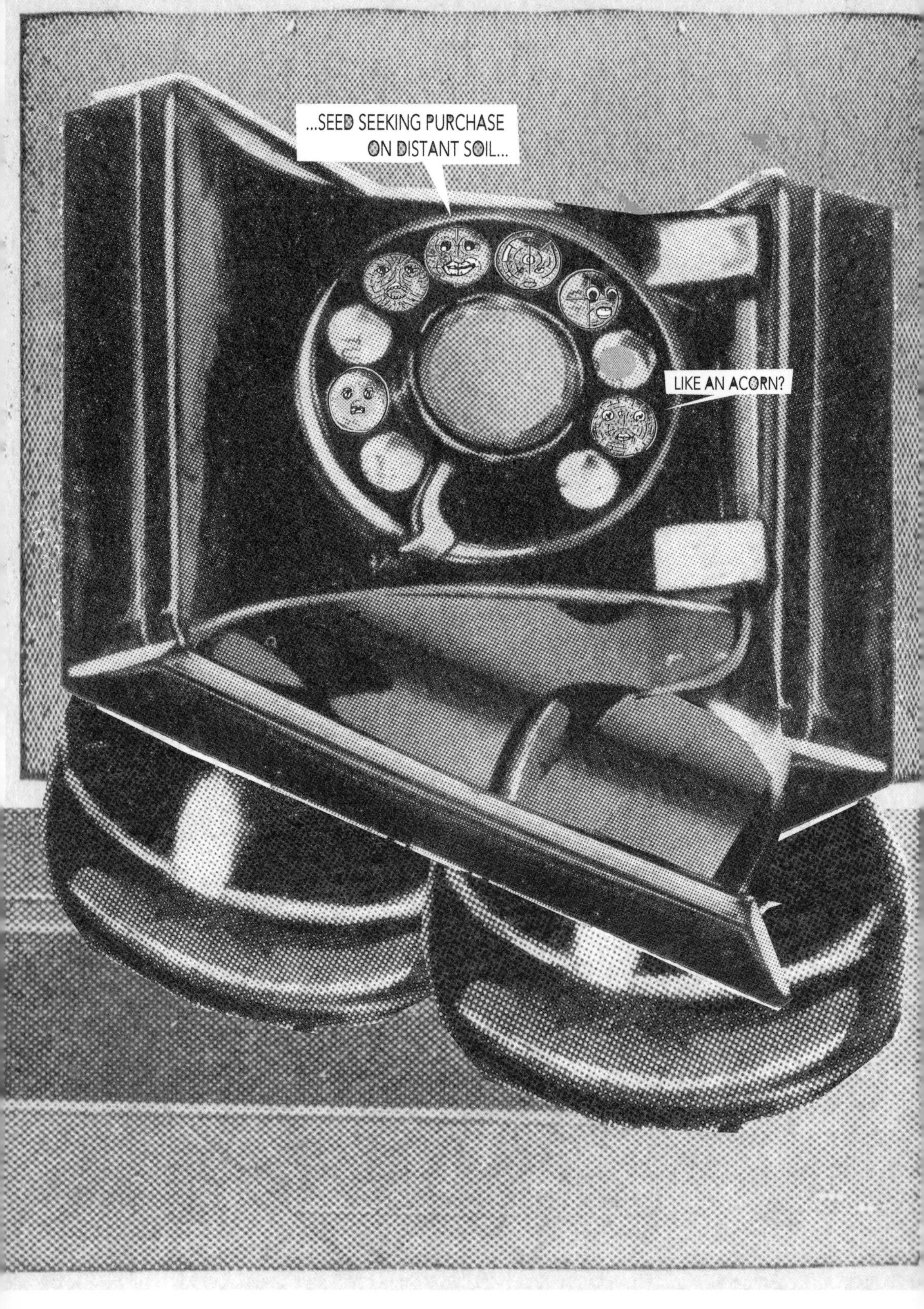
...SEED SEEKING PURCHASE ON DISTANT SOIL...
LIKE AN ACORN?

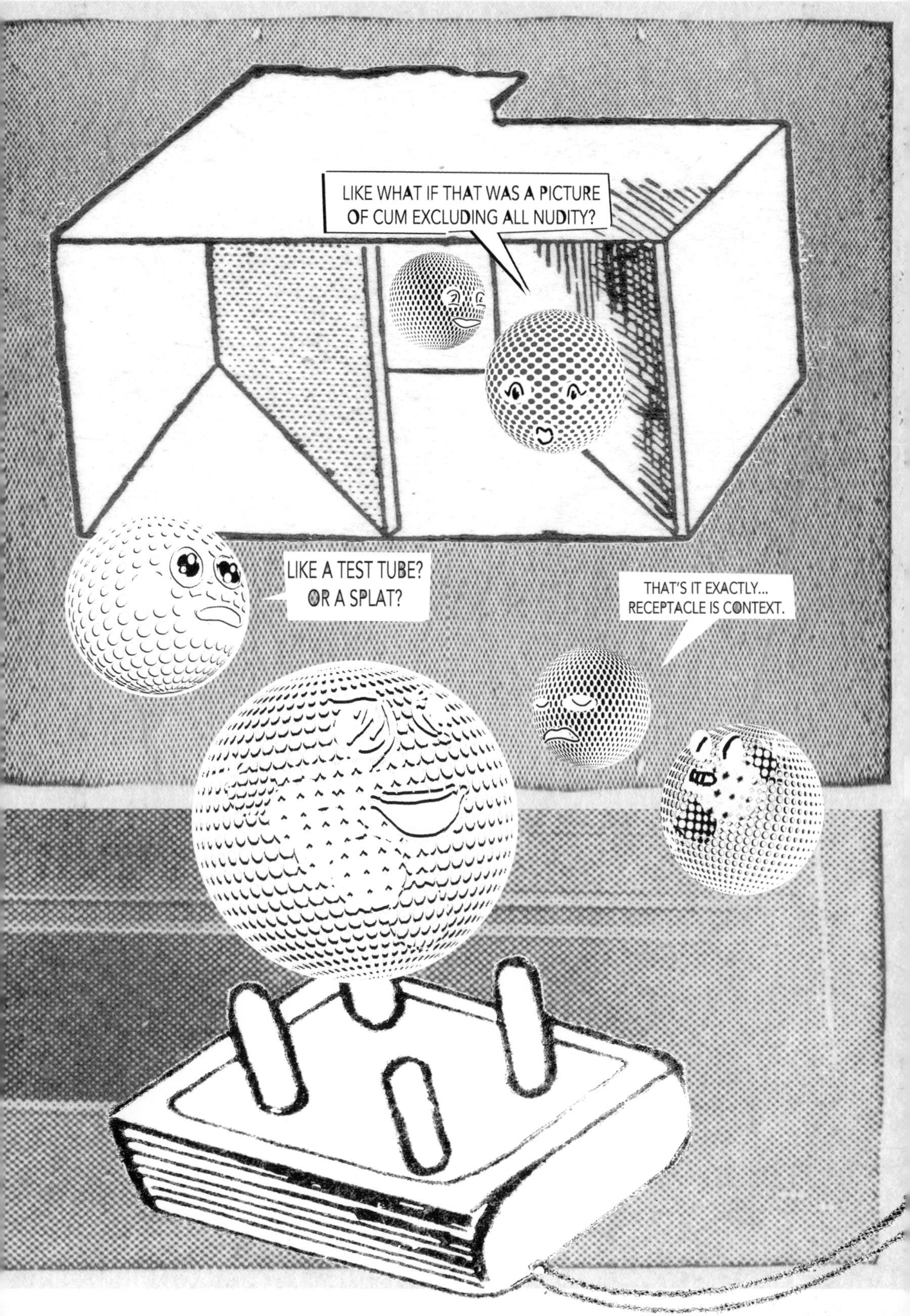
LIKE WHAT IF THAT WAS A PICTURE OF CUM EXCLUDING ALL NUDITY?
LIKE A TEST TUBE? OR A SPLAT?
THAT'S IT EXACTLY... RECEPTACLE IS CONTEXT.

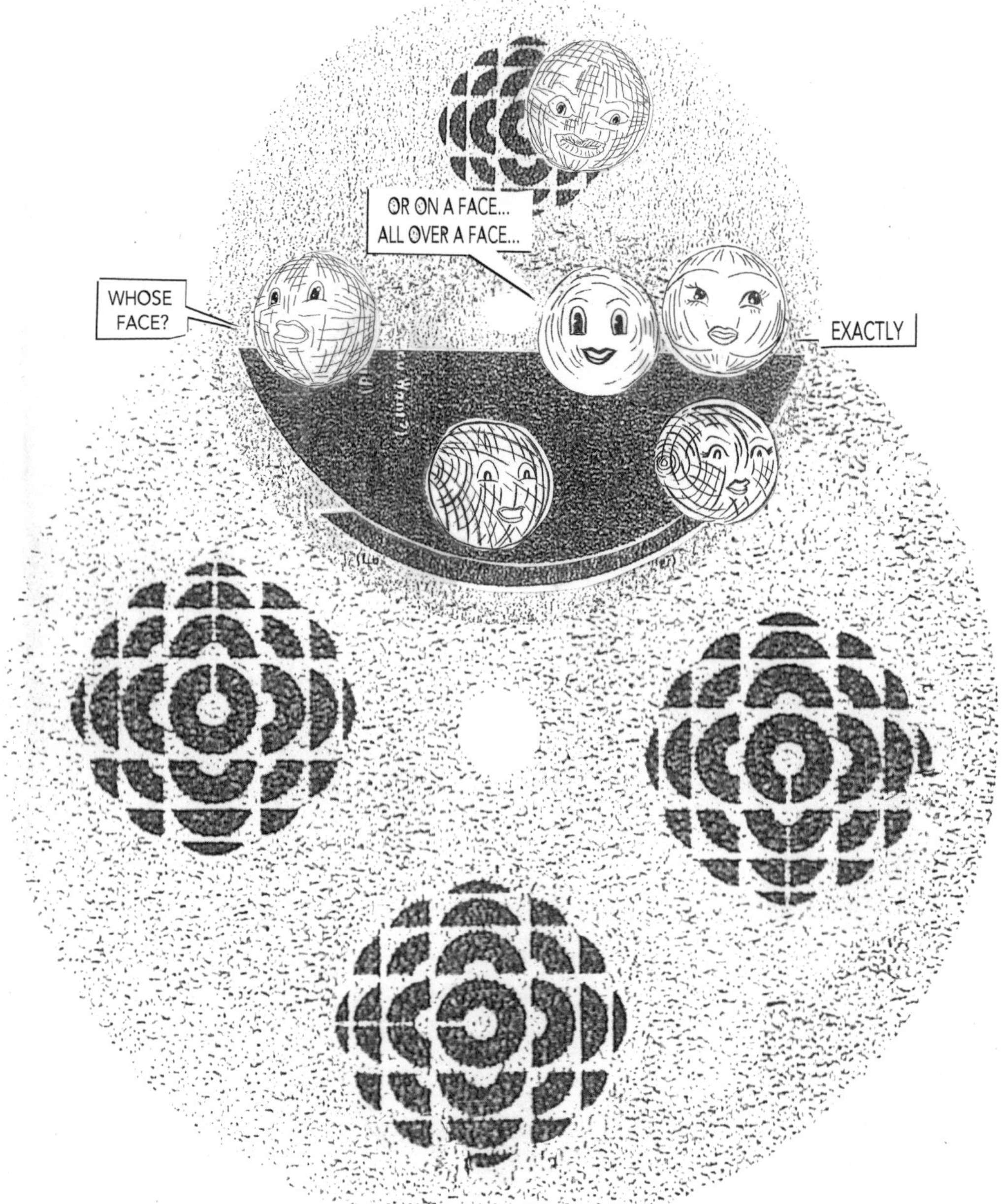
OR ON A FACE...
ALL OVER A FACE...
WHOSE FACE?
EXACTLY

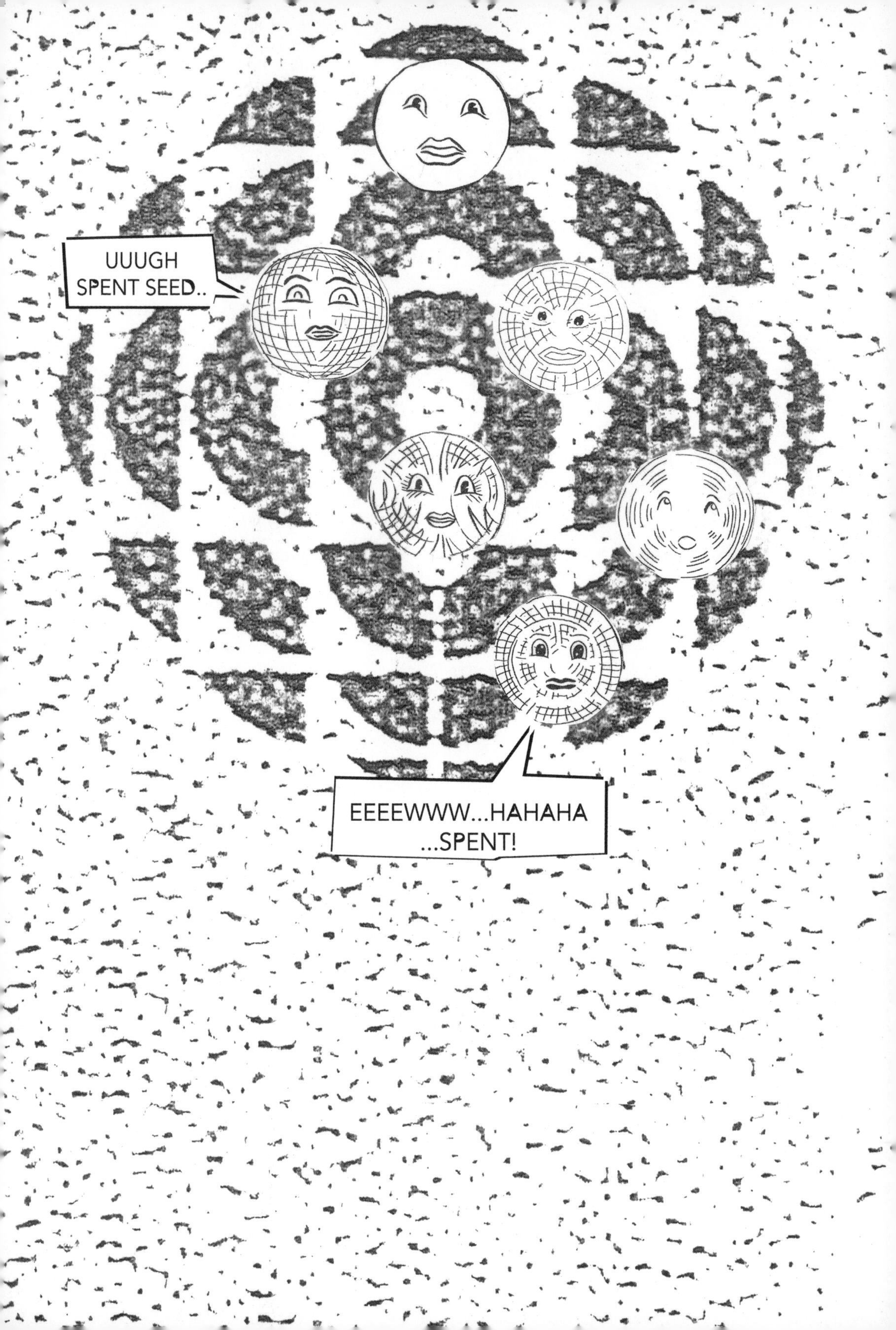
UUUGH SPENT SEED..
EEEEWWW...HAHAHA ...SPENT!

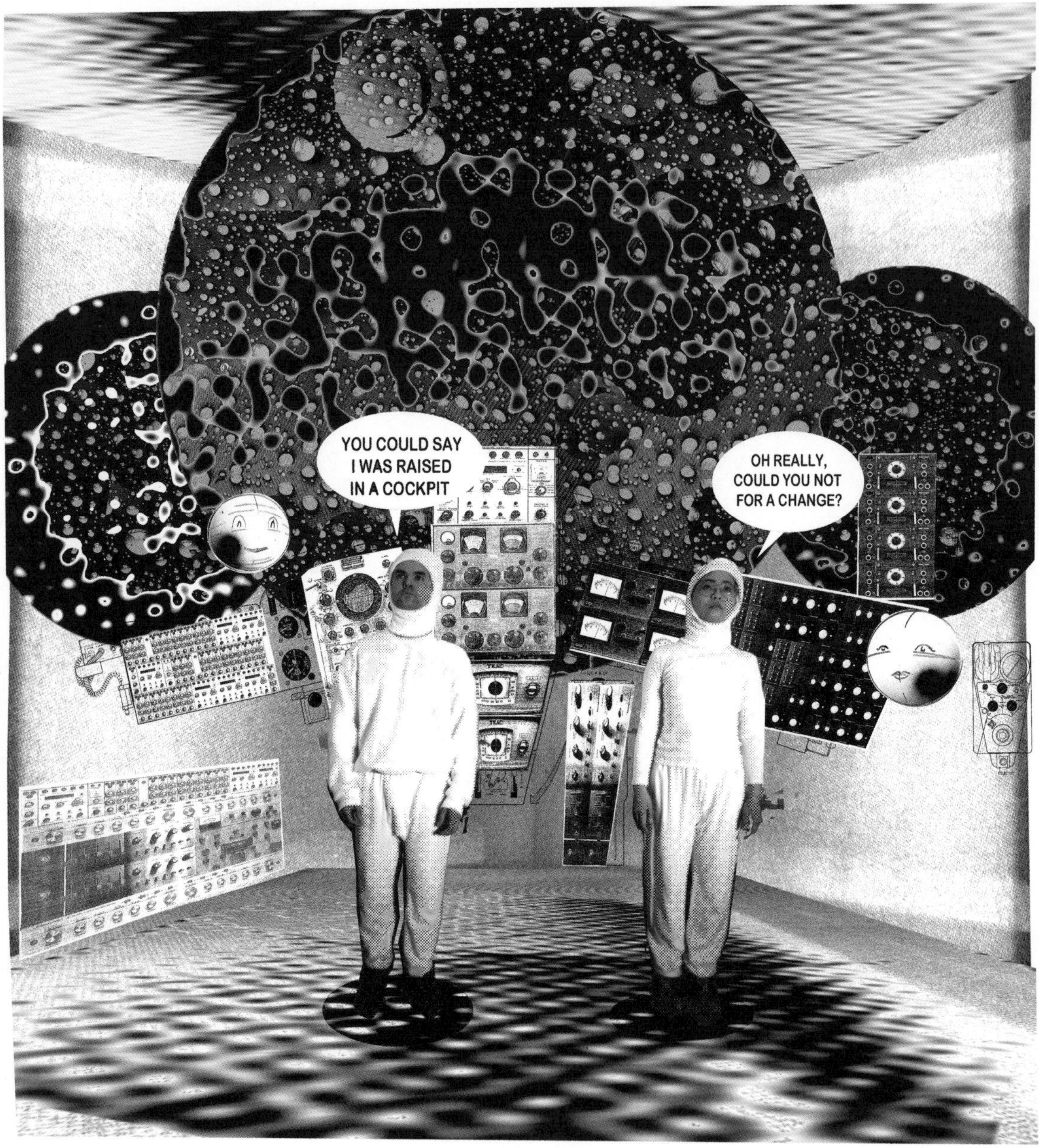
YOU COULD SAY I WAS RAISED IN A COCKPIT
OH REALLY, COULD YOU NOT FOR A CHANGE?

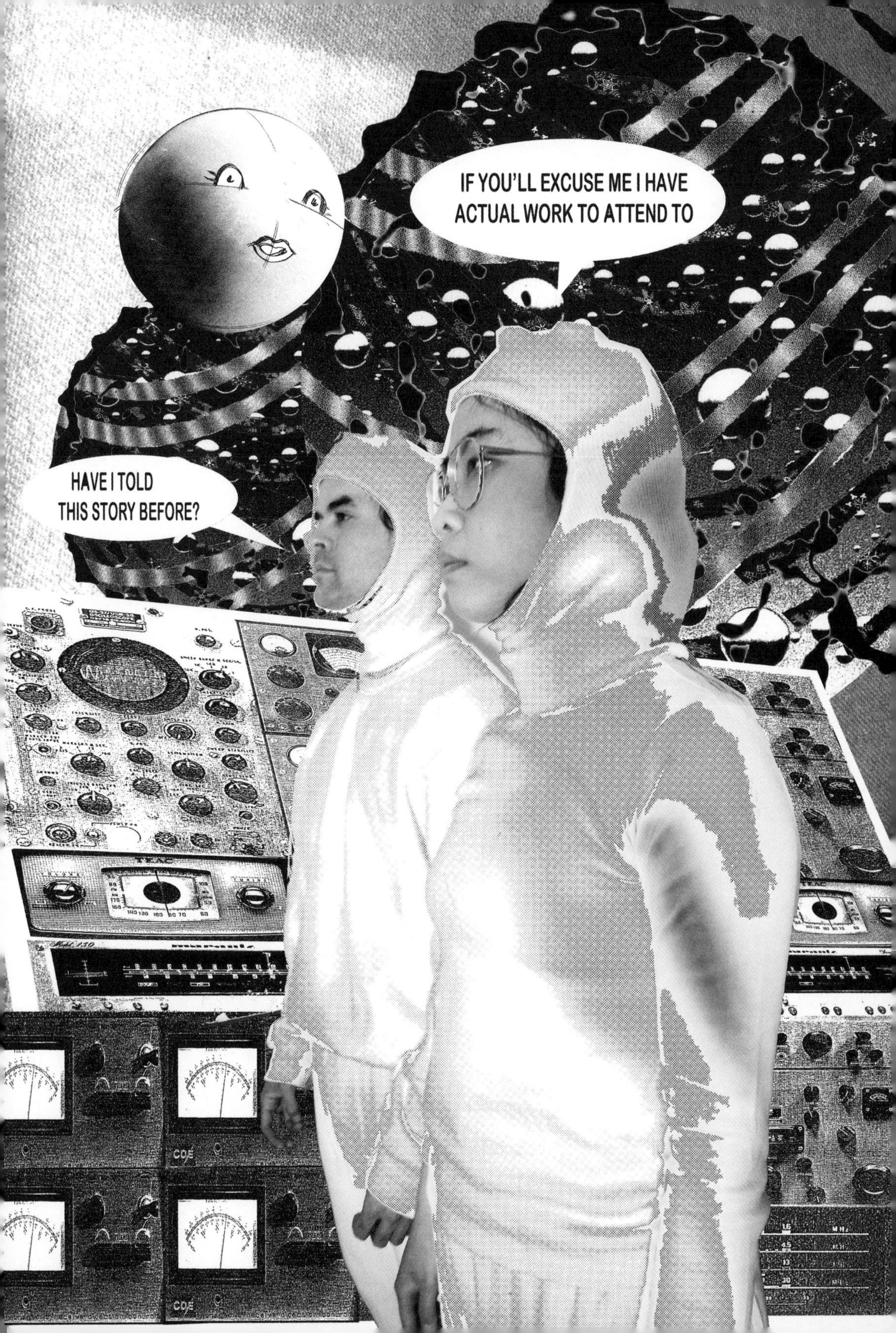
IF YOU'LL EXCUSE ME I HAVE ACTUAL WORK TO ATTEND TO
HAVE I TOLD THIS STORY BEFORE?

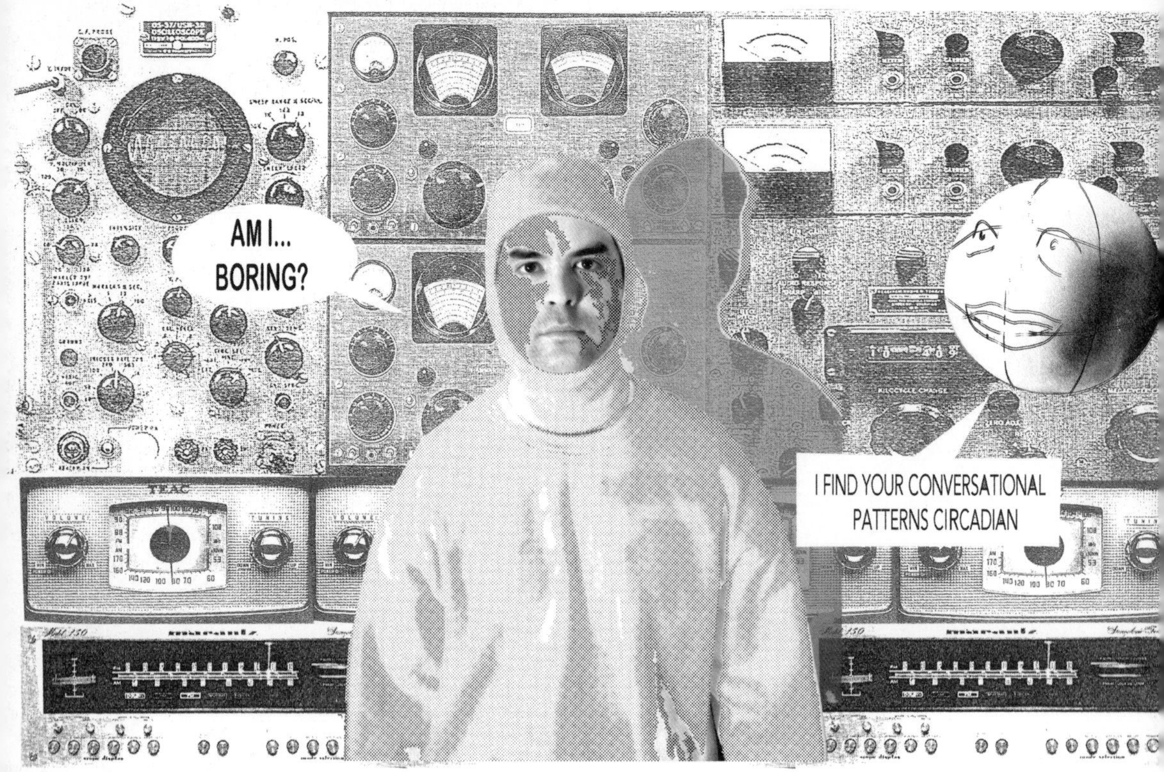
AM I...
BORING?
I FIND YOUR CONVERSATIONAL PATTERNS CIRCADIAN

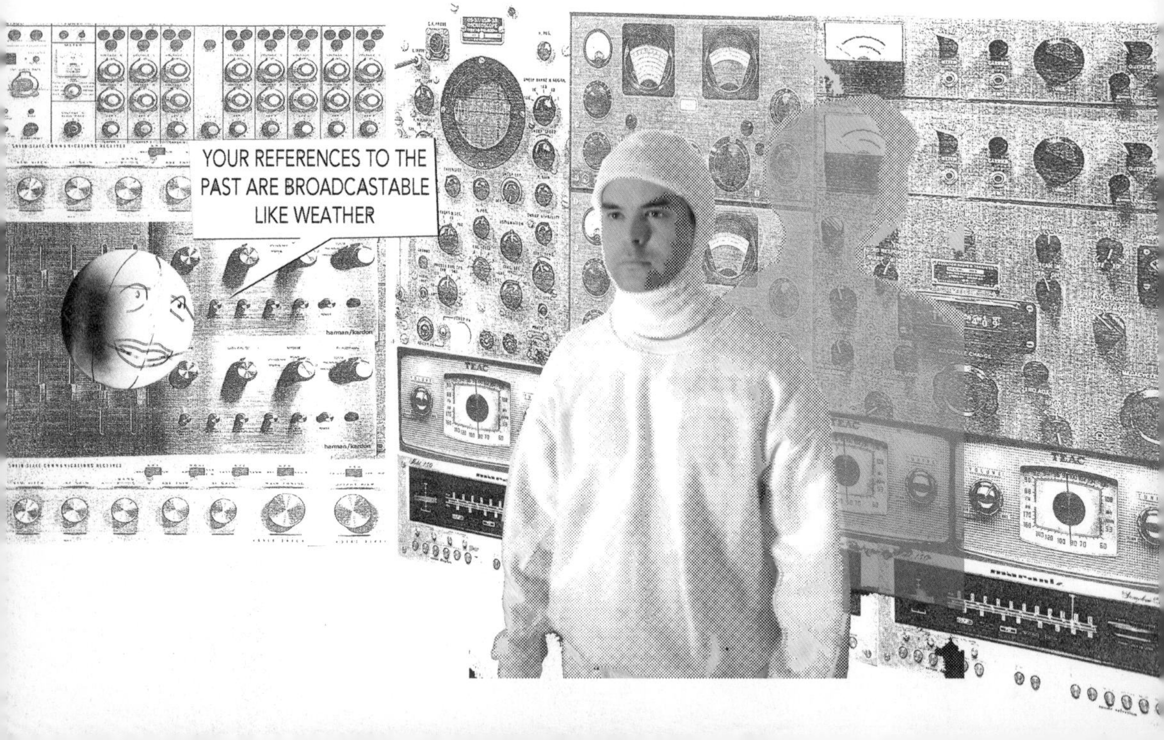
YOUR REFERENCES TO THE PAST ARE BROADCASTABLE LIKE WEATHER

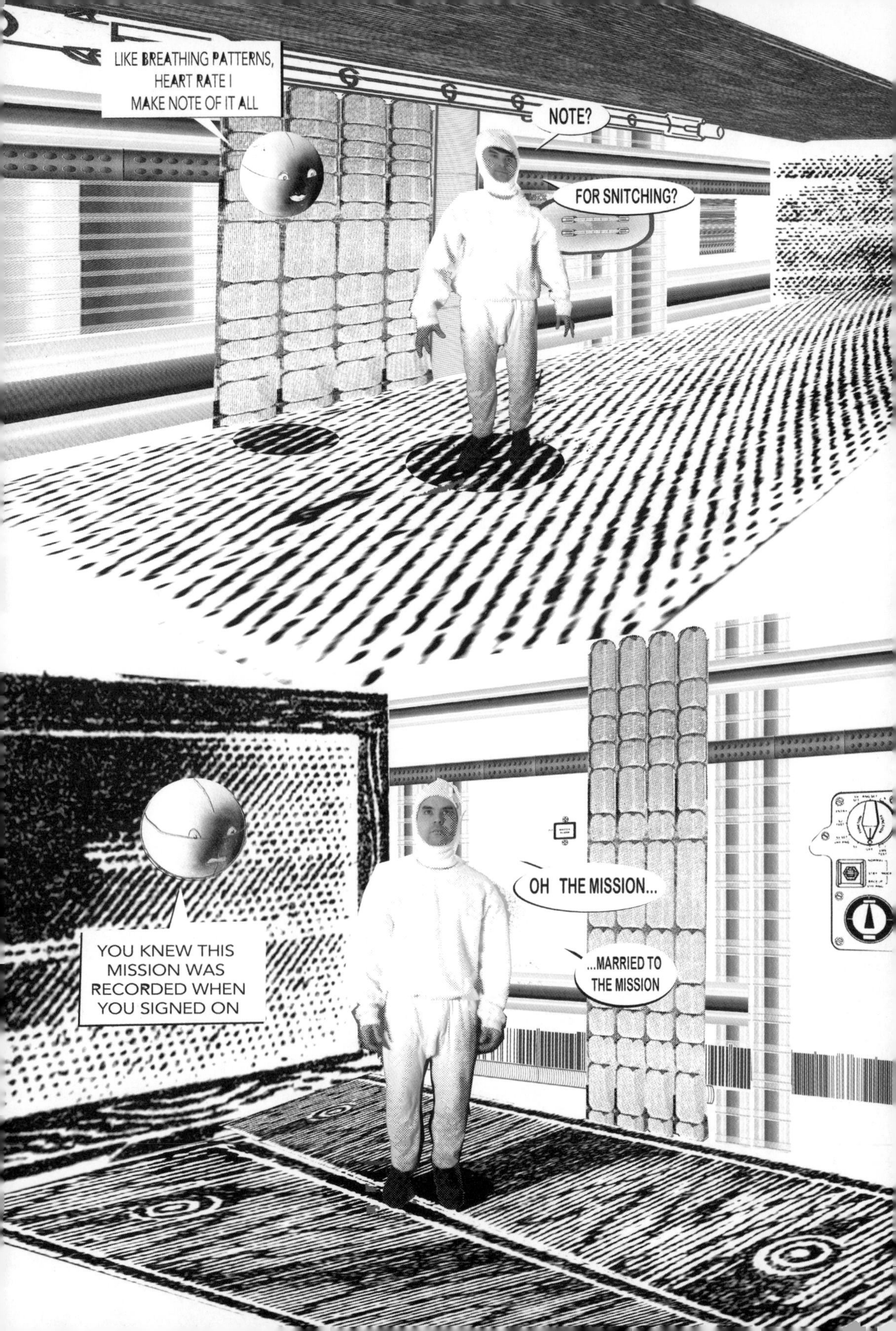
LIKE BREATHING PATTERNS, HEART RATE I MAKE NOTE OF IT ALL
NOTE?
FOR SNITCHING?
YOU KNEW THIS MISSION WAS RECORDED WHEN YOU SIGNED ON
OH THE MISSION...
...MARRIED TO THE MISSION

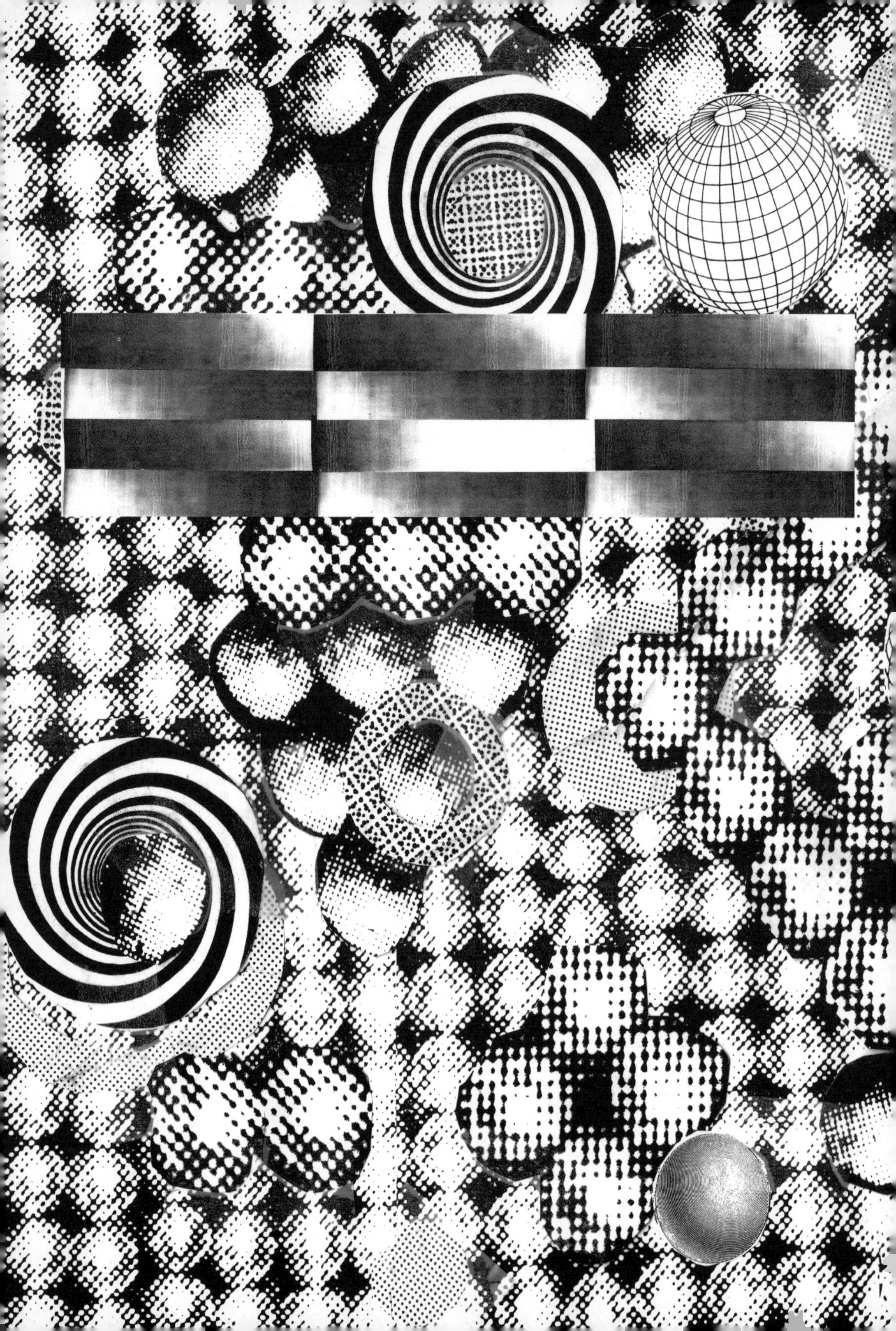

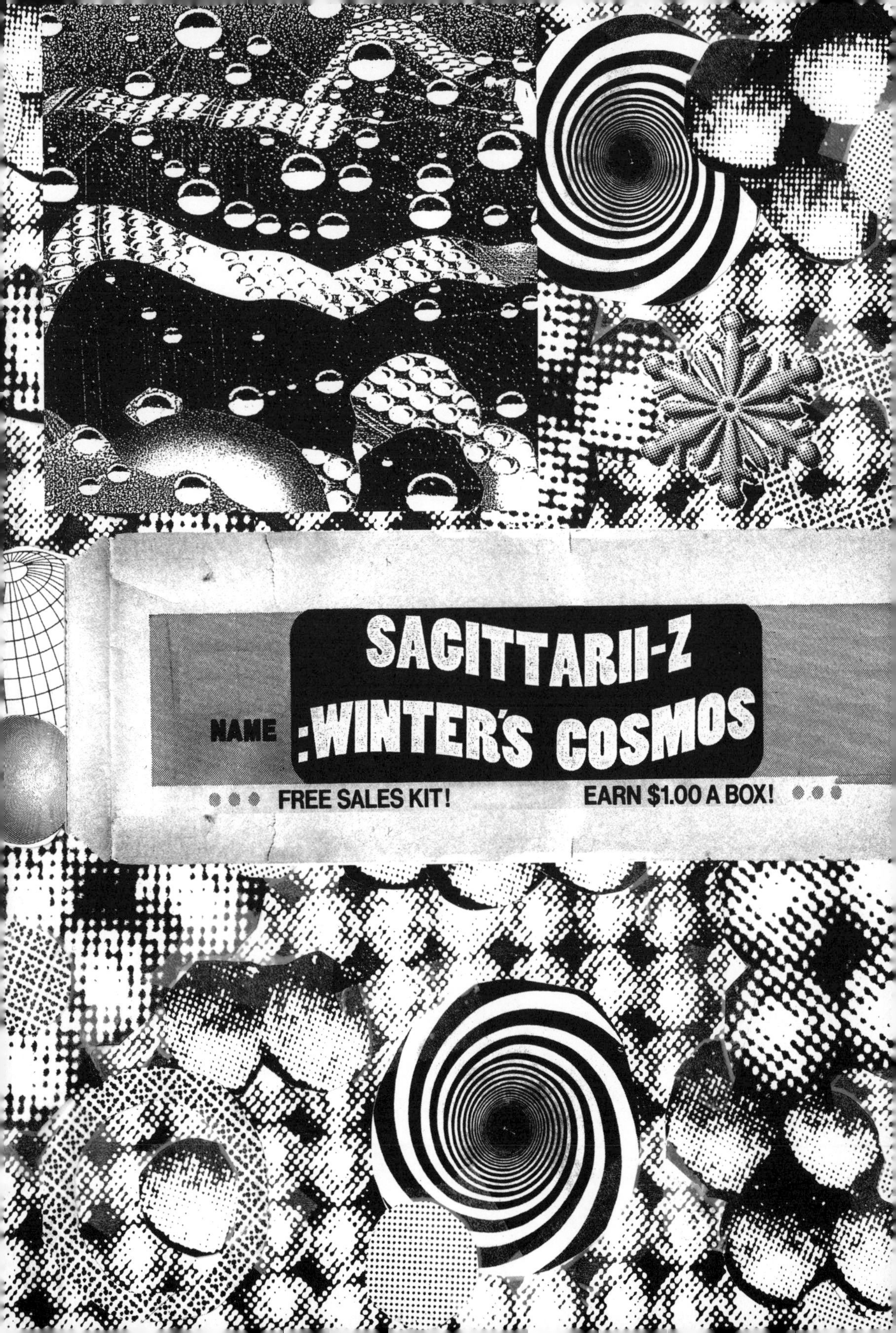
SAGITTARII-Z
NAME :WINTER'S COSMOS
FREE SALES KIT!
EARN $1.00 A BOX!

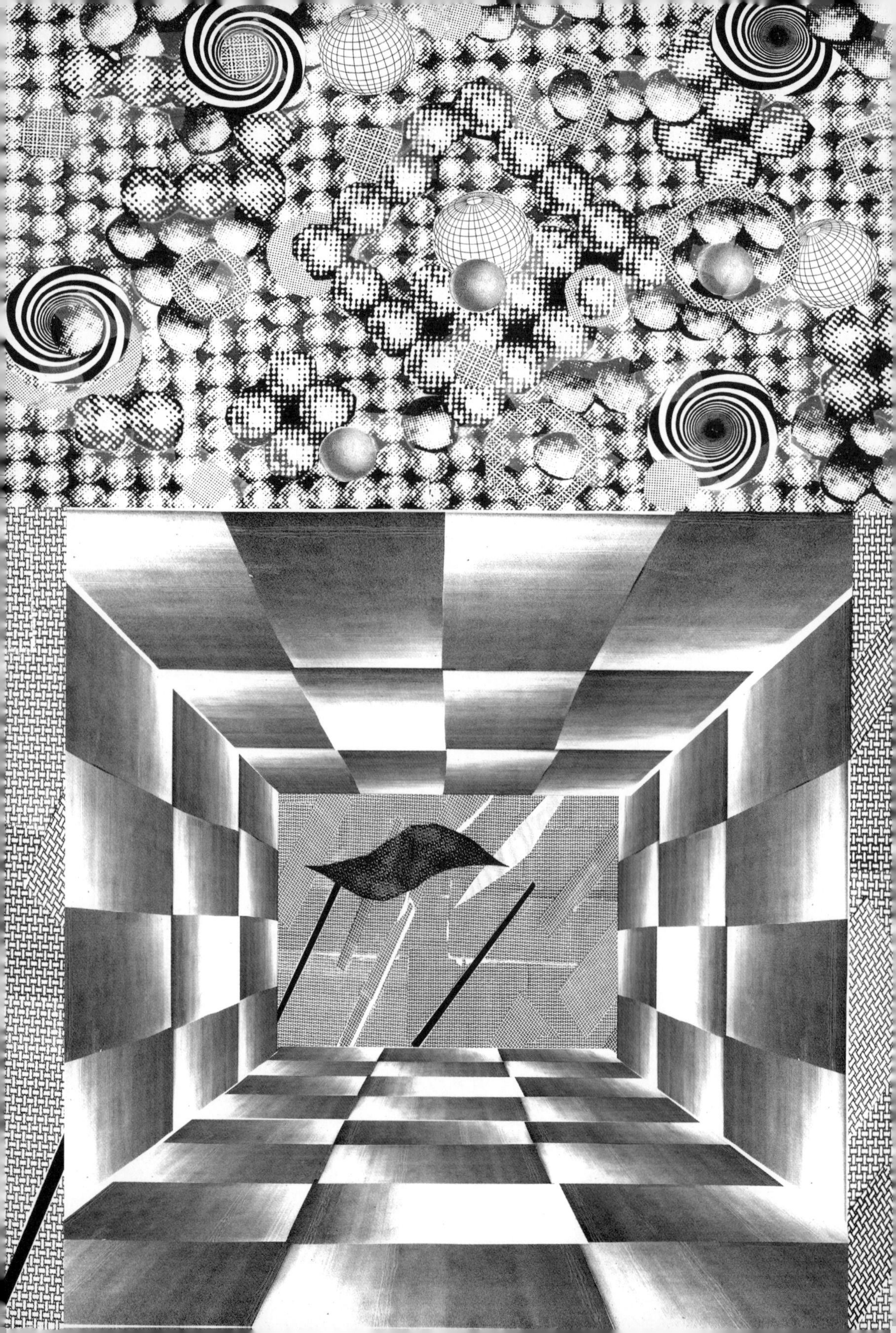

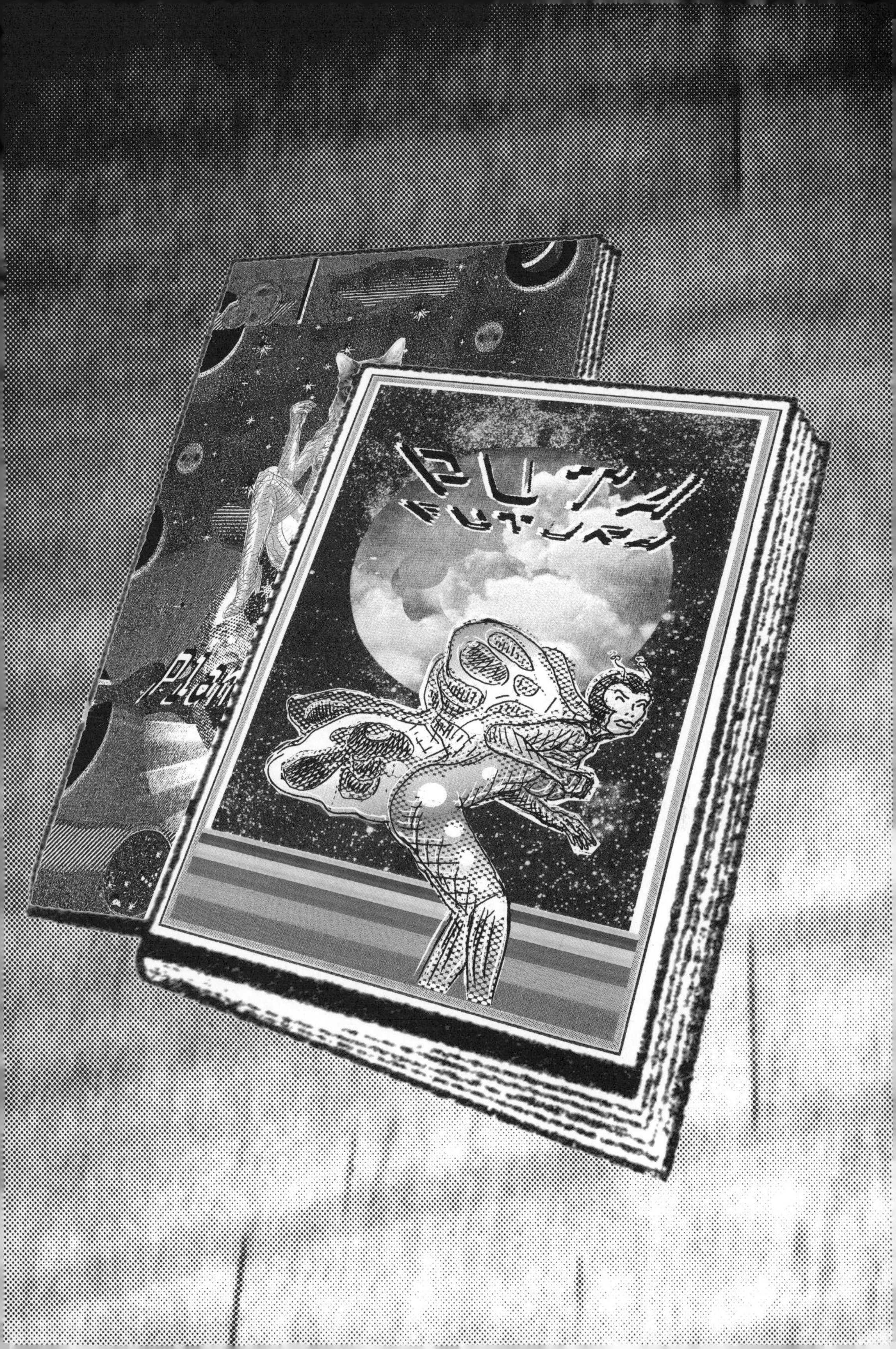
PUTA
FUTURA

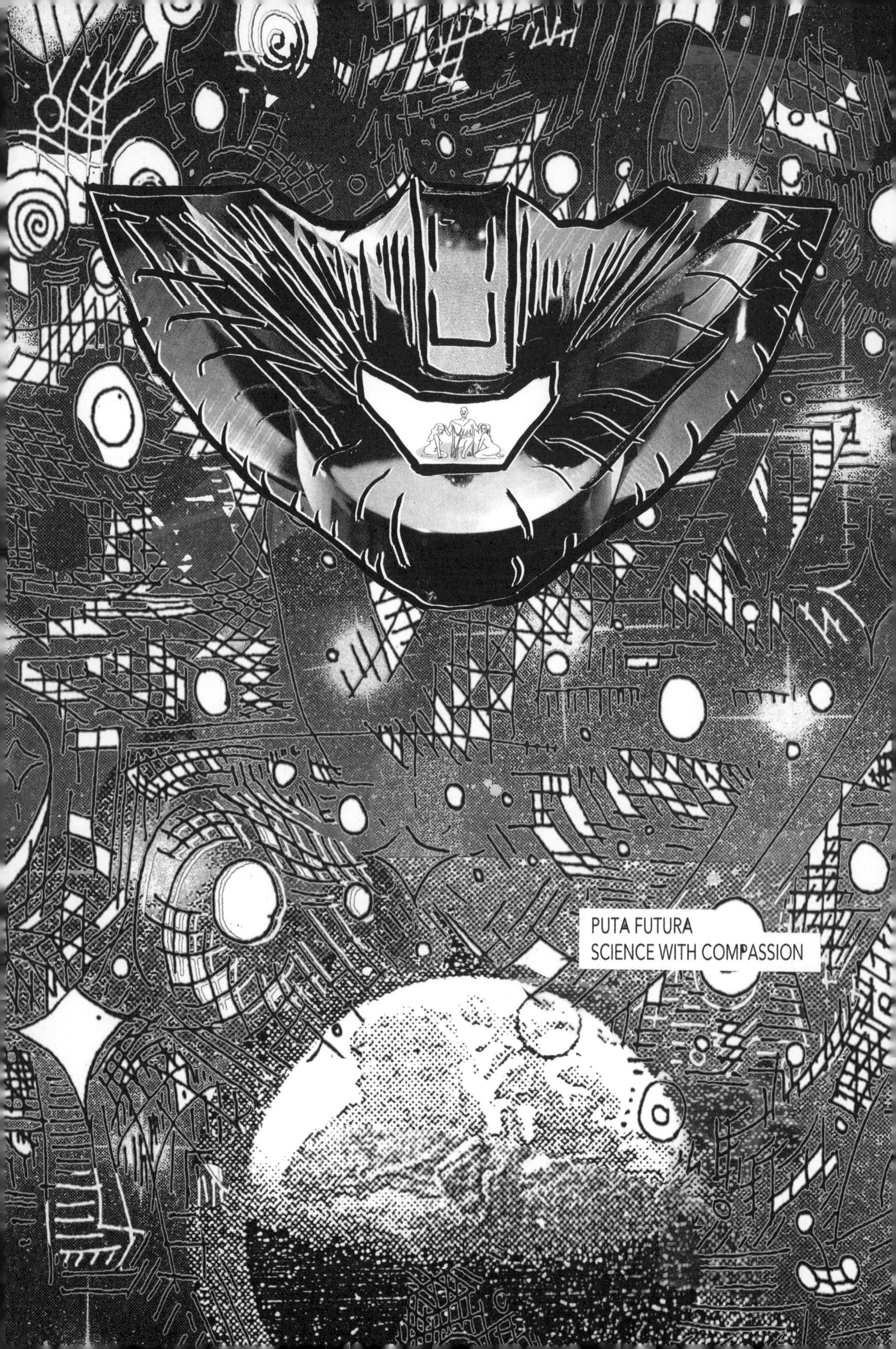
PUTA FUTURA
SCIENCE WITH COMPASSION

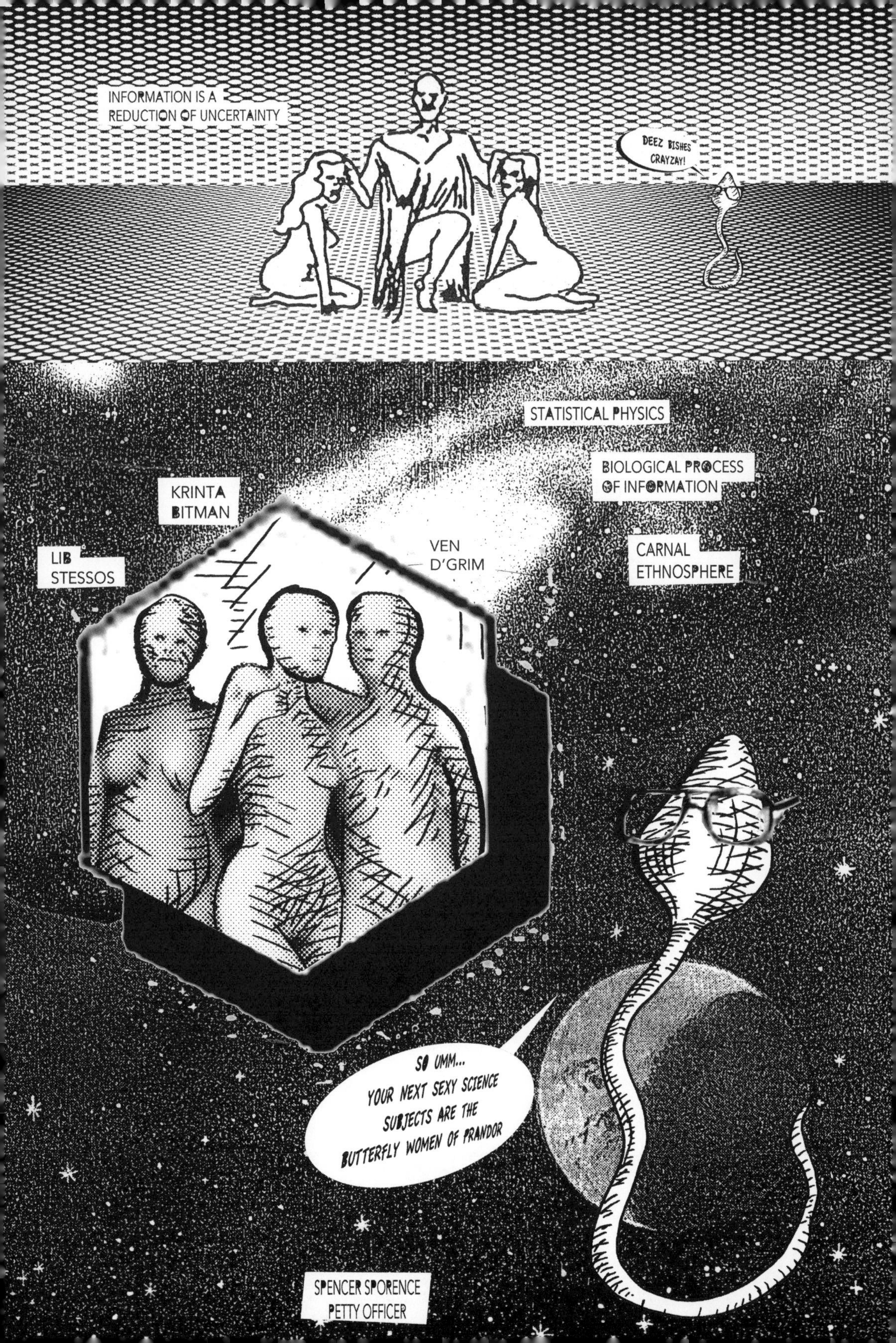

INFORMATION IS A REDUCTION OF UNCERTAINTY
DEEZ BISHES CRAYZAY!
STATISTICAL PHYSICS
BIOLOGICAL PROCESS OF INFORMATION
KRINTA BITMAN
LIB STESSOS
VEN D'GRIM
CARNAL ETHNOSPHERE
SO UMM... YOUR NEXT SEXY SCIENCE SUBJECTS ARE THE BUTTERFLY WOMEN OF PRANDOR
SPENCER SPORENCE PETTY OFFICER

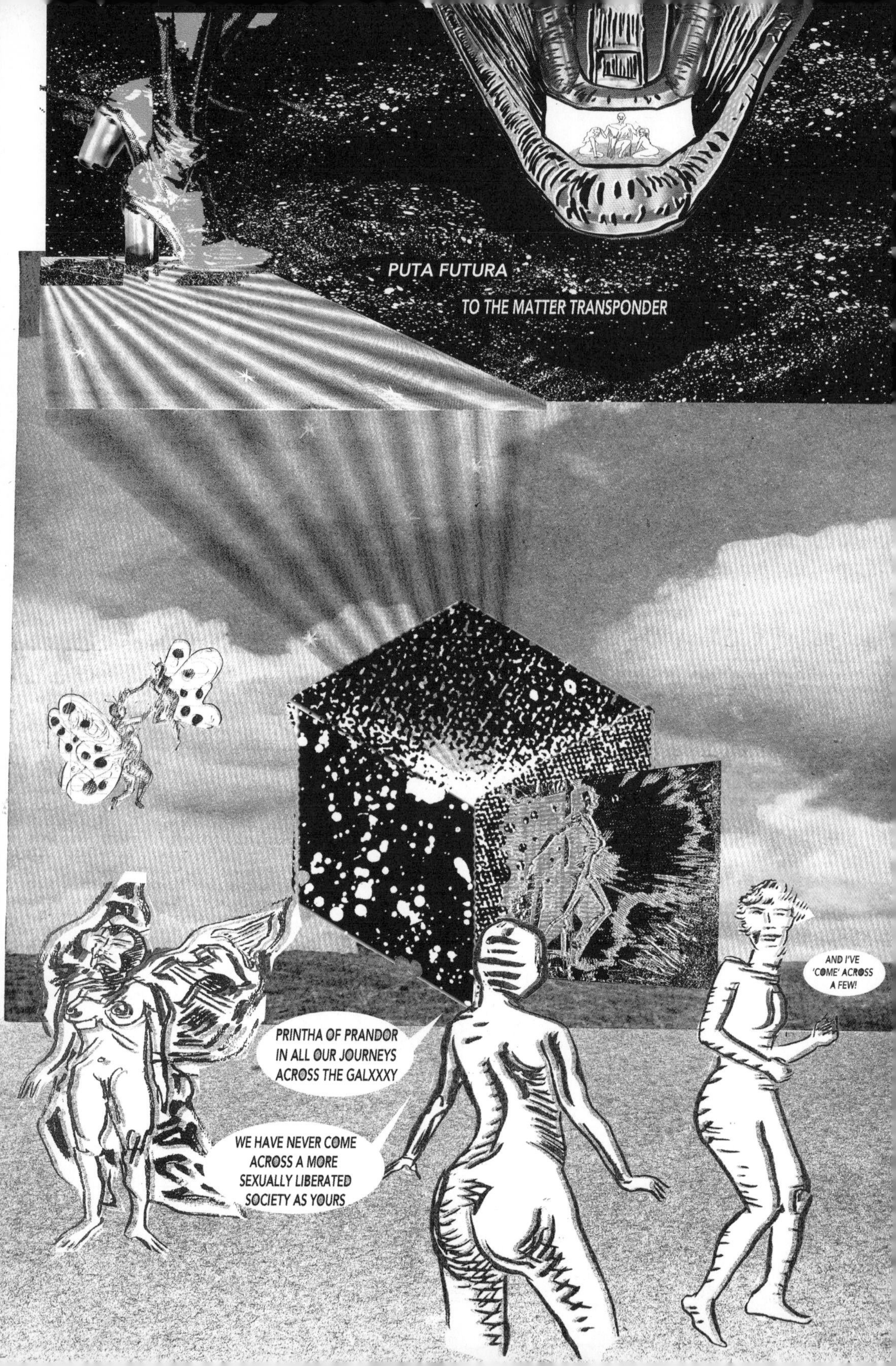
PUTA FUTURA
TO THE MATTER TRANSPONDER
PRINTHA OF PRANDOR IN ALL OUR JOURNEYS ACROSS THE GALXXXY
WE HAVE NEVER COME ACROSS A MORE SEXUALLY LIBERATED SOCIETY AS YOURS
AND I'VE 'COME' ACROSS A FEW!

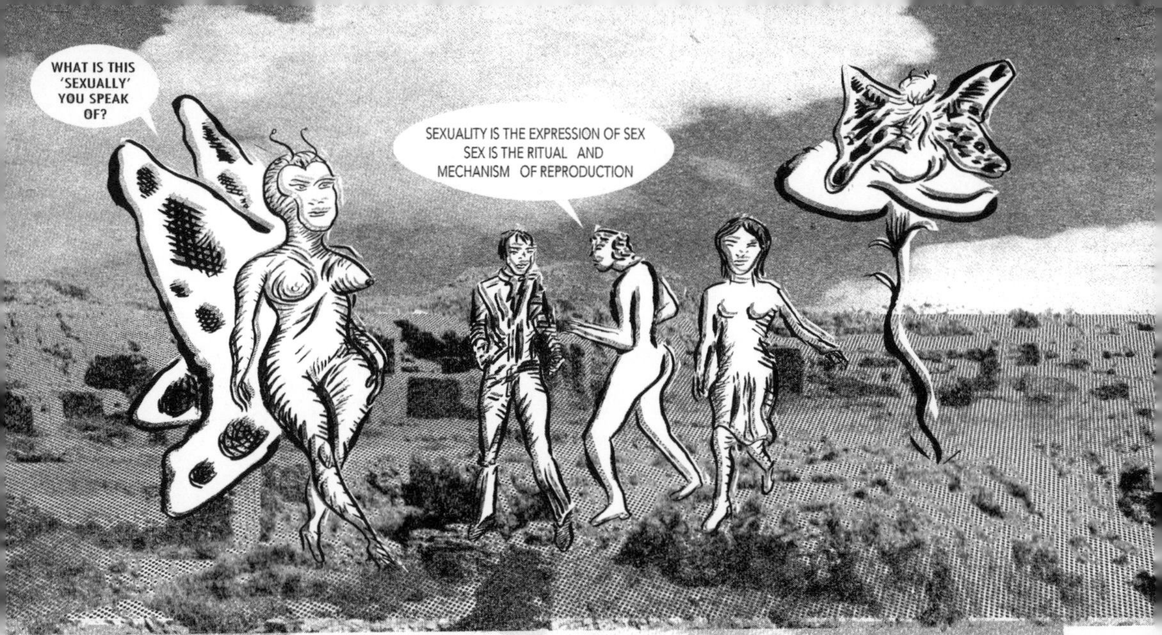
WHAT IS THIS 'SEXUALLY' YOU SPEAK OF?
SEXUALITY IS THE EXPRESSION OF SEX SEX IS THE RITUAL AND MECHANISM OF REPRODUCTION

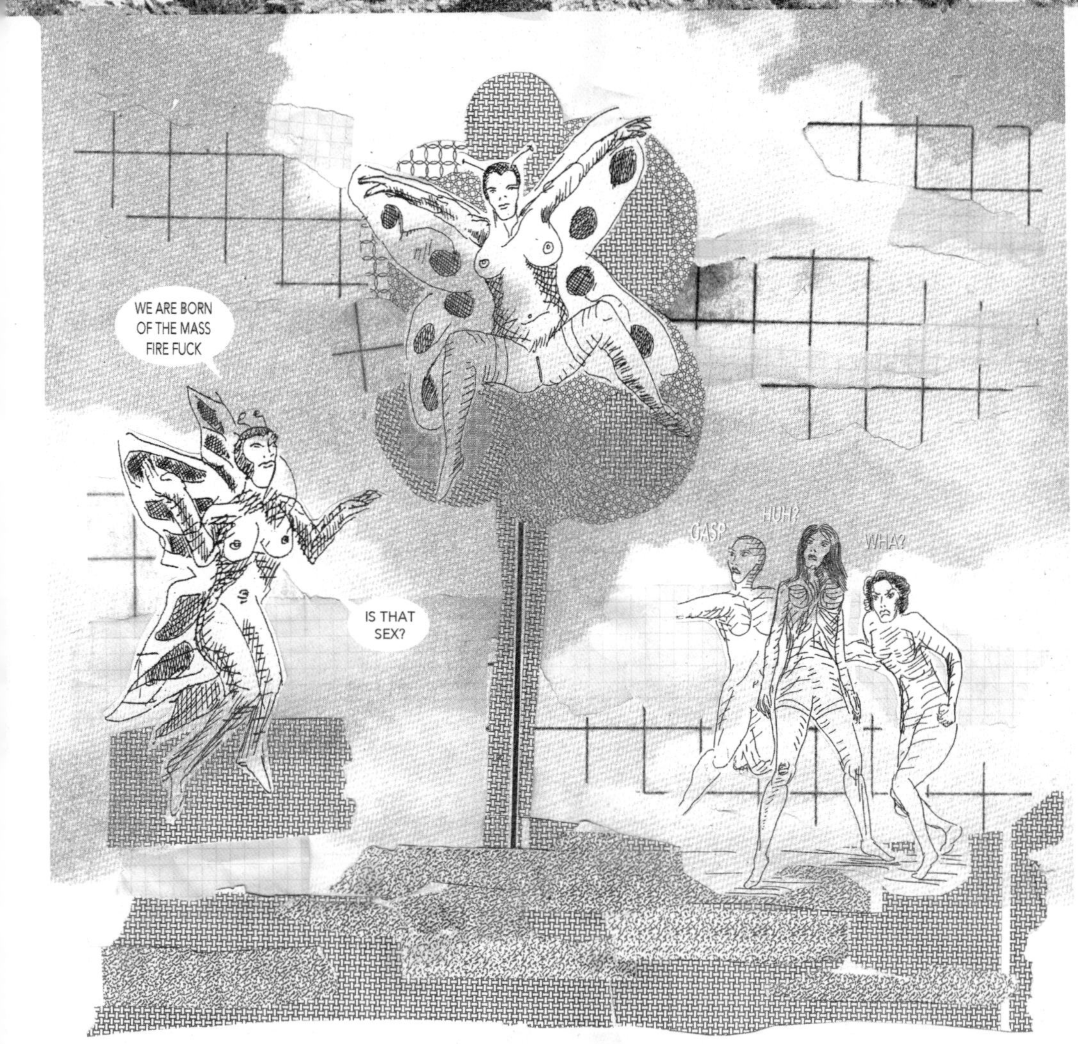
WE ARE BORN OF THE MASS FIRE FUCK
IS THAT SEX?
GASP
HUH?
WHA?

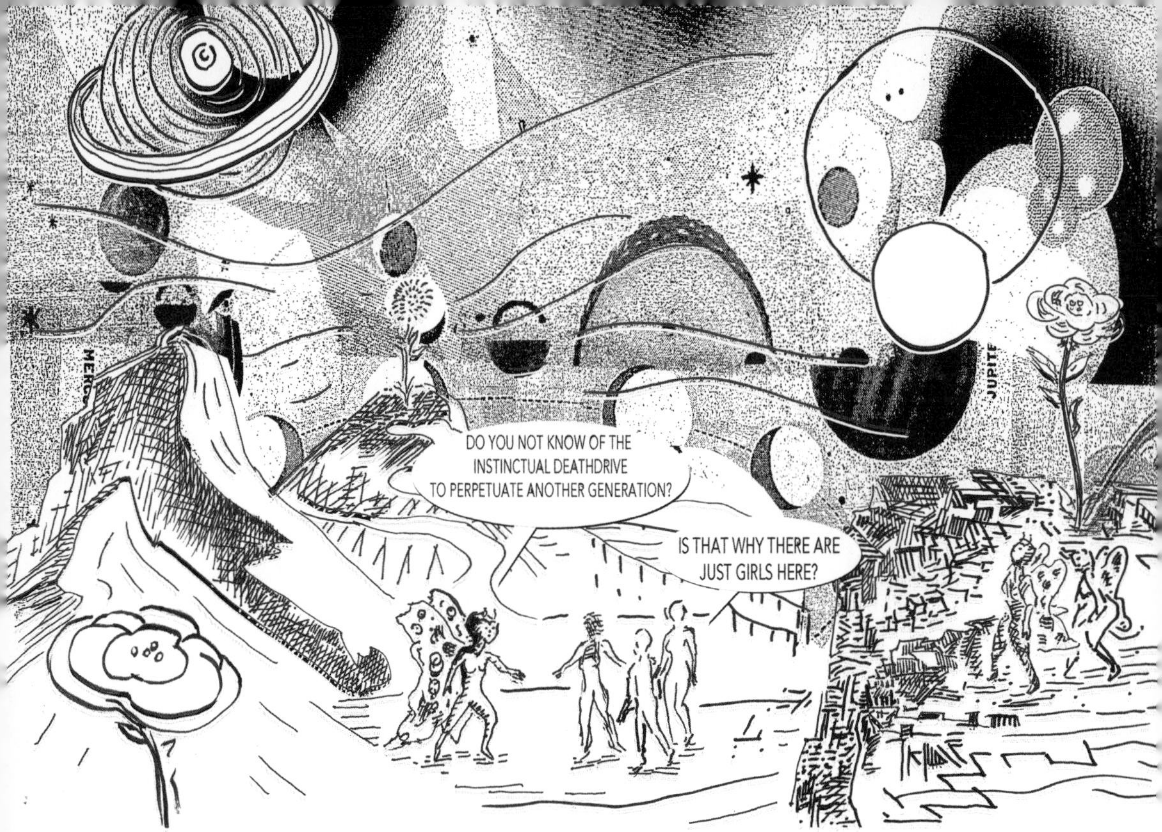
DO YOU NOT KNOW OF THE INSTINCTUAL DEATHDRIVE TO PERPETUATE ANOTHER GENERATION?
IS THAT WHY THERE ARE JUST GIRLS HERE?

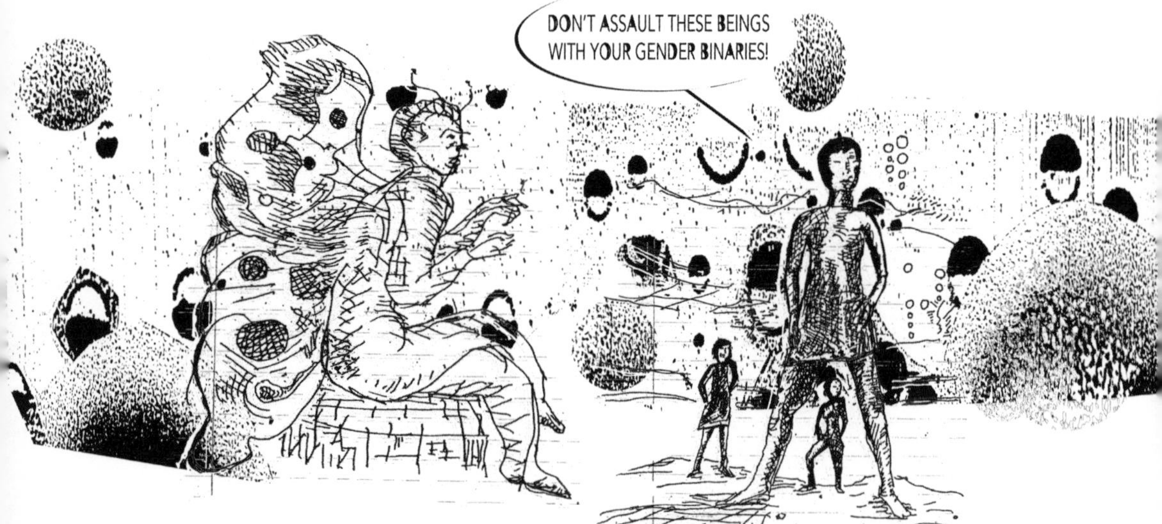
DON'T ASSAULT THESE BEINGS WITH YOUR GENDER BINARIES!

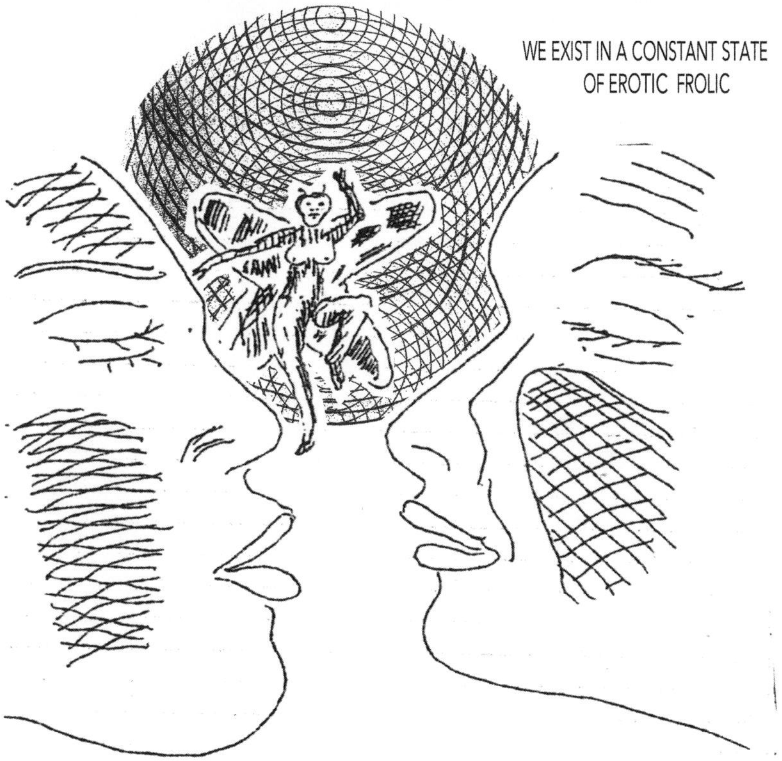
WE EXIST IN A CONSTANT STATE
OF EROTIC FROLIC

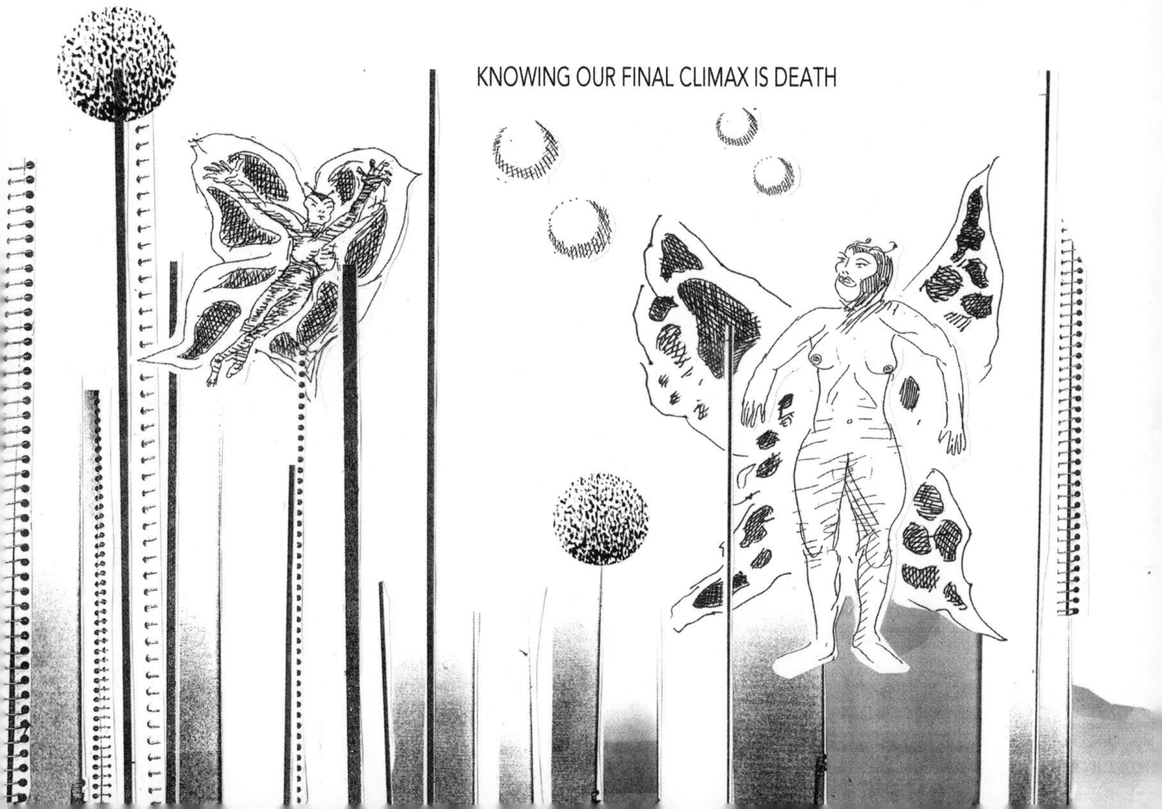
KNOWING OUR FINAL CLIMAX IS DEATH

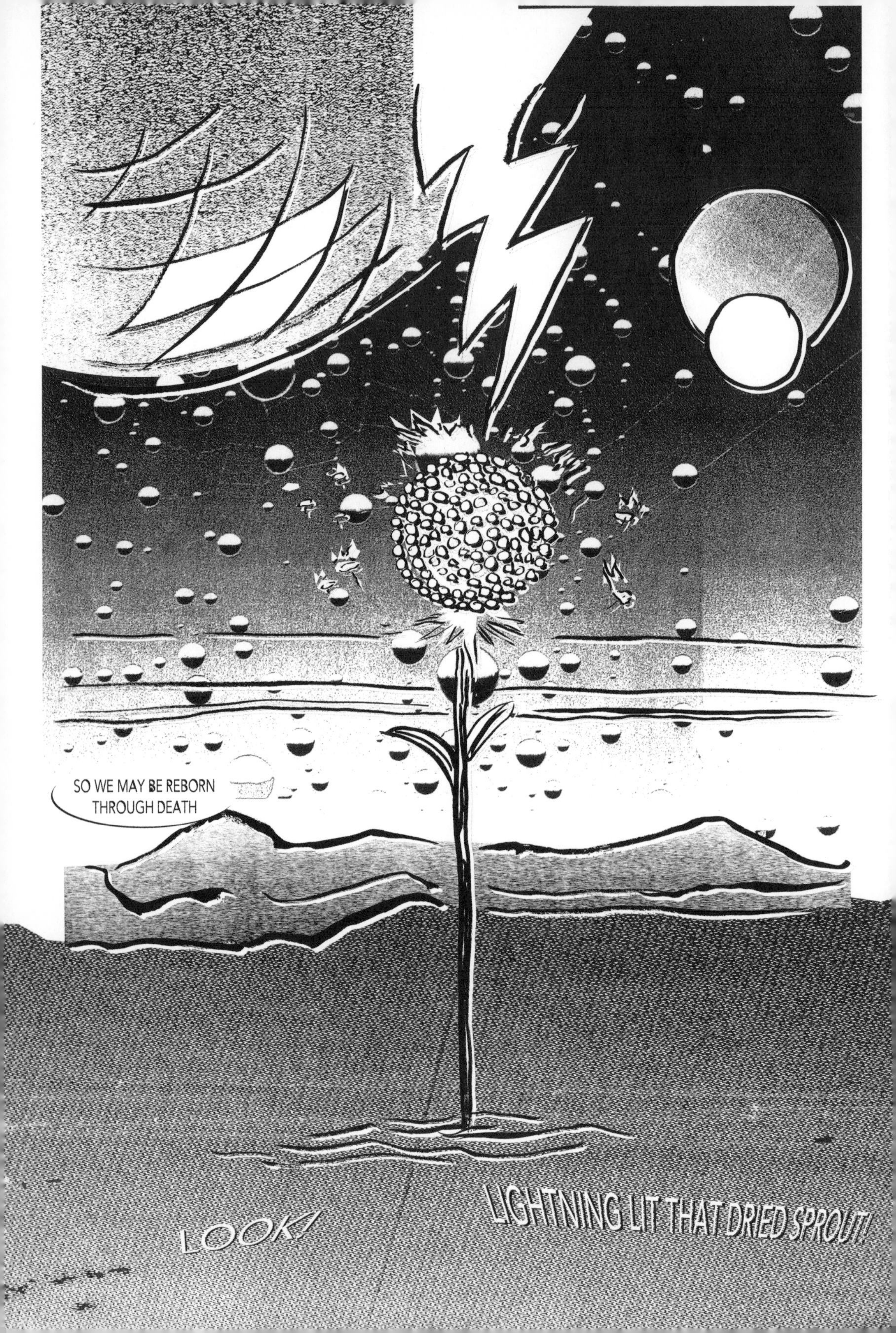
SO WE MAY BE REBORN THROUGH DEATH
LOOK!
LIGHTNING LIT THAT DRIED SPROUT!

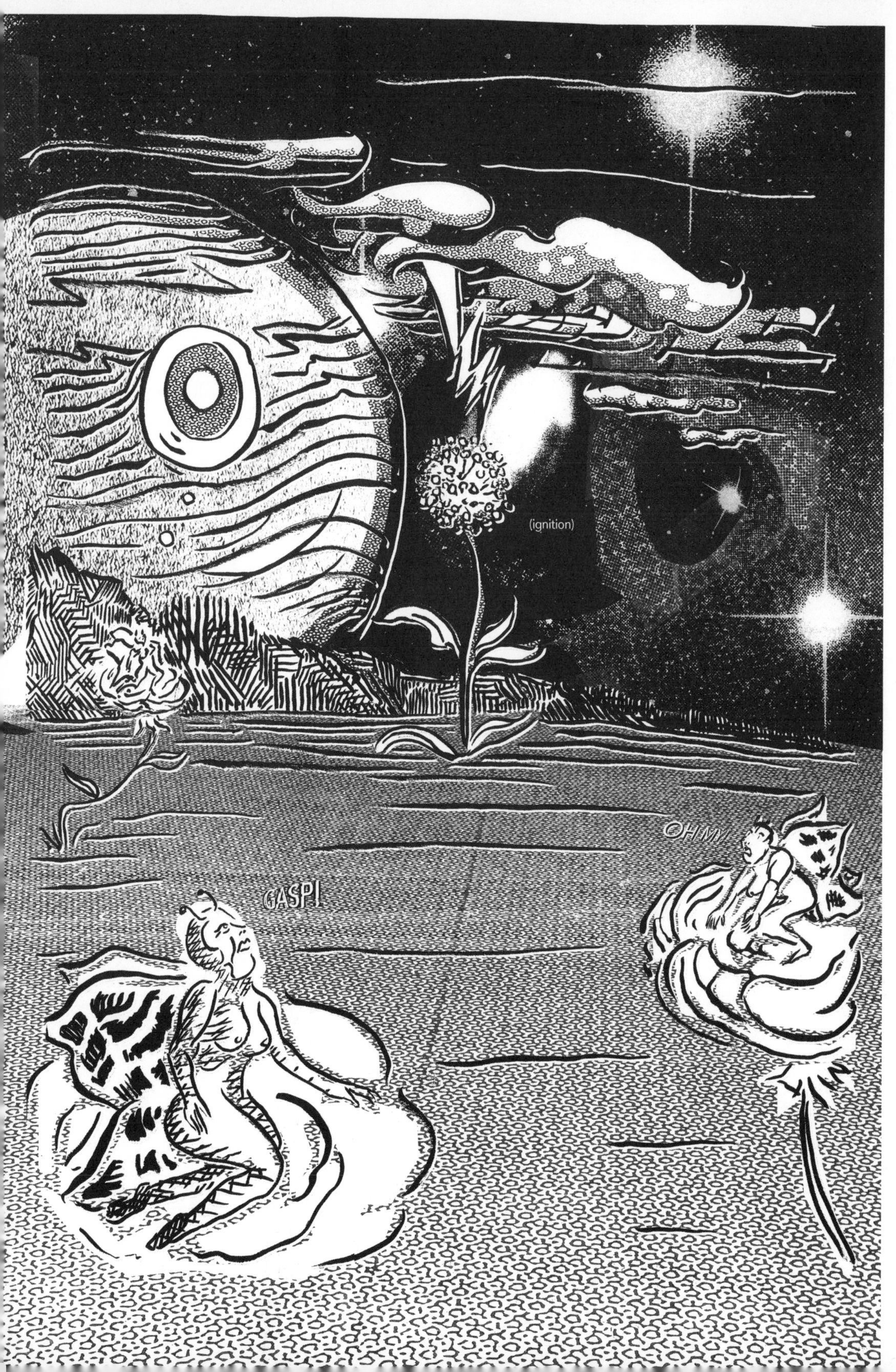
(ignition)
GASP!
OH MY!

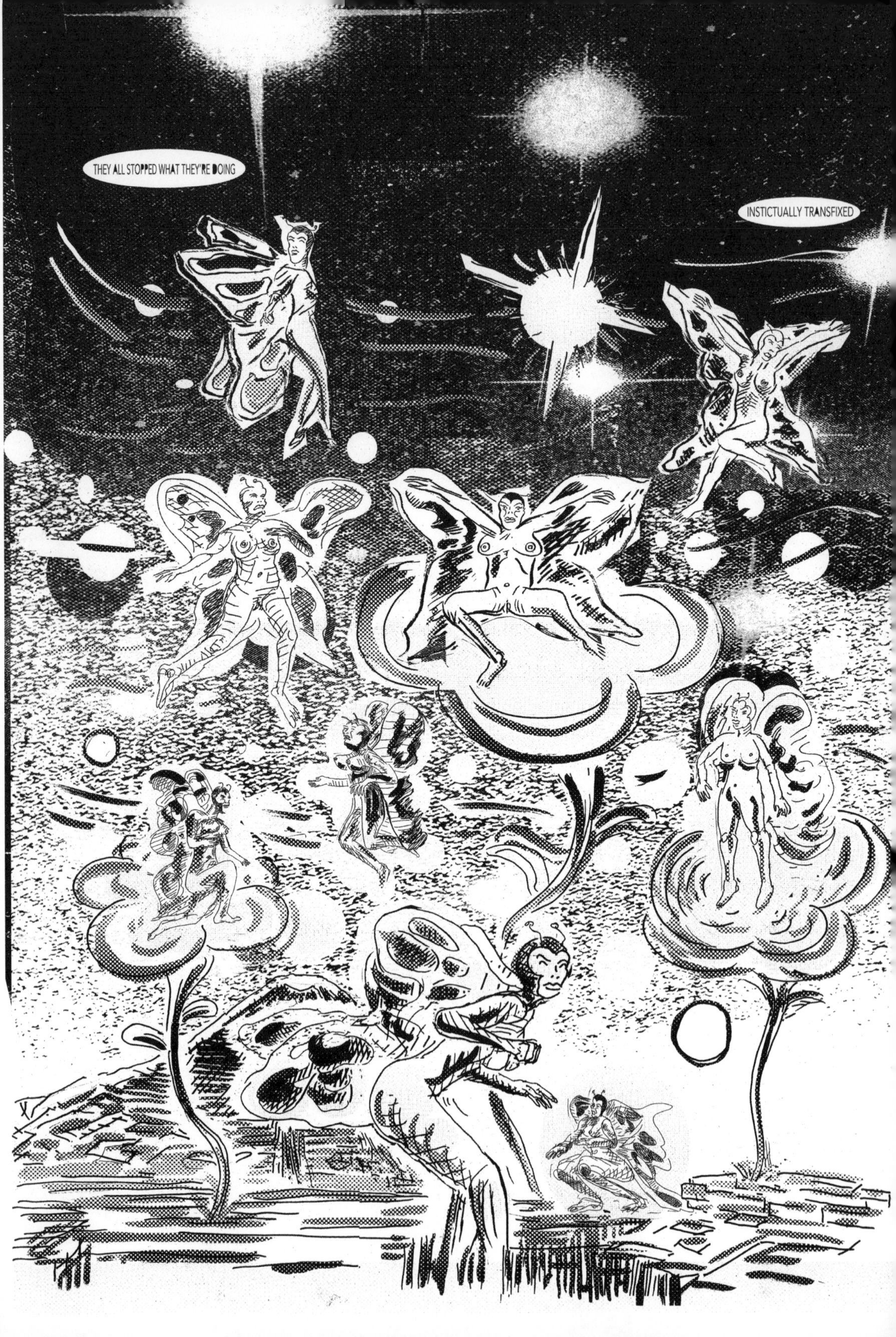
THEY ALL STOPPED WHAT THEY'RE DOING
INSTICTUALLY TRANSFIXED

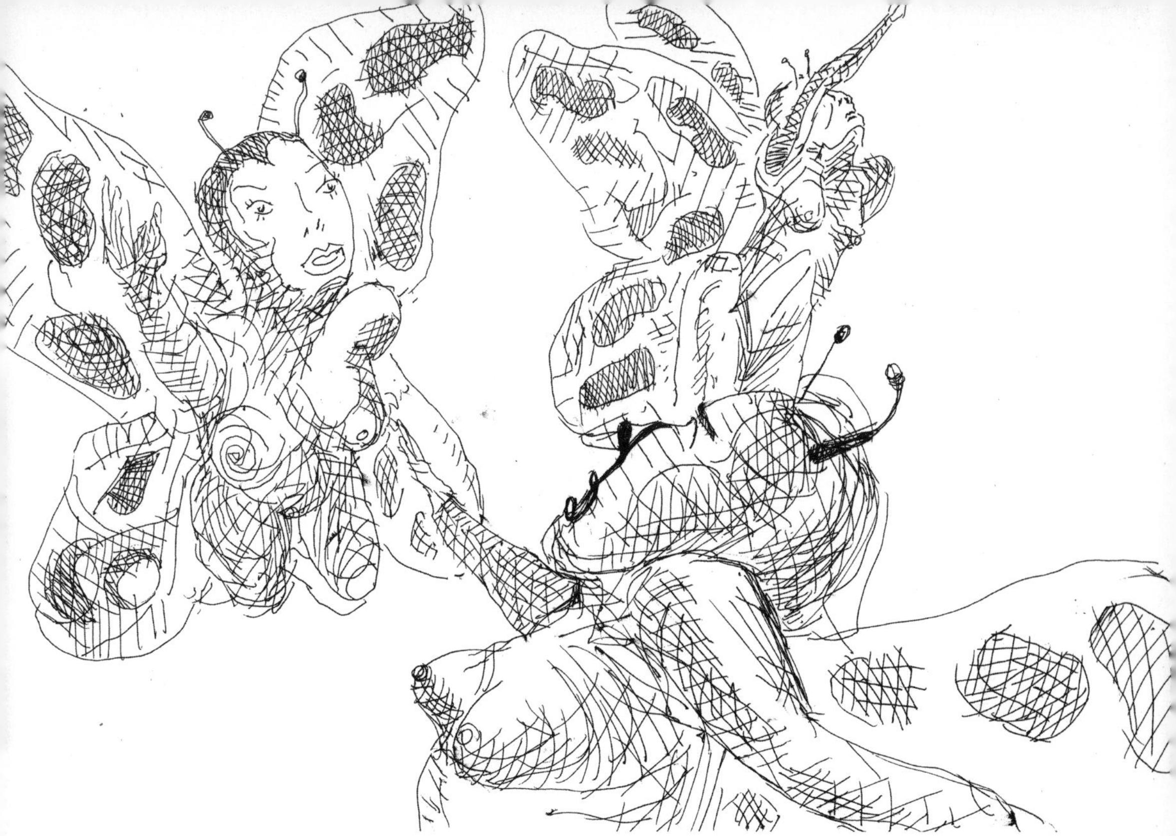

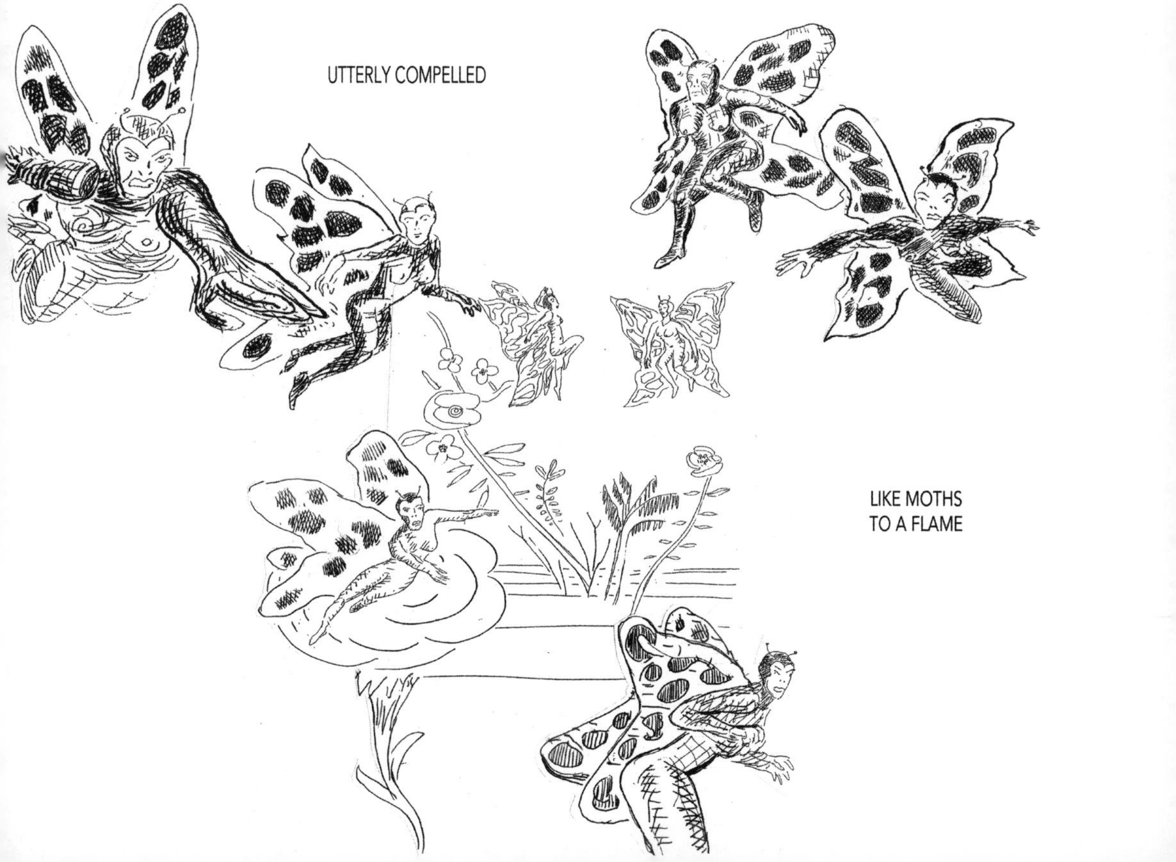
UTTERLY COMPELLED
LIKE MOTHS TO A FLAME

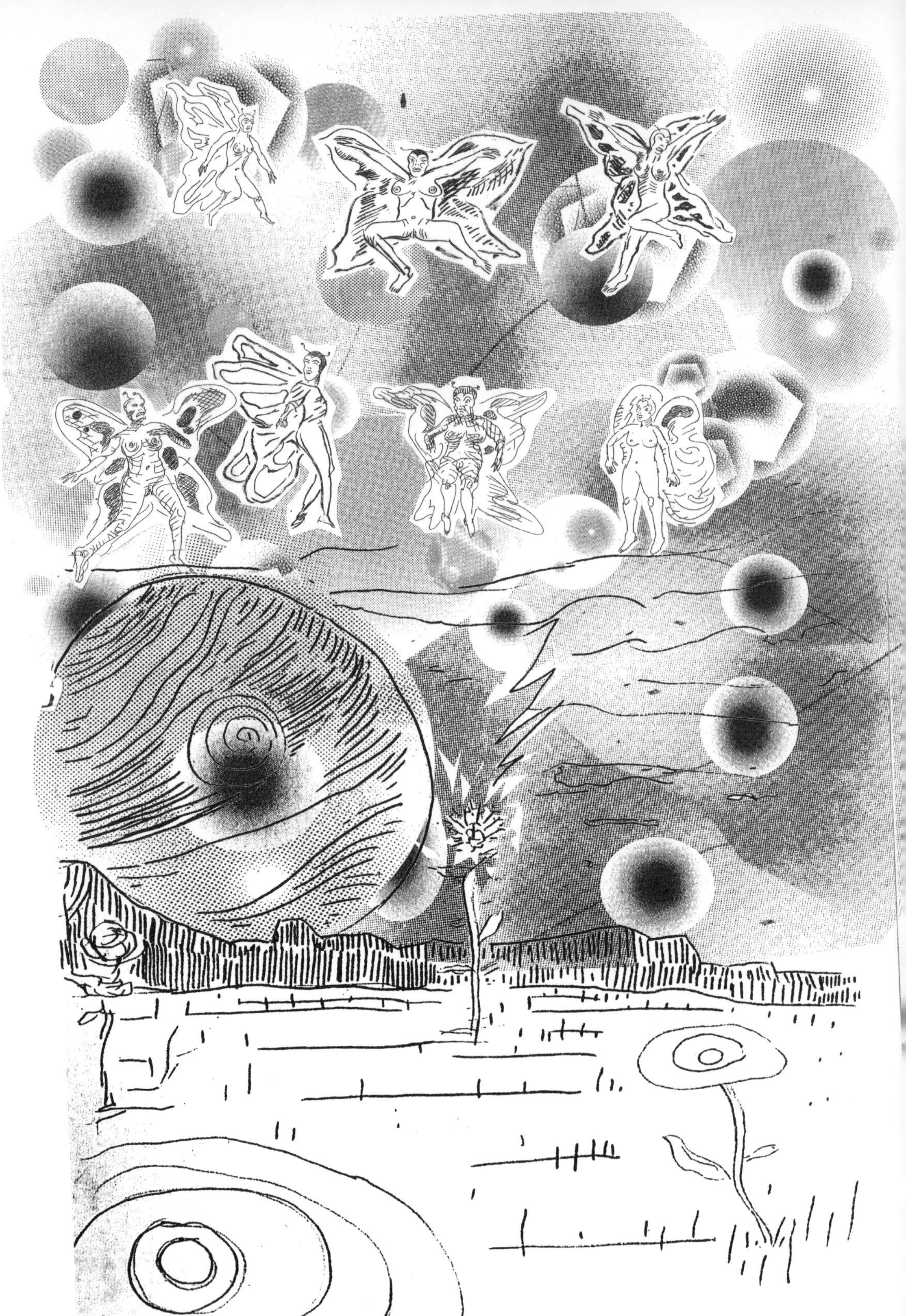

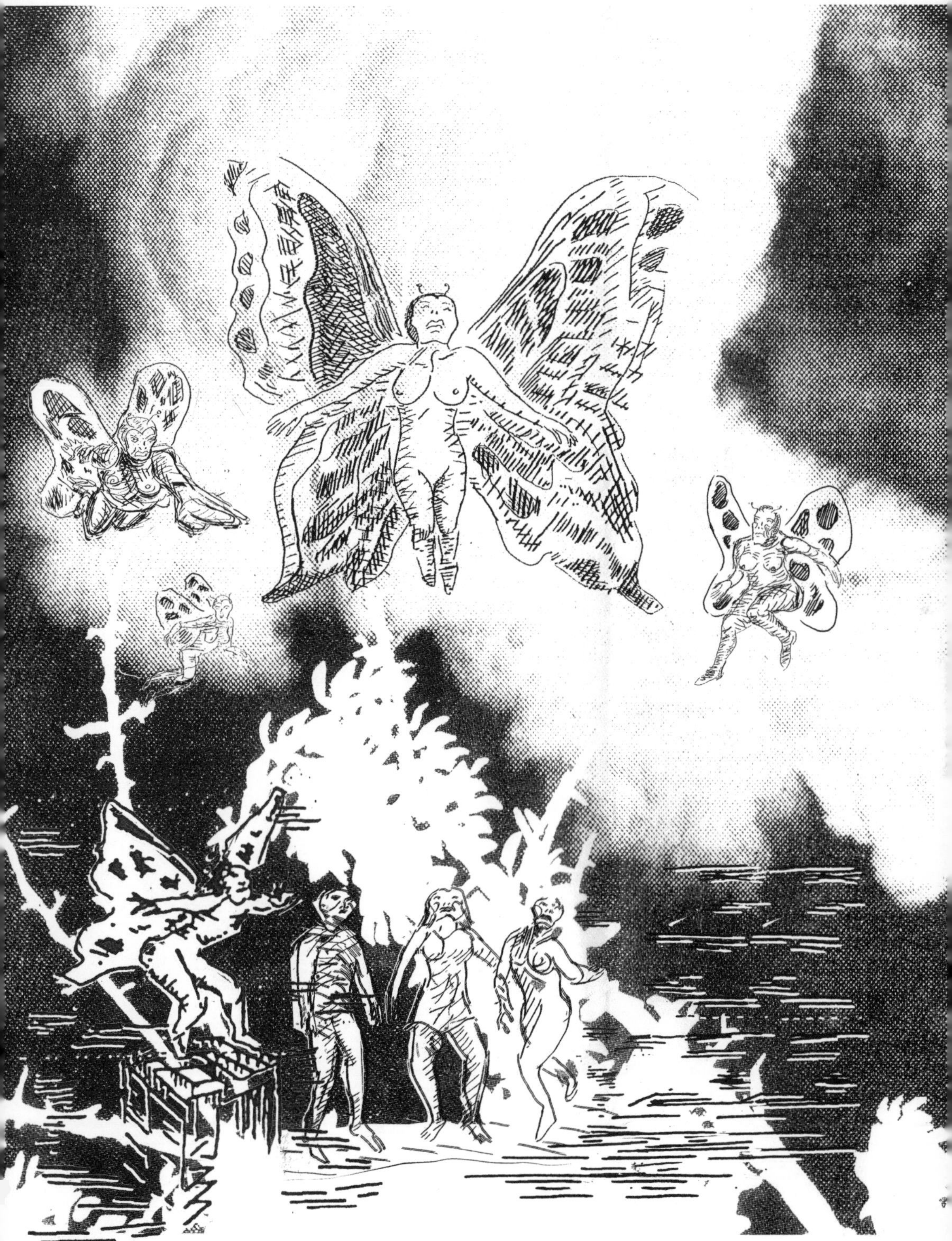

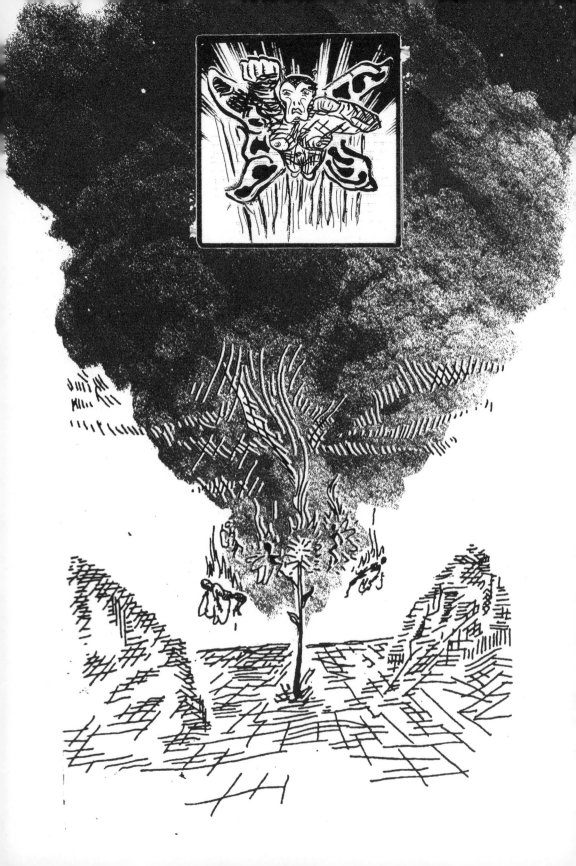

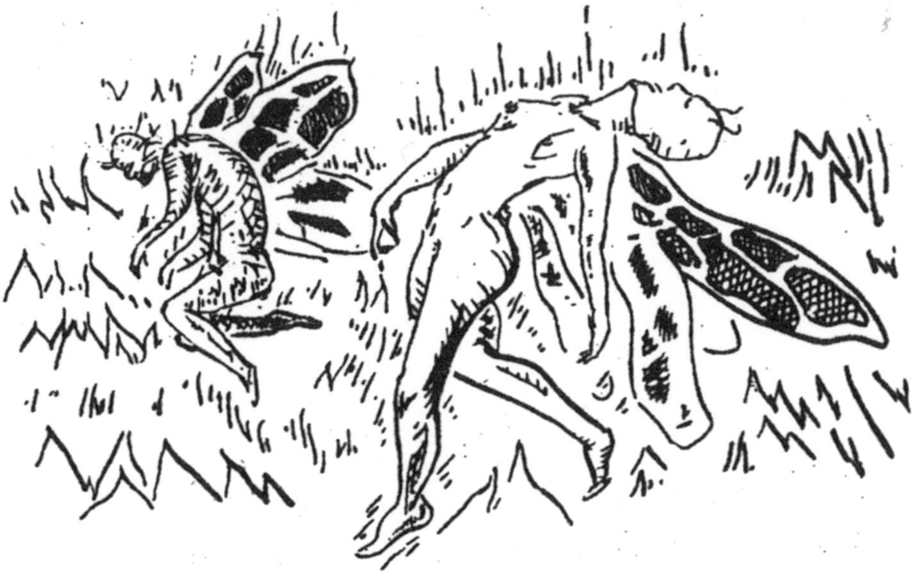

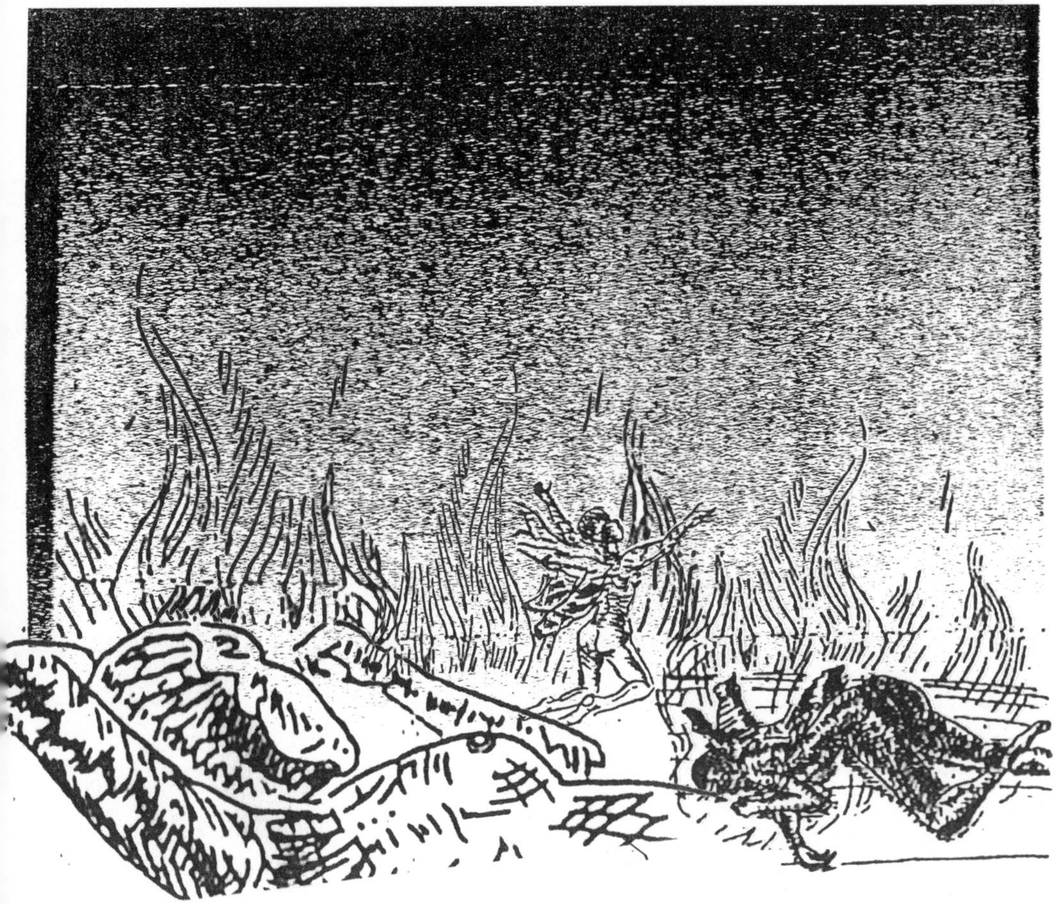

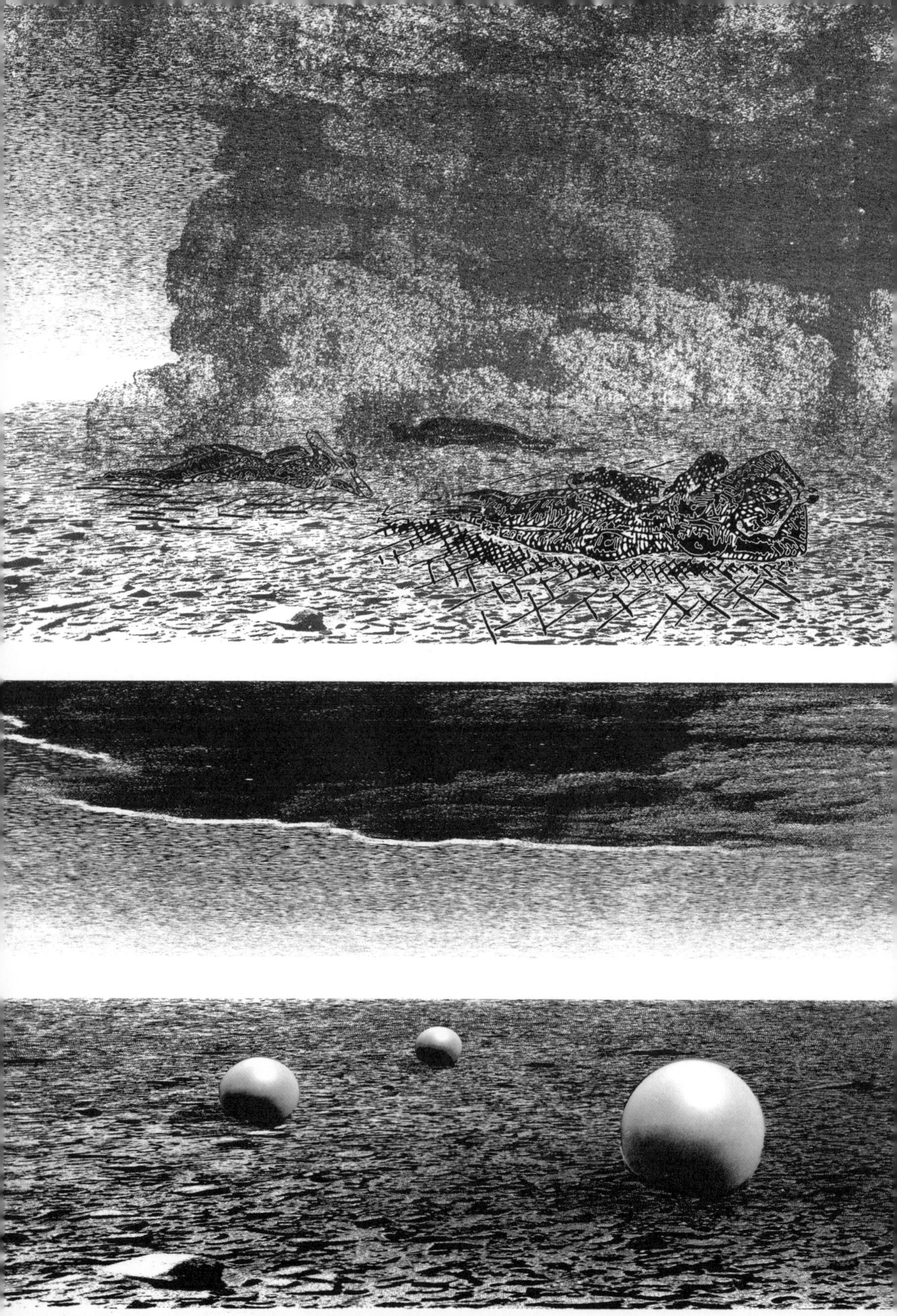

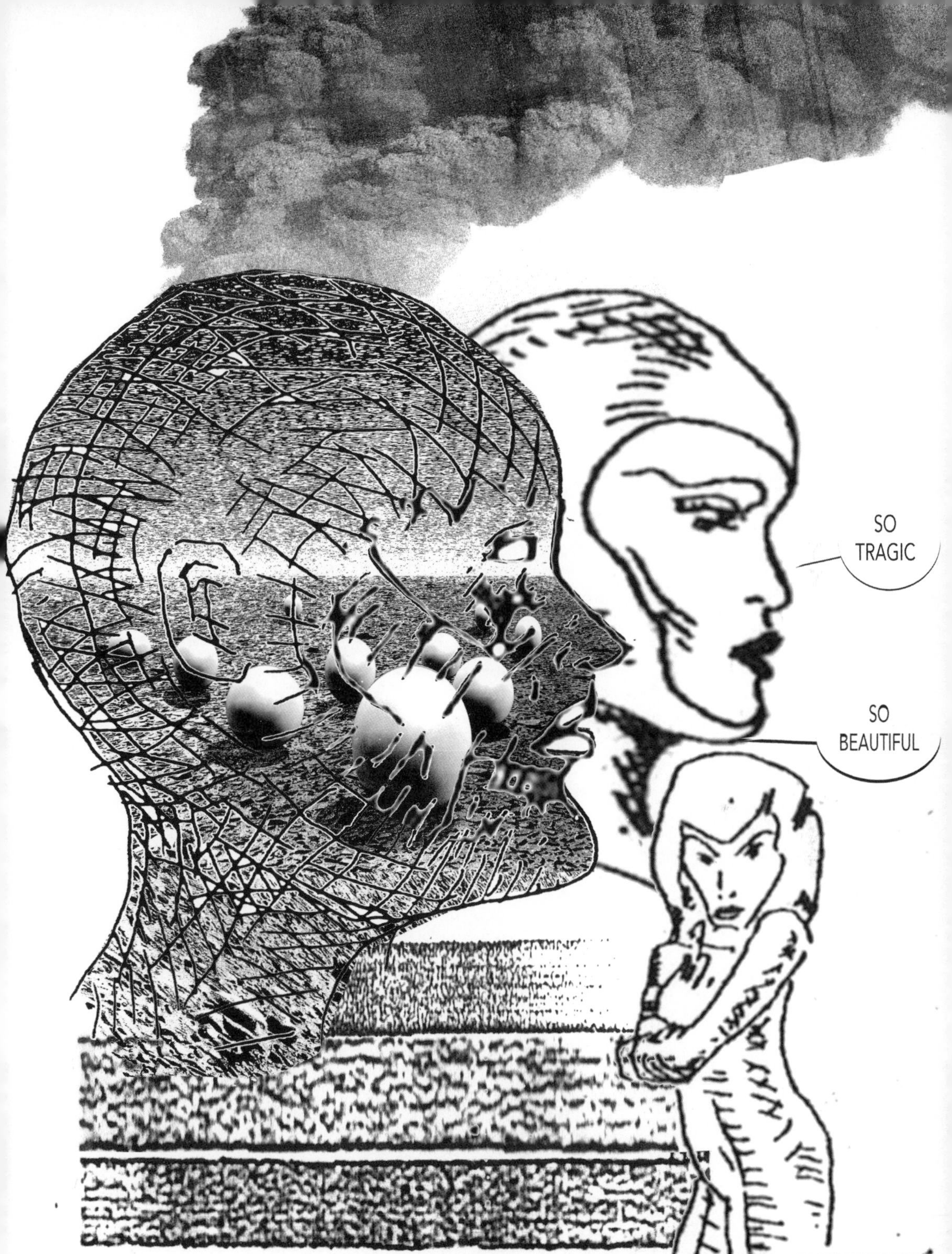
SO TRAGIC
SO BEAUTIFUL

THIS IS THE TRAGEDY THAT BEGETS ANOTHER GENERATION. IT WAS OUR PRIVILEDGE AND SEX SCIENCE DUTY TO BEAR WITNESS

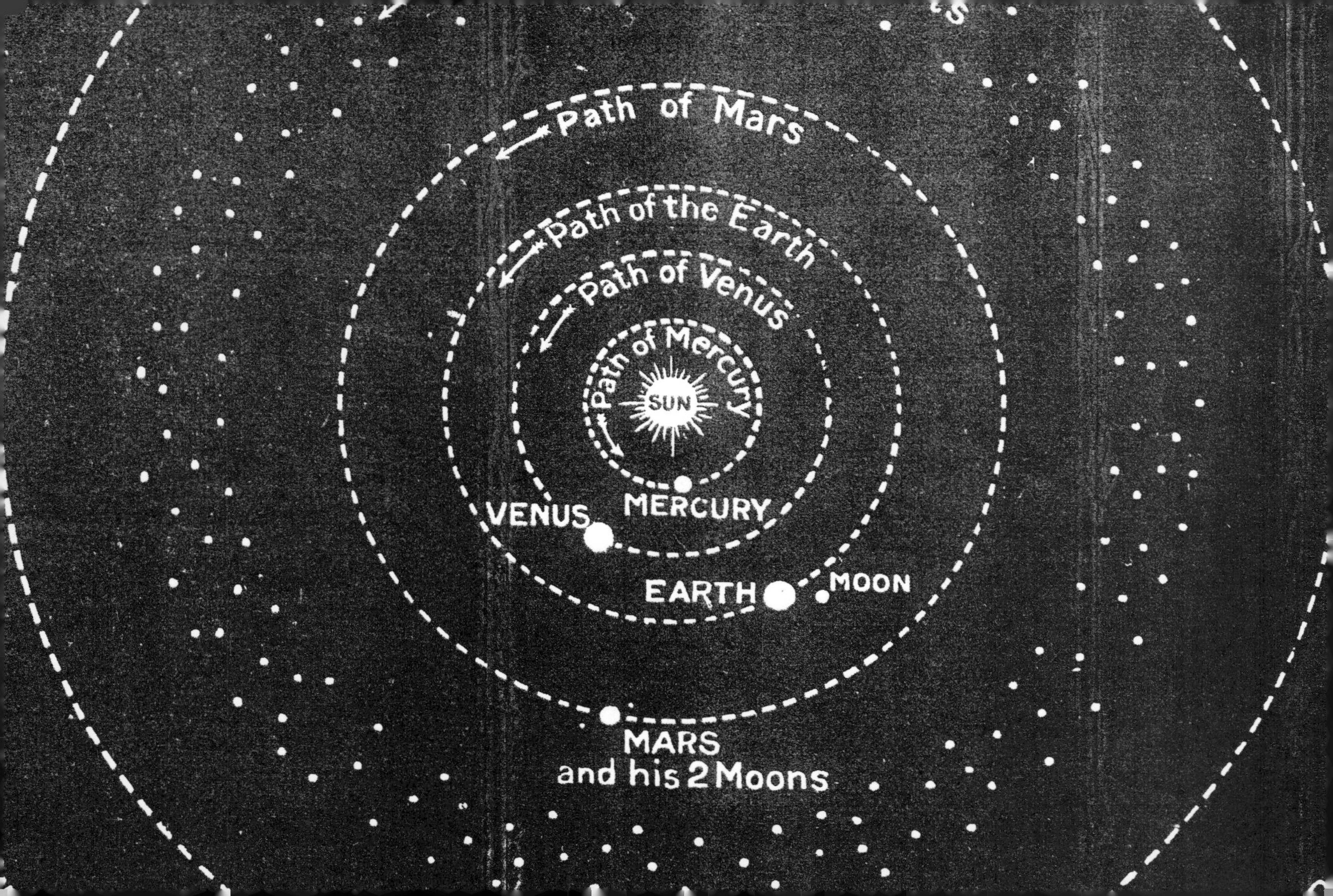
Path of Mars
Path of the Earth
Path of Venus
Path of Mercury
SUN
MERCURY
VENUS
EARTH
MOON
MARS
and his 2 Moons

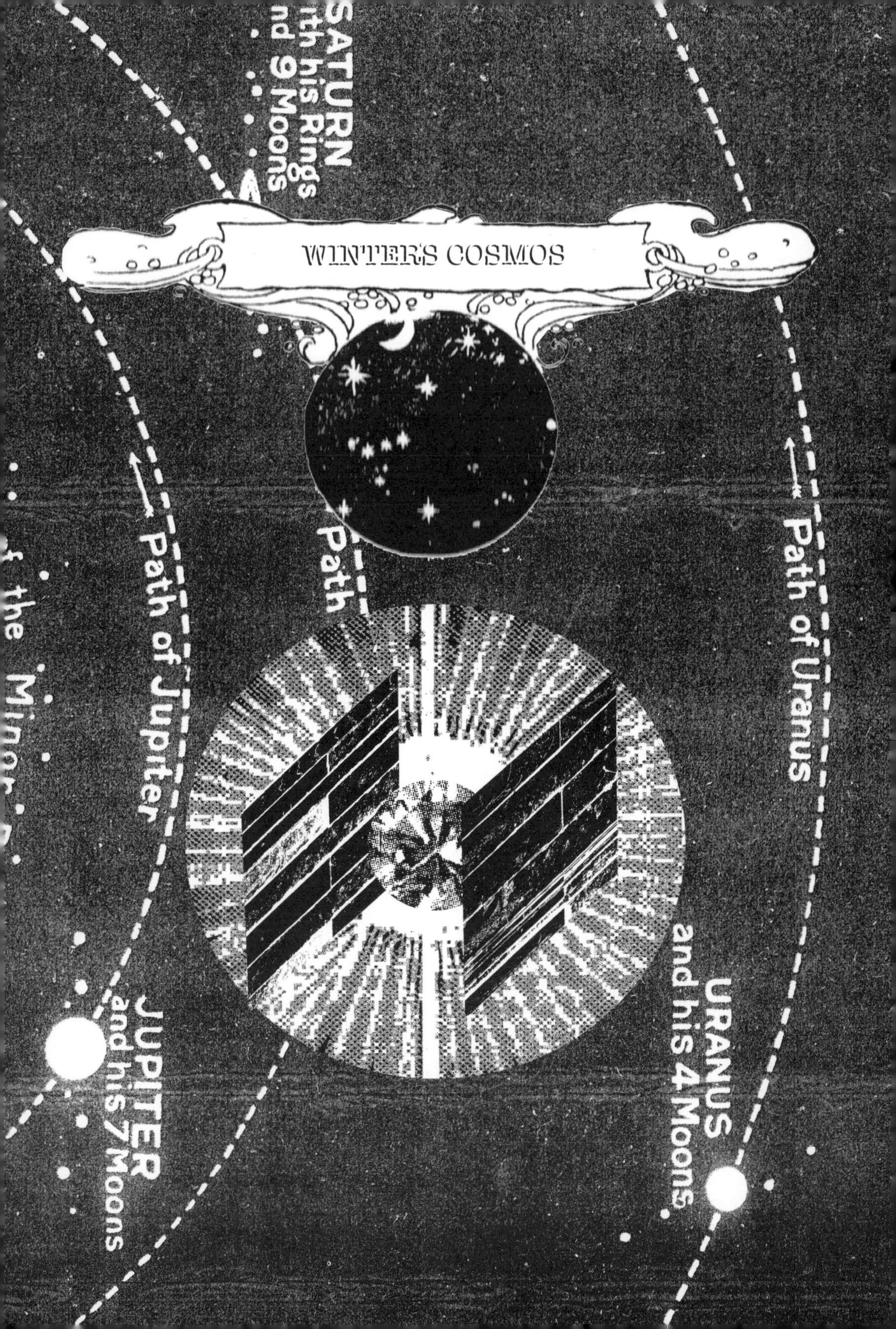

WINTERS COSMOS

SATURN
with his Rings
and 9 Moons

Path of Jupiter

Path of Uranus

Path

of the Minor

JUPITER
and his 7 Moons

URANUS
and his 4 Moons

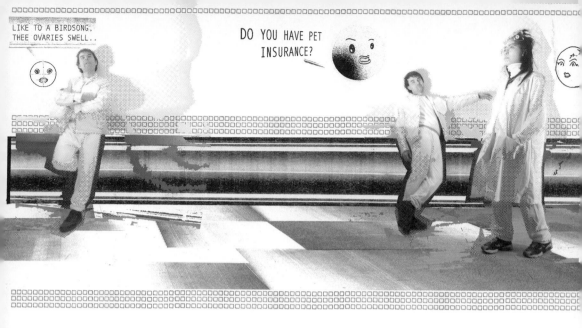

LIKE TO A BIRDSONG,
THEE OVARIES SWELL..

DO YOU HAVE PET
INSURANCE?

CUZ YOUR PUSSY
GETTIN' SMASHED
TONIGHT!

GROAN

gross

ROCK N' ROLL ORIGINALLY

MEANT TO
SEXUALLY COPULATE..

...YOU KNOW?

..TO FUCK.

ROCK AROUND THE CLOCK
WAS SEX ALL NIGHT LONG.

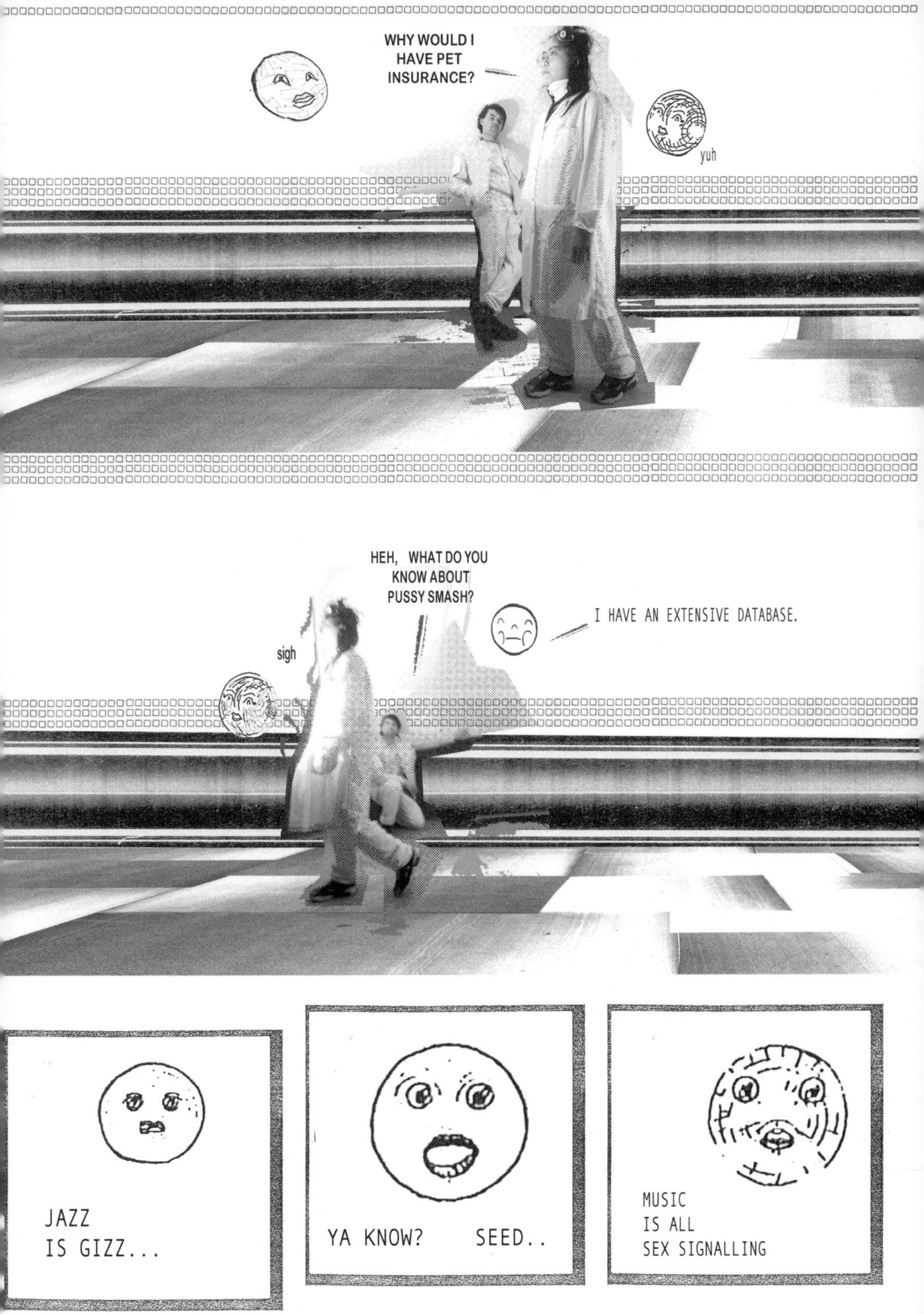
WHY WOULD I HAVE PET INSURANCE?
yuh
HEH, WHAT DO YOU KNOW ABOUT PUSSY SMASH?
I HAVE AN EXTENSIVE DATABASE.
sigh
JAZZ IS GIZZ...
YA KNOW? SEED..
MUSIC IS ALL SEX SIGNALLING

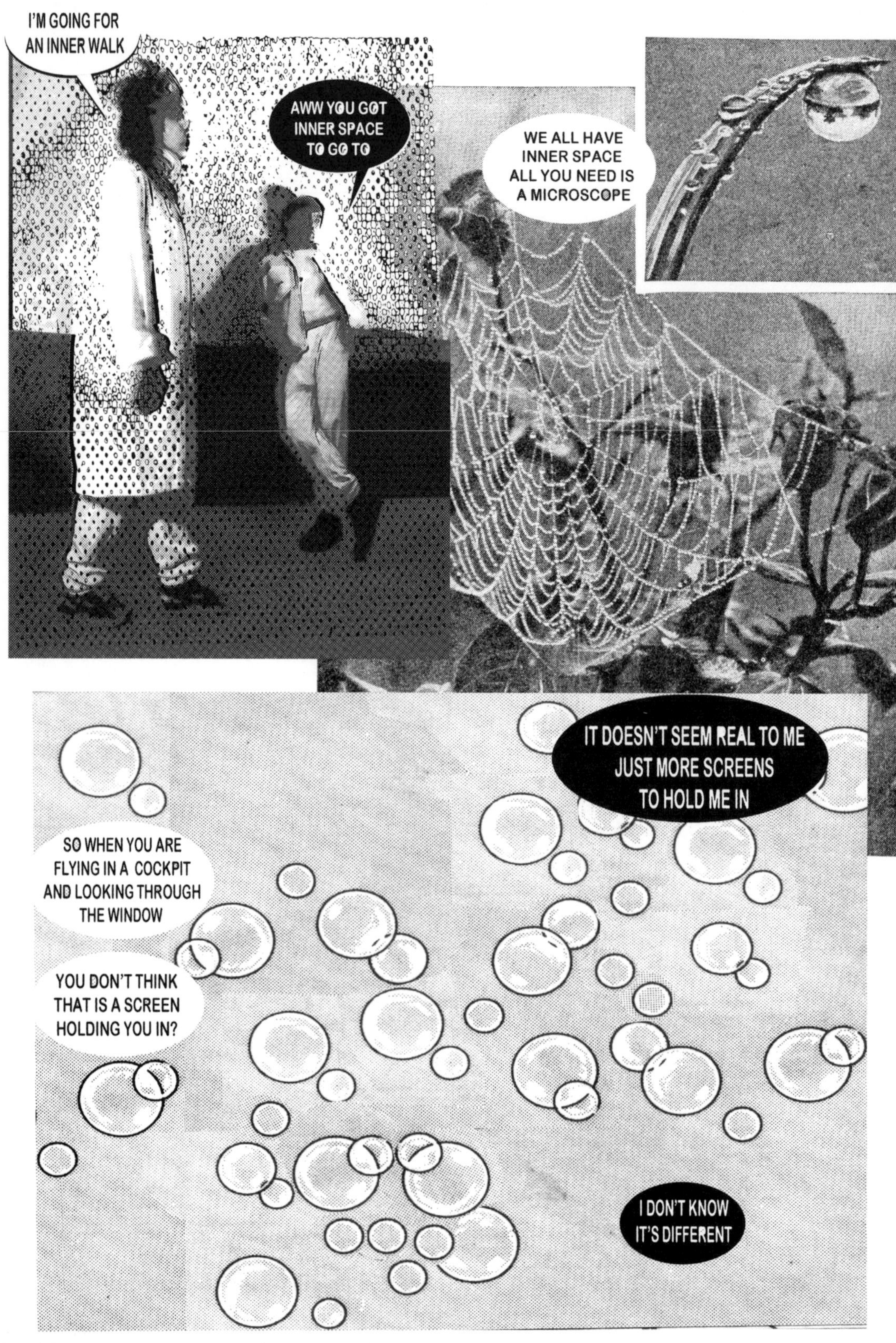
I'M GOING FOR AN INNER WALK
AWW YOU GOT INNER SPACE TO GO TO
WE ALL HAVE INNER SPACE ALL YOU NEED IS A MICROSCOPE
IT DOESN'T SEEM REAL TO ME JUST MORE SCREENS TO HOLD ME IN
SO WHEN YOU ARE FLYING IN A COCKPIT AND LOOKING THROUGH THE WINDOW
YOU DON'T THINK THAT IS A SCREEN HOLDING YOU IN?
I DON'T KNOW IT'S DIFFERENT

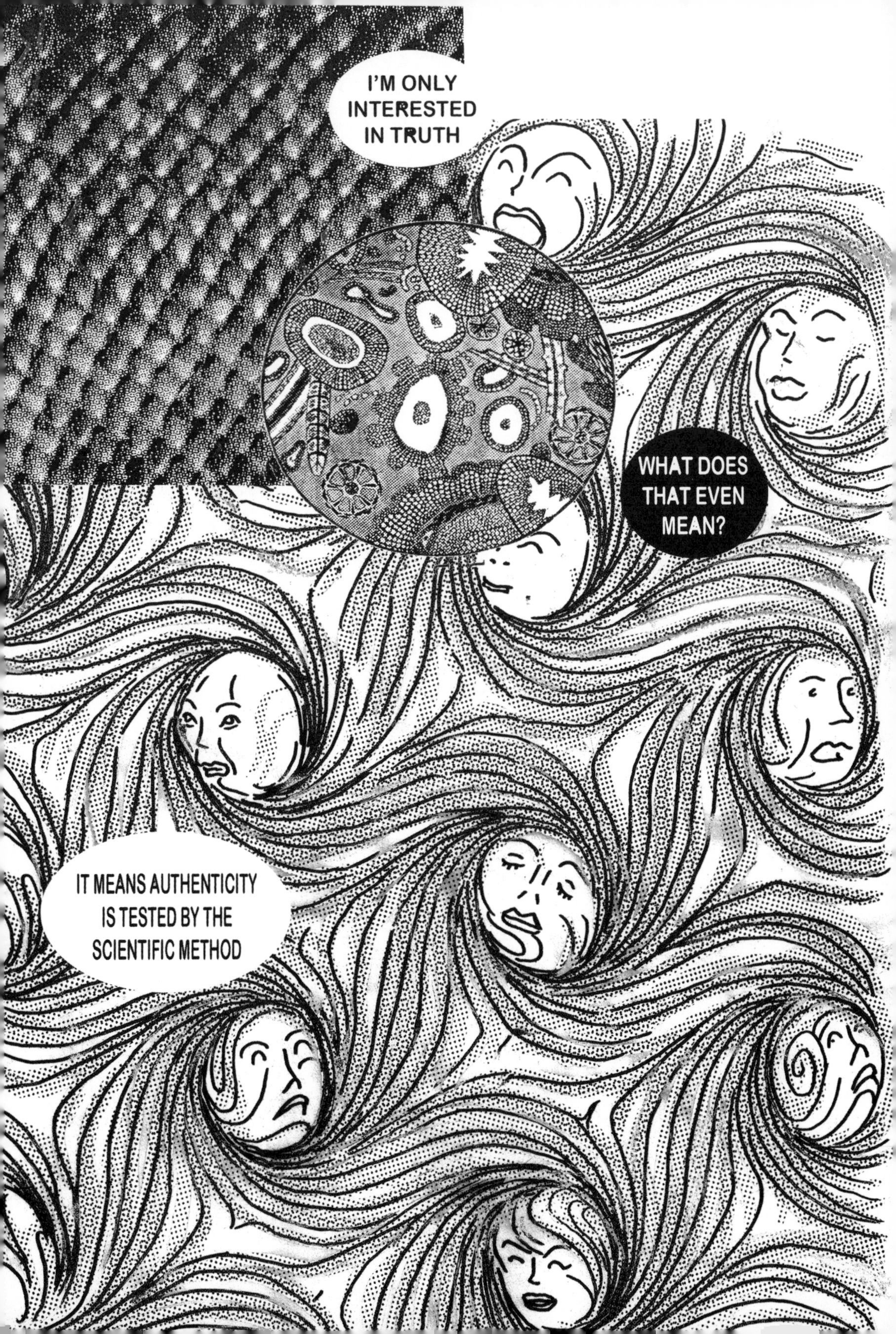
I'M ONLY INTERESTED IN TRUTH
WHAT DOES THAT EVEN MEAN?
IT MEANS AUTHENTICITY IS TESTED BY THE SCIENTIFIC METHOD

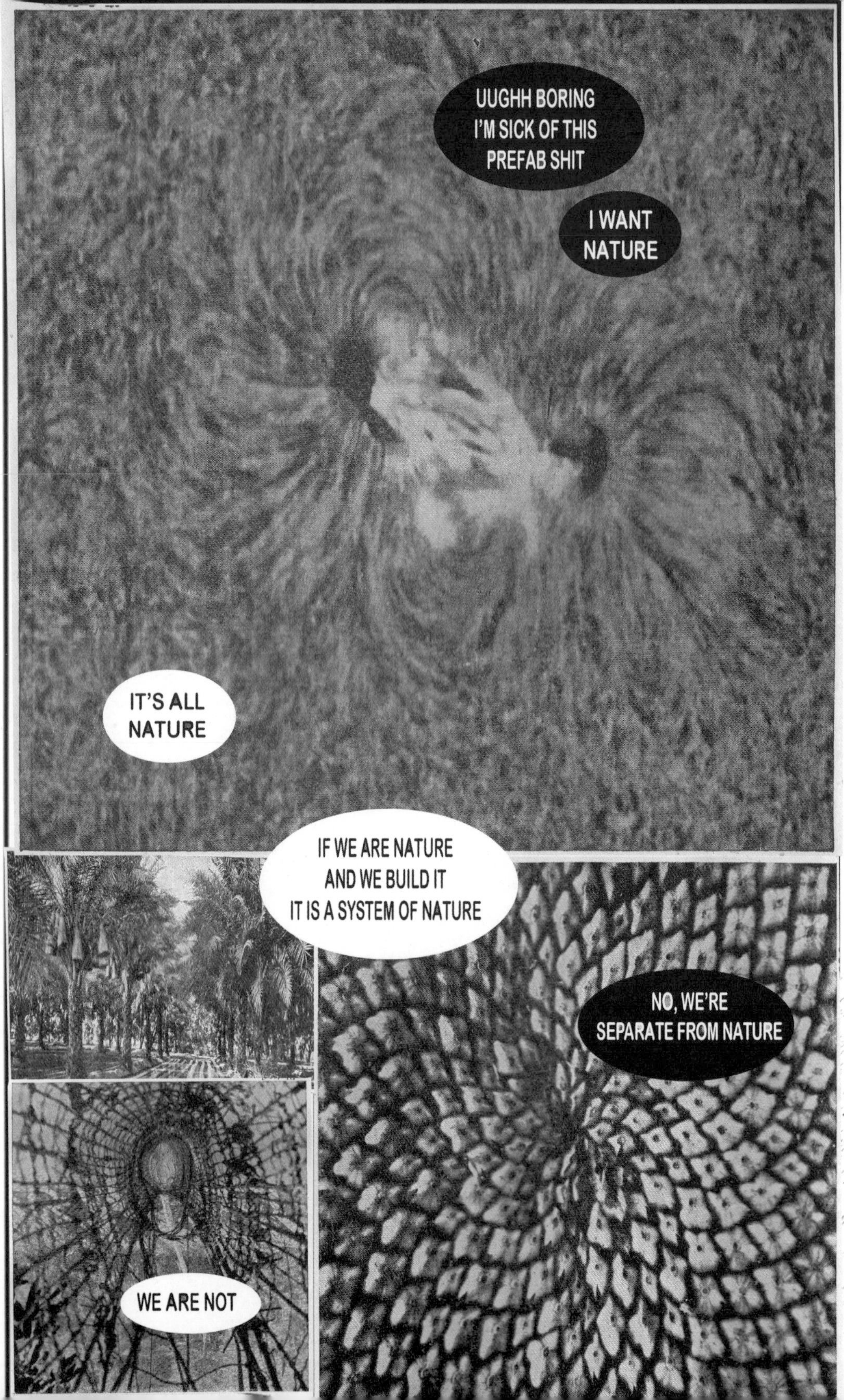
UUGHH BORING
I'M SICK OF THIS
PREFAB SHIT
I WANT
NATURE
IT'S ALL
NATURE
IF WE ARE NATURE
AND WE BUILD IT
IT IS A SYSTEM OF NATURE
NO, WE'RE
SEPARATE FROM NATURE
WE ARE NOT

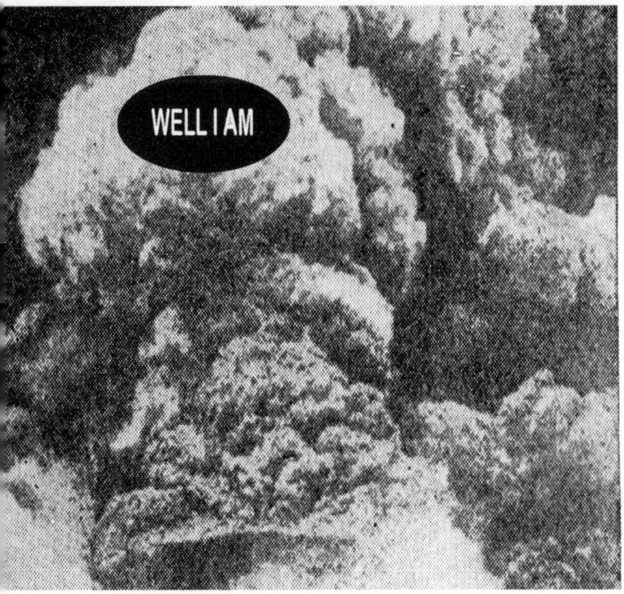
WELL I AM

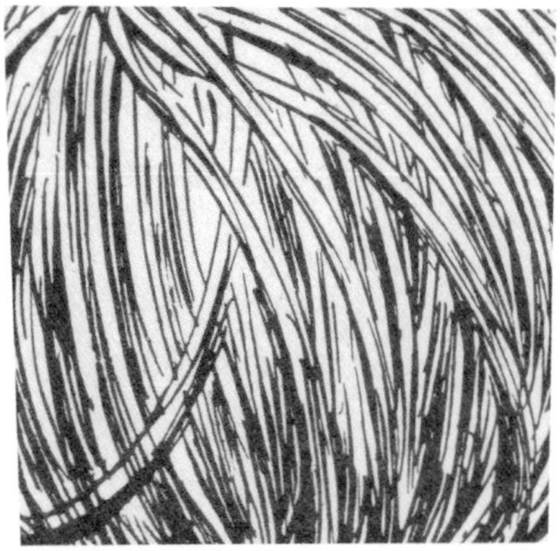

WHEN YOU DIE
YOU WILL ROT

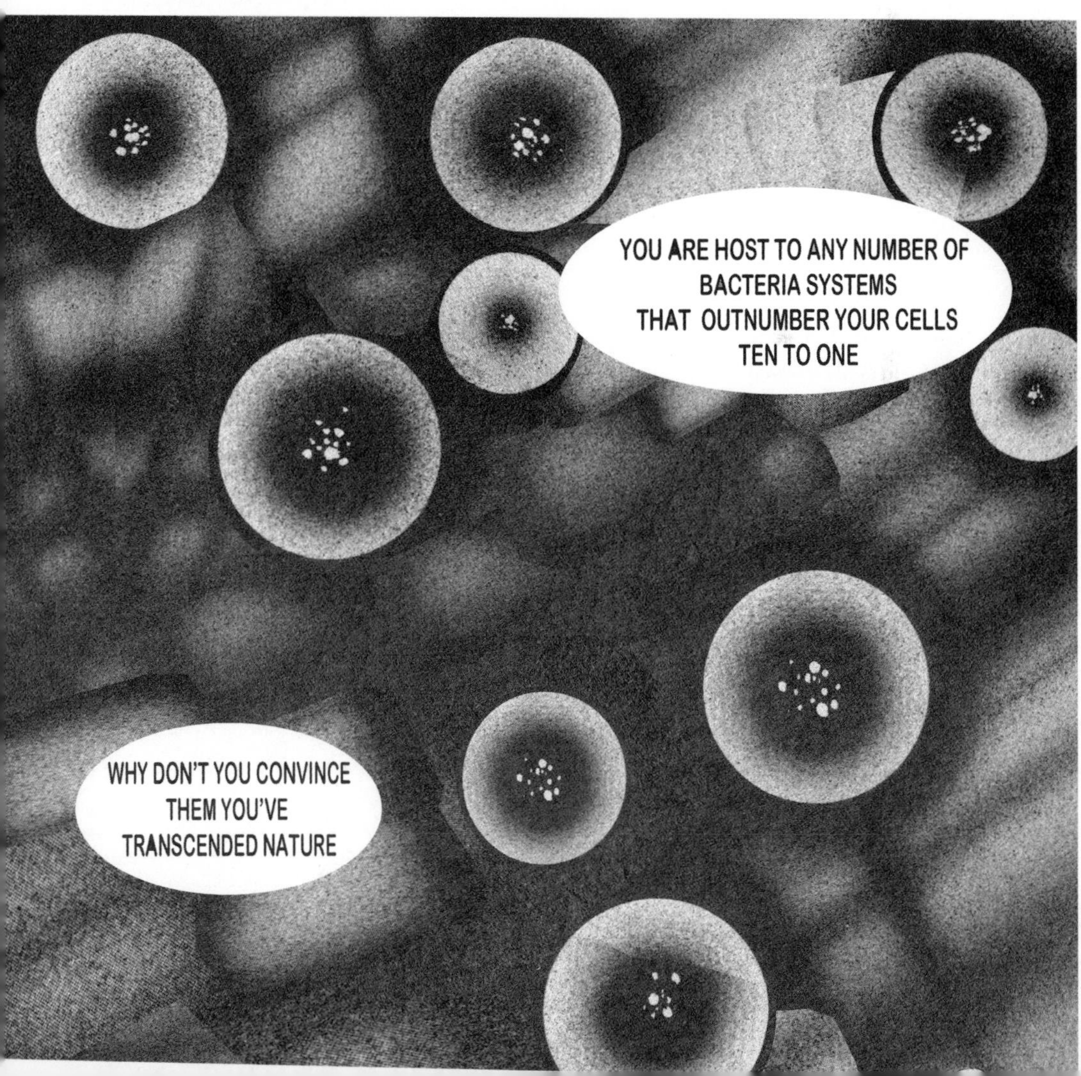
YOU ARE HOST TO ANY NUMBER OF BACTERIA SYSTEMS THAT OUTNUMBER YOUR CELLS TEN TO ONE
WHY DON'T YOU CONVINCE THEM YOU'VE TRANSCENDED NATURE

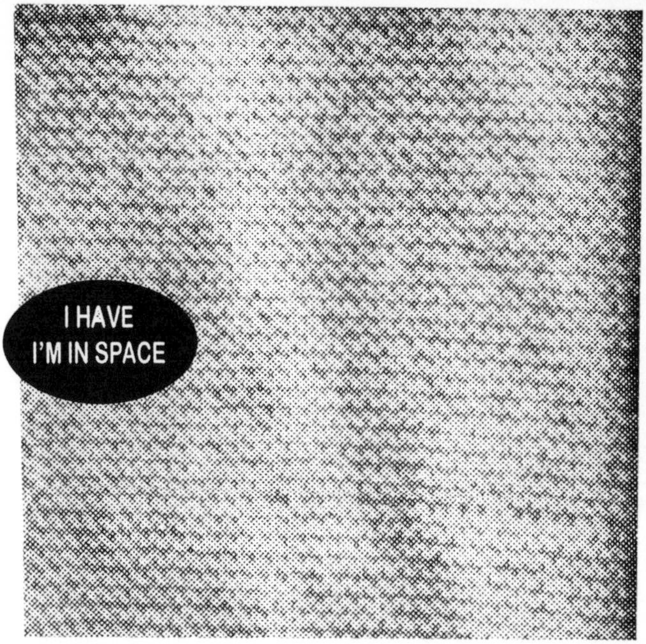
I HAVE
I'M IN SPACE

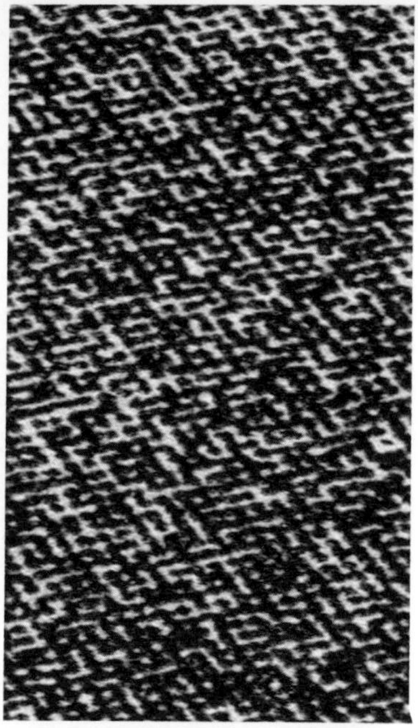

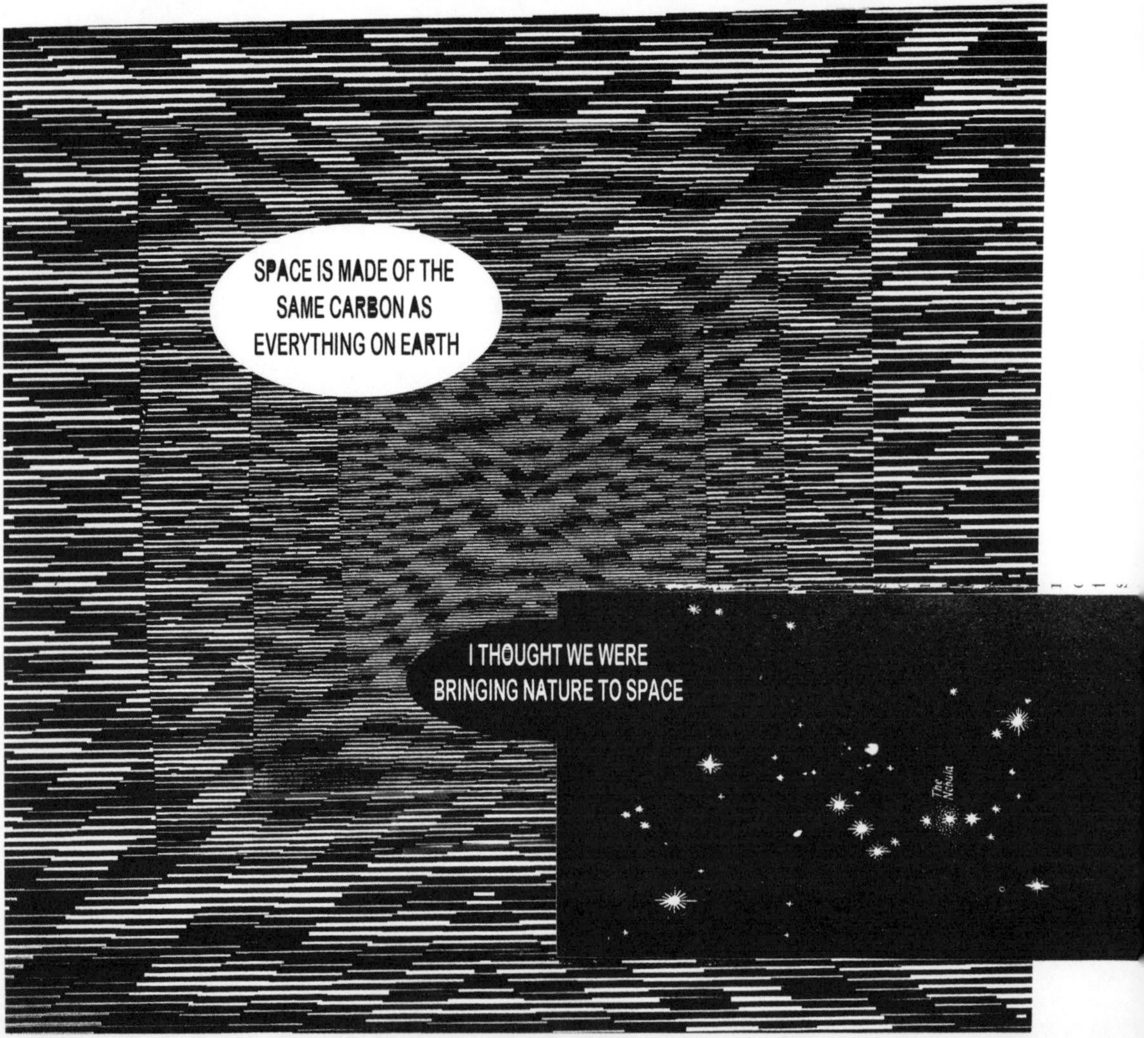
SPACE IS MADE OF THE SAME CARBON AS EVERYTHING ON EARTH
I THOUGHT WE WERE BRINGING NATURE TO SPACE
The Nebula

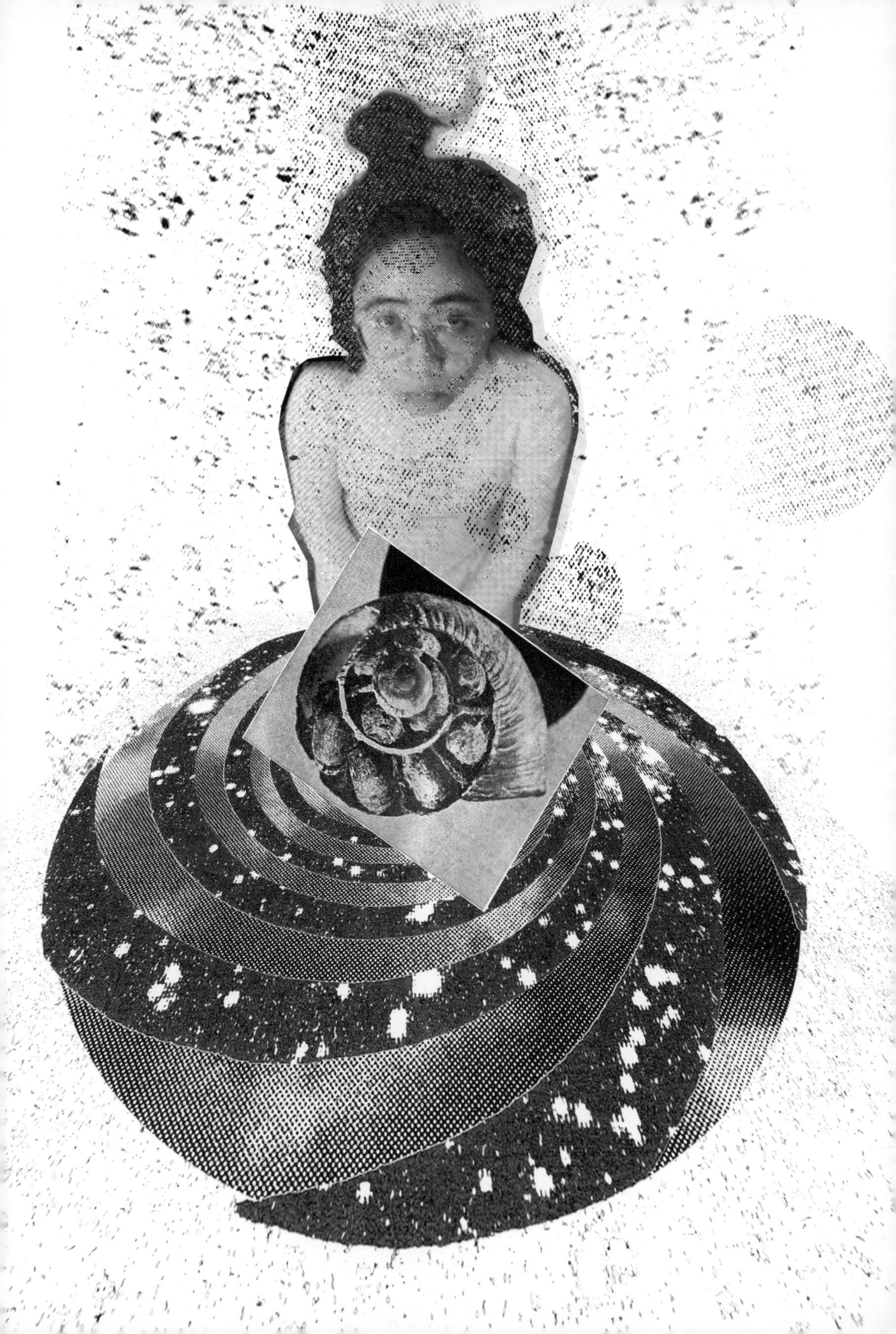

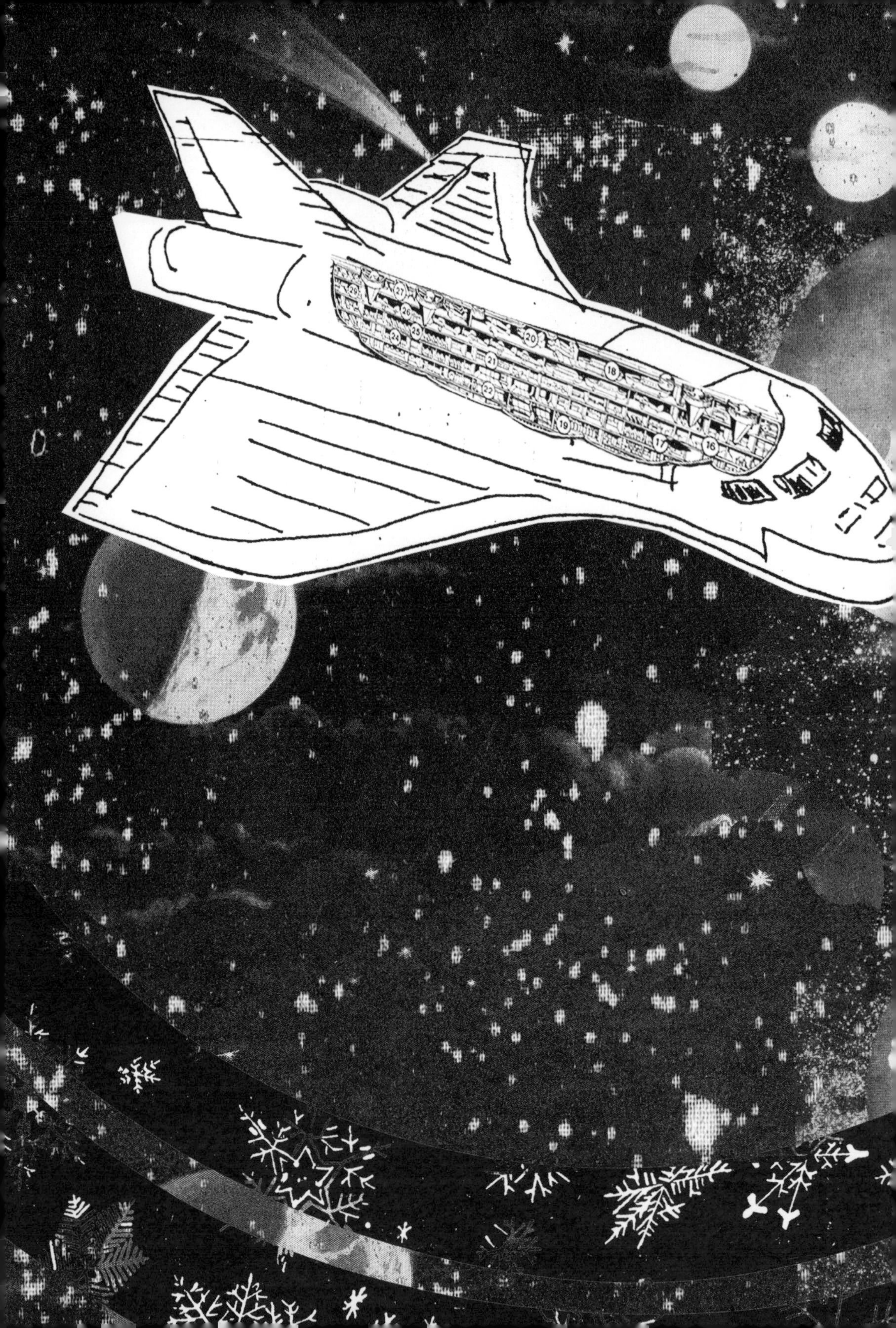

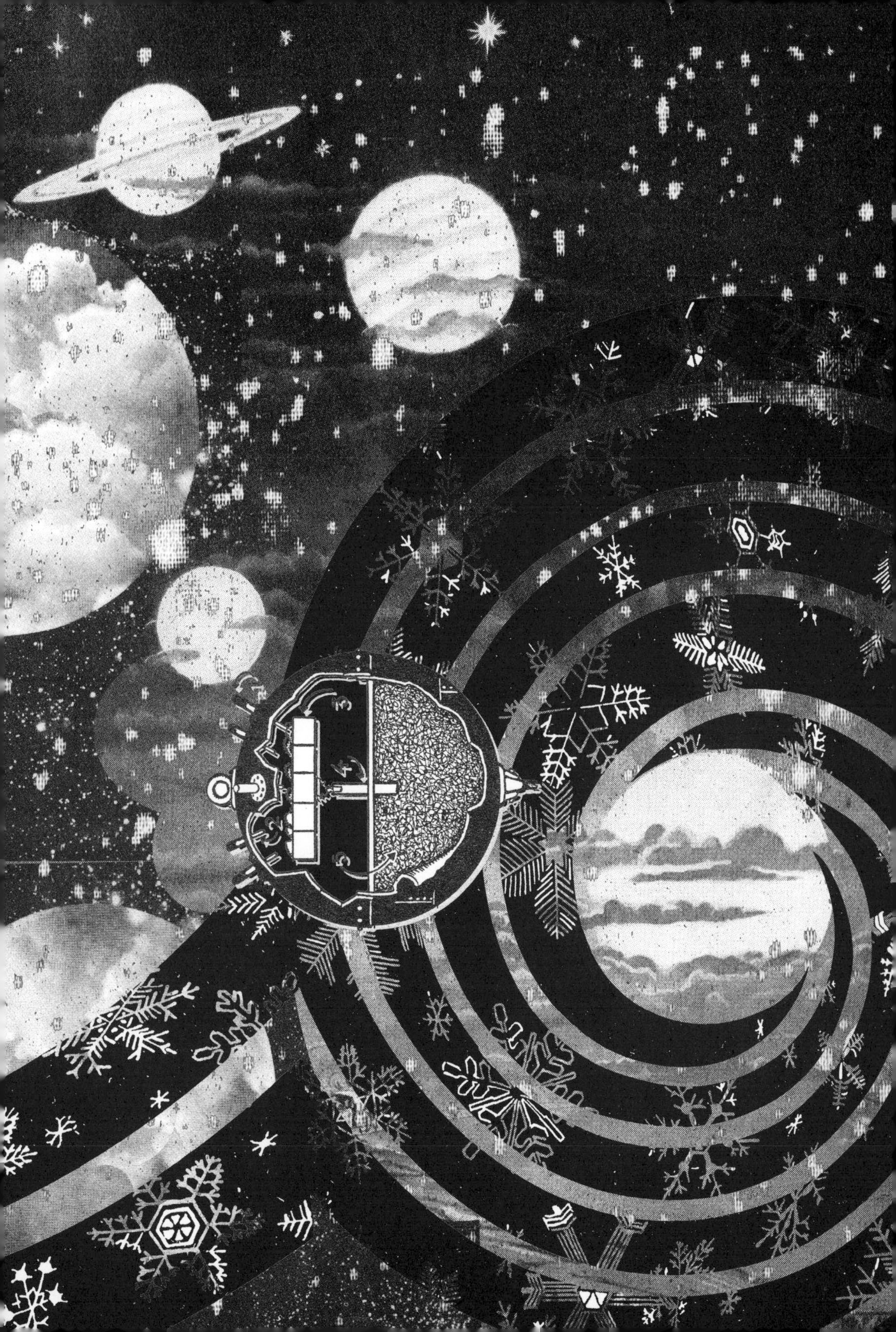

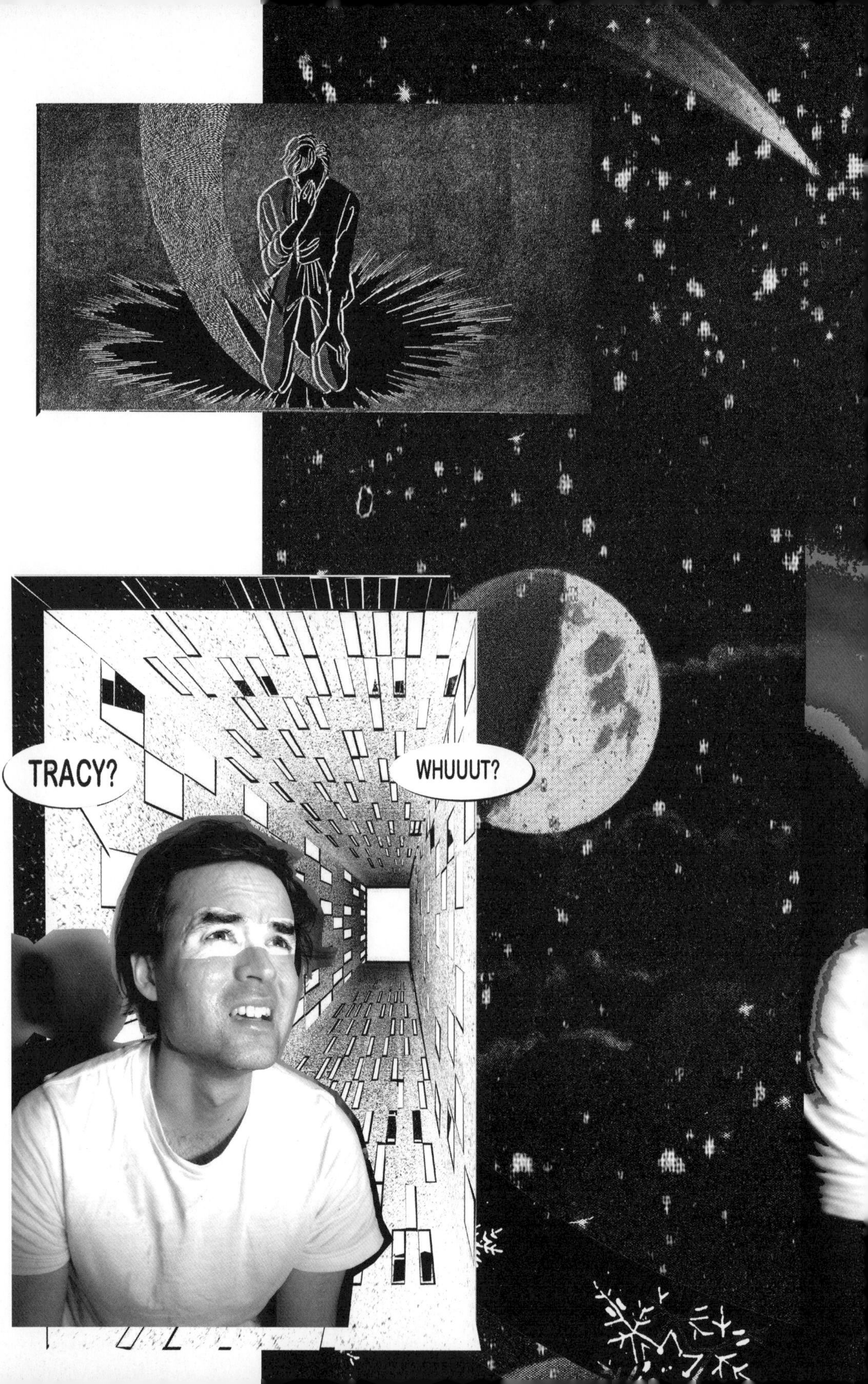
TRACY?
WHUUUT?

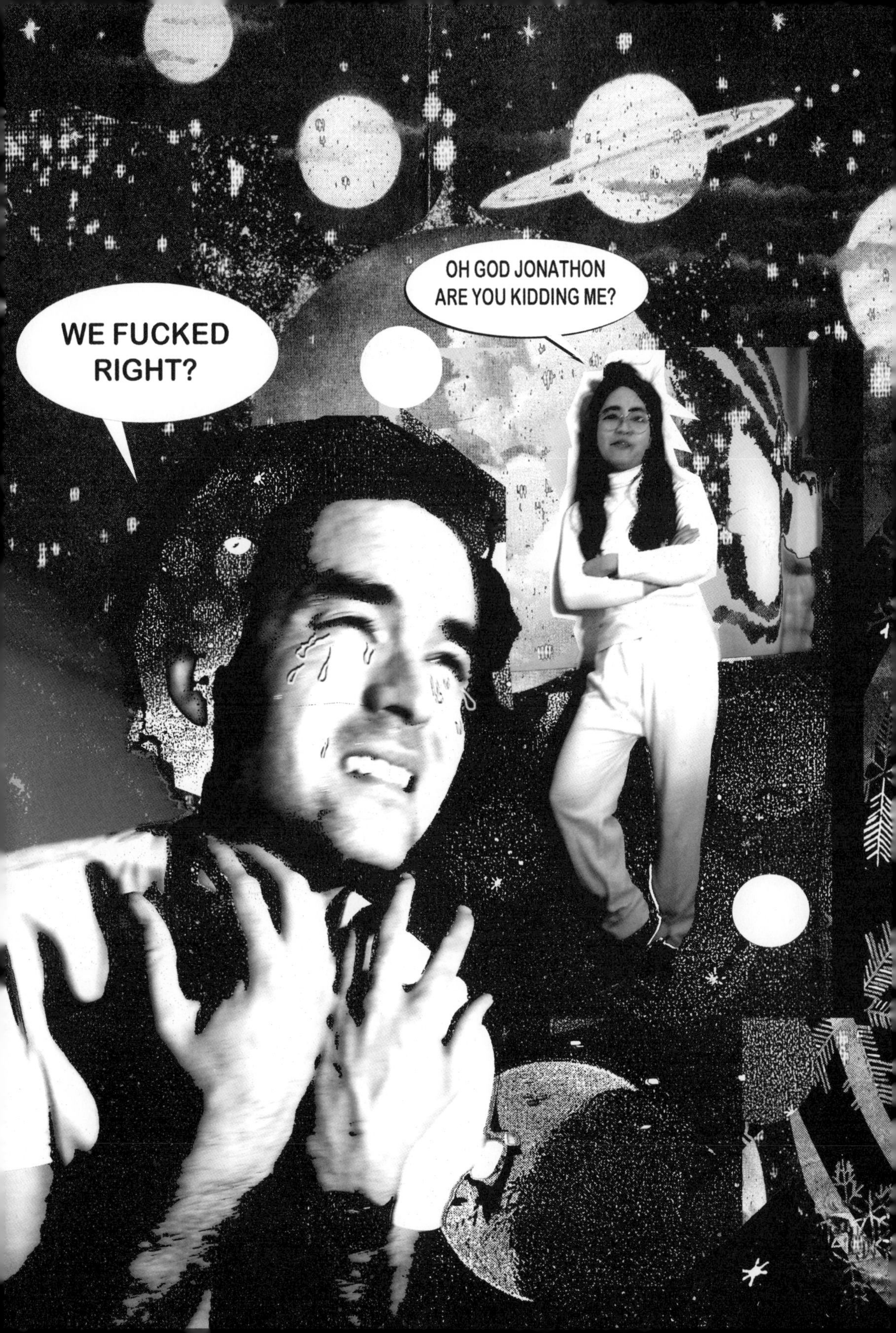
WE FUCKED
RIGHT?
OH GOD JONATHON
ARE YOU KIDDING ME?

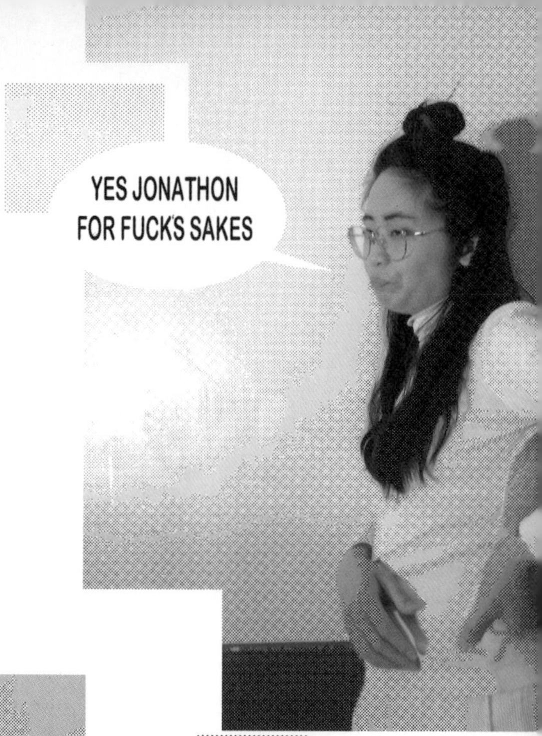
YES JONATHON
FOR FUCK'S SAKES

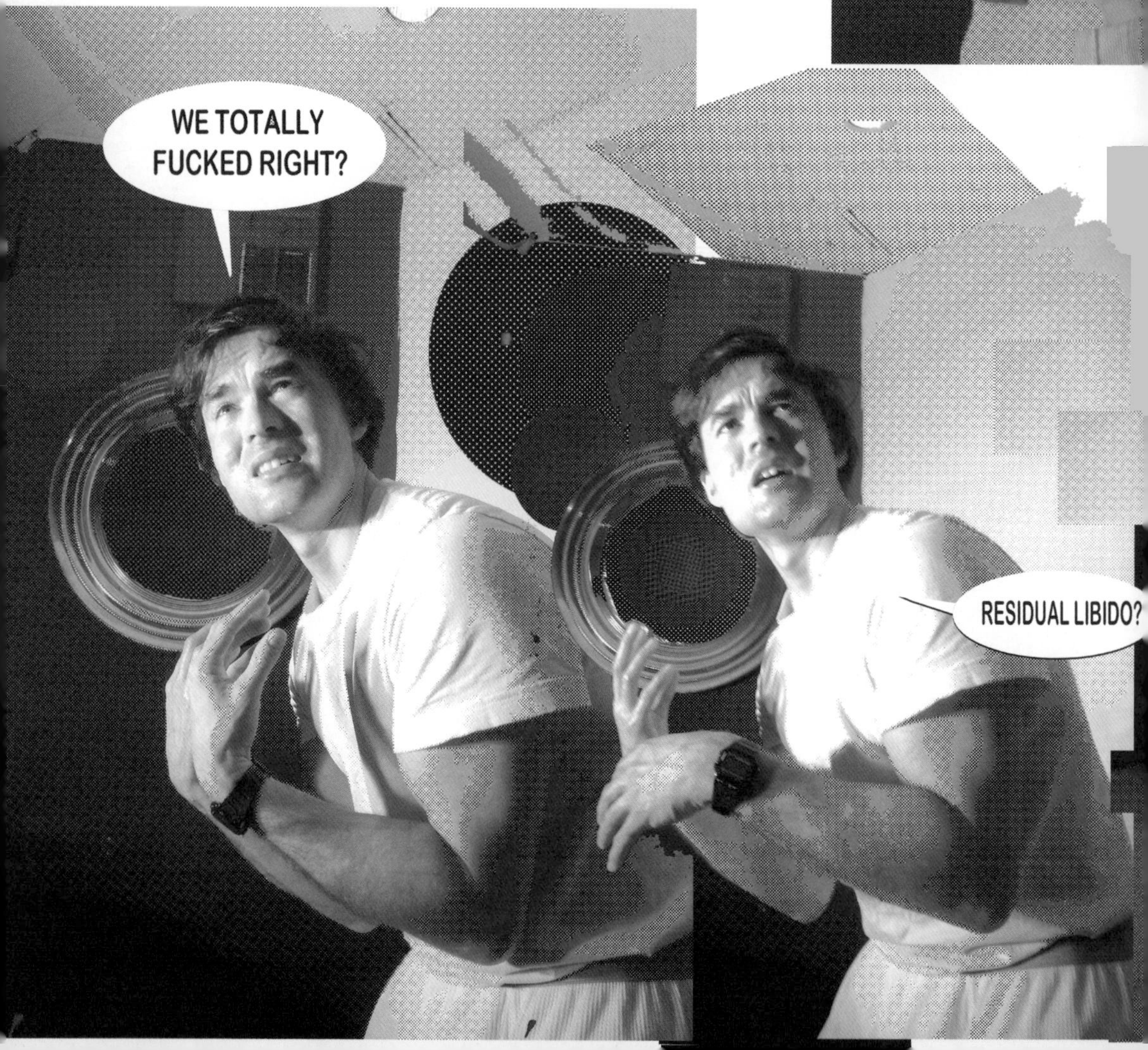
WE TOTALLY
FUCKED RIGHT?
RESIDUAL LIBIDO?

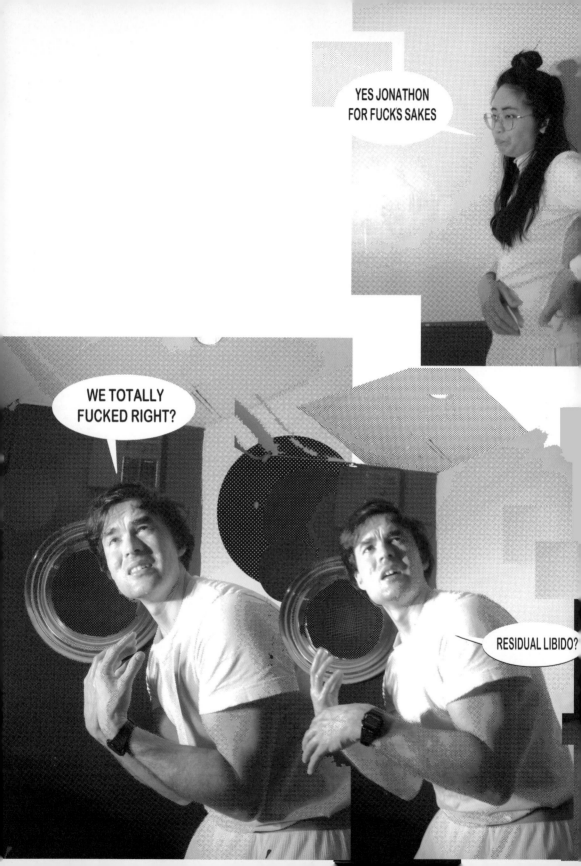

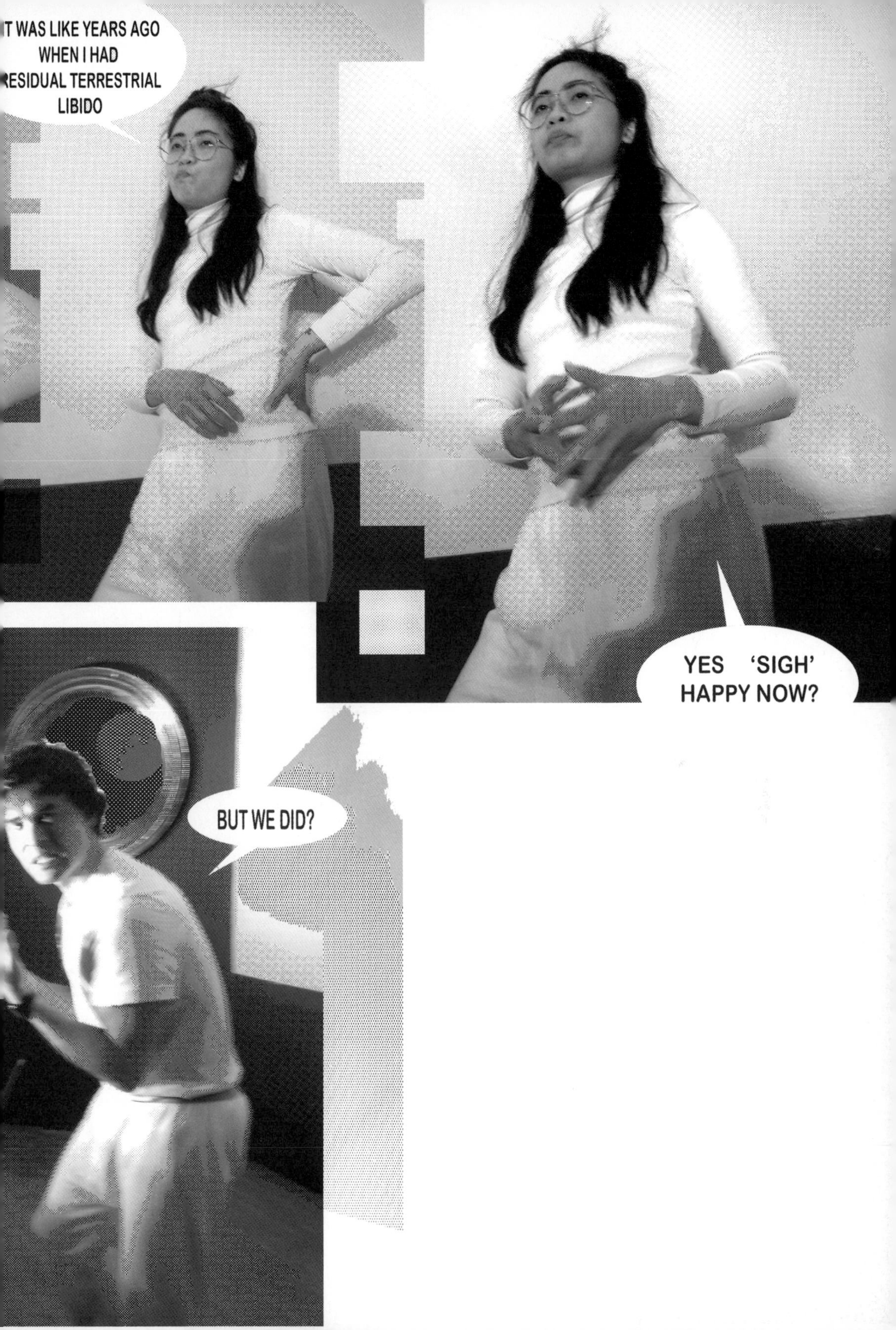
T WAS LIKE YEARS AGO WHEN I HAD ESIDUAL TERRESTRIAL LIBIDO
YES 'SIGH' HAPPY NOW?
BUT WE DID?

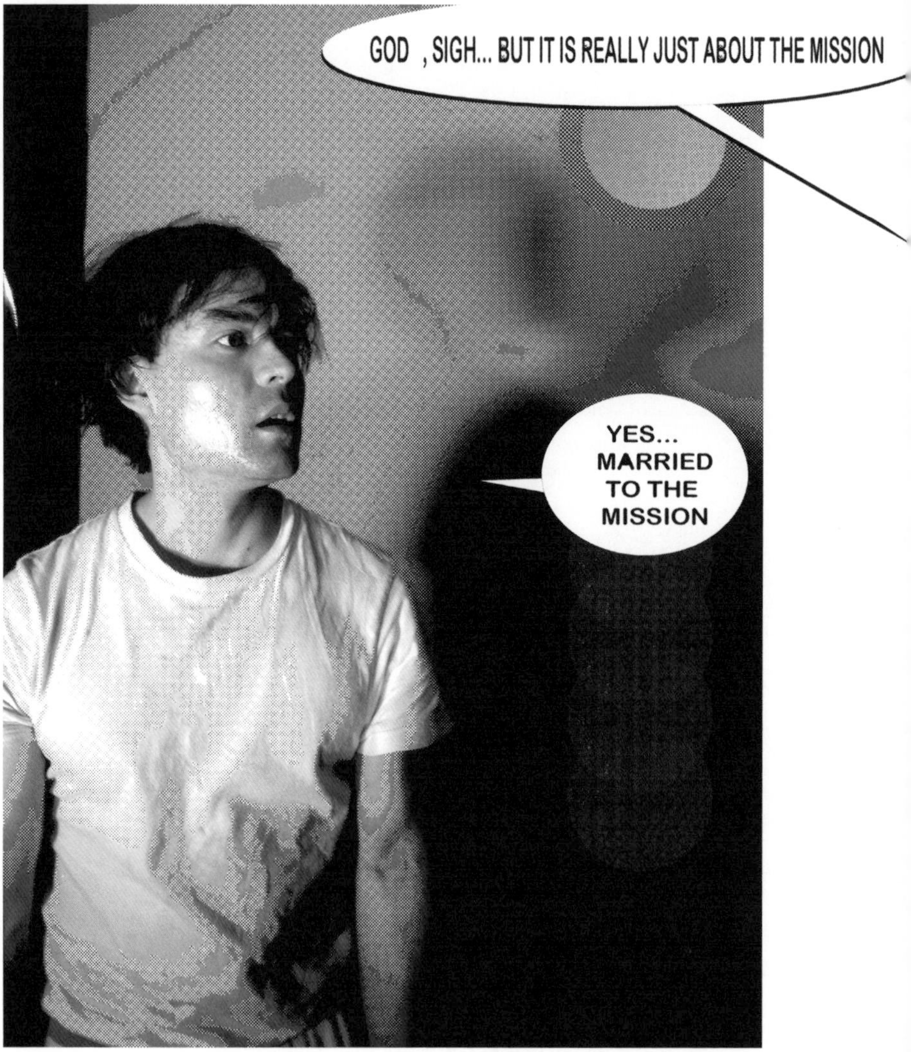
GOD , SIGH... BUT IT IS REALLY JUST ABOUT THE MISSION
YES... MARRIED TO THE MISSION

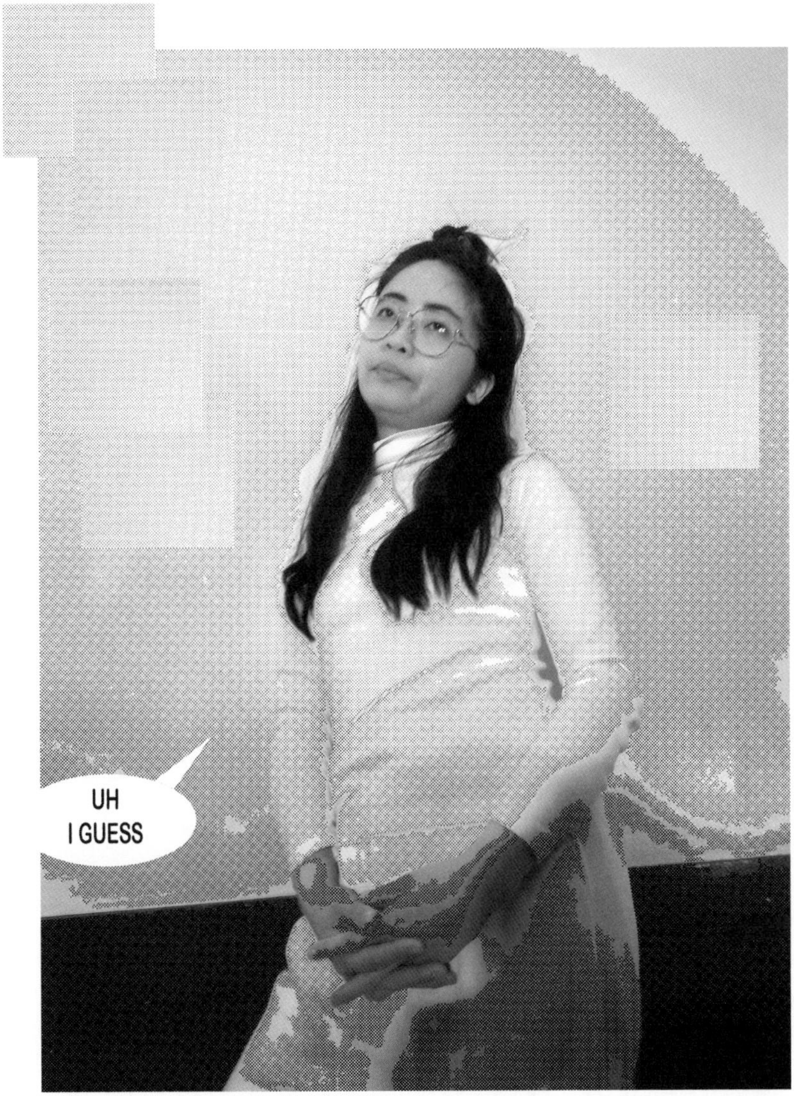
UH
I GUESS

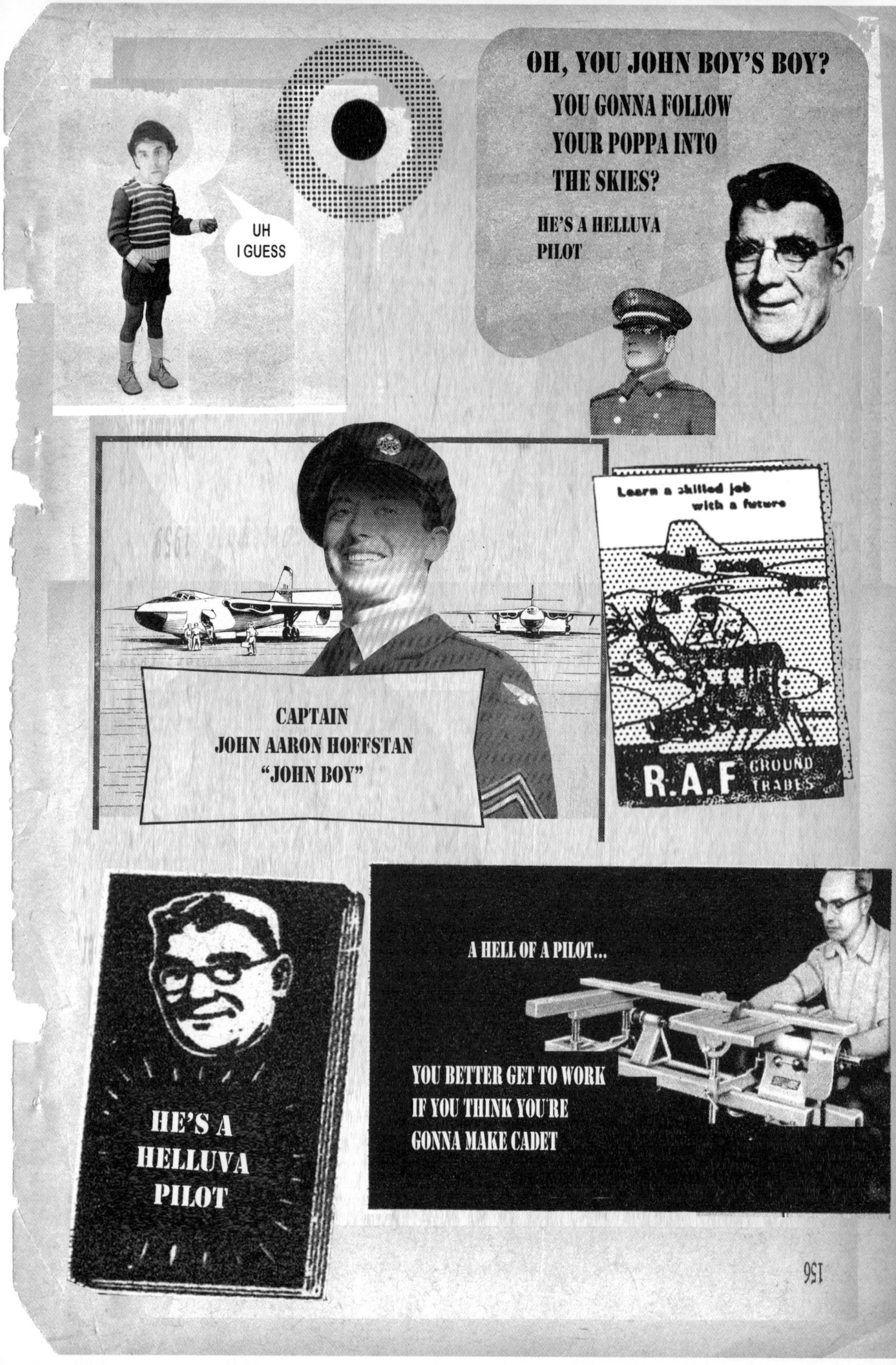

UH
I GUESS
OH, YOU JOHN BOY'S BOY?
YOU GONNA FOLLOW
YOUR POPPA INTO
THE SKIES?
HE'S A HELLUVA
PILOT
CAPTAIN
JOHN AARON HOFFSTAN
"JOHN BOY"
Learn a skilled job
with a future
R.A.F GROUND TRADES
HE'S A
HELLUVA
PILOT
A HELL OF A PILOT...
YOU BETTER GET TO WORK
IF YOU THINK YOU'RE
GONNA MAKE CADET

# DIFFERENT EXERCISES WITH DUMB-BELLS

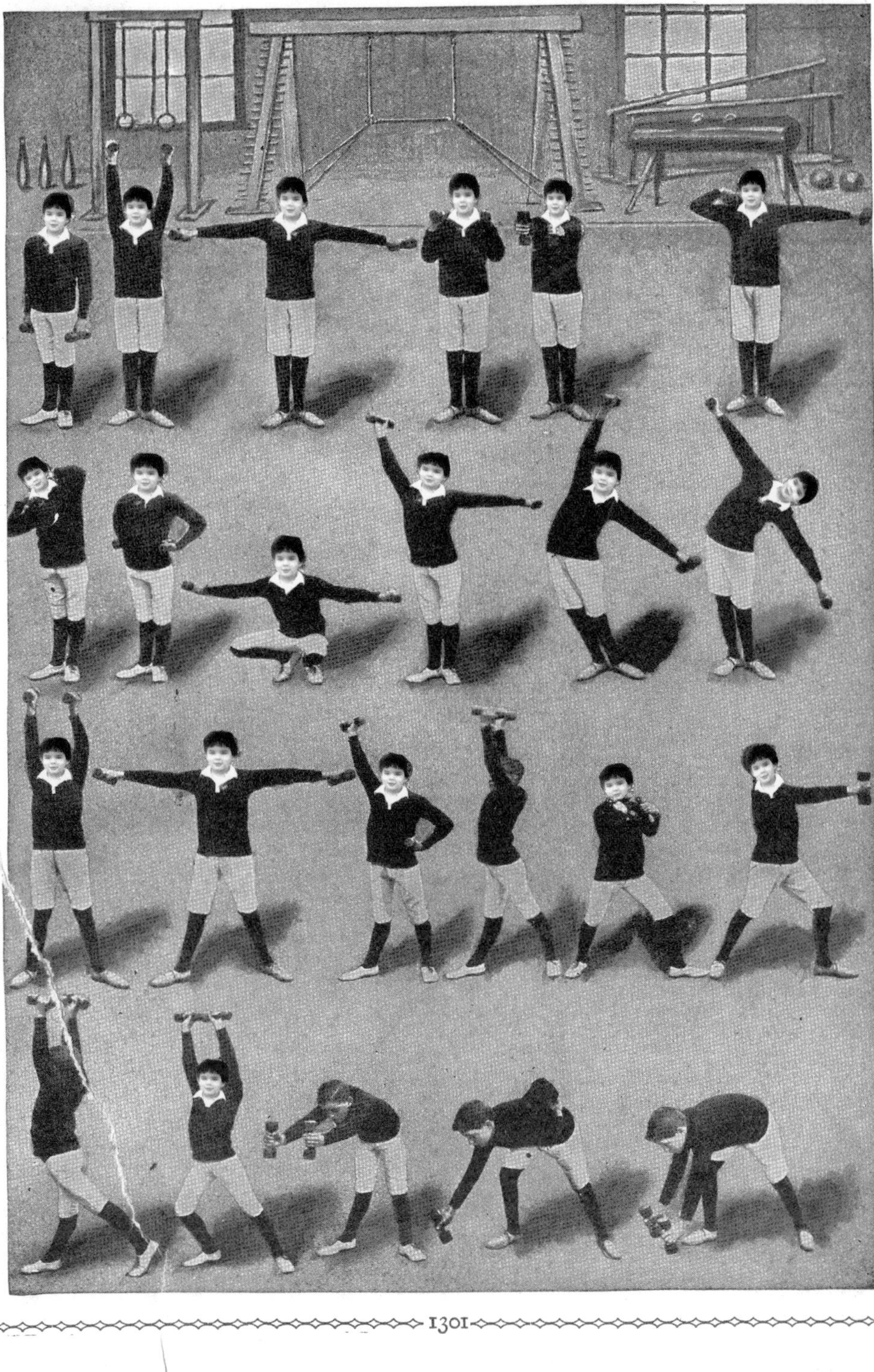

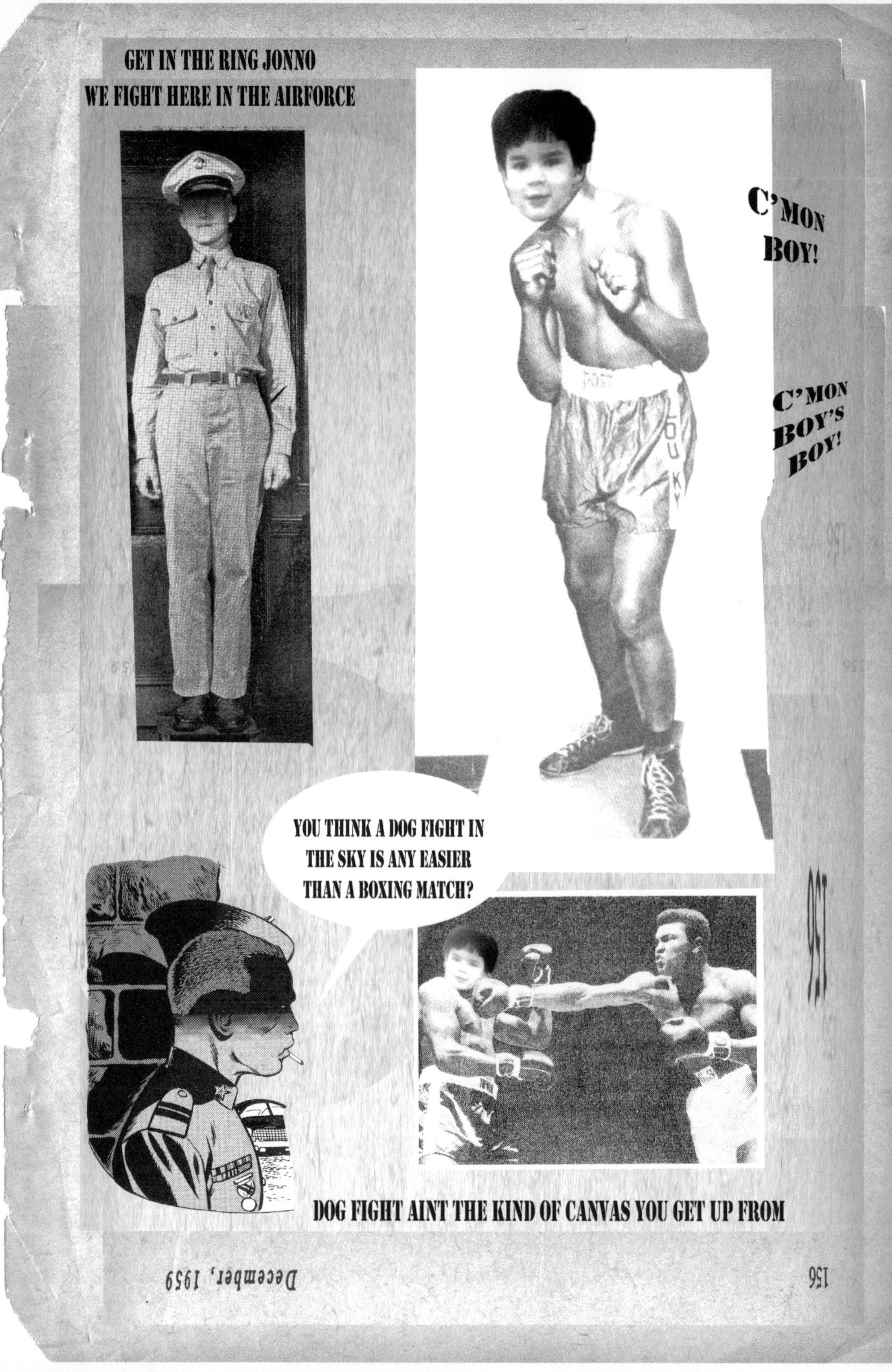

GET IN THE RING JONNO
WE FIGHT HERE IN THE AIRFORCE

C'MON
BOY!

C'MON
BOY'S
BOY!

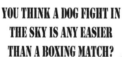

YOU THINK A DOG FIGHT IN
THE SKY IS ANY EASIER
THAN A BOXING MATCH?

DOG FIGHT AINT THE KIND OF CANVAS YOU GET UP FROM

# FORCED INTO RETIREMENT, CAN YOU BELIEVE THAT SHIT?

e girls. Then they

**IT'S ALL VIDEO GAMES**
**ON YOUR GOD DAMN**
**PHONES**

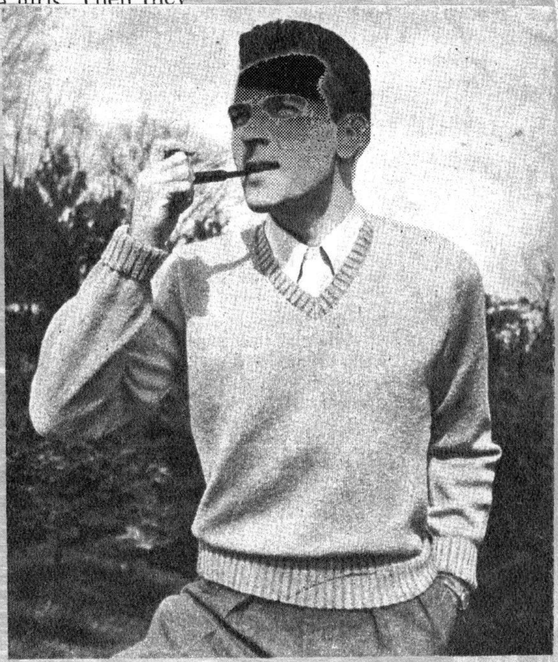

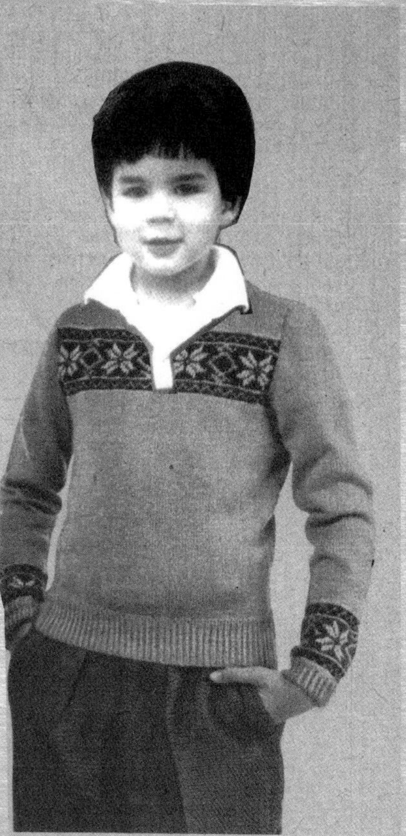

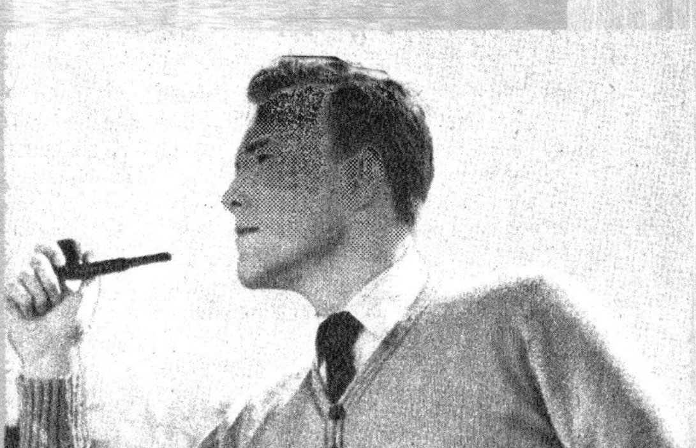

heels clicking.

**VIDEO GAMES TO KILL EACH OTHER**
**FOR WHATEVER GOD DAMN THING**
**THEY CALL A CONFLICT THESE DAYS**

**WAR IS JUST ANOTHER GOD DAMN SCREEN**

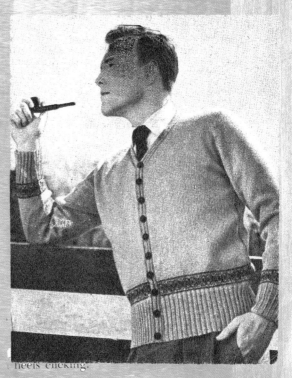

SO WHERE YOU GONNA GO NOW THAT THE SKIES
ARE FOR DRONES AND DIPSHITS JERKIN THEIR
GODDAMN JOYSTICKS?

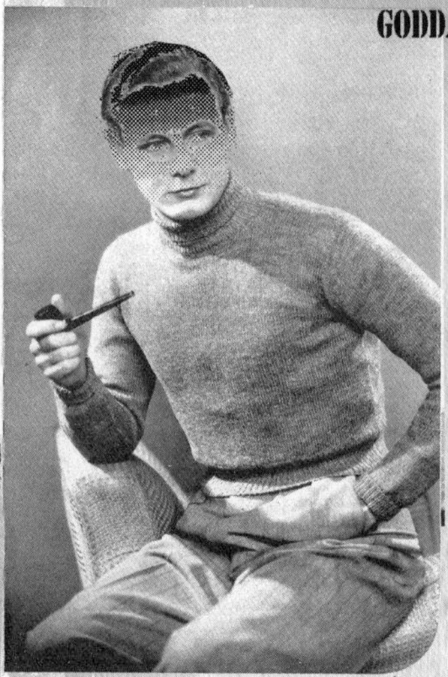

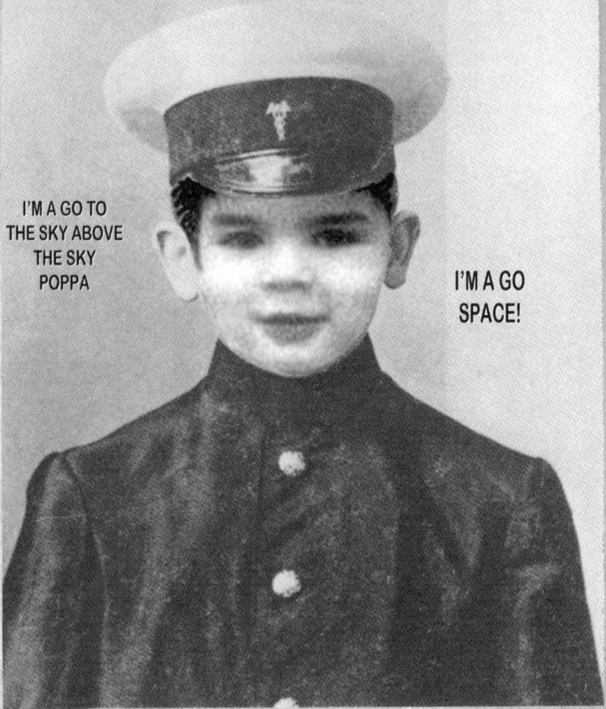
I'M A GO TO THE SKY ABOVE THE SKY POPPA
I'M A GO SPACE!

SPACE AINT NO GODDAMN SKY
THAT SHIT AINT EVEN FLYING

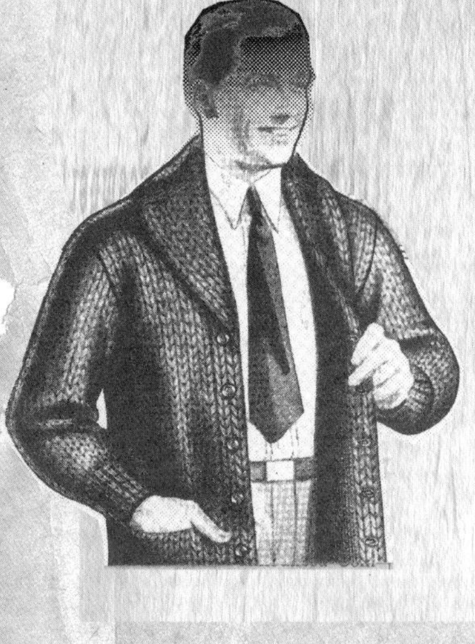

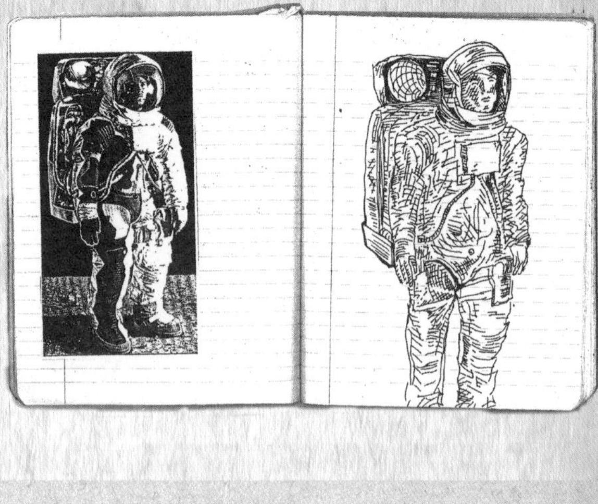

JUST FLOATING AROUND LIKE SOME FRUITY STAR TREK DIPSHITS

**I'M ACCEPTED TO THE STARSEED PROGRAM FATHER**

**OH GREAT
SO THIS PLANET IS FUCKED**

**SO YOU GO FUCK ANOTHER
IS THAT IT?**

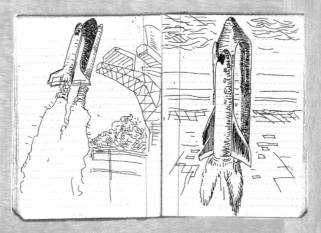

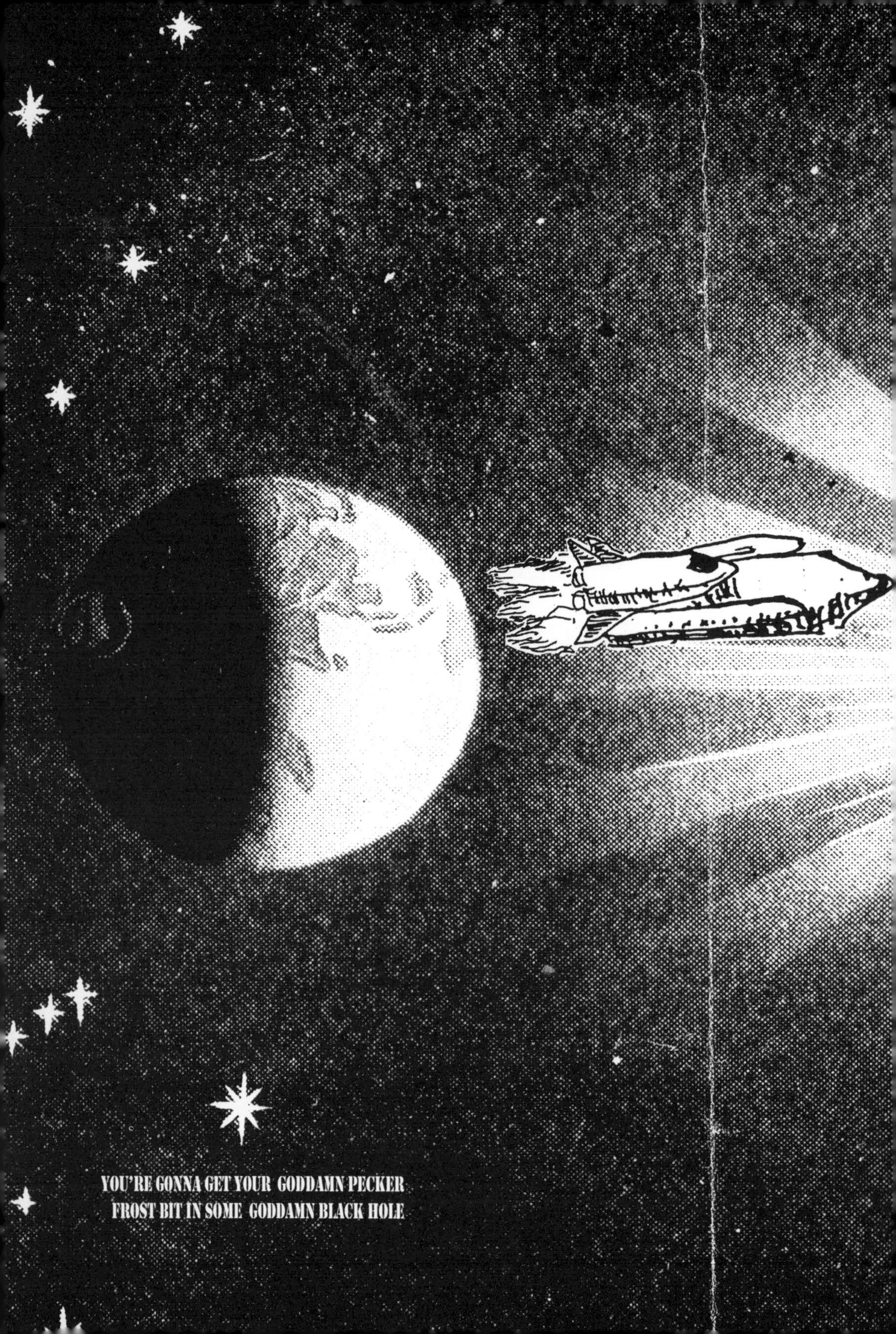
YOU'RE GONNA GET YOUR GODDAMN PECKER
FROST BIT IN SOME GODDAMN BLACK HOLE

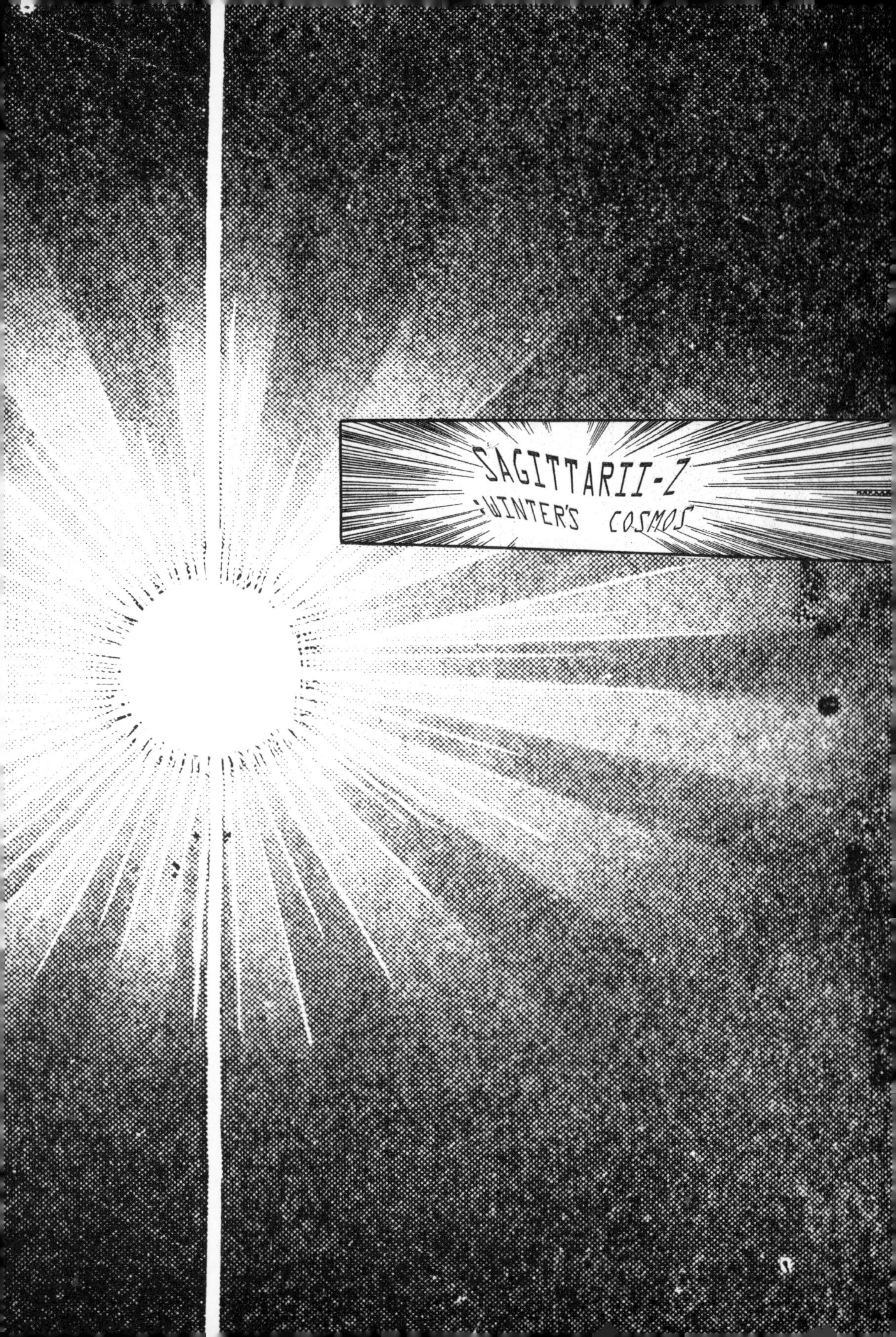
SAGITTARII-Z
: WINTER'S COSMOS

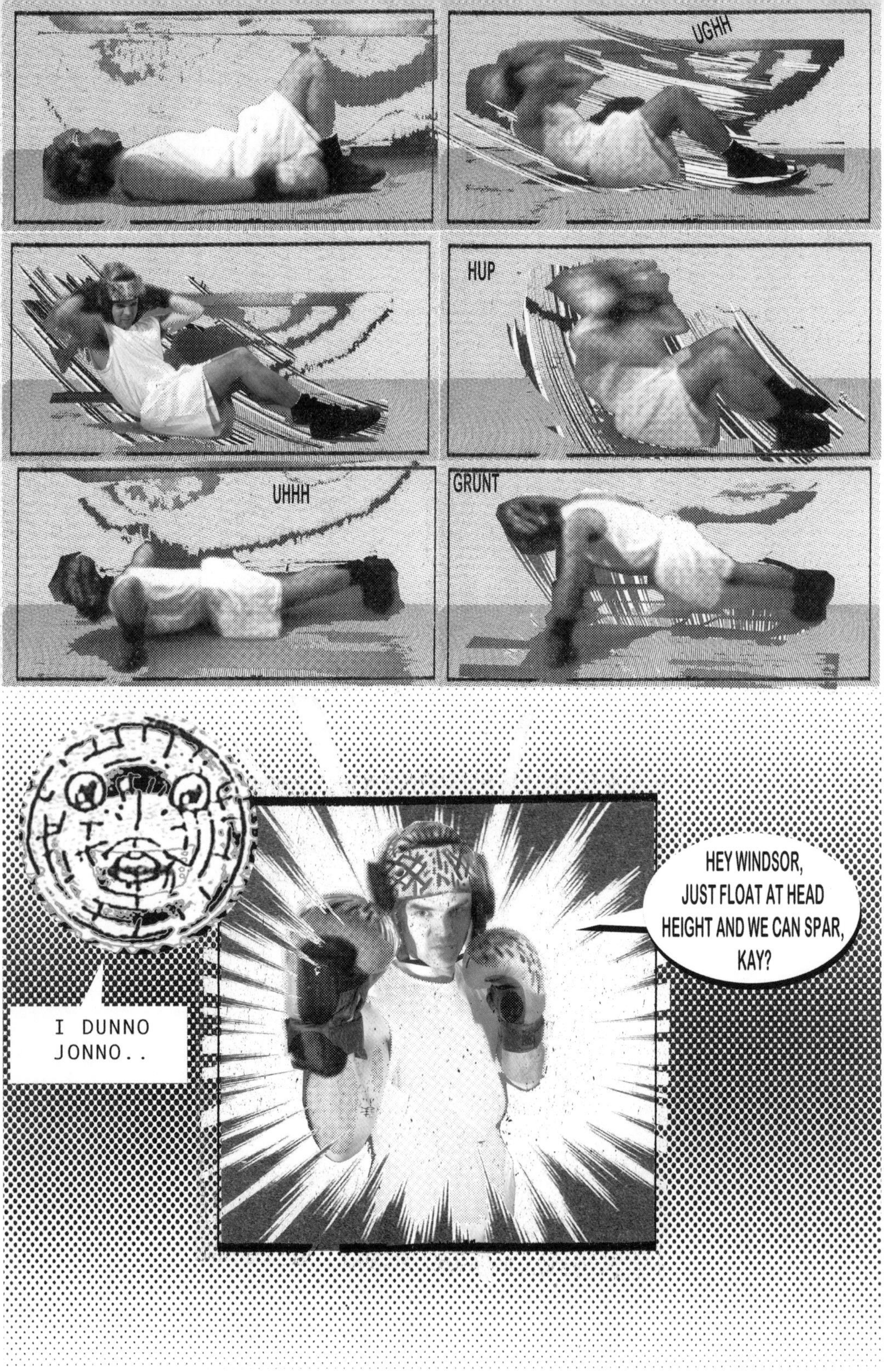
UGHH
HUP
UHHH
GRUNT
I DUNNO JONNO..
HEY WINDSOR, JUST FLOAT AT HEAD HEIGHT AND WE CAN SPAR, KAY?

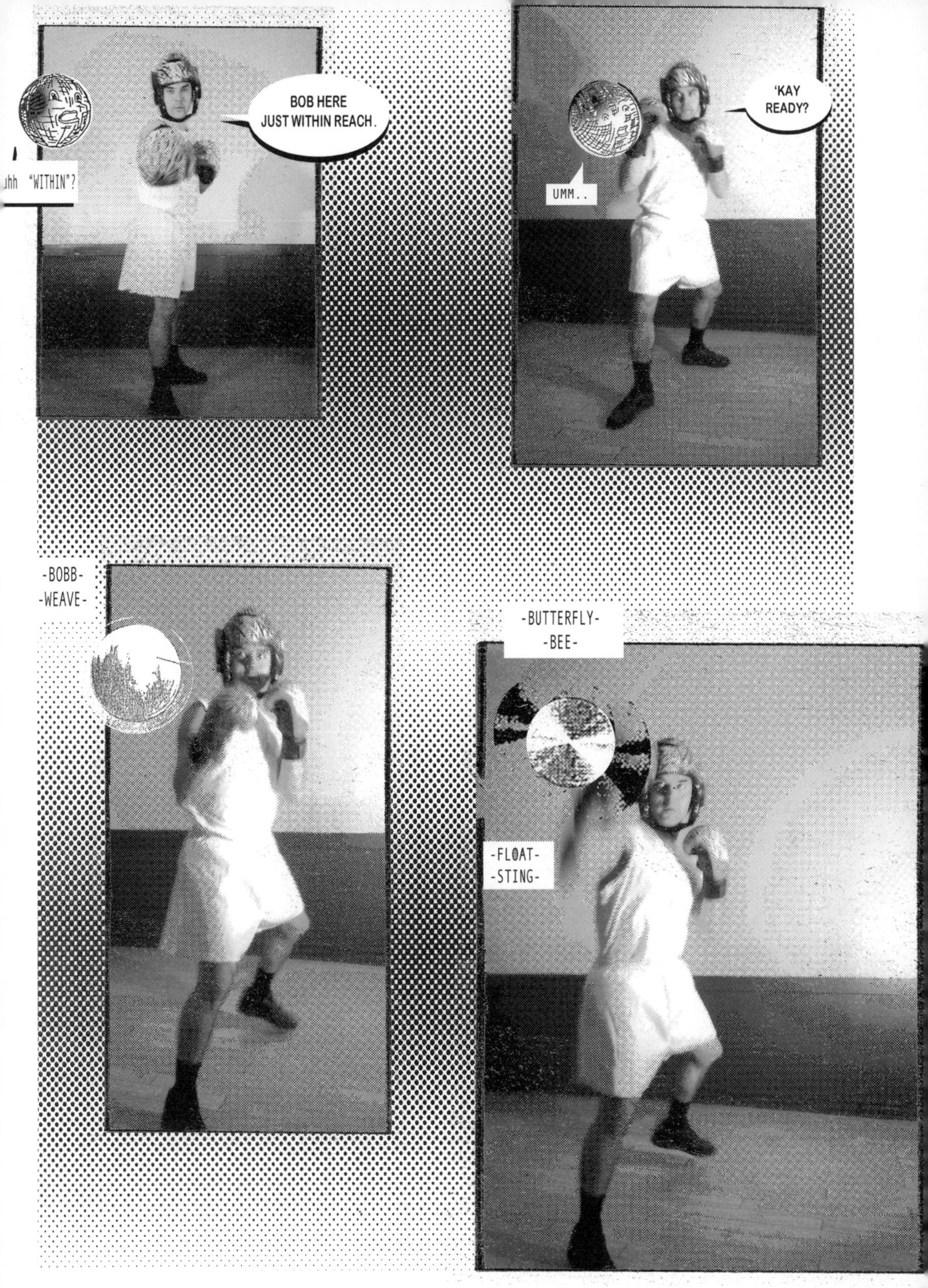
BOB HERE
JUST WITHIN REACH.
uhh "WITHIN"?
'KAY
READY?
UMM..
-BOBB-
-WEAVE-
-BUTTERFLY-
-BEE-
-FLOAT-
-STING-

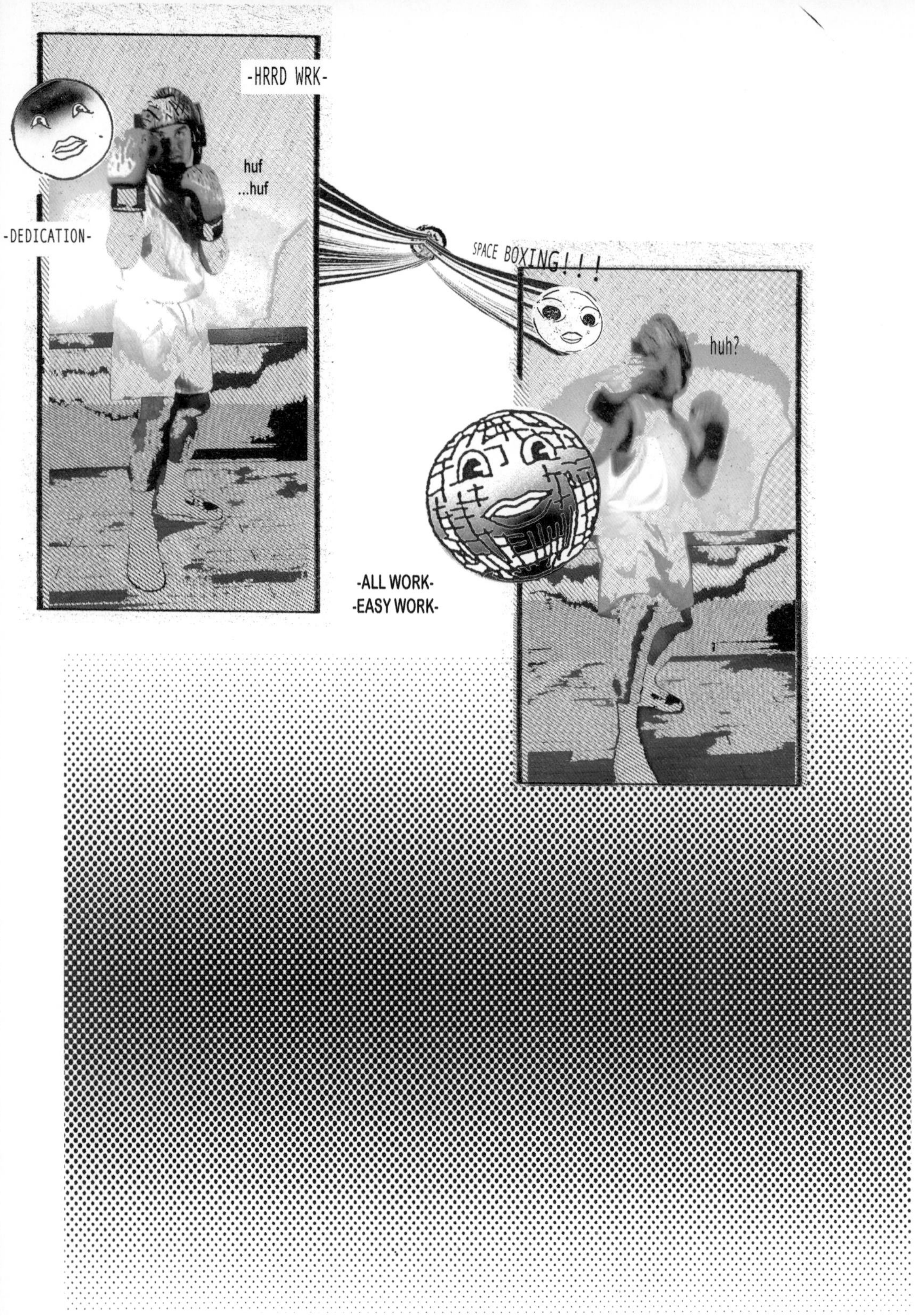

-HRRD WRK-
huf
...huf
-DEDICATION-
SPACE BOXING!!!
huh?
-ALL WORK-
-EASY WORK-

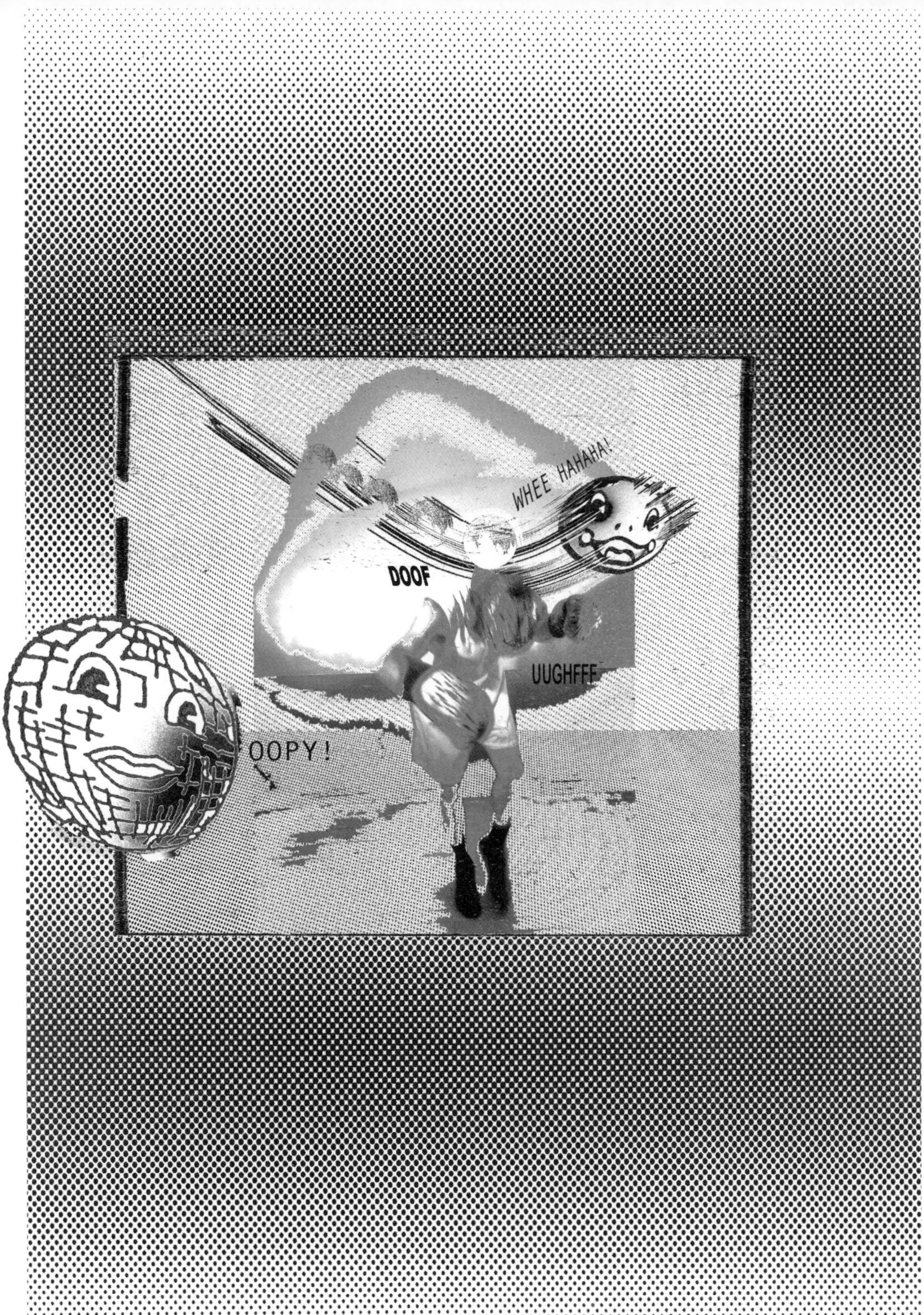
WHEE HAHAHA!
DOOF
UUGHFFF
OOPY!

POINK
OH MY.
WHAT THE FRICK BARRY?
AM I TO DO THAT?.
-BOXIN-
-BOXIN-
-BOX-IN-
THAT'S NOT BOXING!
SUCKER PUNCHING IS NOT BOXING!

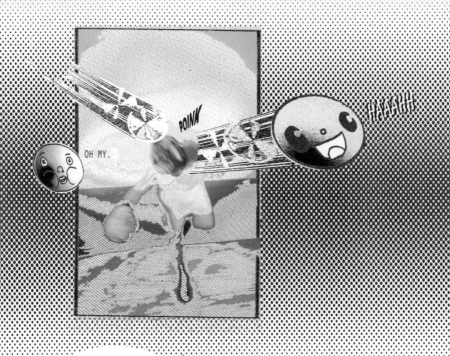

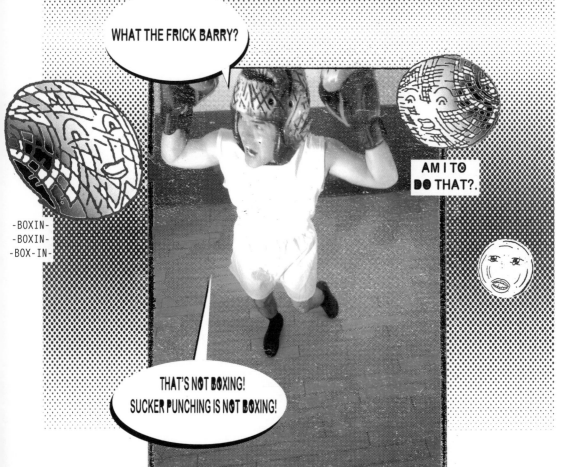

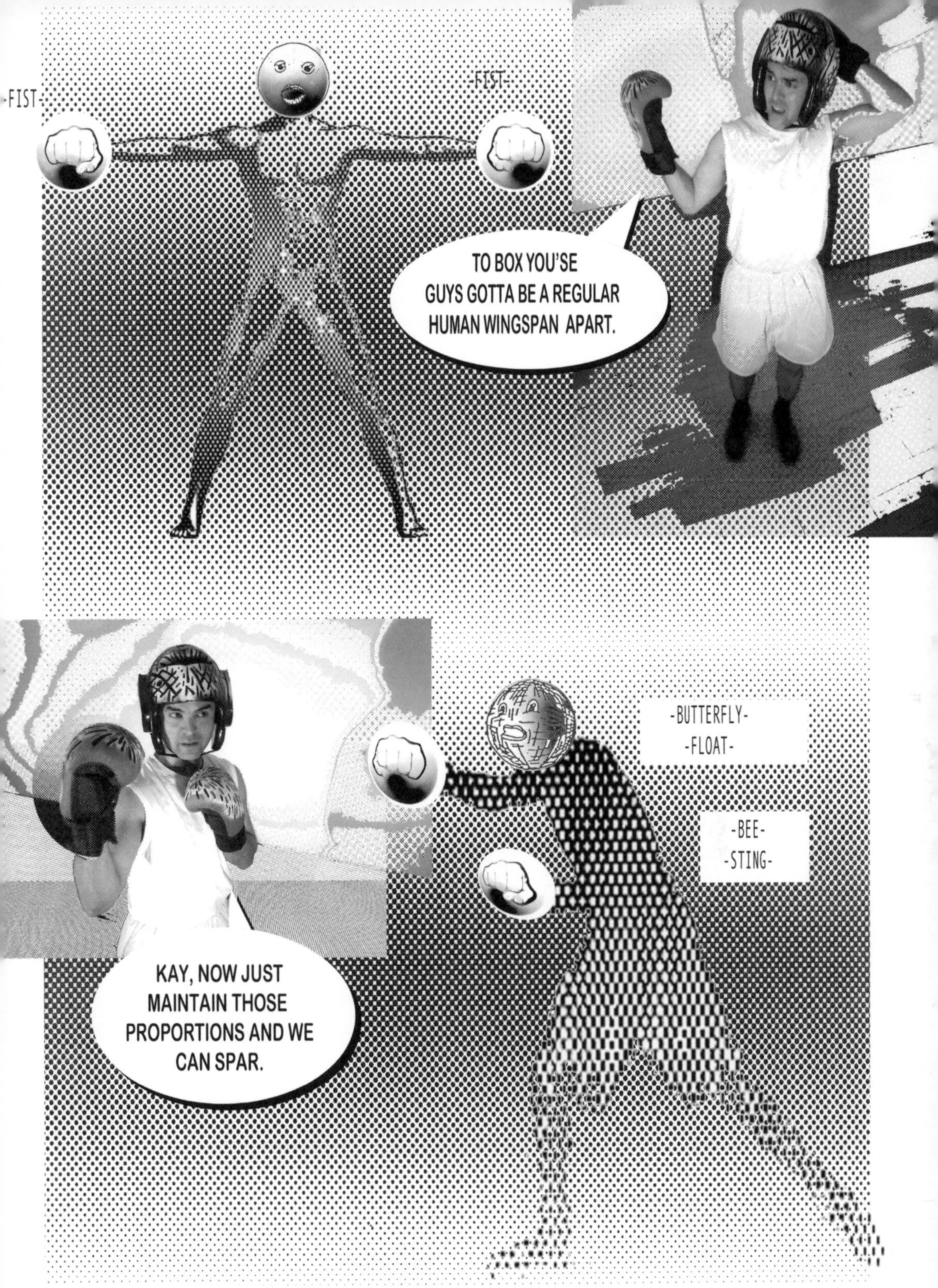
-FIST-
-FIST-
TO BOX YOU'SE GUYS GOTTA BE A REGULAR HUMAN WINGSPAN APART.
-BUTTERFLY-
-FLOAT-
-BEE-
-STING-
KAY, NOW JUST MAINTAIN THOSE PROPORTIONS AND WE CAN SPAR.

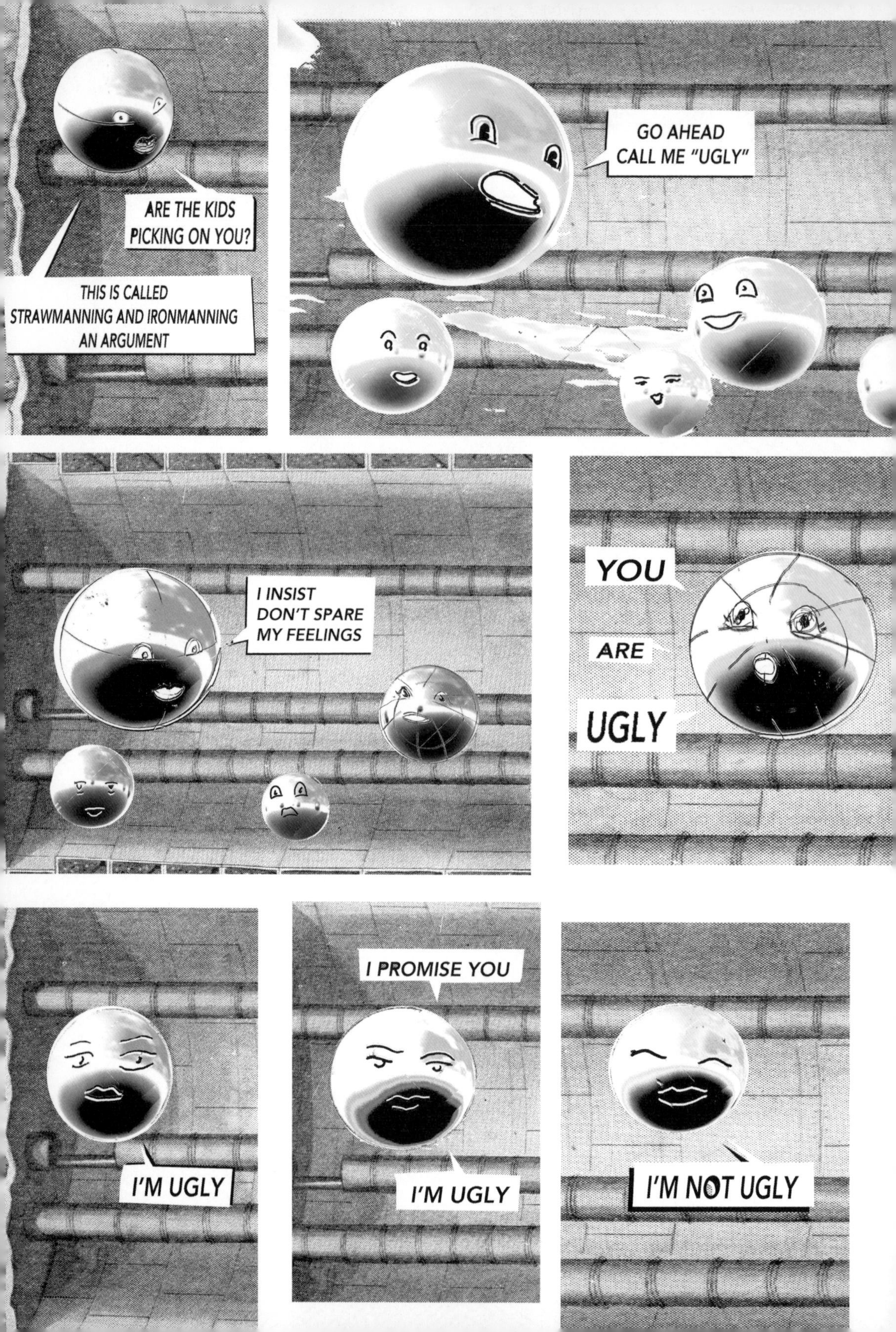
ARE THE KIDS PICKING ON YOU?
THIS IS CALLED STRAWMANNING AND IRONMANNING AN ARGUMENT
GO AHEAD CALL ME "UGLY"
I INSIST DON'T SPARE MY FEELINGS
YOU
ARE
UGLY
I'M UGLY
I PROMISE YOU
I'M UGLY
I'M NOT UGLY

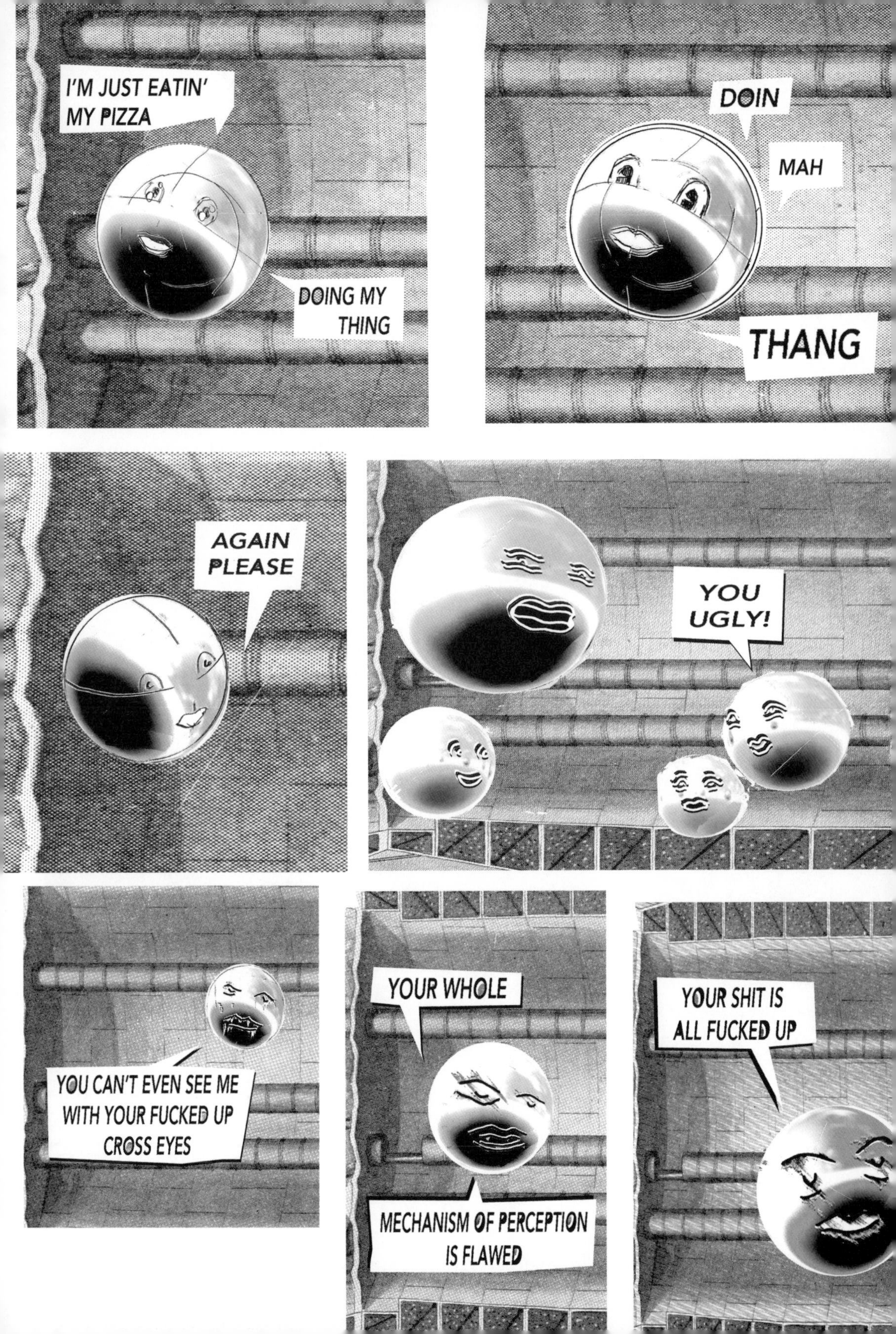
I'M JUST EATIN' MY PIZZA
DOING MY THING
DOIN
MAH
THANG
AGAIN PLEASE
YOU UGLY!
YOU CAN'T EVEN SEE ME WITH YOUR FUCKED UP CROSS EYES
YOUR WHOLE
MECHANISM OF PERCEPTION IS FLAWED
YOUR SHIT IS ALL FUCKED UP

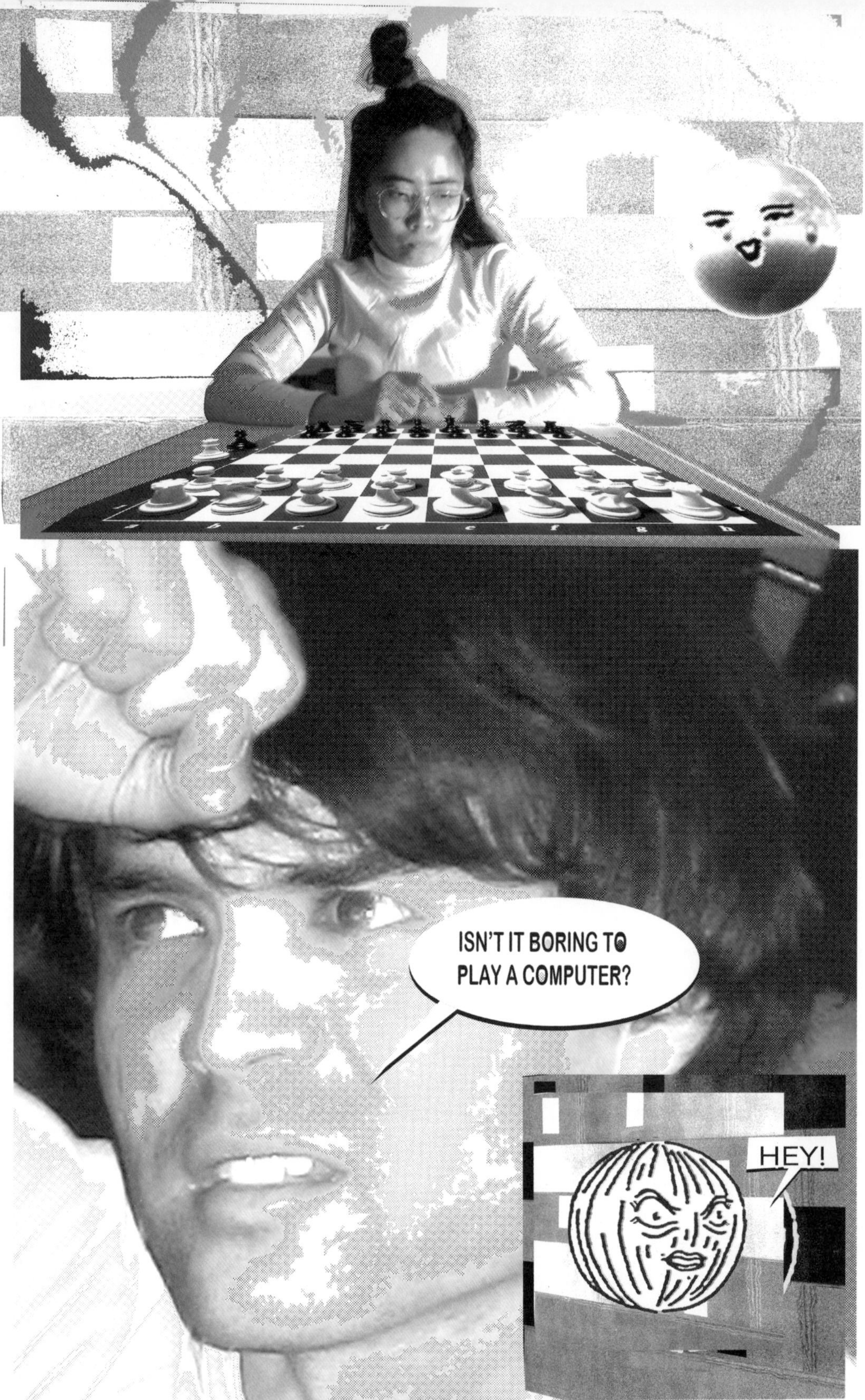
ISN'T IT BORING TO PLAY A COMPUTER?
HEY!

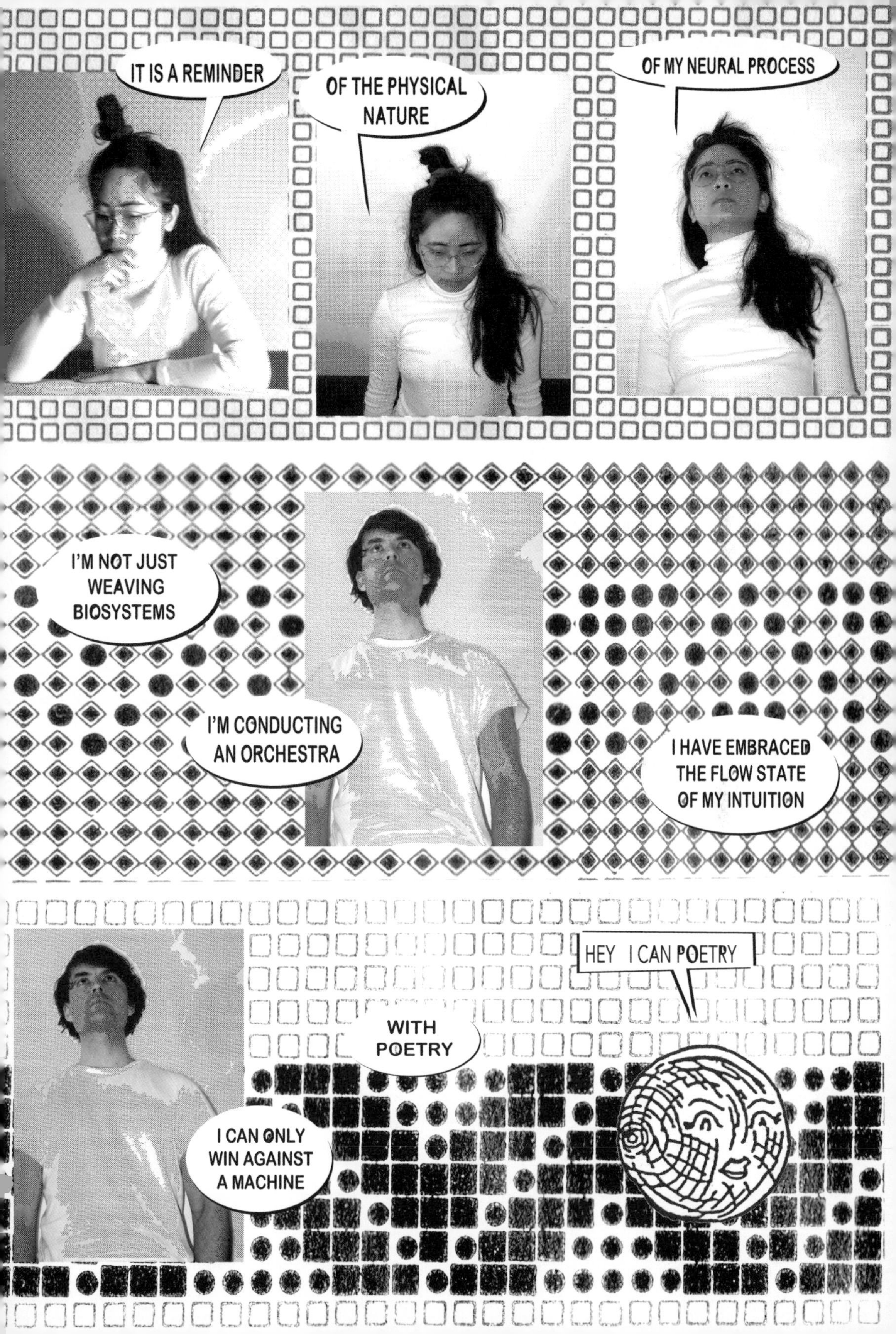
IT IS A REMINDER
OF THE PHYSICAL NATURE
OF MY NEURAL PROCESS
I'M NOT JUST WEAVING BIOSYSTEMS
I'M CONDUCTING AN ORCHESTRA
I HAVE EMBRACED THE FLOW STATE OF MY INTUITION
I CAN ONLY WIN AGAINST A MACHINE
WITH POETRY
HEY I CAN POETRY

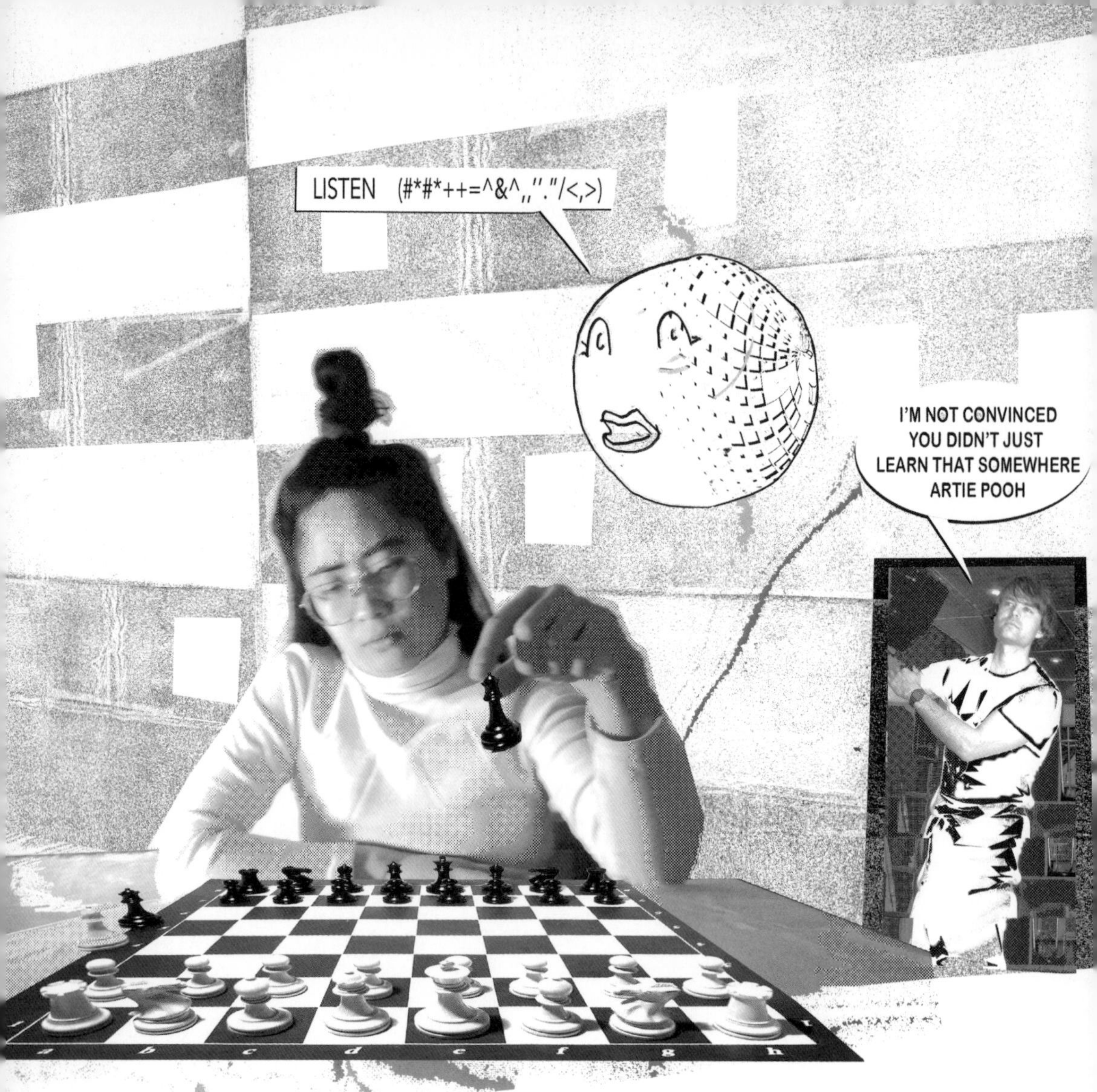
LISTEN (#*#*++=^&^„"."/<,>)
I'M NOT CONVINCED YOU DIDN'T JUST LEARN THAT SOMEWHERE ARTIE POOH

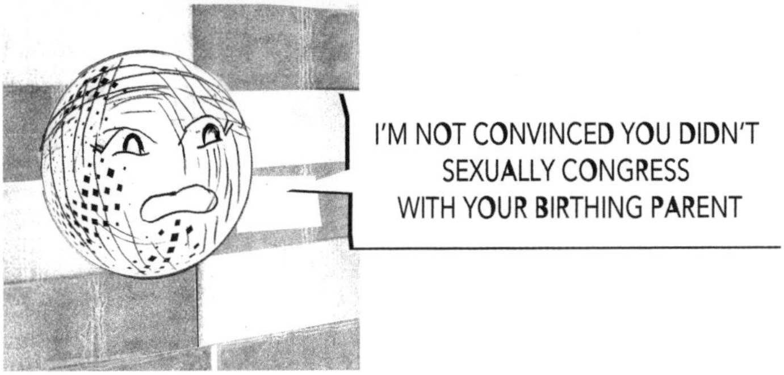
I'M NOT CONVINCED YOU DIDN'T SEXUALLY CONGRESS WITH YOUR BIRTHING PARENT

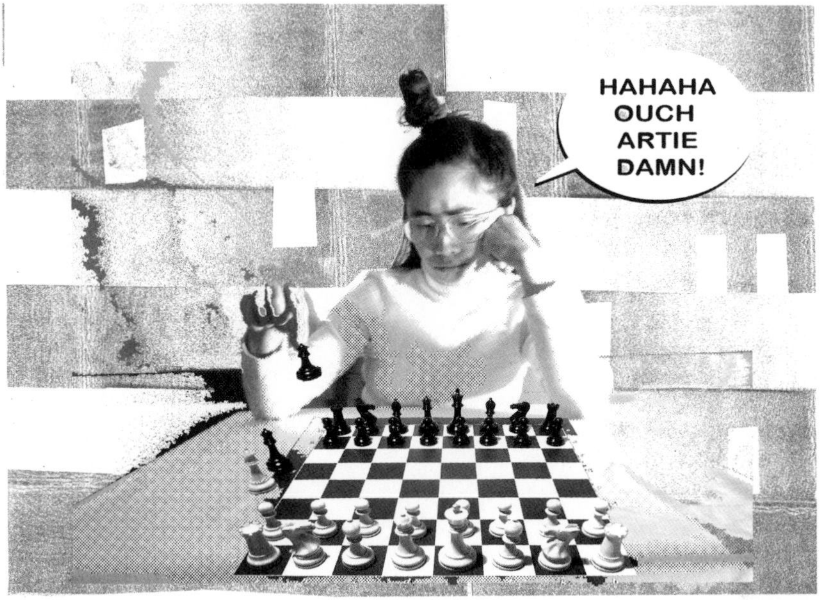
HAHAHA OUCH ARTIE DAMN!

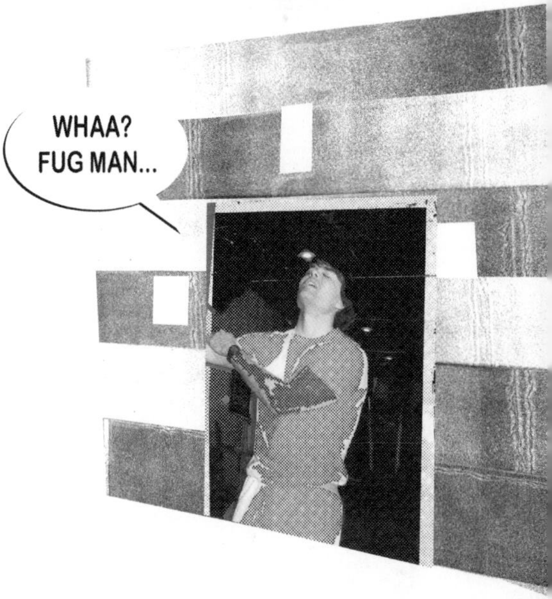
WHAA? FUG MAN...

# thREE inTERIORS

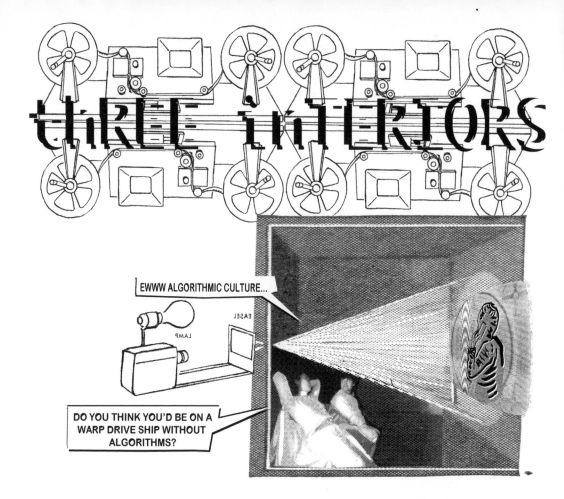

EWWW ALGORITHMIC CULTURE...

LAMP

EASEL

DO YOU THINK YOU'D BE ON A WARP DRIVE SHIP WITHOUT ALGORITHMS?

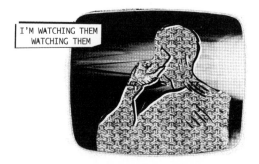

I'M WATCHING THEM WATCHING THEM

YOU NEVER KNOW WHAT'S GOING TO HAPPEN IN THIS ROOM

I'M ALWAYS WATCHING

I GUESS IT MUST BE BORING FOR YOU

WATCHING ME WATCHING

BUT I NEVER KNOW WHAT YOU'LL BE WATCHING

SO WHERE'S THE THIRD INTERIOR?
WHITE OF THE EYE
OPTIC NERVE
to the Brain
IRIS
LENS
EYE SOCKET
IT'S SUGGESTED, A SHADOW OF THE GAZED
I GUESS WHEN YOU ARE A COUPLE YOU DON'T BOTHER WATCHING YOUR ASSIGNED ROOM
SINGLE GUYS LIKE US HAVE TIME TO BOTHER
OH I'M NOT A SINGLE GUY I'M AN ALGORITHM

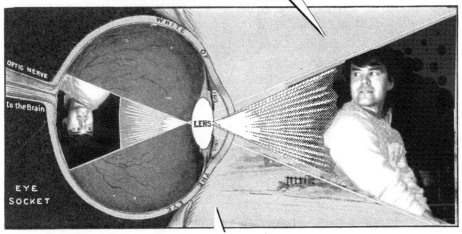

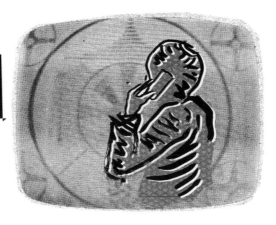

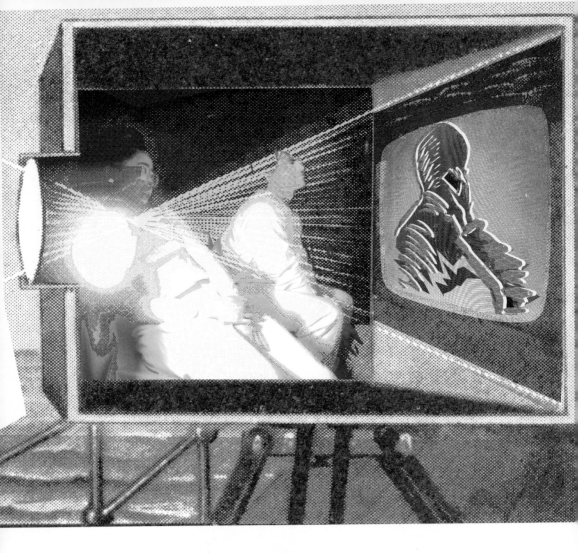

WHA?
REALLY?

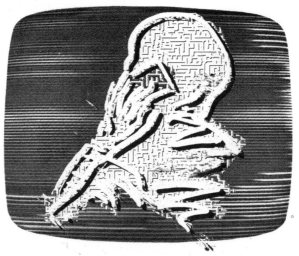

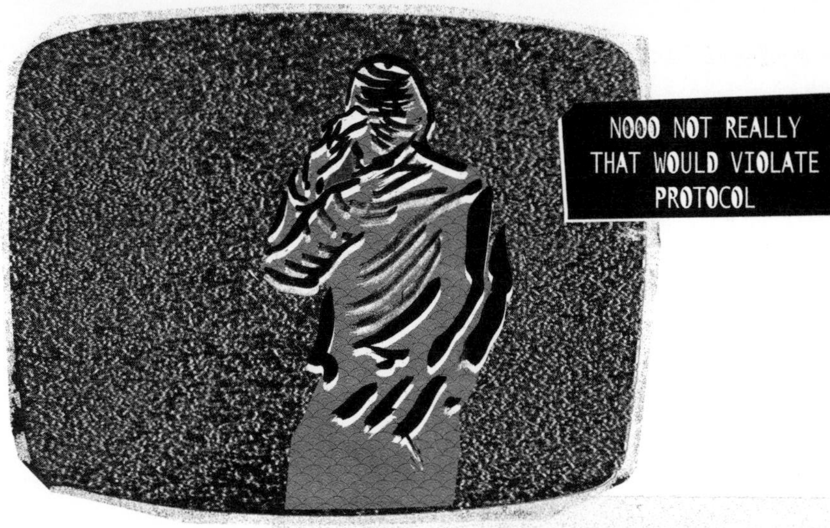
NOOO NOT REALLY
THAT WOULD VIOLATE
PROTOCOL

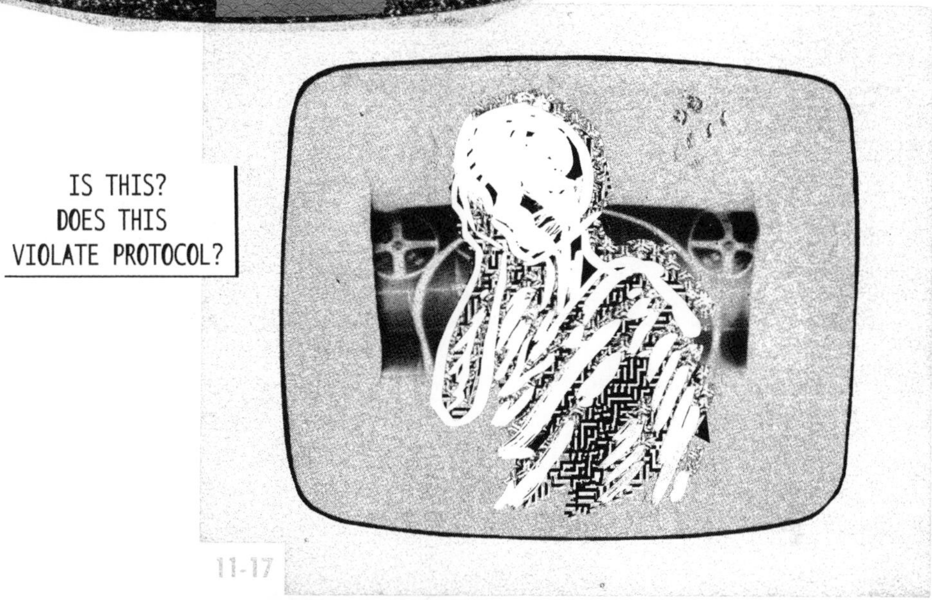
IS THIS?
DOES THIS
VIOLATE PROTOCOL?
11-17

Fig. O C1A open.

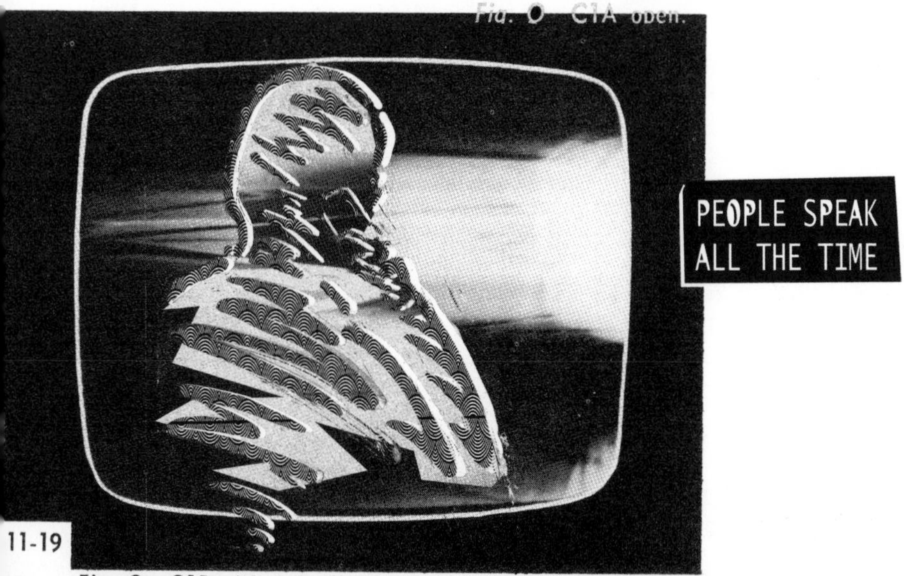
PEOPLE SPEAK
ALL THE TIME
11-19

Fig. Q Ç1B reduced.

BUT BETWEEN WATCHER AND WATCHED?
THAT SEEMS UNUSUAL AT LEAST IF NOT A VIOLATION
LOOK, SOME PEOPLE DON'T EVEN BOTHER TO WATCH
WE ARE TWO PEOPLE THAT BOTHER TALKING TO EACH OTHER
I DON'T SEE HOW THAT DETRACTS FROM ANYTHING
IF ANYTHING WE PROBABLY GET MORE WATCHING DONE ANYHOW
DO YOU KNOW YOUR WATCHER?
OH GOODNESS NO

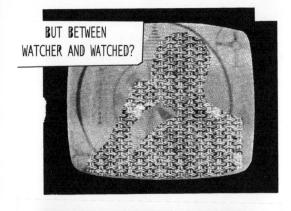

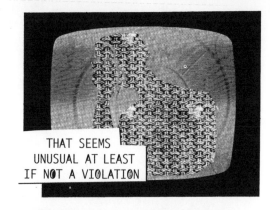

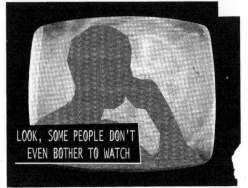

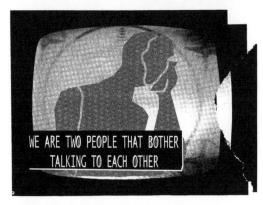

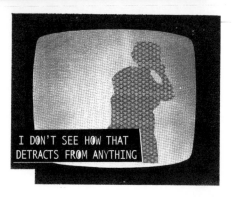

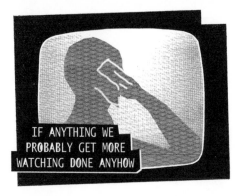

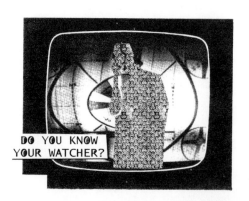

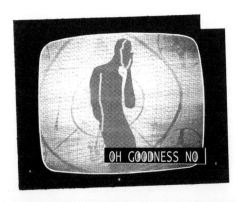

WHAT DO YOU THINK THEY ARE DOING?
JERKIN' IT PROBS
YA THINK?

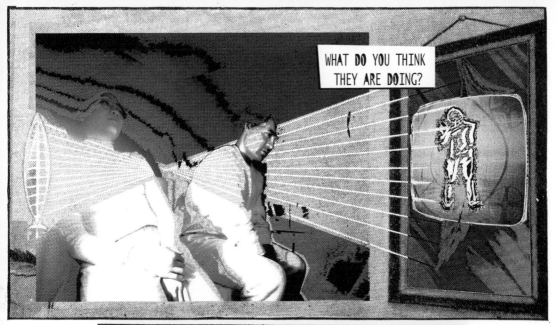

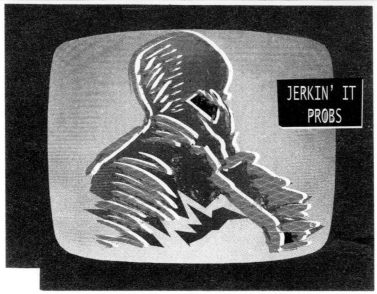

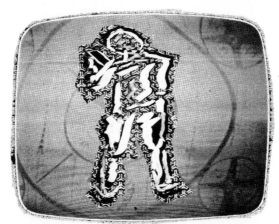

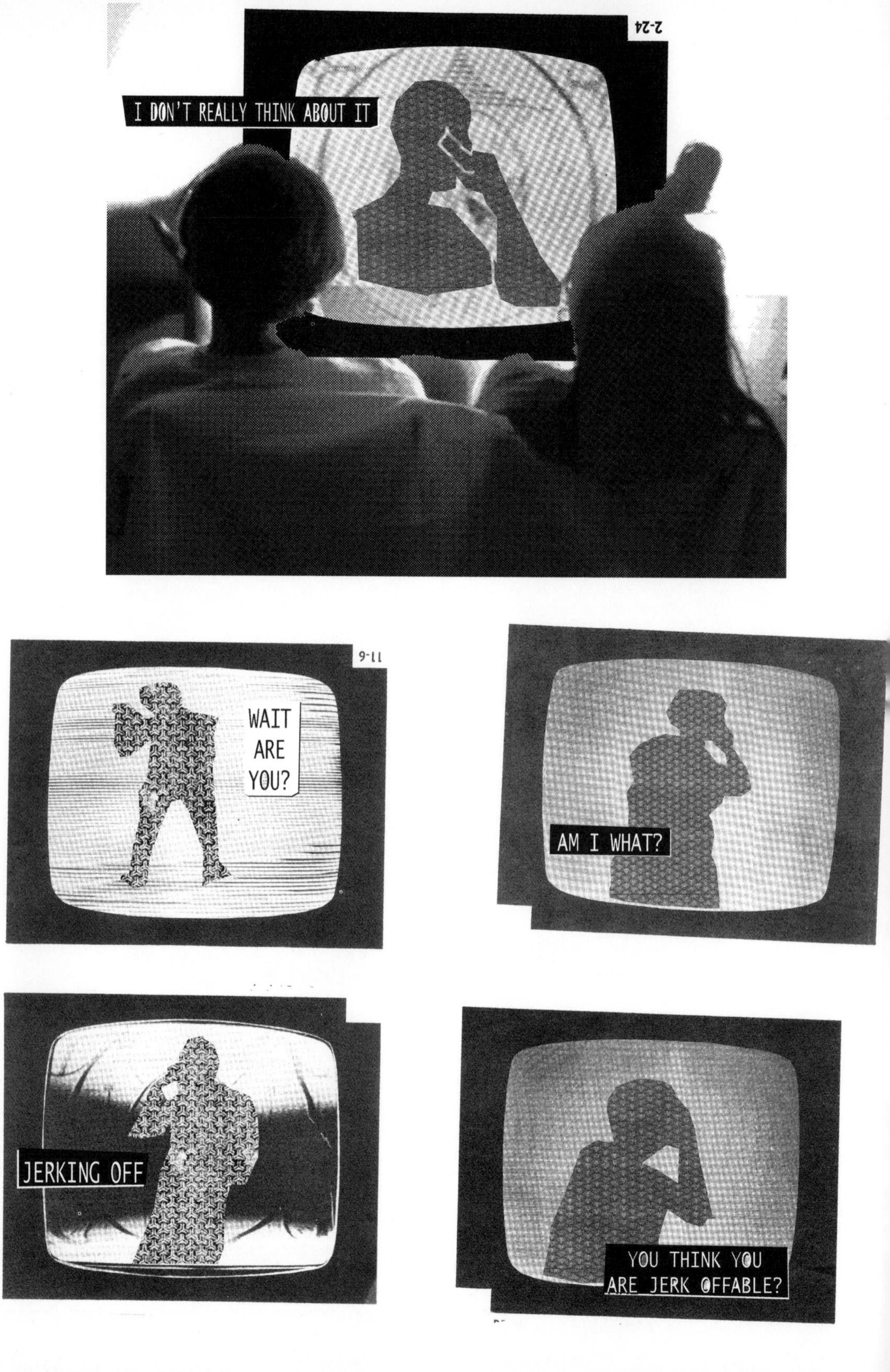
I DON'T REALLY THINK ABOUT IT
WAIT ARE YOU?
AM I WHAT?
JERKING OFF
YOU THINK YOU ARE JERK OFFABLE?

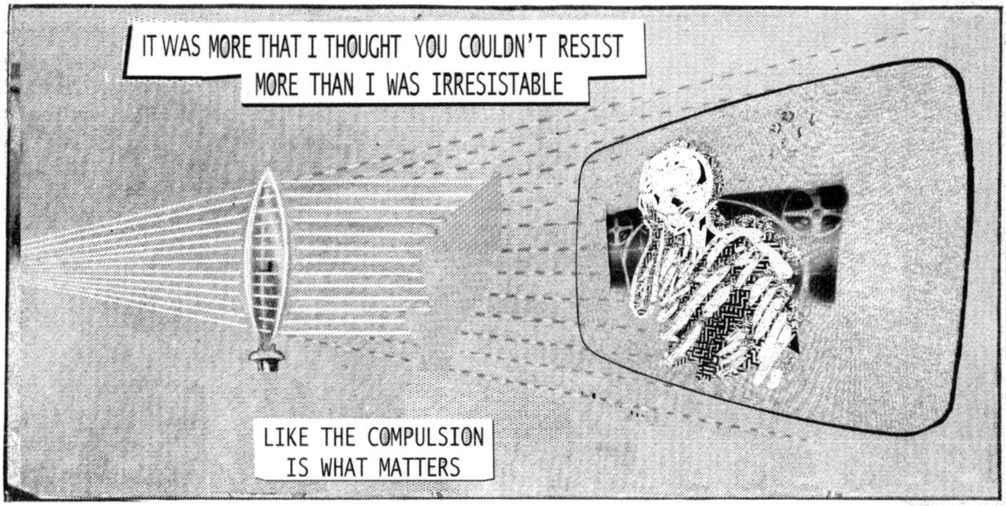
IT WAS MORE THAT I THOUGHT YOU COULDN'T RESIST
MORE THAN I WAS IRRESISTABLE
LIKE THE COMPULSION
IS WHAT MATTERS

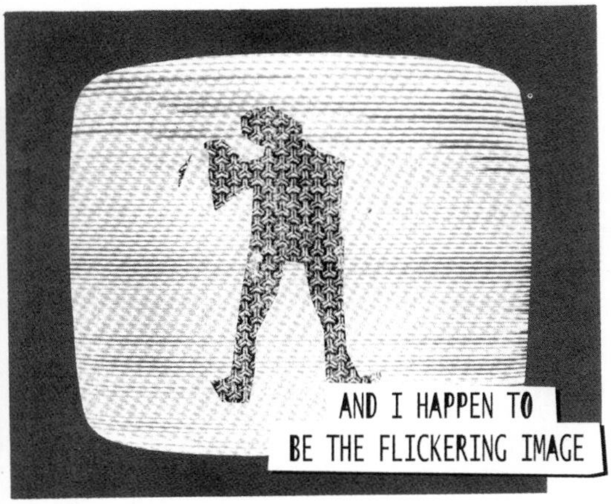
AND I HAPPEN TO
BE THE FLICKERING IMAGE

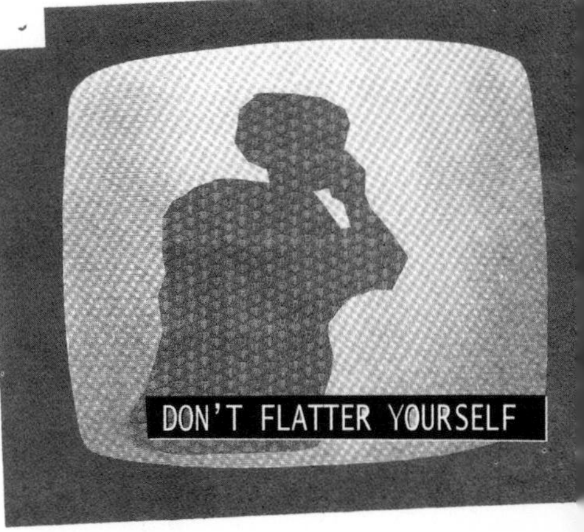
DON'T FLATTER YOURSELF

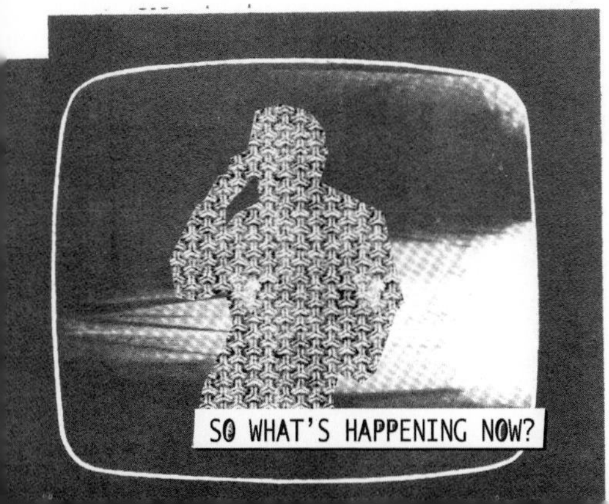
SO WHAT'S HAPPENING NOW?

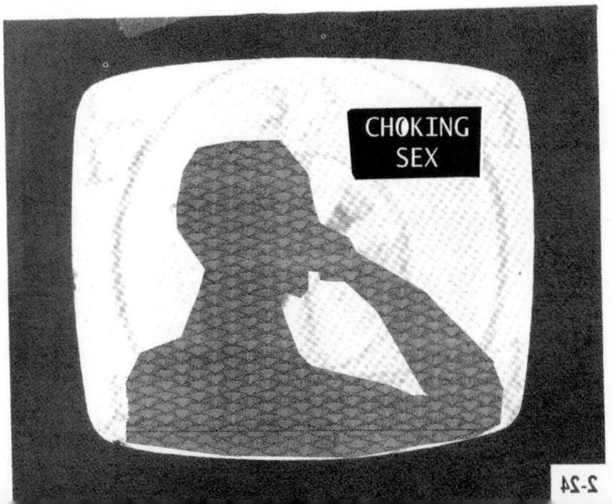
CHOKING
SEX

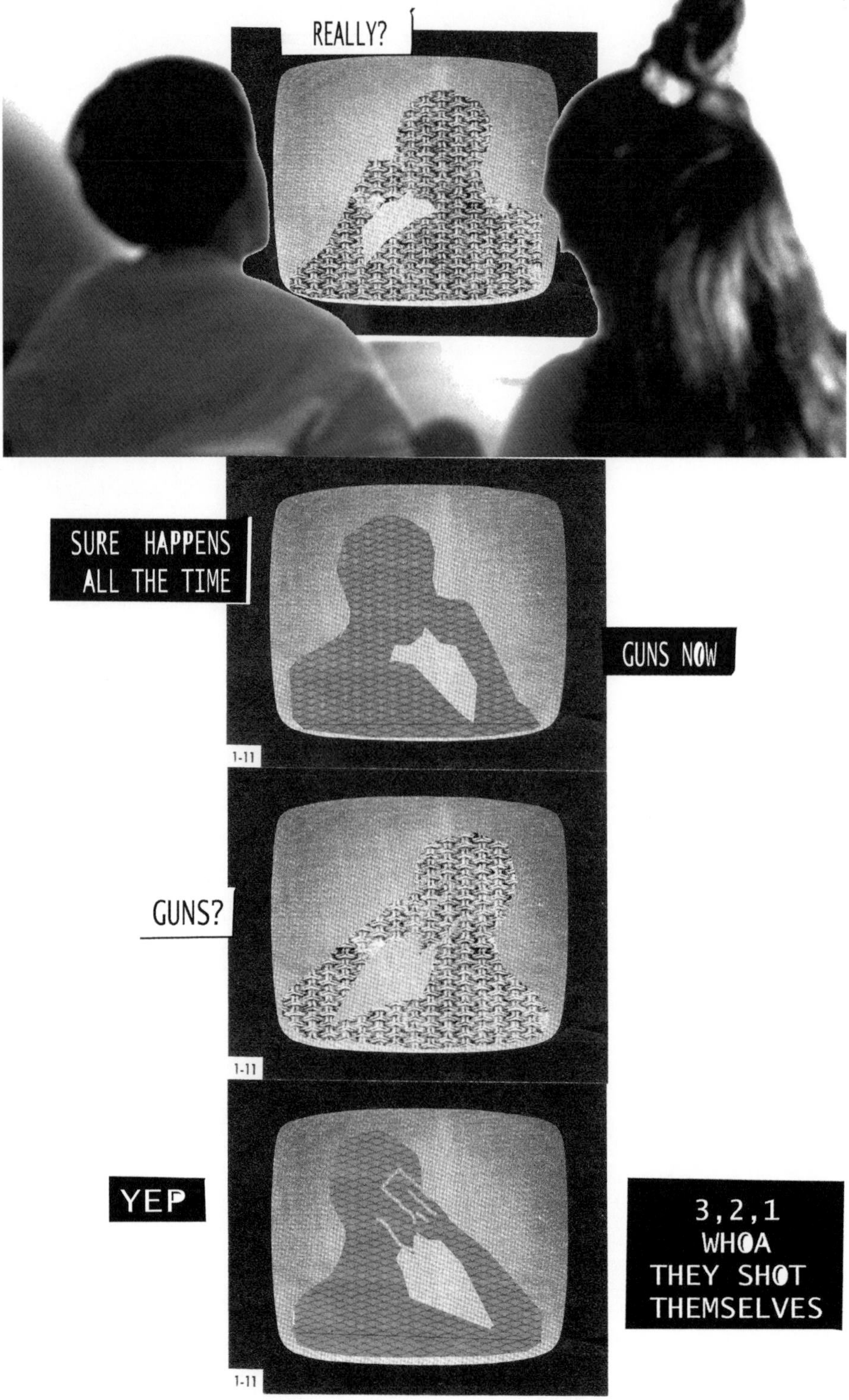
REALLY?
SURE HAPPENS ALL THE TIME
GUNS NOW
1-11
GUNS?
1-11
YEP
3,2,1 WHOA THEY SHOT THEMSELVES
1-11

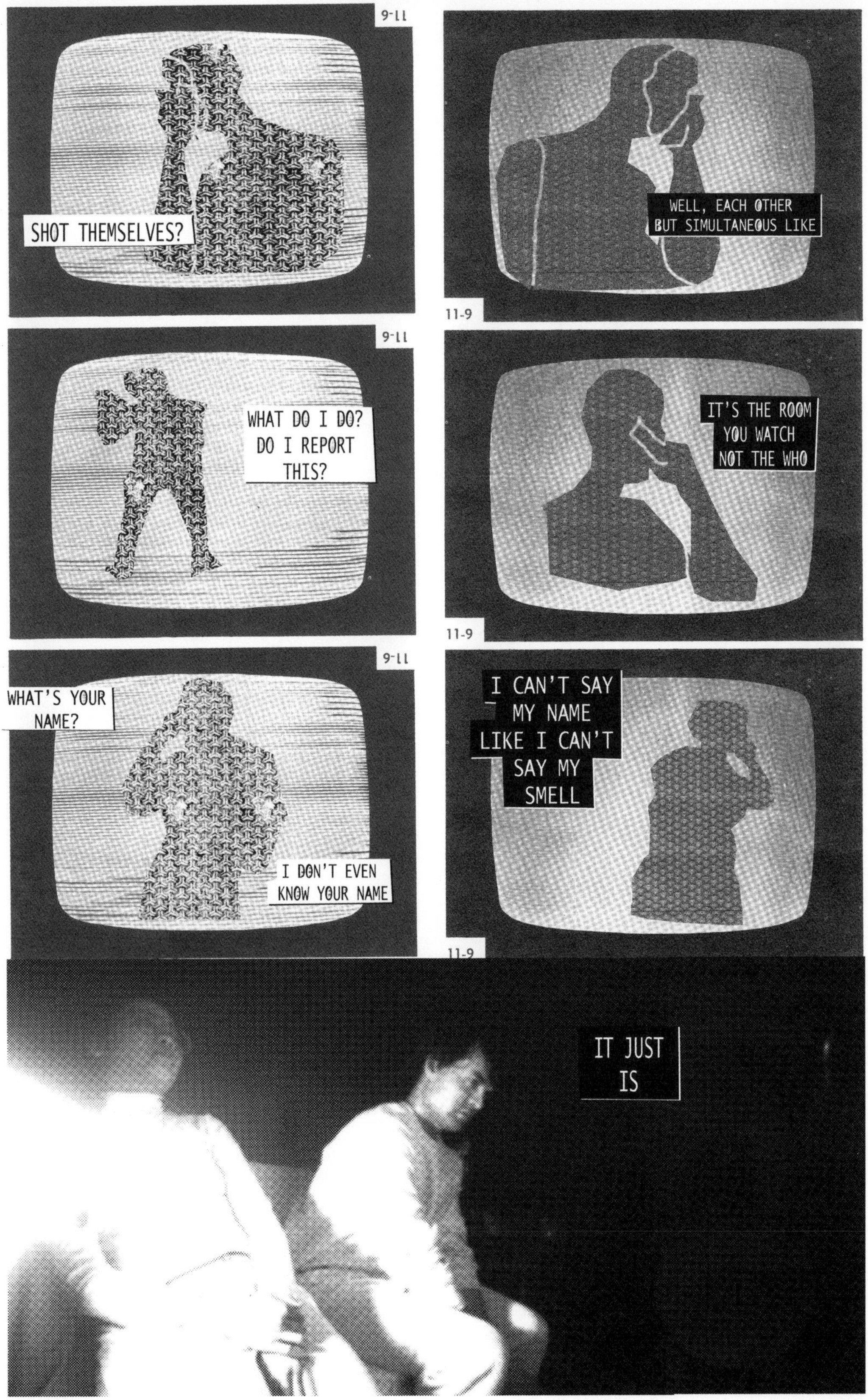
11-9
SHOT THEMSELVES?
WELL, EACH OTHER BUT SIMULTANEOUS LIKE
11-9
11-9
WHAT DO I DO? DO I REPORT THIS?
IT'S THE ROOM YOU WATCH NOT THE WHO
11-9
11-9
WHAT'S YOUR NAME?
I DON'T EVEN KNOW YOUR NAME
I CAN'T SAY MY NAME LIKE I CAN'T SAY MY SMELL
11-9
IT JUST IS

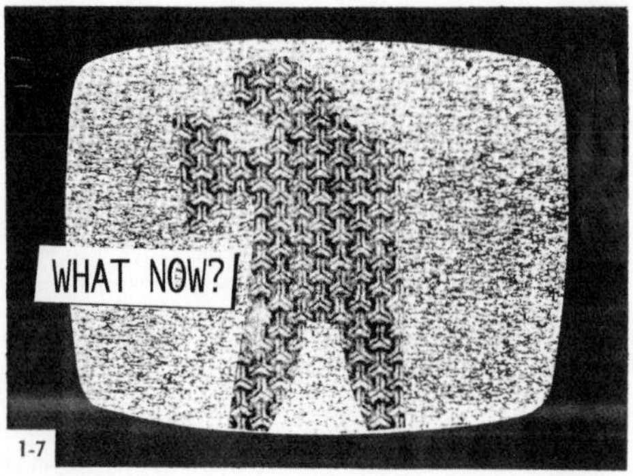
WHAT NOW?
1-7

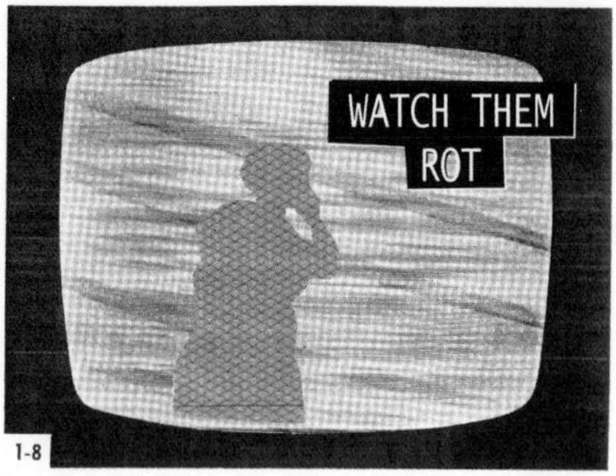
WATCH THEM ROT
1-8

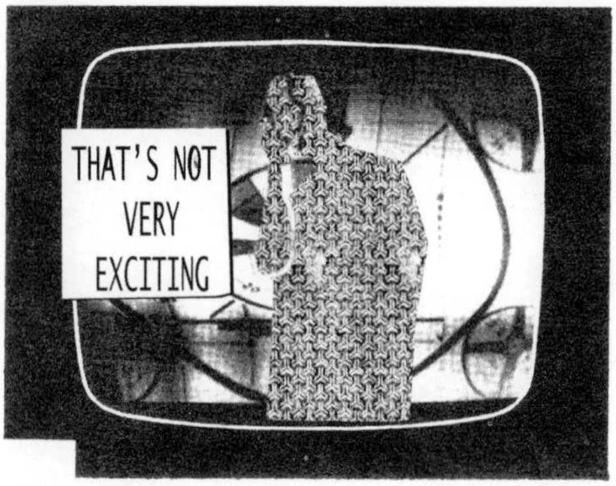
THAT'S NOT VERY EXCITING

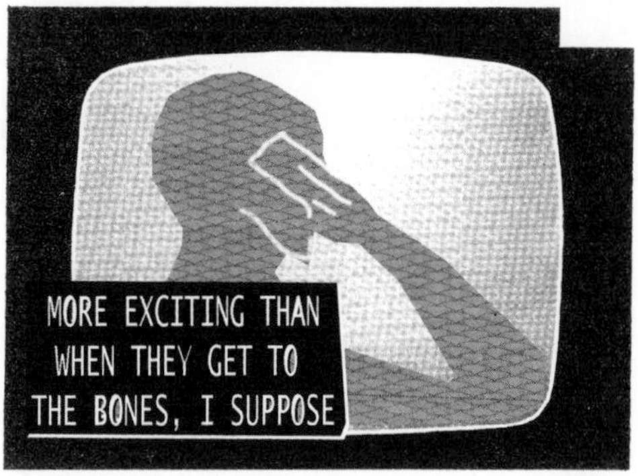
MORE EXCITING THAN WHEN THEY GET TO THE BONES, I SUPPOSE

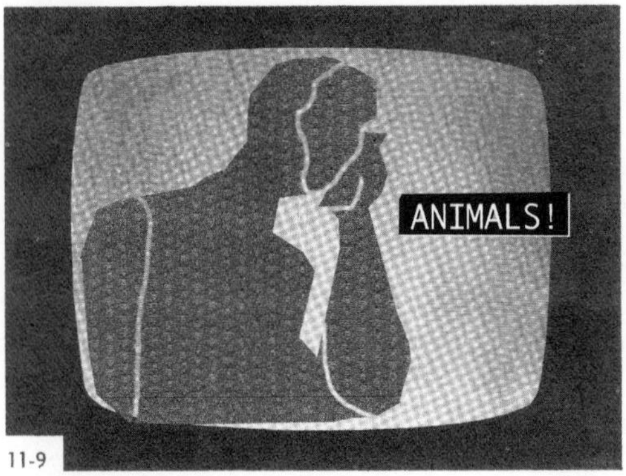
ANIMALS!
11-9

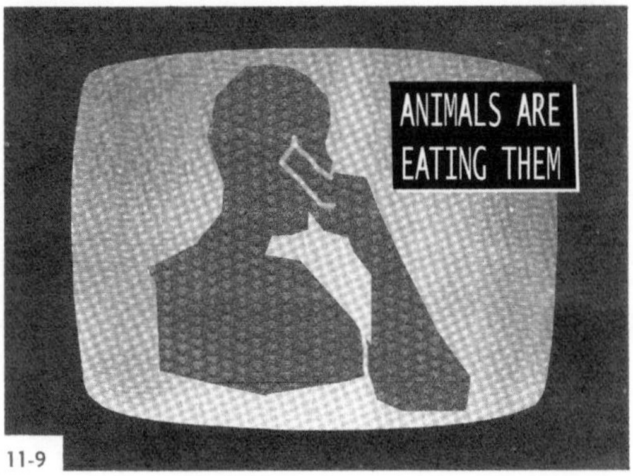
ANIMALS ARE EATING THEM
11-9

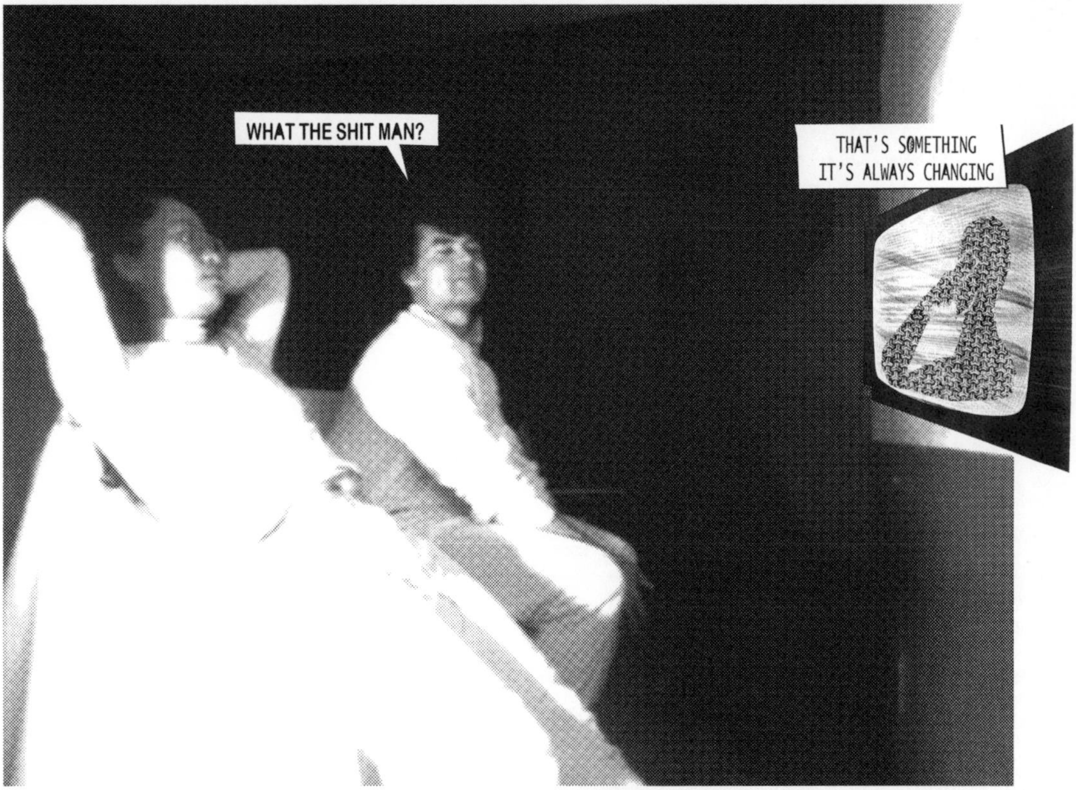
WHAT THE SHIT MAN?
THAT'S SOMETHING
IT'S ALWAYS CHANGING

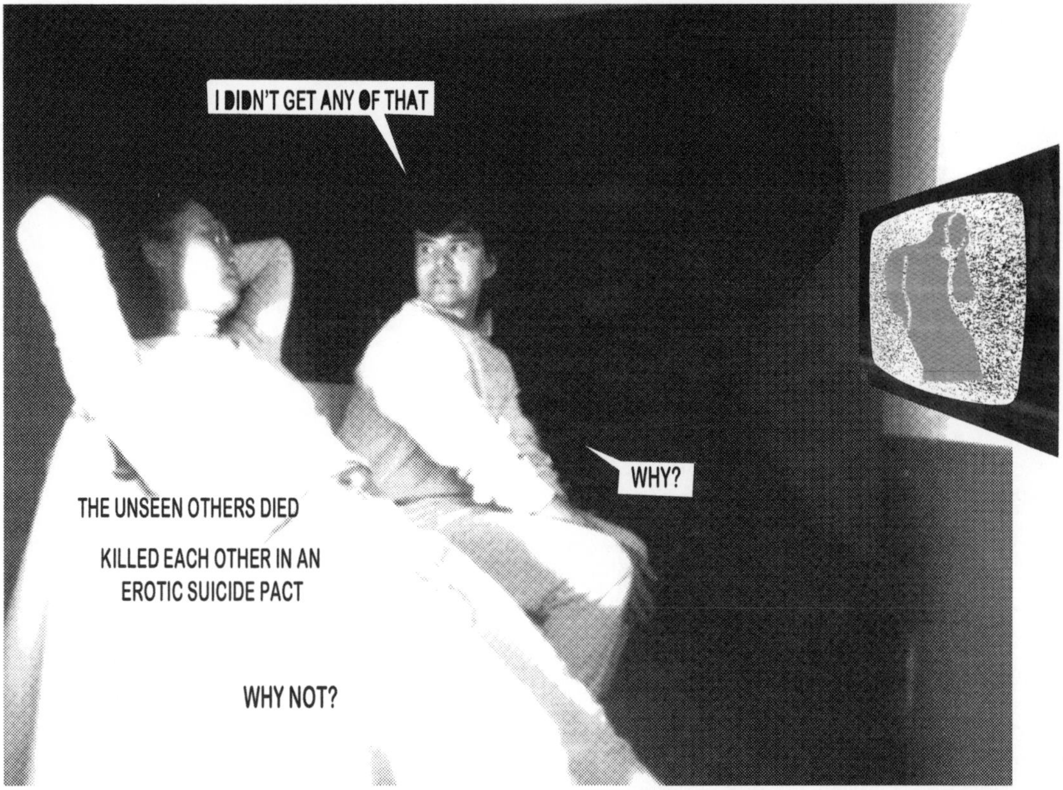
I DIDN'T GET ANY OF THAT
WHY?
THE UNSEEN OTHERS DIED
KILLED EACH OTHER IN AN
EROTIC SUICIDE PACT
WHY NOT?

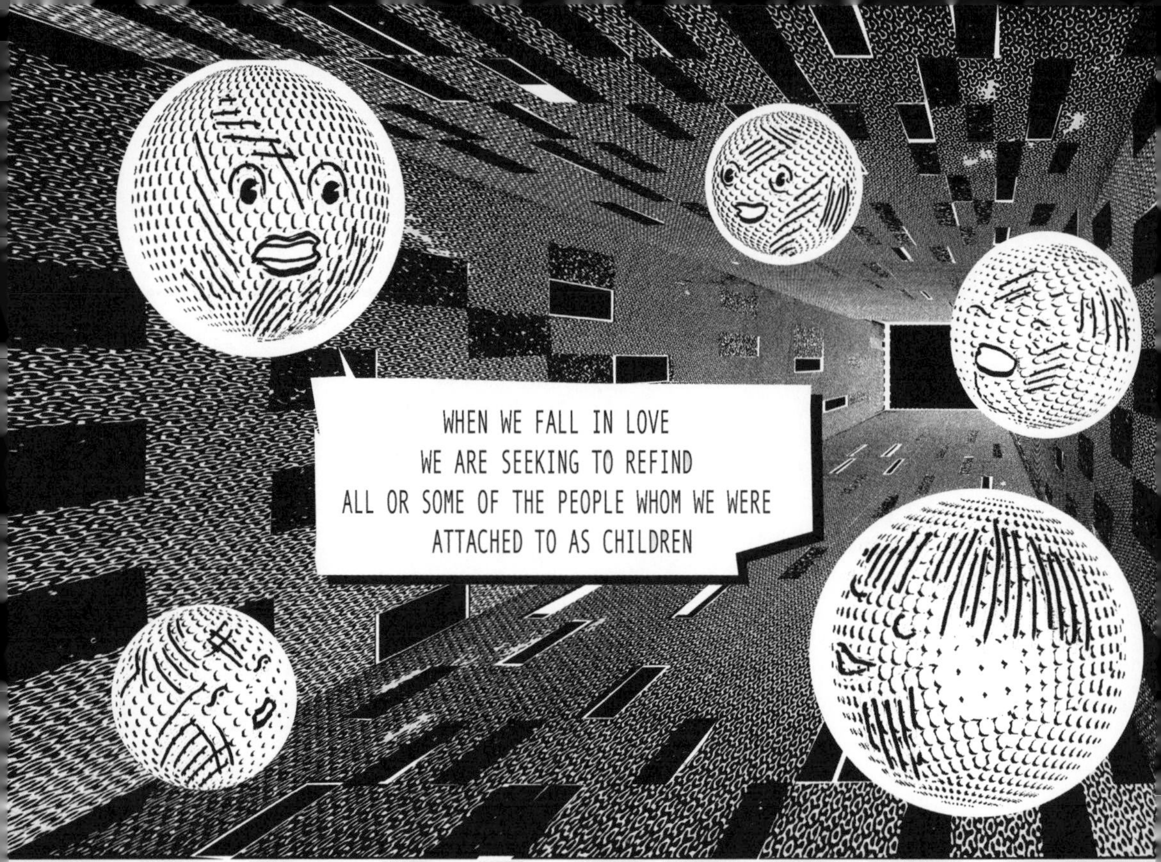
WHEN WE FALL IN LOVE
WE ARE SEEKING TO REFIND
ALL OR SOME OF THE PEOPLE WHOM WE WERE
ATTACHED TO AS CHILDREN

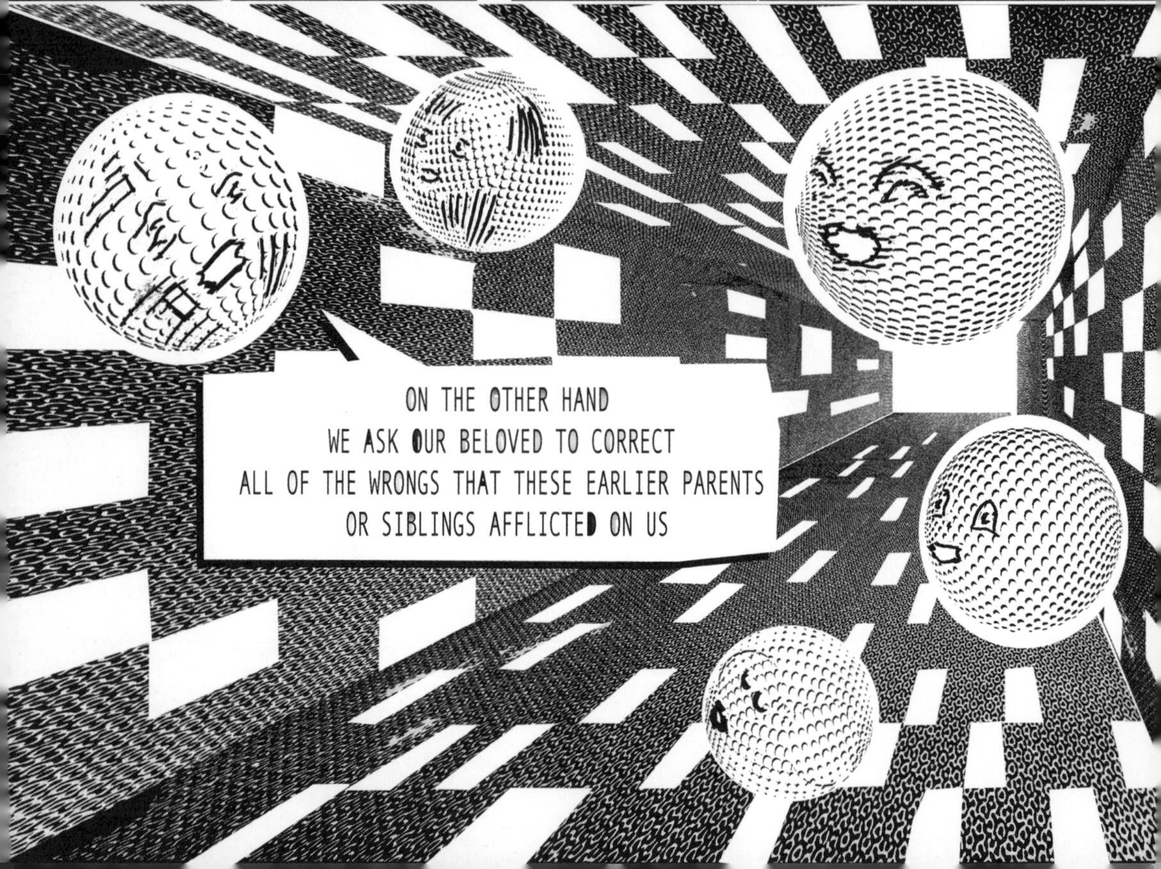
ON THE OTHER HAND
WE ASK OUR BELOVED TO CORRECT
ALL OF THE WRONGS THAT THESE EARLIER PARENTS
OR SIBLINGS AFFLICTED ON US

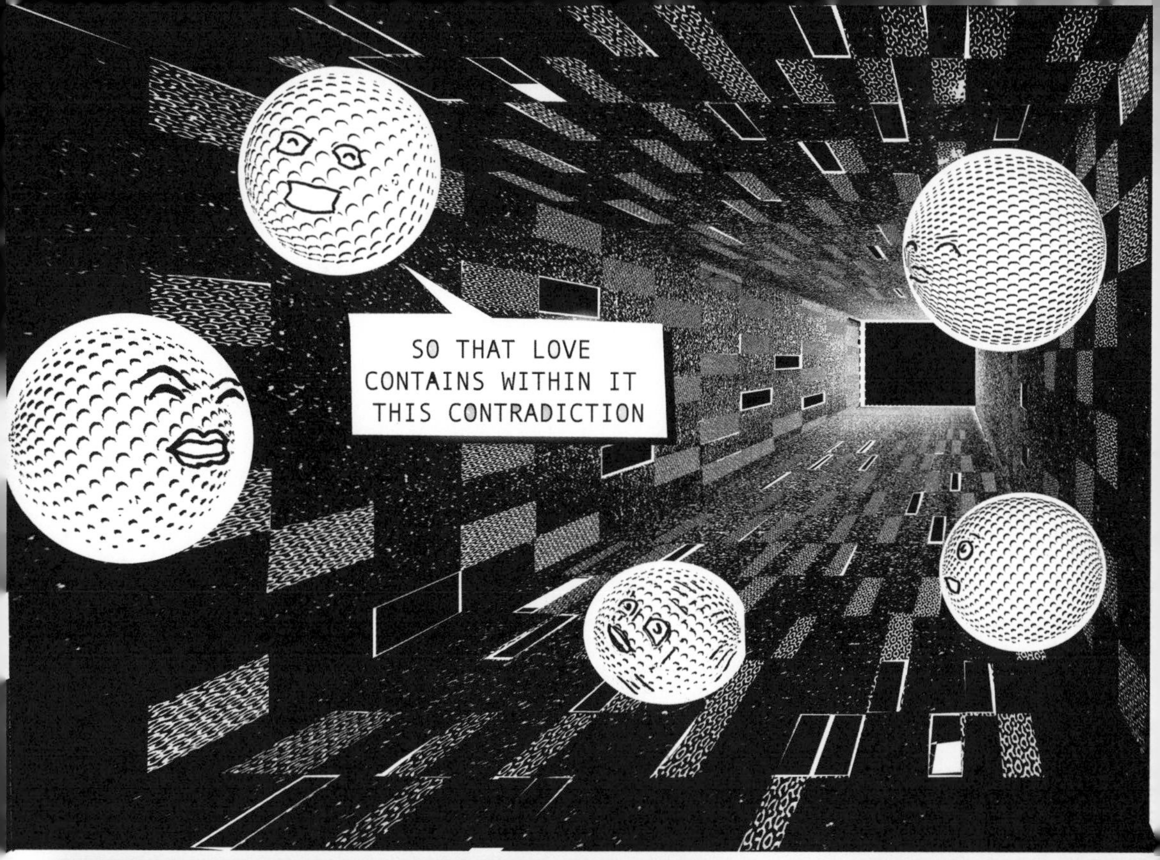
SO THAT LOVE CONTAINS WITHIN IT THIS CONTRADICTION

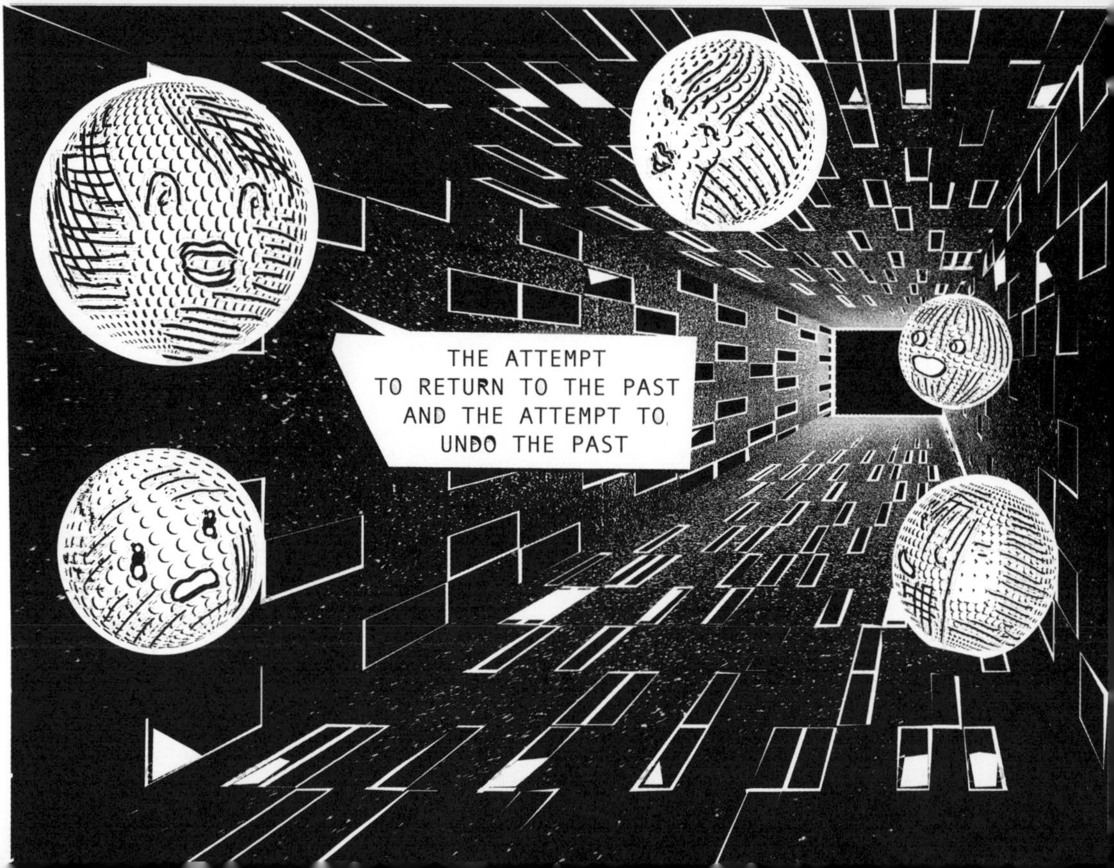
THE ATTEMPT TO RETURN TO THE PAST AND THE ATTEMPT TO UNDO THE PAST

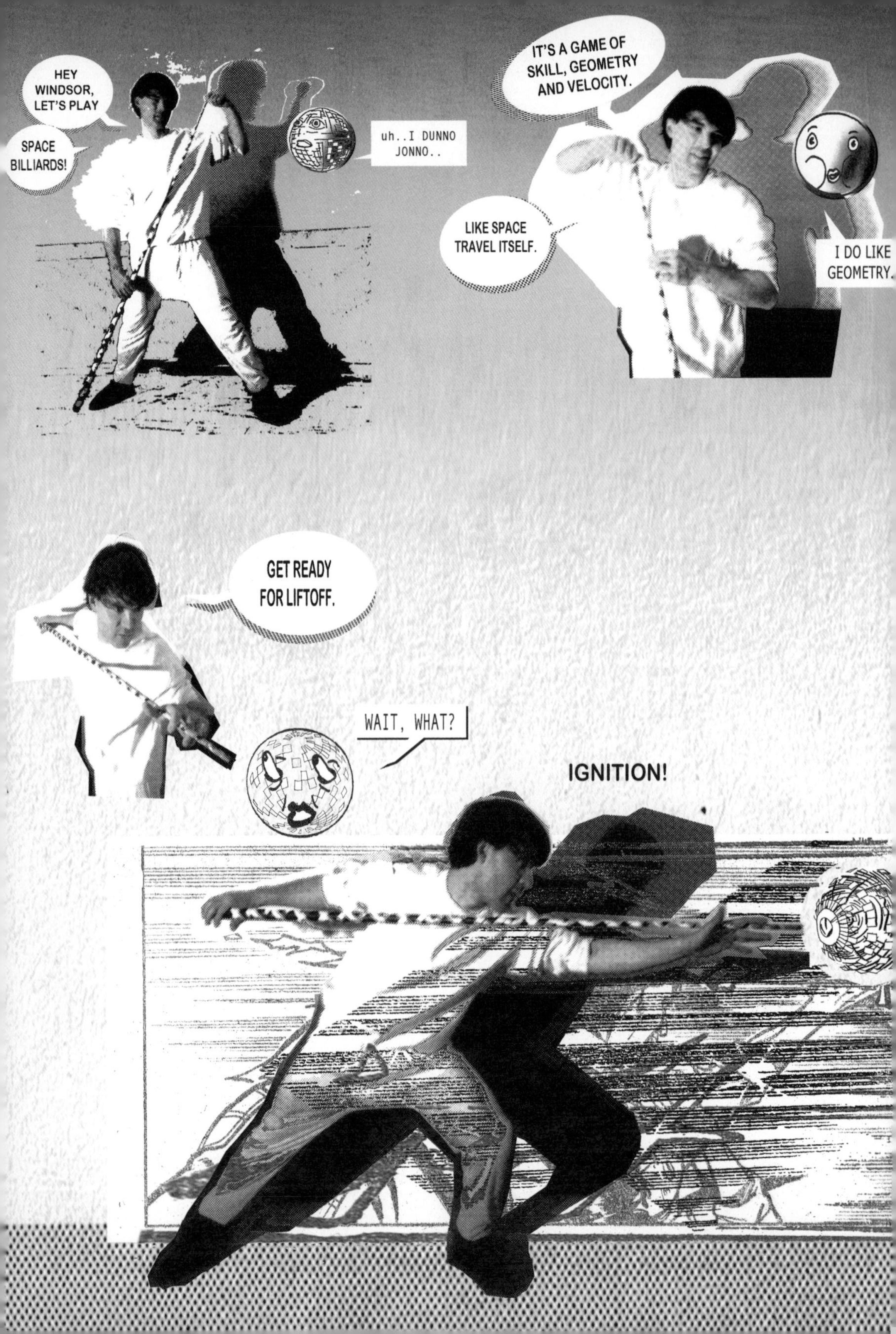
HEY WINDSOR, LET'S PLAY
SPACE BILLIARDS!
uh..I DUNNO JONNO..
IT'S A GAME OF SKILL, GEOMETRY AND VELOCITY.
LIKE SPACE TRAVEL ITSELF.
I DO LIKE GEOMETRY.
GET READY FOR LIFTOFF.
WAIT, WHAT?
IGNITION!

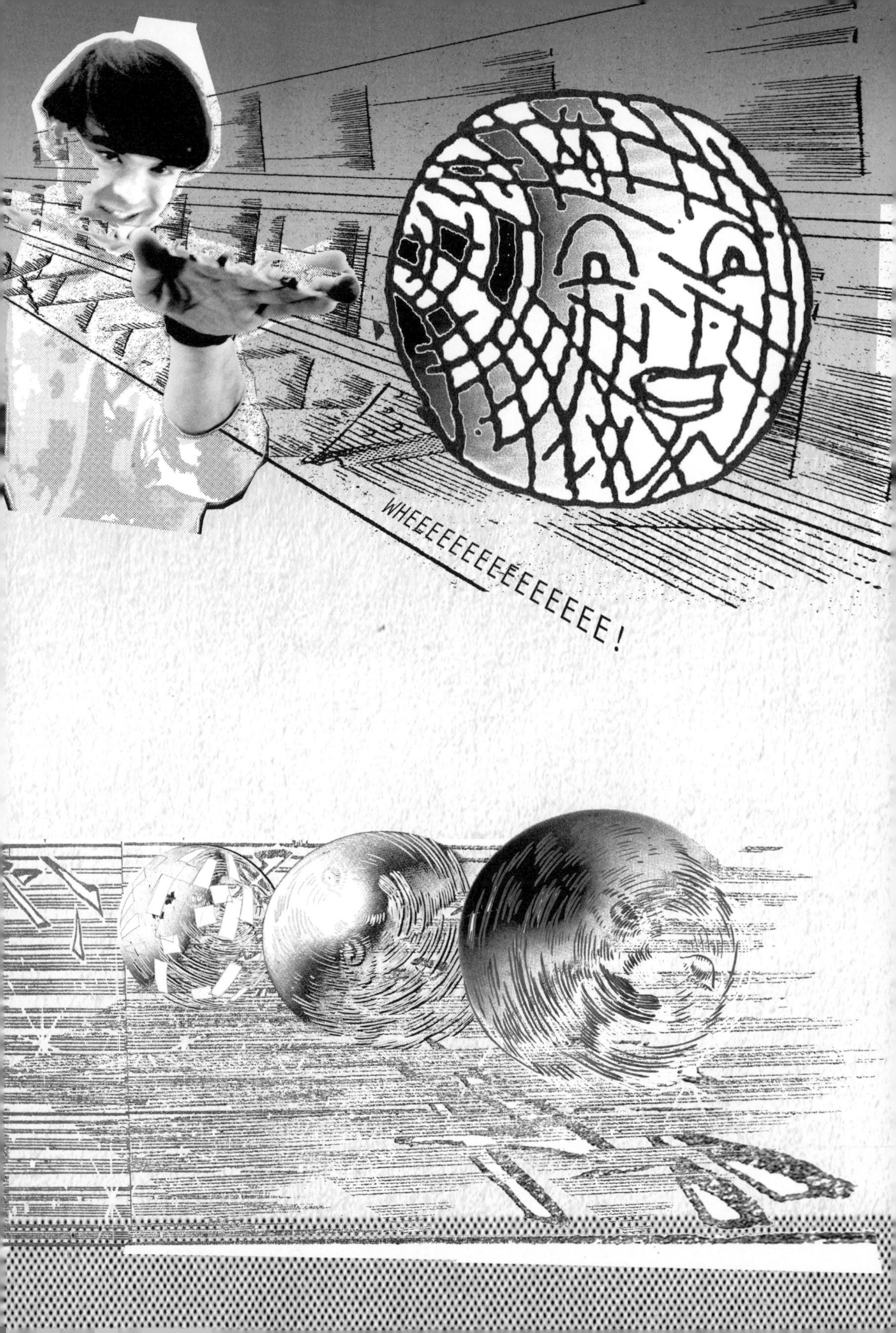
WHEEEEEEEEEEEEEEEEE!

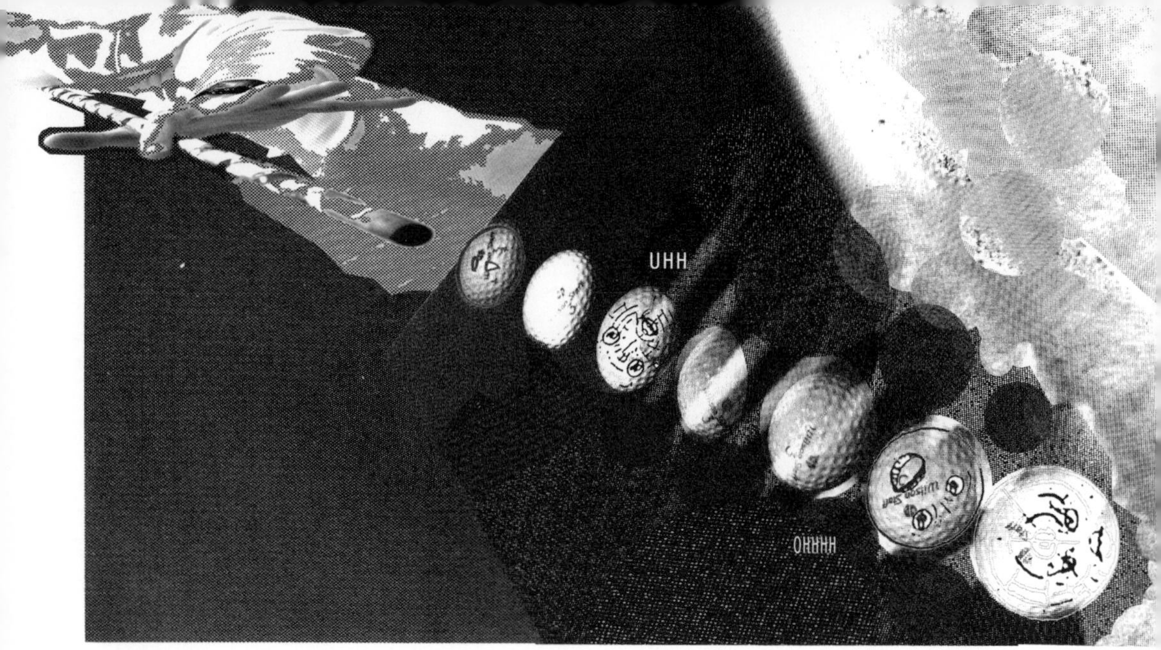
UHH

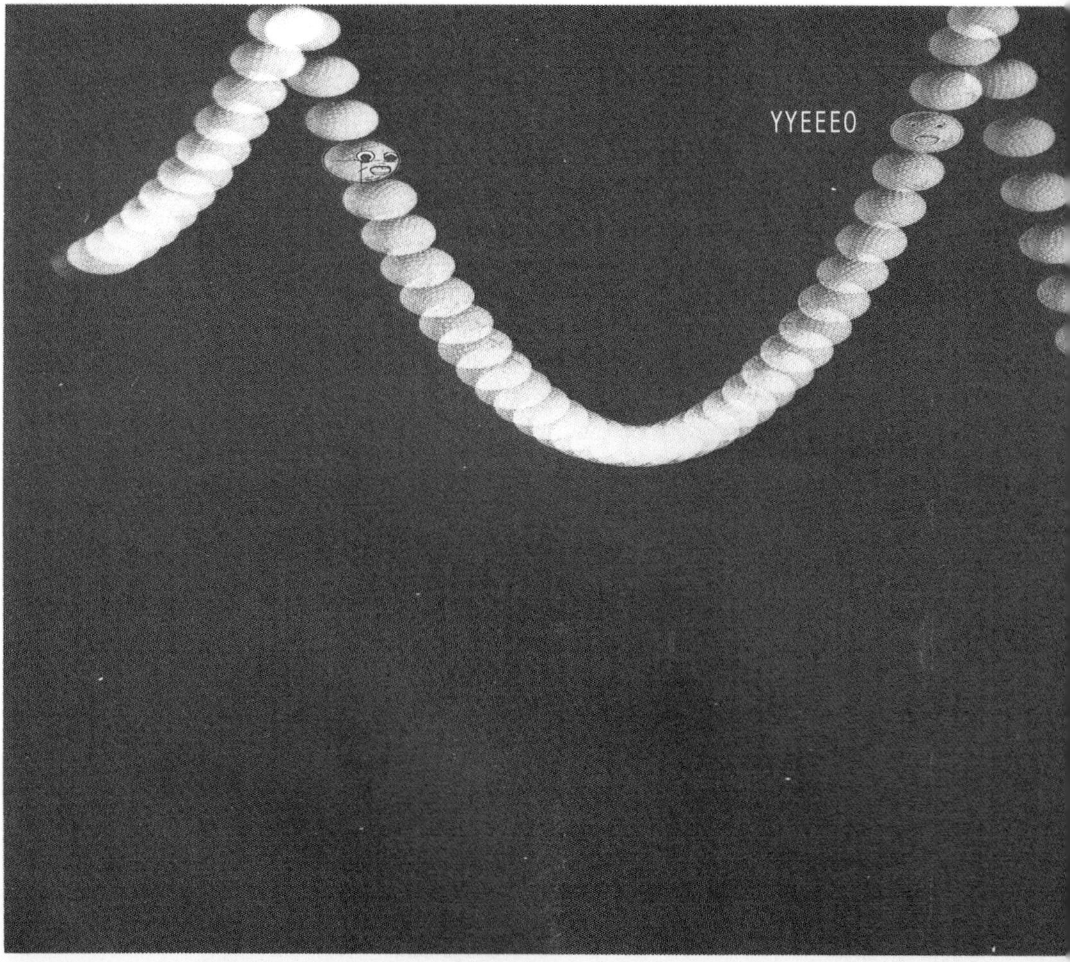
YYEEEO

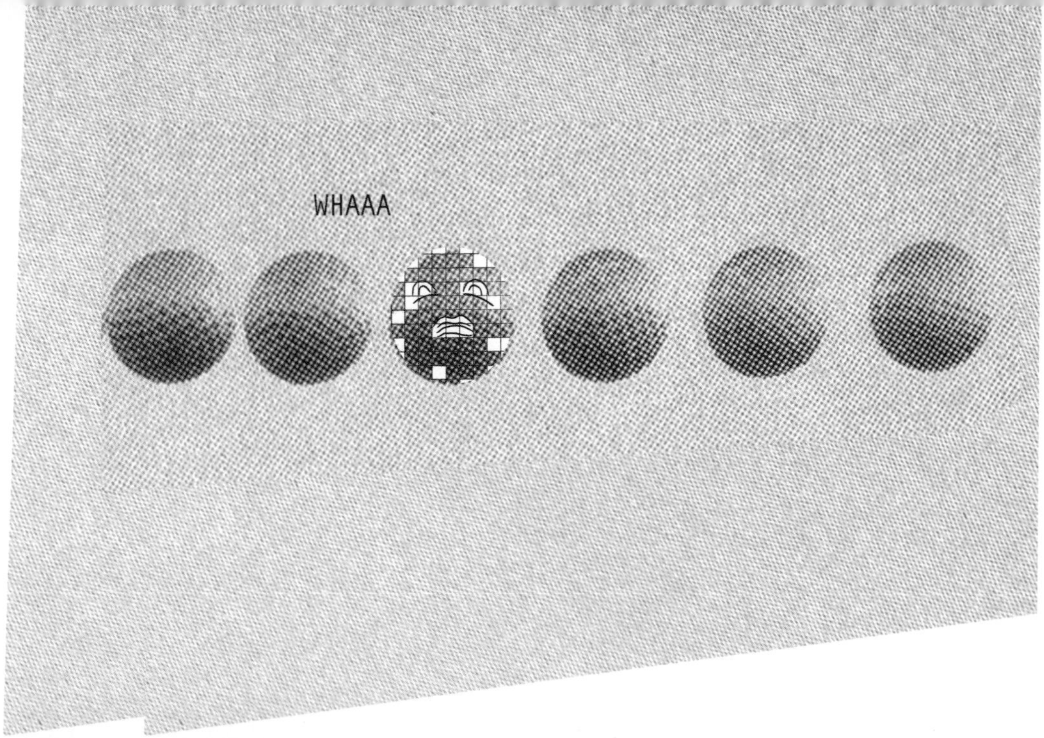
WHAAA

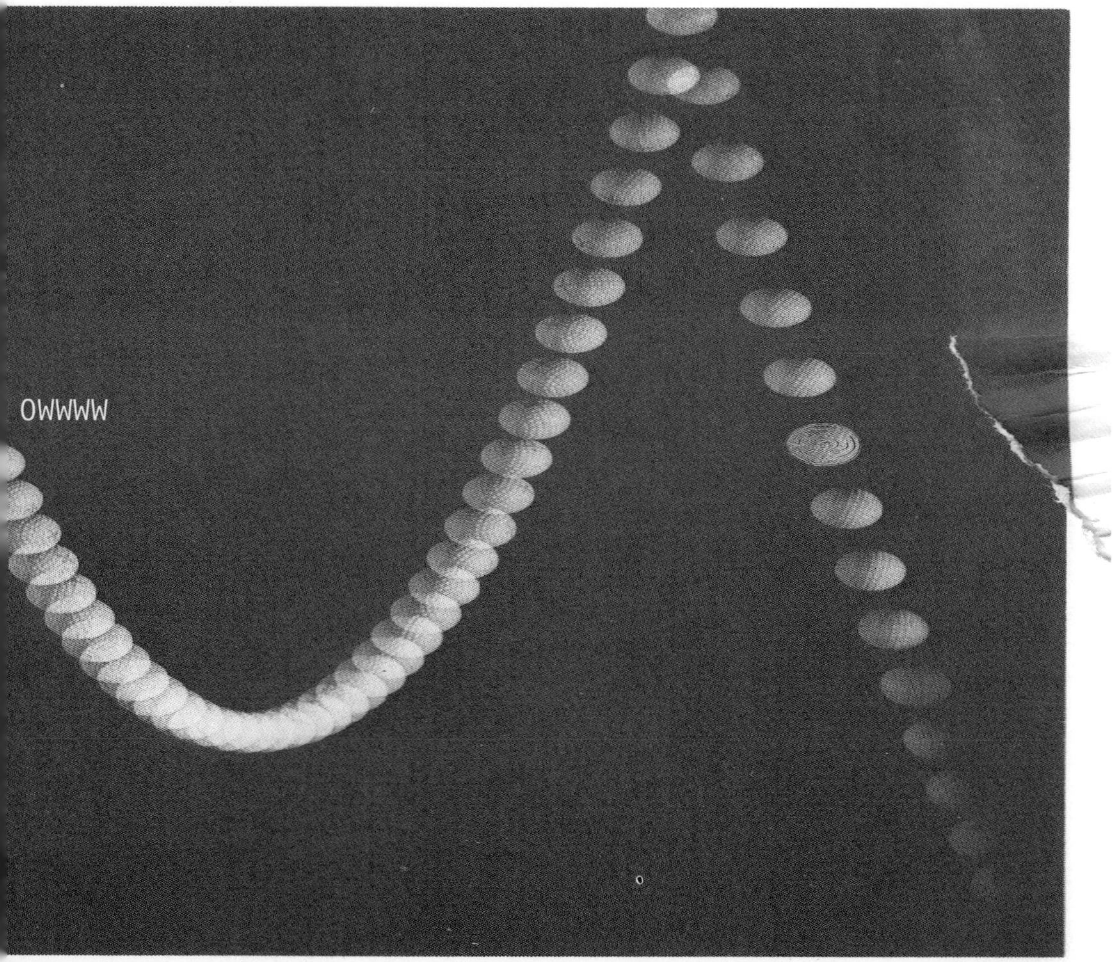
OWWWW

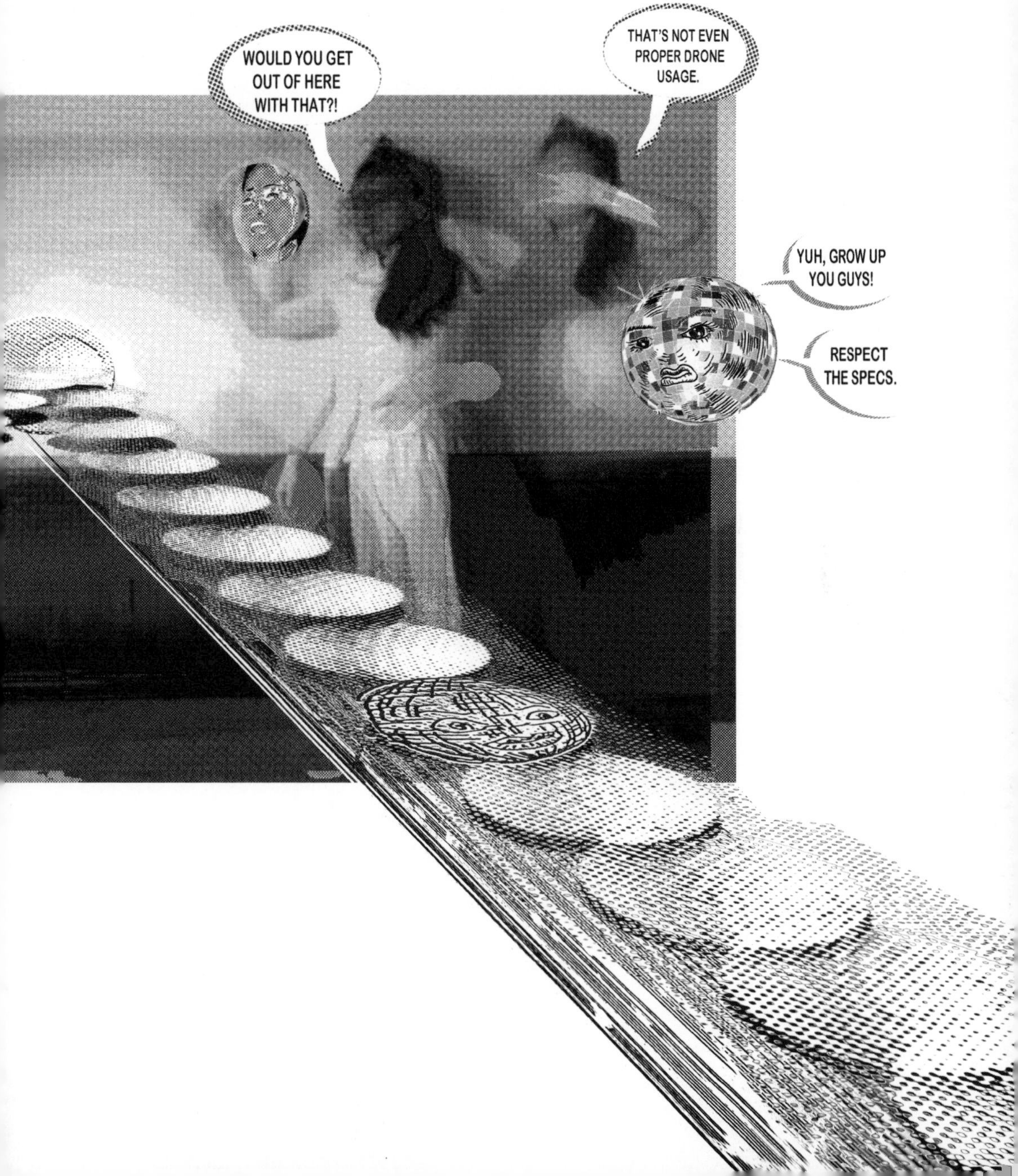
WOULD YOU GET OUT OF HERE WITH THAT?!
THAT'S NOT EVEN PROPER DRONE USAGE.
YUH, GROW UP YOU GUYS!
RESPECT THE SPECS.

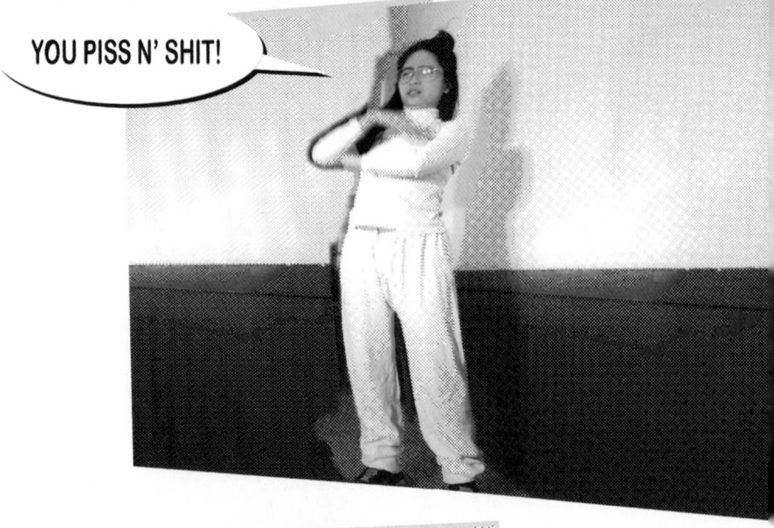
YOU PISS N' SHIT!

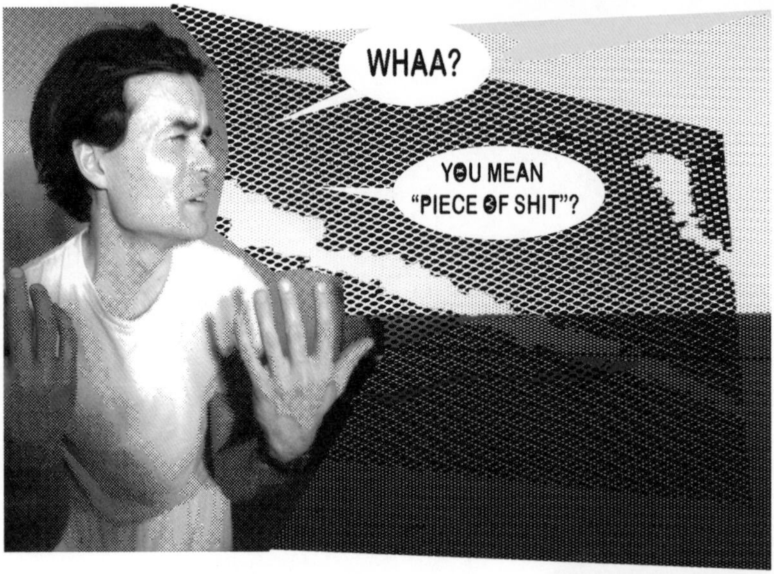
WHAA?
YOU MEAN "PIECE OF SHIT"?

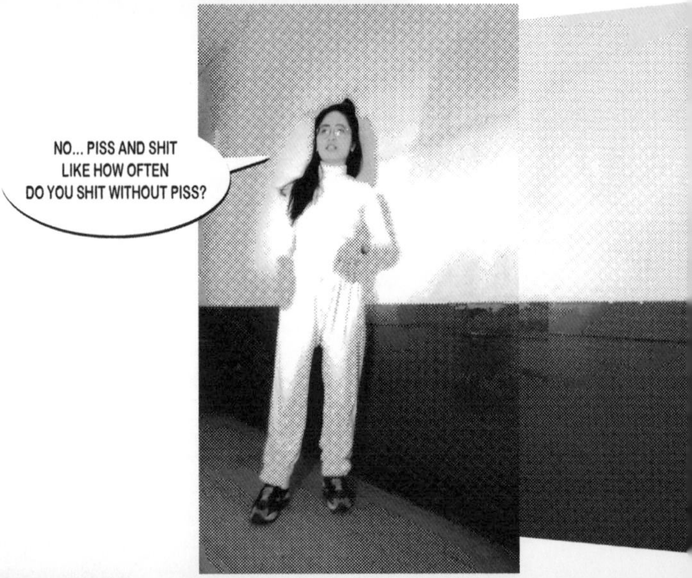
NO... PISS AND SHIT LIKE HOW OFTEN DO YOU SHIT WITHOUT PISS?

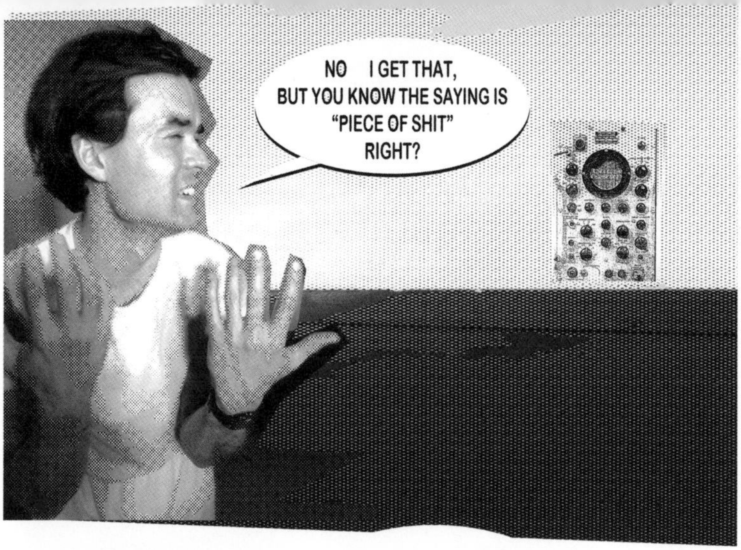
NO I GET THAT,
BUT YOU KNOW THE SAYING IS
“PIECE OF SHIT”
RIGHT?

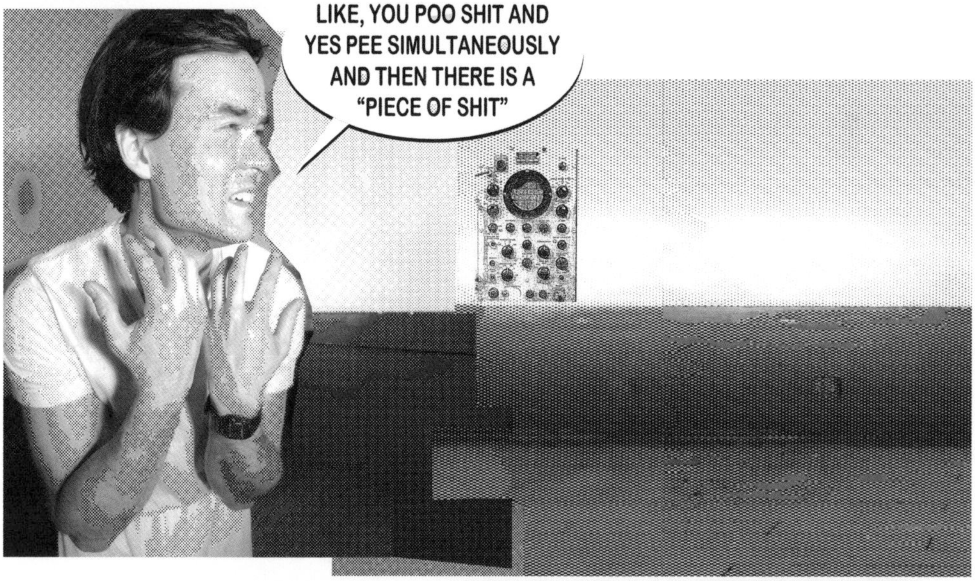
LIKE, YOU POO SHIT AND
YES PEE SIMULTANEOUSLY
AND THEN THERE IS A
“PIECE OF SHIT”

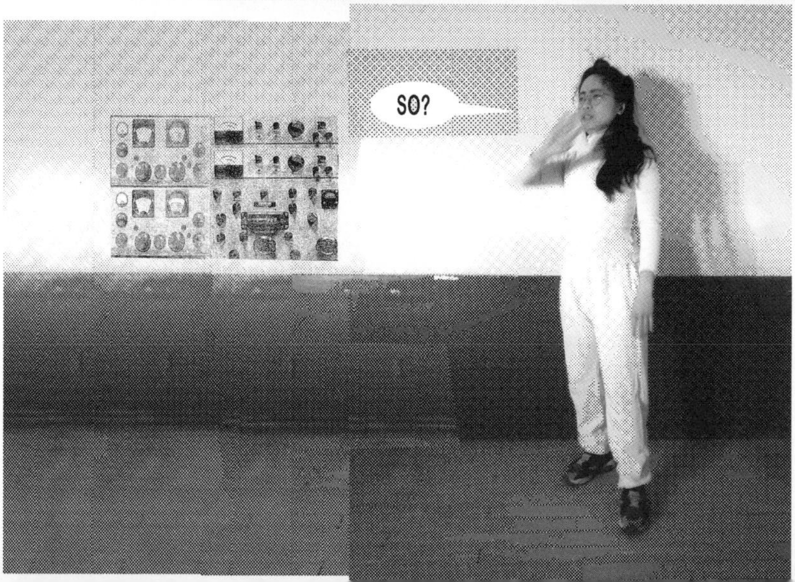
SO?

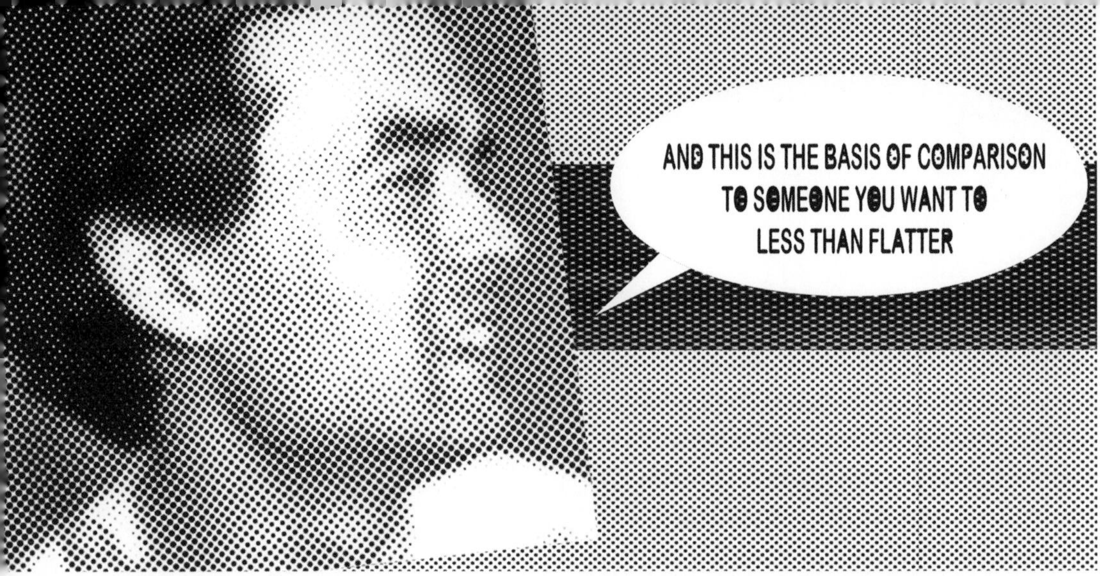
AND THIS IS THE BASIS OF COMPARISON
TO SOMEONE YOU WANT TO
LESS THAN FLATTER

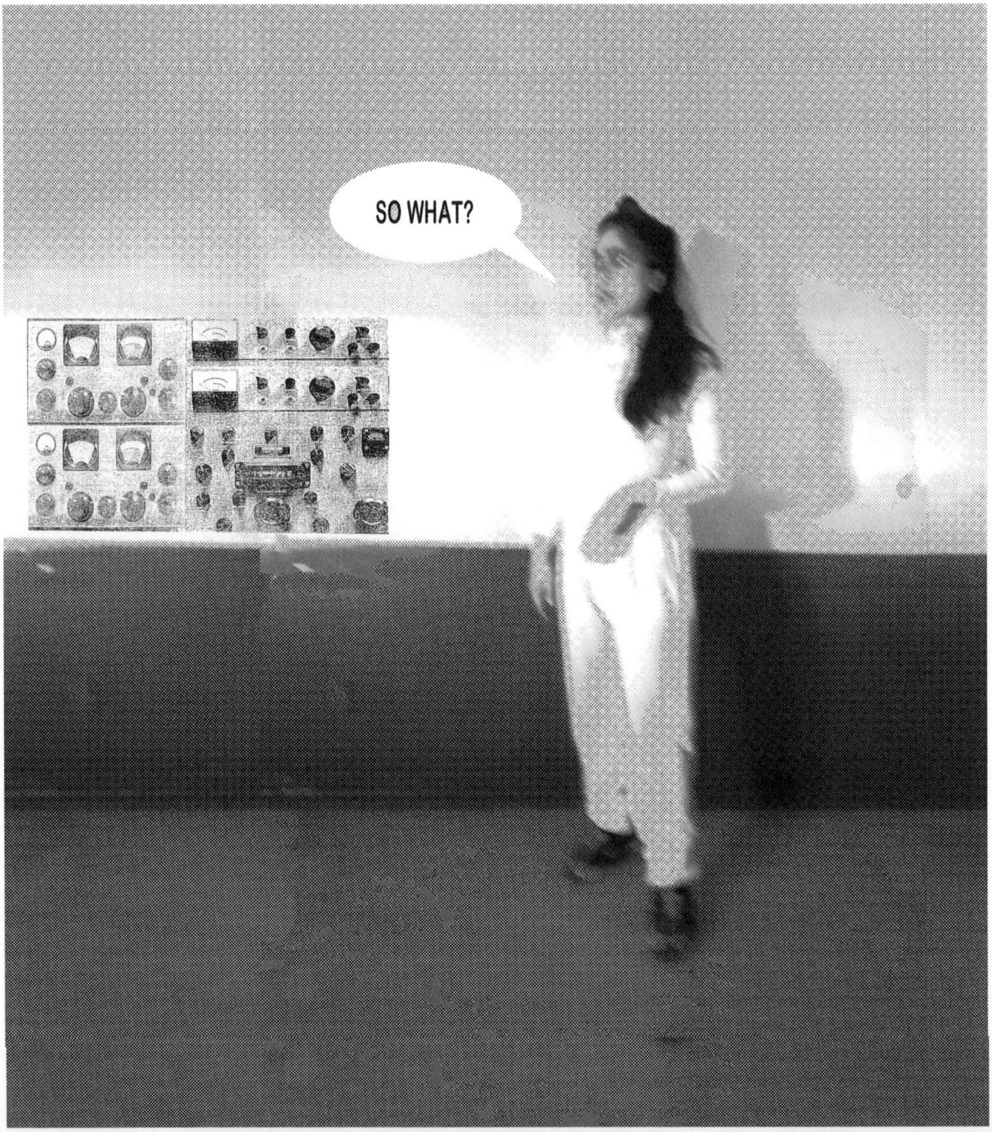
SO WHAT?

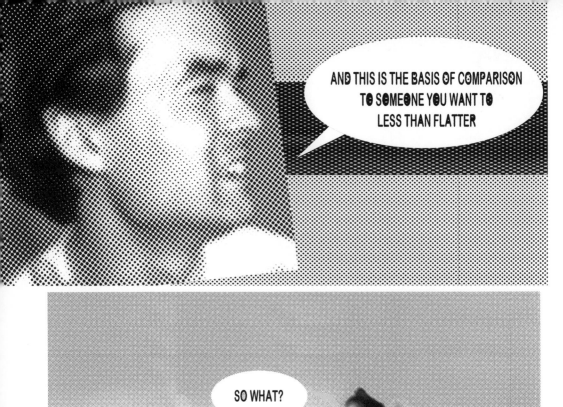

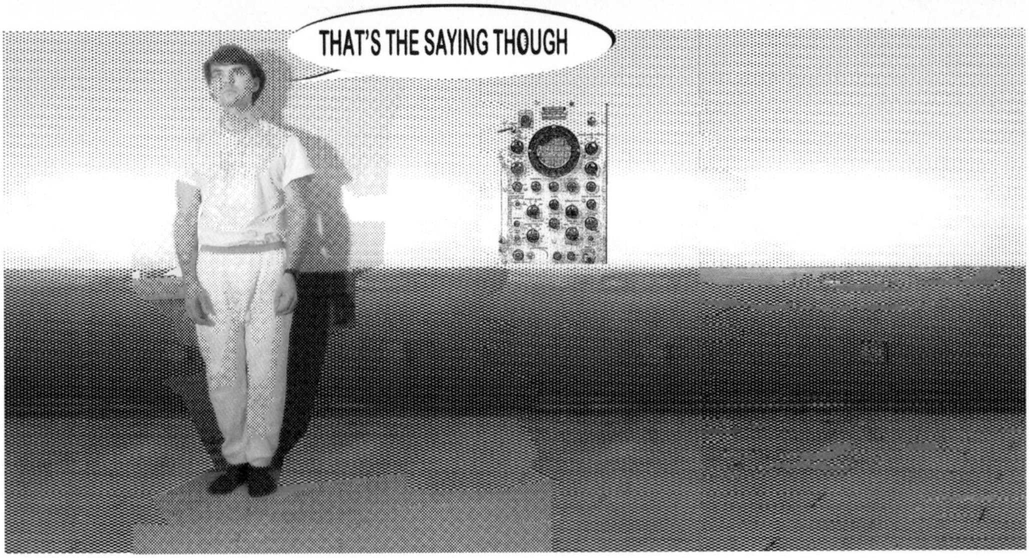
THAT'S THE SAYING THOUGH

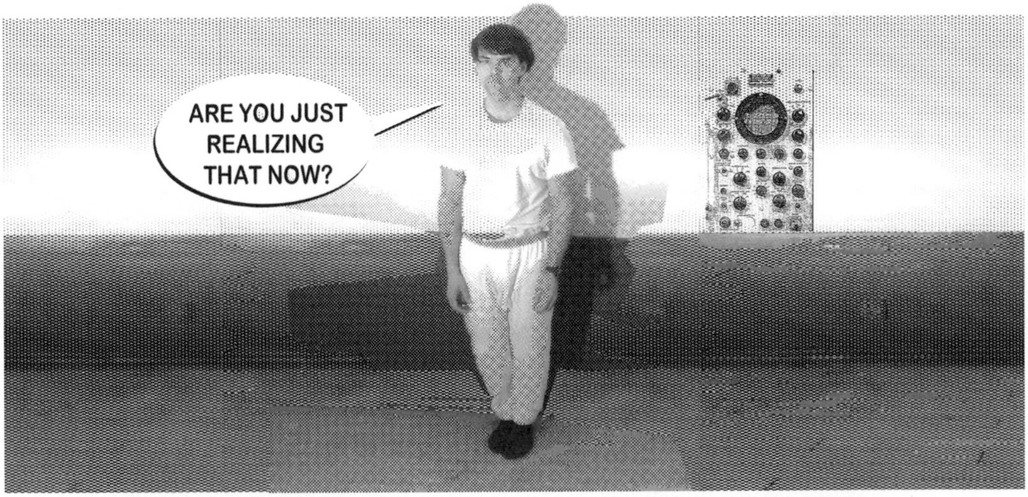
ARE YOU JUST REALIZING THAT NOW?

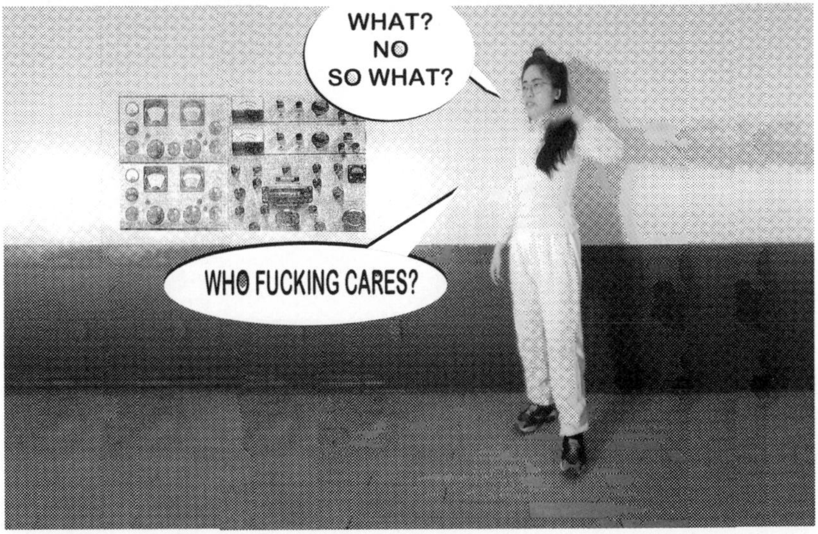
WHAT? NO SO WHAT?
WHO FUCKING CARES?

HAHAHA
YOUR WHOLE FUCKING LIFE
YOU PISS'N SHIT!
YOU BOTH!!

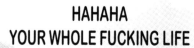

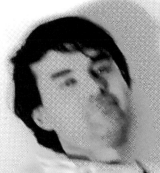

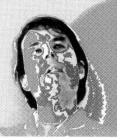

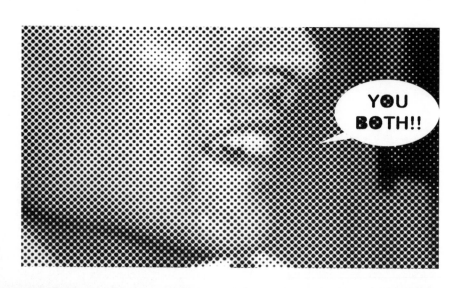

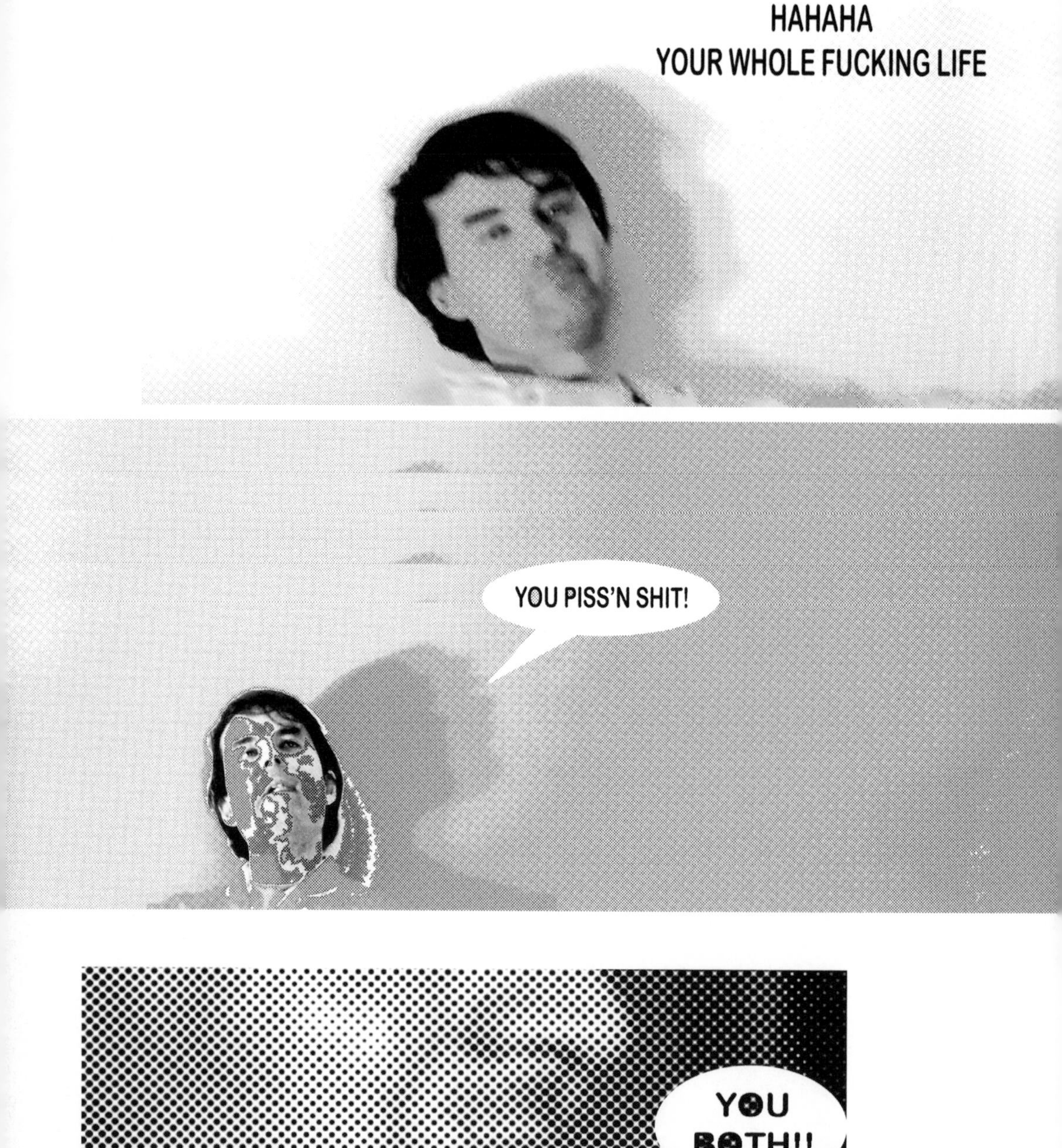

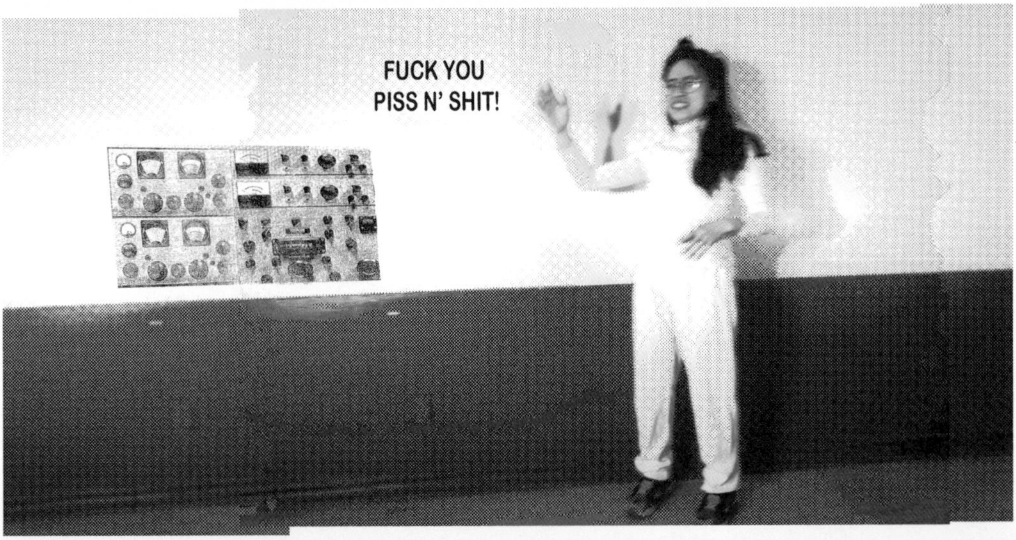
FUCK YOU
PISS N' SHIT!

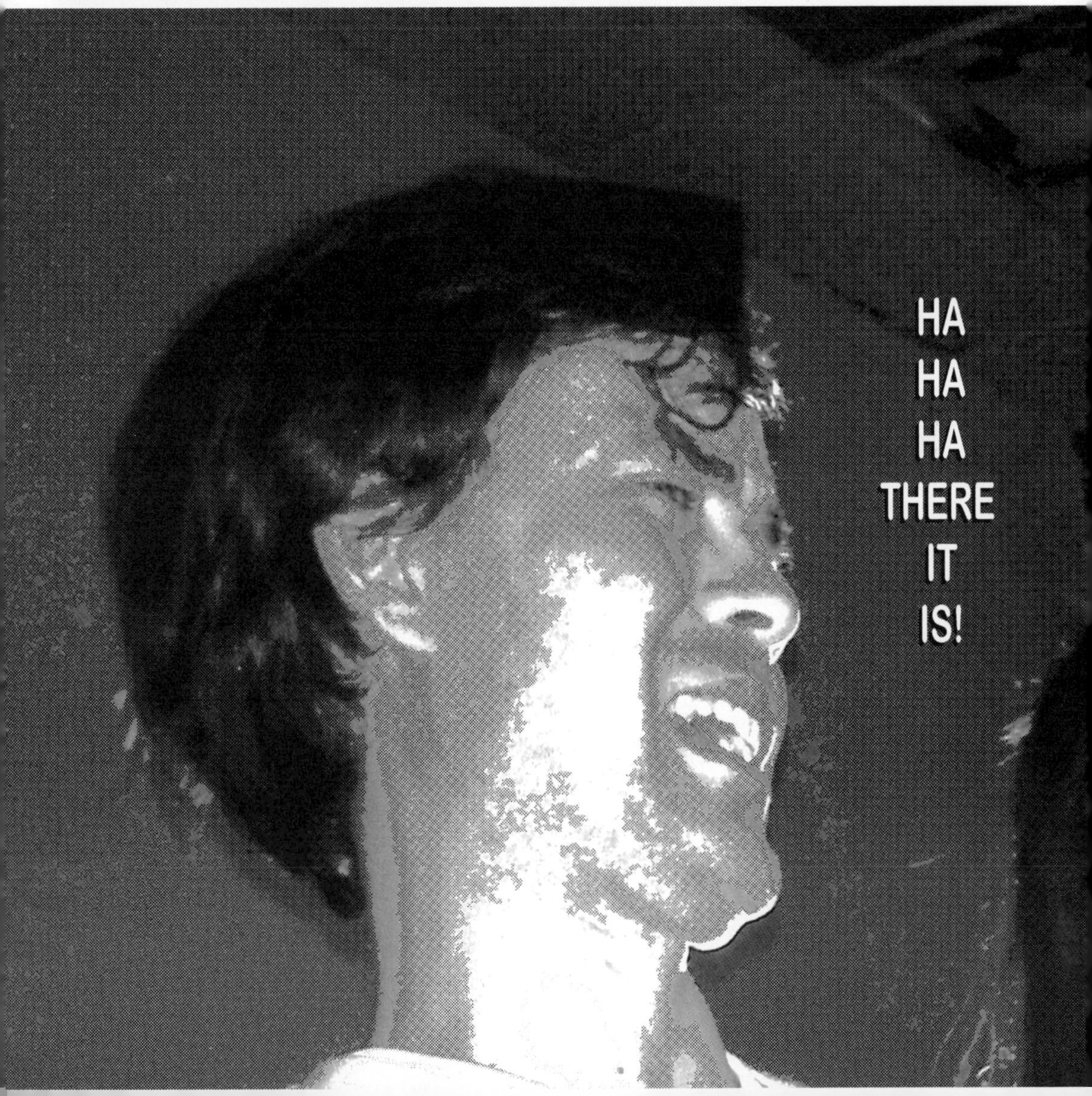
HA
HA
HA
THERE
IT
IS!

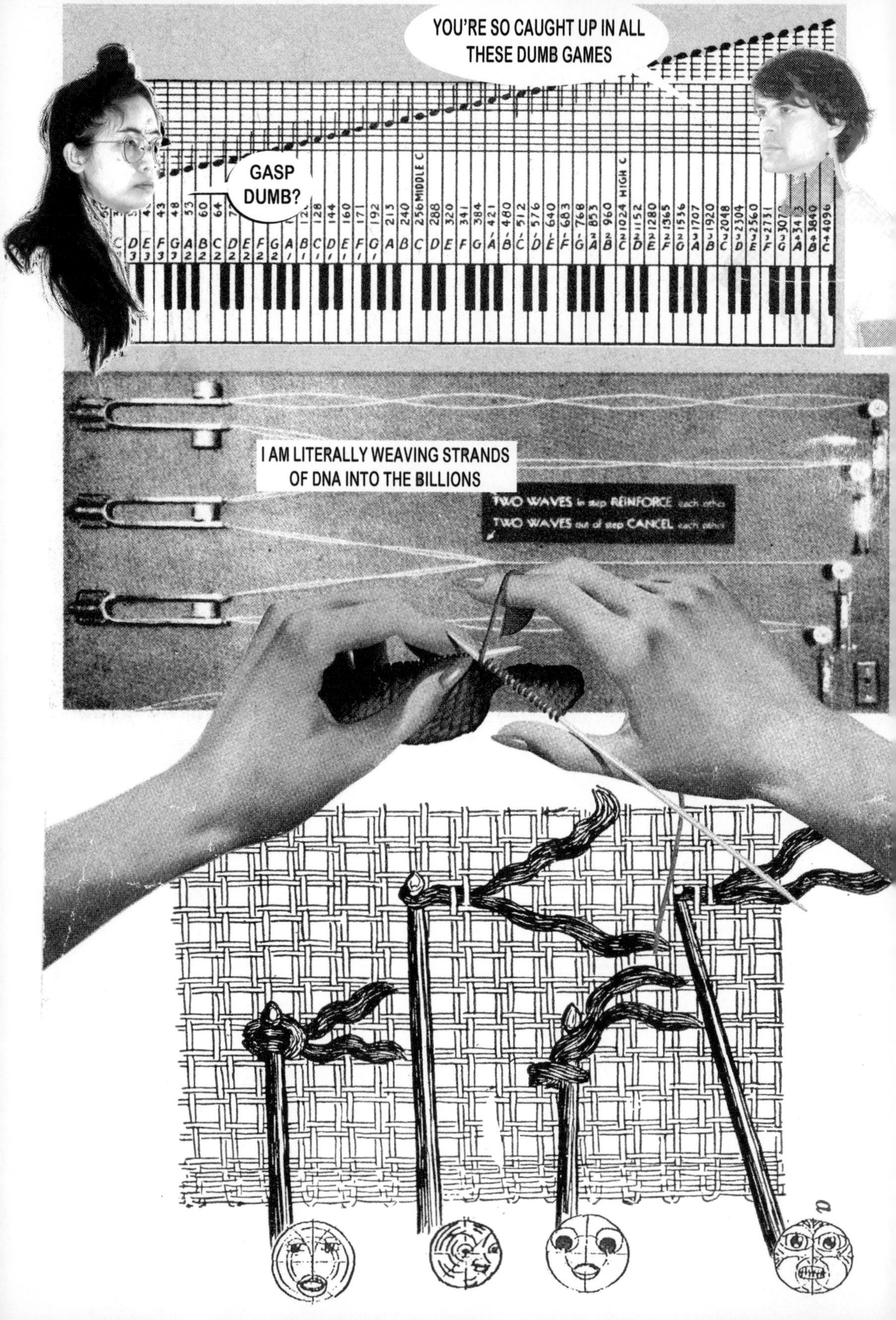
YOU'RE SO CAUGHT UP IN ALL THESE DUMB GAMES
GASP DUMB?
I AM LITERALLY WEAVING STRANDS OF DNA INTO THE BILLIONS
TWO WAVES in step REINFORCE each other
TWO WAVES out of step CANCEL each other

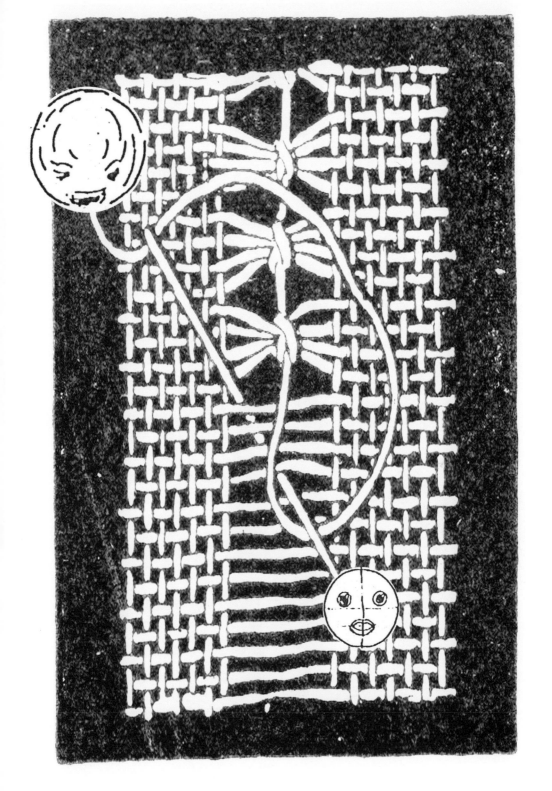

EVERYTHING I DO IS A GAMEFIED INTERFACE WITH MY PRIMARY TASK

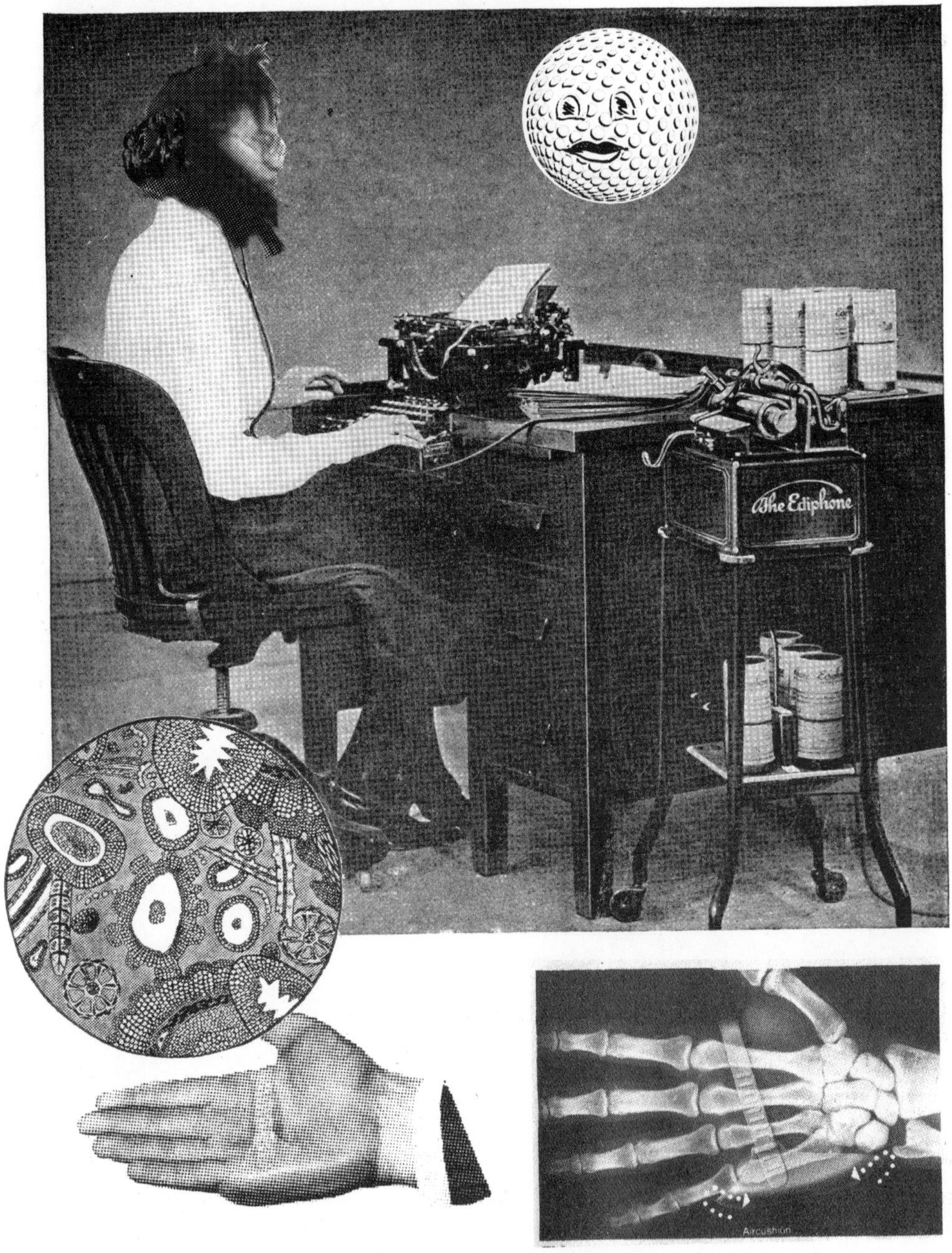
The Ediphone
Aircushion

YOU GET TO SPEND YOUR TIME FREAKING OUT

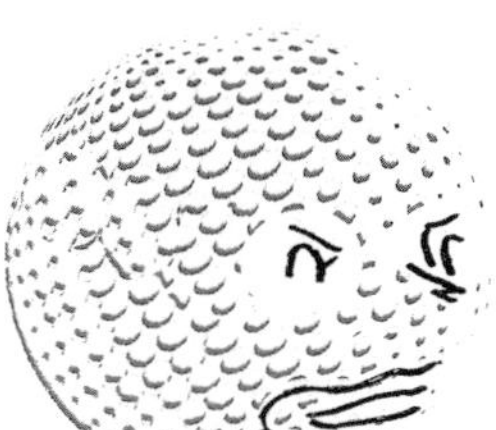

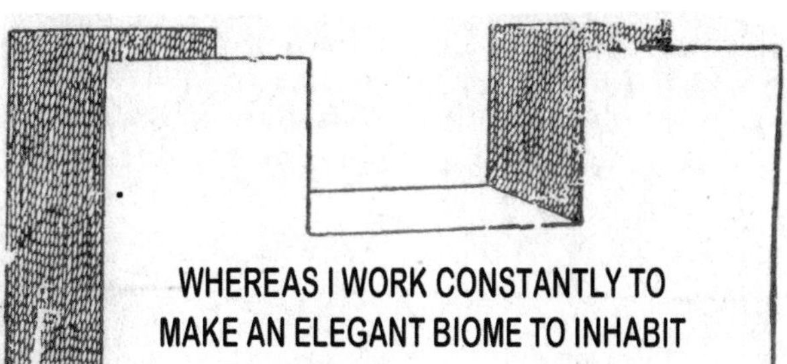
WHEREAS I WORK CONSTANTLY TO
MAKE AN ELEGANT BIOME TO INHABIT

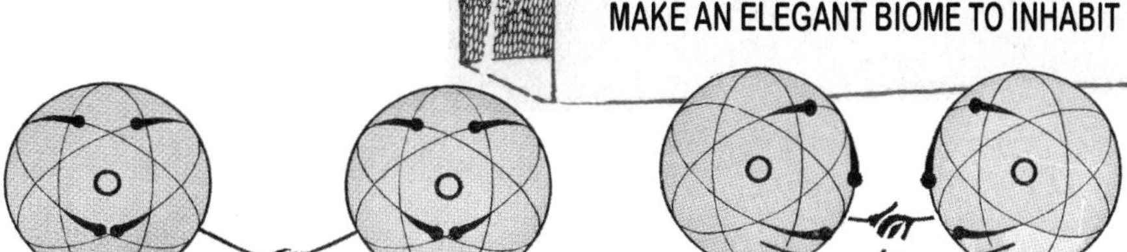

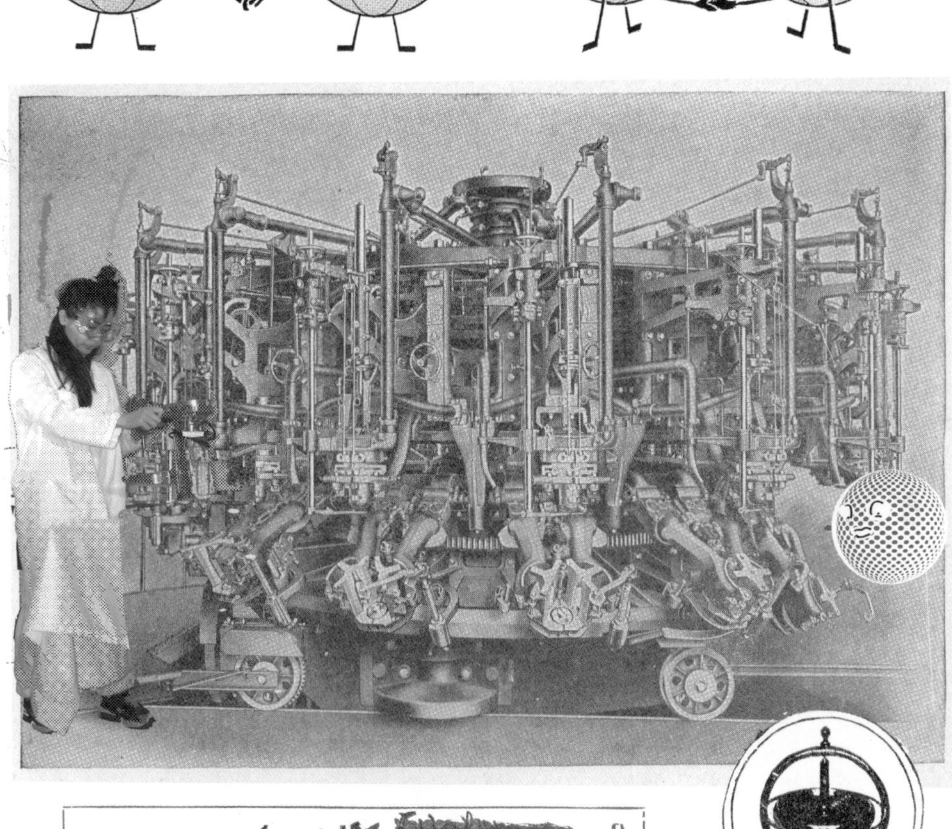

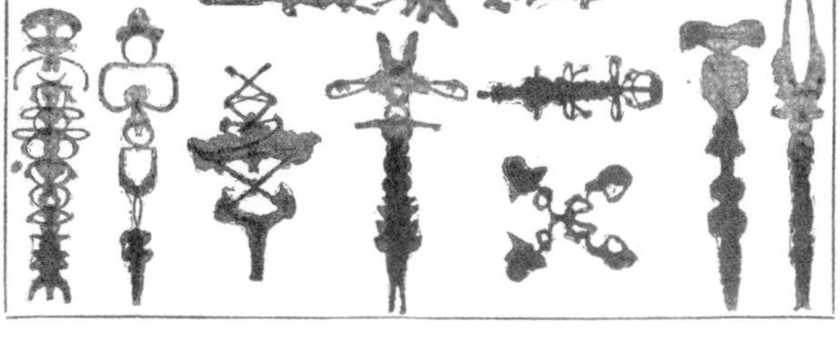

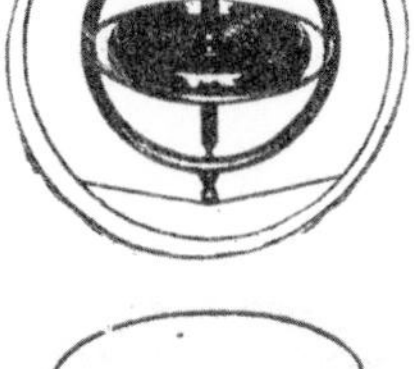

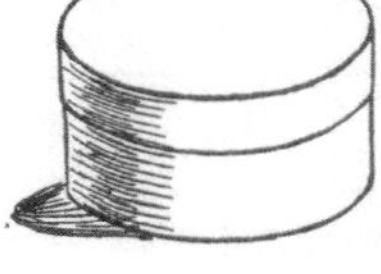

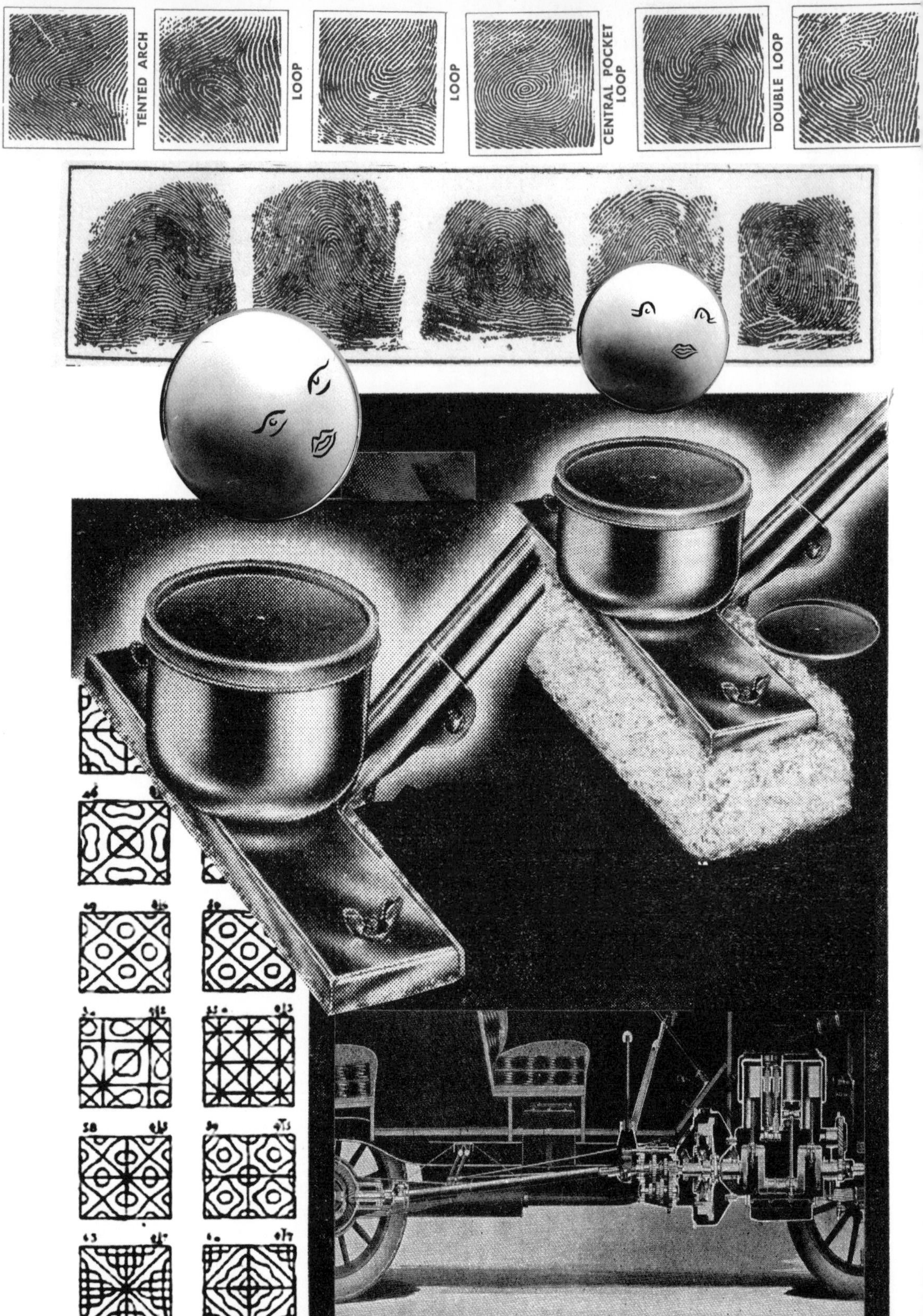
TENTED ARCH
LOOP
LOOP
CENTRAL POCKET LOOP
DOUBLE LOOP

I AM MAKING
A WORLD
BEAUTIFUL

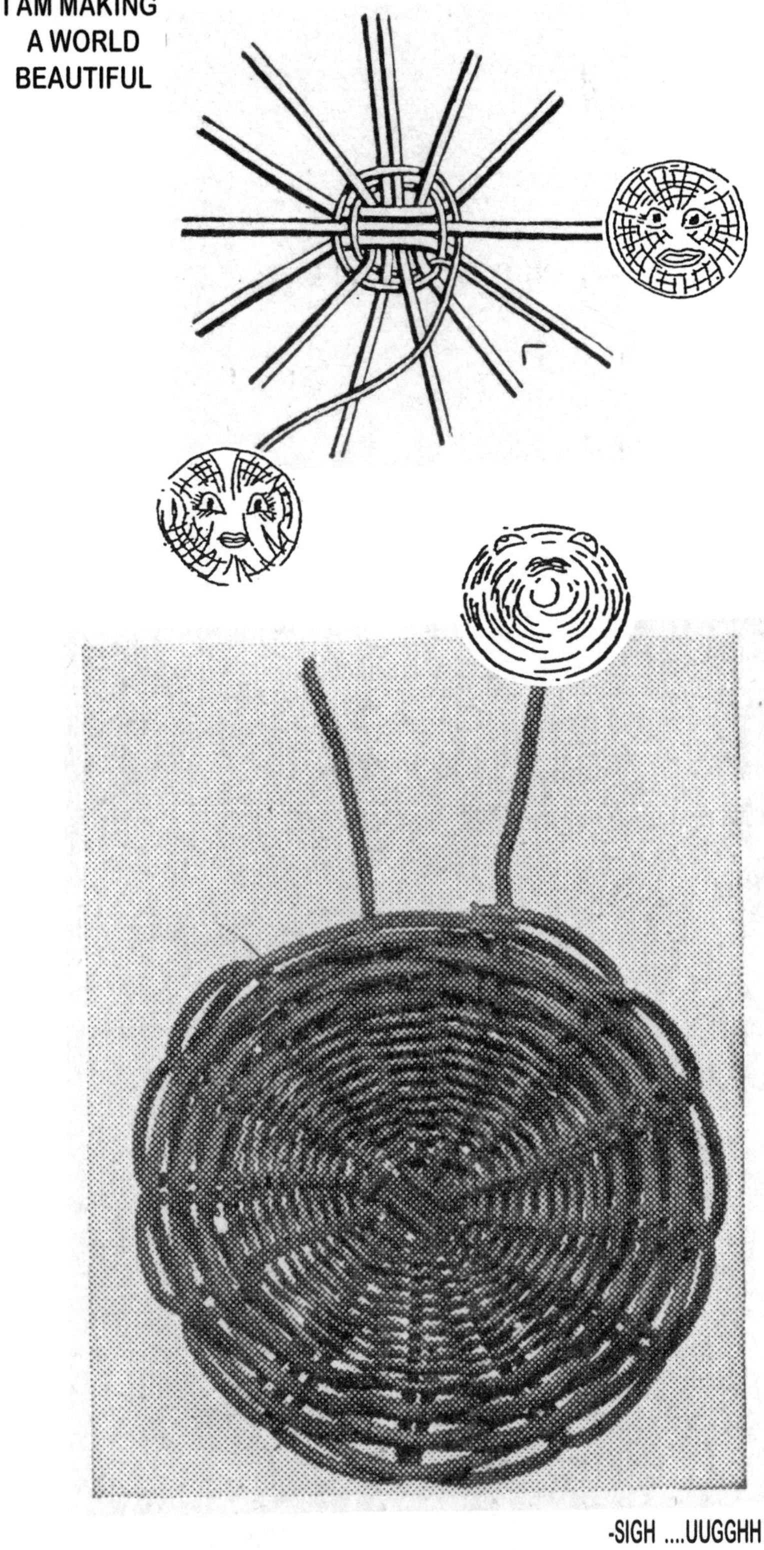

-SIGH ....UUGGHH DUMB...

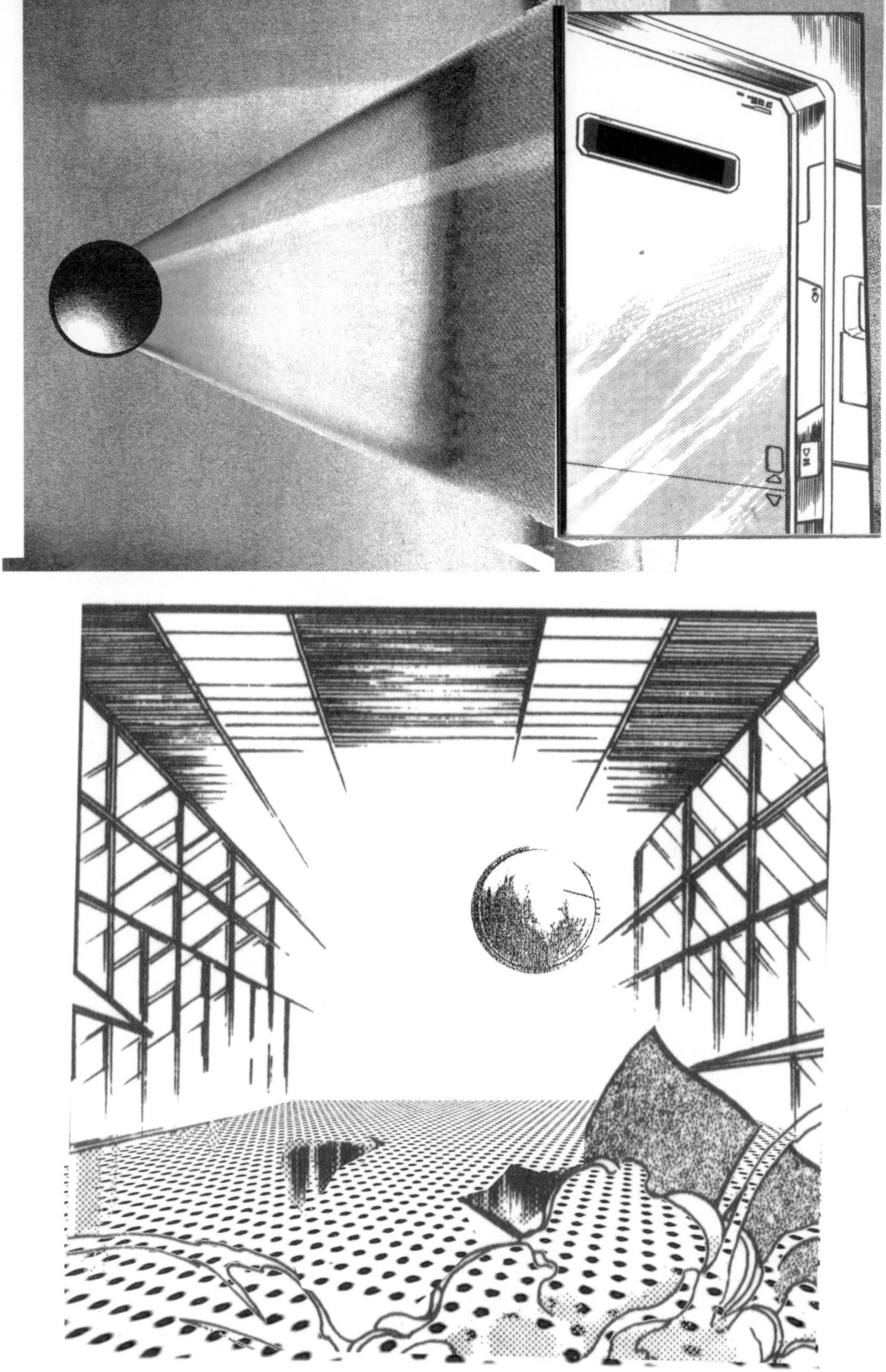

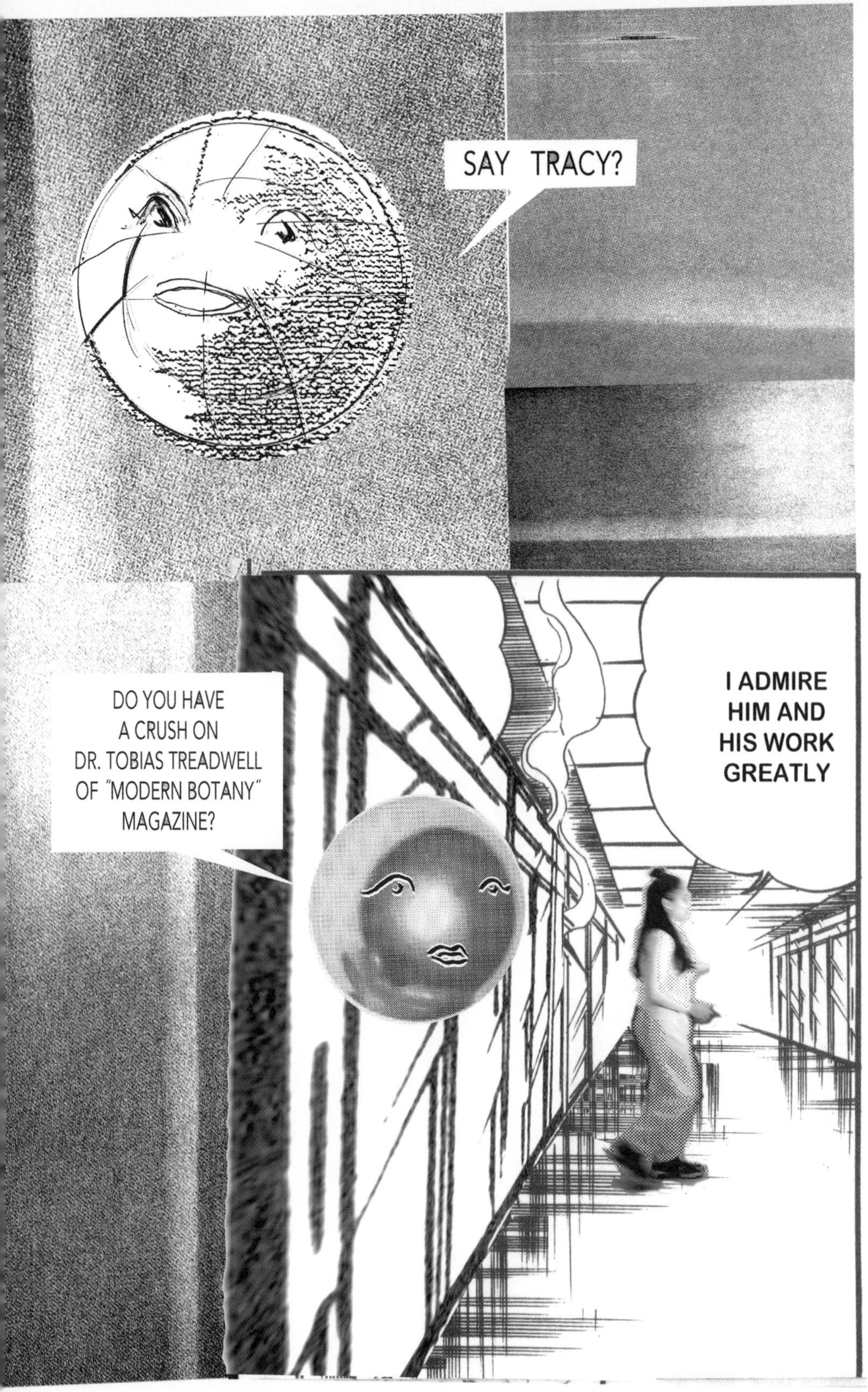
SAY TRACY?
DO YOU HAVE A CRUSH ON DR. TOBIAS TREADWELL OF "MODERN BOTANY" MAGAZINE?
I ADMIRE HIM AND HIS WORK GREATLY

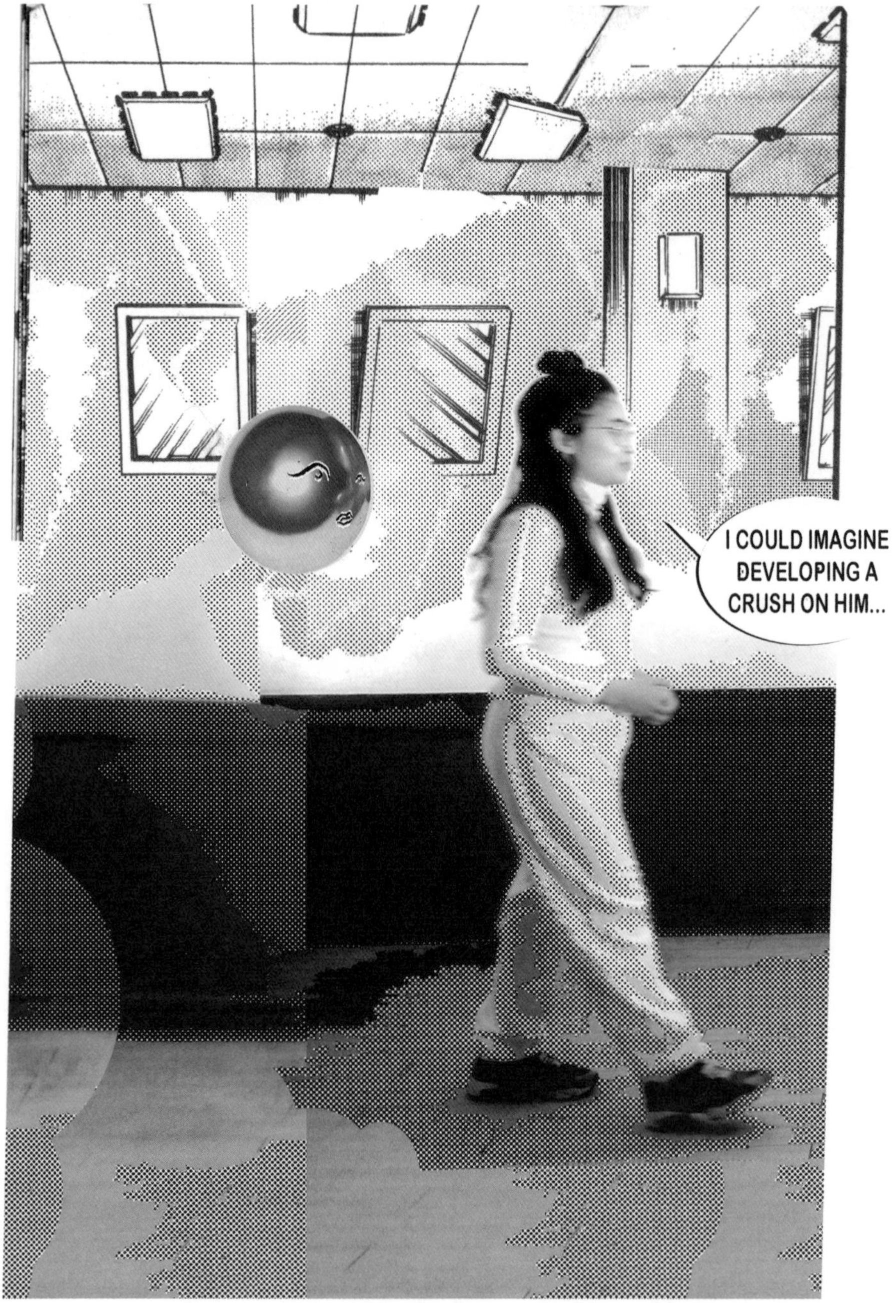
I COULD IMAGINE DEVELOPING A CRUSH ON HIM...

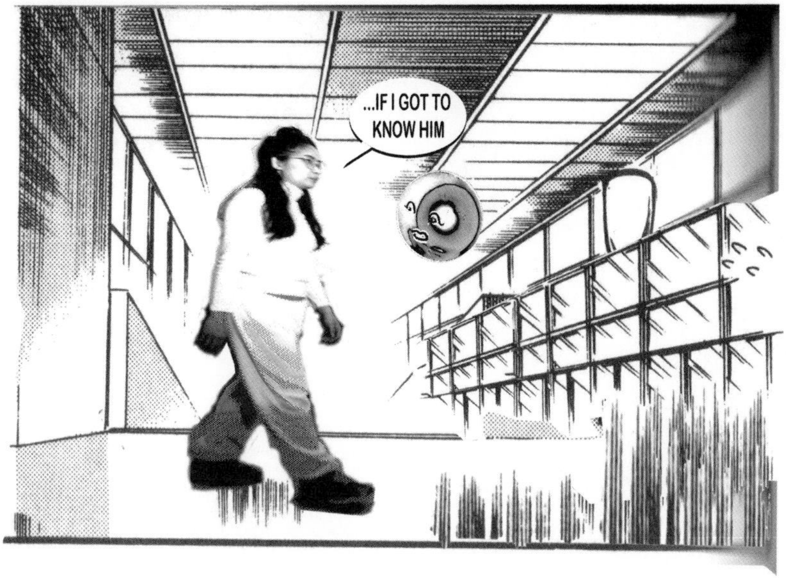
...IF I GOT TO KNOW HIM

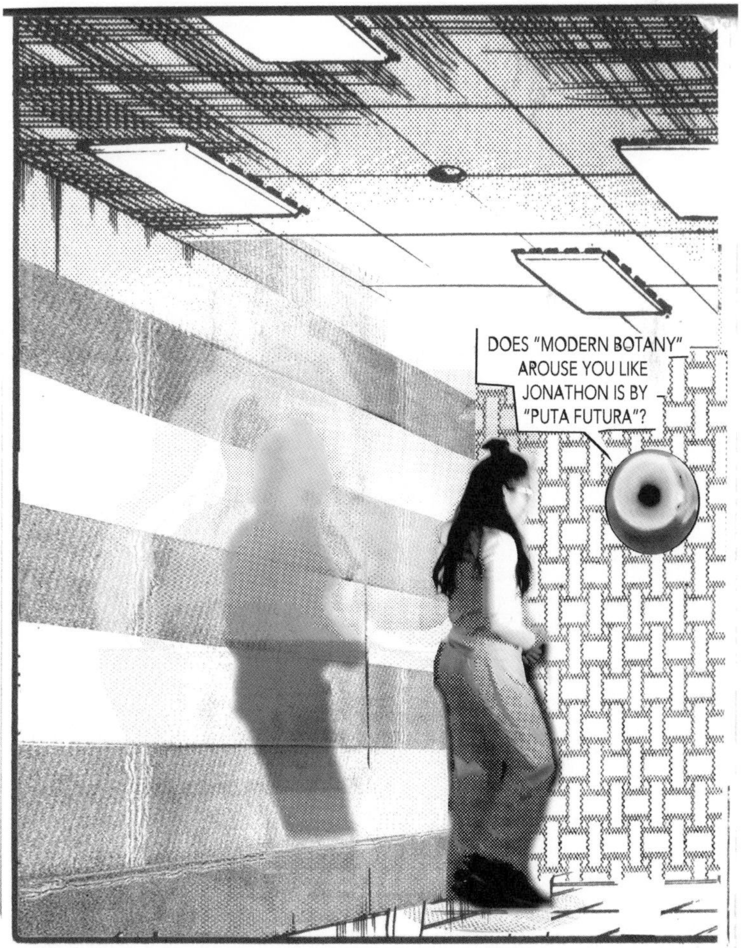
DOES "MODERN BOTANY" AROUSE YOU LIKE JONATHON IS BY "PUTA FUTURA"?

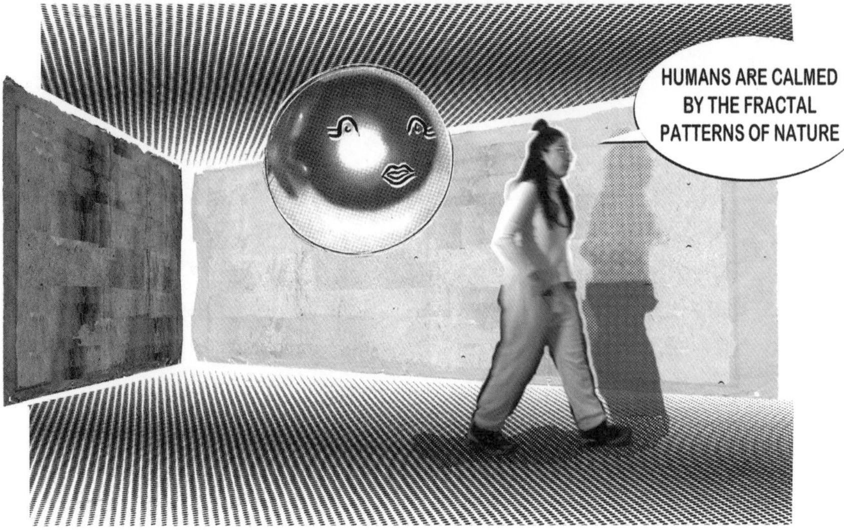
HUMANS ARE CALMED BY THE FRACTAL PATTERNS OF NATURE

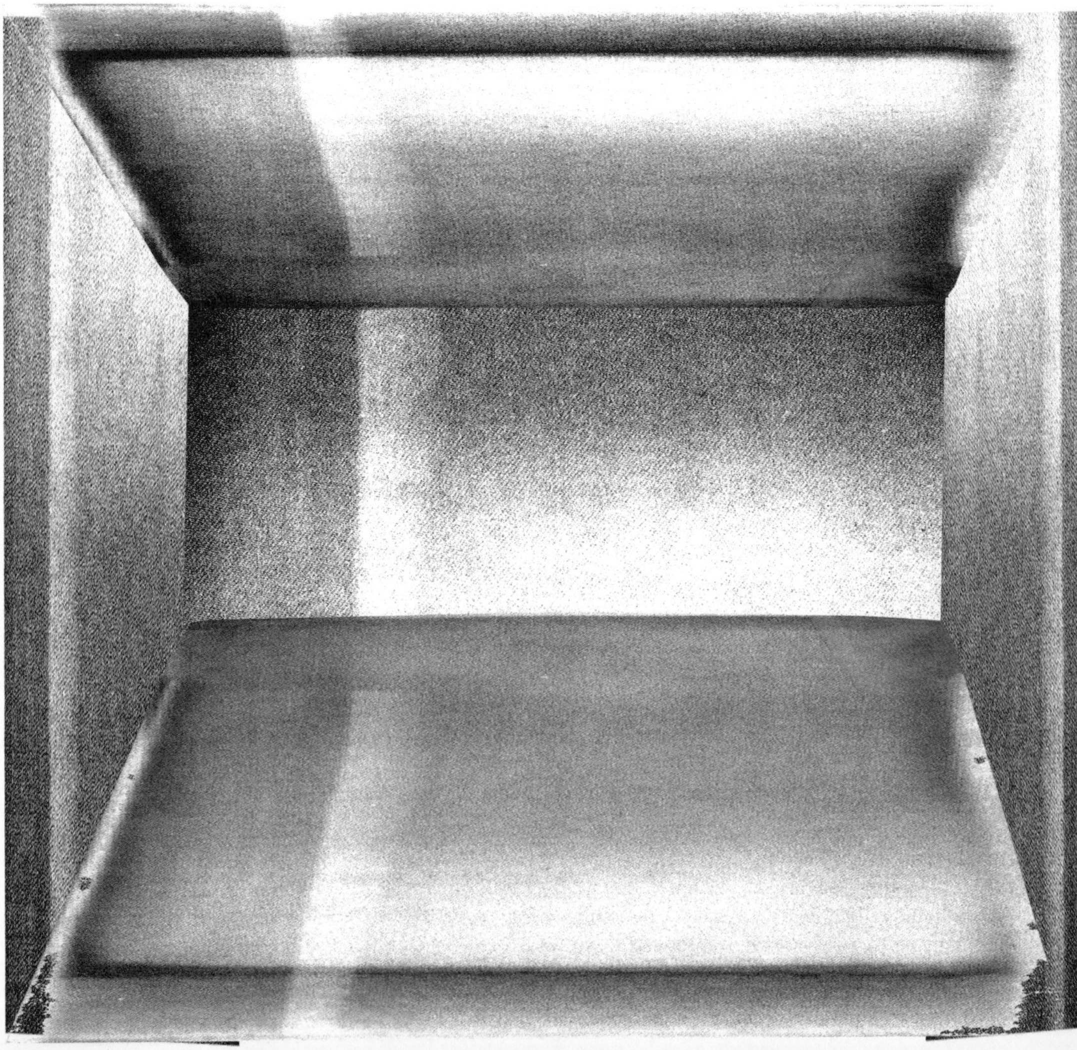

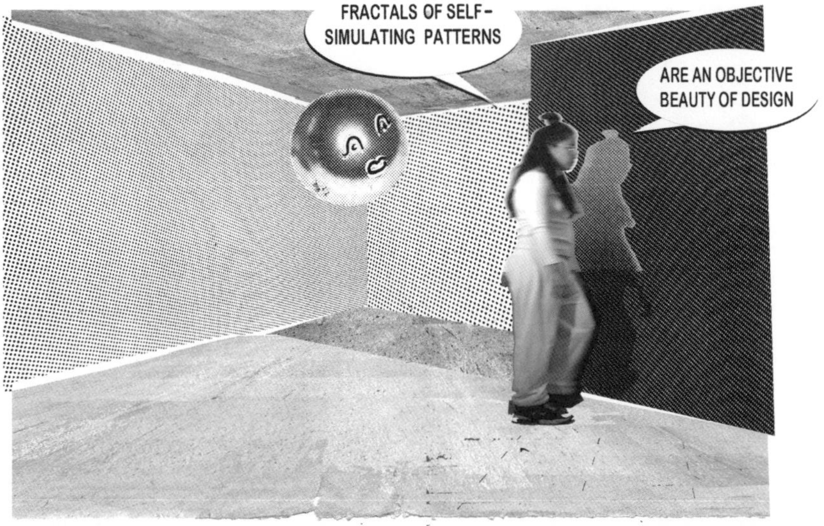
FRACTALS OF SELF-
SIMULATING PATTERNS
ARE AN OBJECTIVE
BEAUTY OF DESIGN

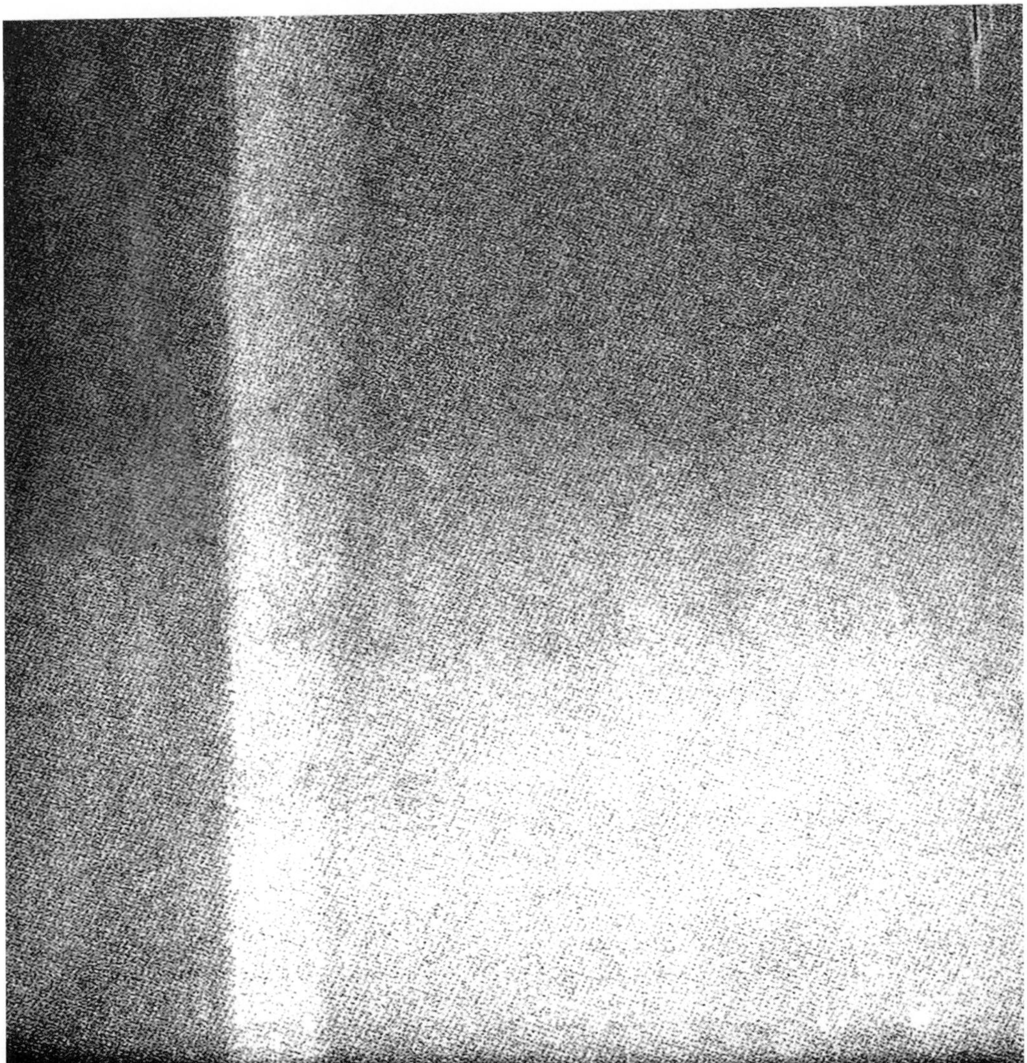

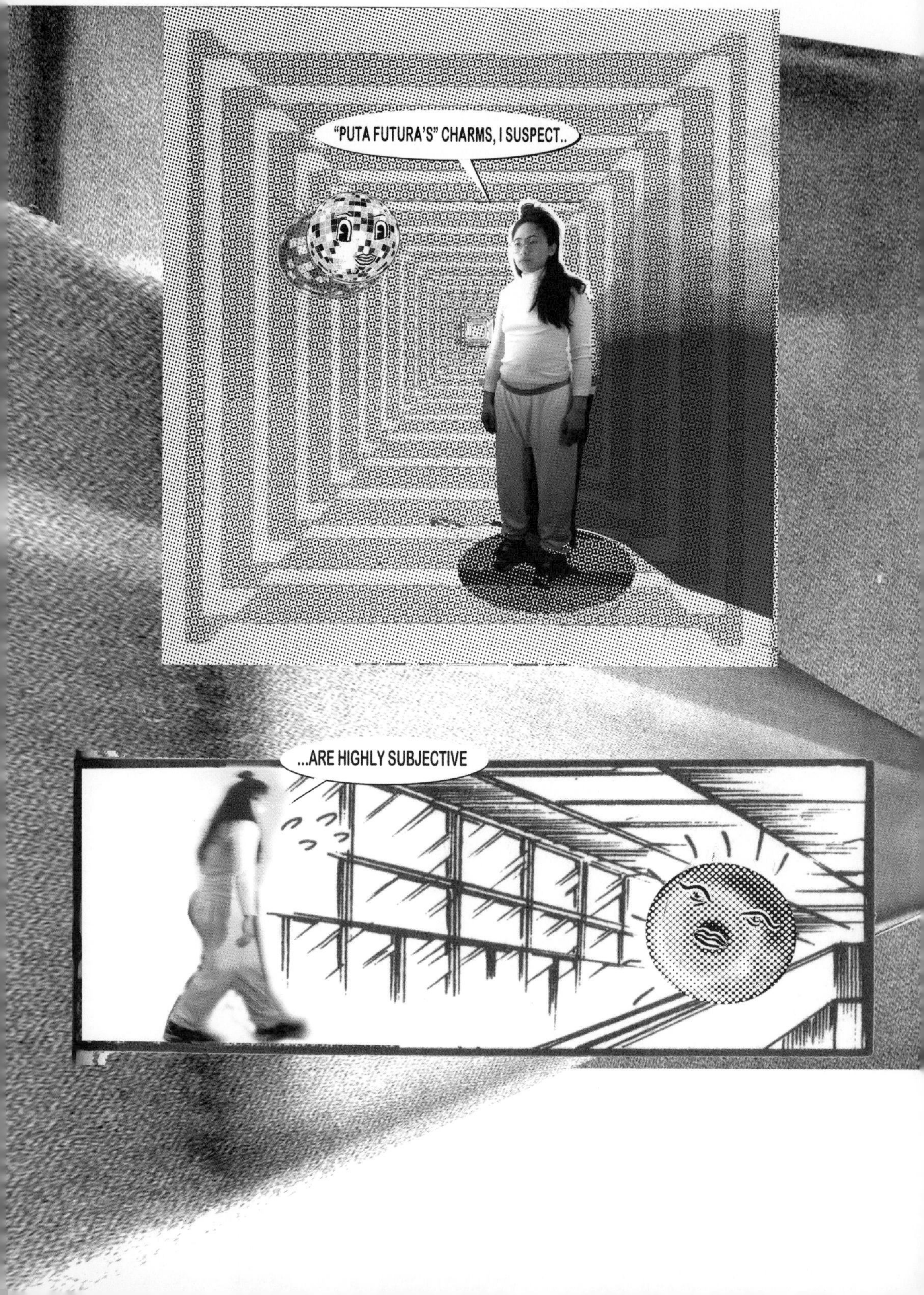
"PUTA FUTURA'S" CHARMS, I SUSPECT..
...ARE HIGHLY SUBJECTIVE

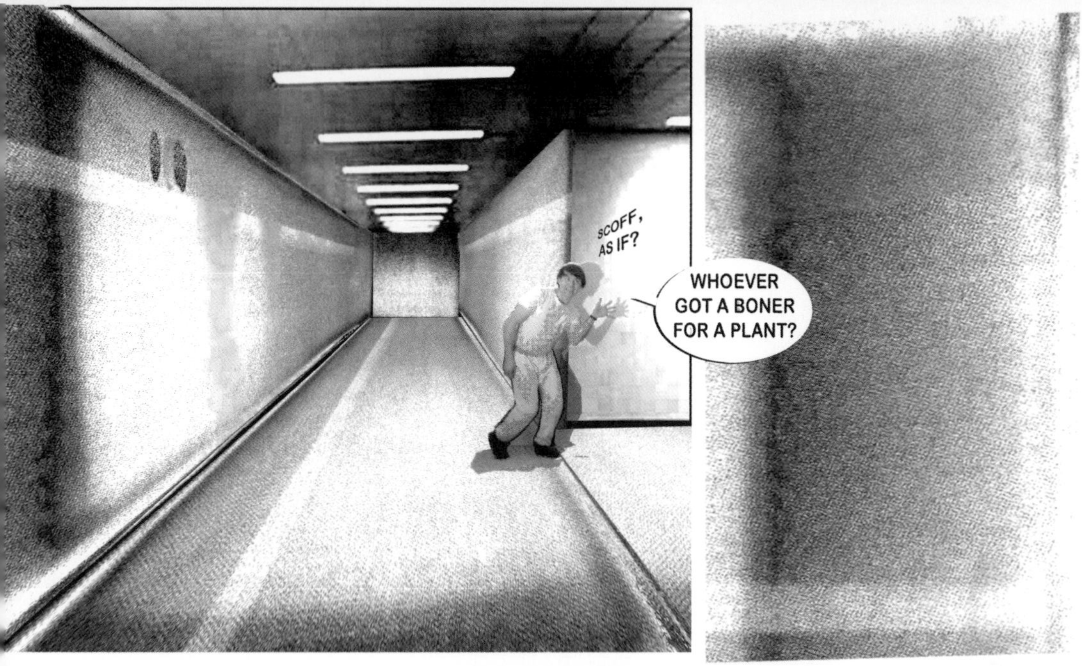
SCOFF, AS IF?
WHOEVER GOT A BONER FOR A PLANT?

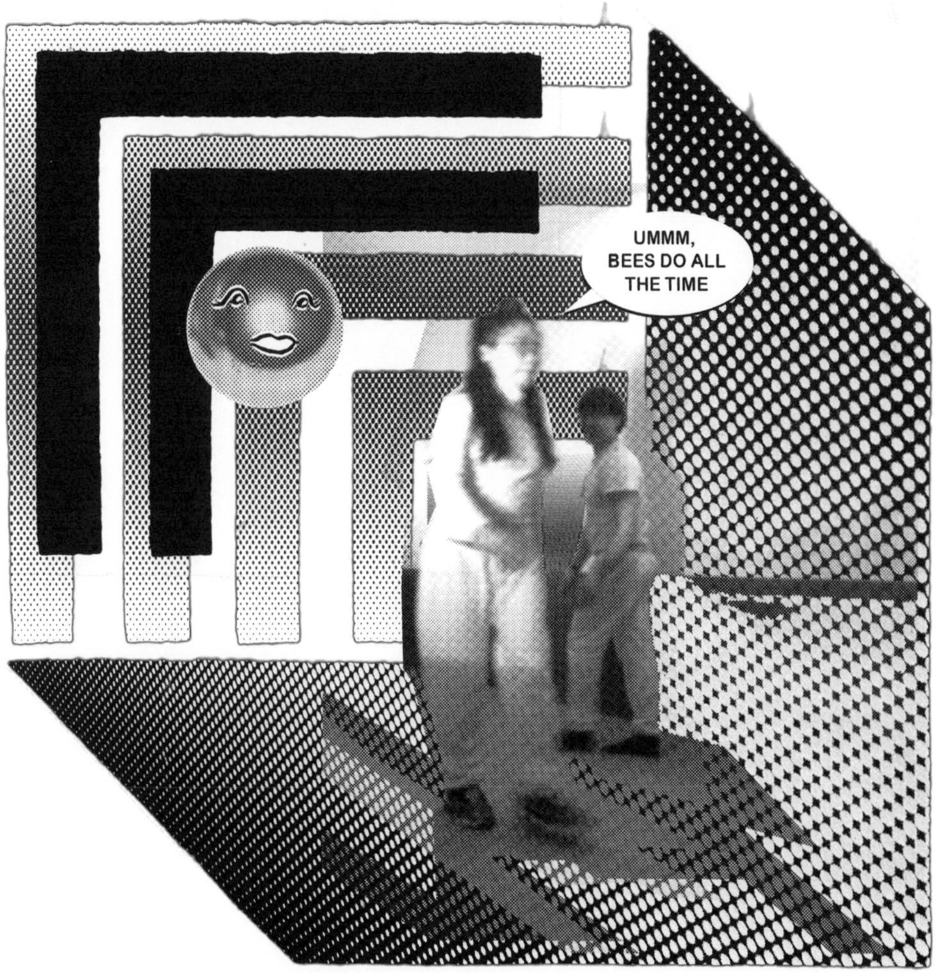
UMMM, BEES DO ALL THE TIME

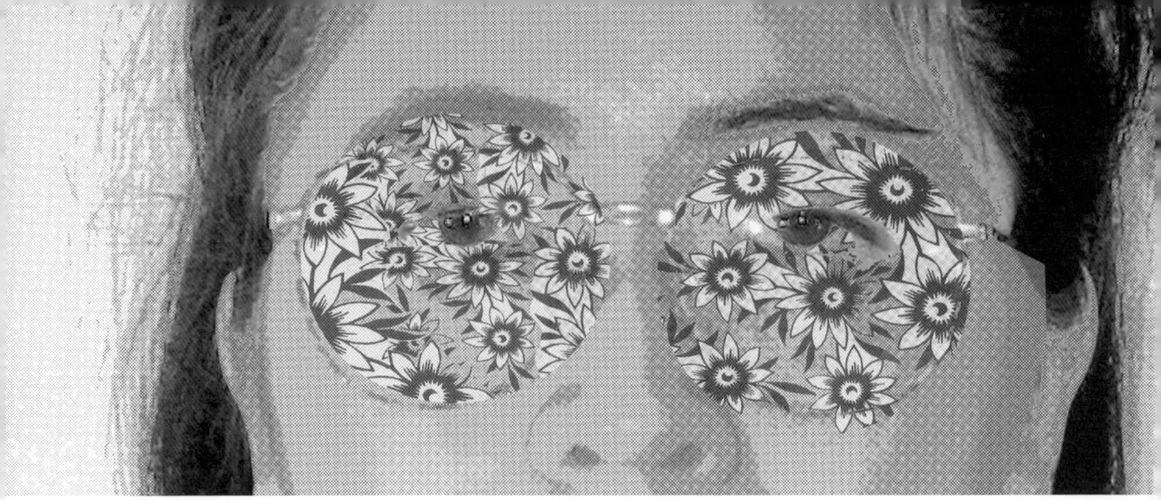

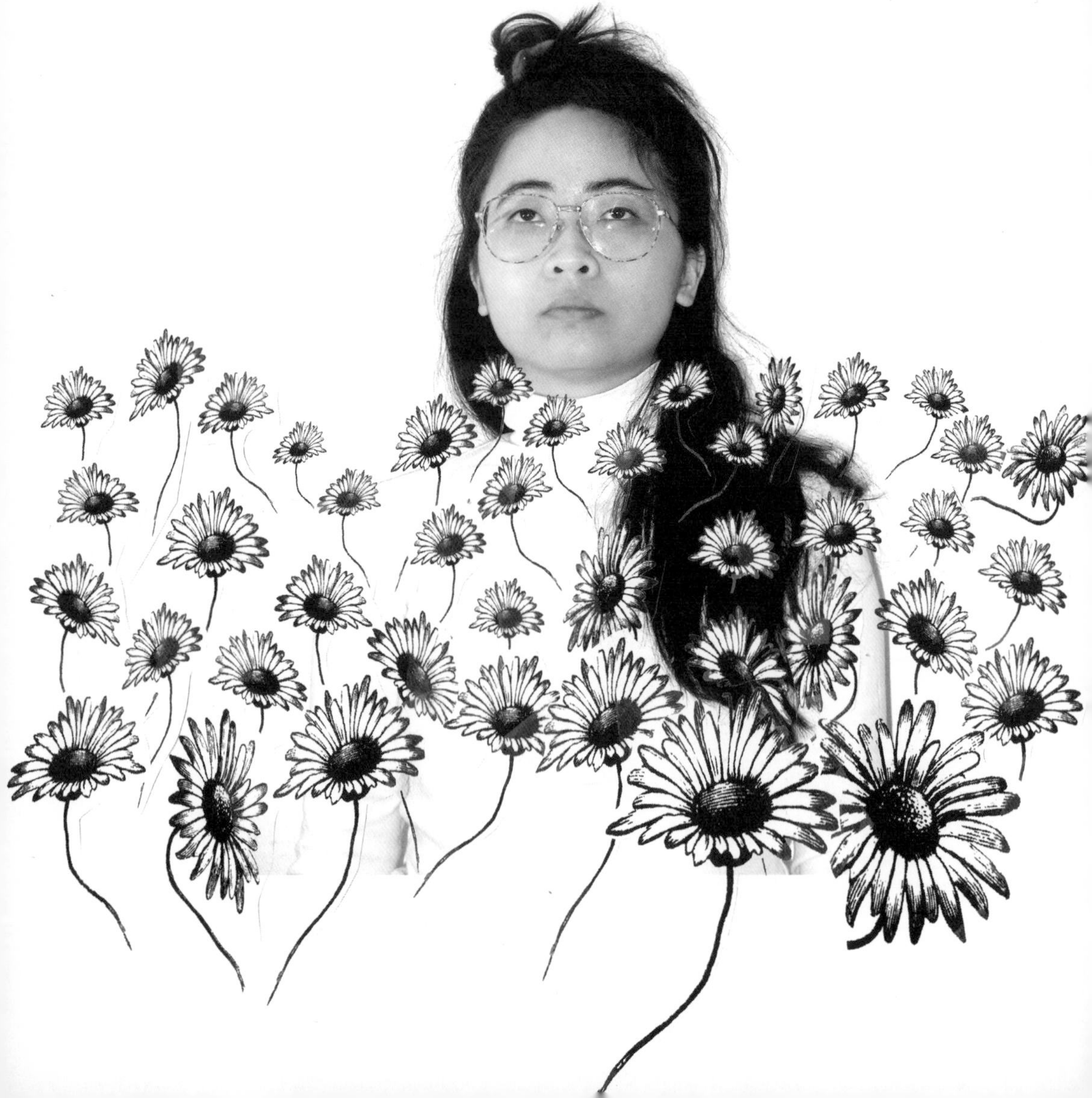

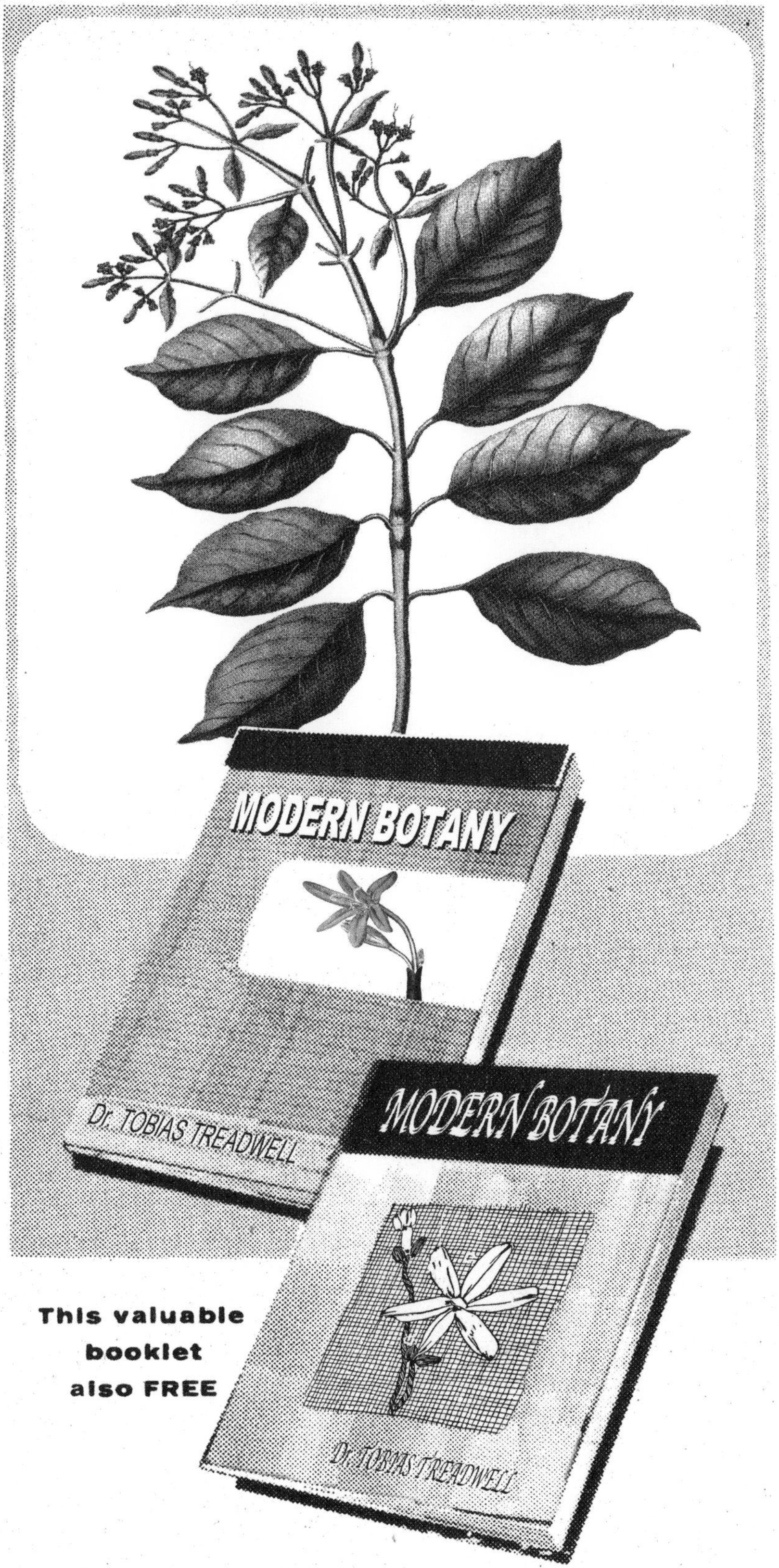
MODERN BOTANY
Dr. TOBIAS TREADWELL
MODERN BOTANY
Dr. TOBIAS TREADWELL
This valuable booklet also FREE

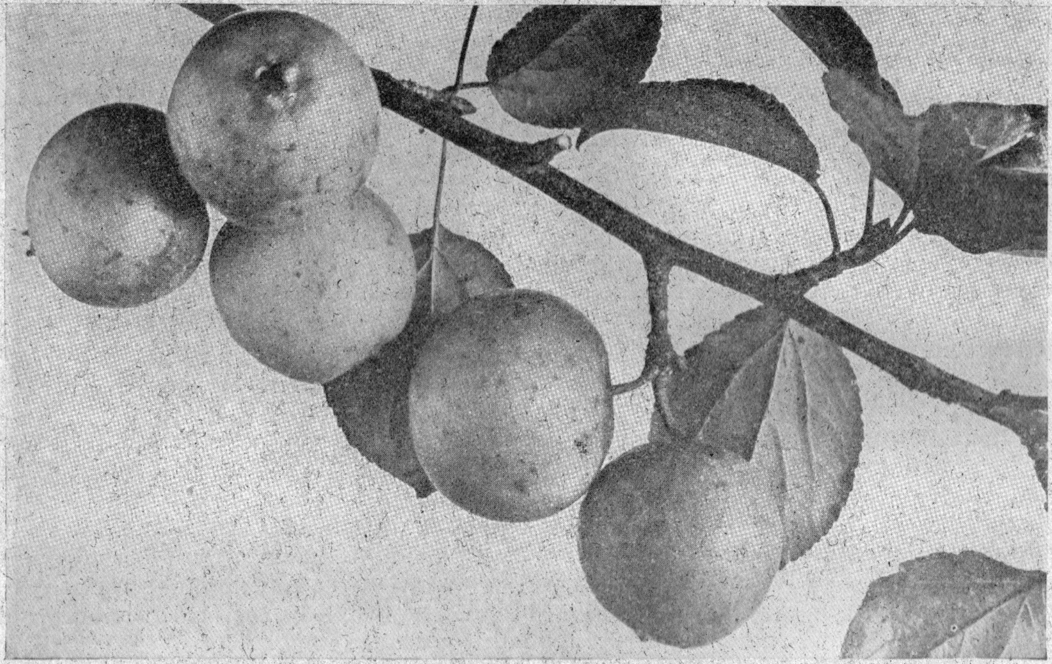

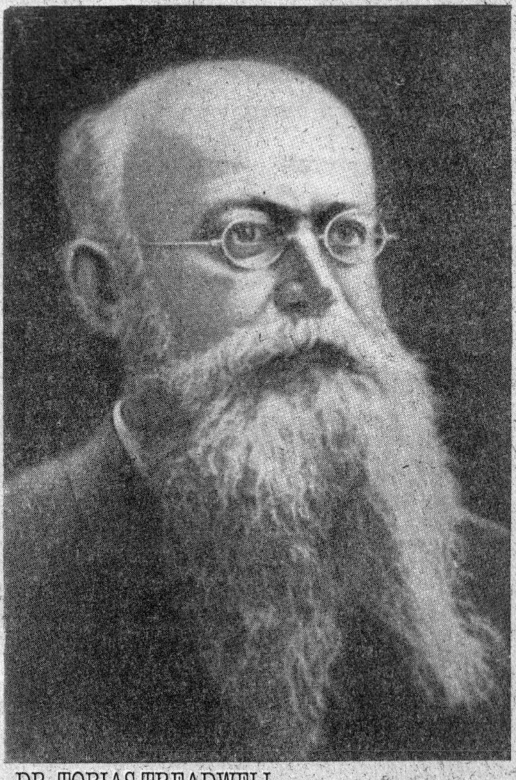

DR. TOBIAS TREADWELL

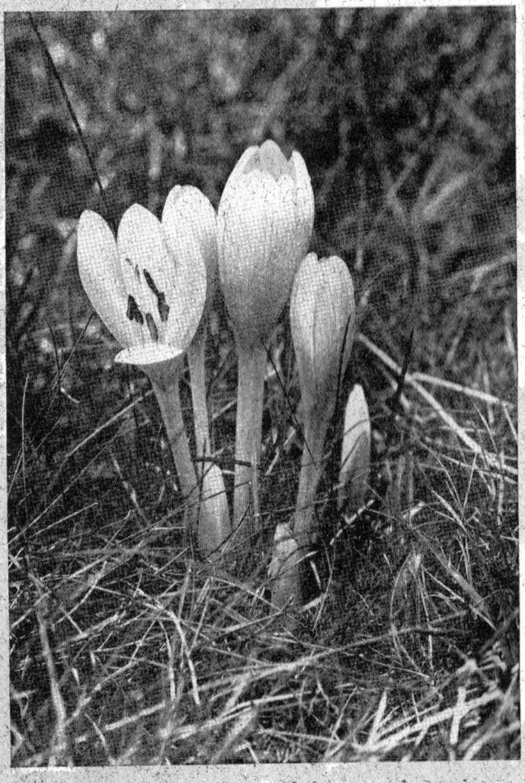

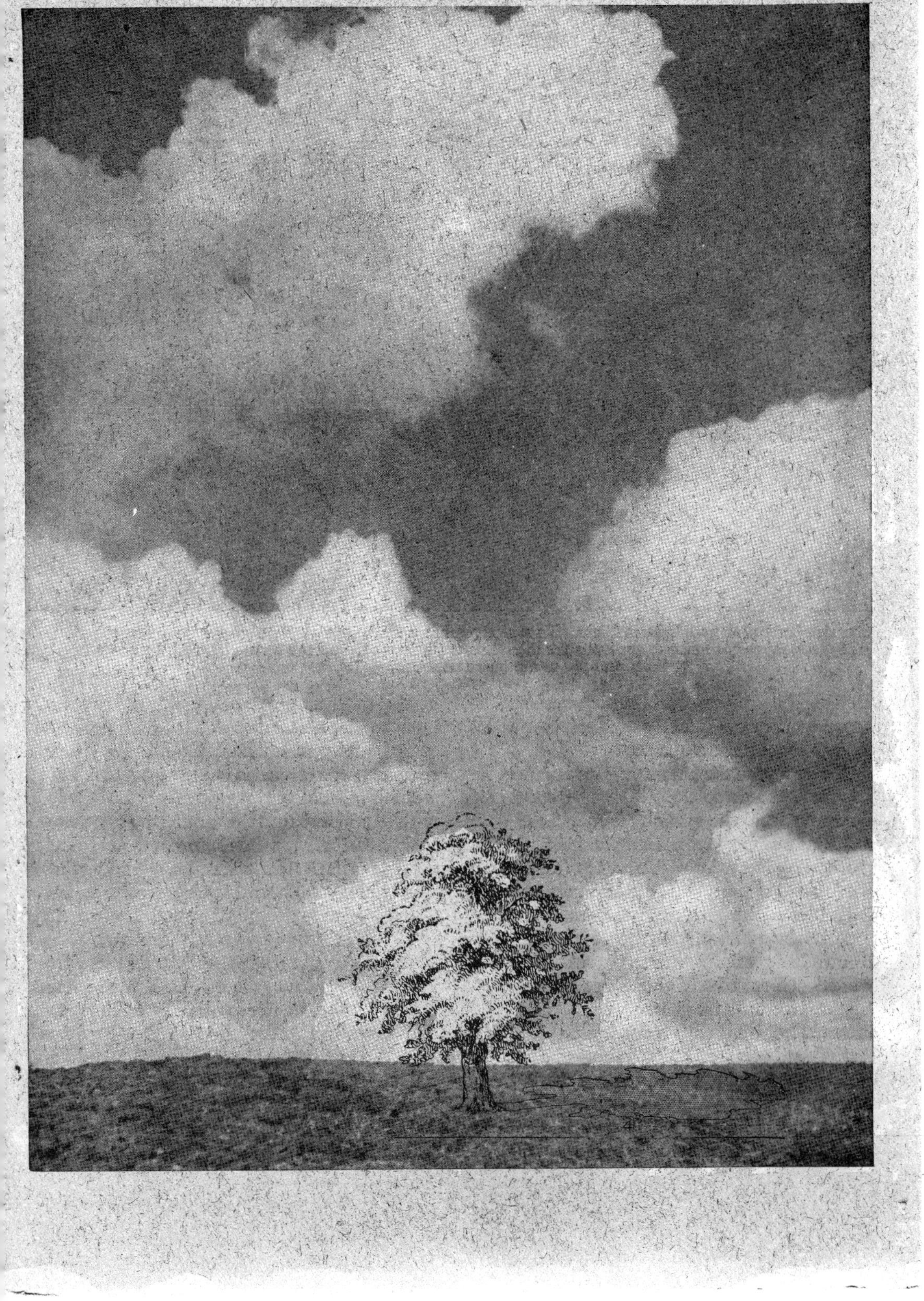

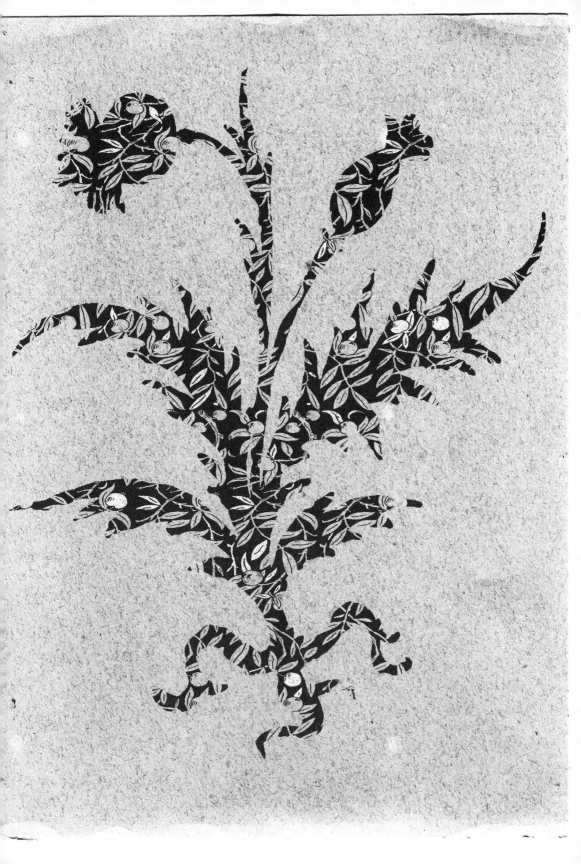

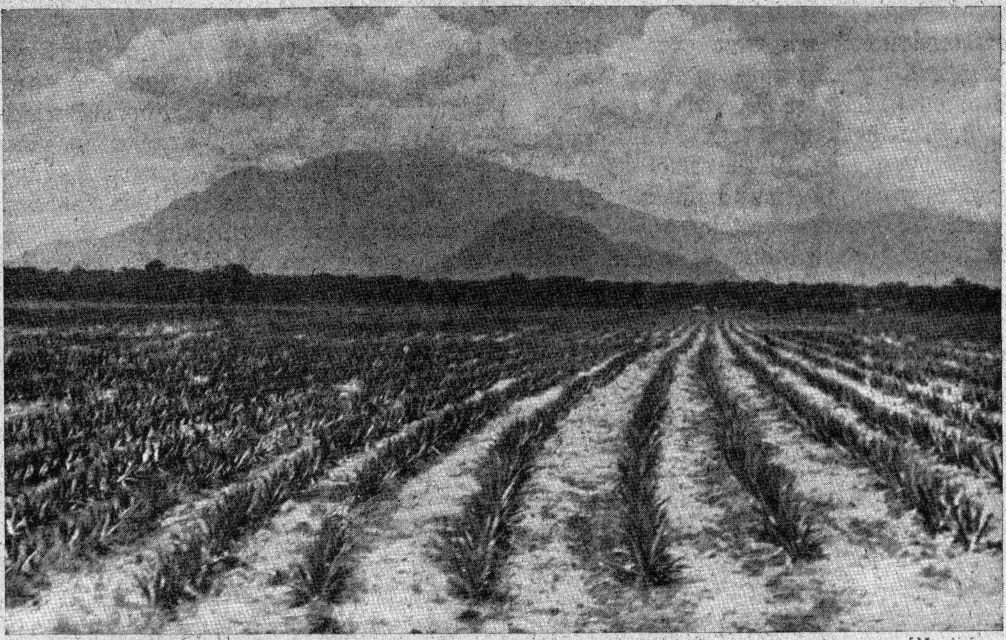

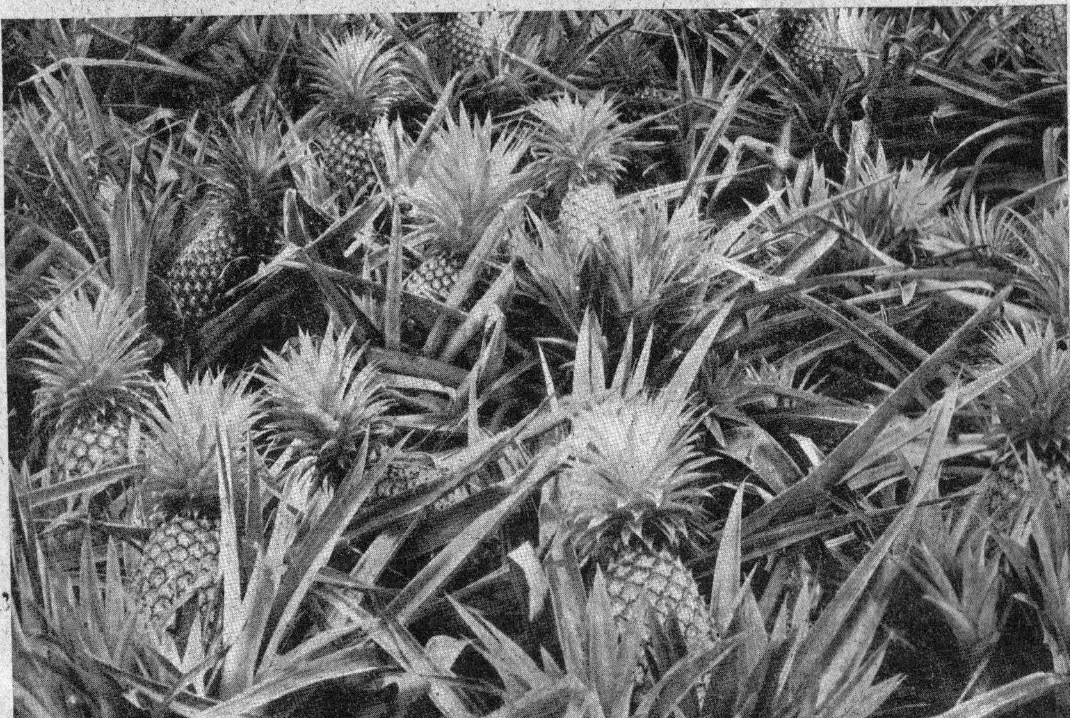

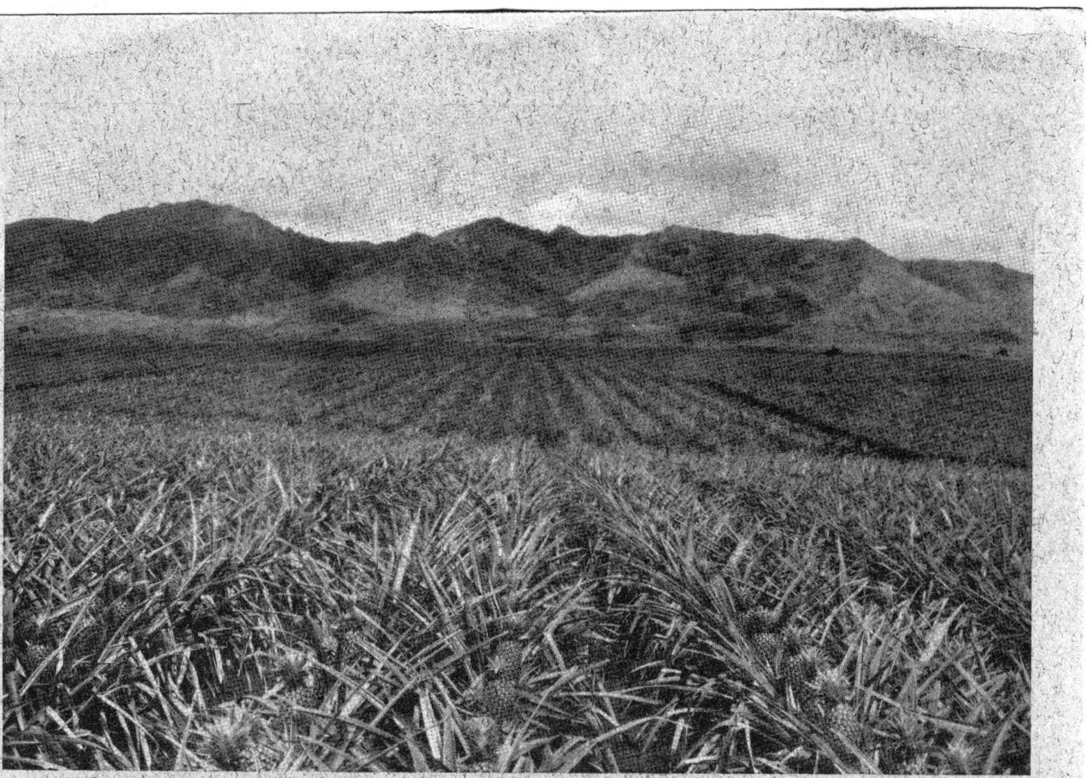

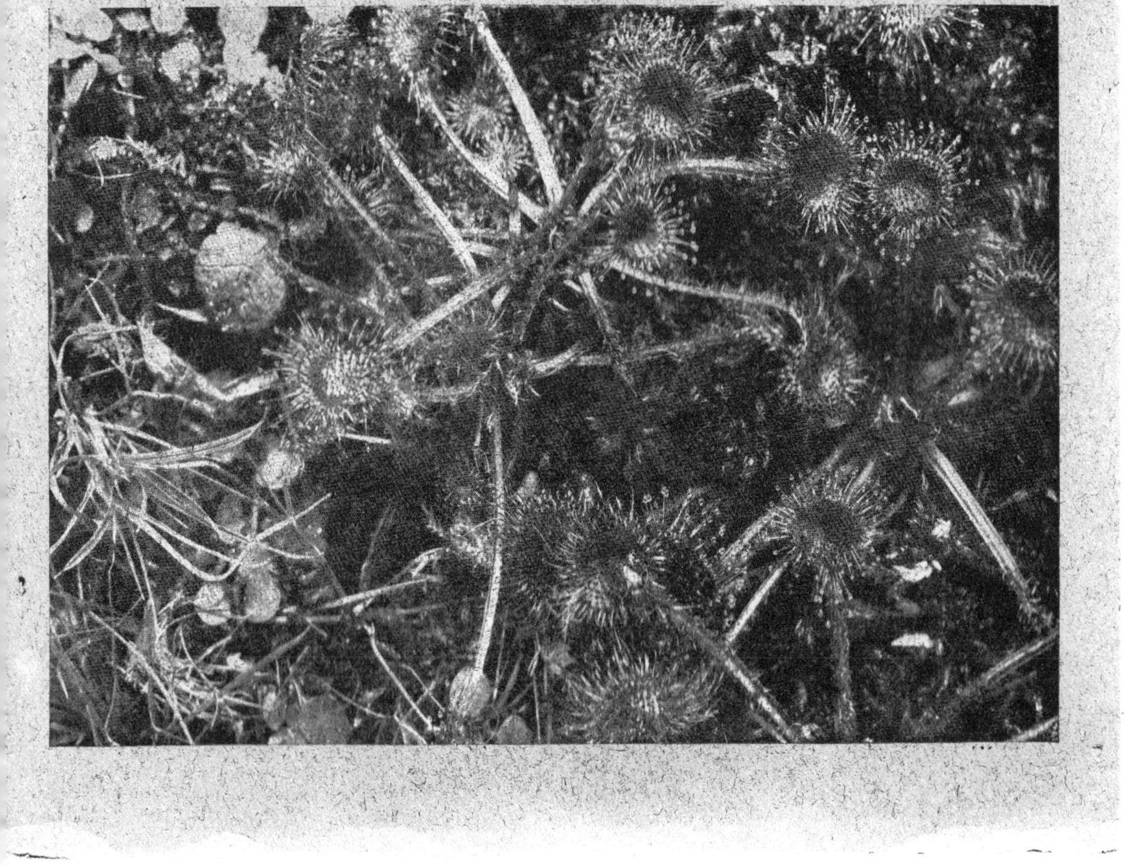

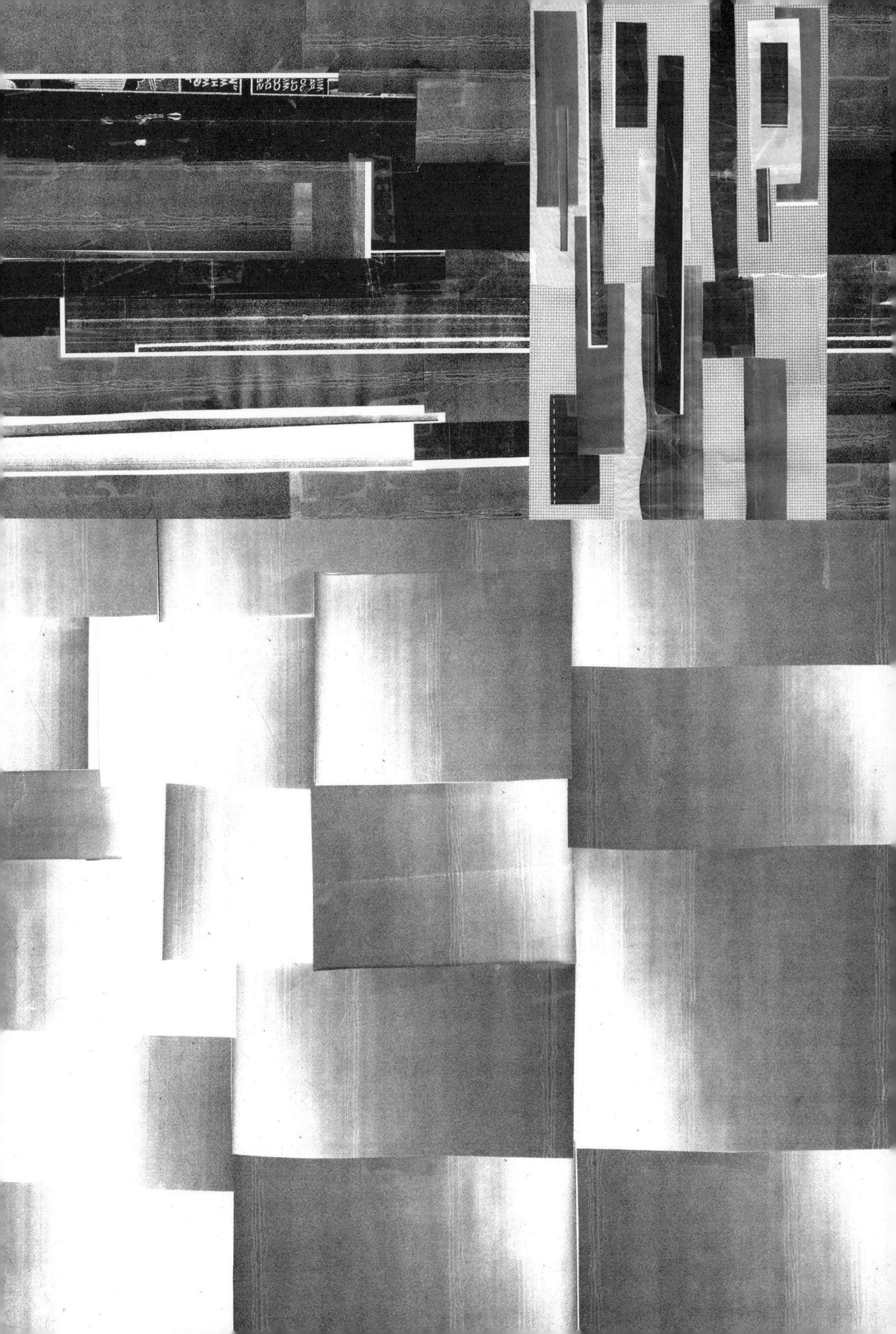

# I WAS BORN FROM SCIENCE FOR SCIENCE

## A SURROGATE CARRIER OF A FROZEN EGG

DR. CYNTHIA NGUYEN

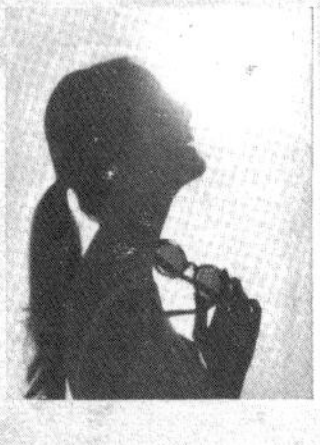

## SCIENCE IS BASED ON REASON

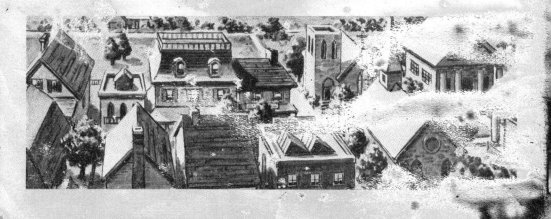

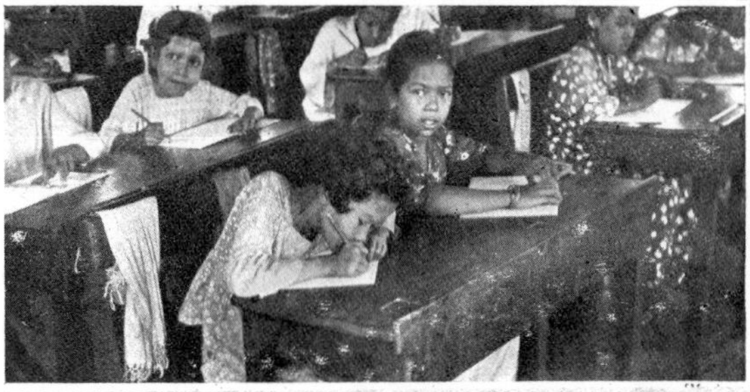

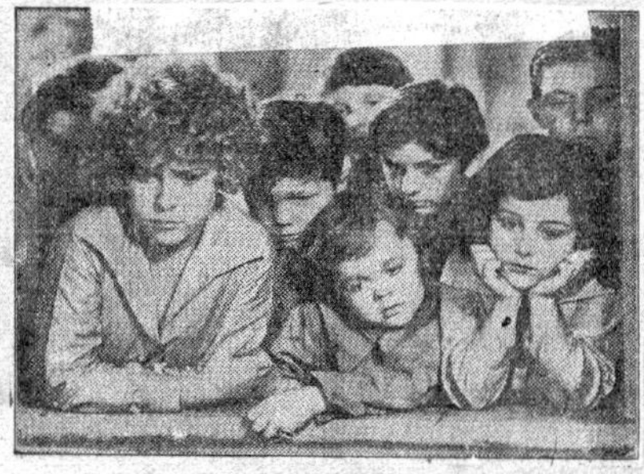

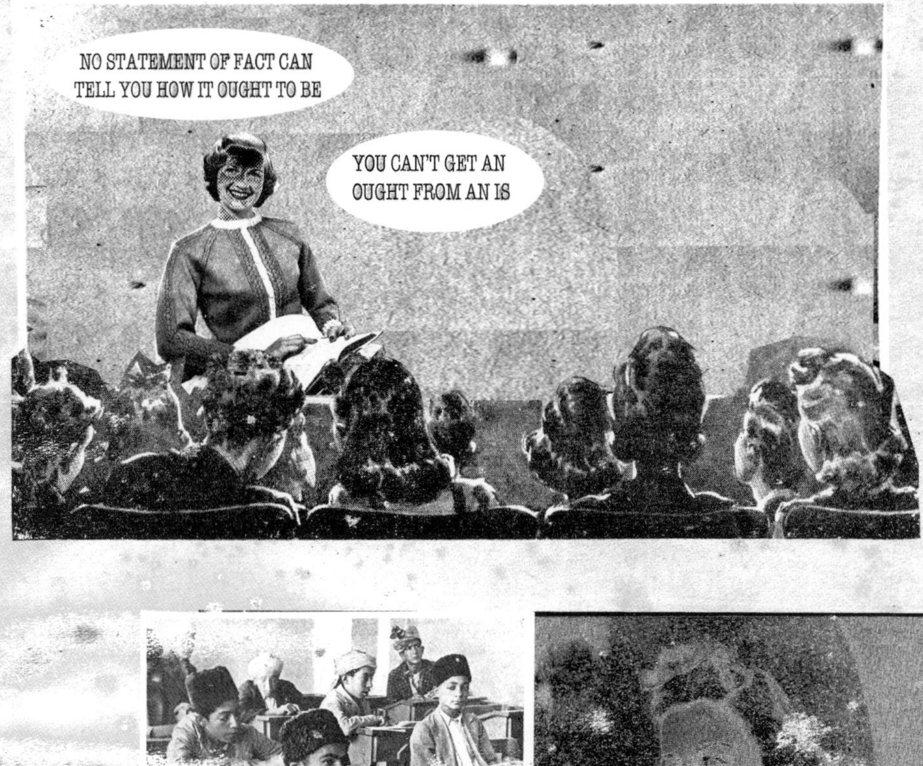
NO STATEMENT OF FACT CAN TELL YOU HOW IT OUGHT TO BE
YOU CAN'T GET AN OUGHT FROM AN IS

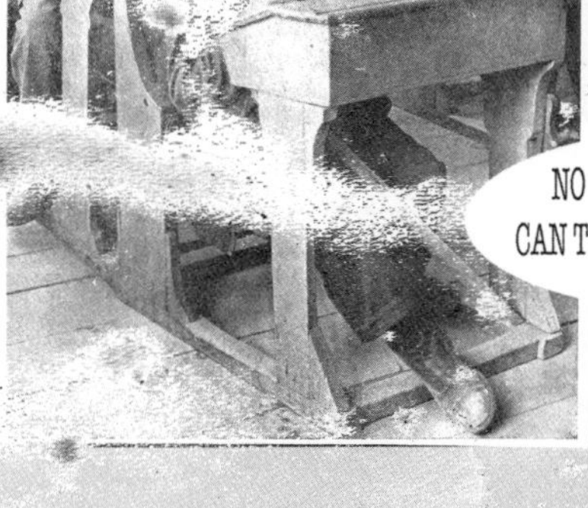

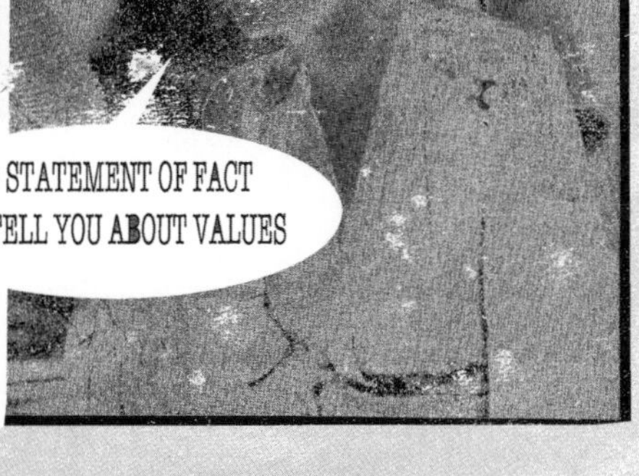
NO STATEMENT OF FACT CAN TELL YOU ABOUT VALUES

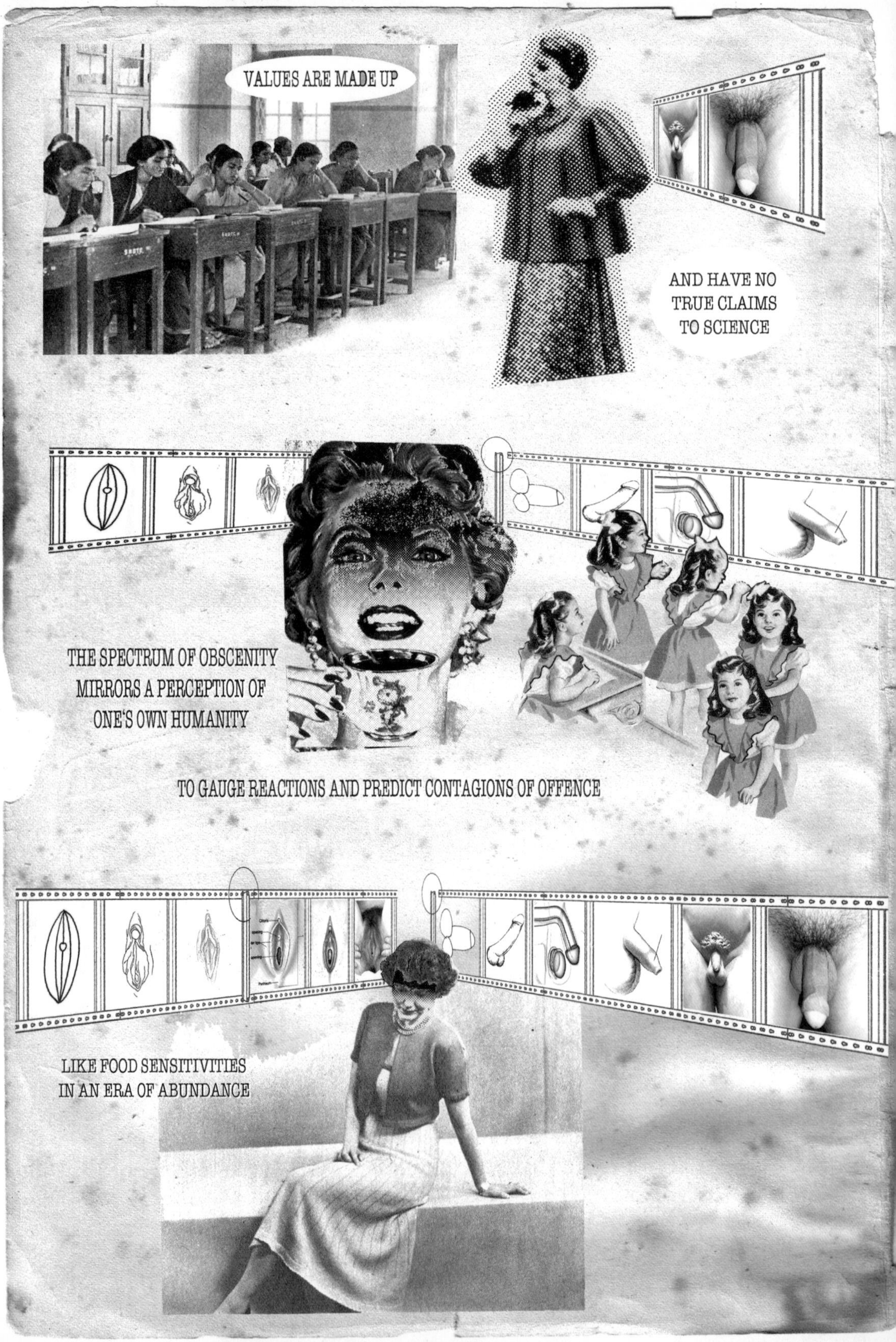
VALUES ARE MADE UP
AND HAVE NO TRUE CLAIMS TO SCIENCE
THE SPECTRUM OF OBSCENITY MIRRORS A PERCEPTION OF ONE'S OWN HUMANITY
TO GAUGE REACTIONS AND PREDICT CONTAGIONS OF OFFENCE
LIKE FOOD SENSITIVITIES IN AN ERA OF ABUNDANCE

IN THIS TIME OF INCREASING SECURITY ACTUAL VIOLENCE IS DISTANT AND ABSTRACT SO WE INDULGE IN PERCEPTIONS OF MICRO AGGRESSIONS

WE FIND REASONS FOR OUR CONSTANT STATE OF STRESS

PIONEER OF THE SPECTRUM OF OBSCENITY IN WHICH THE SUBJECT ENGAGES WITH IMAGES OF THE HUMAN VAGINA RENDERED IN A VARIETY OF WAYS FROM DOODLE TO GLOSSY PHOTO

THIS IS USED TO GAUGE REACTIONS AND PREDICT CONTAGIONS OF OFFENCE

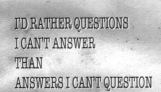

I'D RATHER QUESTIONS
I CAN'T ANSWER
THAN
ANSWERS I CAN'T QUESTION

THE PENIS IS
OVERT, COMEDIC
OR THREATENING

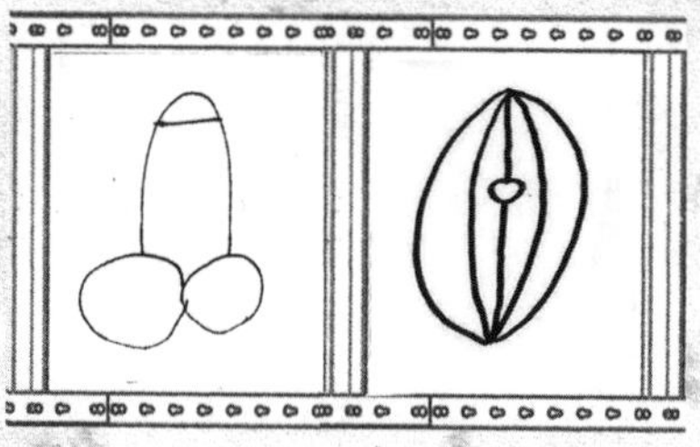

THE VAGINA IS THE
PATH FROM WHENCE
WE CAME

THE MYSTERY
OF SELF

REPRESSED AND DENIED
COVERT BUT NOT A VISUAL FOCUS

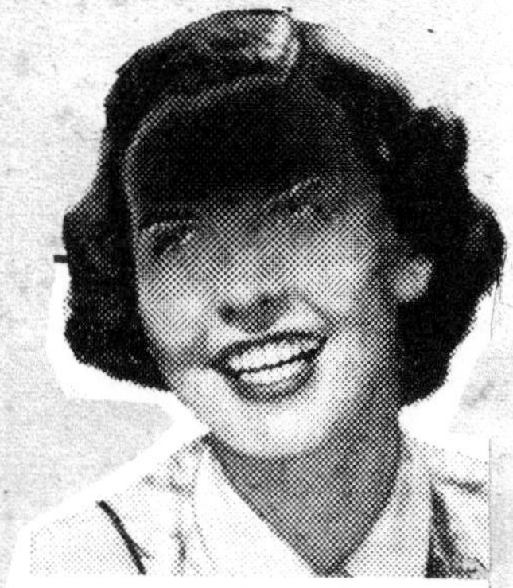

OFFENCE TEMPERATURE
OF THE ETHNOSPHERE
AND ITS AFFECT ON THE BIOSPHERE

DATA SYNTHESIS

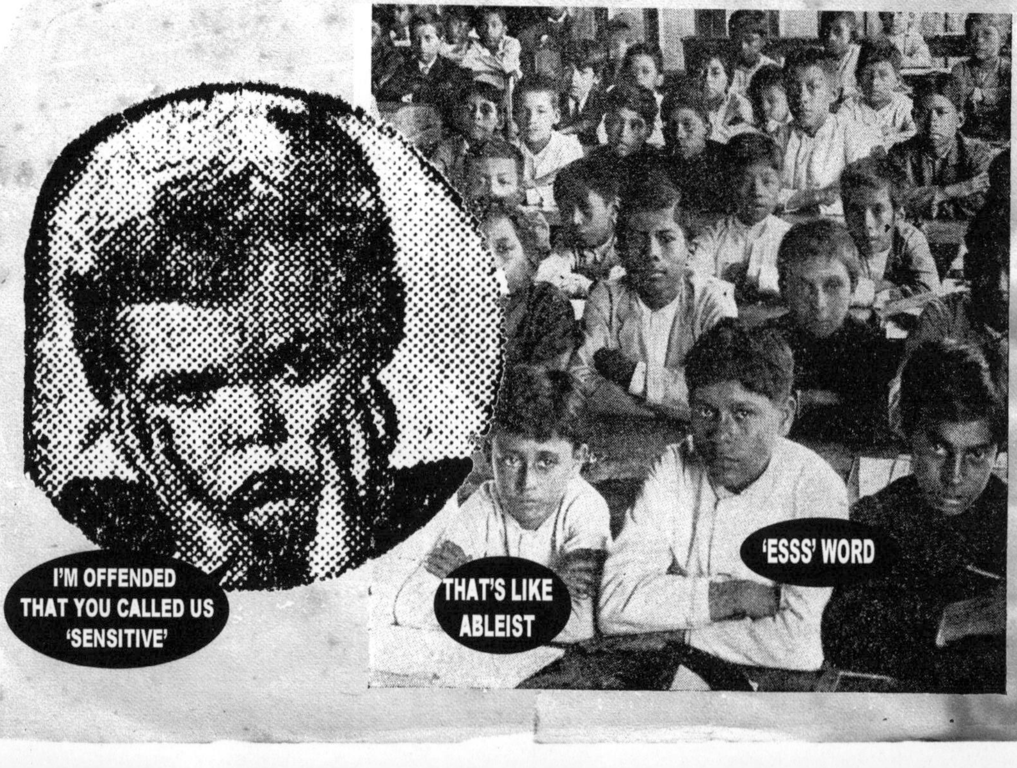
I'M OFFENDED
THAT YOU CALLED US
'SENSITIVE'
THAT'S LIKE
ABLEIST
'ESSS' WORD

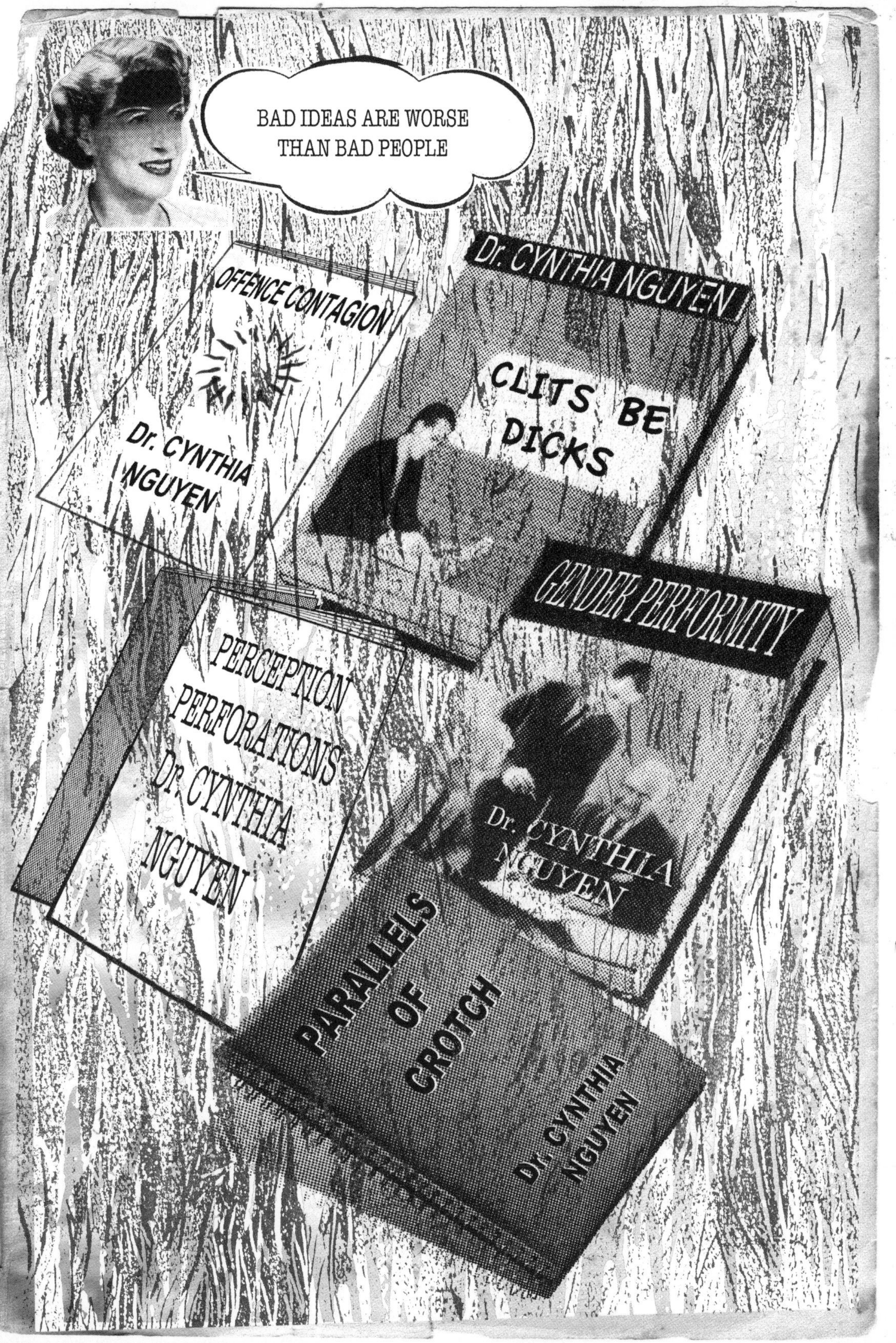
BAD IDEAS ARE WORSE THAN BAD PEOPLE
OFFENCE CONTAGION
Dr. CYNTHIA NGUYEN
Dr. CYNTHIA NGUYEN
CLITS BE DICKS
GENDER PERFORMITY
Dr. CYNTHIA NGUYEN
PERCEPTION PERFORATIONS
Dr. CYNTHIA NGUYEN
PARALLELS OF CROTCH
Dr. CYNTHIA NGUYEN

Imaging if you will,
those who dance and those who do not.

Dance is a unifying activity of great benefit.

Yet if the situation of dance was somehow instantly visited upon the nondancing population they would experience the velocity of the rhythmic movement as assault

That perspective is less apropos when in an actual discotheque.

Those who experience offense within a club of comedy,
a place dedicated to
puncturing the balloon of expectation
as de rigueur…

might compare to those who take offence to a
basketball player missing a free throw.

A violation of your demanded sentimentality.

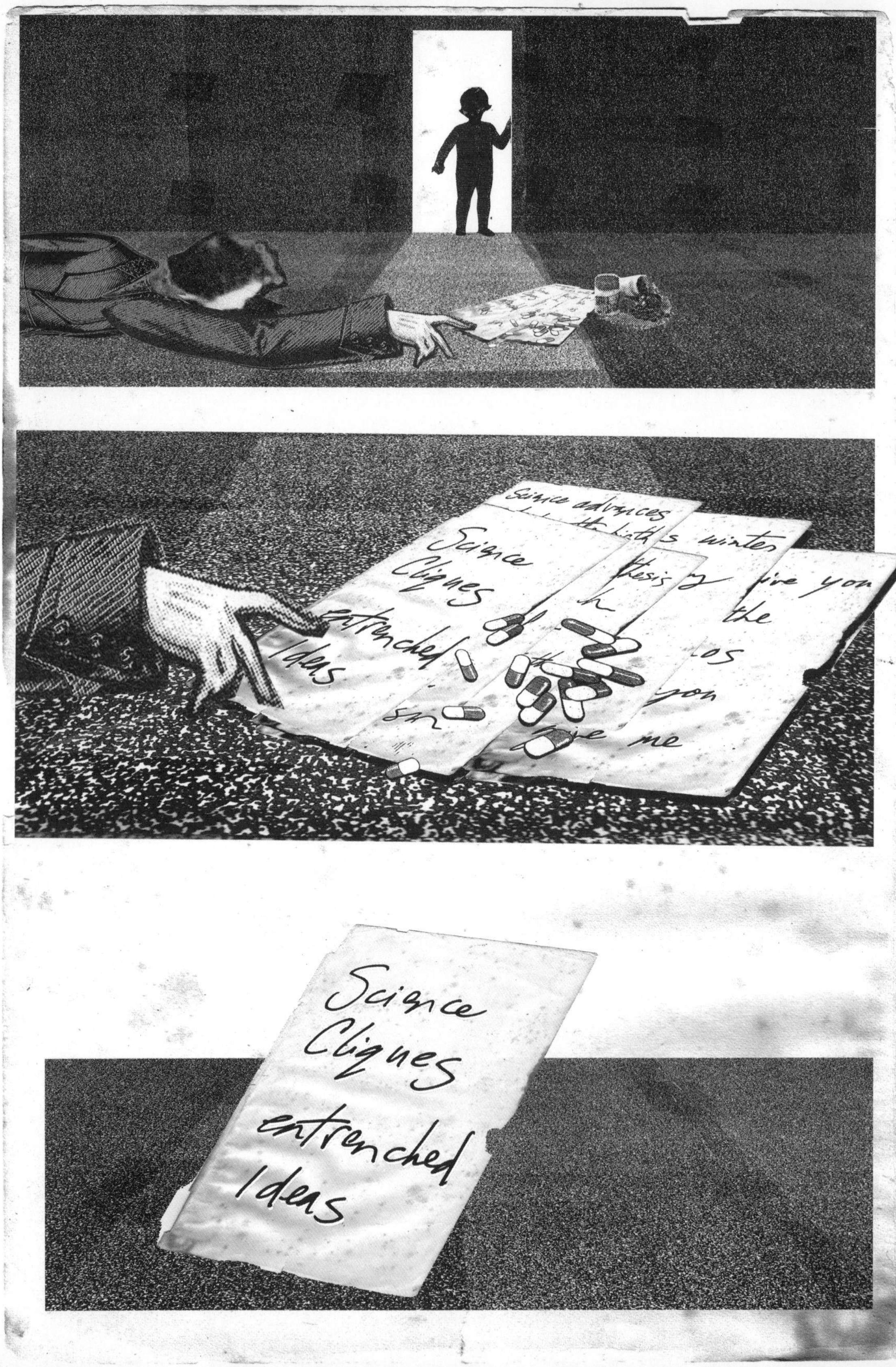

Science advances
Science
Cliques
entrenched
Ideas
Science
Cliques
entrenched
Ideas

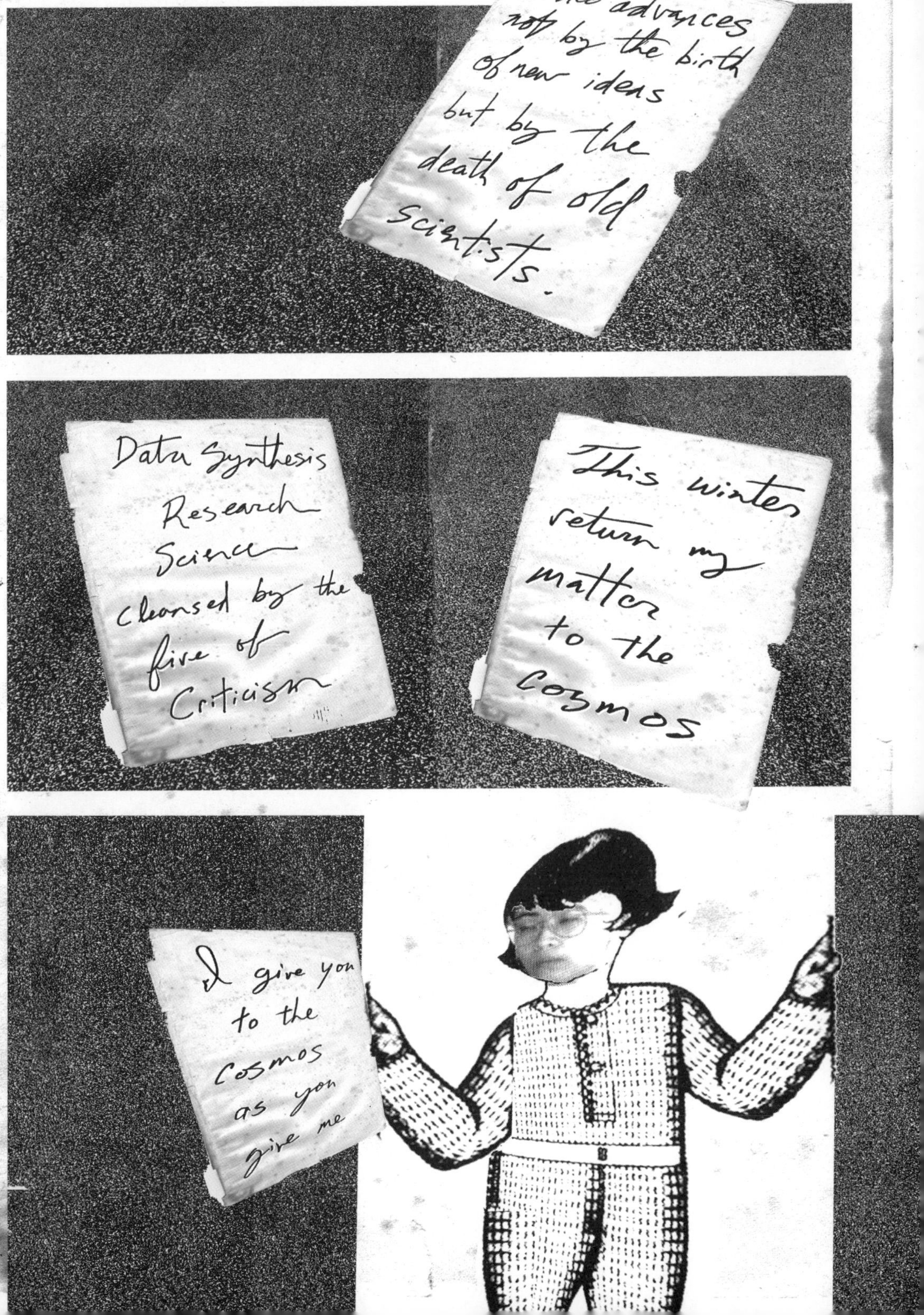

Science advances not by the birth of new ideas but by the death of old scientists.
Data Synthesis Research Science Cleansed by the fire of Criticism
This winter return my matter to the Cosmos
I give you to the Cosmos as you give me

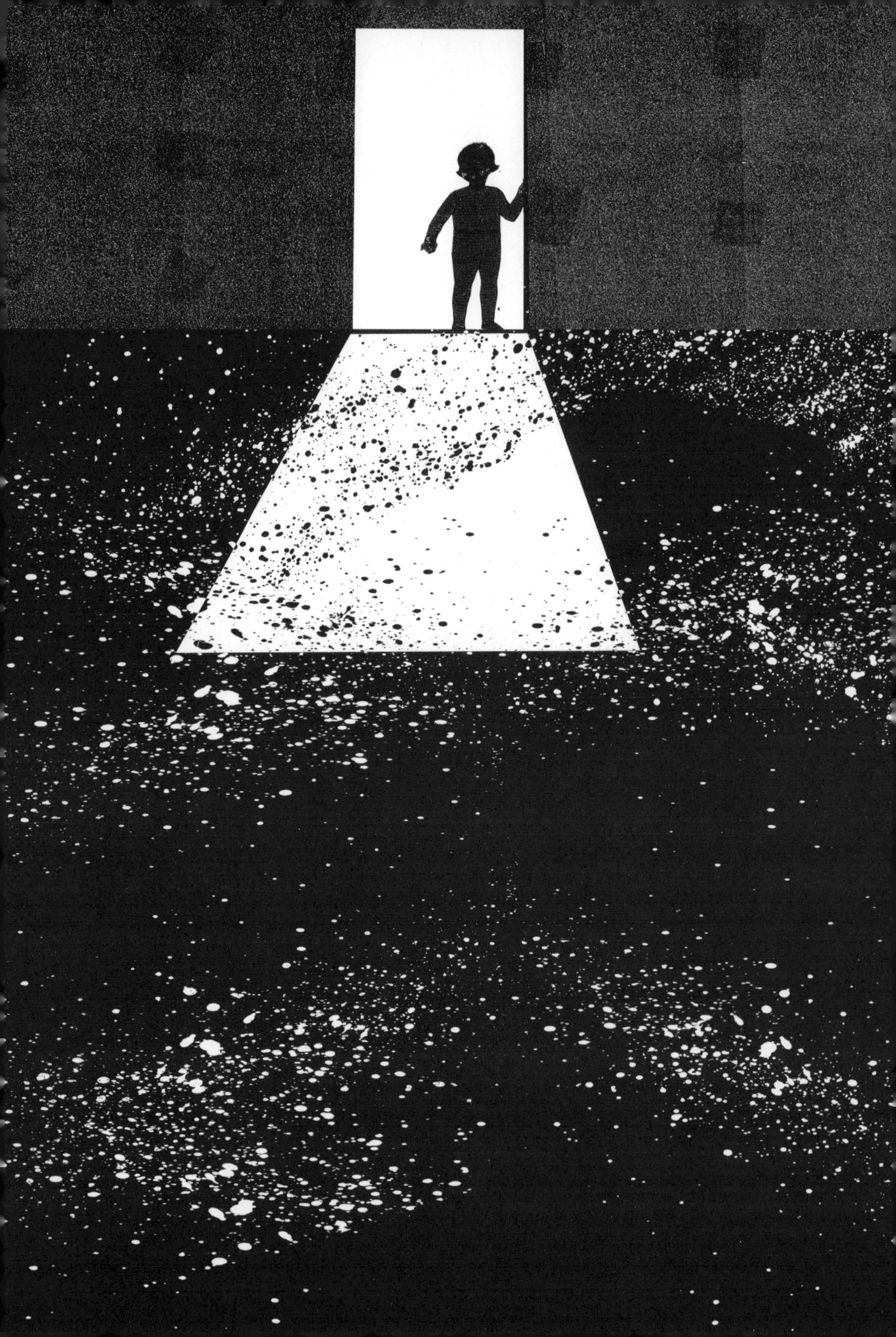

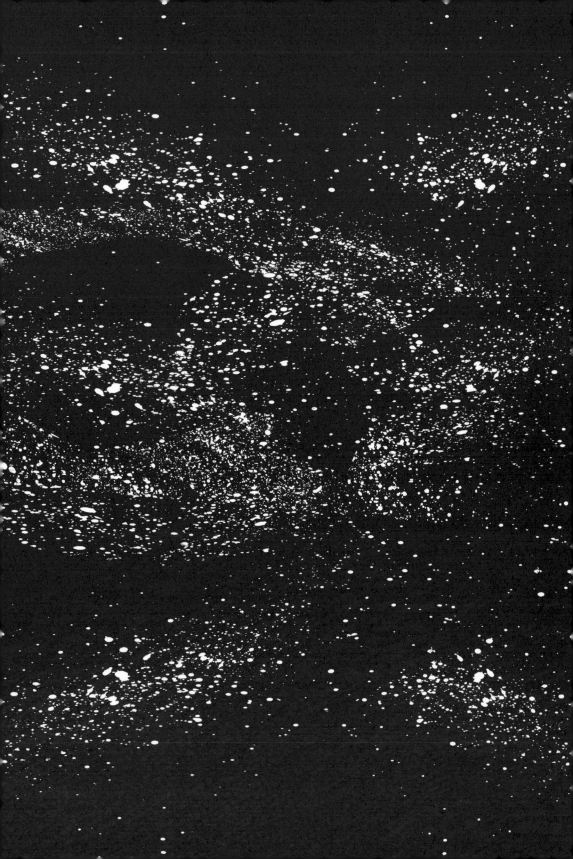

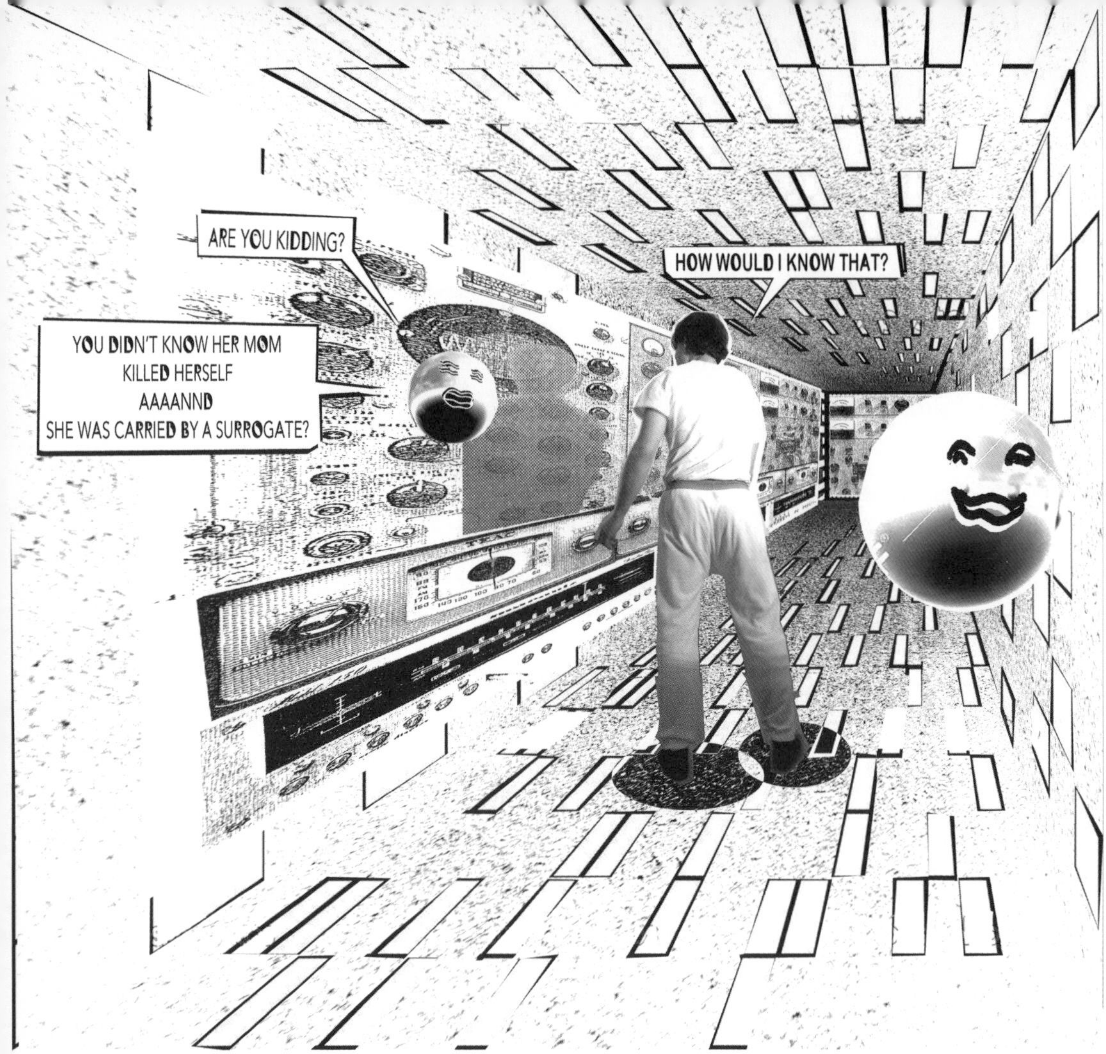
ARE YOU KIDDING?
YOU DIDN'T KNOW HER MOM
KILLED HERSELF
AAAANND
SHE WAS CARRIED BY A SURROGATE?
HOW WOULD I KNOW THAT?

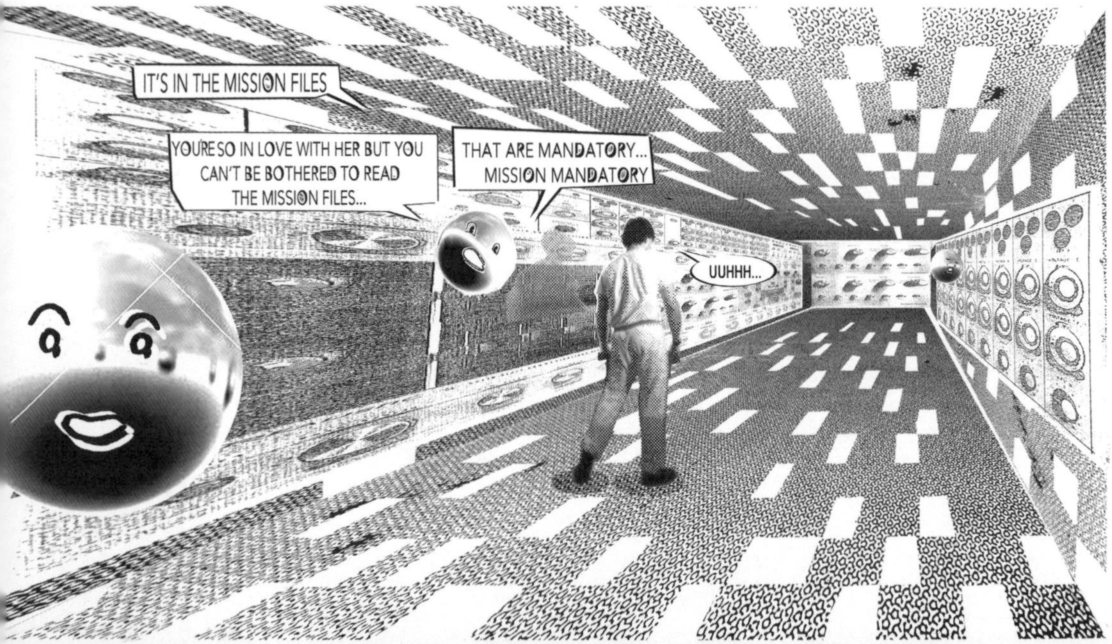
IT'S IN THE MISSION FILES
YOU'RE SO IN LOVE WITH HER BUT YOU
CAN'T BE BOTHERED TO READ
THE MISSION FILES...
THAT ARE MANDATORY...
MISSION MANDATORY
UUHHH...

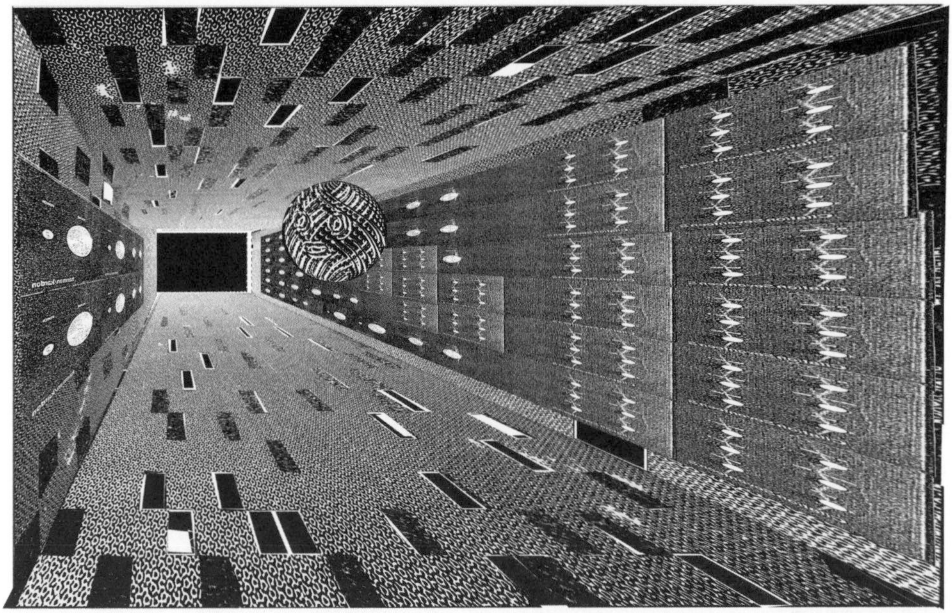

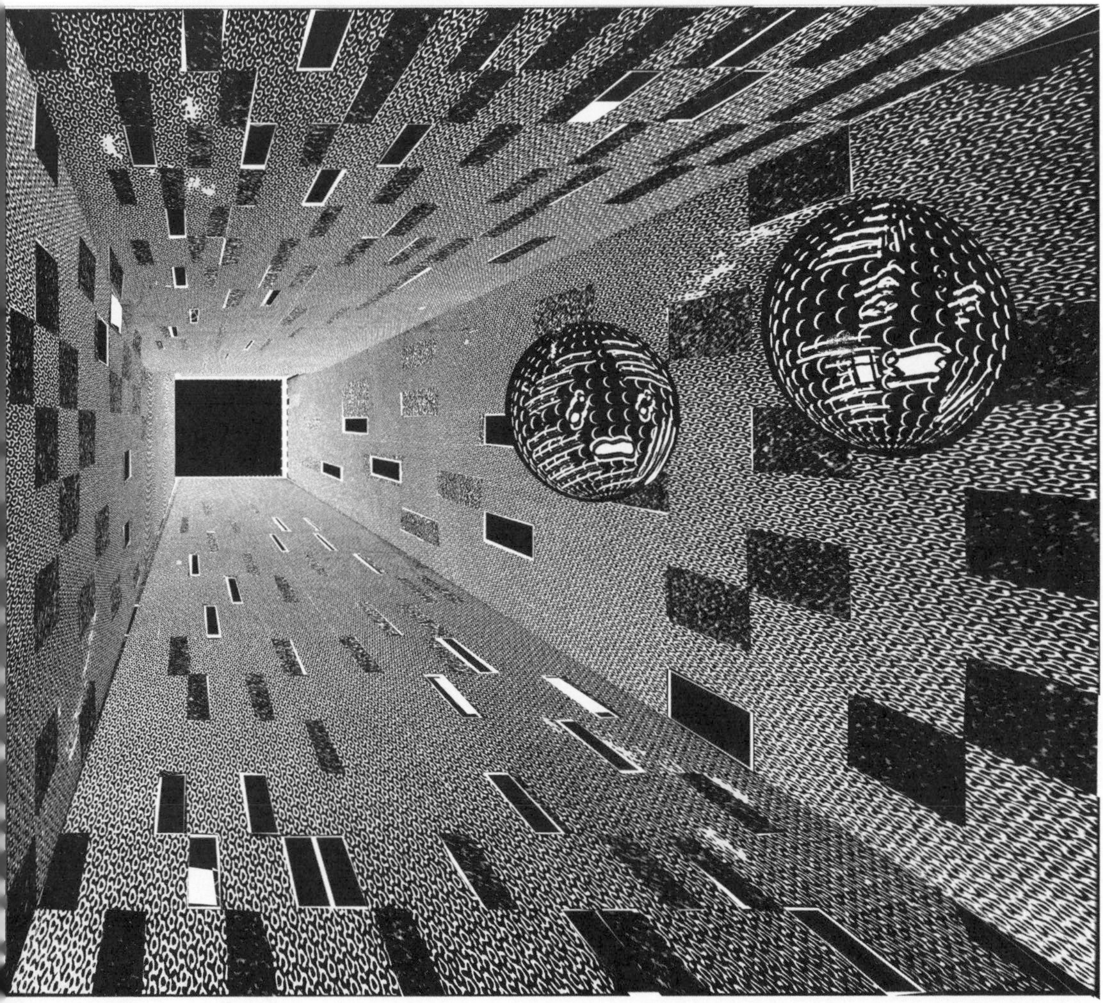

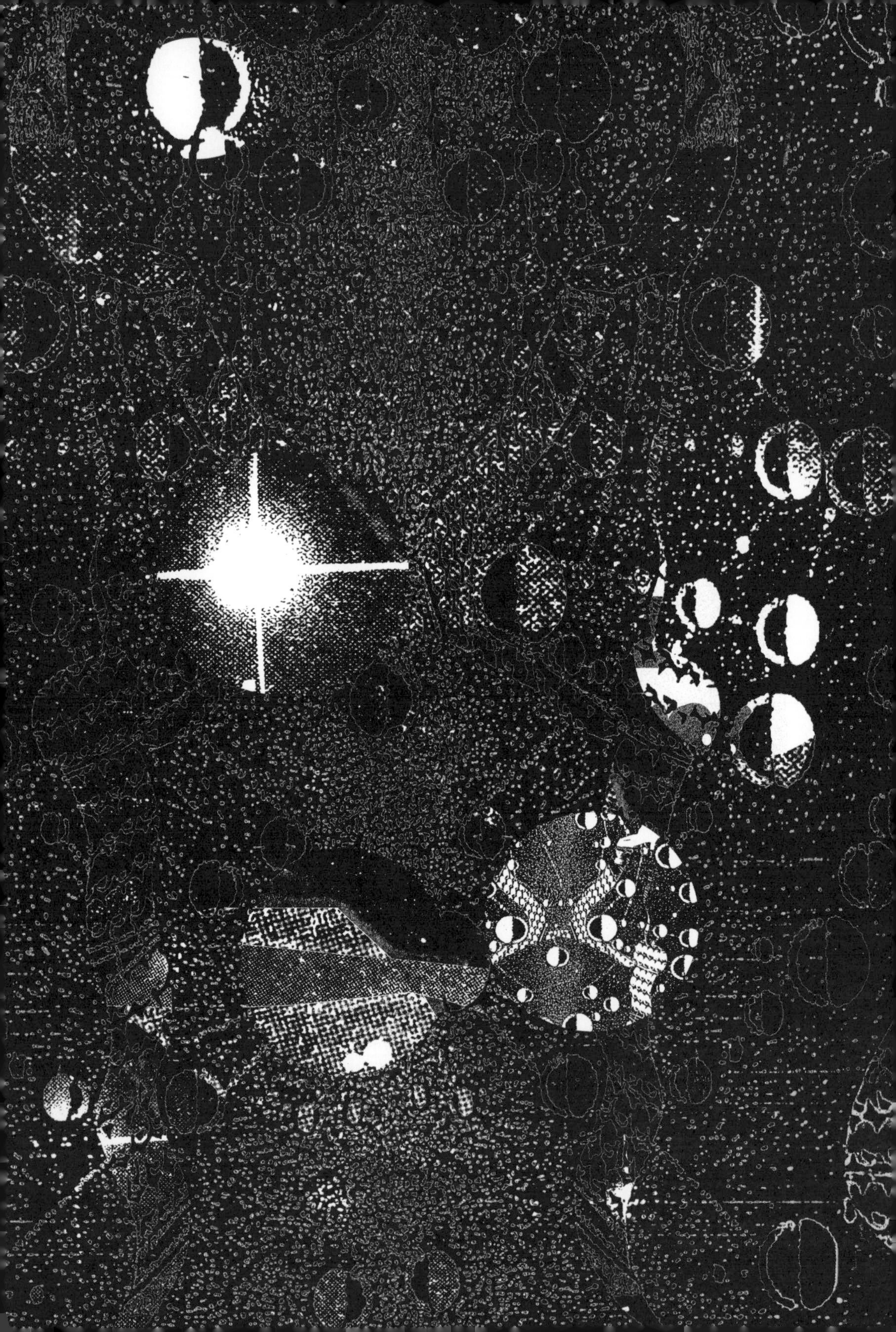

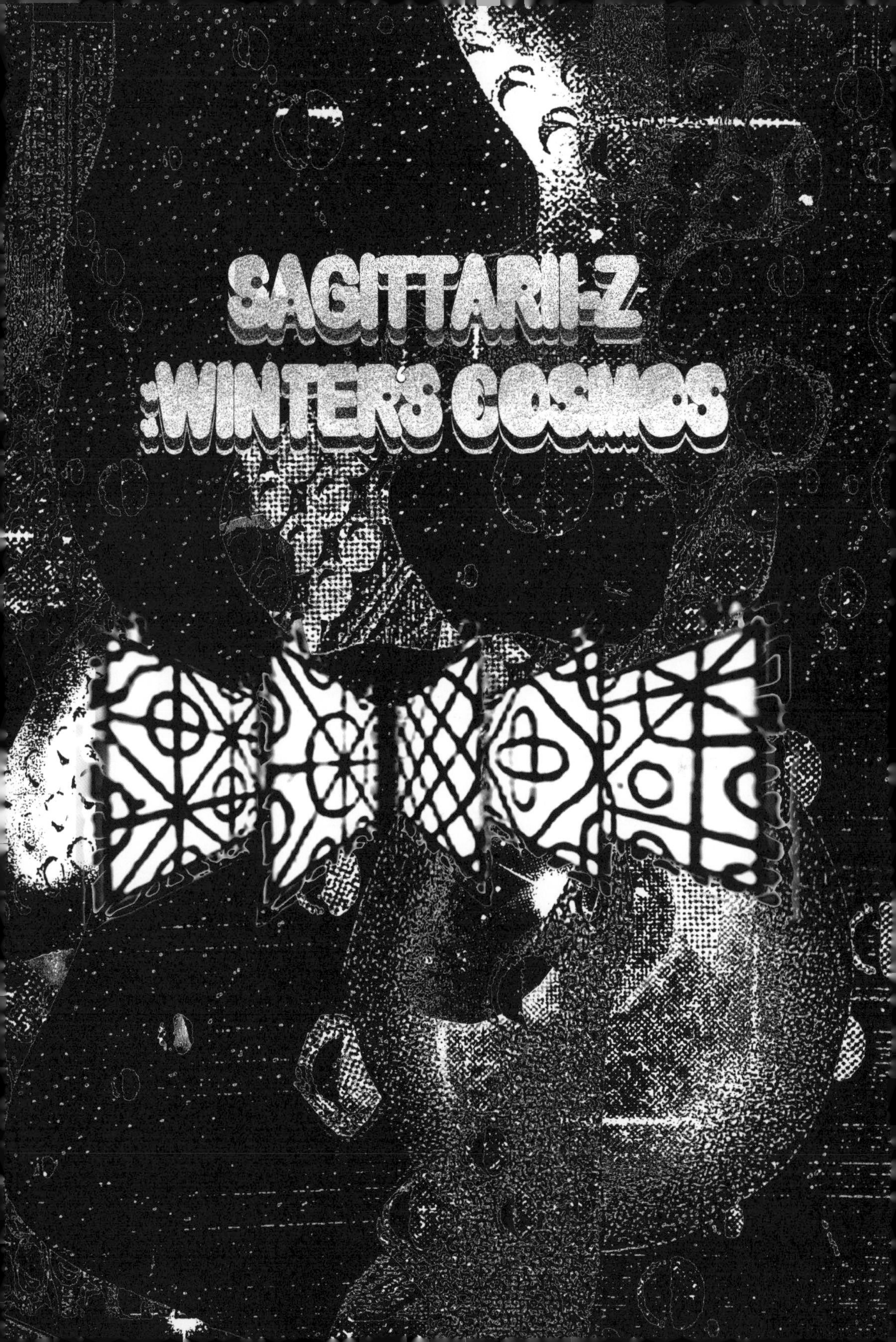
SAGITTARII-Z
:WINTER'S COSMOS

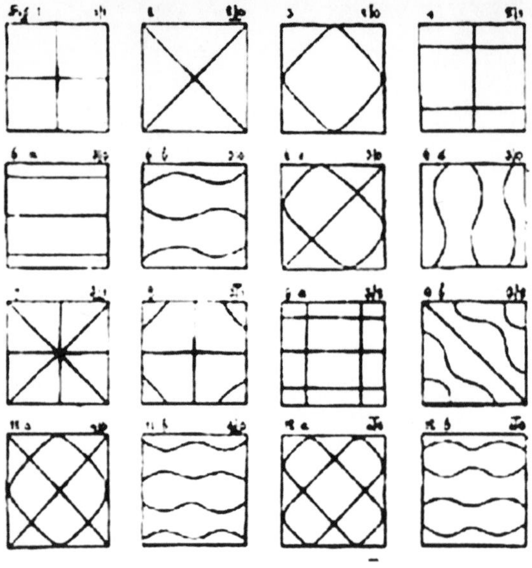

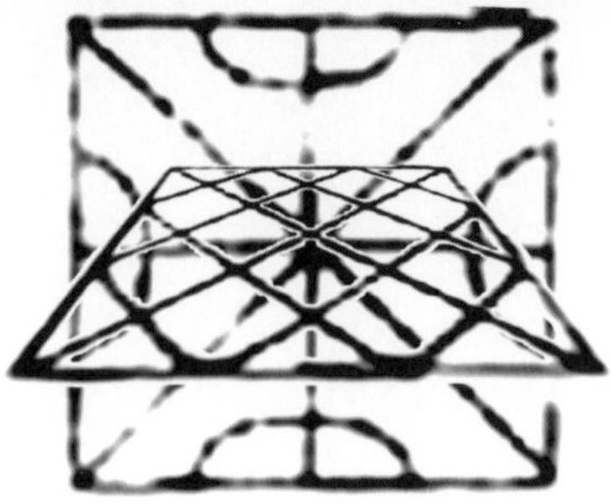

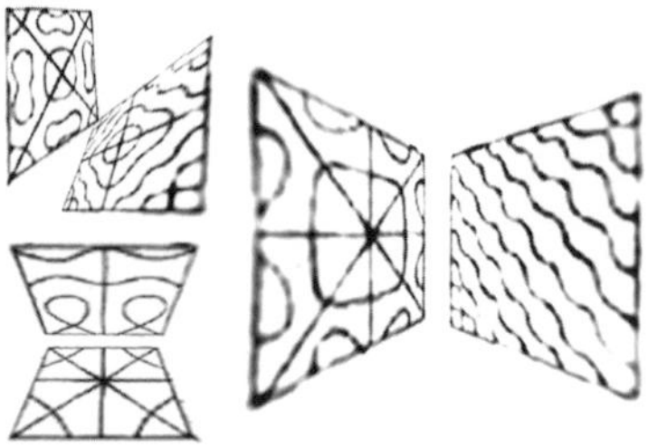

ERNST CHLADNI, 1756-1827 GERMAN PHYSICIST AND MUSICIAN

CHLADNI SHOWS THE MODES OF VIBRATION OF A RIGID SURFACE

WHEN RESONATING A PLATE OR MEMBRANE IS DIVIDED INTO REGIONS
THAT VIBRATE IN OPPOSITE DIRECTIONS

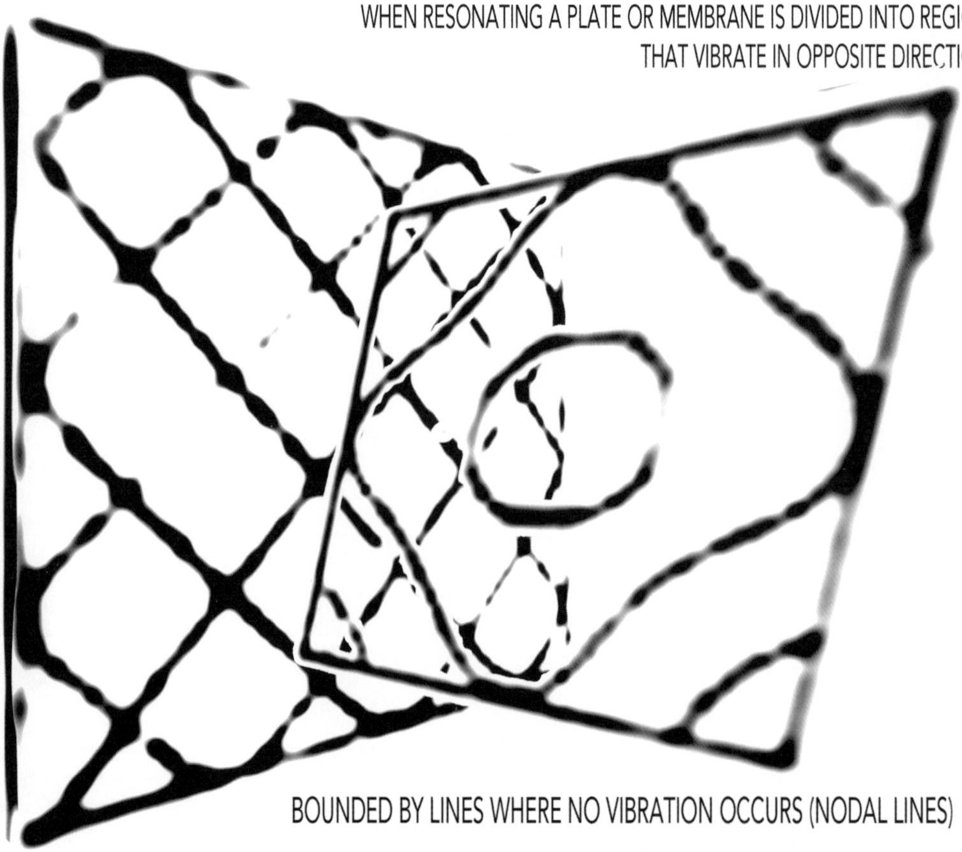

BOUNDED BY LINES WHERE NO VIBRATION OCCURS (NODAL LINES)

THE PLATE WAS BOWED UNTIL IT REACHED RESONANCE, WHEN THE VIBRATION
CAUSES SOUND TO MOVE AND CONCENTRATE ALONG NODAL LINES

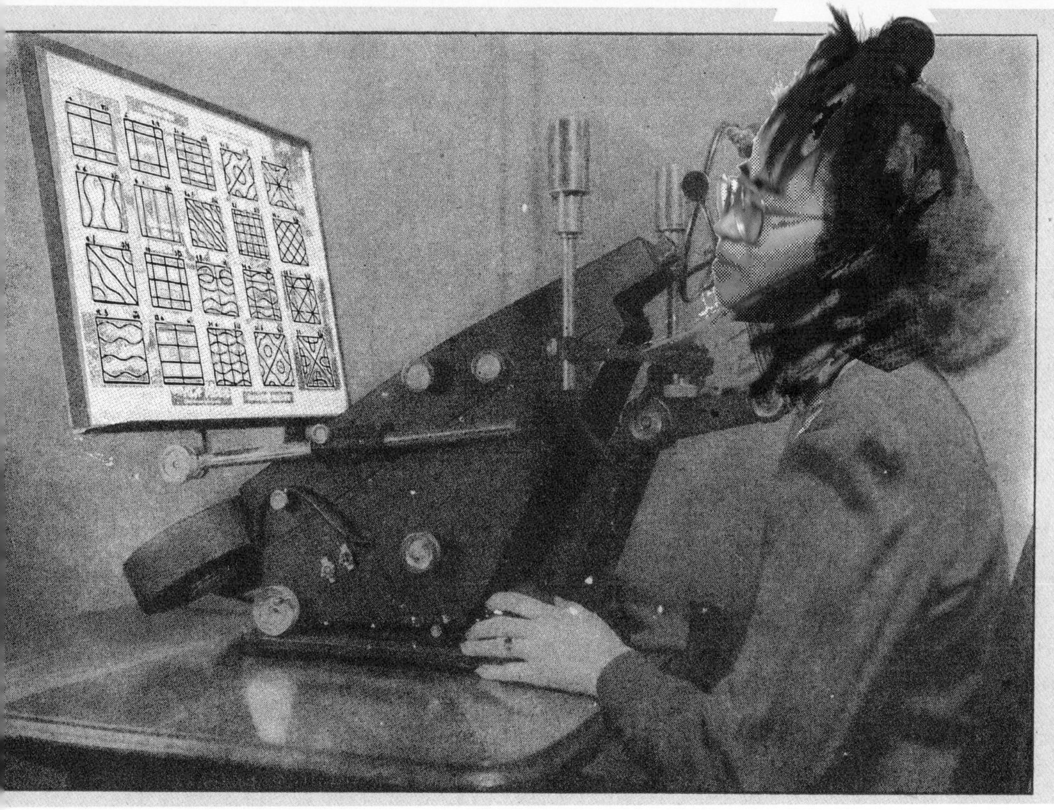

WHERE THE SURFACE IS STILL OUTLINING NODAL LINES, CHLADNI FIGURES

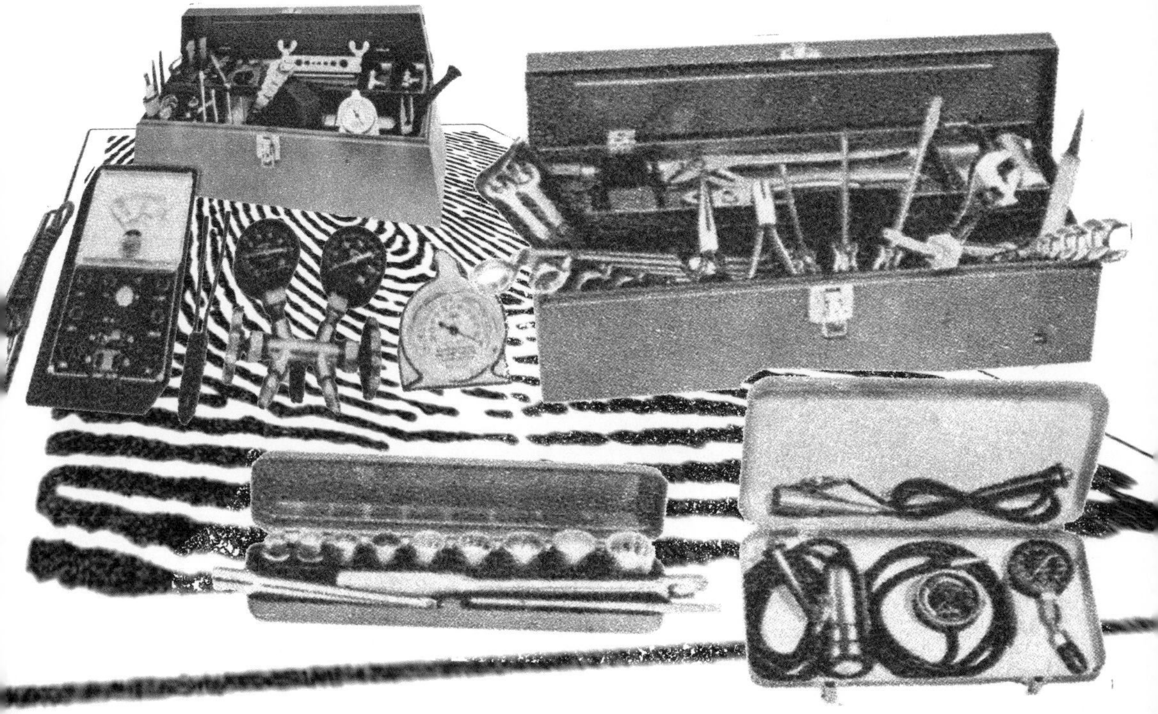

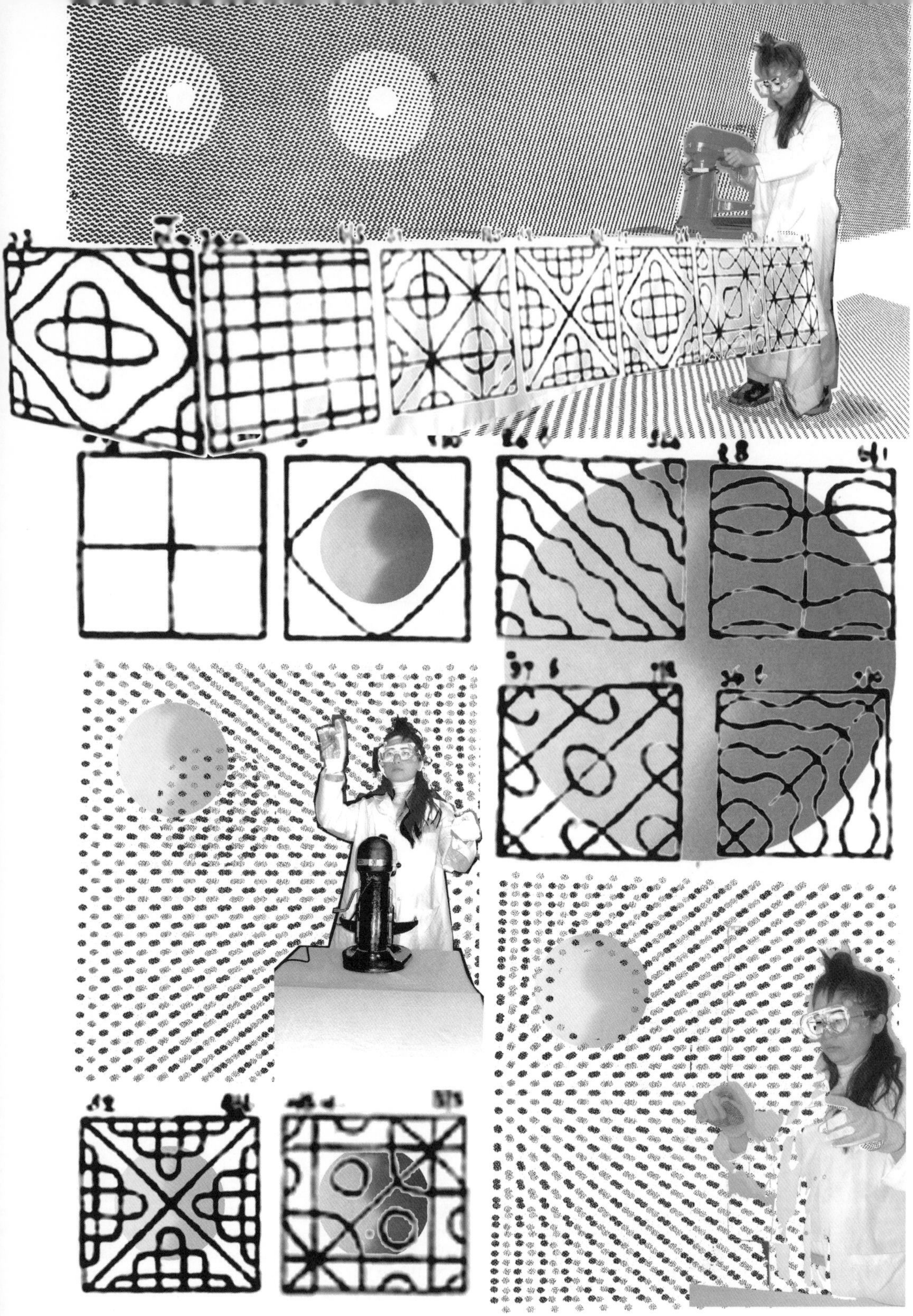

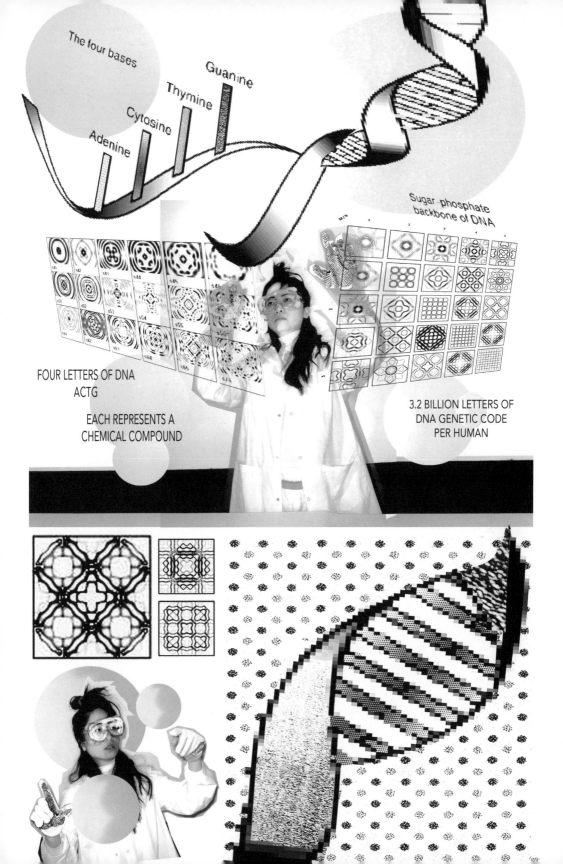

The four bases

Guanine

Thymine

Cytosine

Adenine

Sugar -phosphate
backbone of DNA

FOUR LETTERS OF DNA
ACTG

EACH REPRESENTS A
CHEMICAL COMPOUND

3.2 BILLION LETTERS OF
DNA GENETIC CODE
PER HUMAN

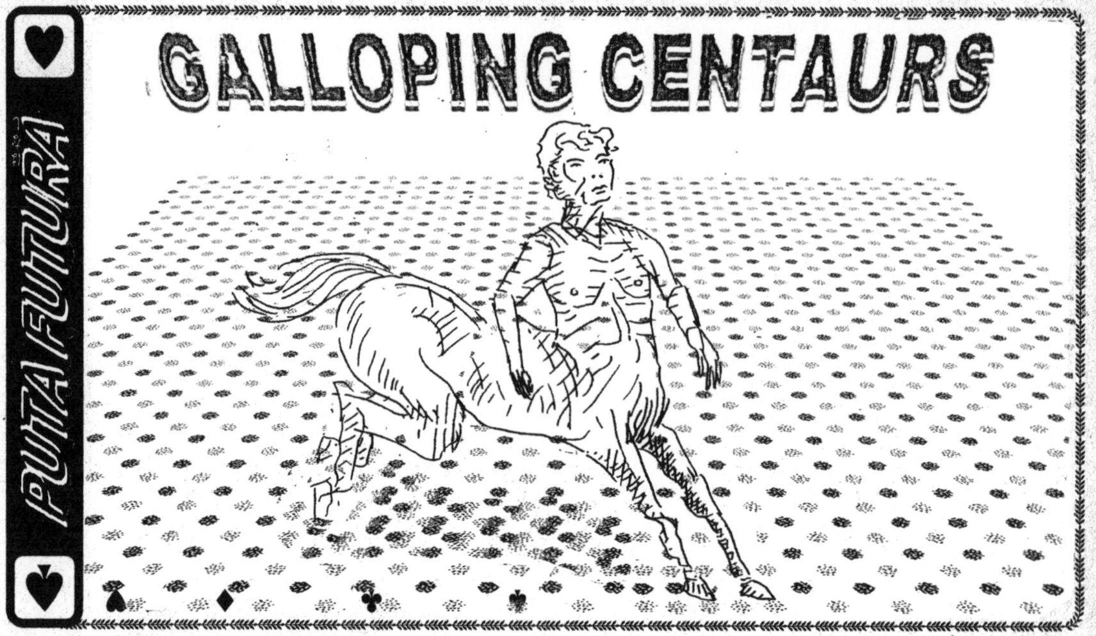
GALLOPING CENTAURS
PUNTA FUTURA

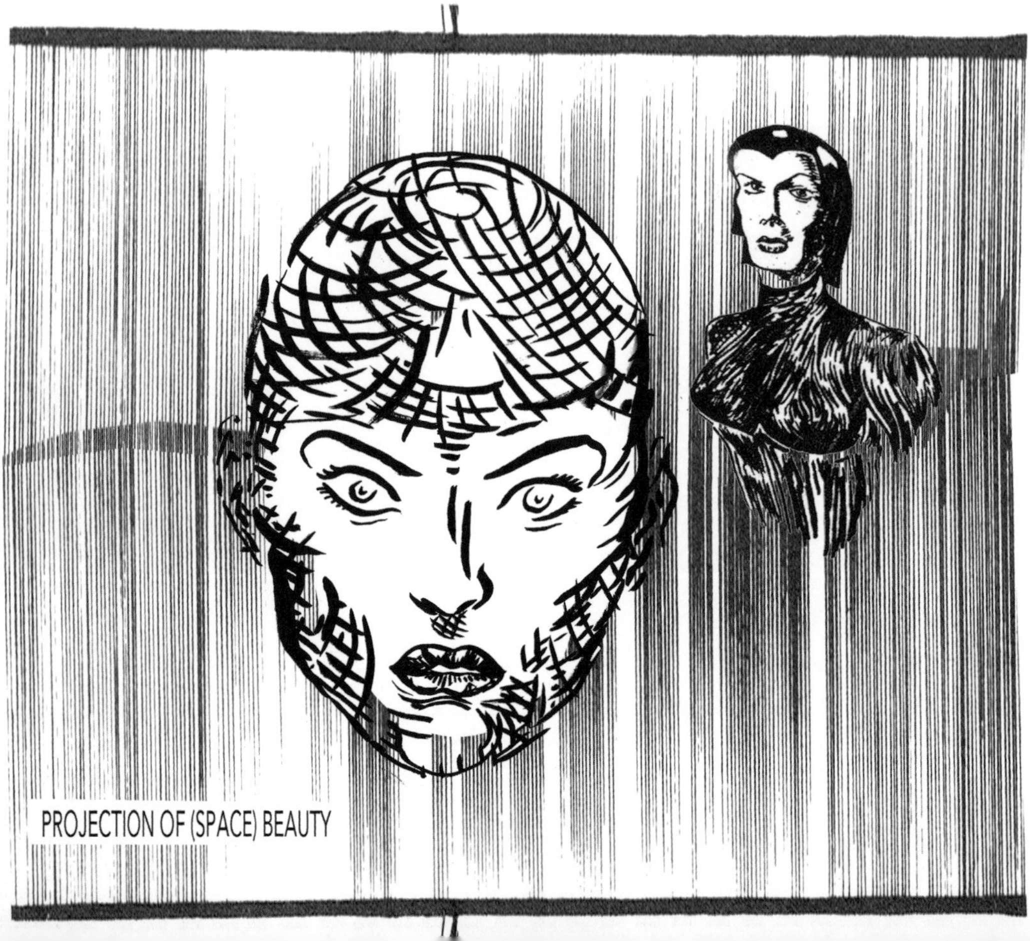

PROJECTION OF (SPACE) BEAUTY

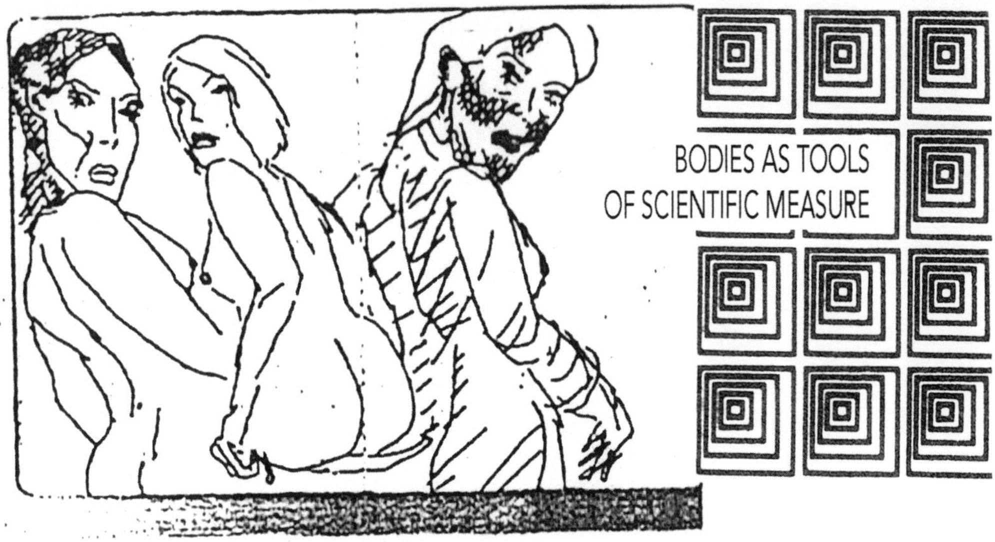
BODIES AS TOOLS
OF SCIENTIFIC MEASURE

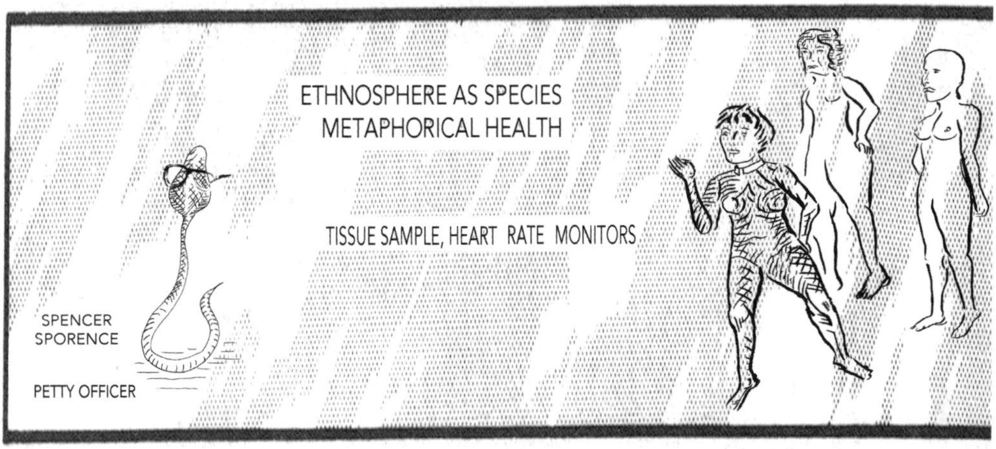
ETHNOSPHERE AS SPECIES
METAPHORICAL HEALTH
TISSUE SAMPLE, HEART RATE MONITORS
SPENCER
SPORENCE
PETTY OFFICER

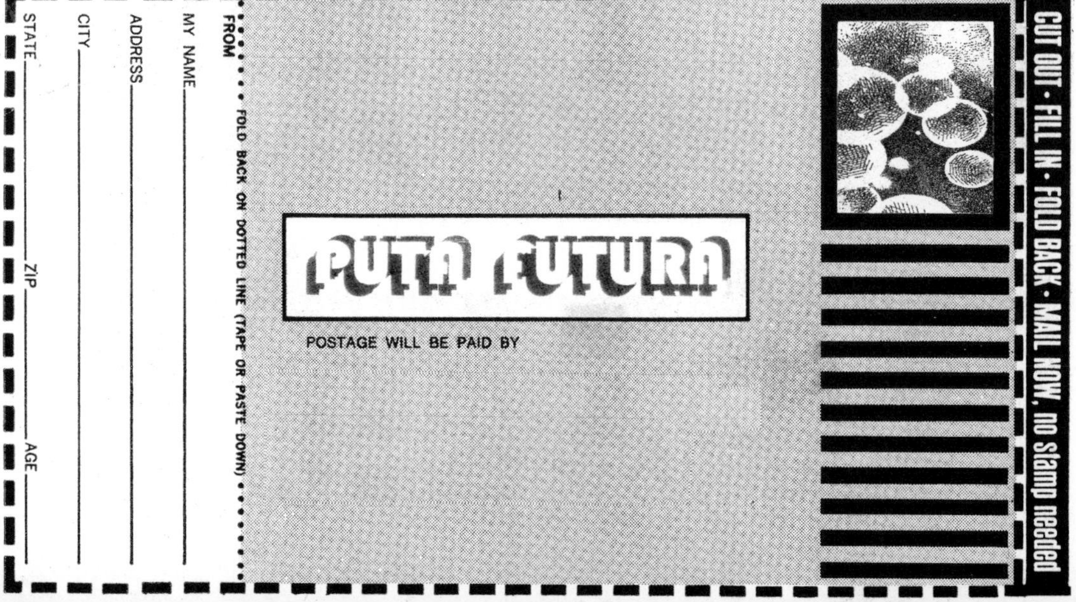
FROM
MY NAME
ADDRESS
CITY
STATE
ZIP
AGE
FOLD BACK ON DOTTED LINE (TAPE OR PASTE DOWN)
PUTA FUTURA
POSTAGE WILL BE PAID BY
CUT OUT • FILL IN • FOLD BACK • MAIL NOW, no stamp needed

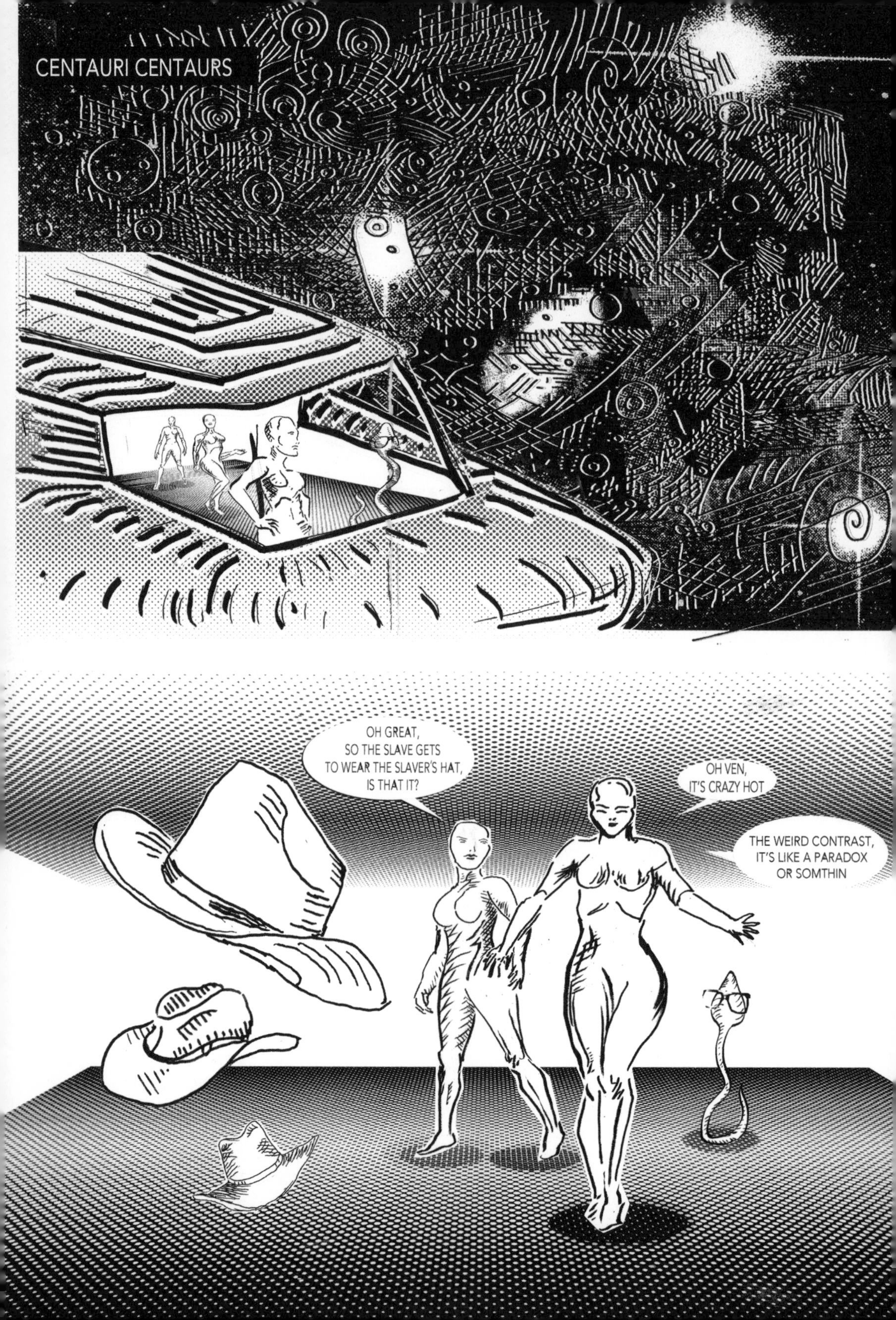

CENTAURI CENTAURS
OH GREAT, SO THE SLAVE GETS TO WEAR THE SLAVER'S HAT, IS THAT IT?
OH VEN, IT'S CRAZY HOT
THE WEIRD CONTRAST, IT'S LIKE A PARADOX OR SOMTHIN

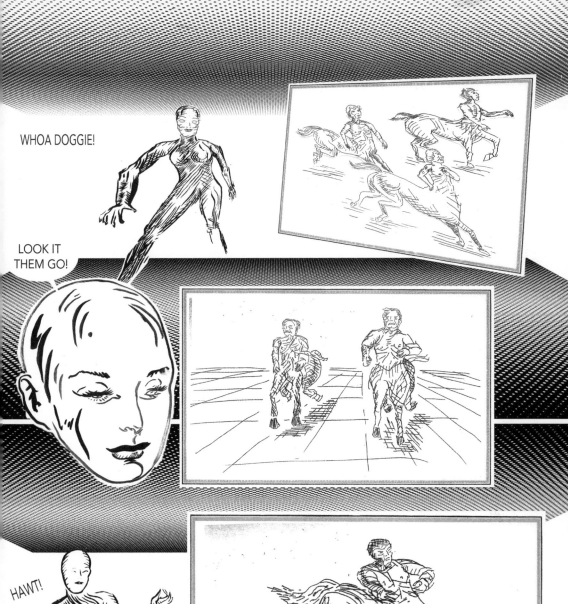

WHOA DOGGIE!

LOOK IT
THEM GO!

HAWT!

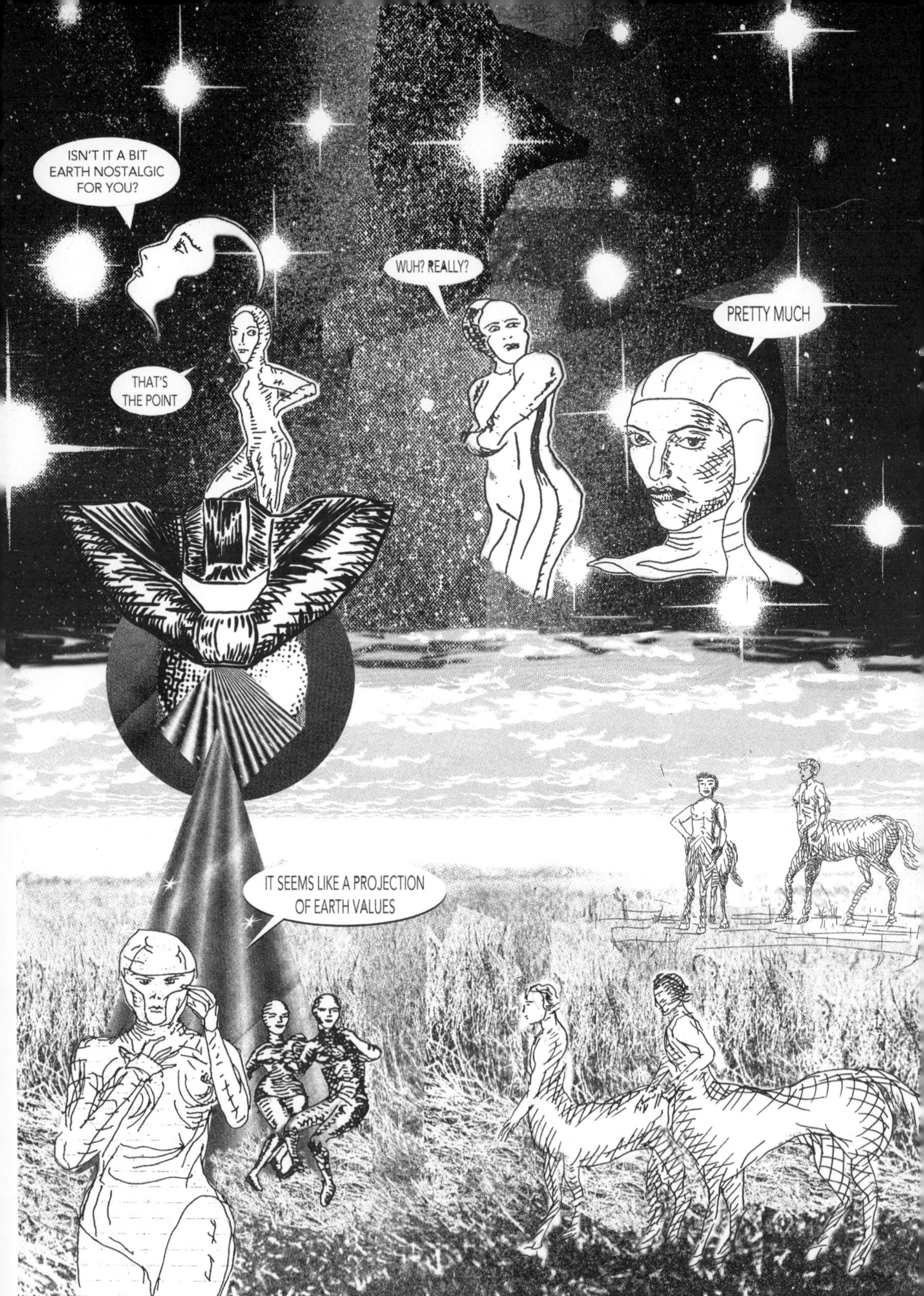
ISN'T IT A BIT EARTH NOSTALGIC FOR YOU?
THAT'S THE POINT
WUH? REALLY?
PRETTY MUCH
IT SEEMS LIKE A PROJECTION OF EARTH VALUES

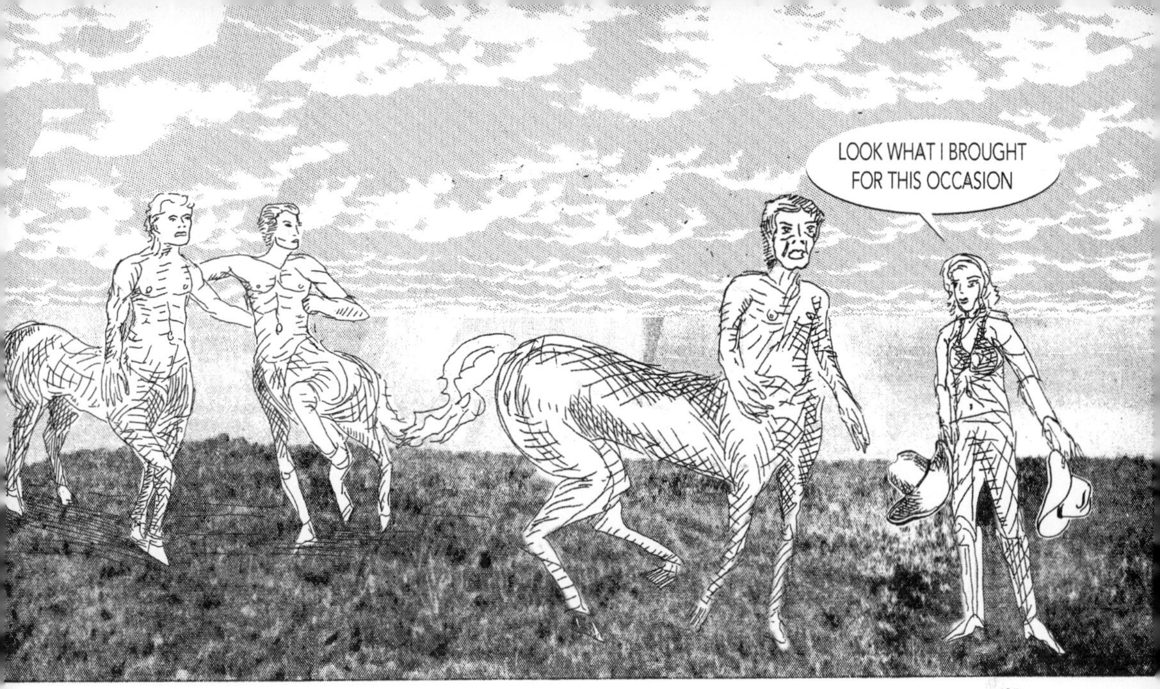
LOOK WHAT I BROUGHT FOR THIS OCCASION

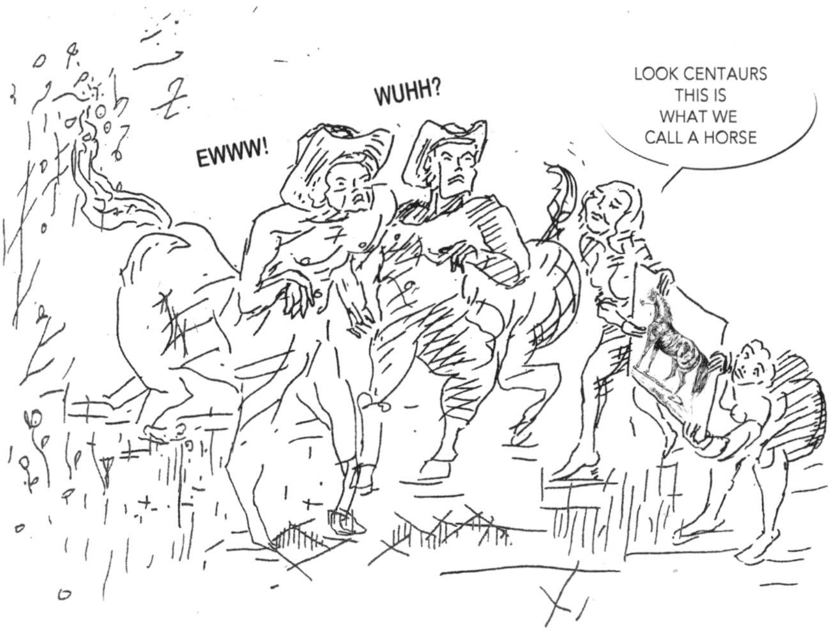
EWWW!
WUHH?
LOOK CENTAURS THIS IS WHAT WE CALL A HORSE

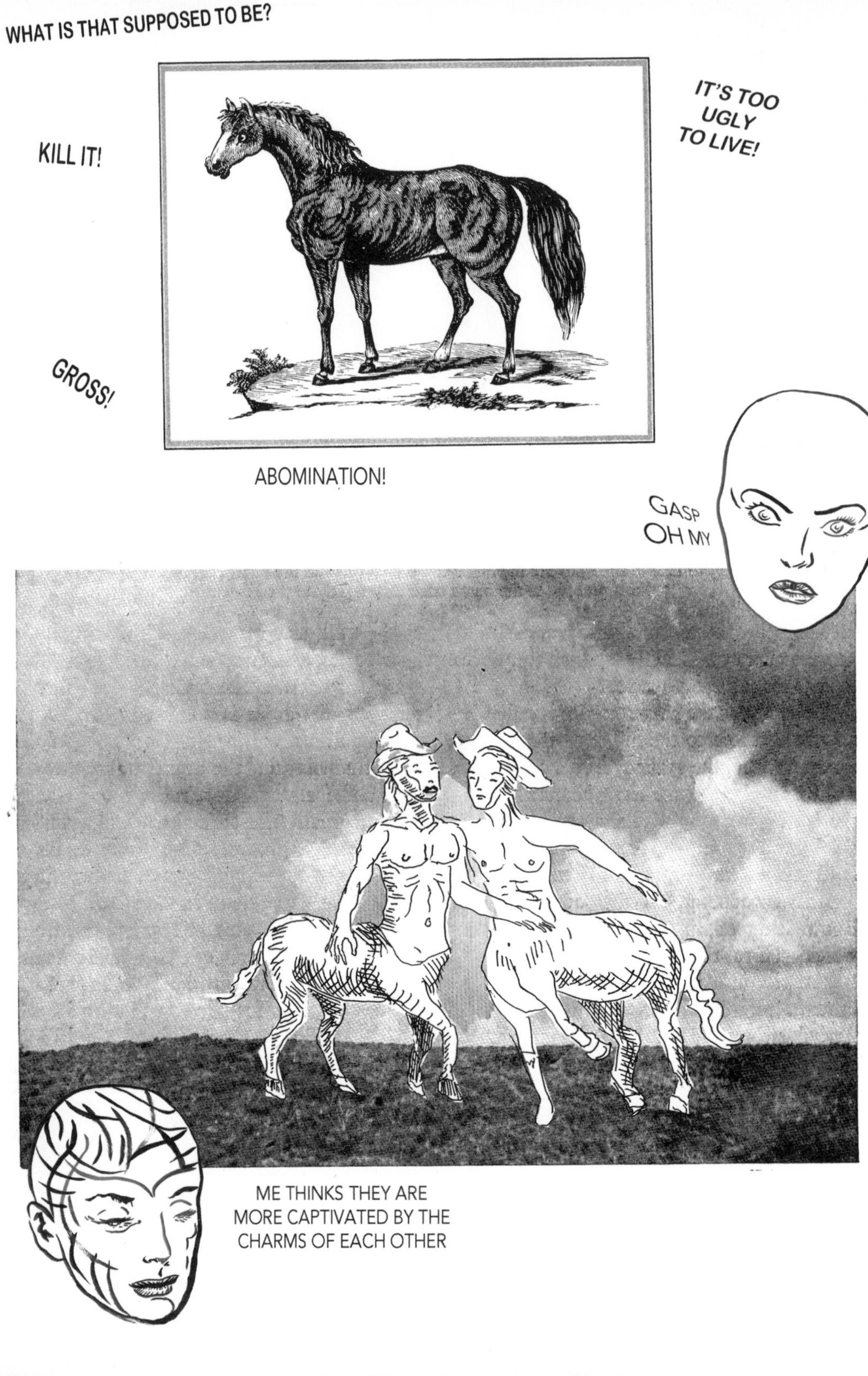
WHAT IS THAT SUPPOSED TO BE?
KILL IT!
IT'S TOO UGLY TO LIVE!
GROSS!
ABOMINATION!
GASP OH MY
ME THINKS THEY ARE MORE CAPTIVATED BY THE CHARMS OF EACH OTHER

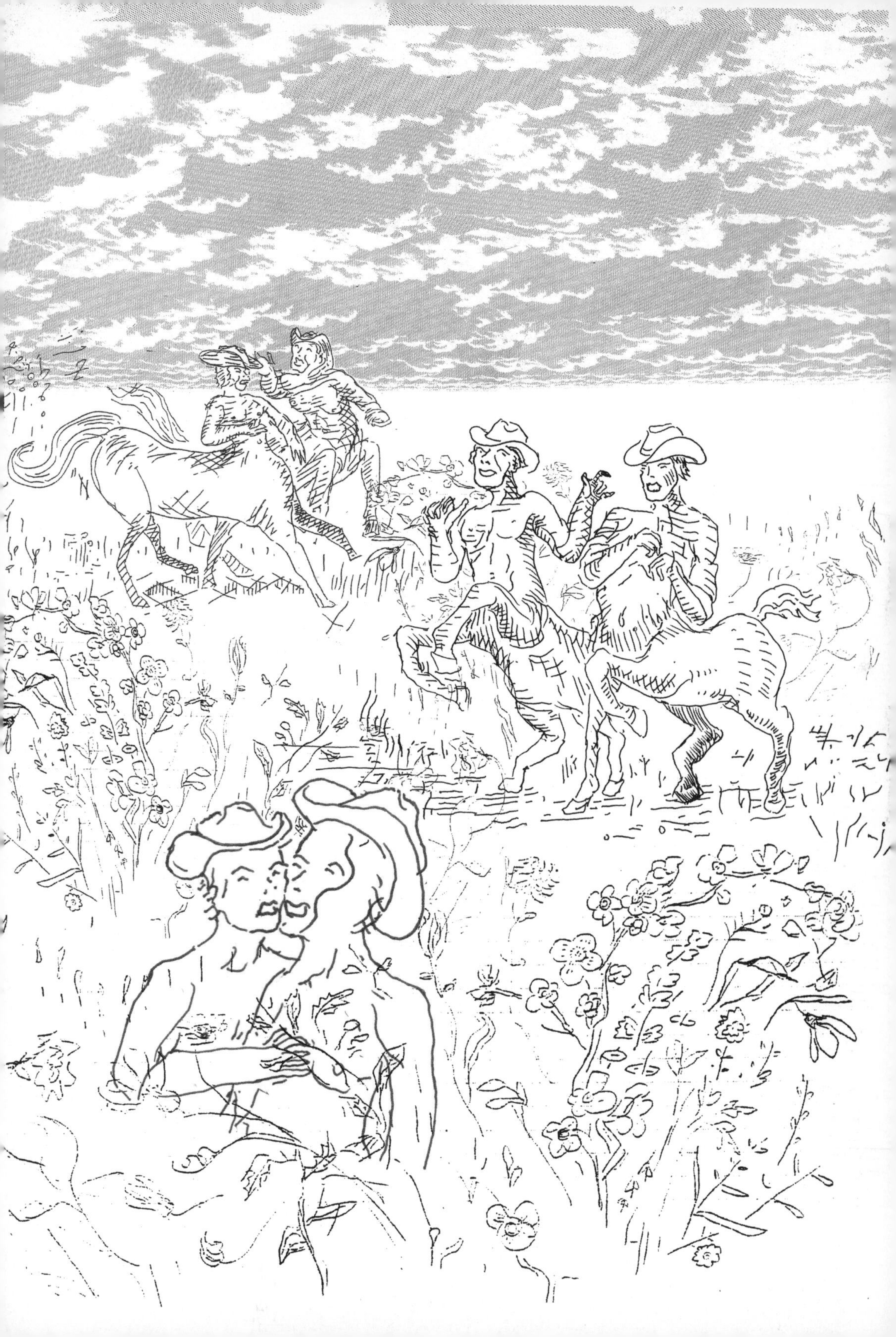

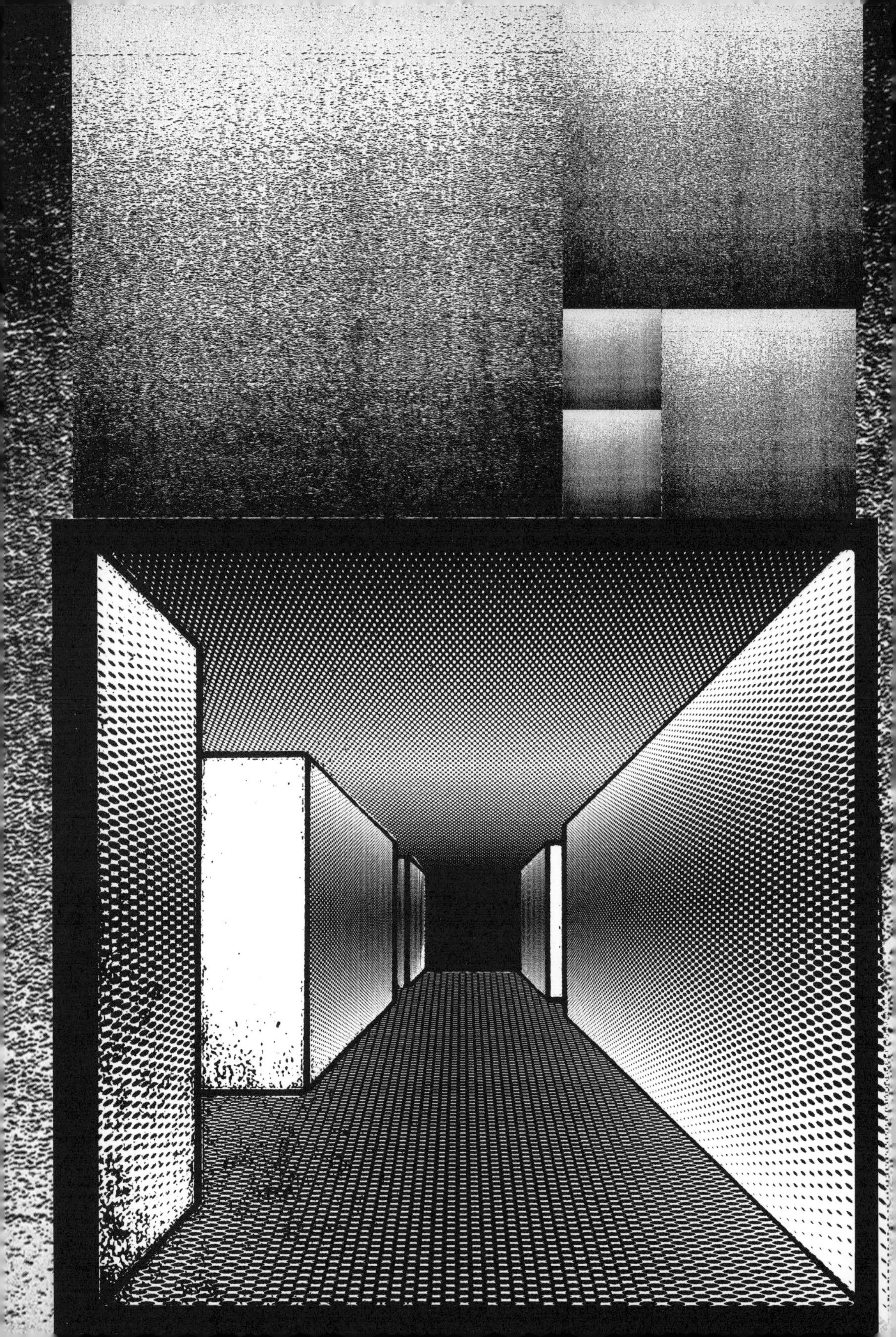

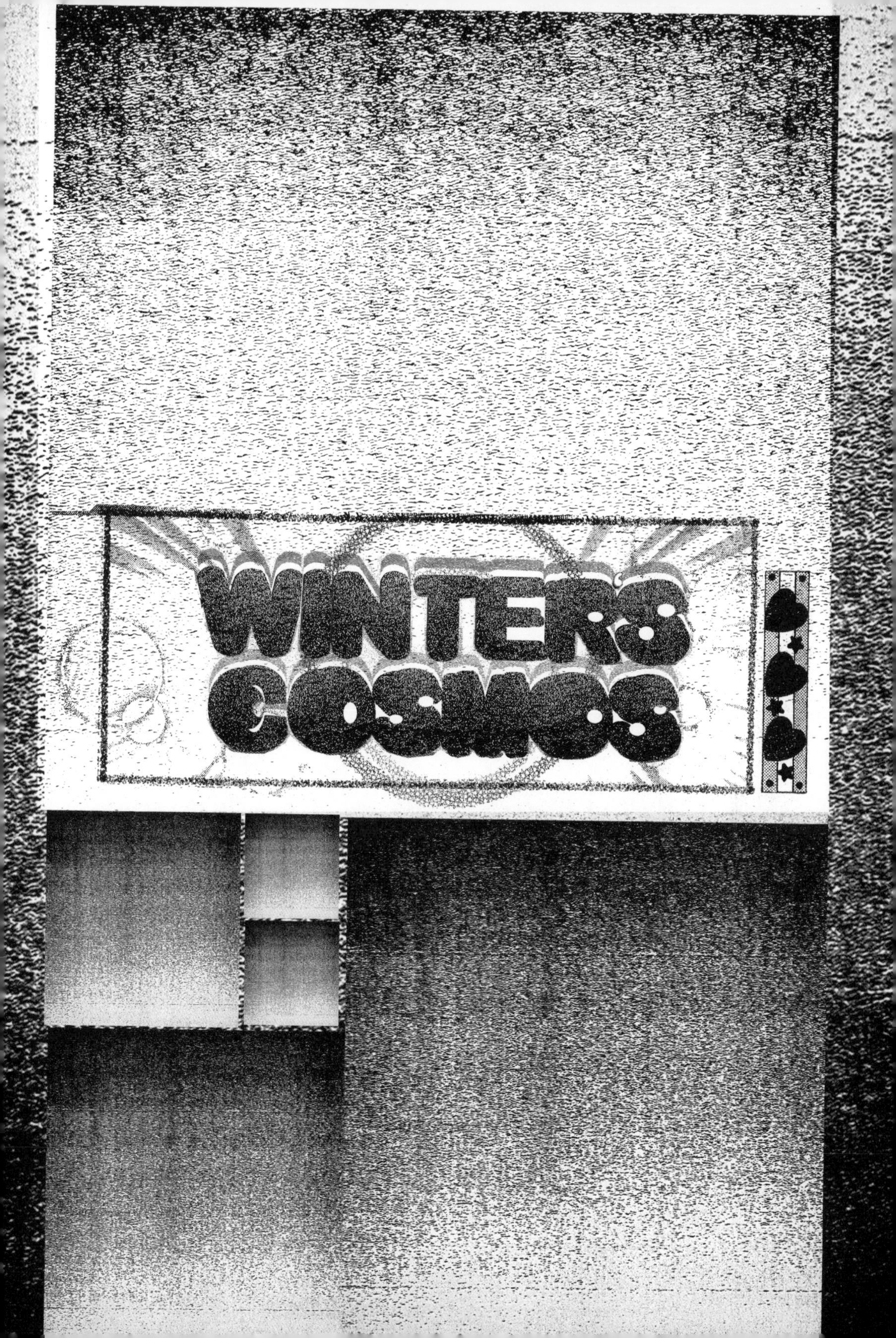
WINTER'S
COSMOS

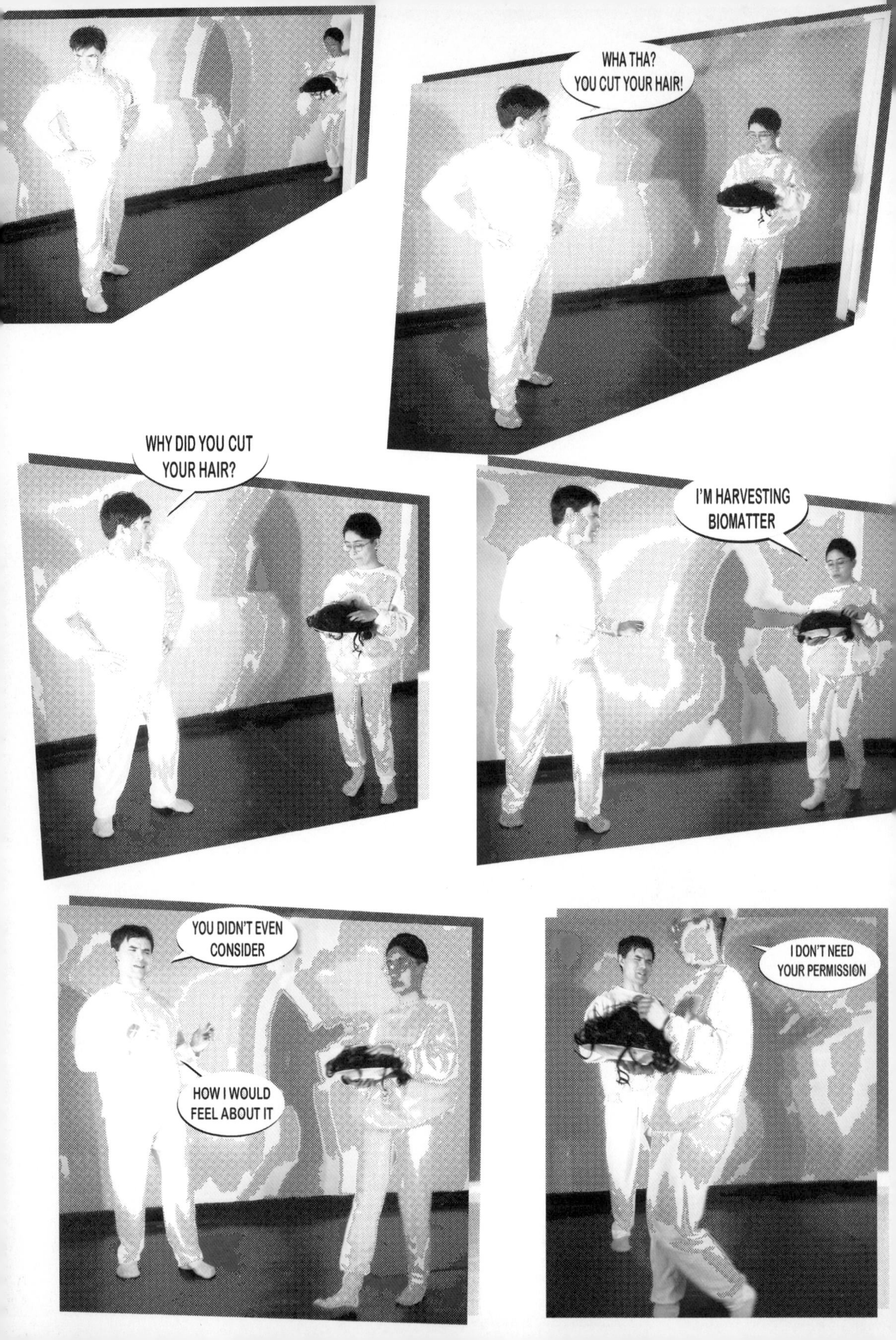
WHA THA? YOU CUT YOUR HAIR!
WHY DID YOU CUT YOUR HAIR?
I'M HARVESTING BIOMATTER
YOU DIDN'T EVEN CONSIDER
HOW I WOULD FEEL ABOUT IT
I DON'T NEED YOUR PERMISSION

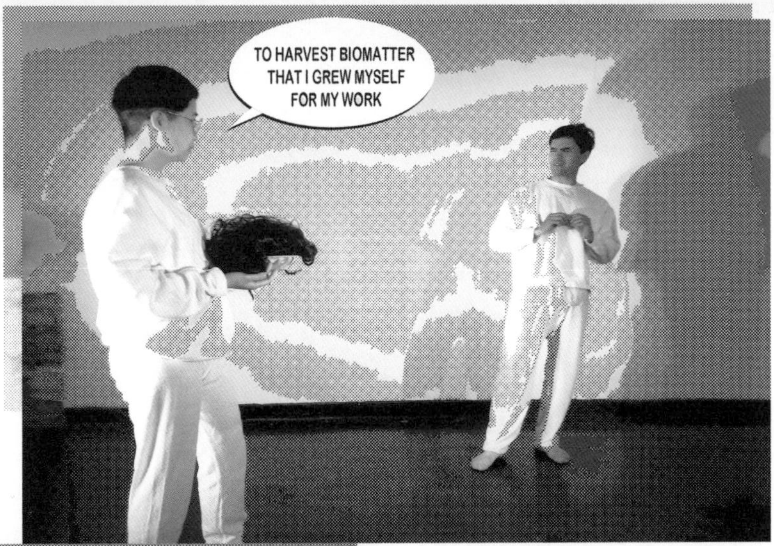
TO HARVEST BIOMATTER THAT I GREW MYSELF FOR MY WORK

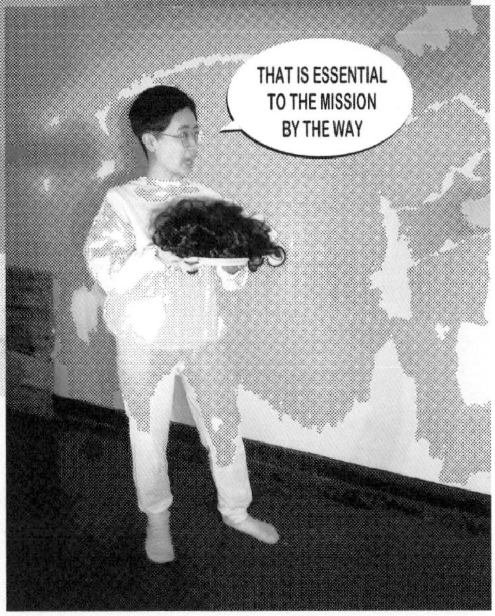
THAT IS ESSENTIAL TO THE MISSION BY THE WAY

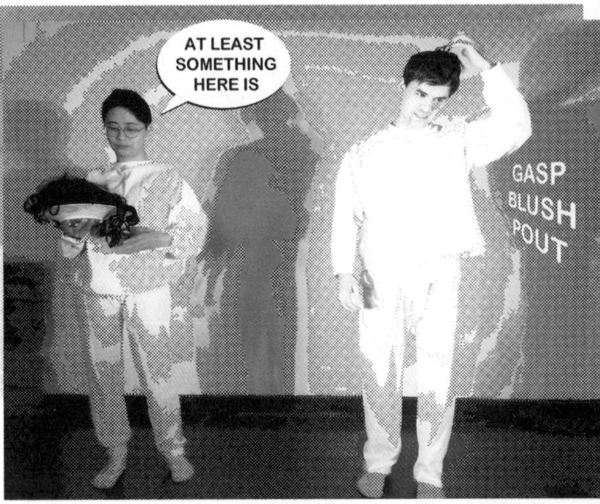
AT LEAST SOMETHING HERE IS
GASP
BLUSH
POUT

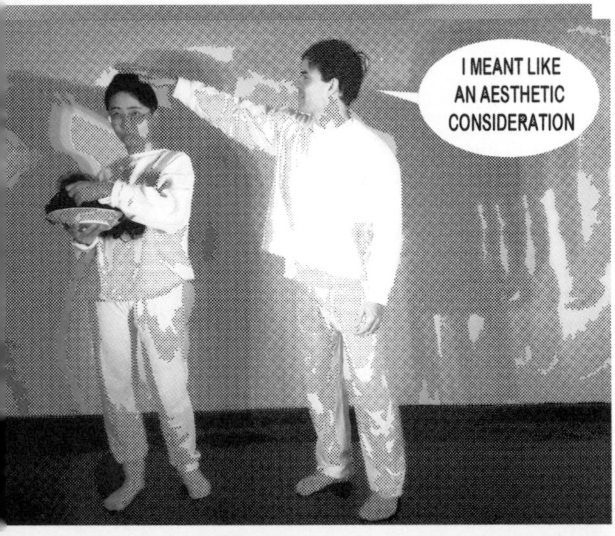
I MEANT LIKE AN AESTHETIC CONSIDERATION

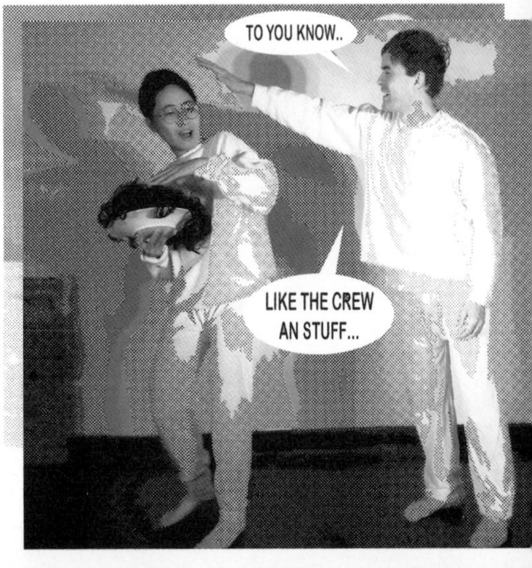
TO YOU KNOW..
LIKE THE CREW AN STUFF...

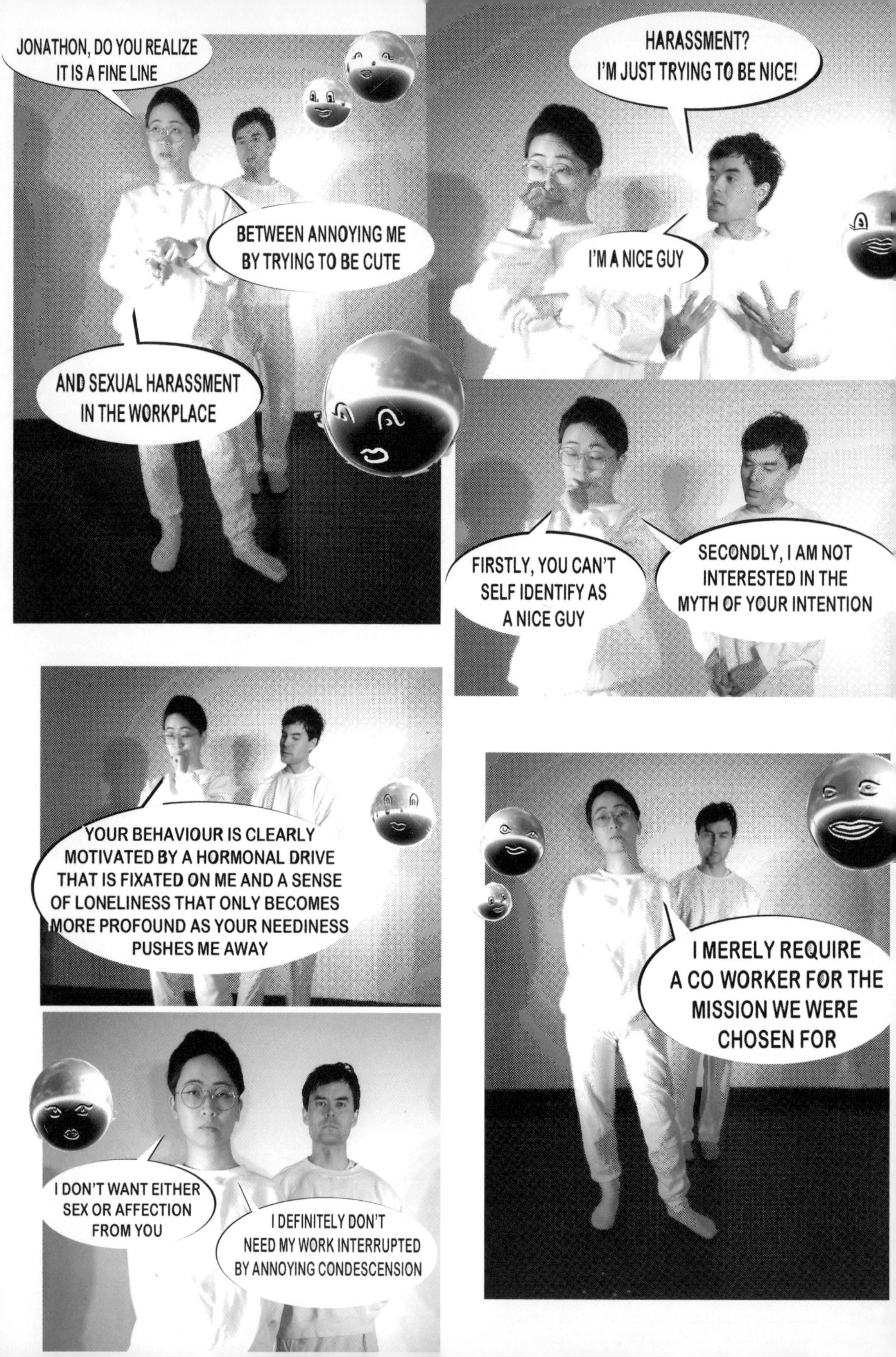
JONATHON, DO YOU REALIZE IT IS A FINE LINE
BETWEEN ANNOYING ME BY TRYING TO BE CUTE
AND SEXUAL HARASSMENT IN THE WORKPLACE
HARASSMENT? I'M JUST TRYING TO BE NICE!
I'M A NICE GUY
FIRSTLY, YOU CAN'T SELF IDENTIFY AS A NICE GUY
SECONDLY, I AM NOT INTERESTED IN THE MYTH OF YOUR INTENTION
YOUR BEHAVIOUR IS CLEARLY MOTIVATED BY A HORMONAL DRIVE THAT IS FIXATED ON ME AND A SENSE OF LONELINESS THAT ONLY BECOMES MORE PROFOUND AS YOUR NEEDINESS PUSHES ME AWAY
I DON'T WANT EITHER SEX OR AFFECTION FROM YOU
I DEFINITELY DON'T NEED MY WORK INTERRUPTED BY ANNOYING CONDESCENSION
I MERELY REQUIRE A CO WORKER FOR THE MISSION WE WERE CHOSEN FOR

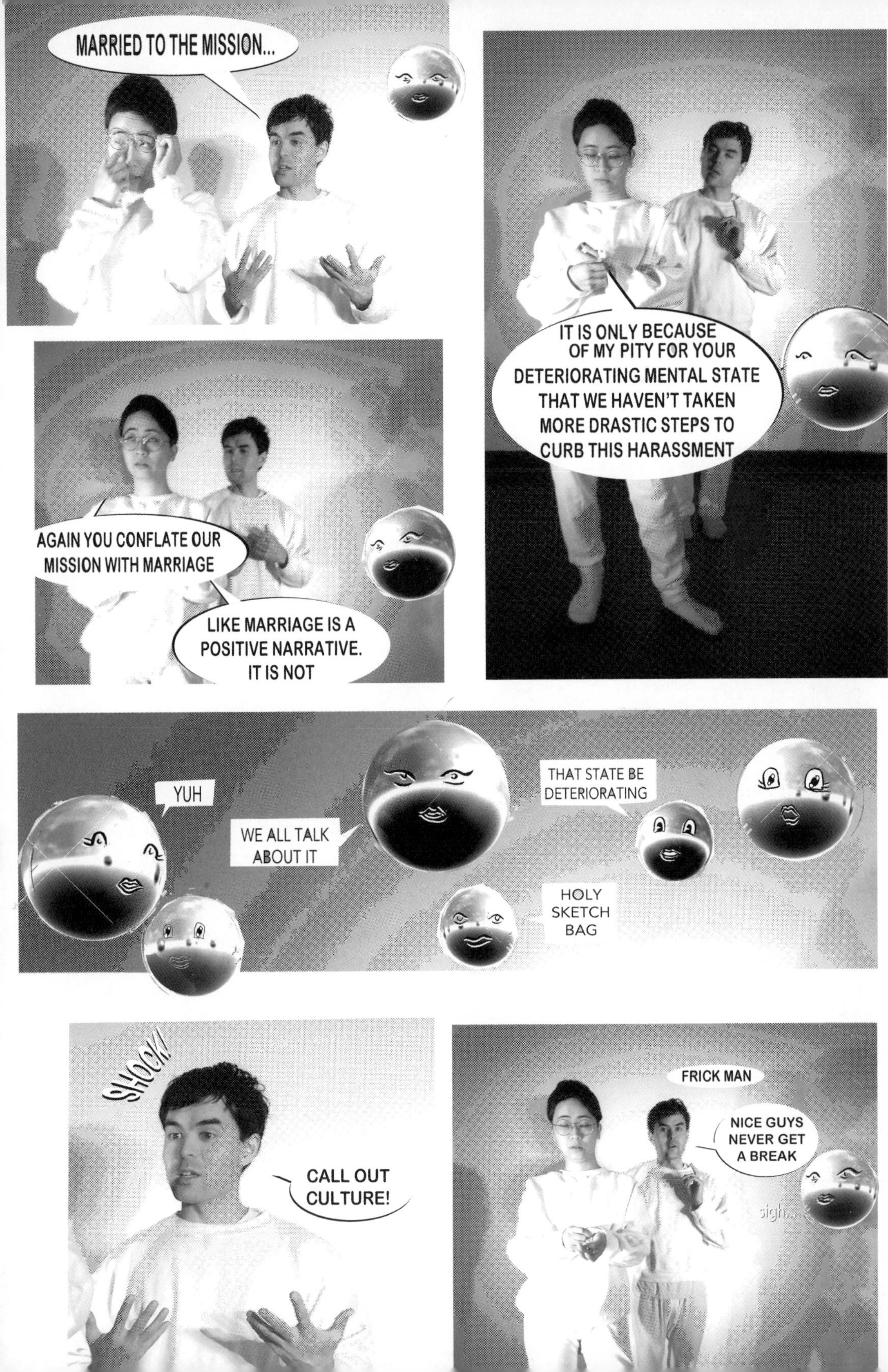

MARRIED TO THE MISSION...
AGAIN YOU CONFLATE OUR MISSION WITH MARRIAGE
LIKE MARRIAGE IS A POSITIVE NARRATIVE. IT IS NOT
IT IS ONLY BECAUSE OF MY PITY FOR YOUR DETERIORATING MENTAL STATE THAT WE HAVEN'T TAKEN MORE DRASTIC STEPS TO CURB THIS HARASSMENT
YUH
WE ALL TALK ABOUT IT
THAT STATE BE DETERIORATING
HOLY SKETCH BAG
SHOCK!
CALL OUT CULTURE!
FRICK MAN
NICE GUYS NEVER GET A BREAK
sigh...

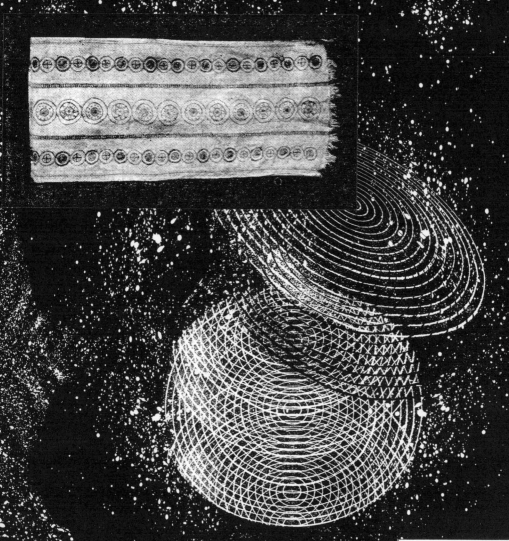

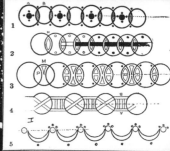

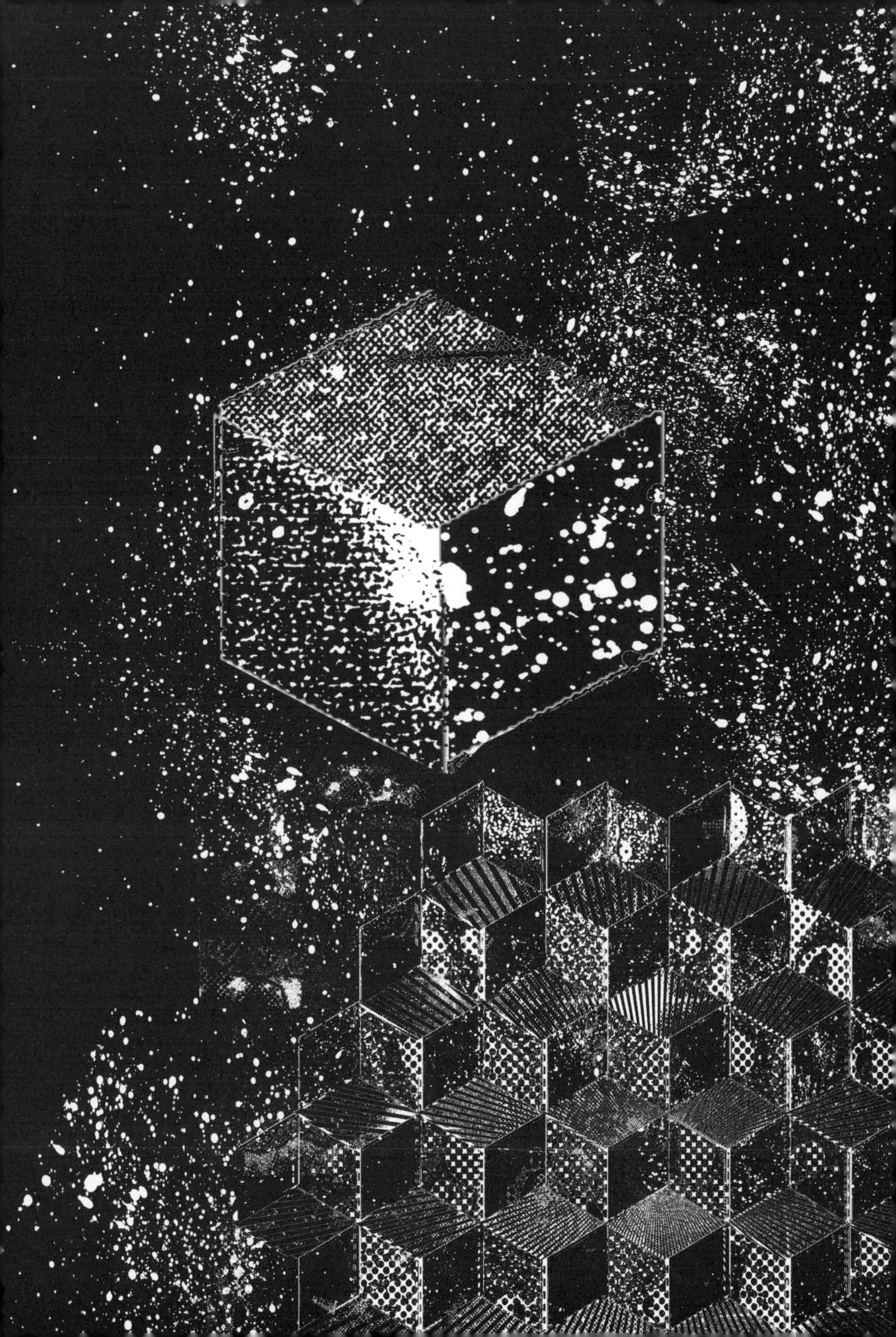

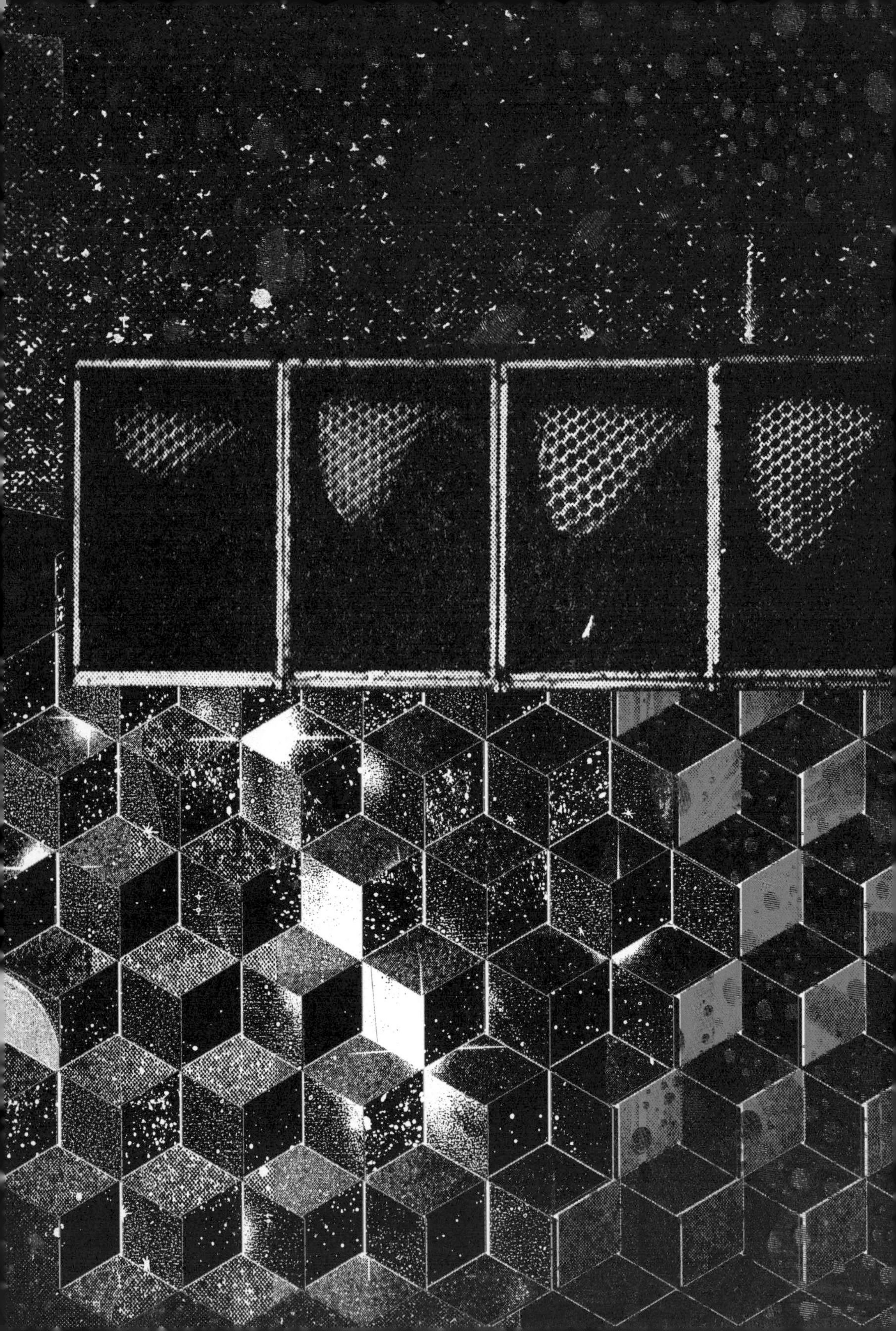

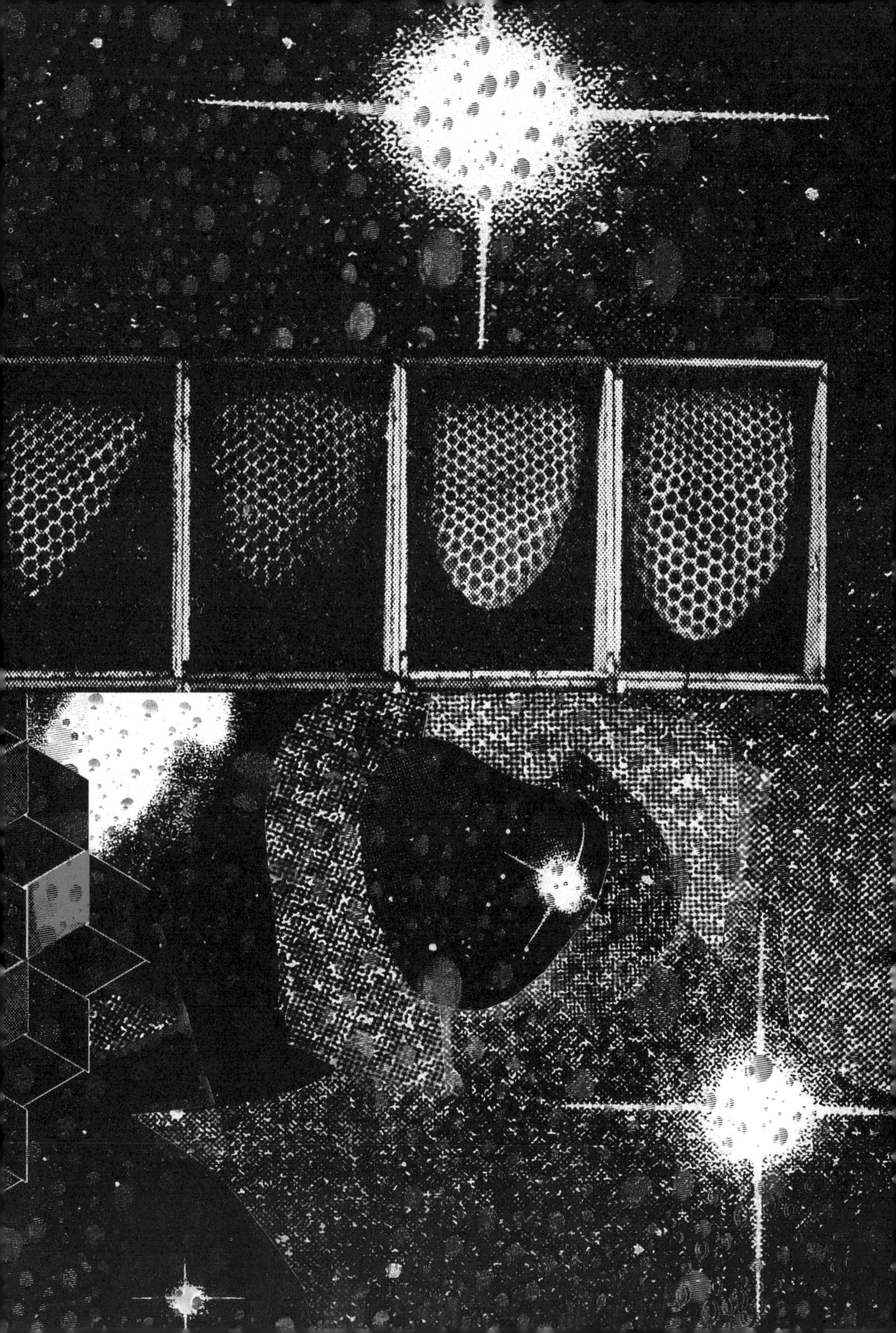

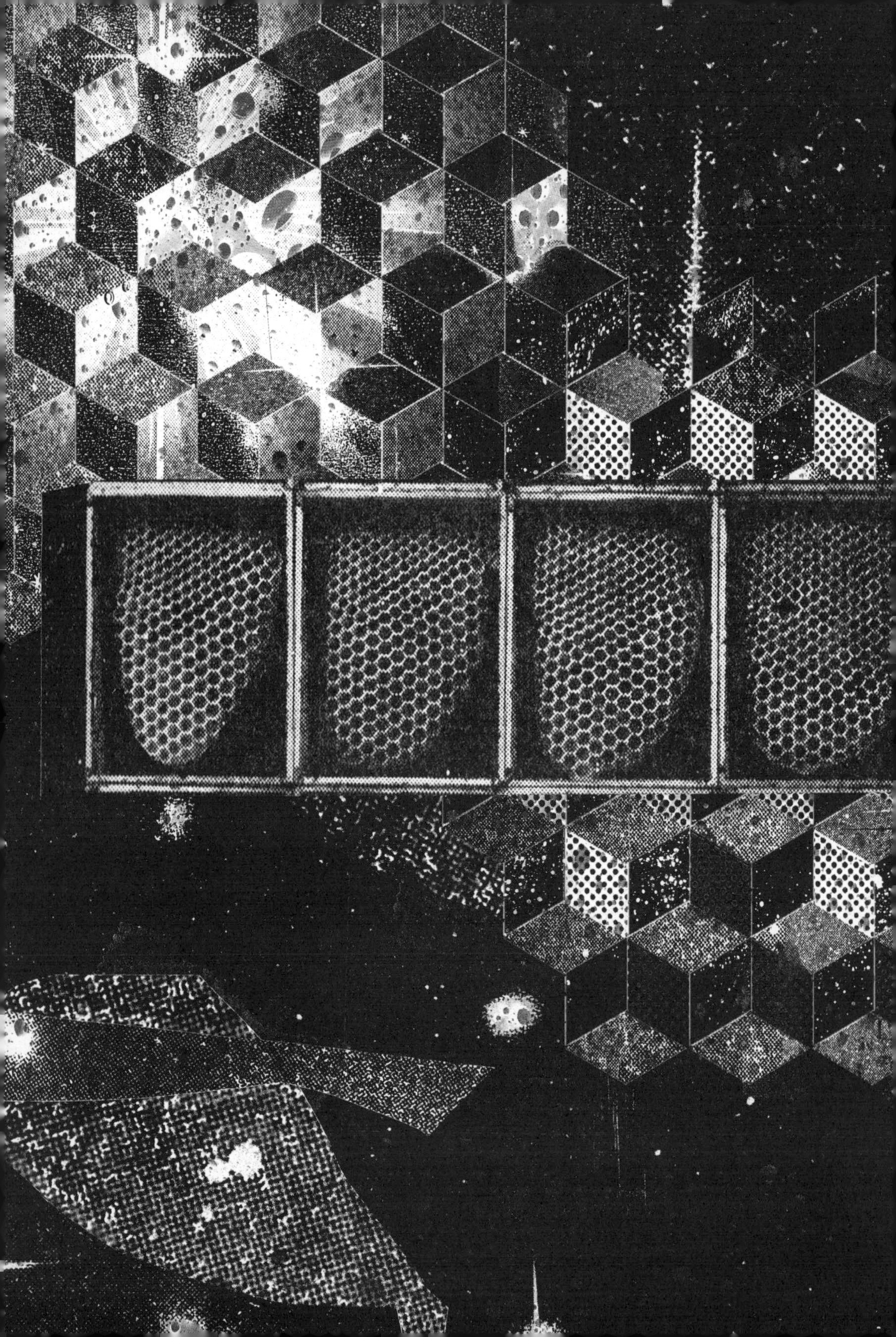

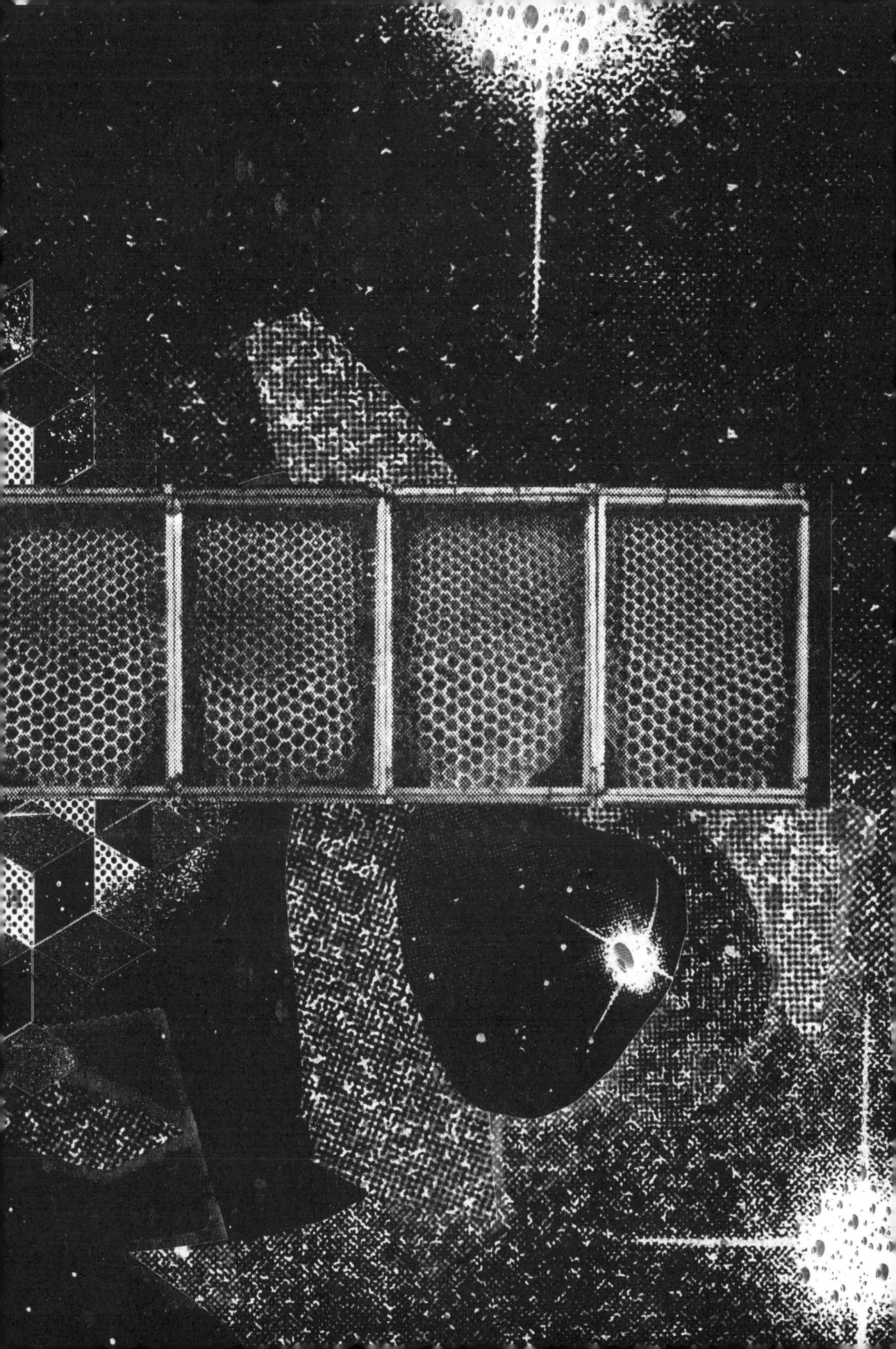

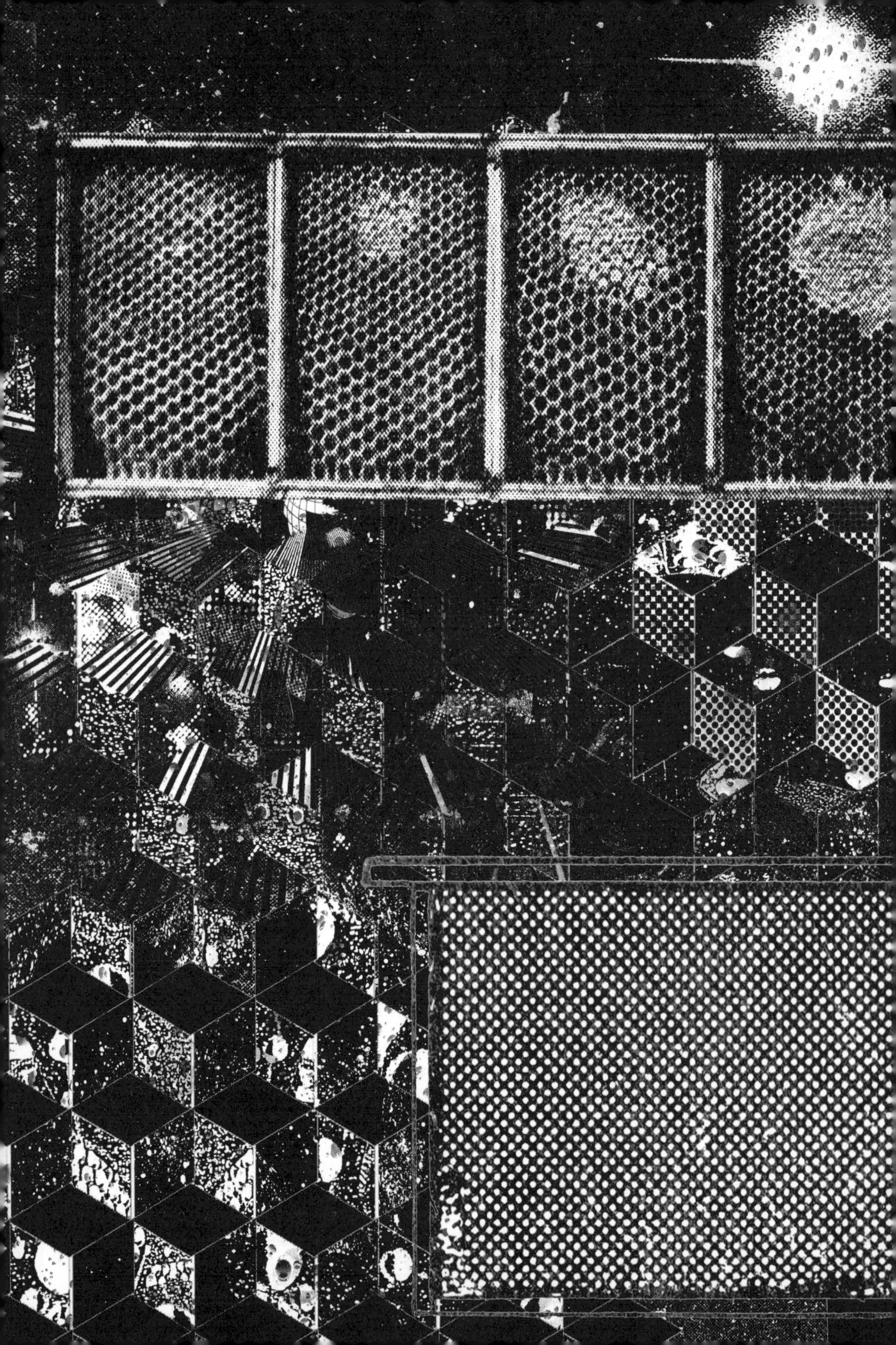

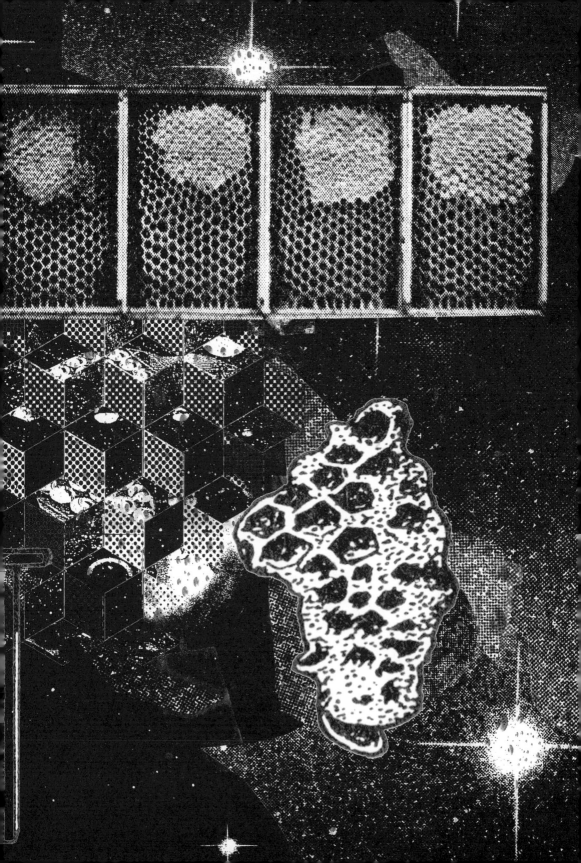

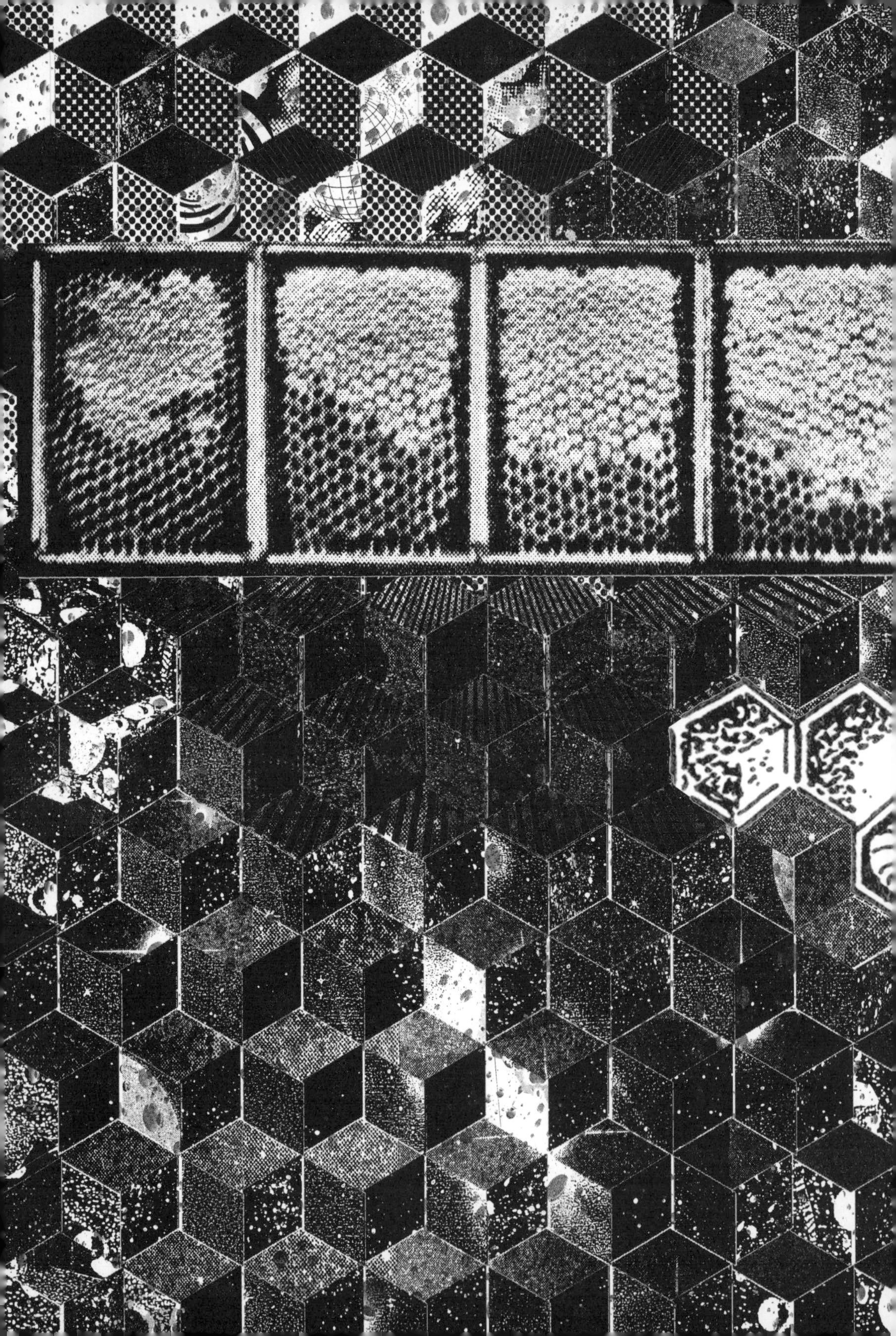

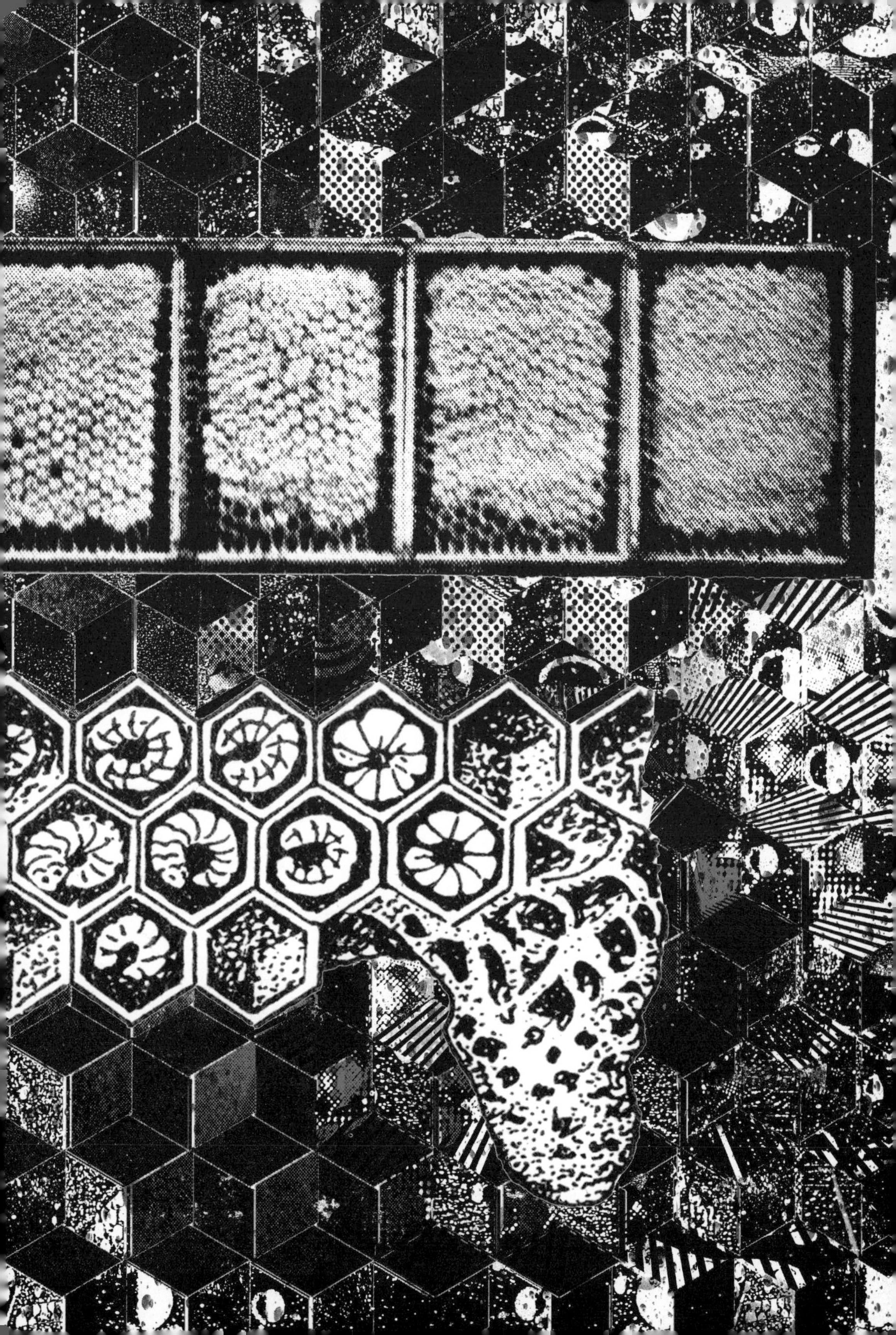

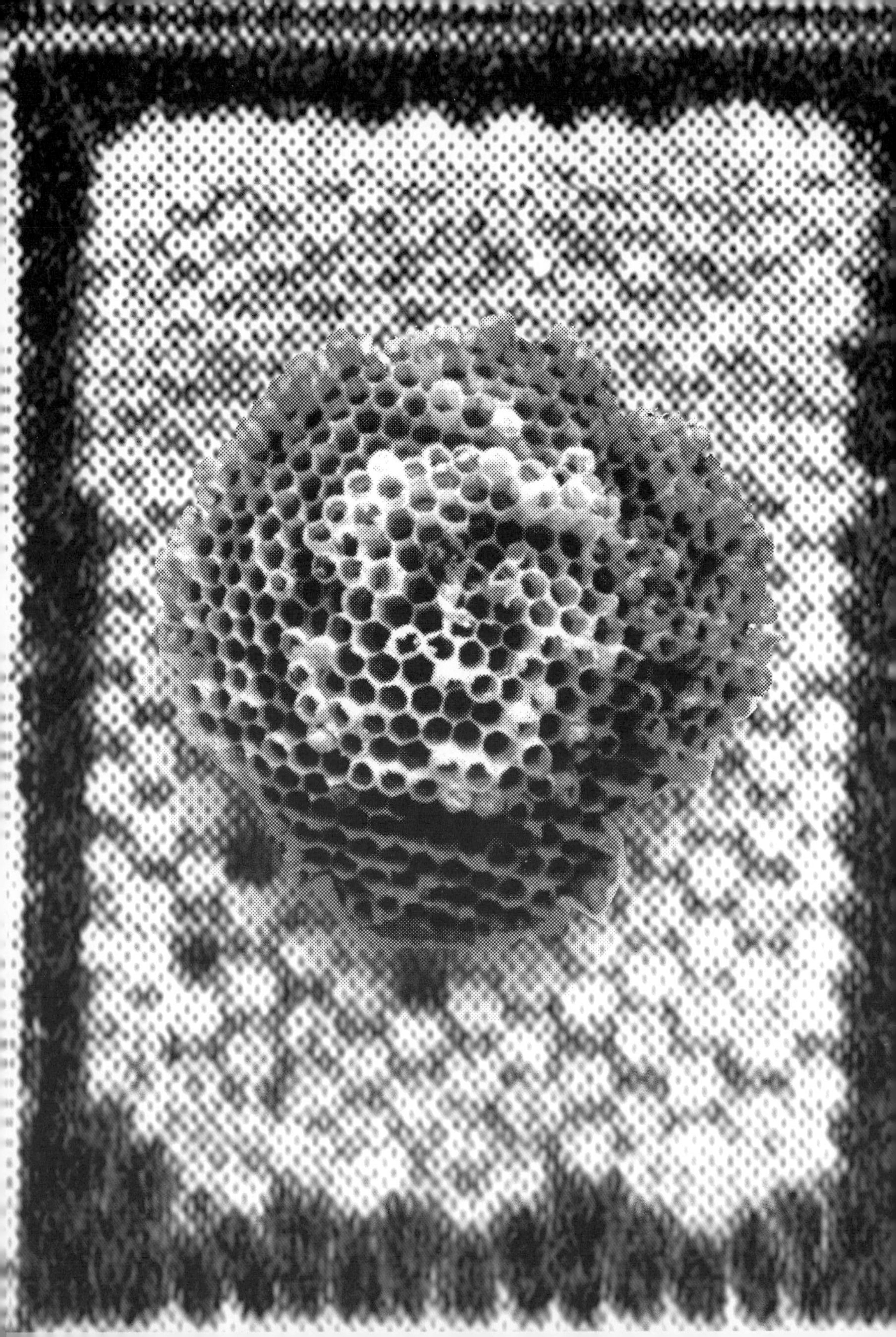

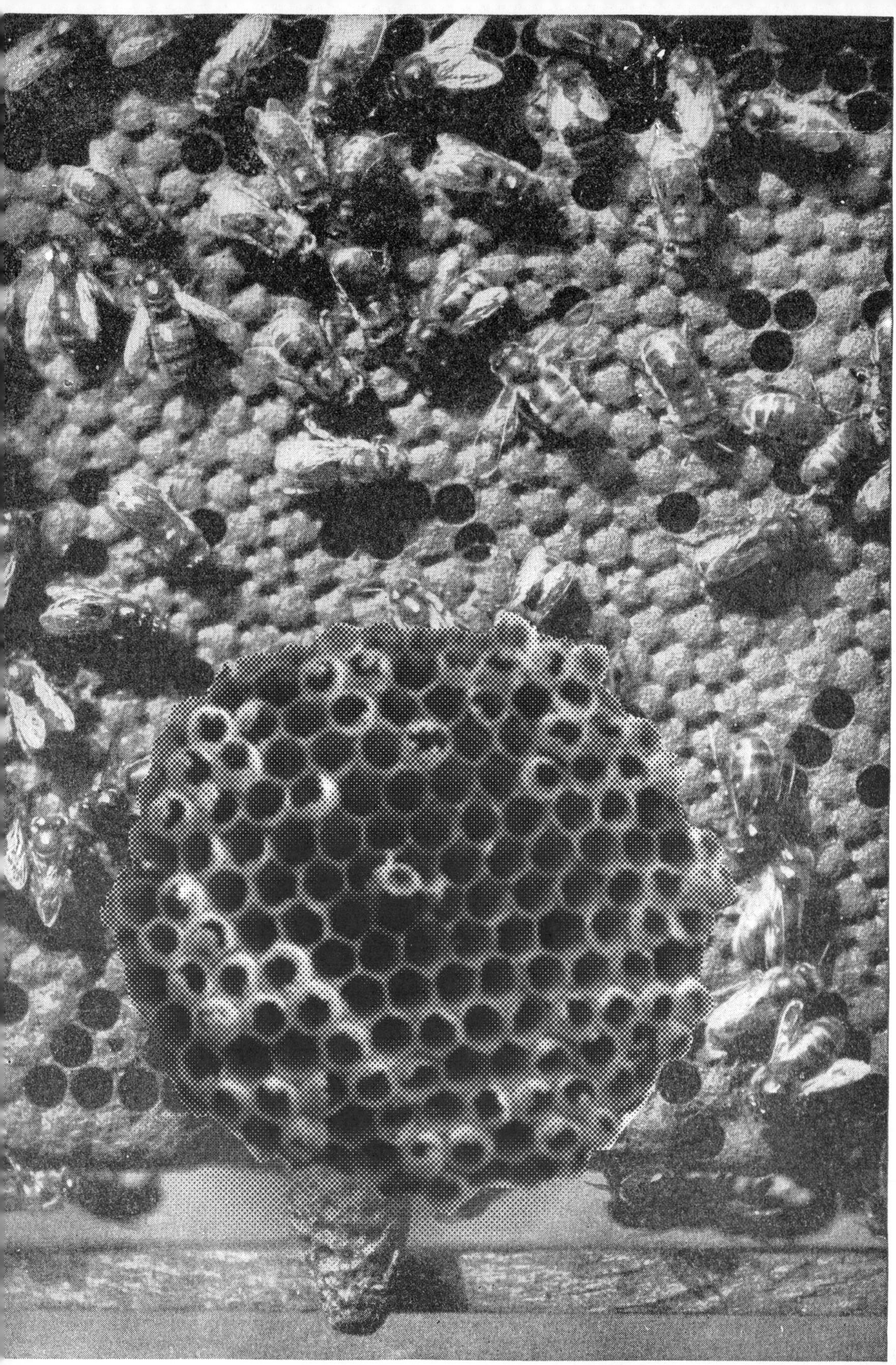

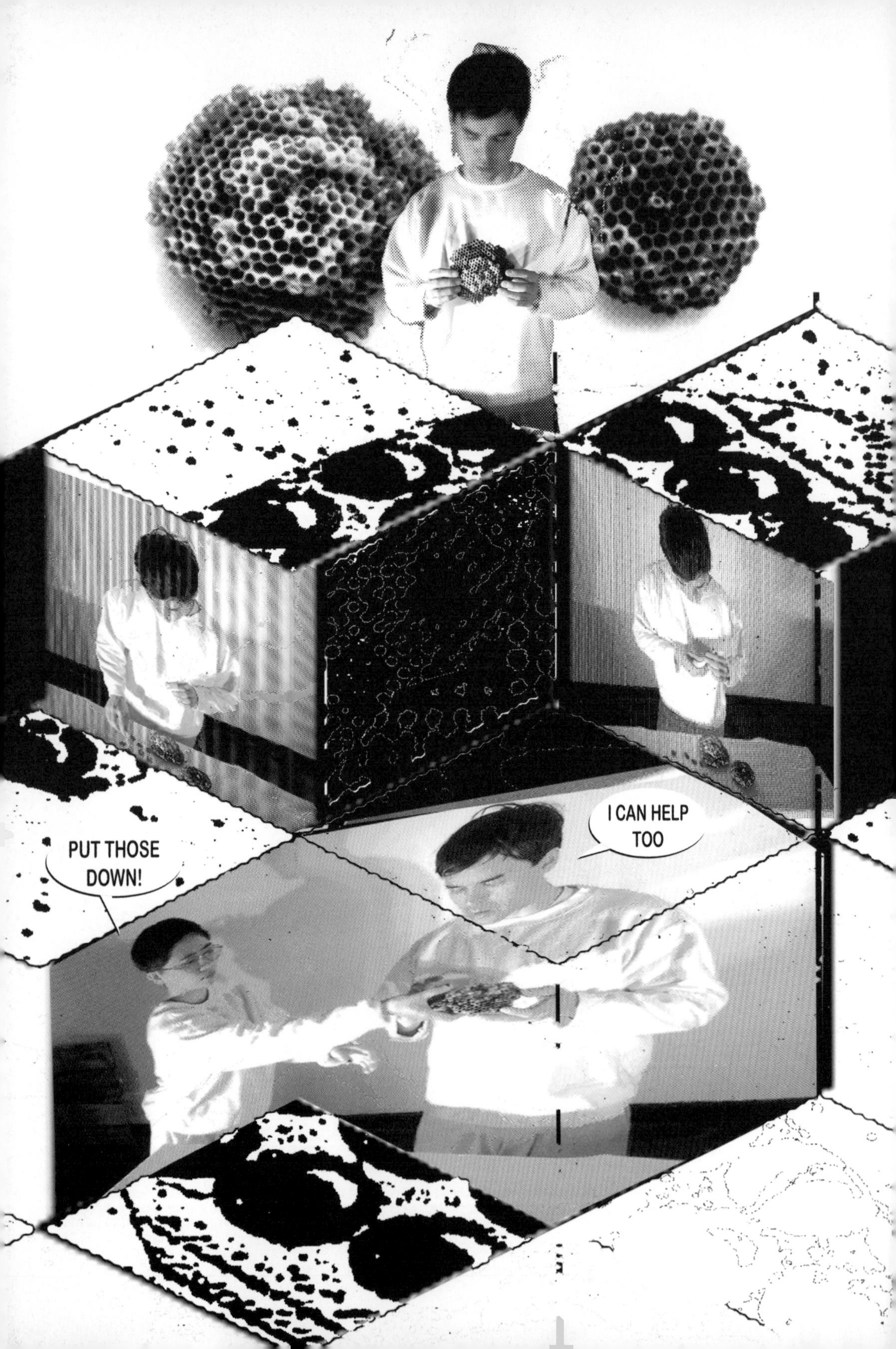
PUT THOSE DOWN!
I CAN HELP TOO

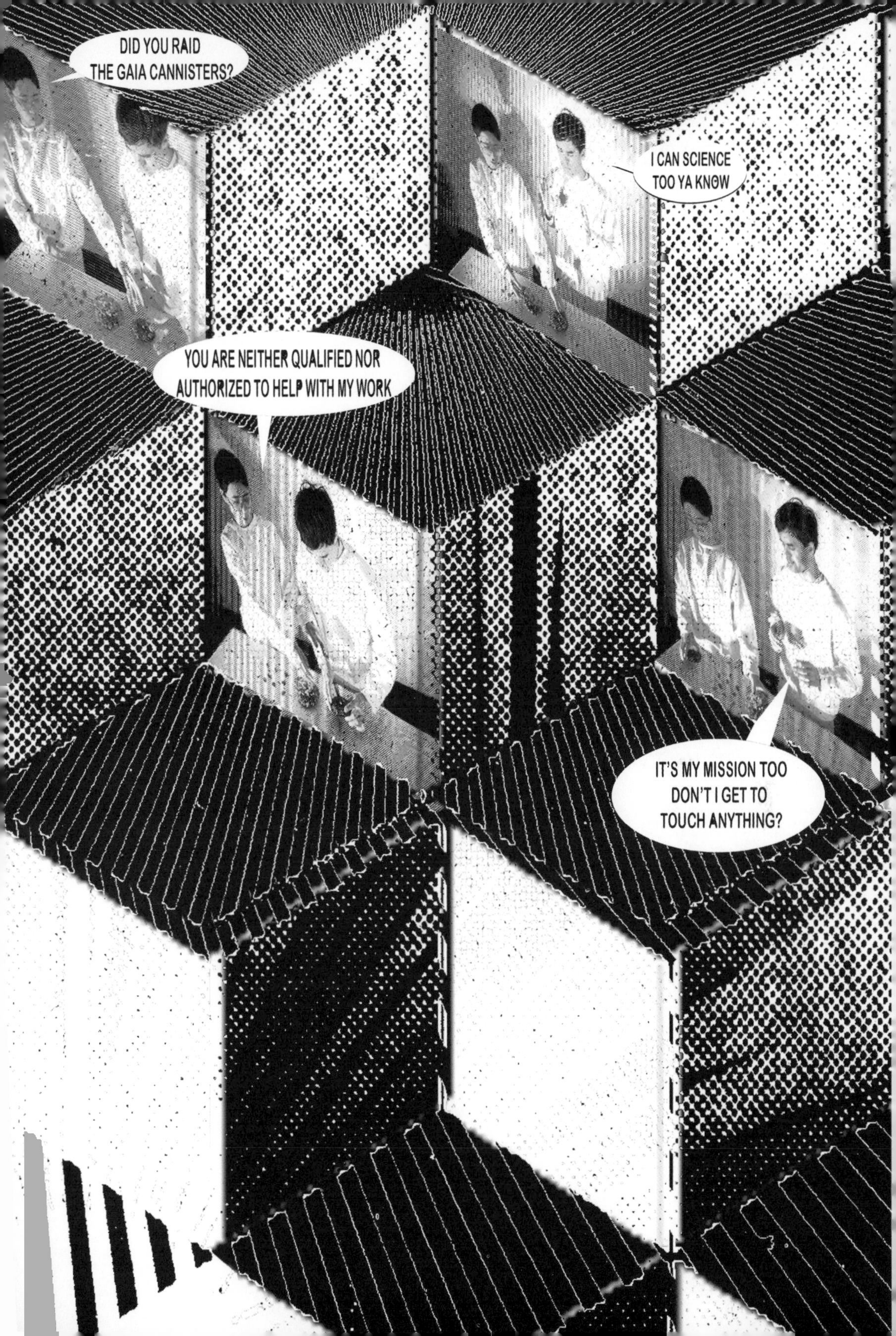
DID YOU RAID THE GAIA CANNISTERS?
I CAN SCIENCE TOO YA KNOW
YOU ARE NEITHER QUALIFIED NOR AUTHORIZED TO HELP WITH MY WORK
IT'S MY MISSION TOO DON'T I GET TO TOUCH ANYTHING?

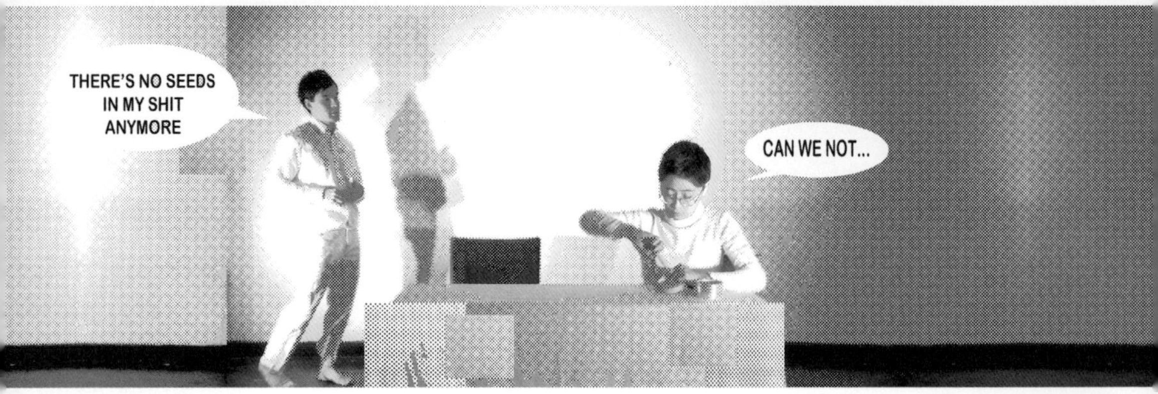
THERE'S NO SEEDS IN MY SHIT ANYMORE
CAN WE NOT...

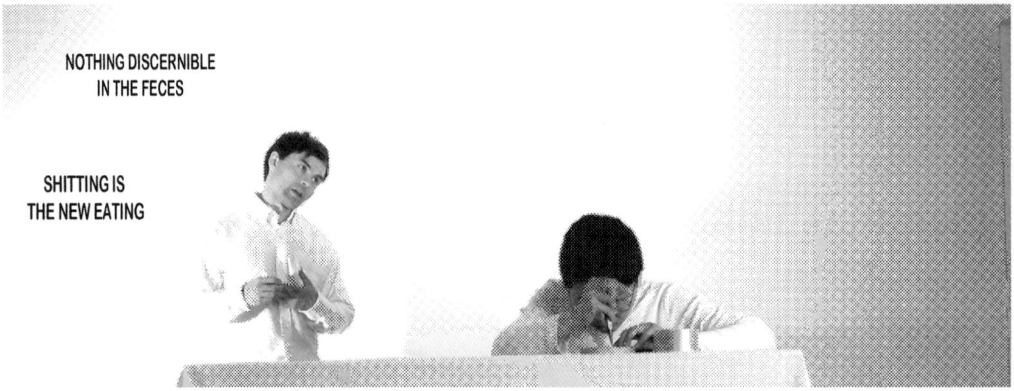
NOTHING DISCERNIBLE IN THE FECES
SHITTING IS THE NEW EATING

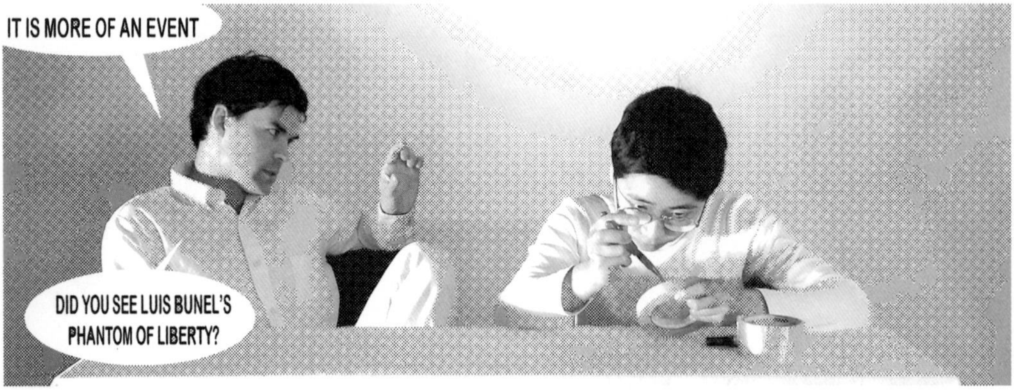
IT IS MORE OF AN EVENT
DID YOU SEE LUIS BUNEL'S PHANTOM OF LIBERTY?

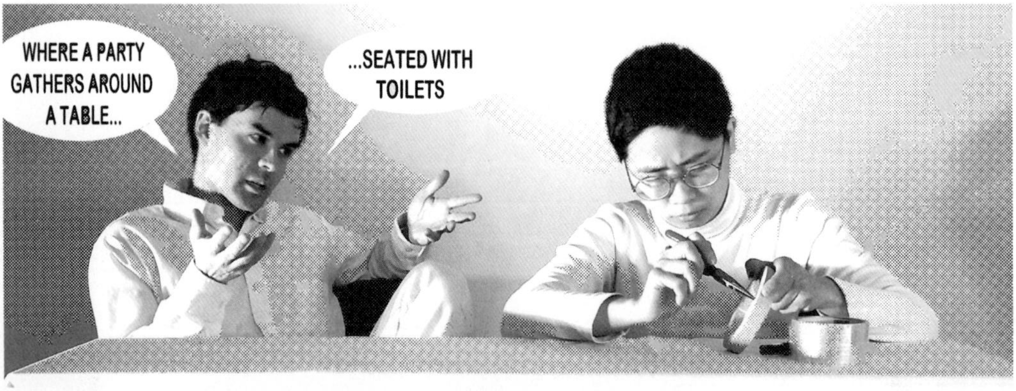
WHERE A PARTY GATHERS AROUND A TABLE...
...SEATED WITH TOILETS

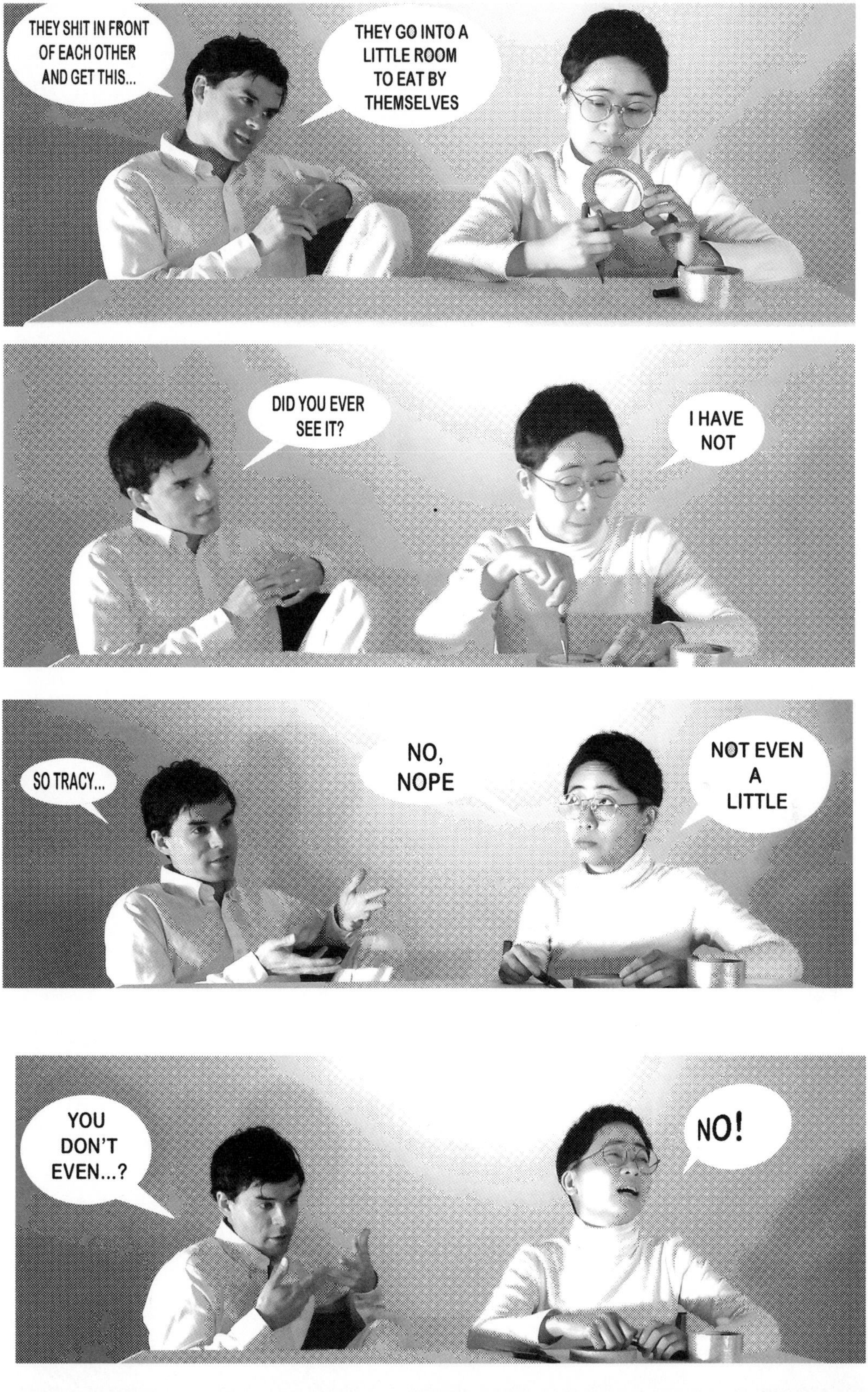
THEY SHIT IN FRONT OF EACH OTHER AND GET THIS...
THEY GO INTO A LITTLE ROOM TO EAT BY THEMSELVES
DID YOU EVER SEE IT?
I HAVE NOT
SO TRACY...
NO, NOPE
NOT EVEN A LITTLE
YOU DON'T EVEN...?
NO!

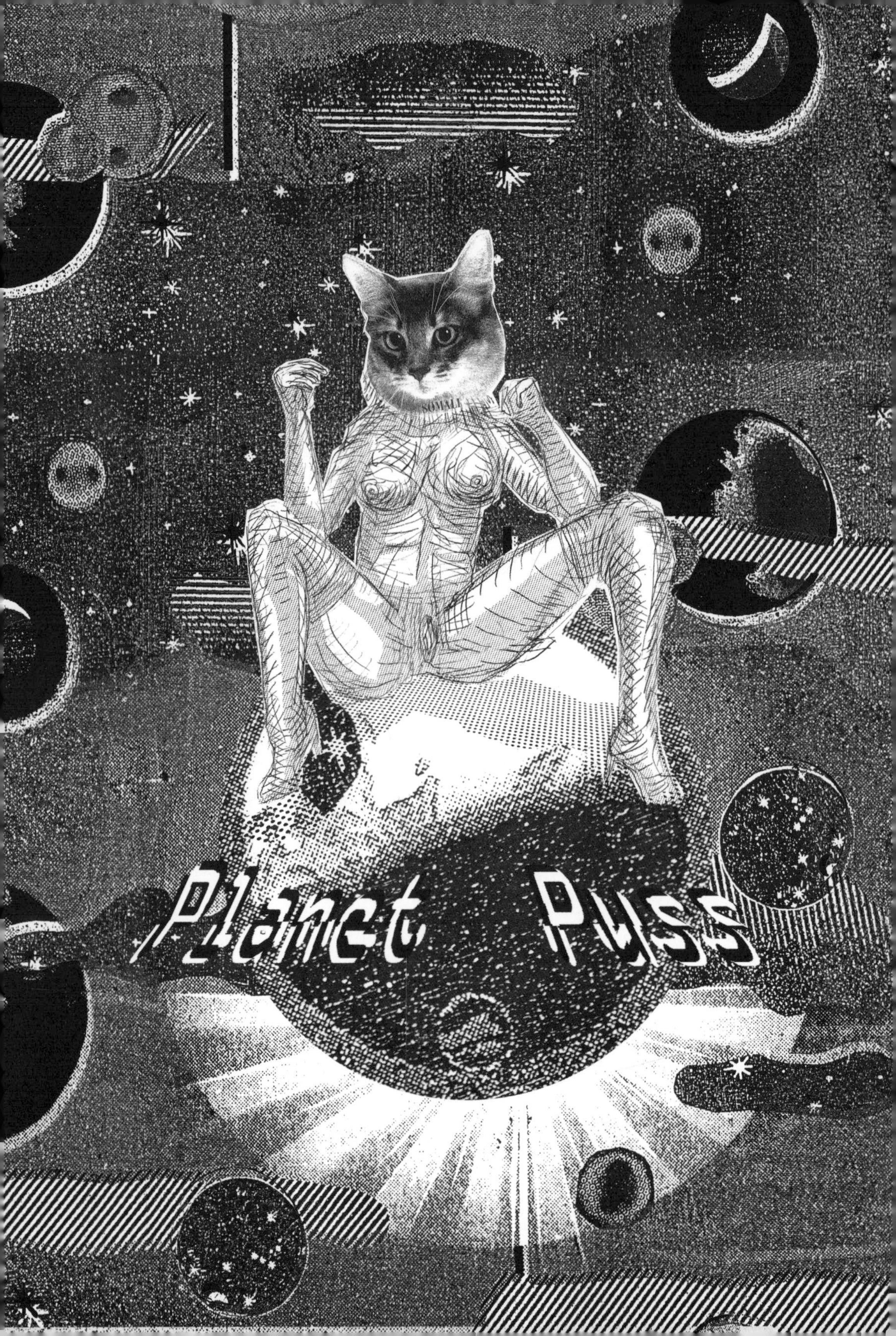
Planet Puss

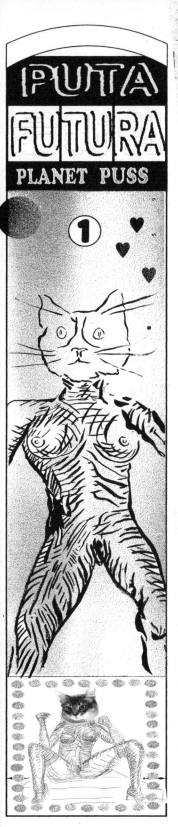

# PUTA FUTURA
## PLANET PUSS

**1**

MISSION TO ENGAGE IN SEXUAL CULTURE

PANCOSMIC
SEXUAL CULTURE

CULTURE IS A MECHANISM
TO INCREASE INTELLIGENCE

ANTHROPOLOGY OF THE CROTCH

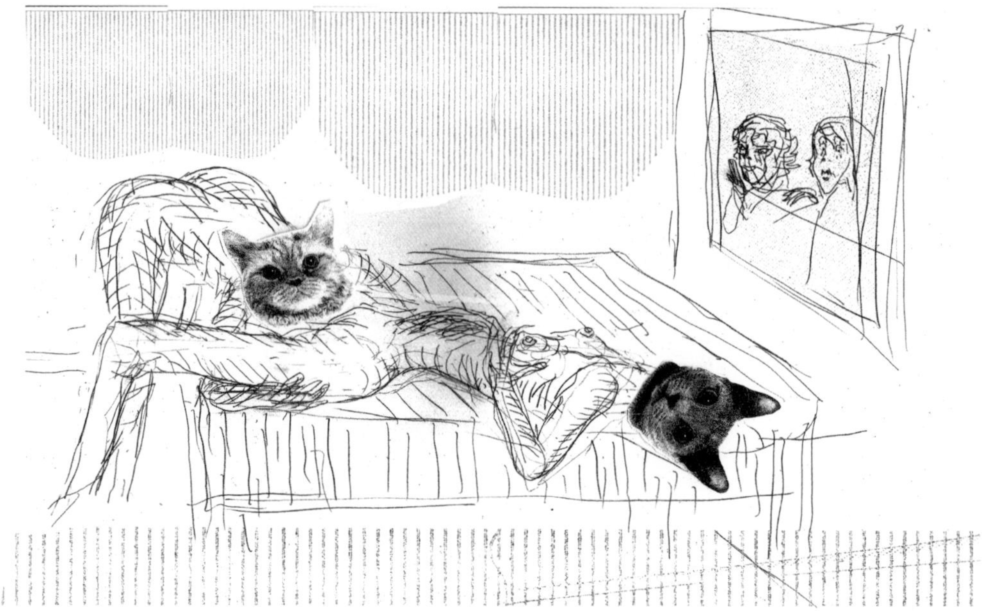

WELL THIS IS PROBABLY PRETTY EARTHIST BUT THE INHABITANTS OF PLANET PUSS LOOK LIKE CUTE KITTY CATS

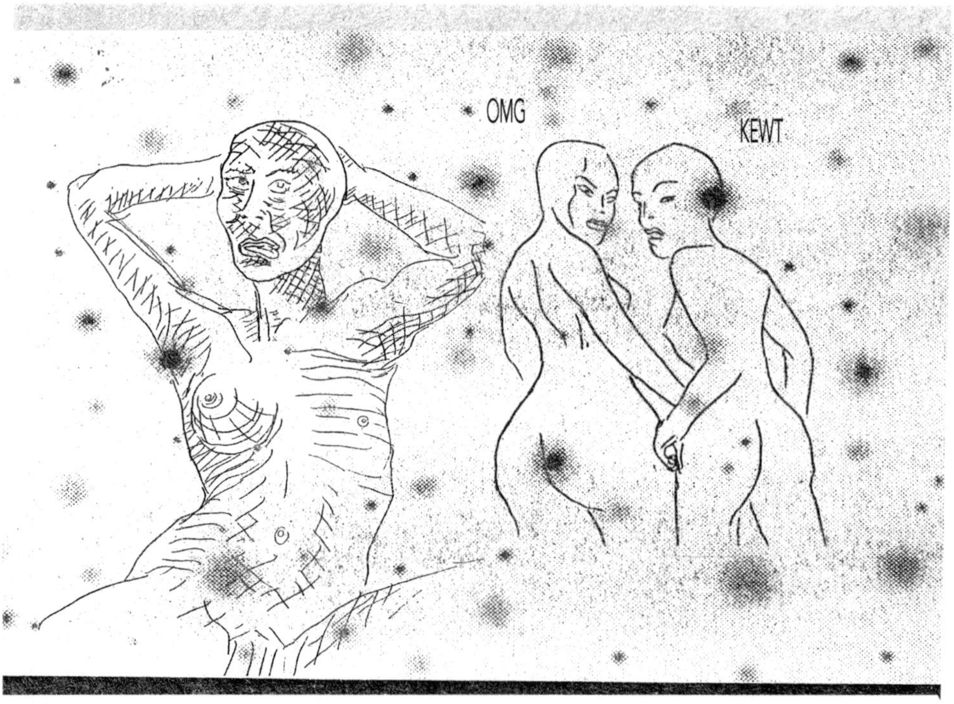
OMG
KEWT

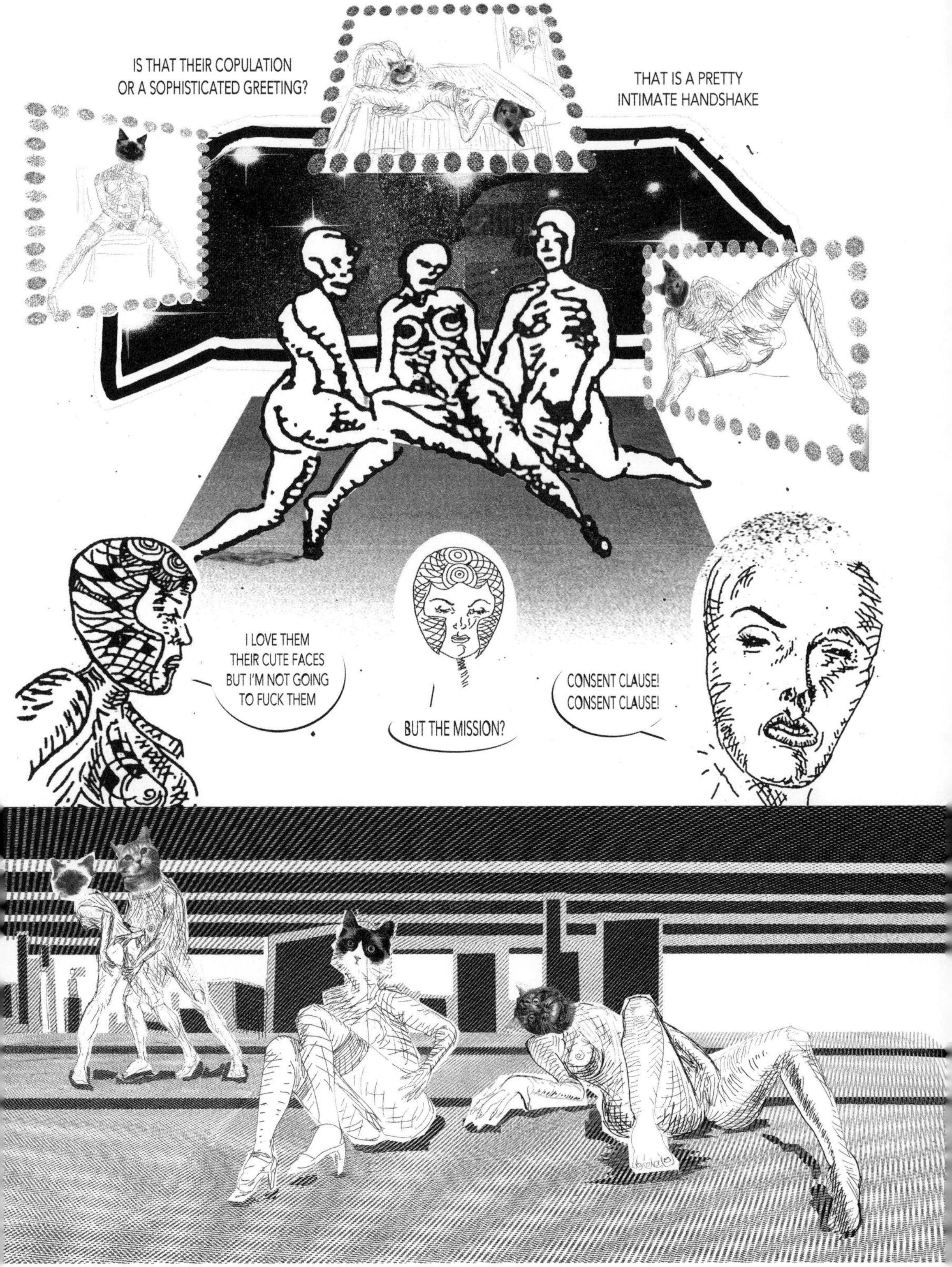
IS THAT THEIR COPULATION OR A SOPHISTICATED GREETING?
THAT IS A PRETTY INTIMATE HANDSHAKE
I LOVE THEM THEIR CUTE FACES BUT I'M NOT GOING TO FUCK THEM
BUT THE MISSION?
CONSENT CLAUSE! CONSENT CLAUSE!

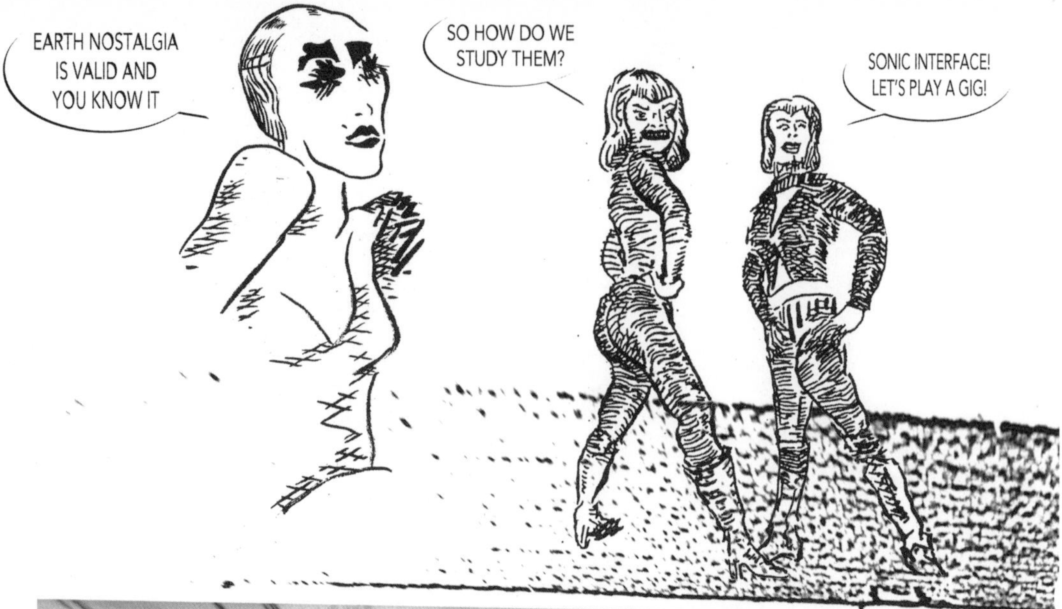
EARTH NOSTALGIA IS VALID AND YOU KNOW IT
SO HOW DO WE STUDY THEM?
SONIC INTERFACE! LET'S PLAY A GIG!

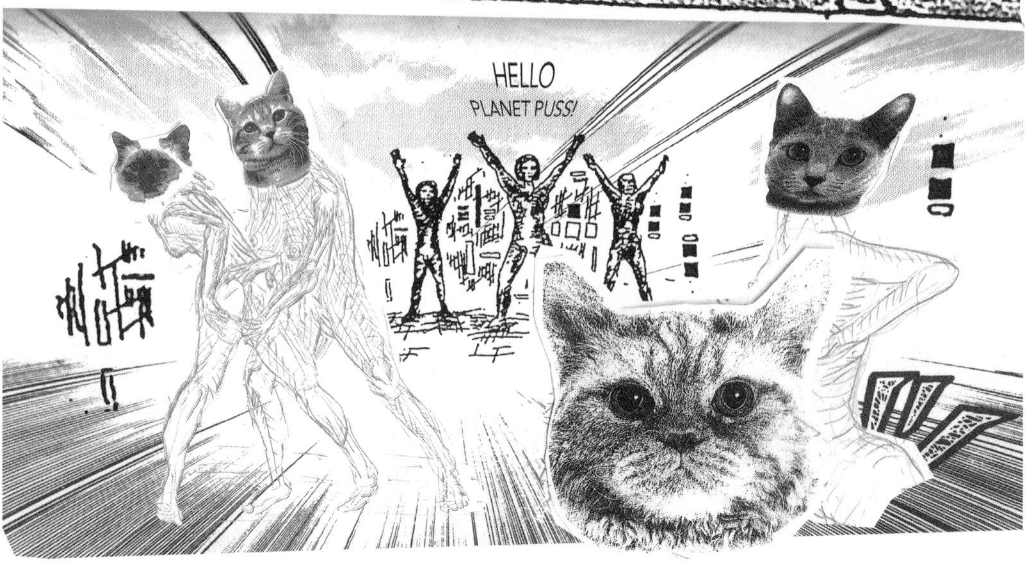
HELLO PLANET *PUSS!*

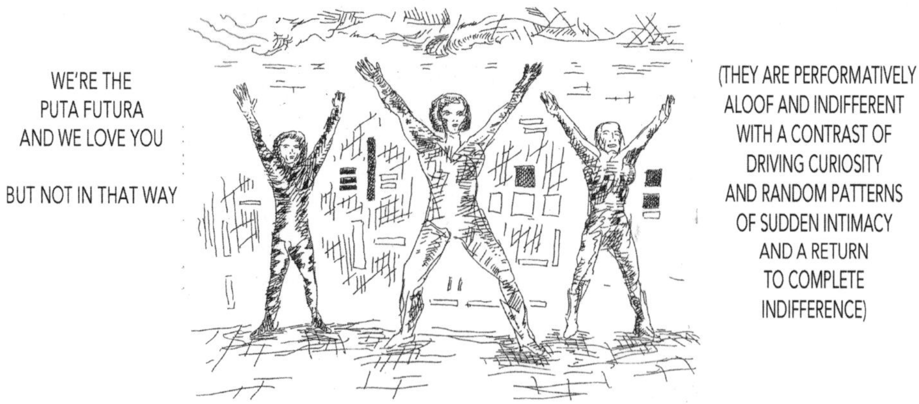
WE'RE THE PUTA FUTURA AND WE LOVE YOU
BUT NOT IN THAT WAY
(THEY ARE PERFORMATIVELY ALOOF AND INDIFFERENT WITH A CONTRAST OF DRIVING CURIOSITY AND RANDOM PATTERNS OF SUDDEN INTIMACY AND A RETURN TO COMPLETE INDIFFERENCE)

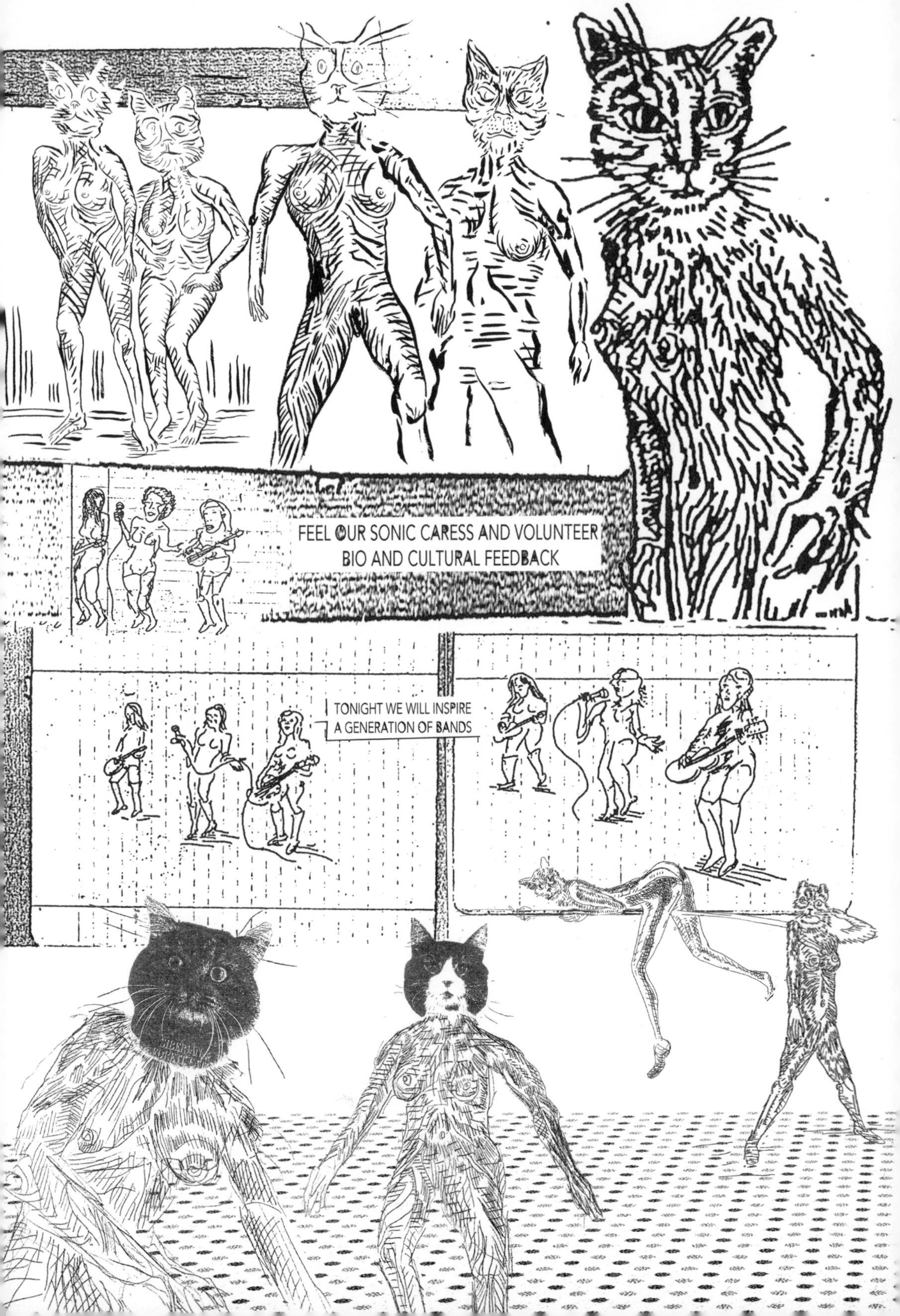

FEEL OUR SONIC CARESS AND VOLUNTEER BIO AND CULTURAL FEEDBACK
TONIGHT WE WILL INSPIRE A GENERATION OF BANDS

CYSTER CYST CHECK

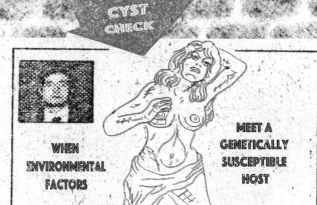

WHEN ENVIRONMENTAL FACTORS

MEET A GENETICALLY SUSCEPTIBLE HOST

80% OF BREAST CANCER CASES ARE DISCOVERED WHEN THE WOMAN FEELS A LUMP.

YOU DON'T WANT THIS TO HAPPEN   DO YOU BRO!

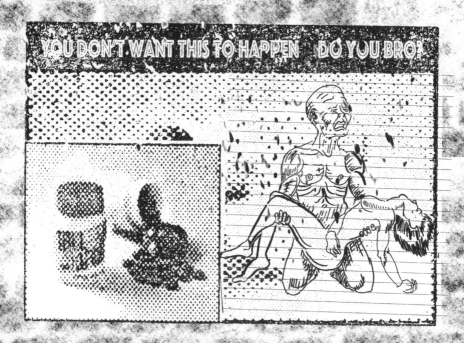

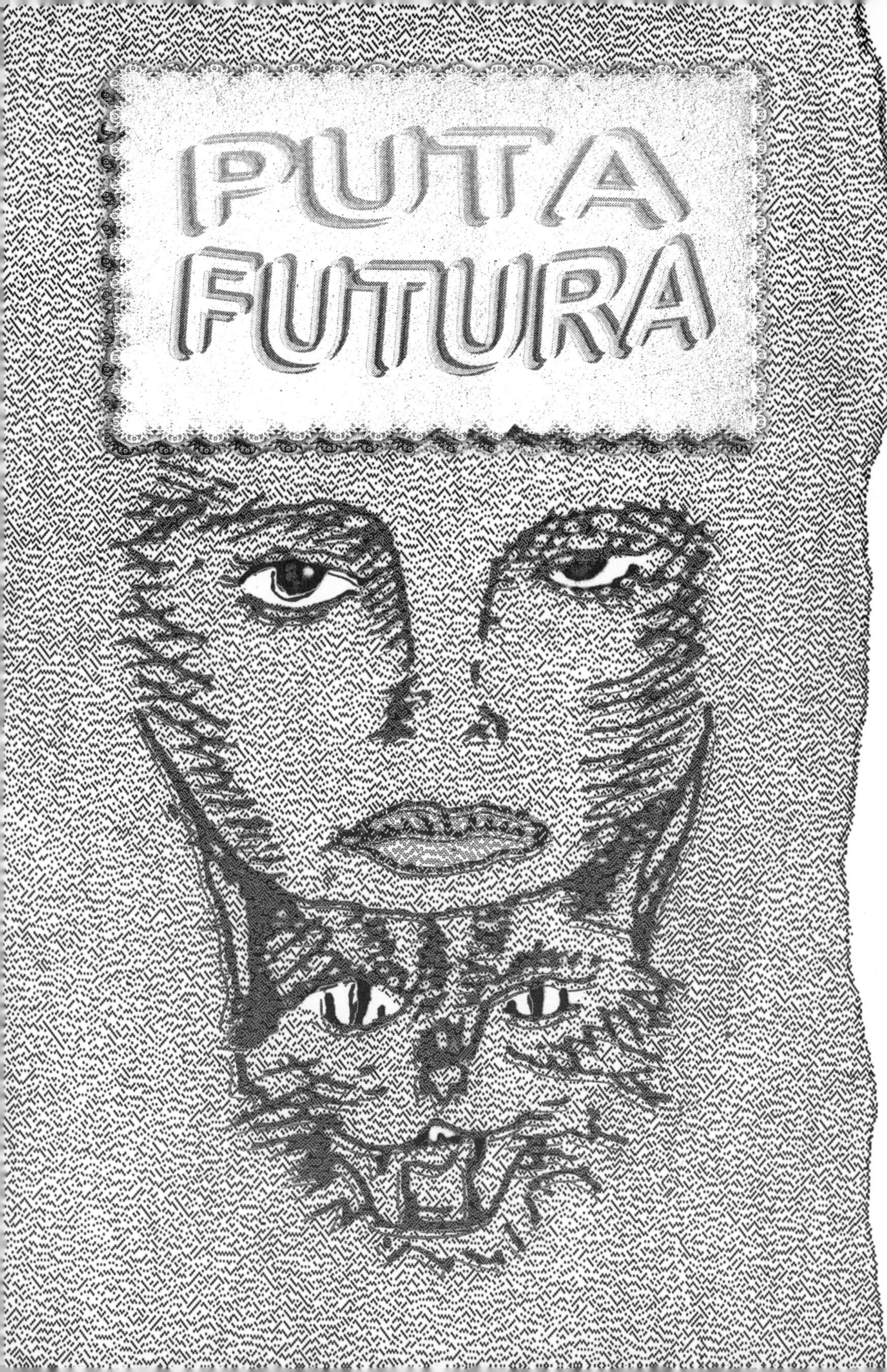
PUTA
FUTURA

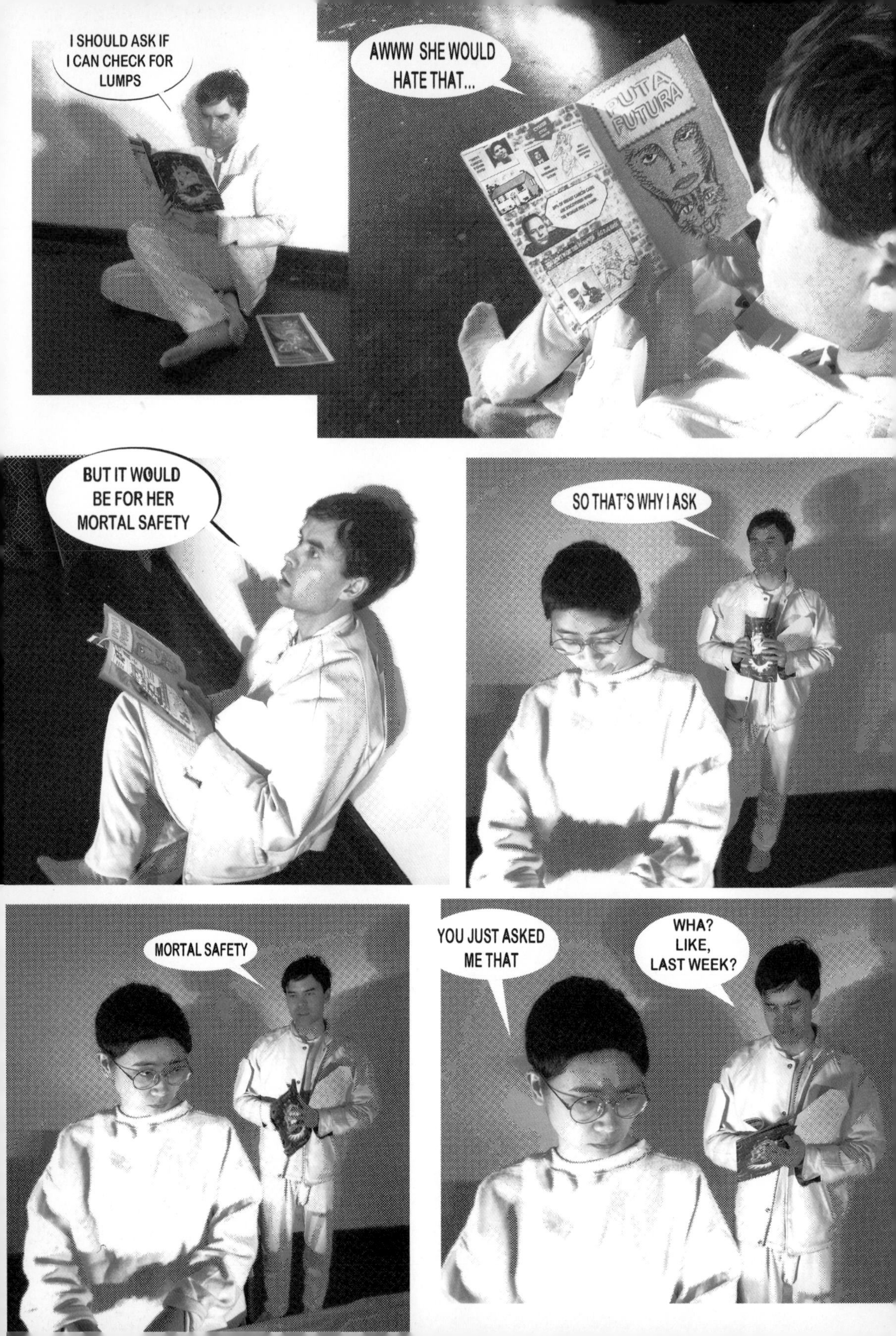
I SHOULD ASK IF I CAN CHECK FOR LUMPS
AWWW SHE WOULD HATE THAT...
PUTA FUTURA
BUT IT WOULD BE FOR HER MORTAL SAFETY
SO THAT'S WHY I ASK
MORTAL SAFETY
YOU JUST ASKED ME THAT
WHA? LIKE, LAST WEEK?

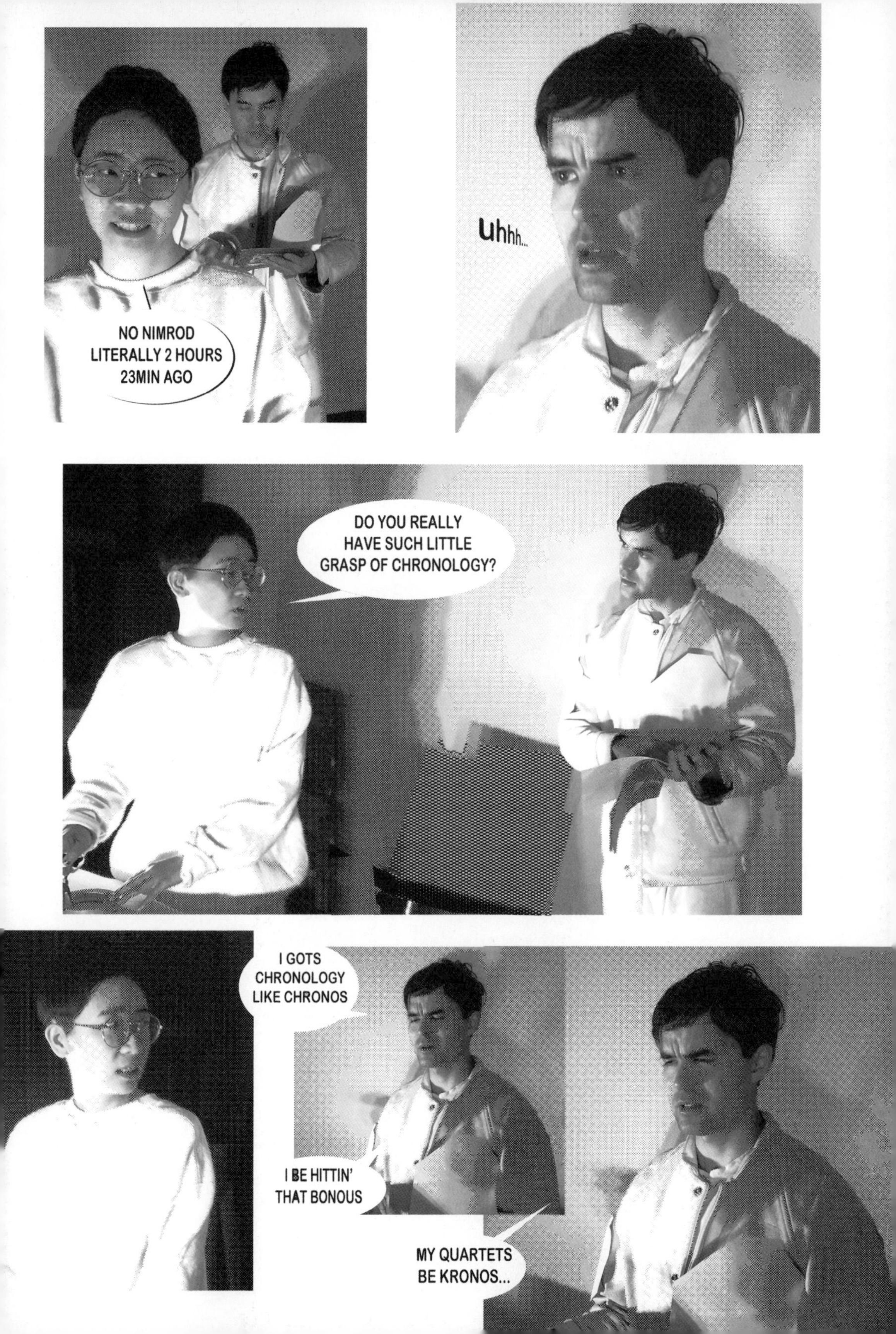
NO NIMROD
LITERALLY 2 HOURS
23MIN AGO
Uhhh...
DO YOU REALLY
HAVE SUCH LITTLE
GRASP OF CHRONOLOGY?
I GOTS
CHRONOLOGY
LIKE CHRONOS
I BE HITTIN'
THAT BONOUS
MY QUARTETS
BE KRONOS...

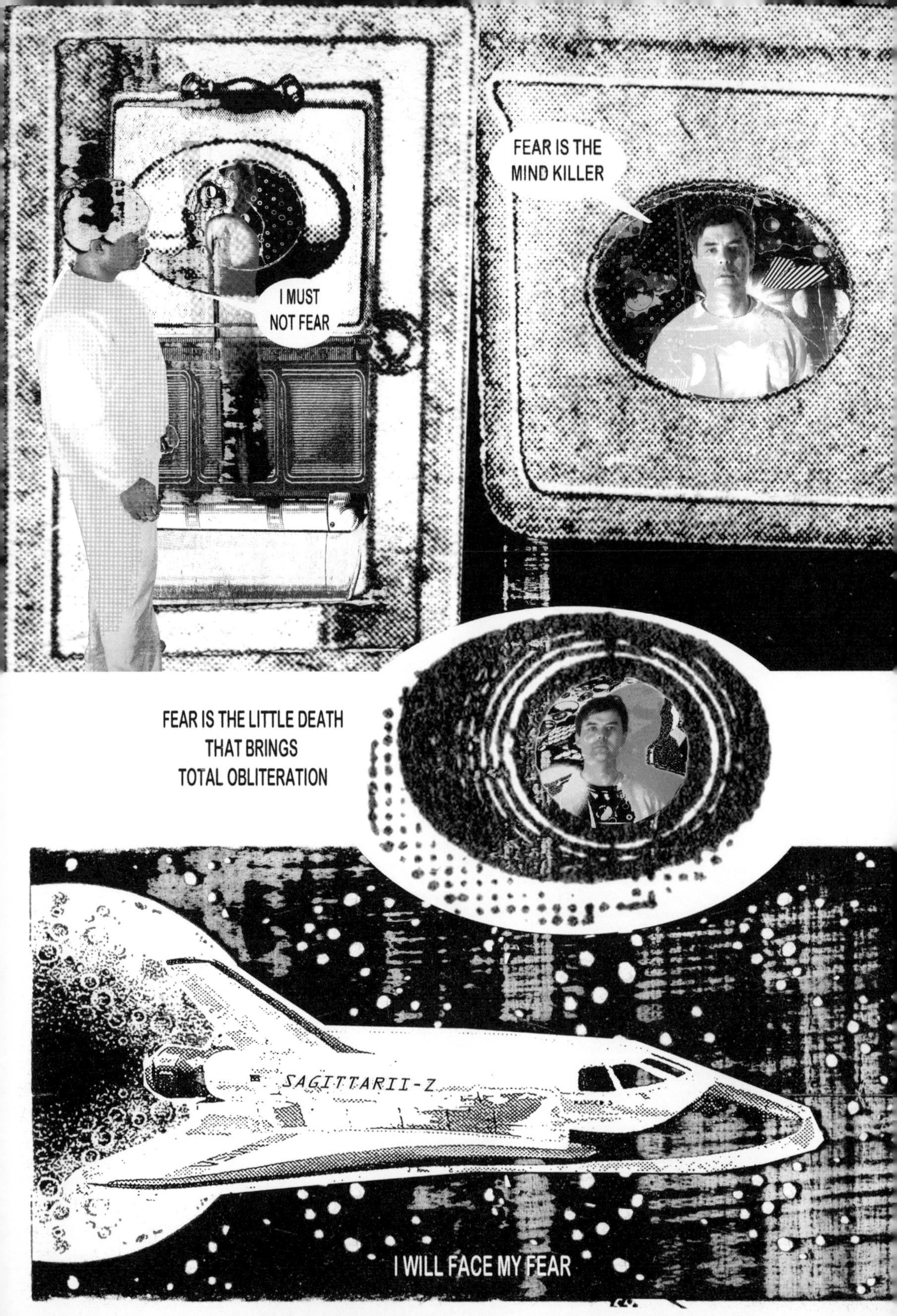
I MUST NOT FEAR
FEAR IS THE MIND KILLER
FEAR IS THE LITTLE DEATH THAT BRINGS TOTAL OBLITERATION
SAGITTARII-Z
I WILL FACE MY FEAR

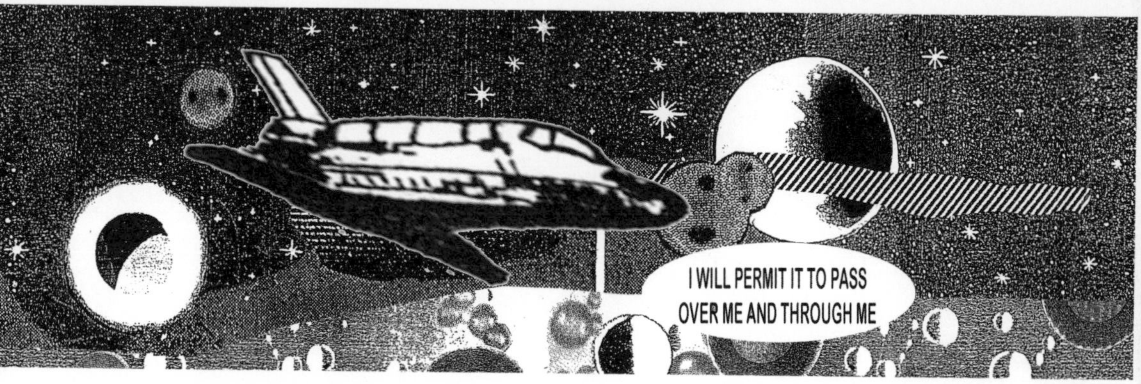
I WILL PERMIT IT TO PASS
OVER ME AND THROUGH ME

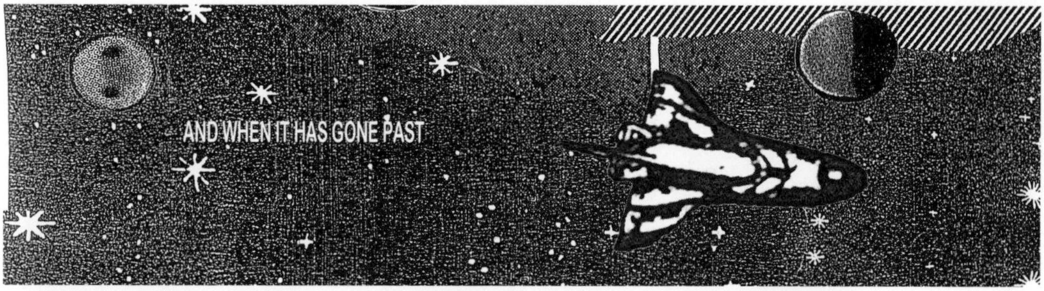
AND WHEN IT HAS GONE PAST

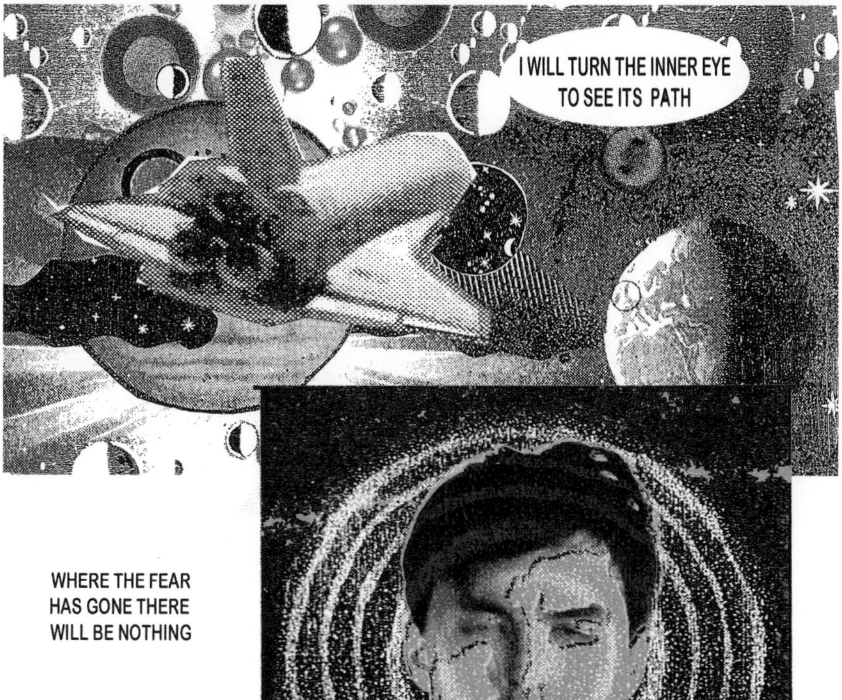
I WILL TURN THE INNER EYE
TO SEE ITS PATH

WHERE THE FEAR
HAS GONE THERE
WILL BE NOTHING

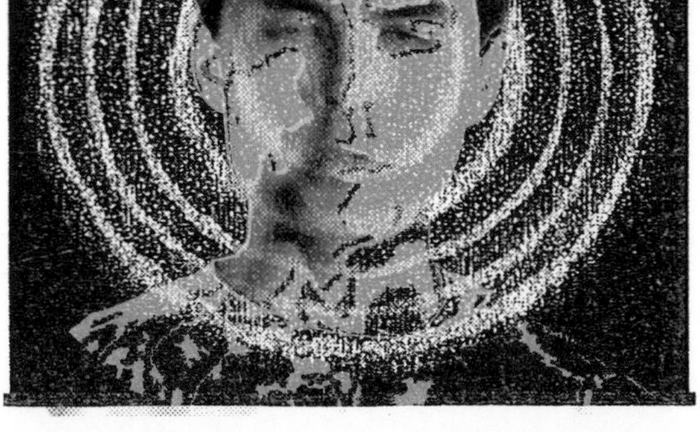

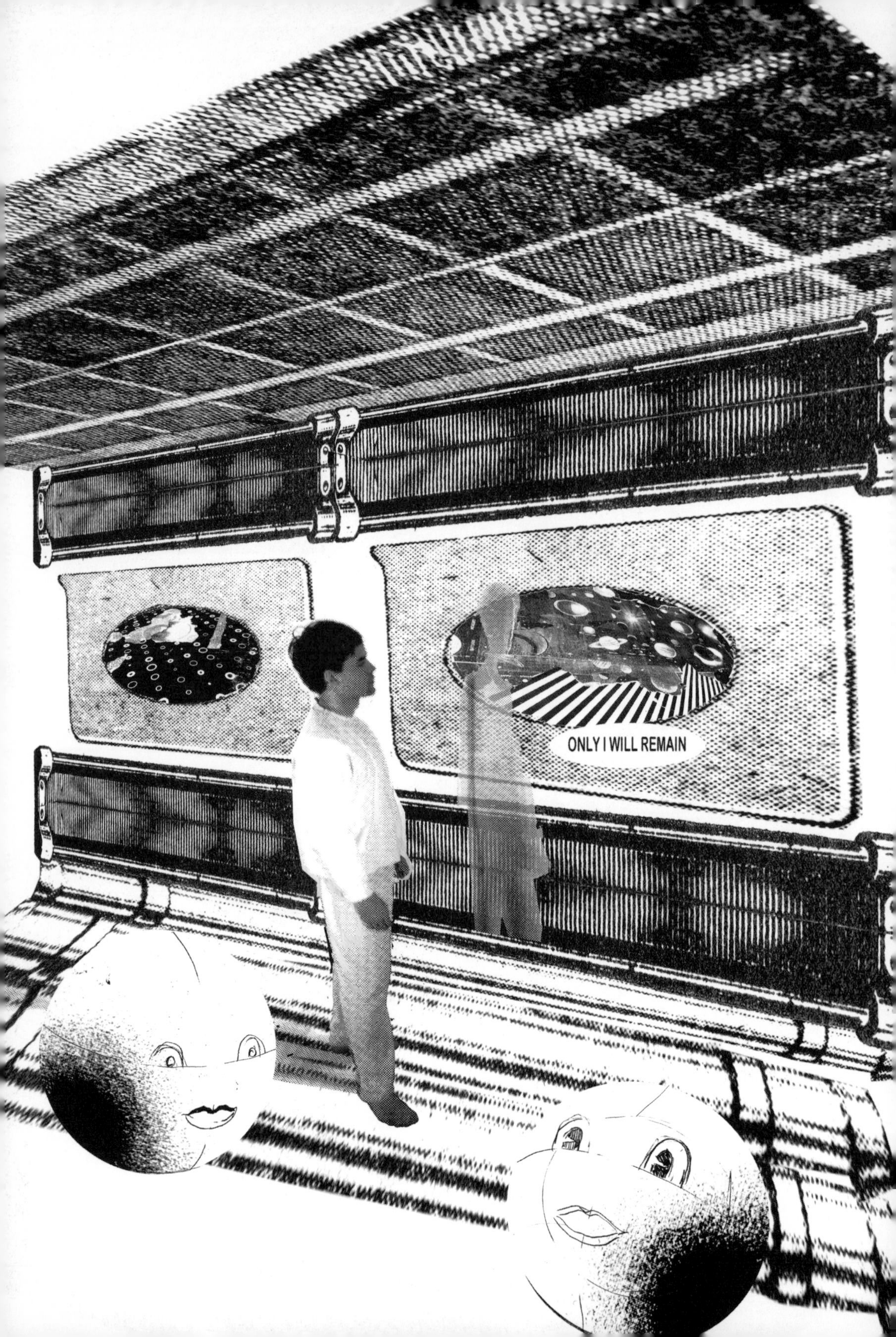
ONLY I WILL REMAIN

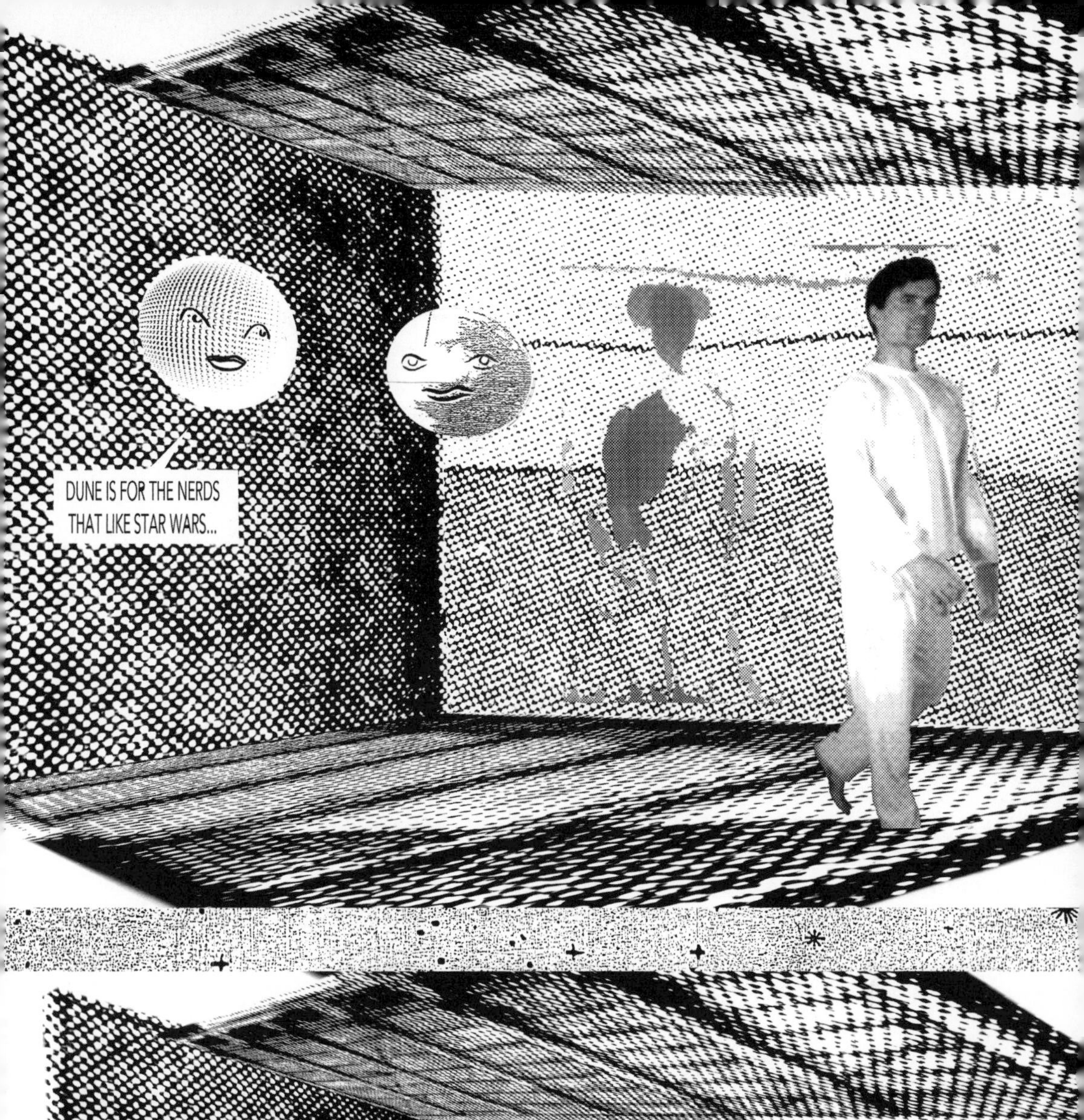
DUNE IS FOR THE NERDS THAT LIKE STAR WARS...

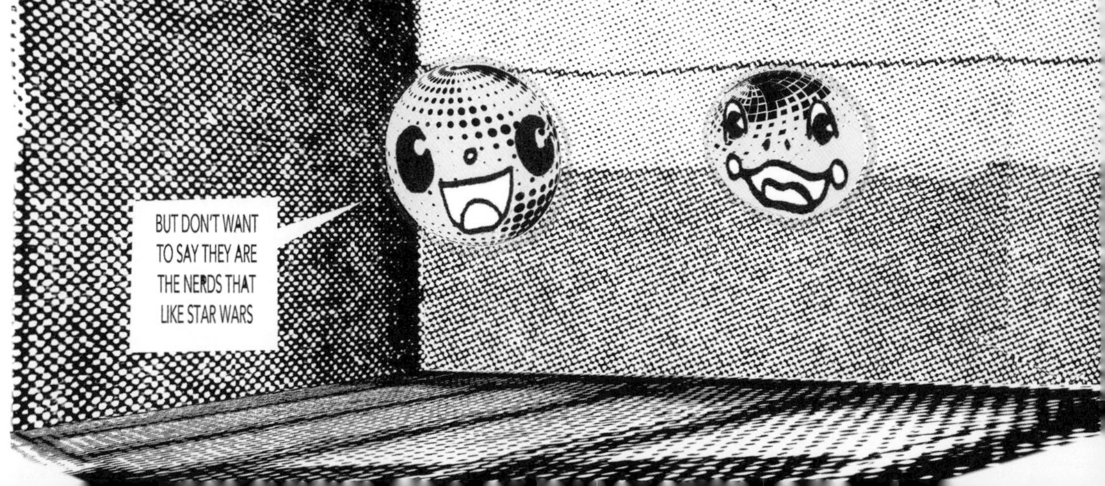
BUT DON'T WANT TO SAY THEY ARE THE NERDS THAT LIKE STAR WARS

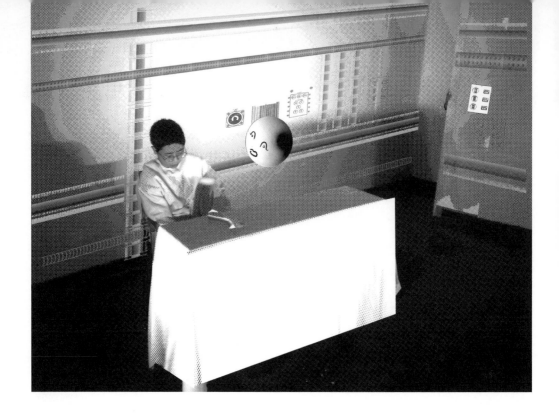

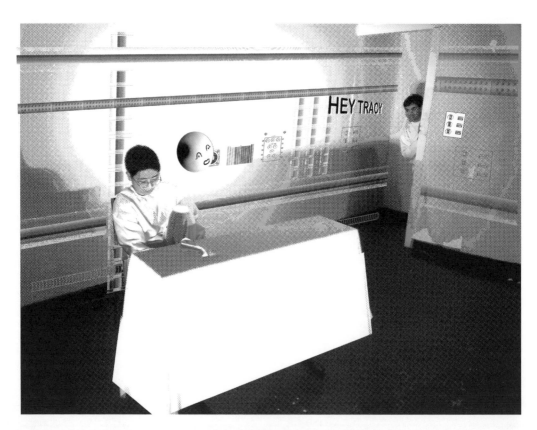

HEY TRACY

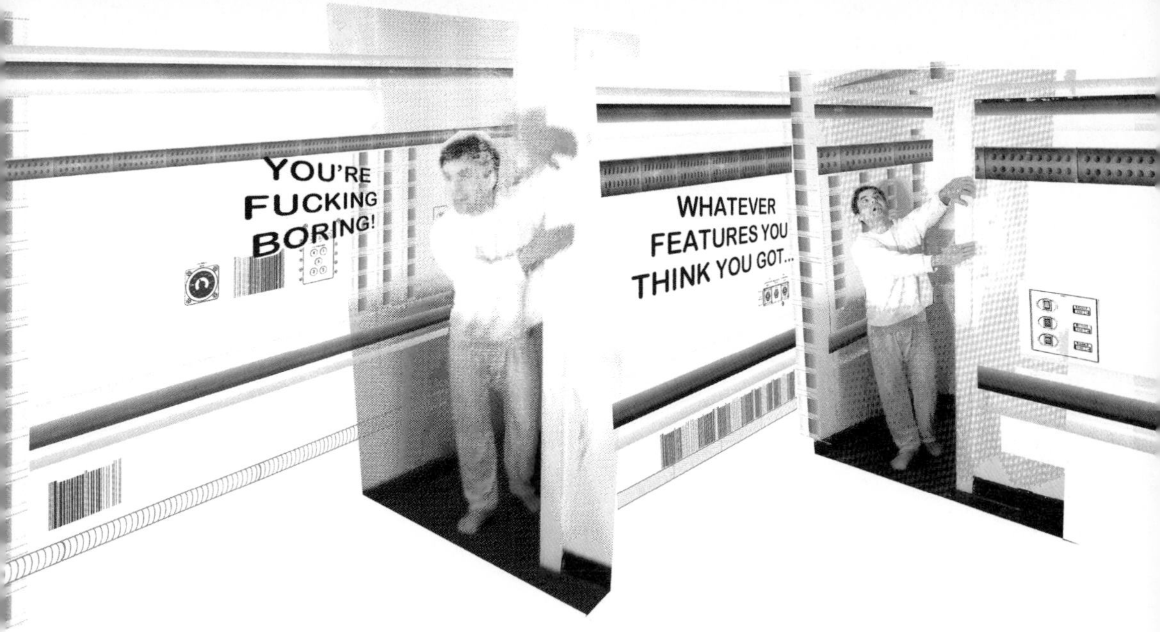
YOU'RE FUCKING BORING!
WHATEVER FEATURES YOU THINK YOU GOT...

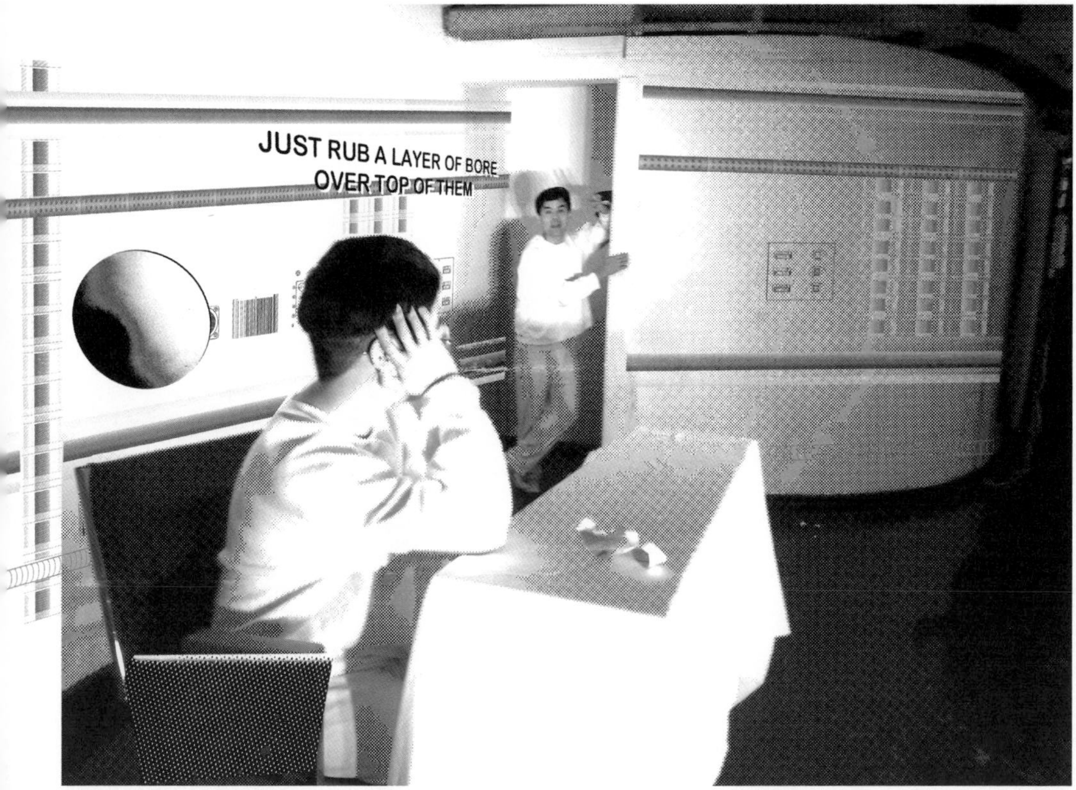
JUST RUB A LAYER OF BORE OVER TOP OF THEM

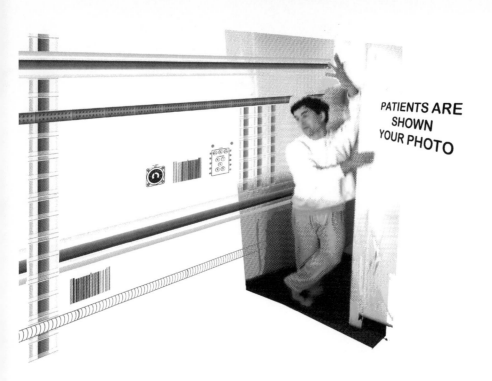

PATIENTS ARE SHOWN YOUR PHOTO

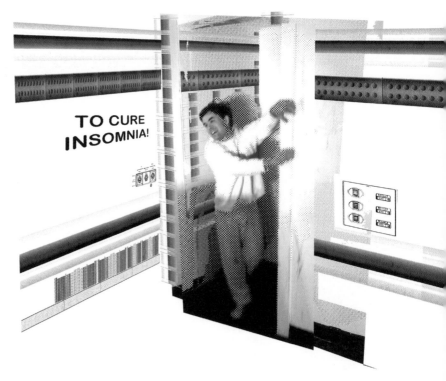

TO CURE INSOMNIA!

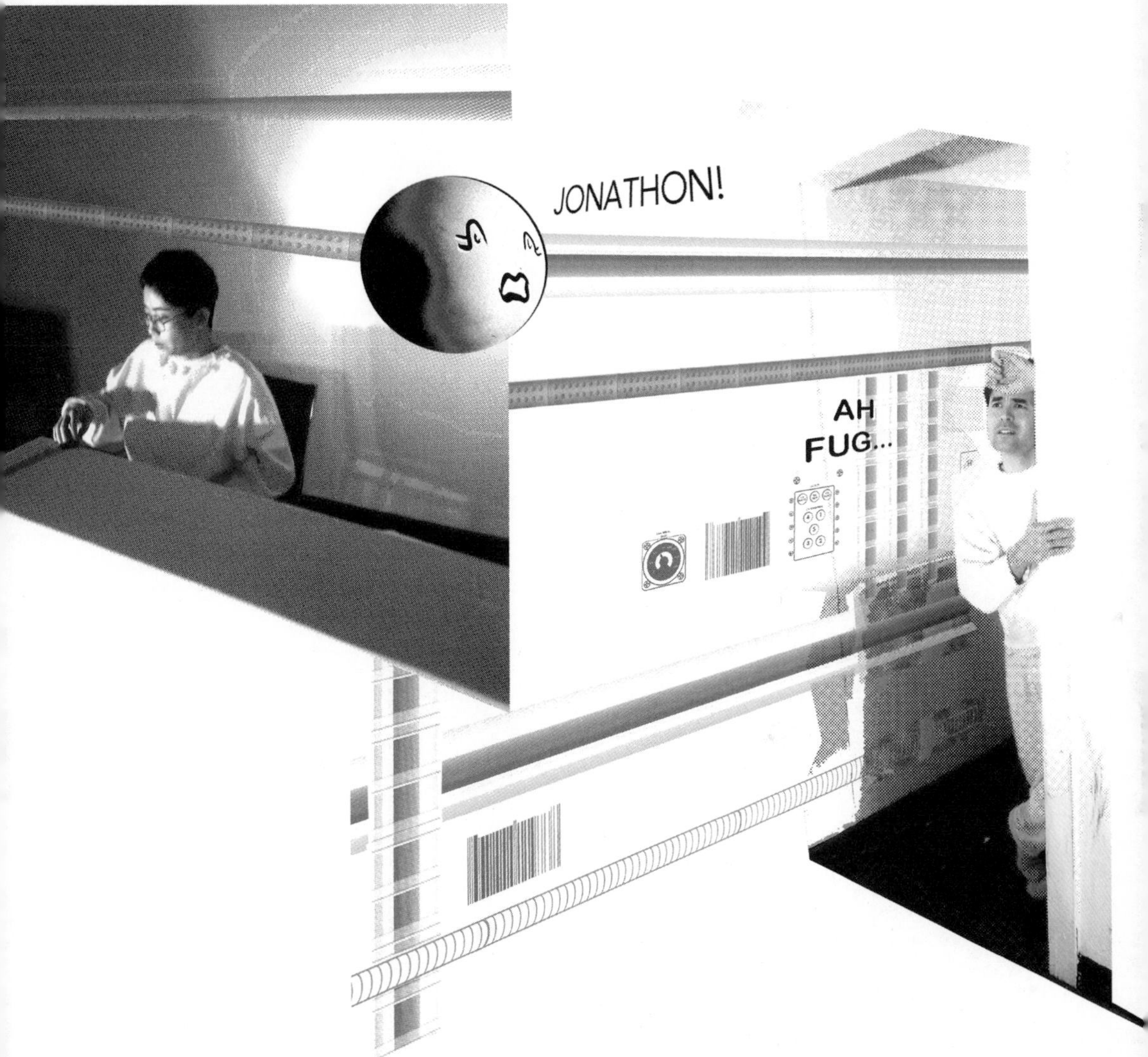
JONATHON!
AH
FUG...

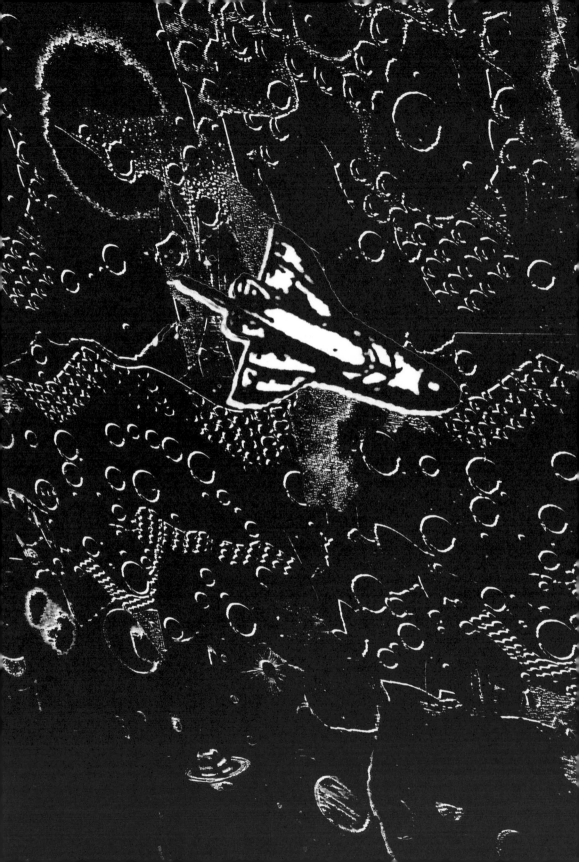

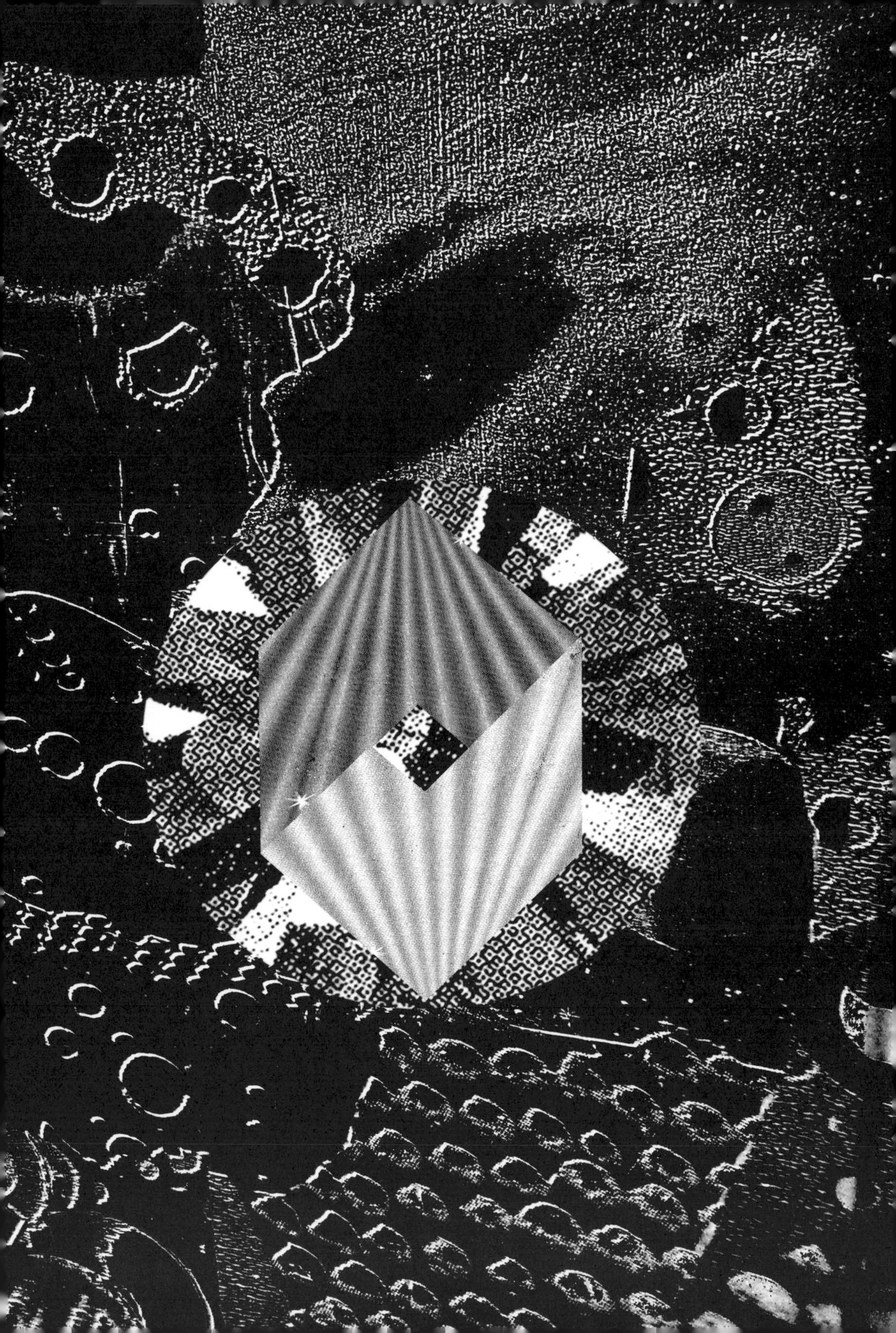

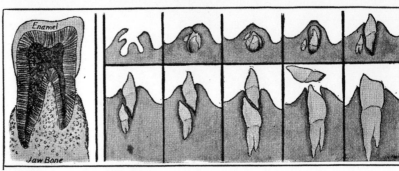

Enamel
Jaw Bone
THE MODERN DIET HAS MADE WISDOM TEETH SUPERFLUOUS
WE'VE EVOLVED
I HAVE MY OWN BIOMATTER TO HARVEST
OWW AHHHG

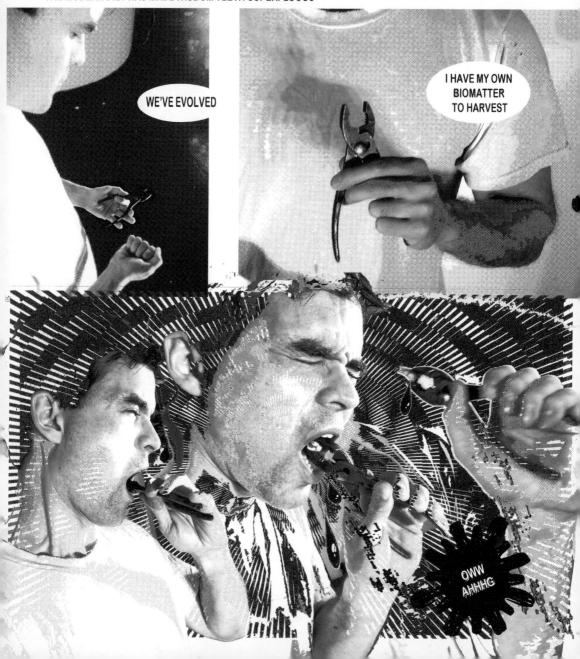

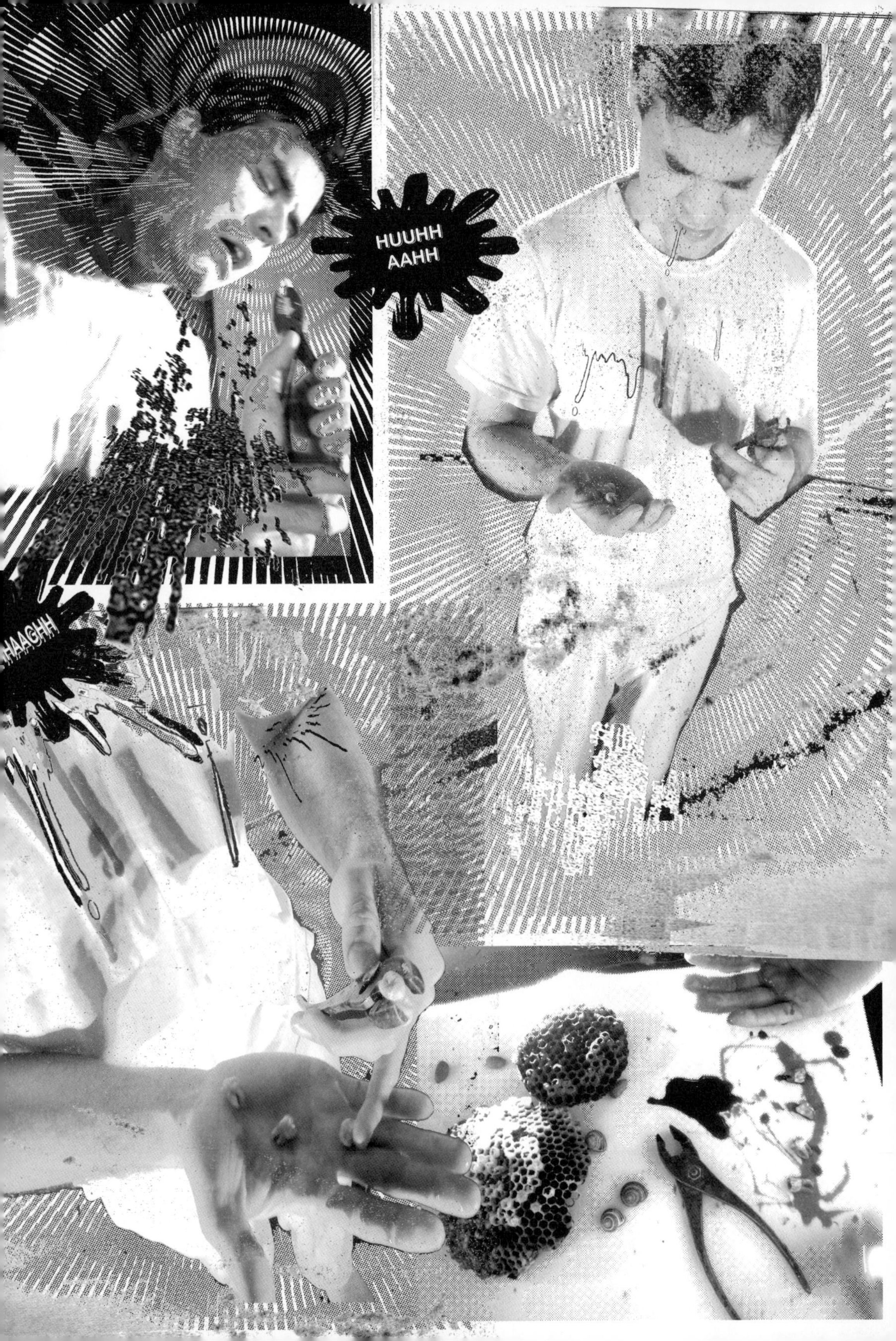
HUUHH
AAHH
HAAGHH

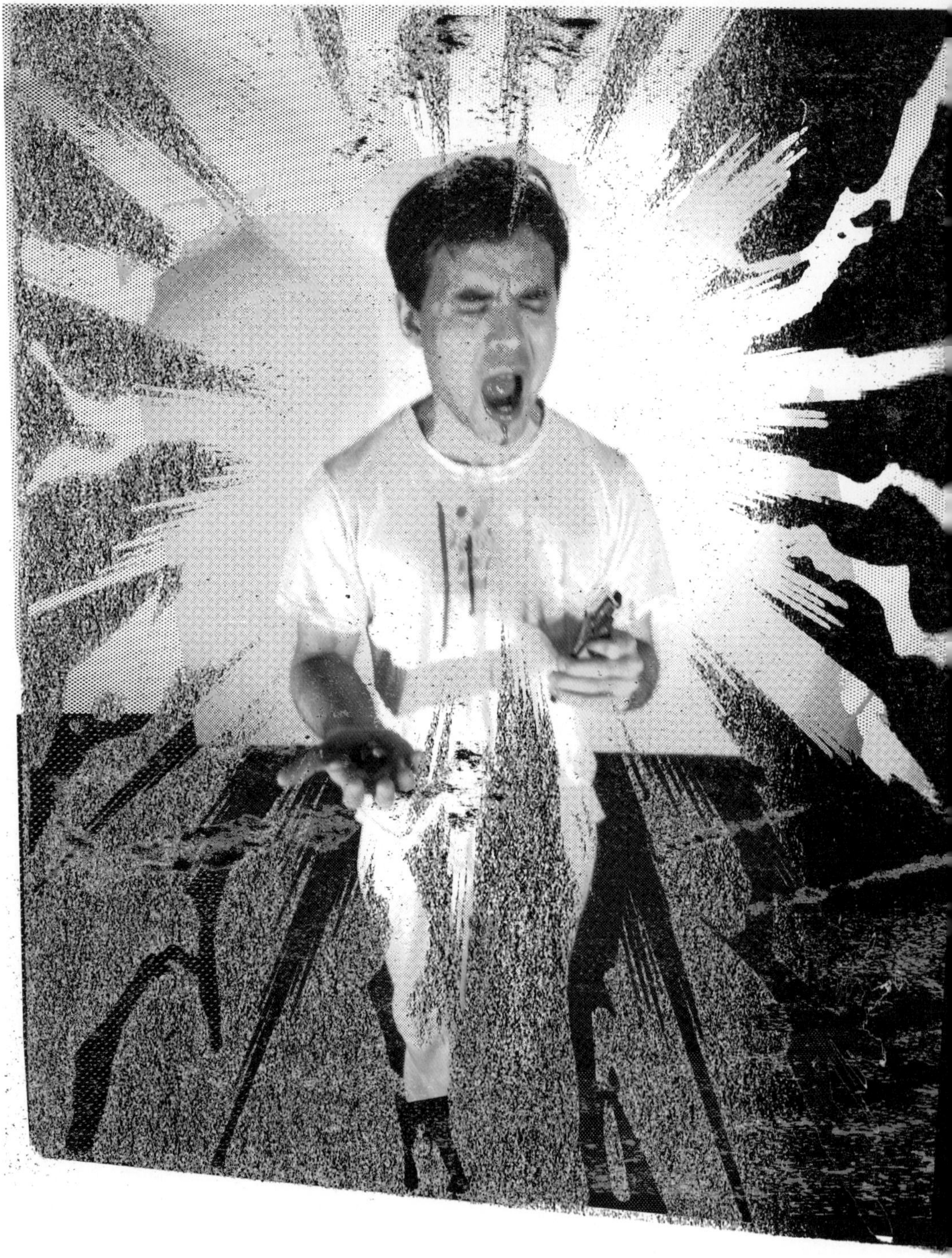

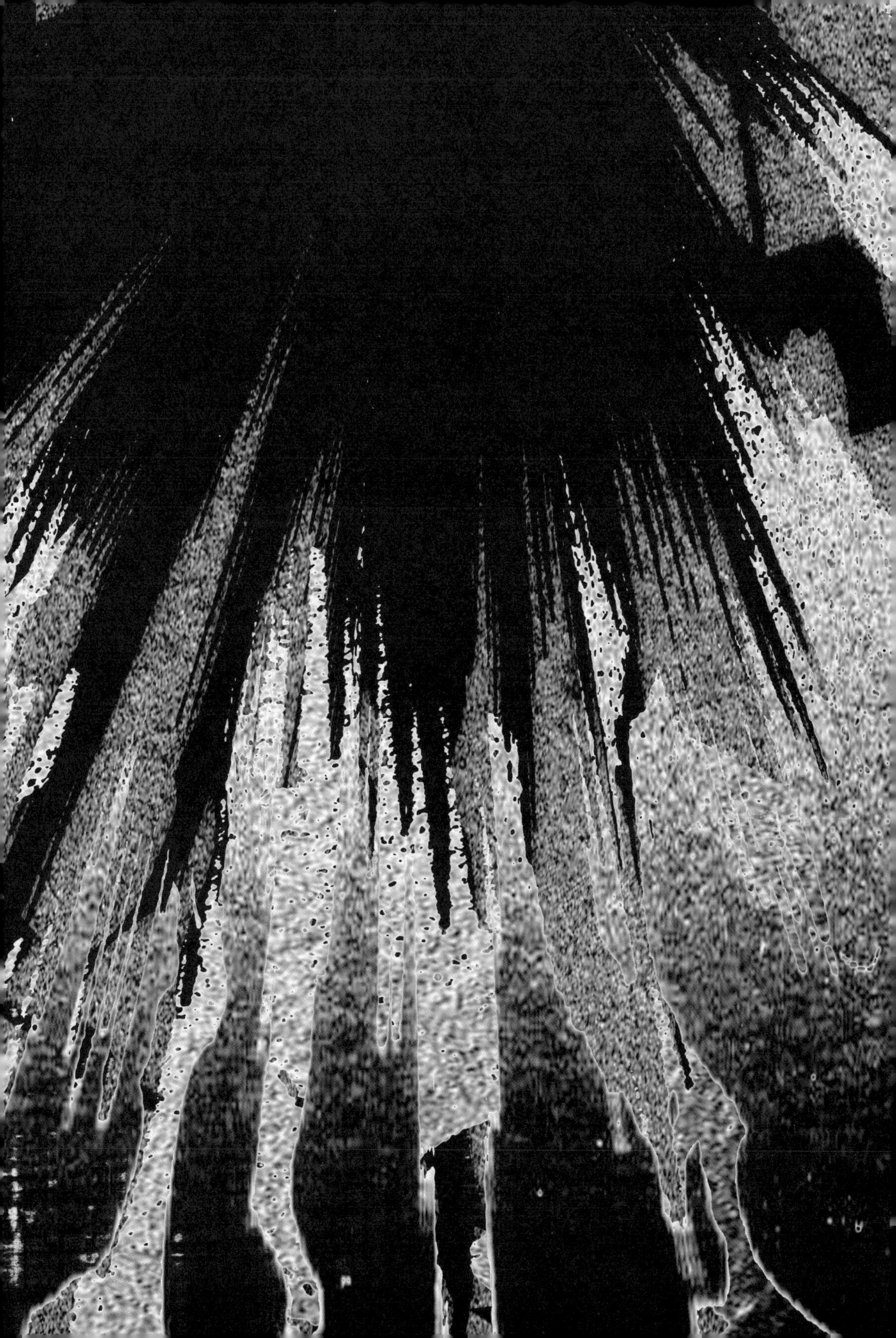

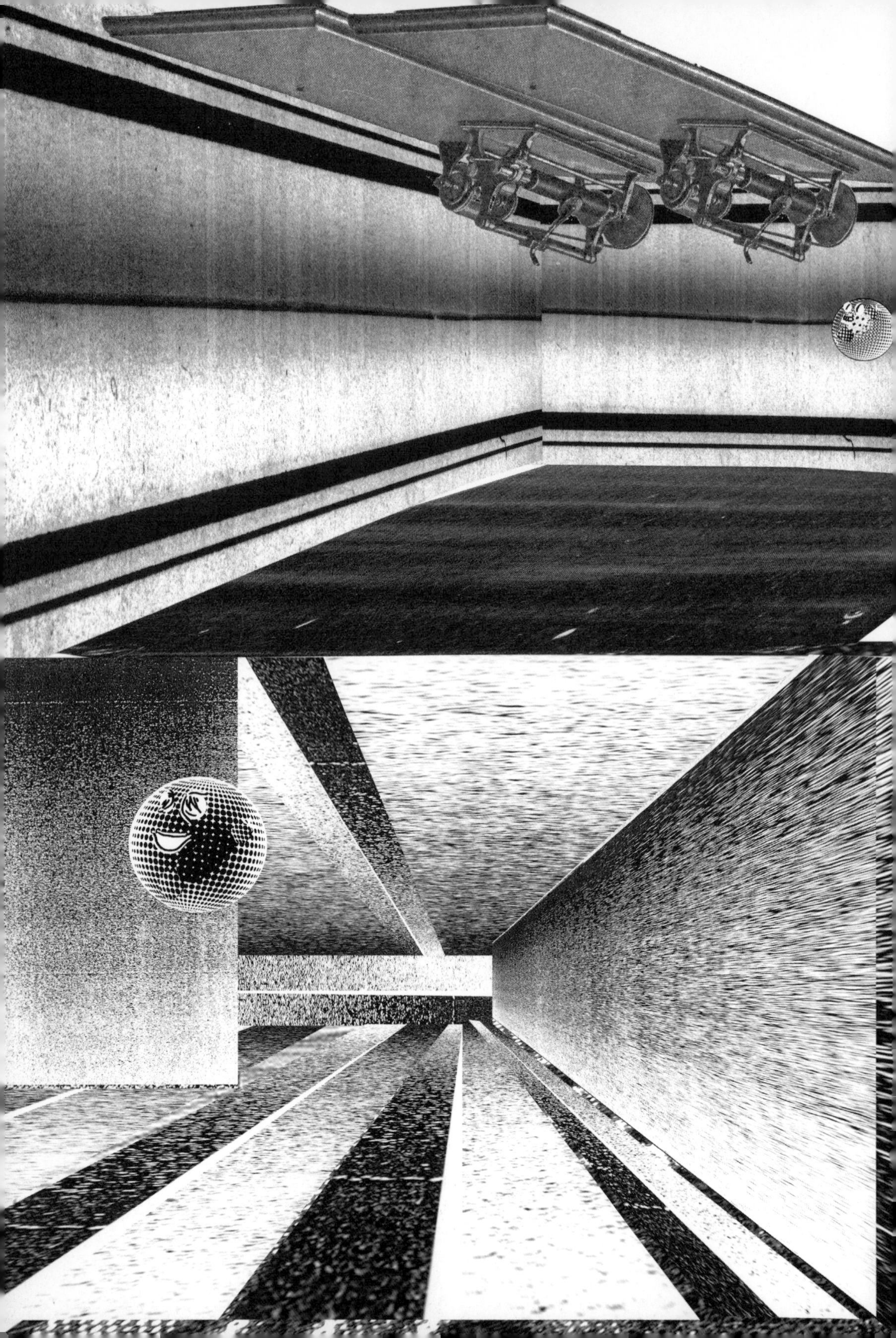

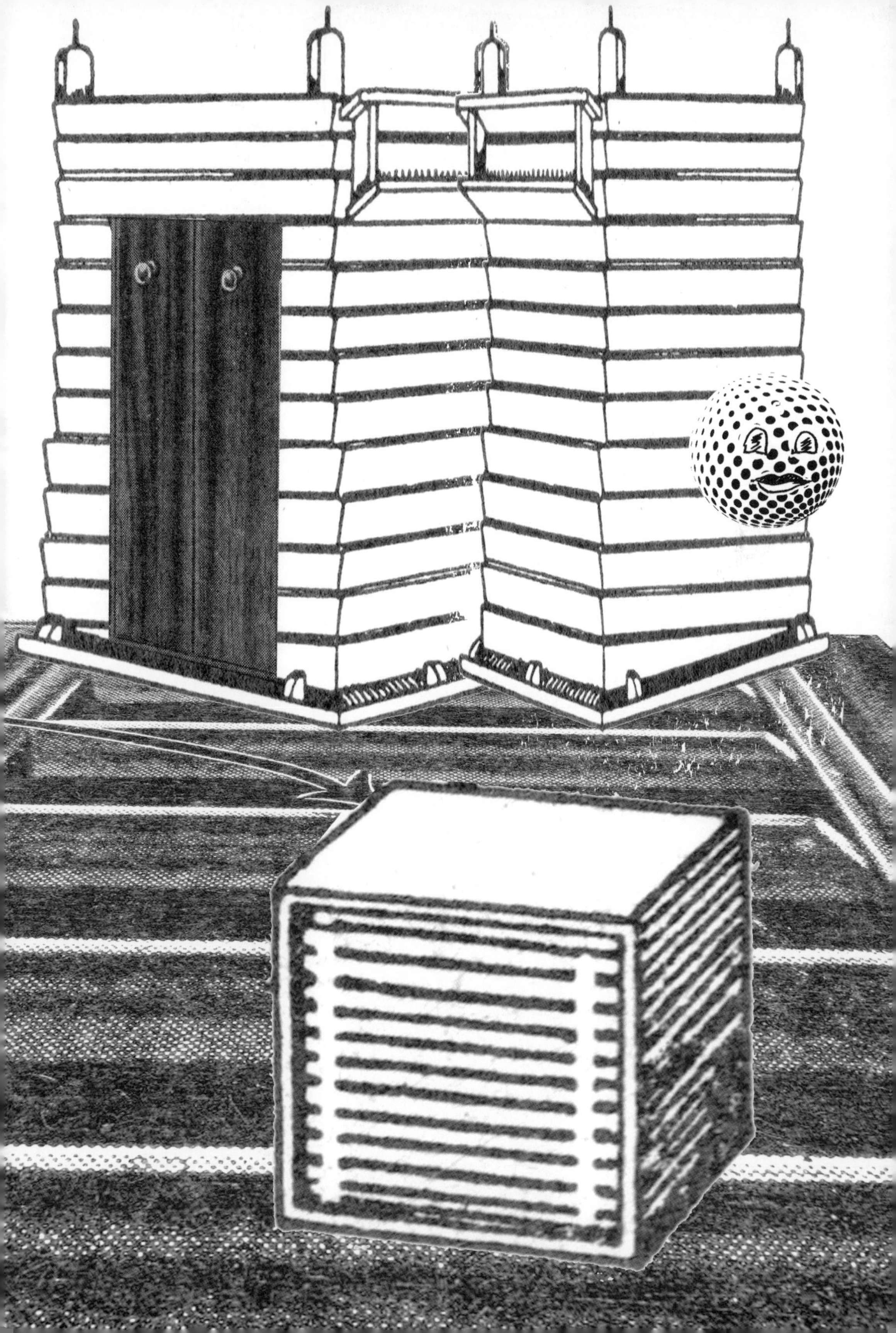

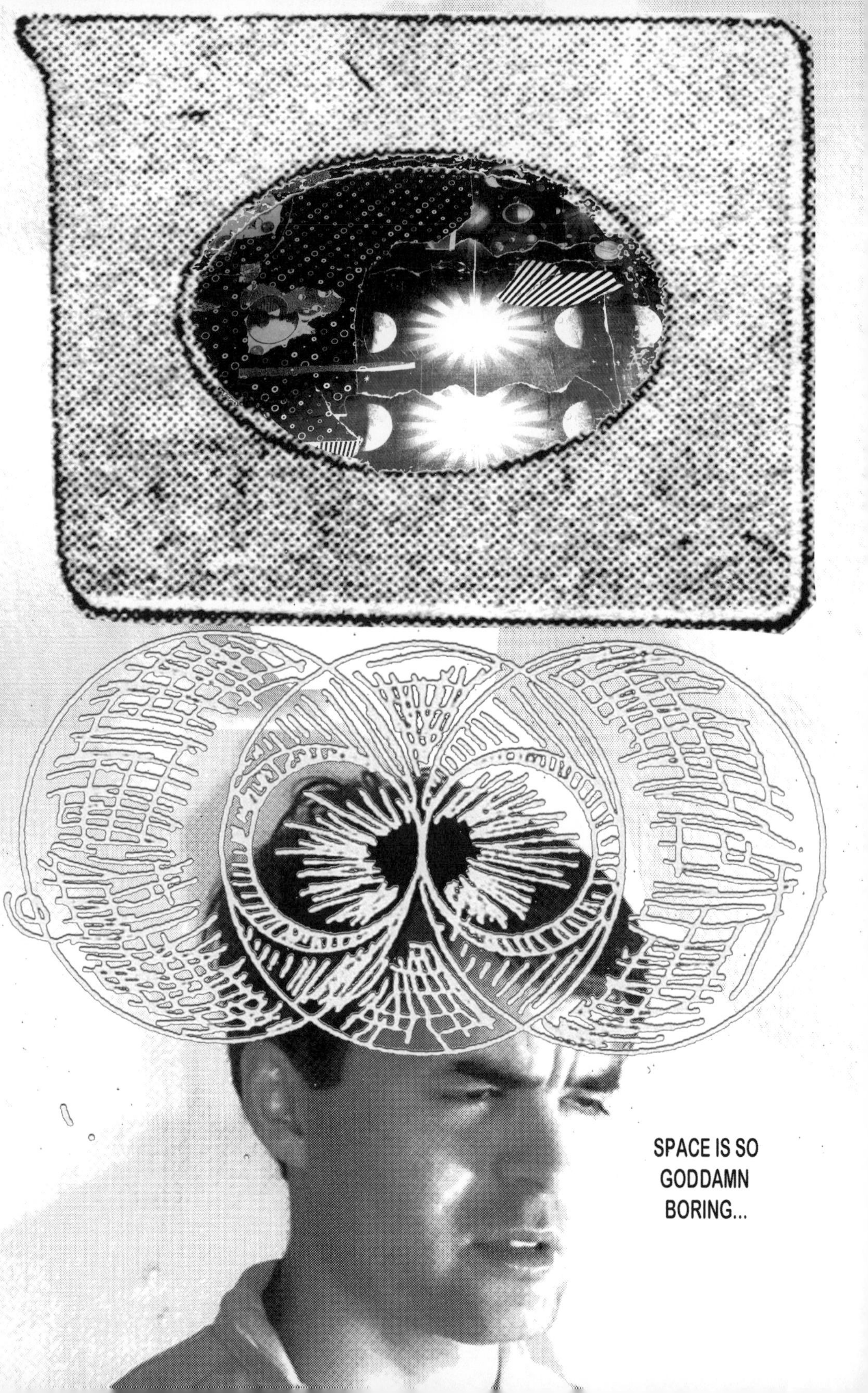
SPACE IS SO GODDAMN BORING...

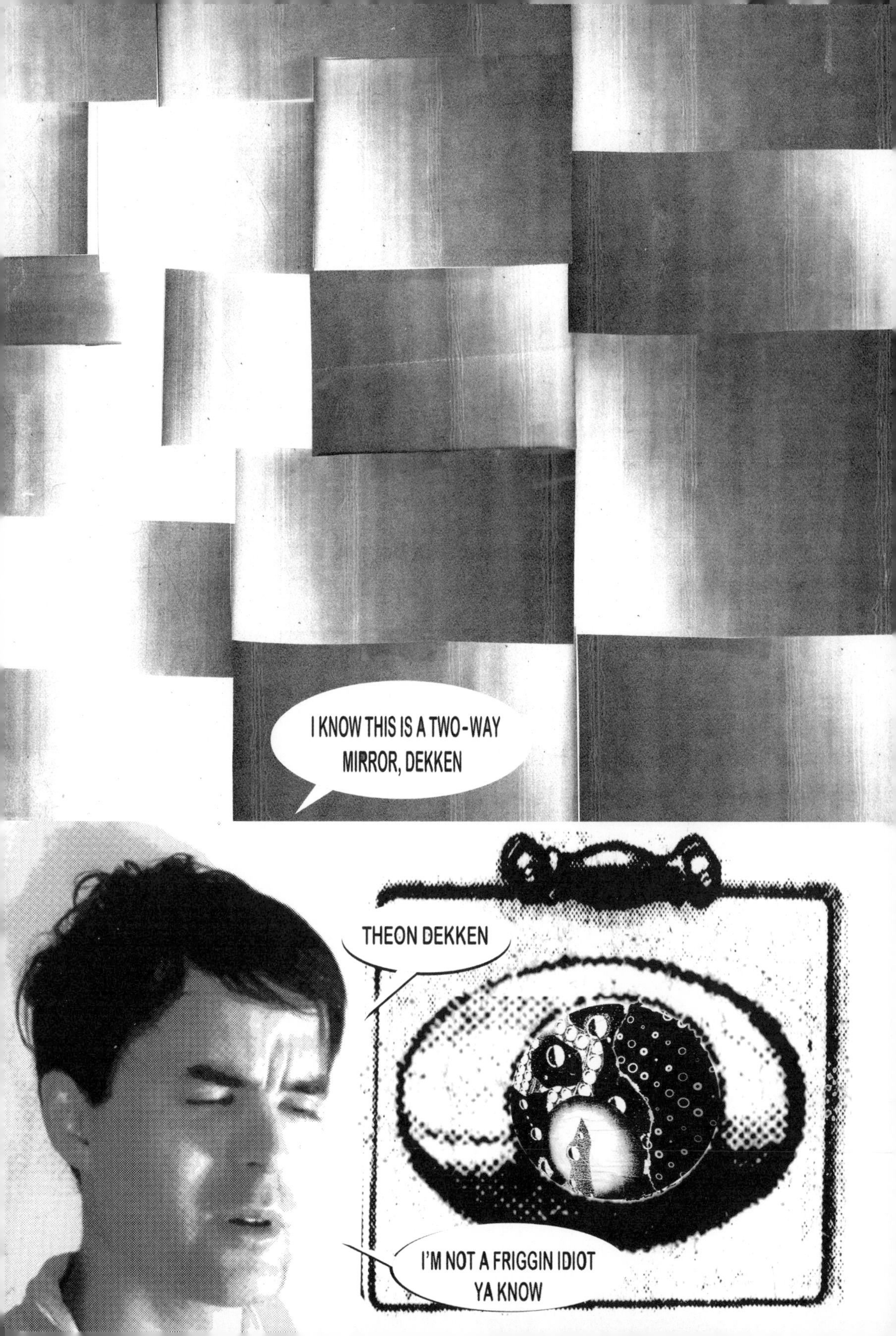
I KNOW THIS IS A TWO-WAY
MIRROR, DEKKEN
THEON DEKKEN
I'M NOT A FRIGGIN IDIOT
YA KNOW

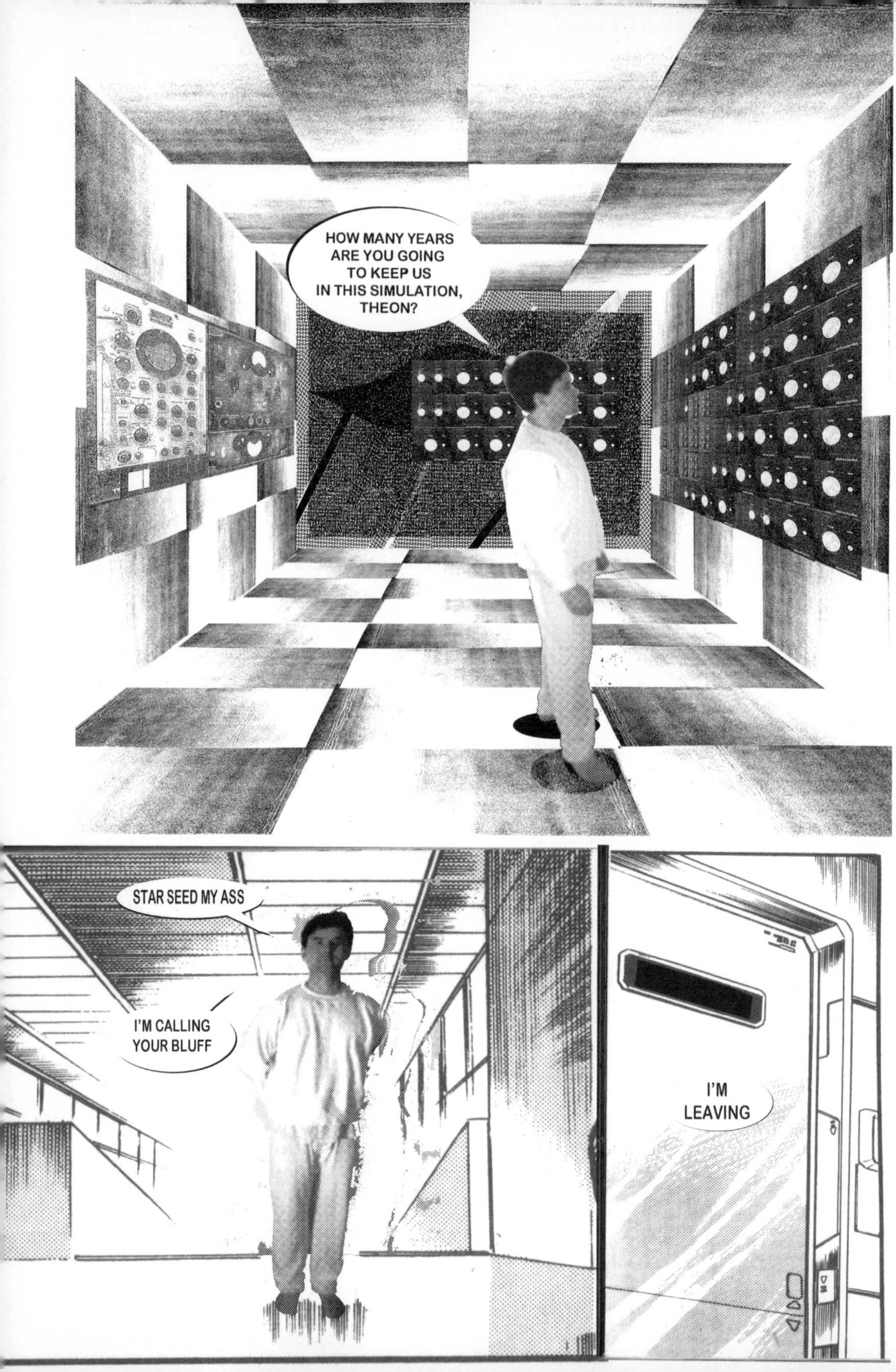
HOW MANY YEARS ARE YOU GOING TO KEEP US IN THIS SIMULATION, THEON?
STAR SEED MY ASS
I'M CALLING YOUR BLUFF
I'M LEAVING

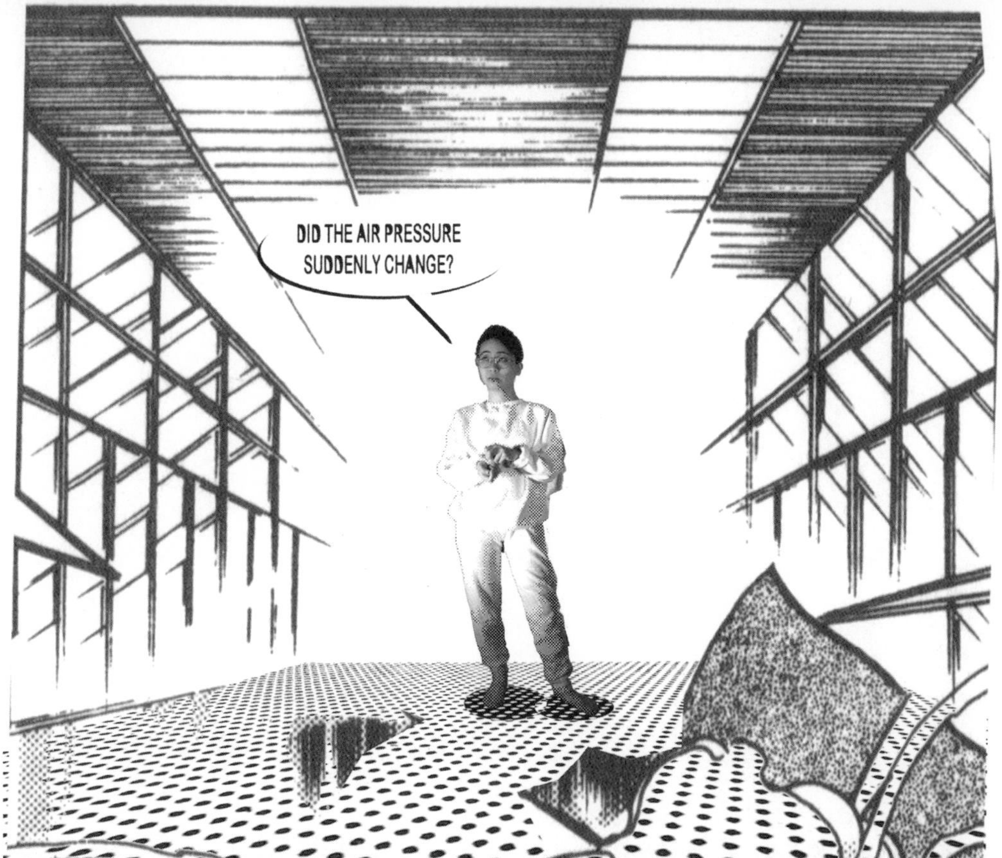
DID THE AIR PRESSURE
SUDDENLY CHANGE?

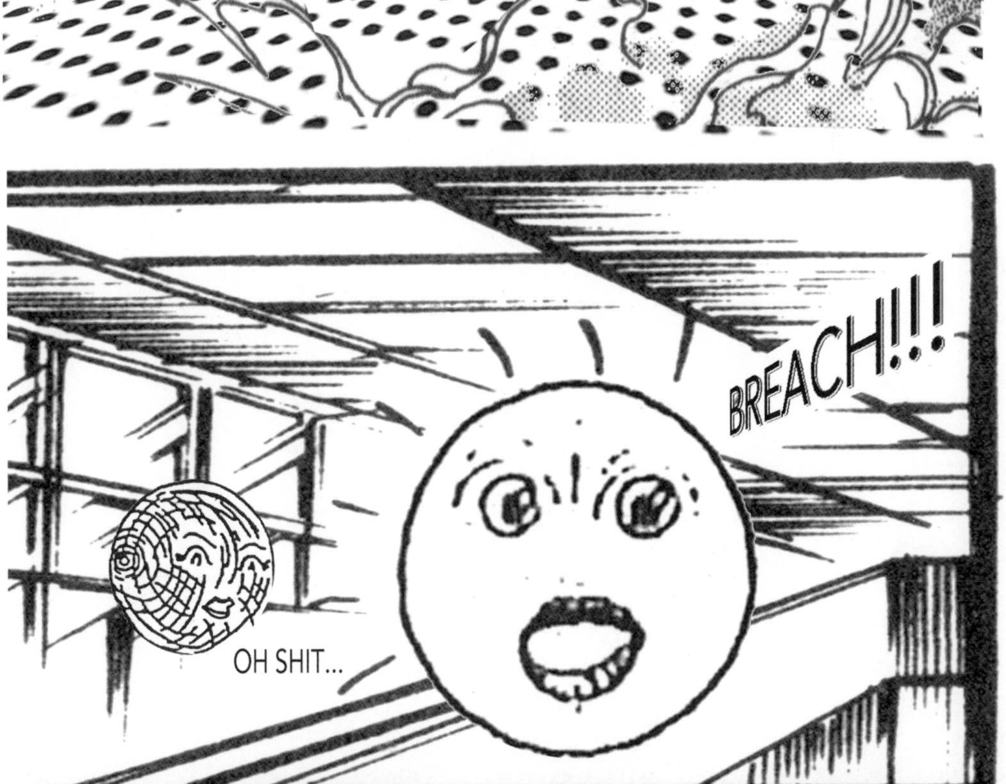
BREACH!!!
OH SHIT...

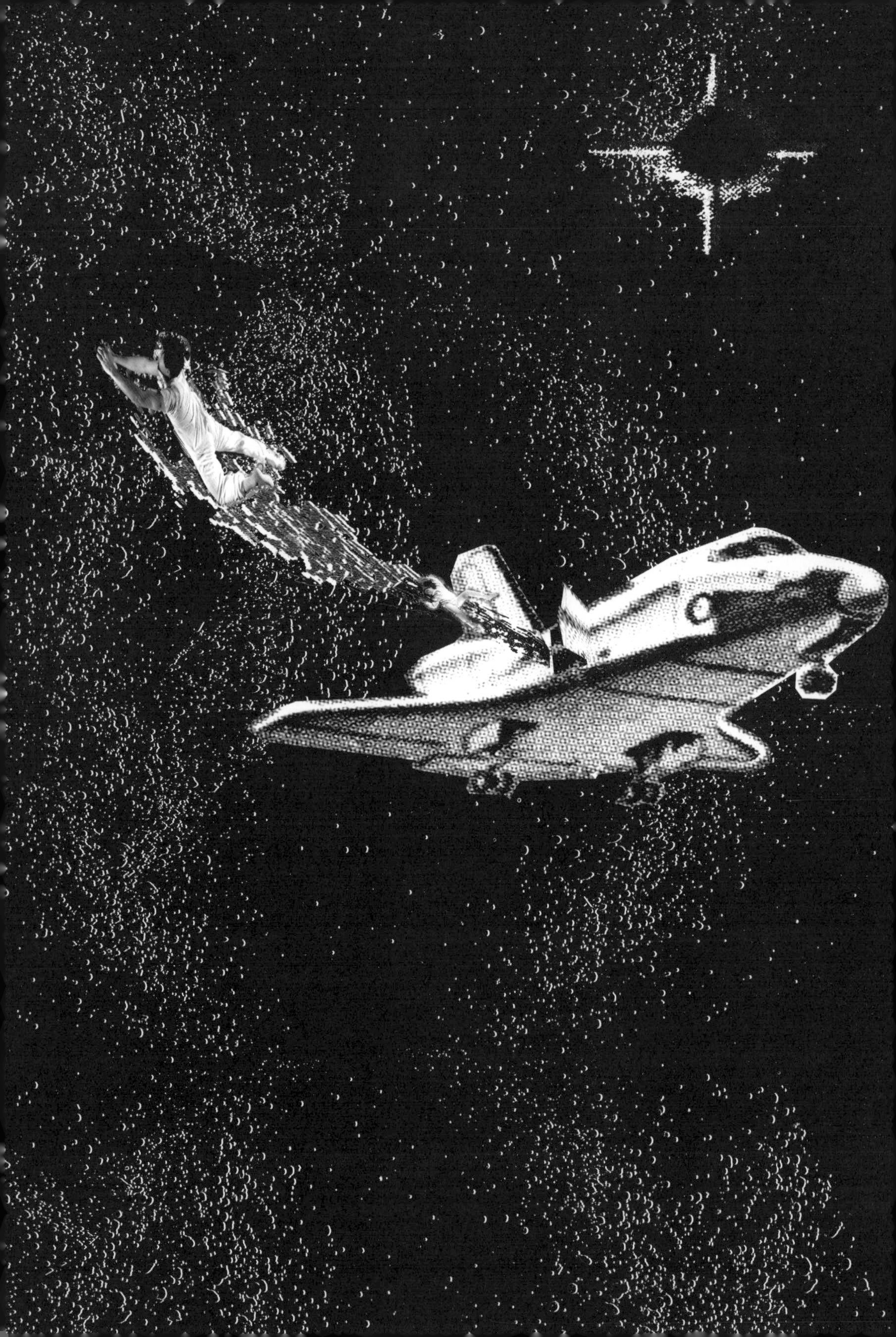

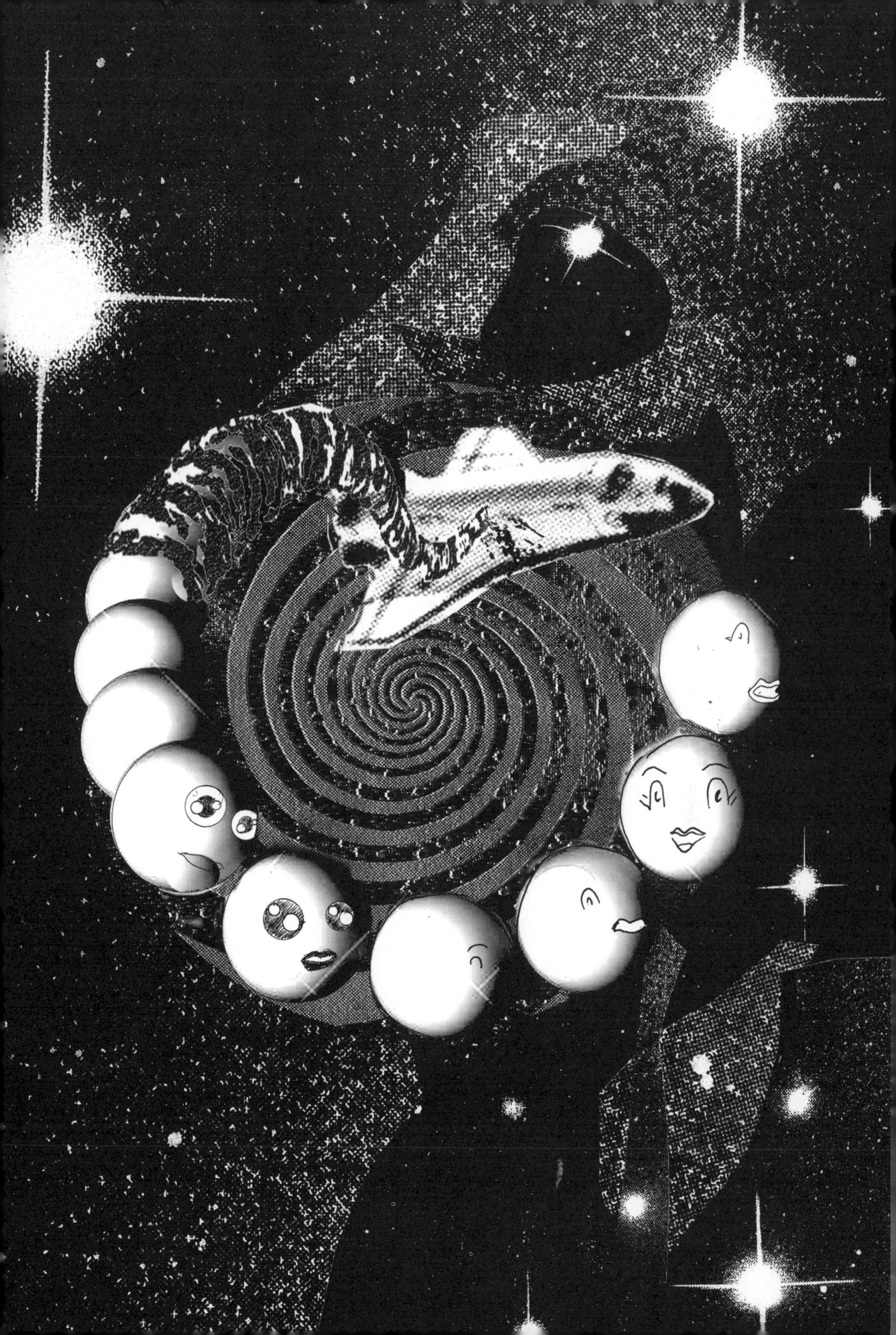

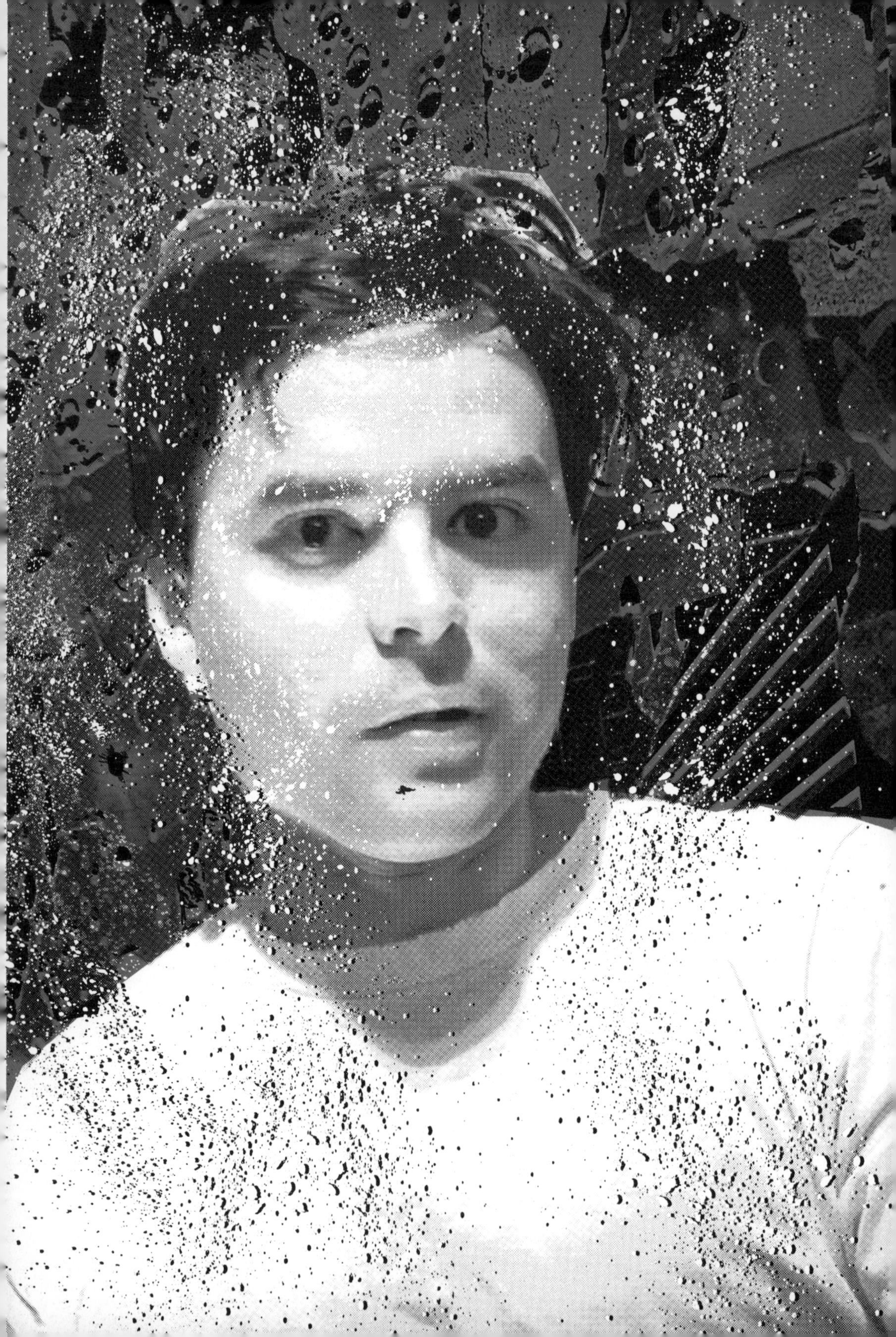

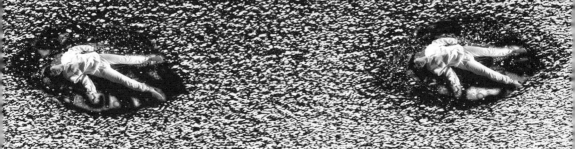

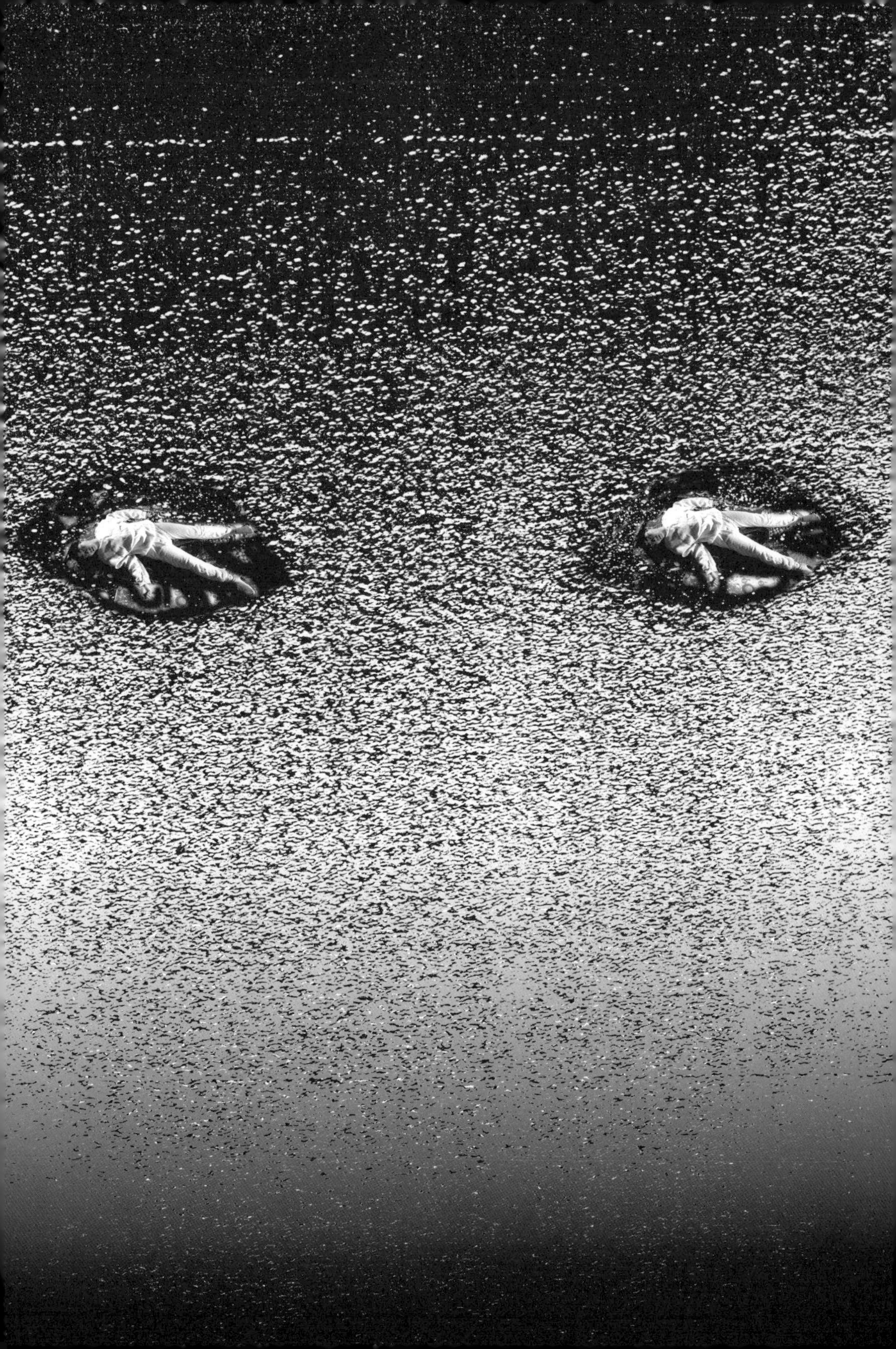

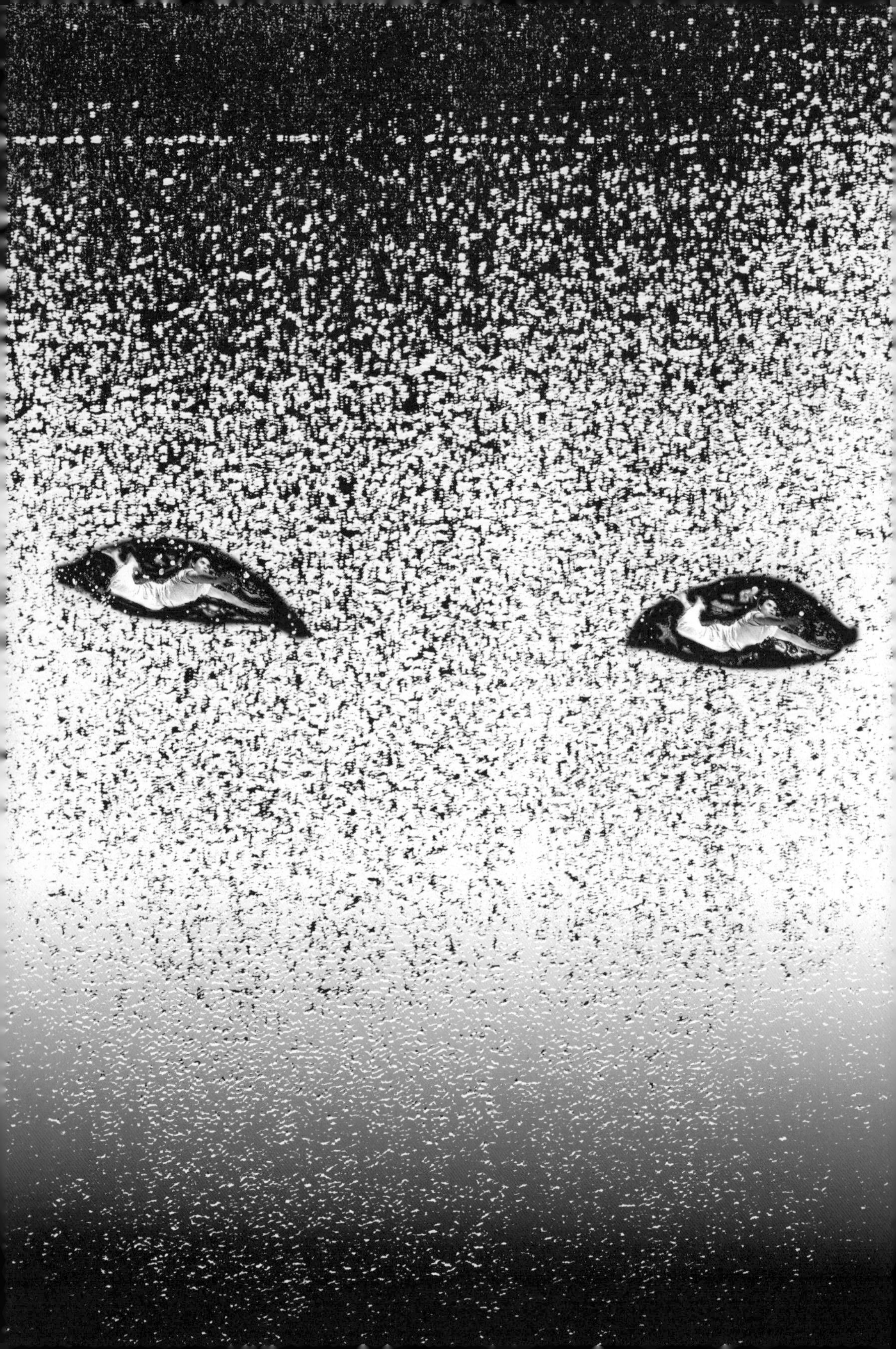

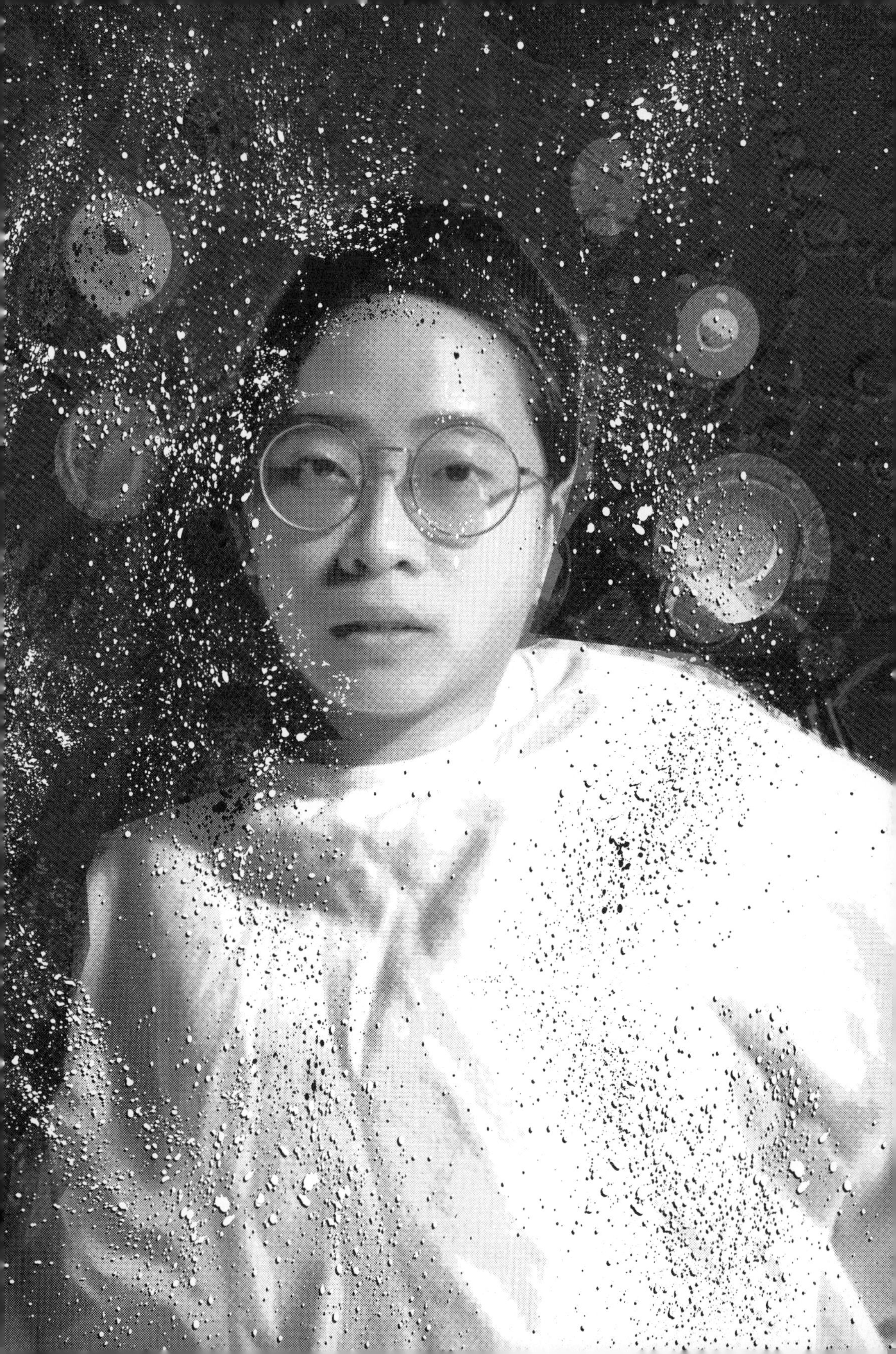

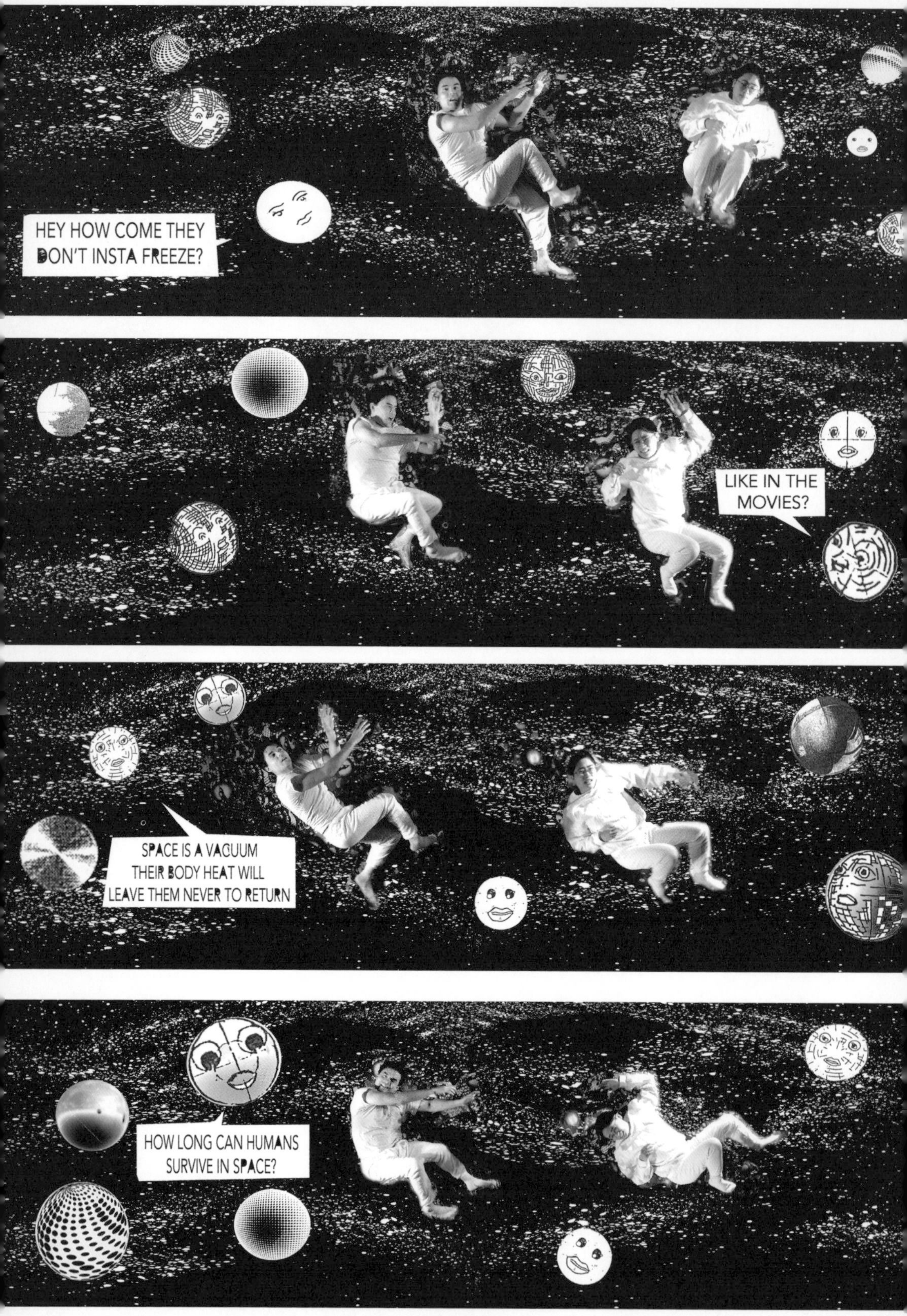
HEY HOW COME THEY DON'T INSTA FREEZE?
LIKE IN THE MOVIES?
SPACE IS A VACUUM THEIR BODY HEAT WILL LEAVE THEM NEVER TO RETURN
HOW LONG CAN HUMANS SURVIVE IN SPACE?

MAYBE 1 TO 3 MINUTES
BUT THEY HAVE BRAIN ACTIVITY FOR 7 MIN AFTER DEATH
EWWW GROSS

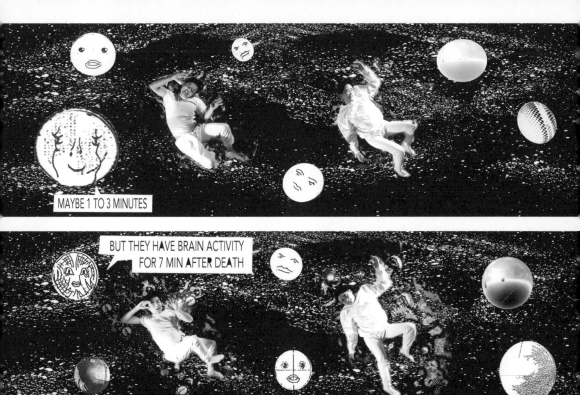

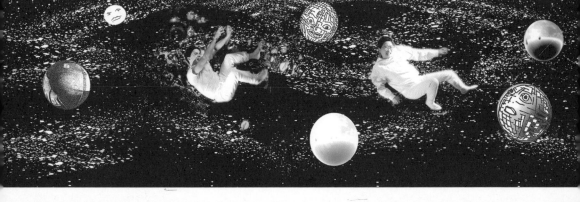

WHAT DO YOU THINK
THEY ARE THINKING ABOUT?
I CAN SPACE BILLIARDS US
TO BECOME CONSTELLATIONS!
UH HUH
WHATEVER...

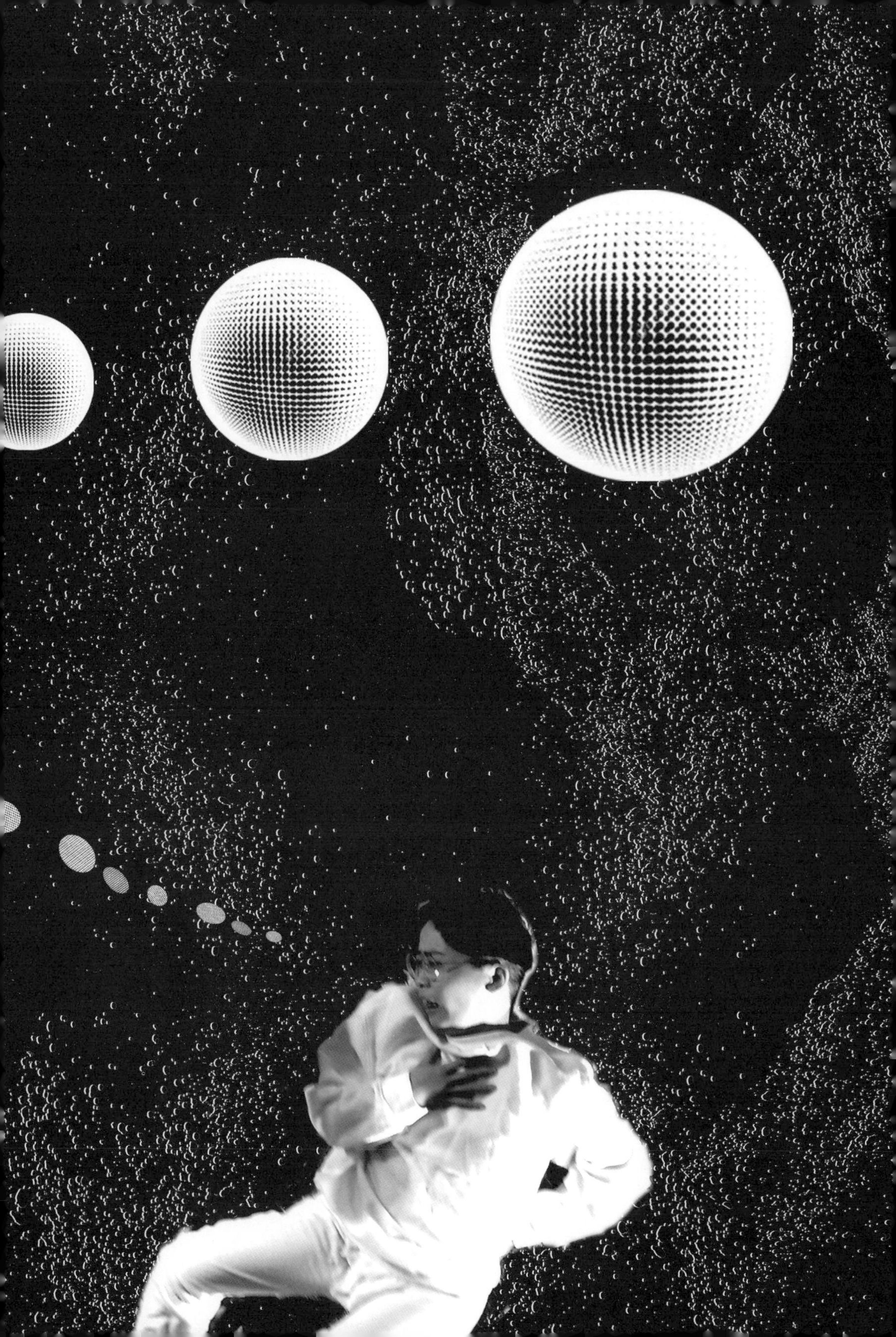

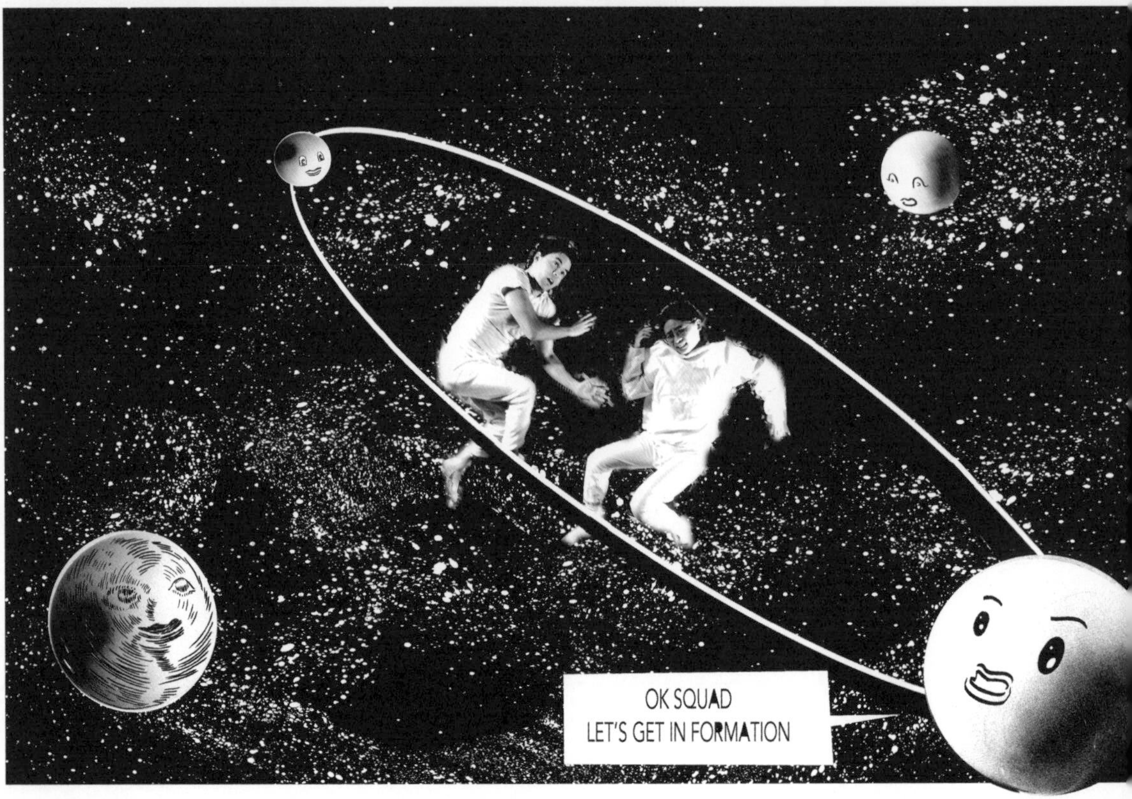
OK SQUAD
LET'S GET IN FORMATION

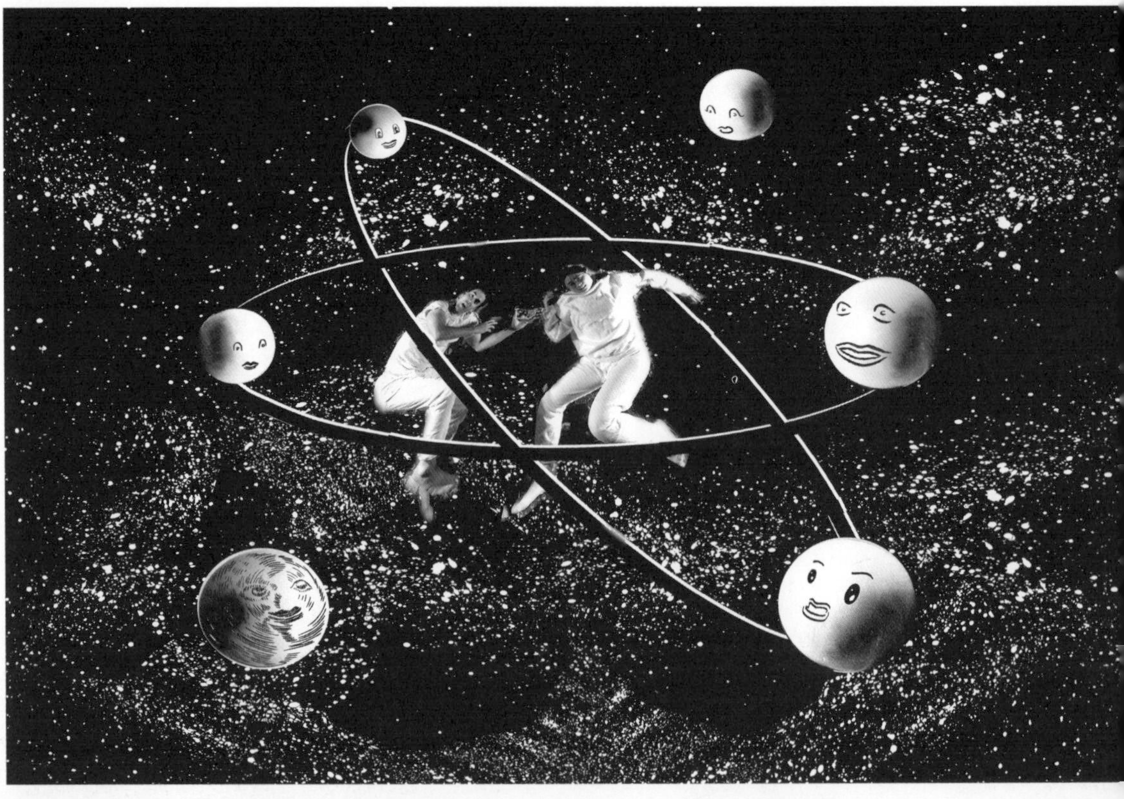

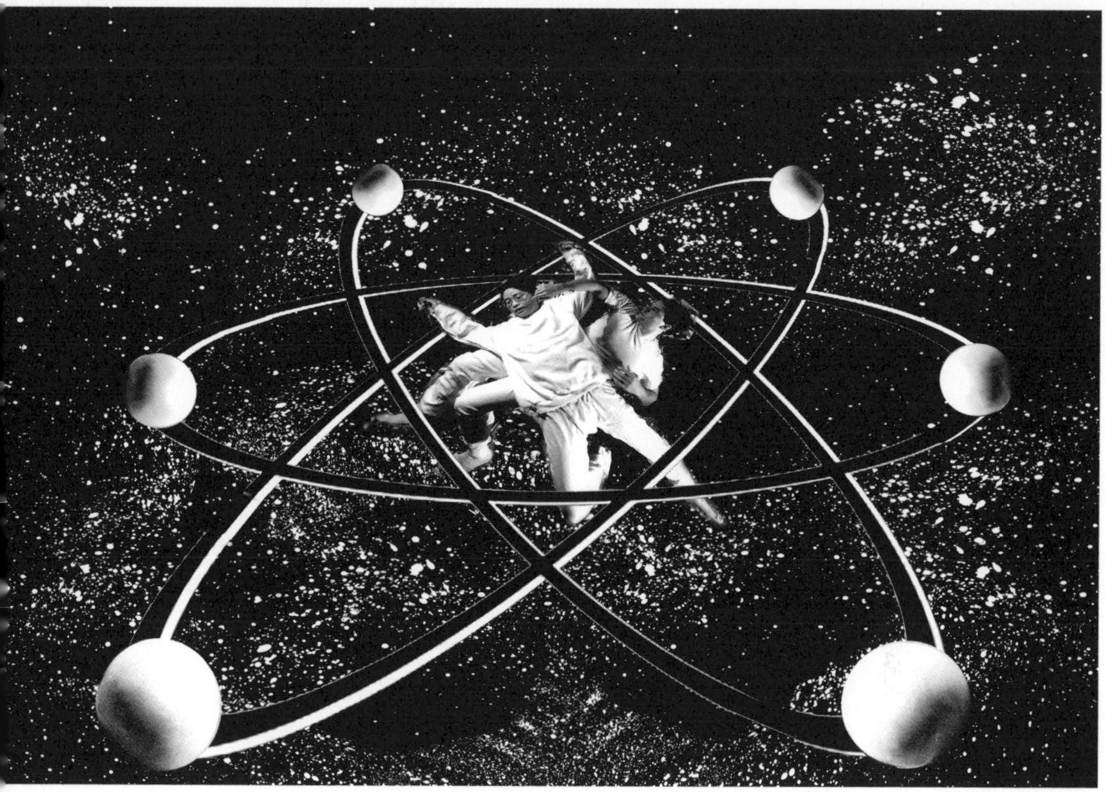

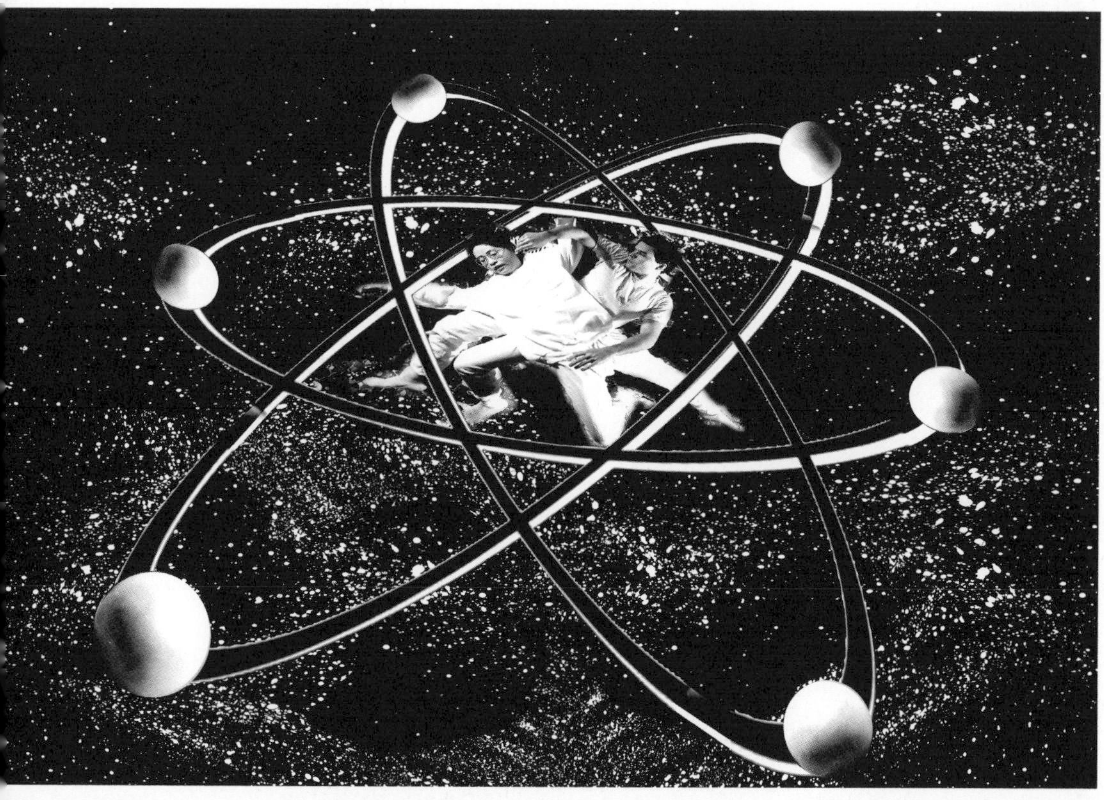

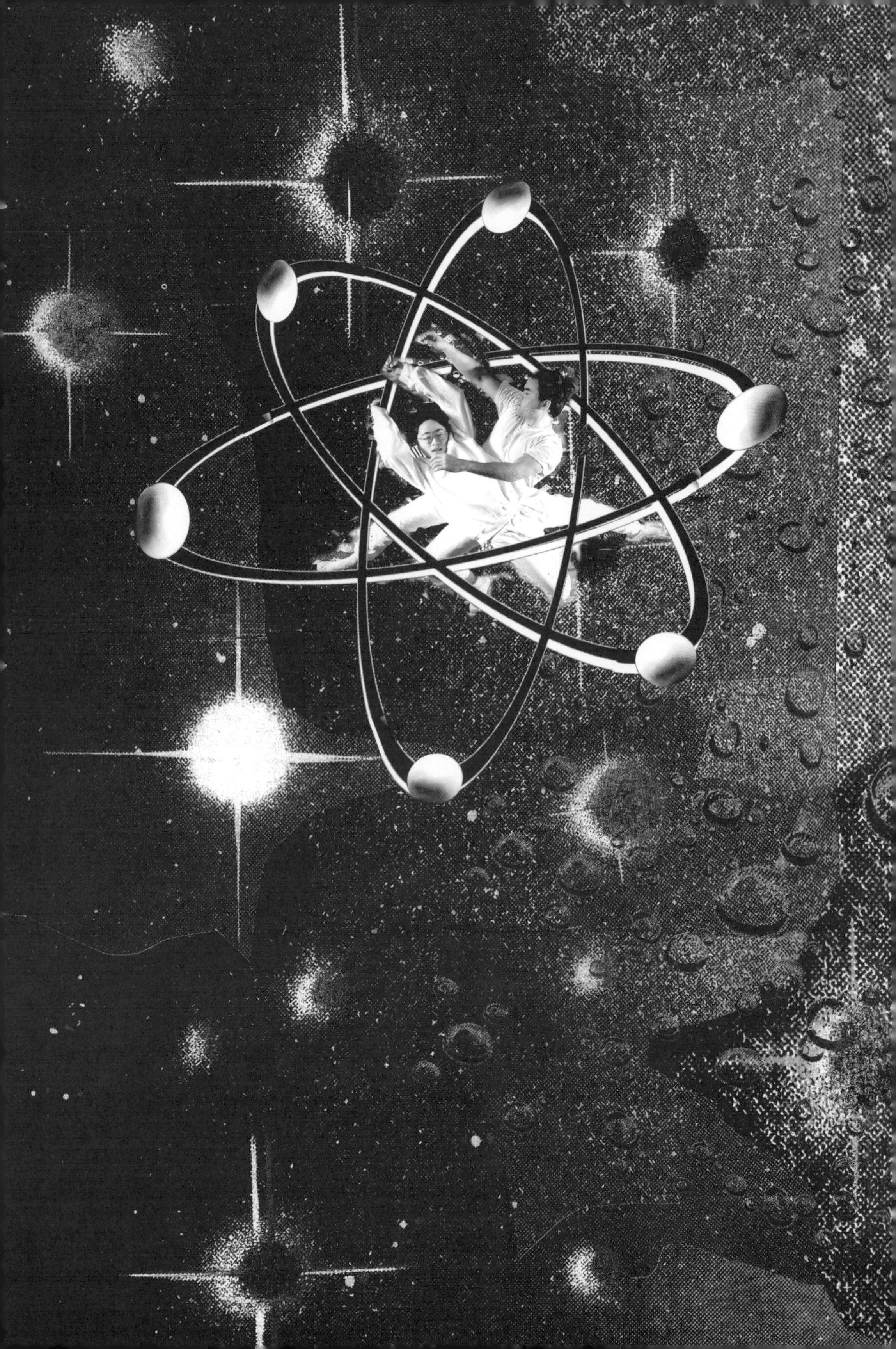

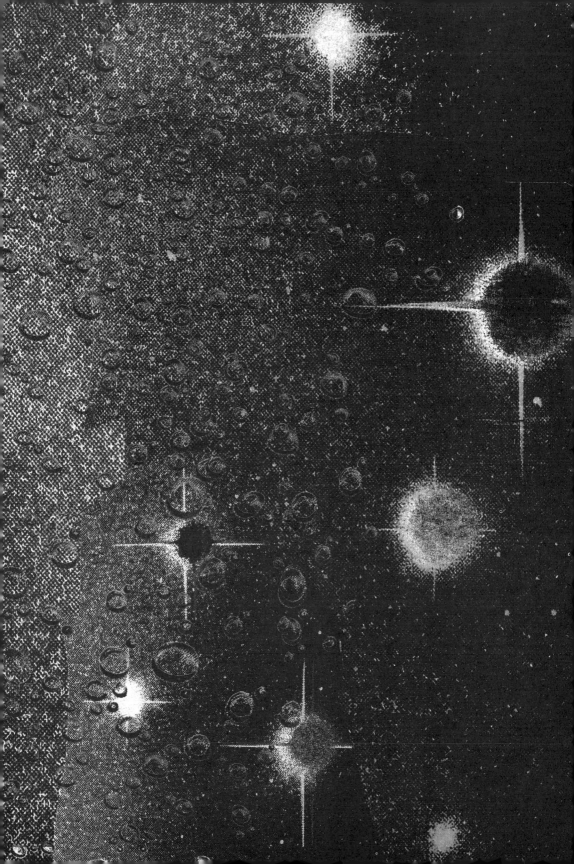

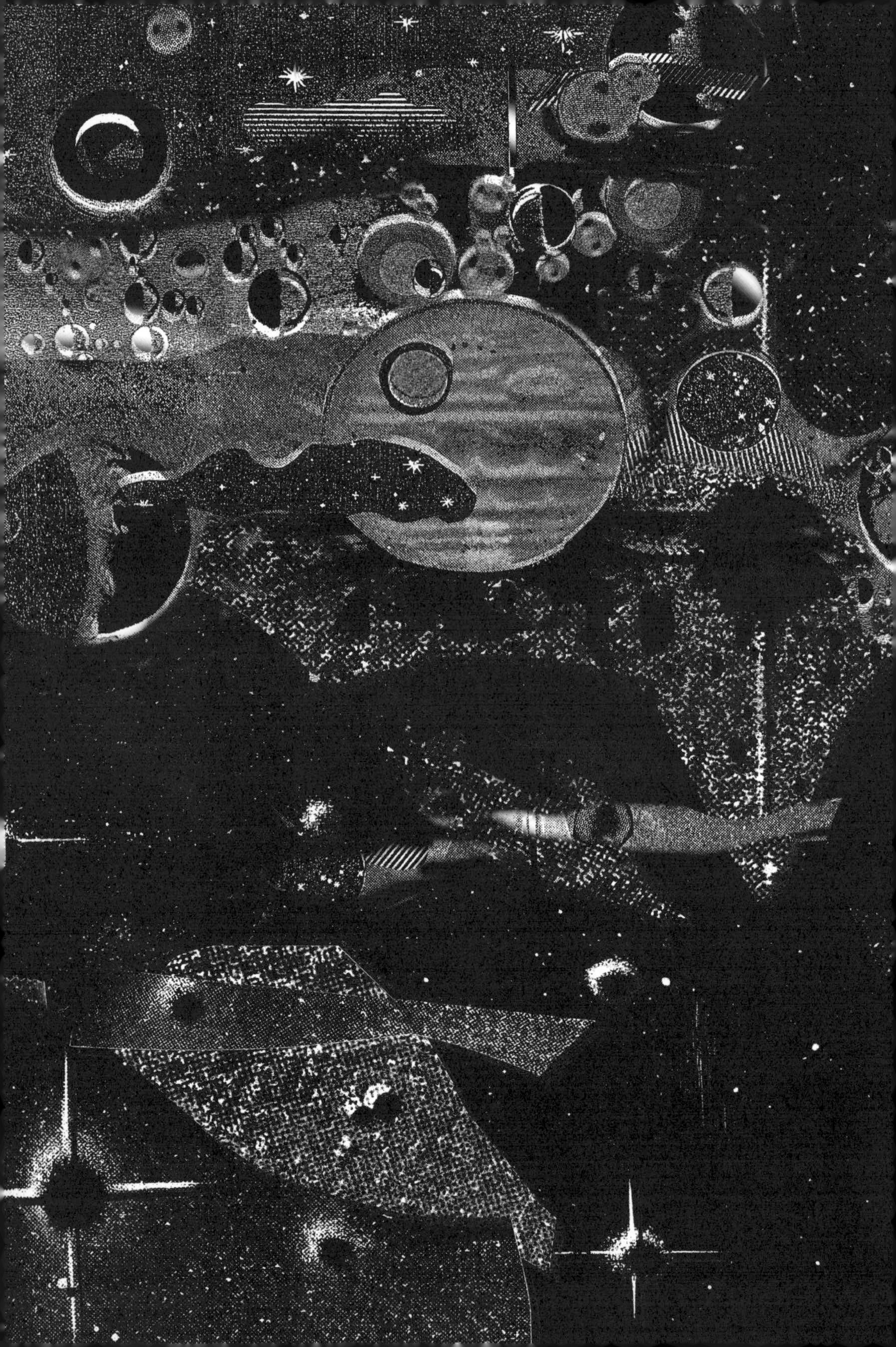

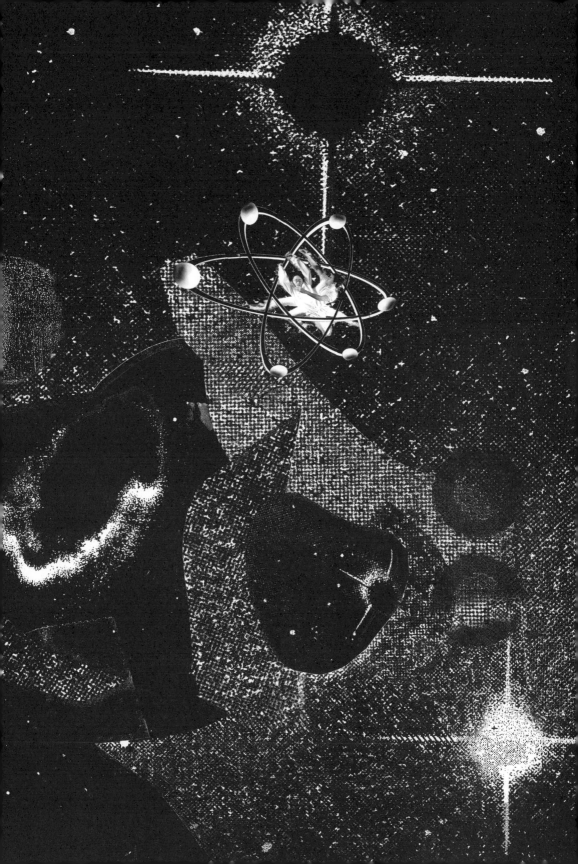

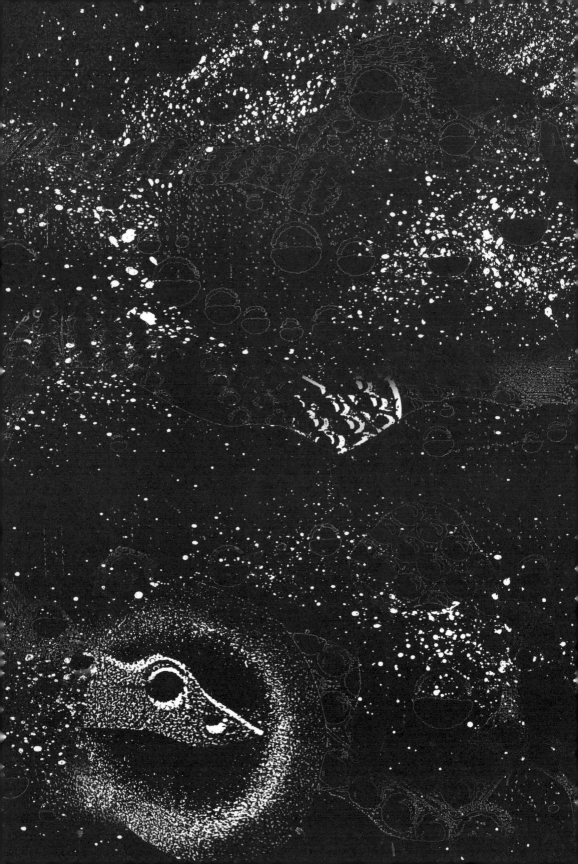

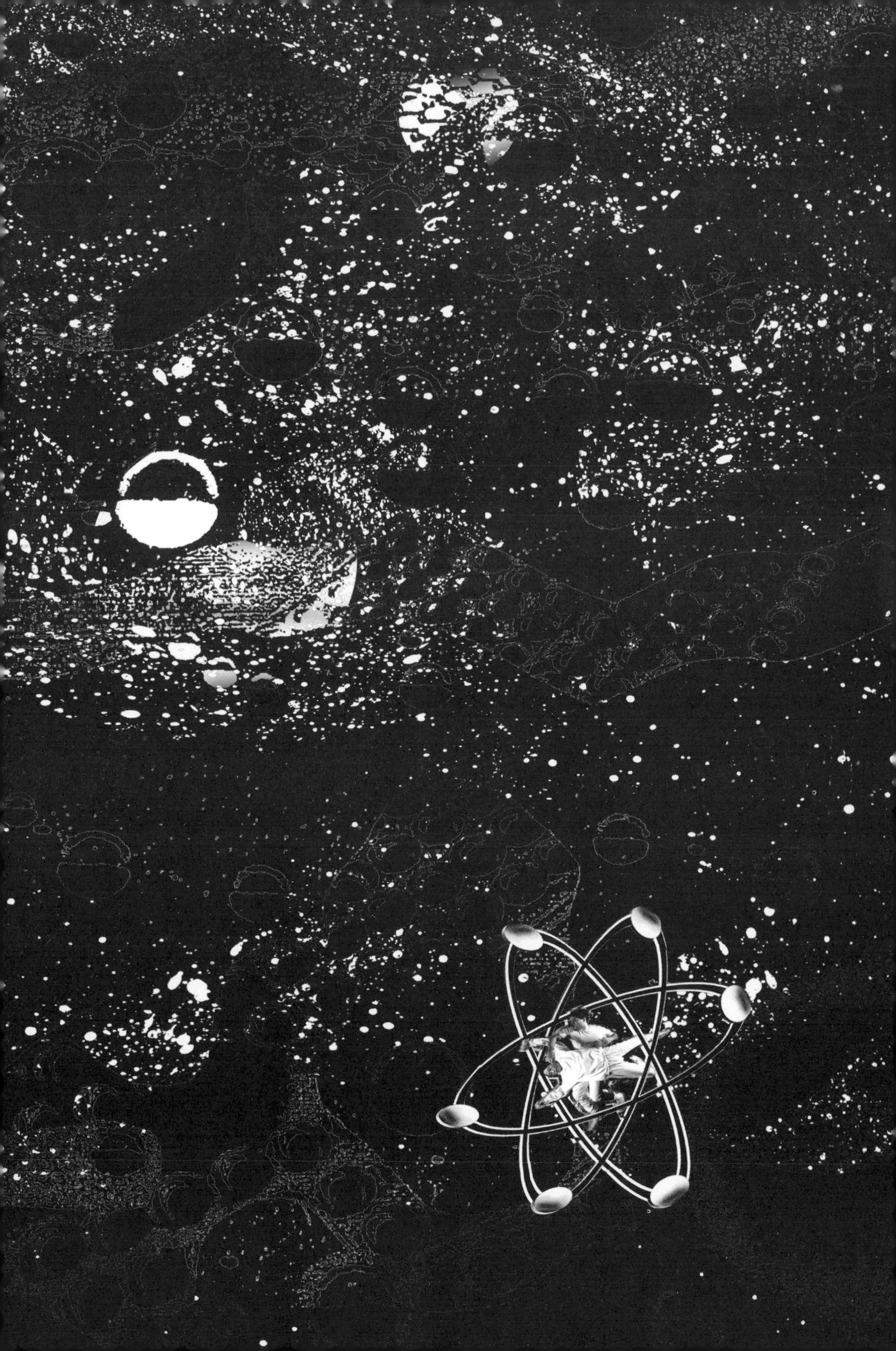

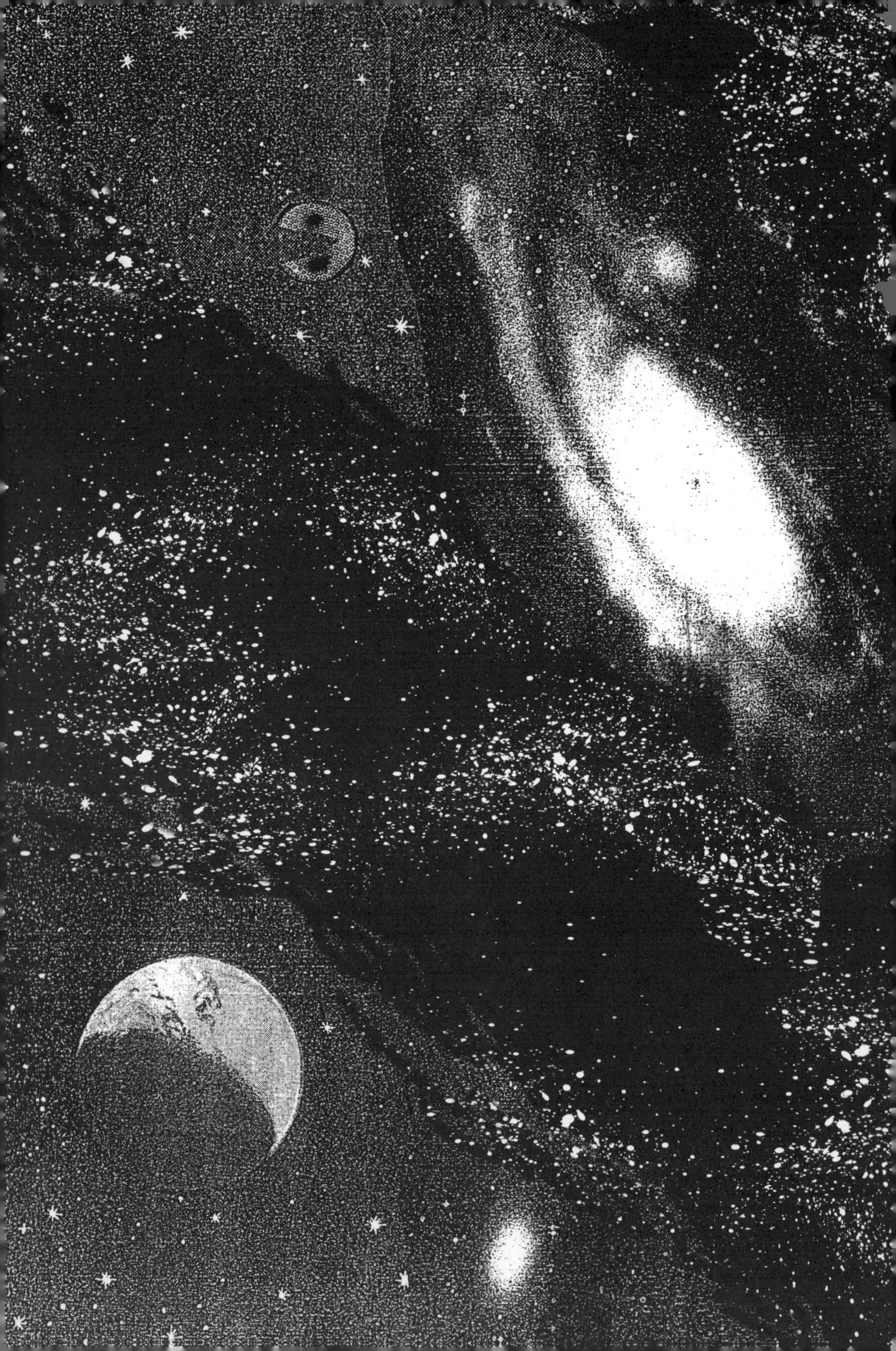

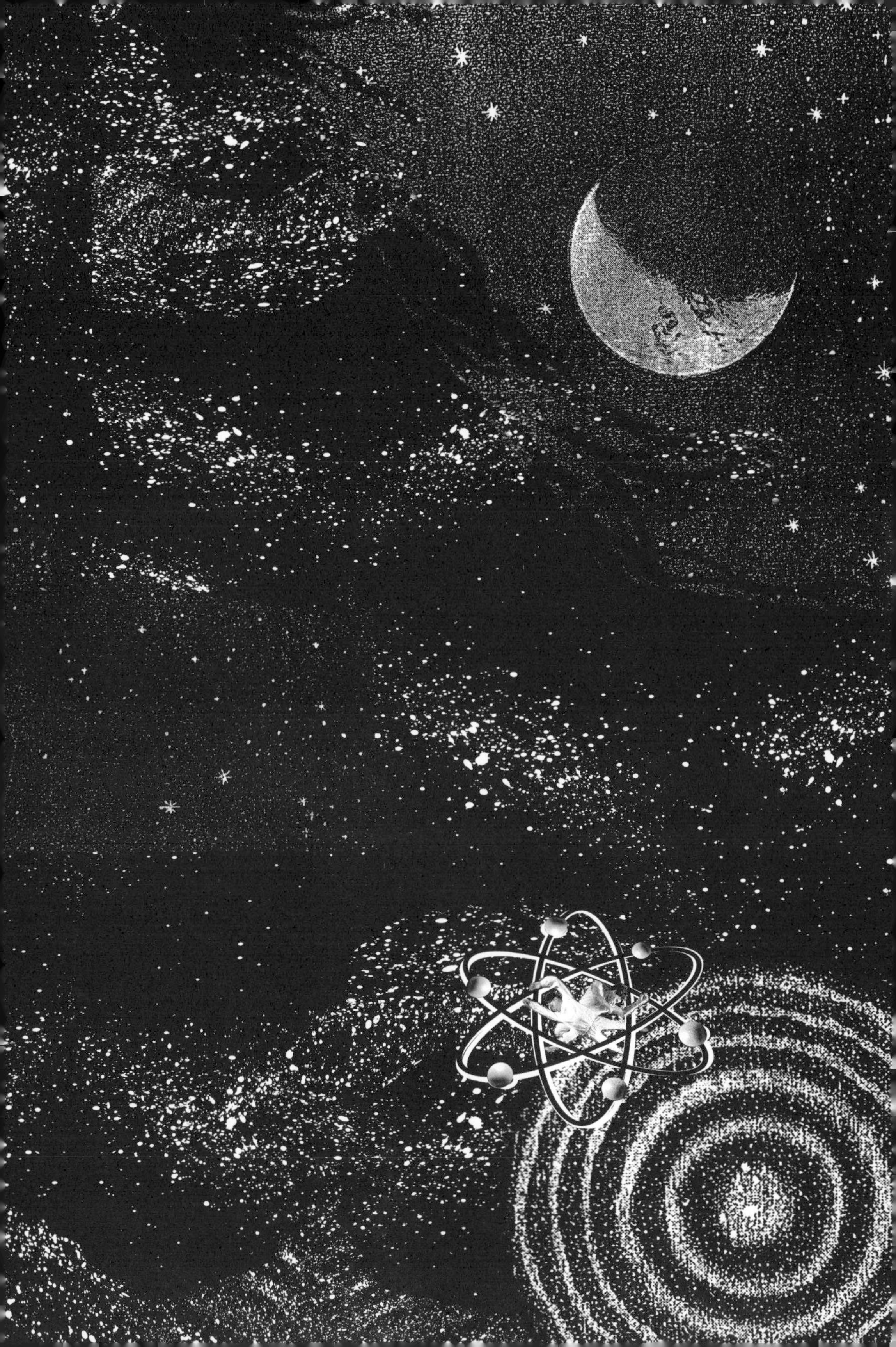

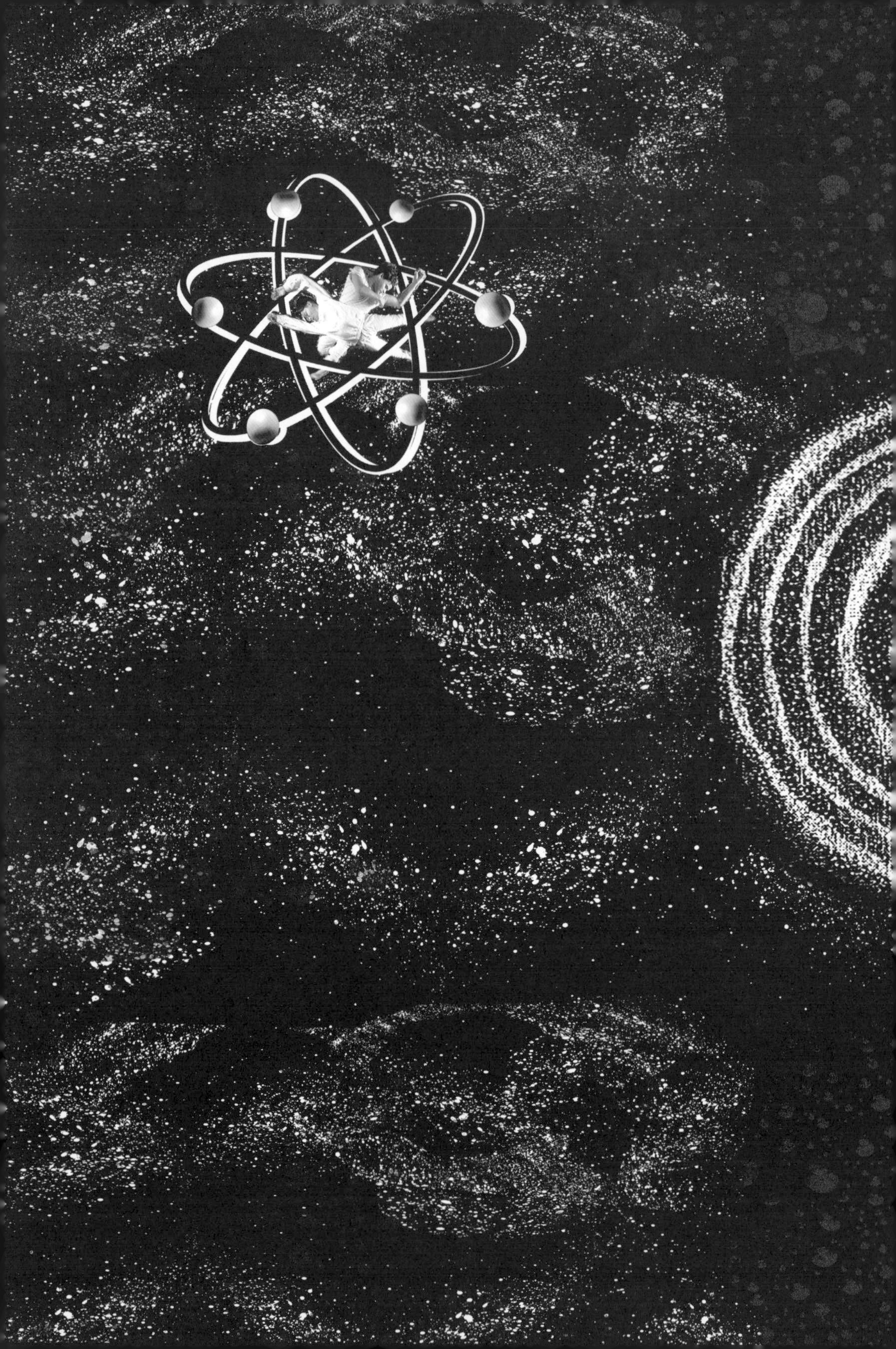

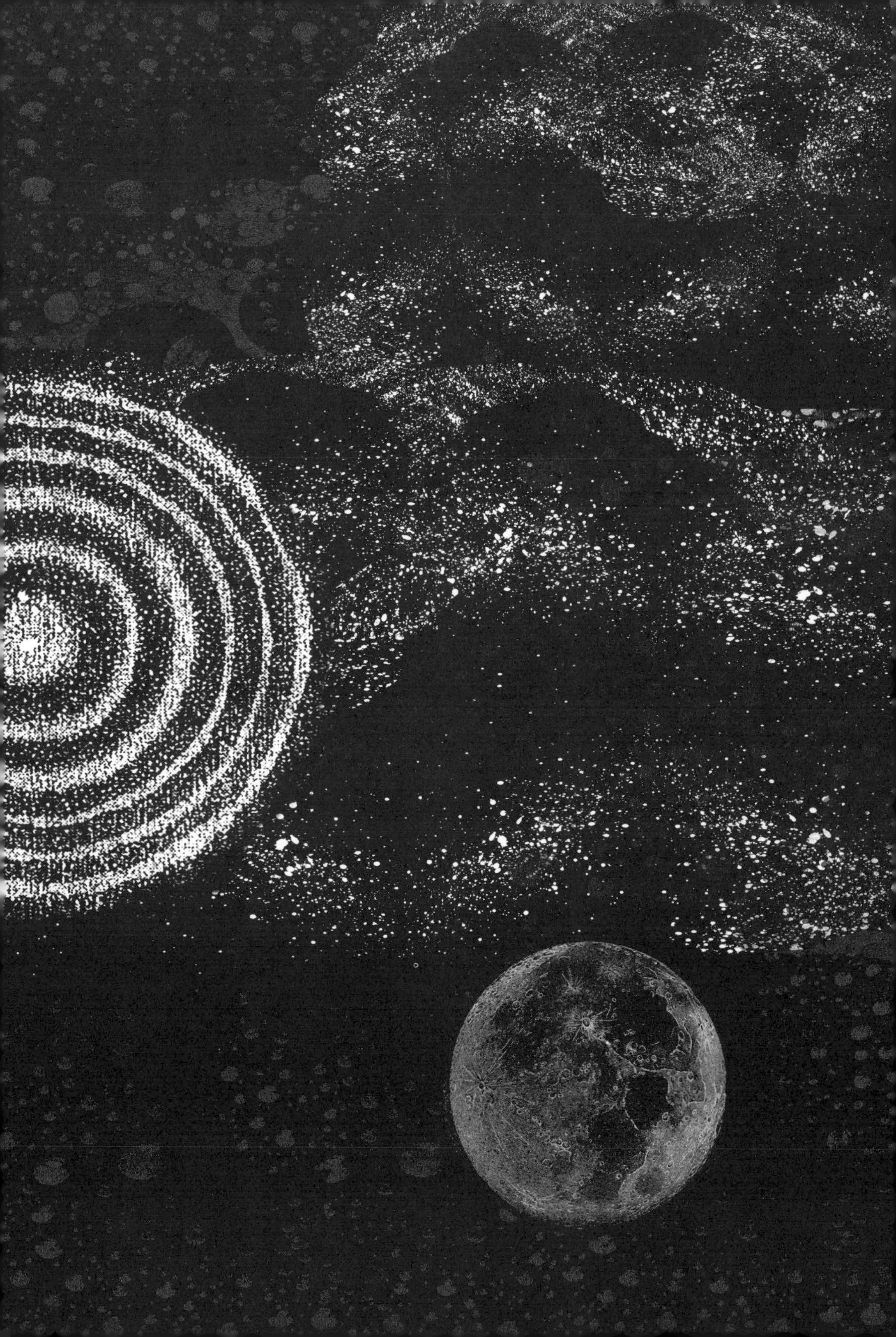

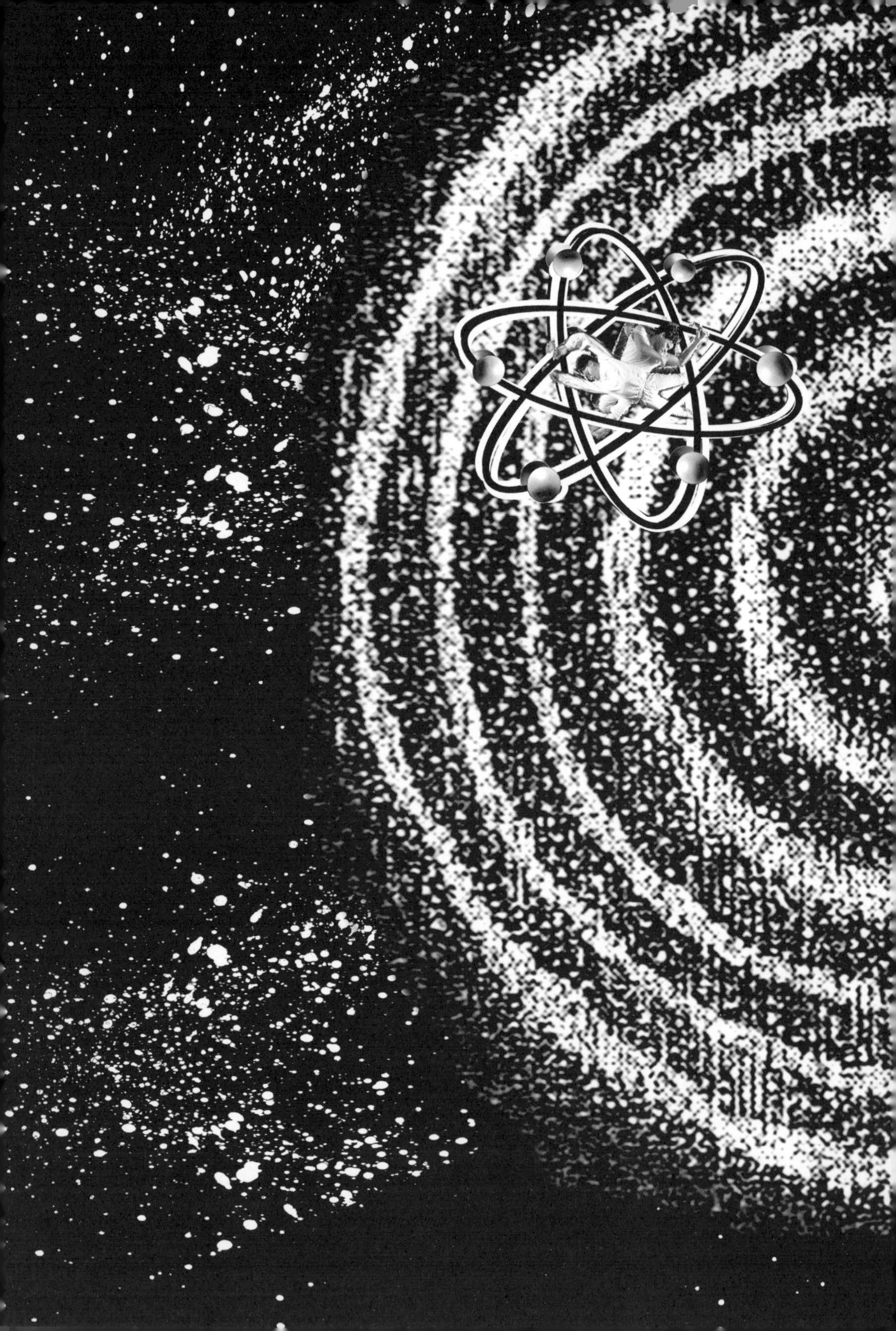

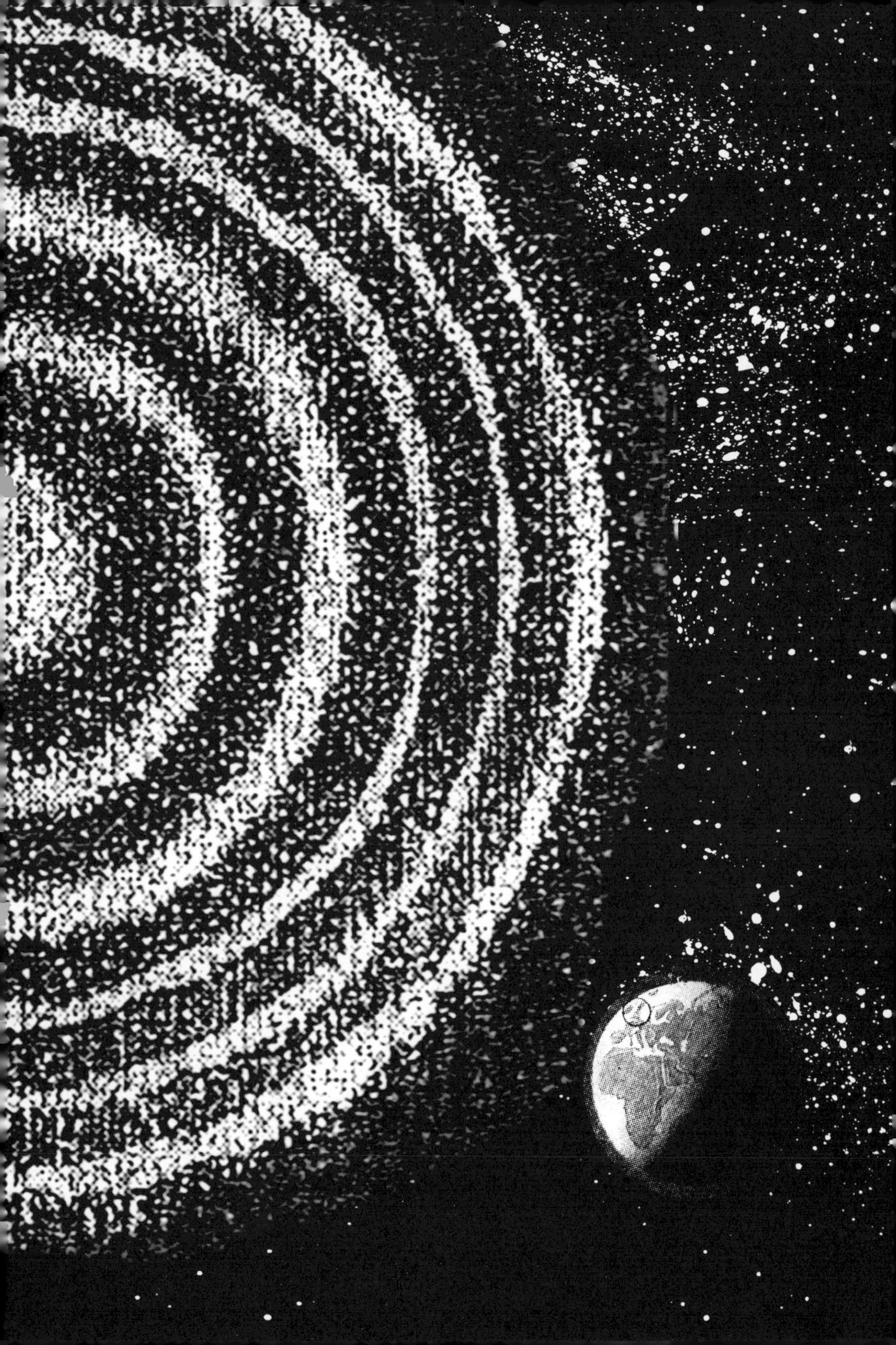

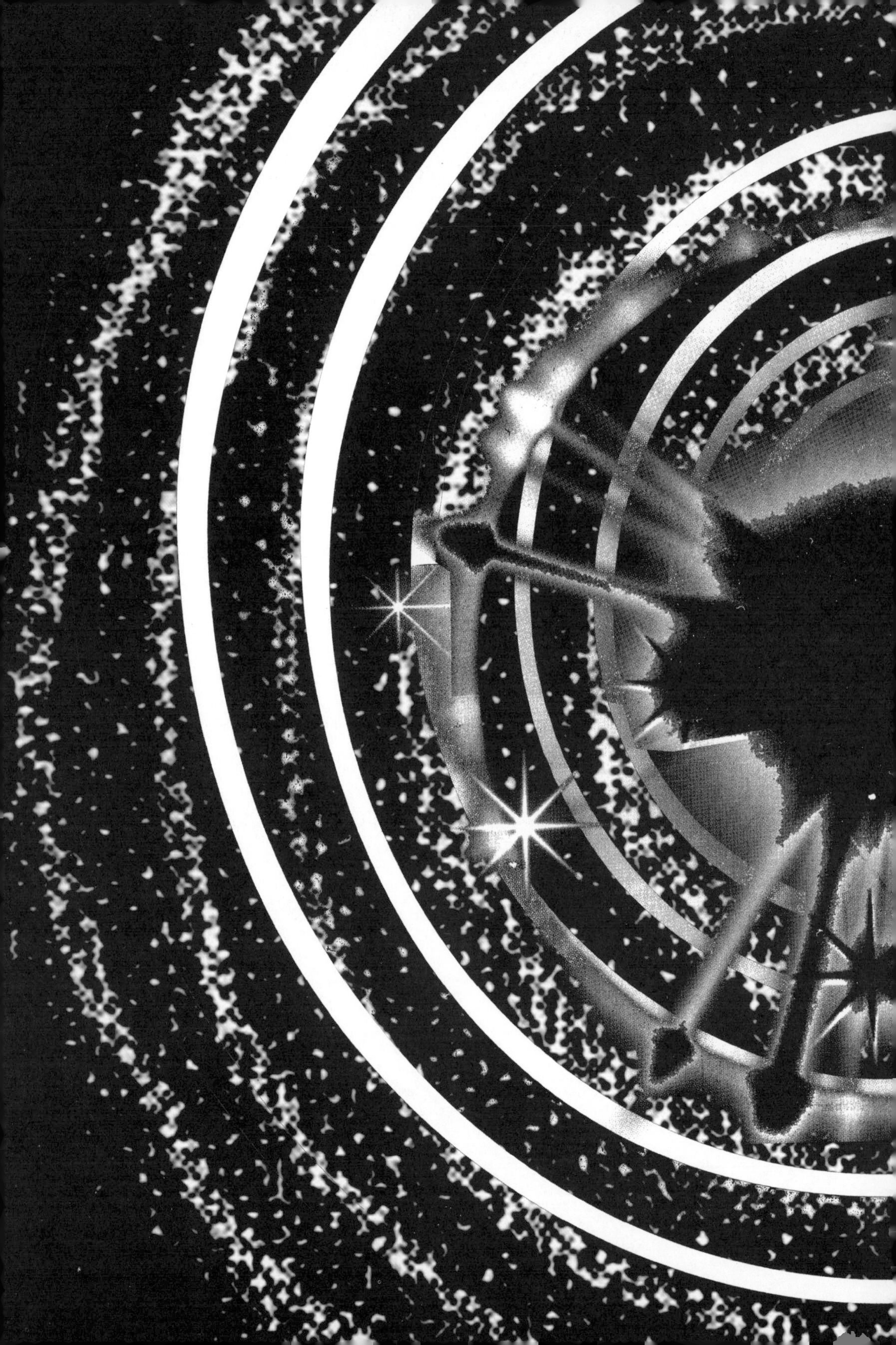

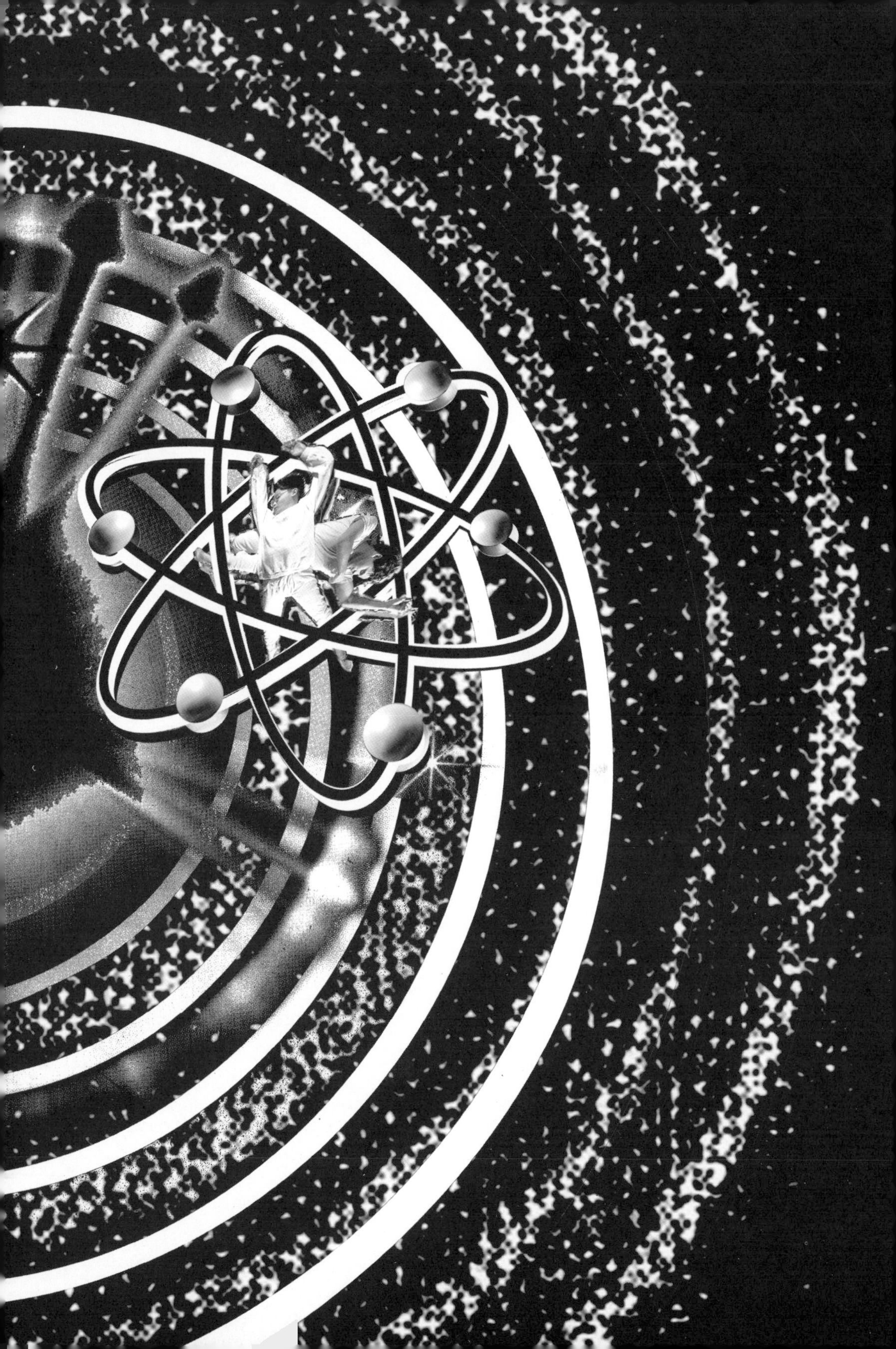

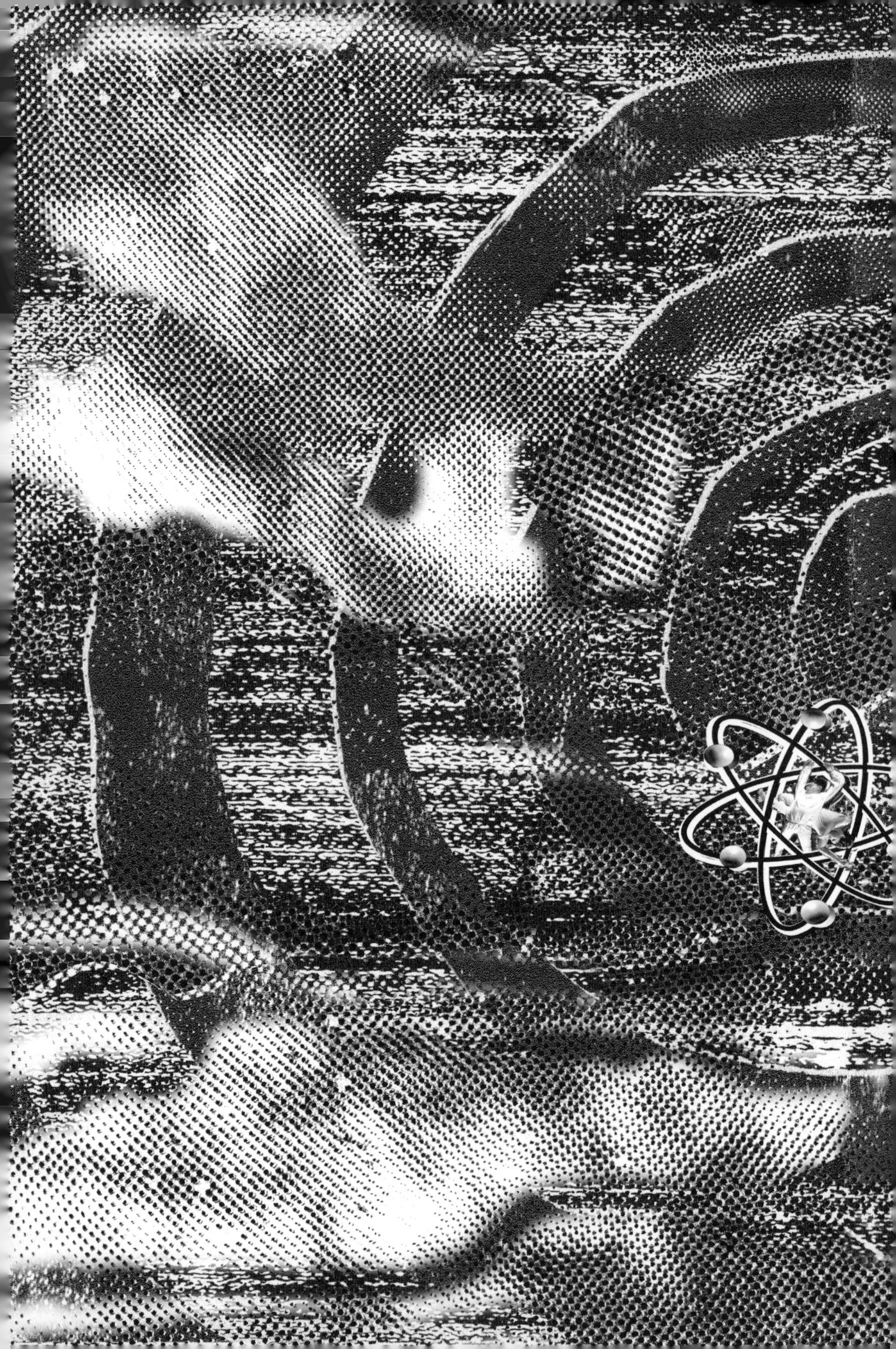

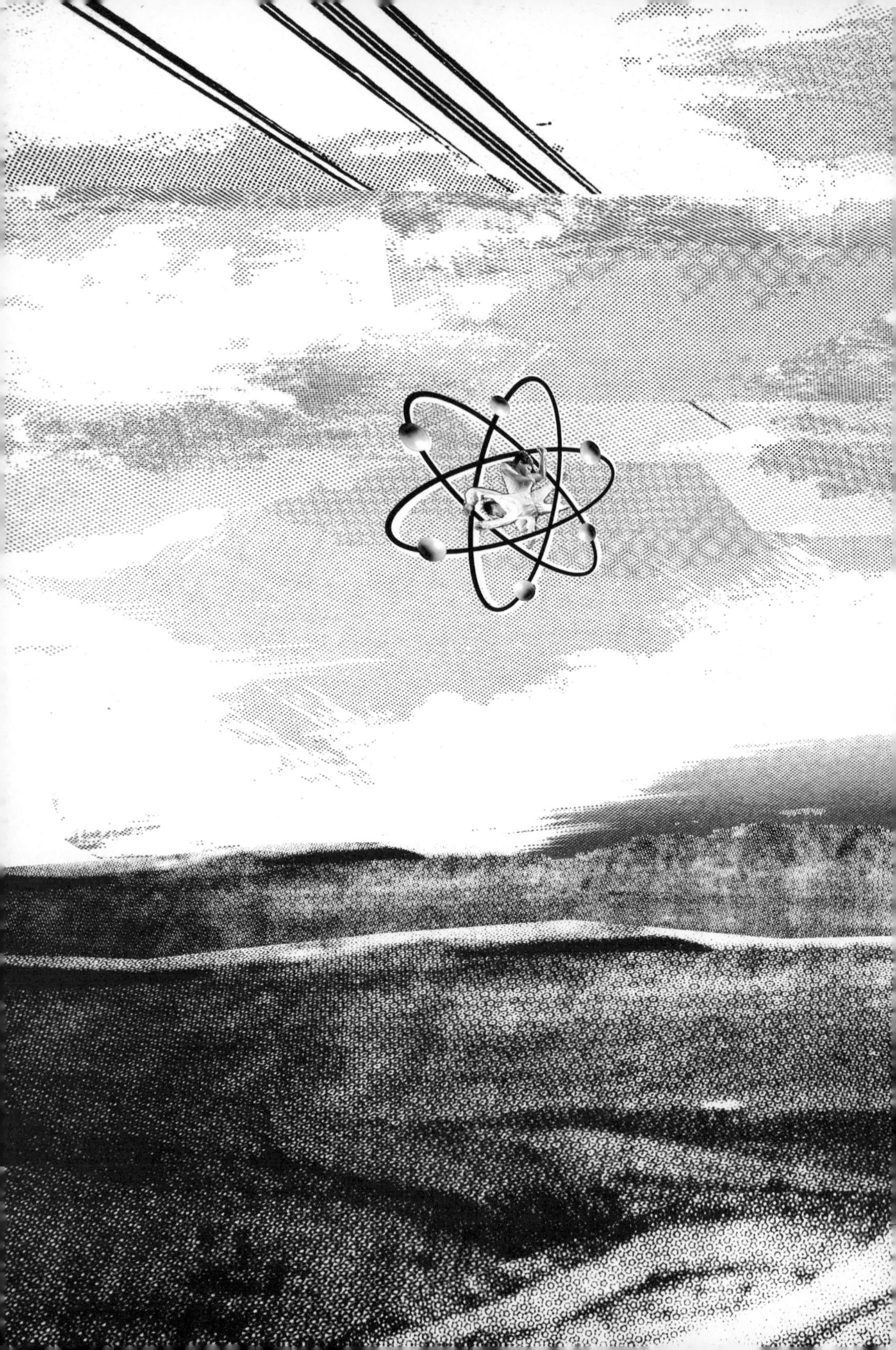

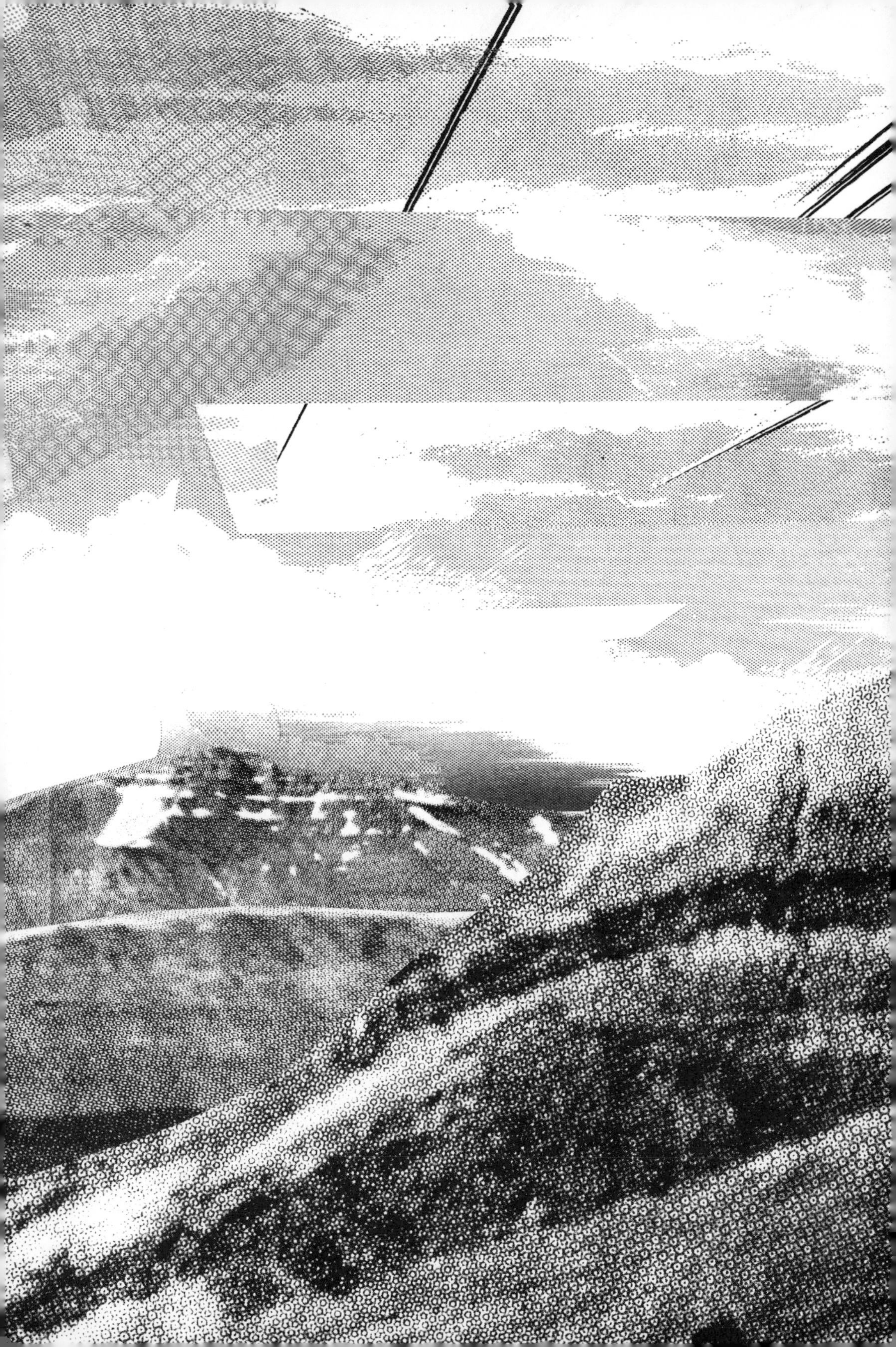

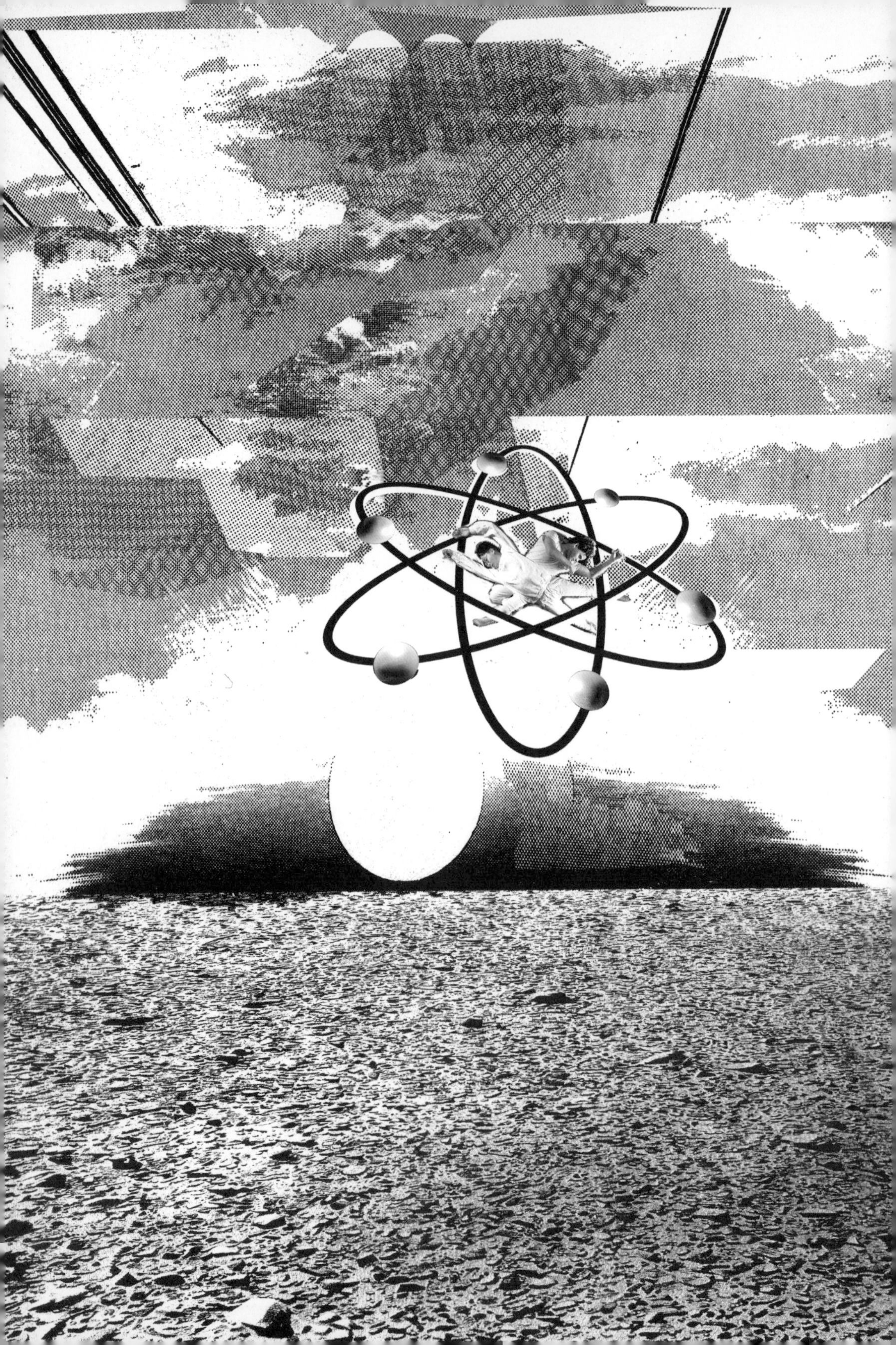

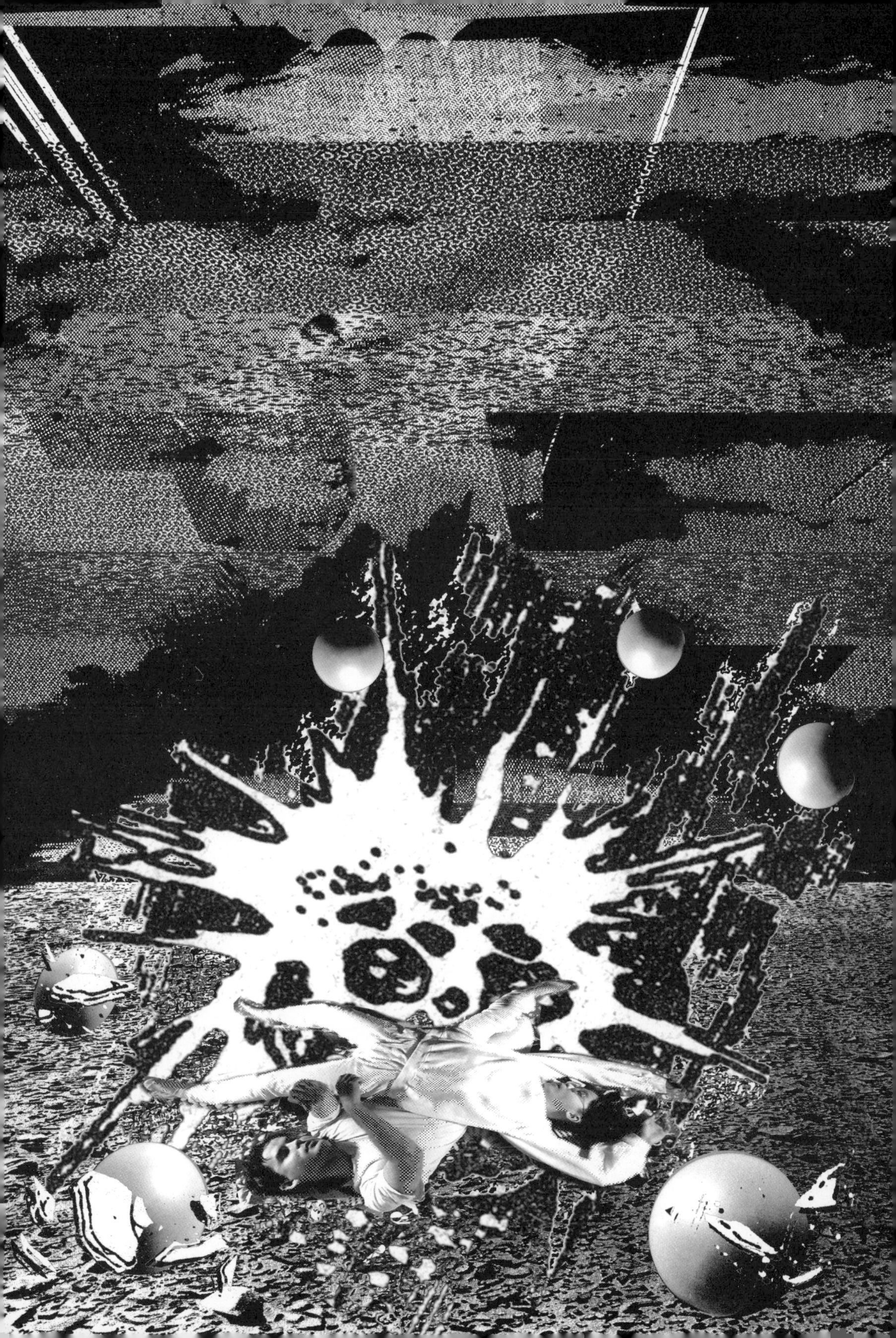

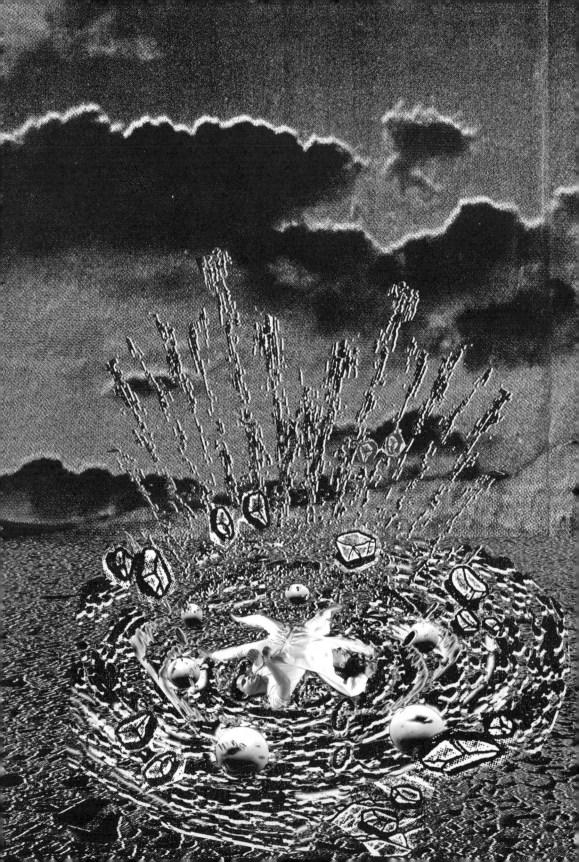

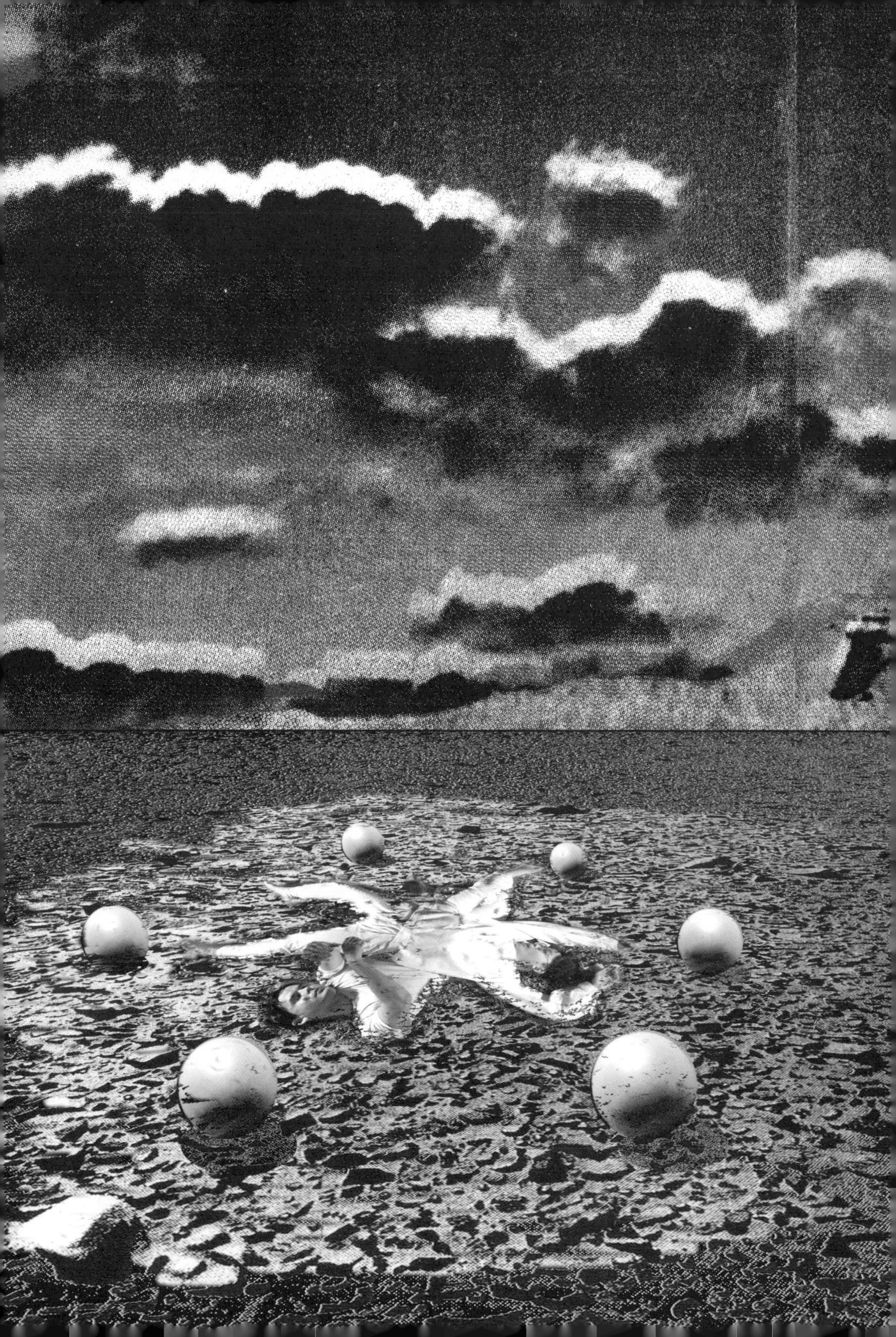

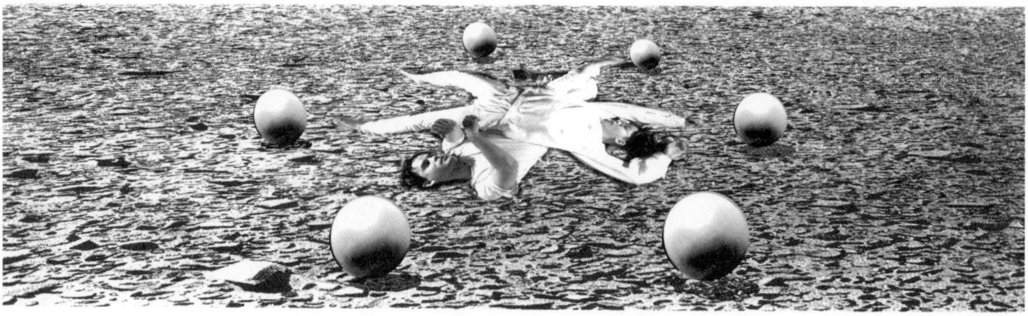

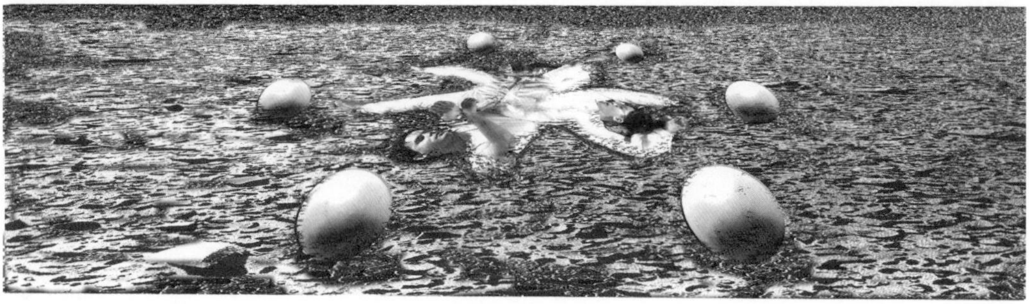

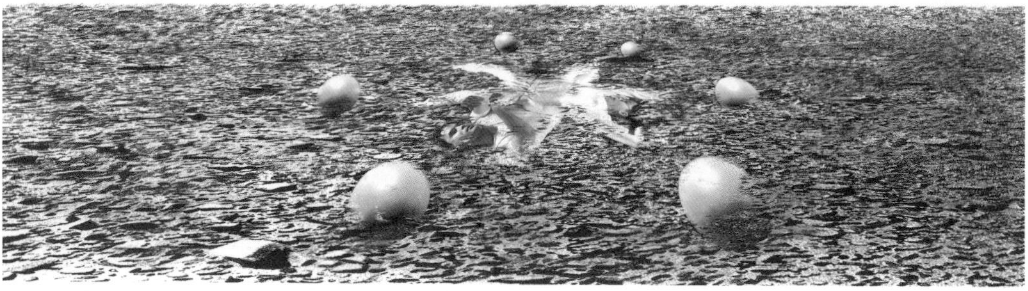

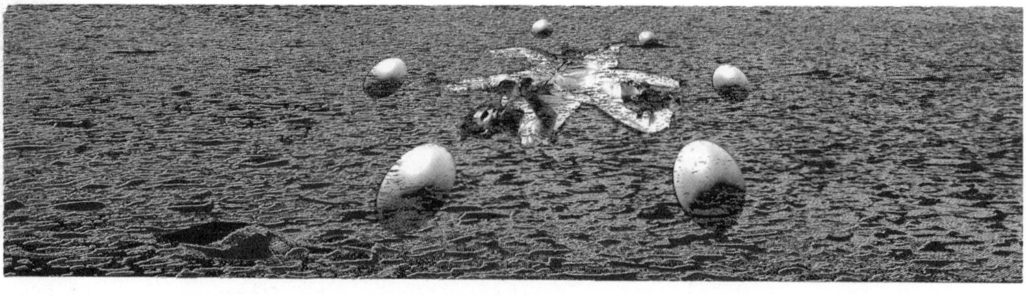

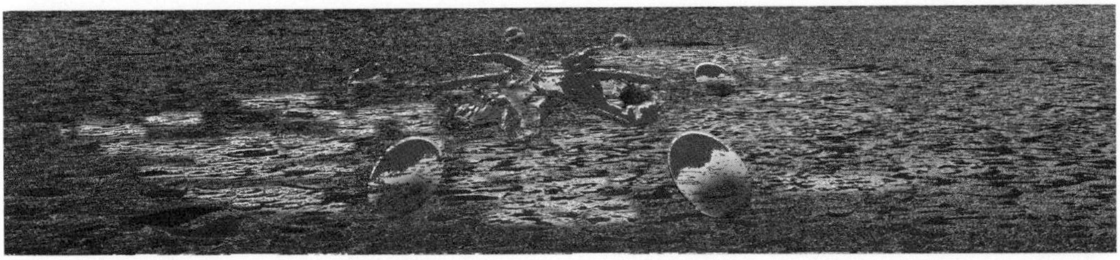
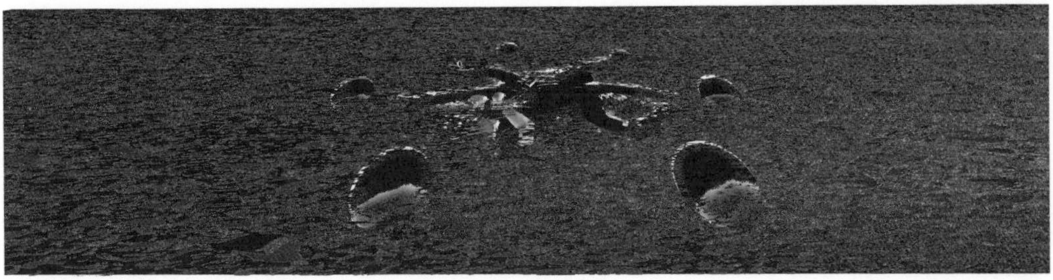
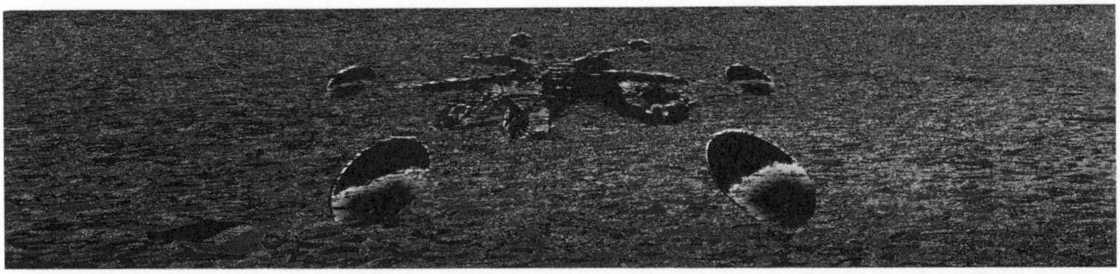
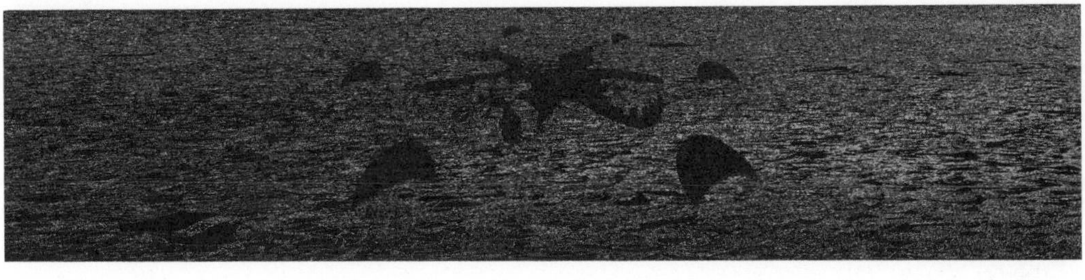

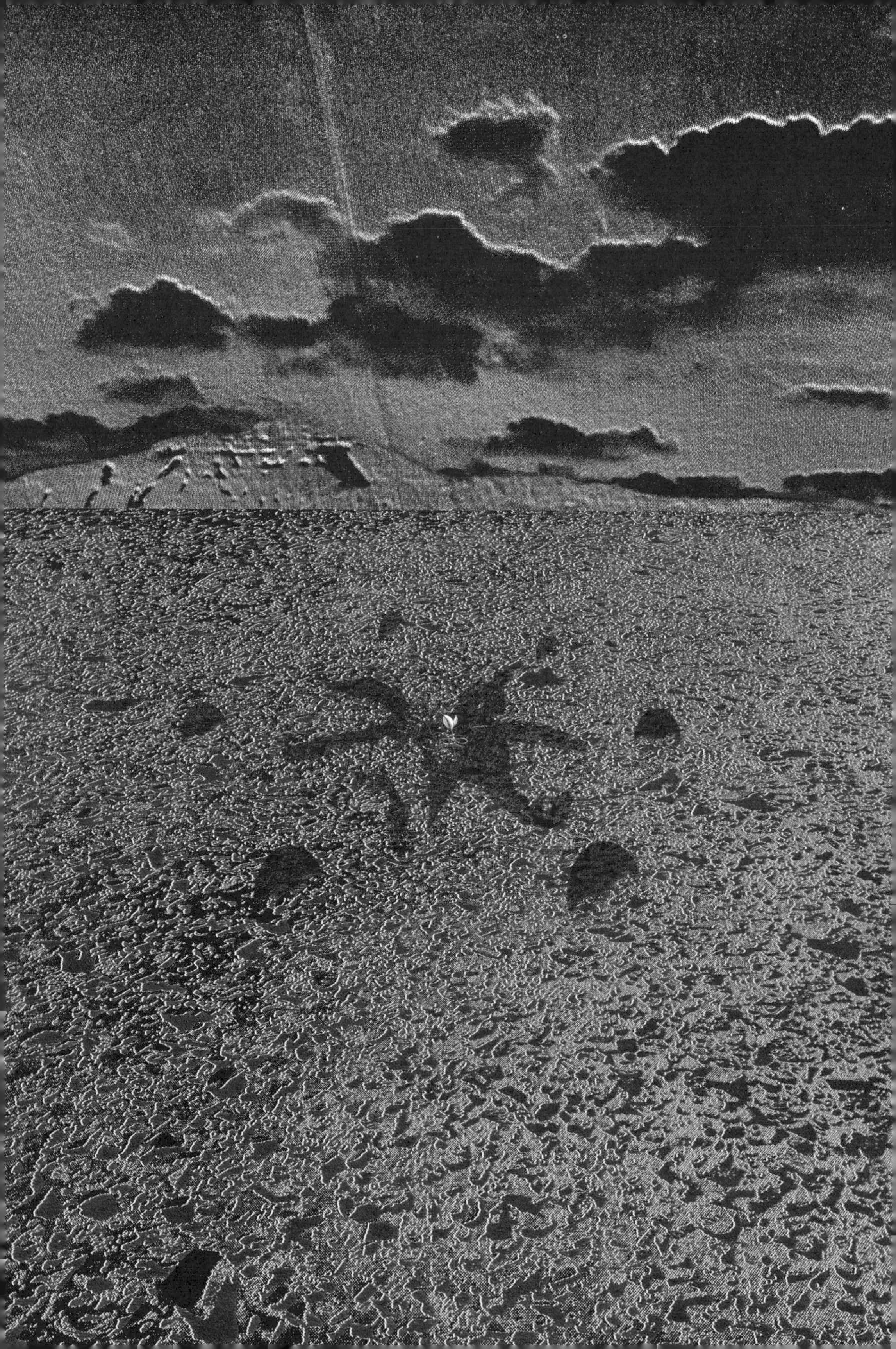

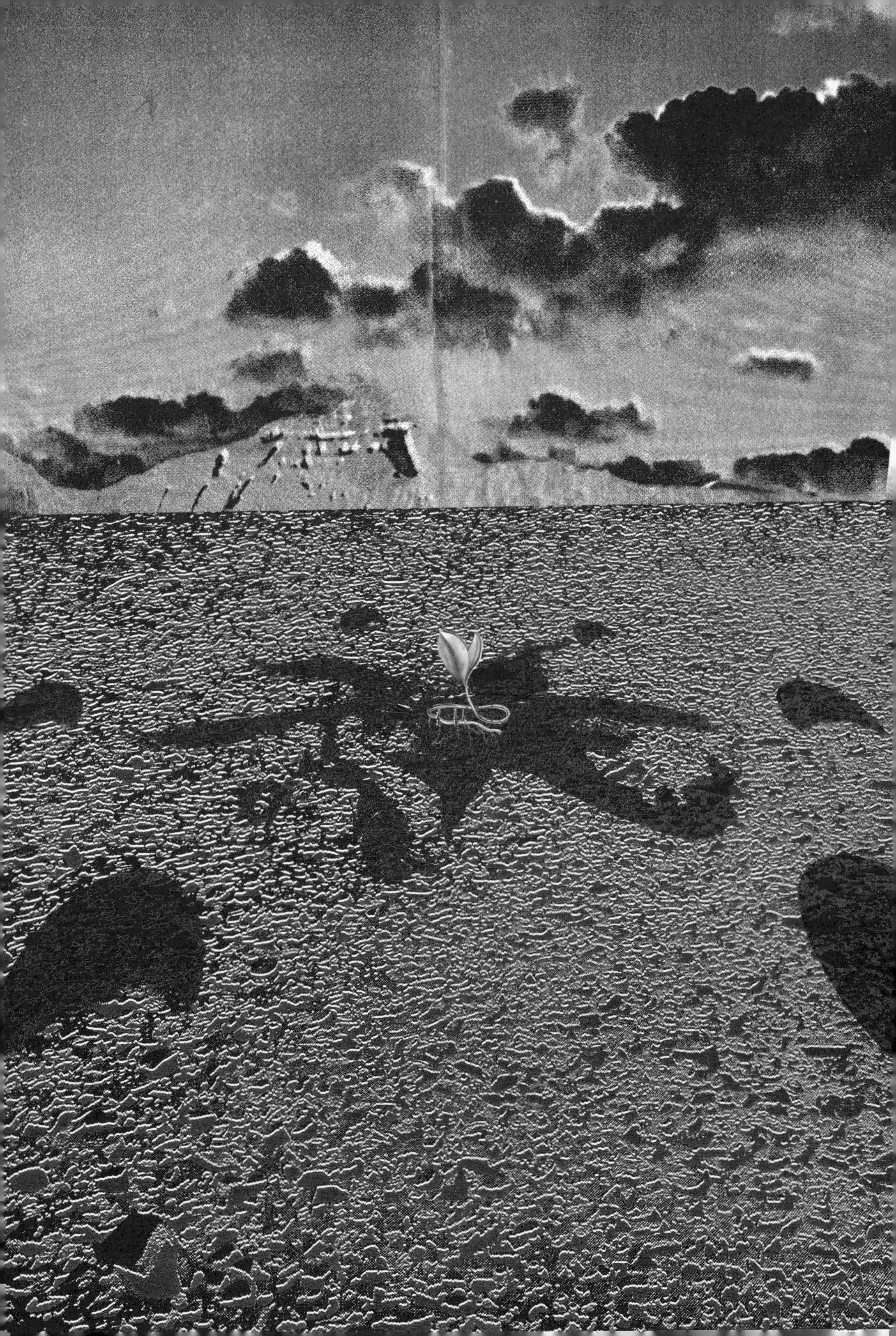

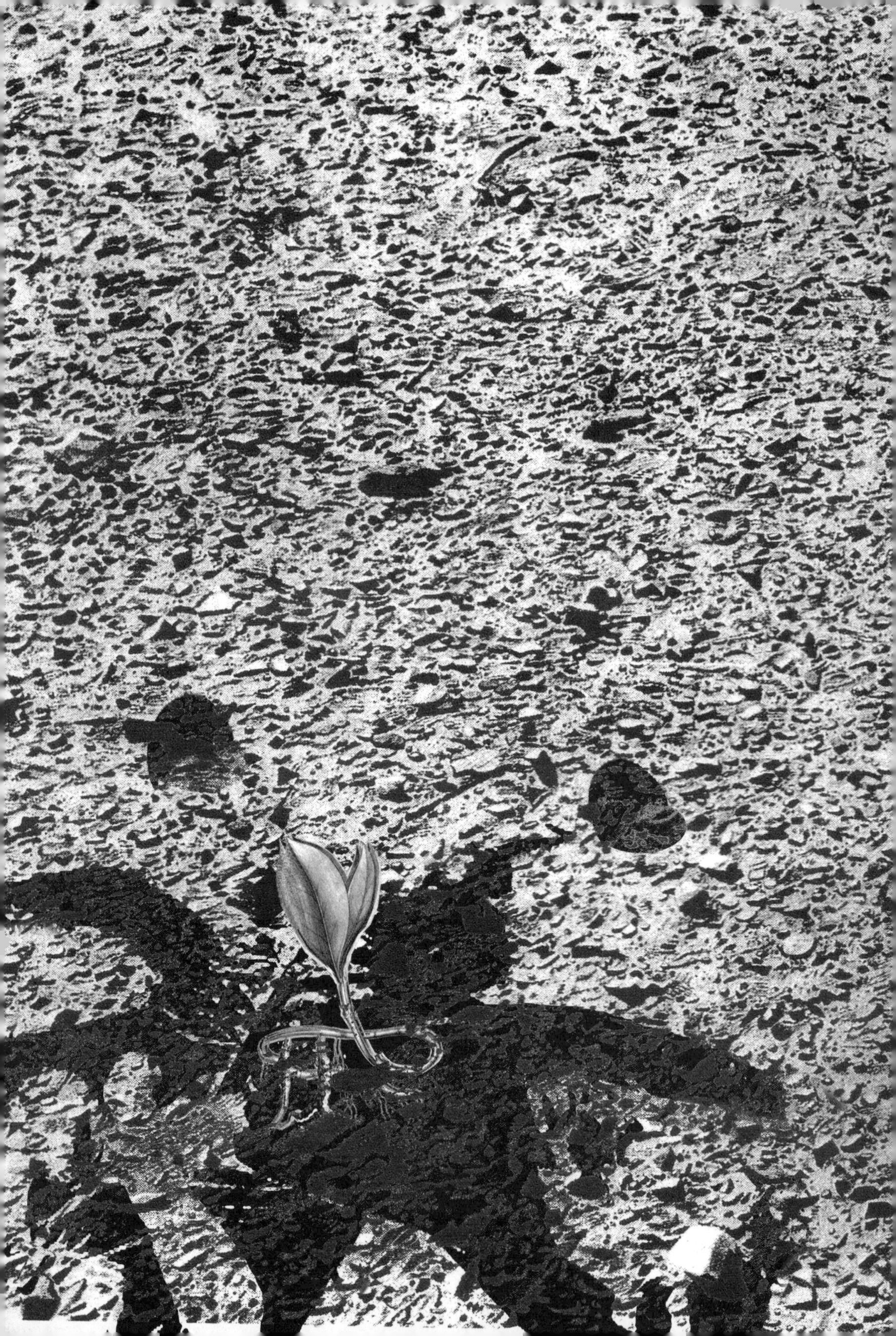

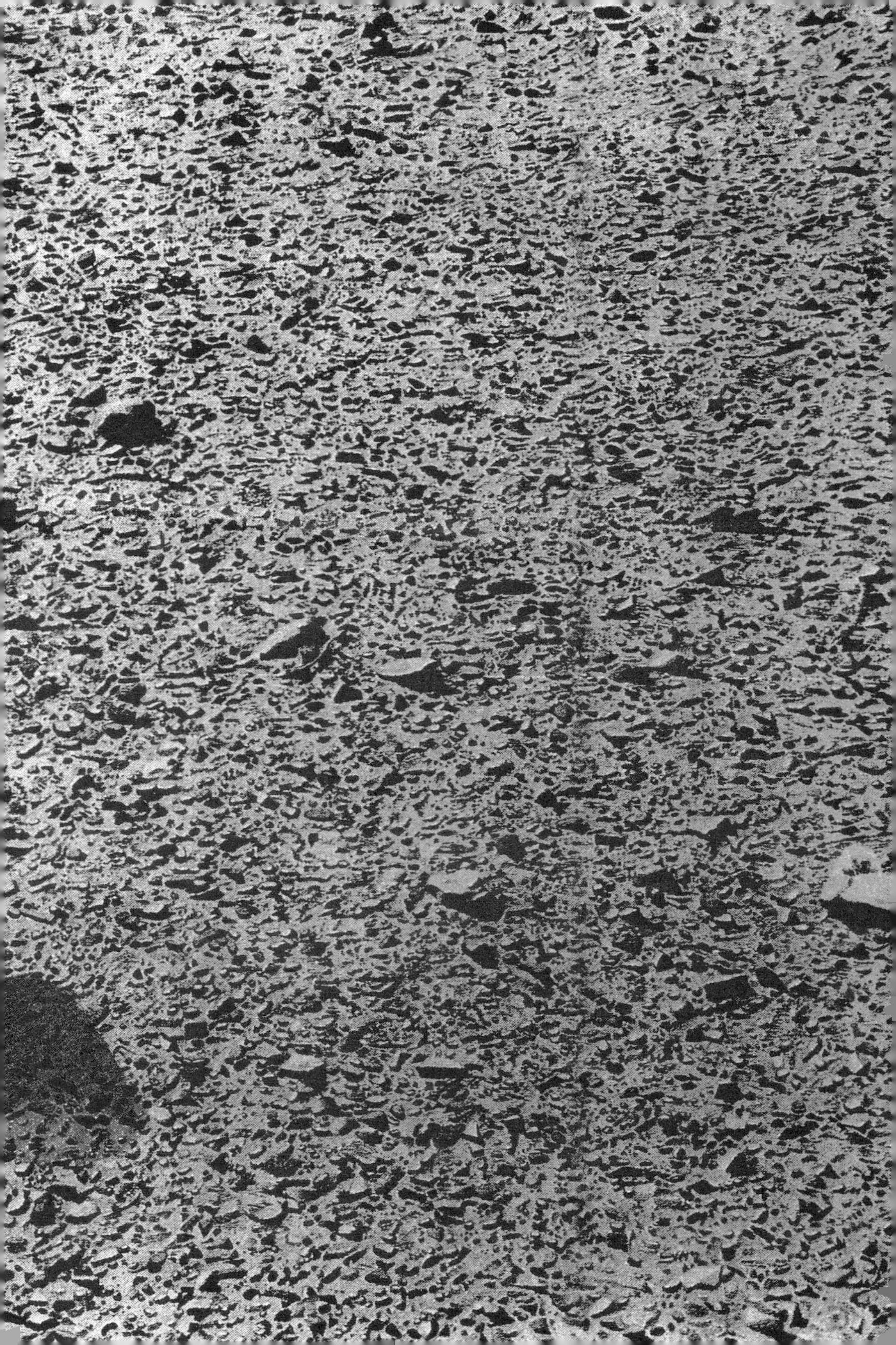

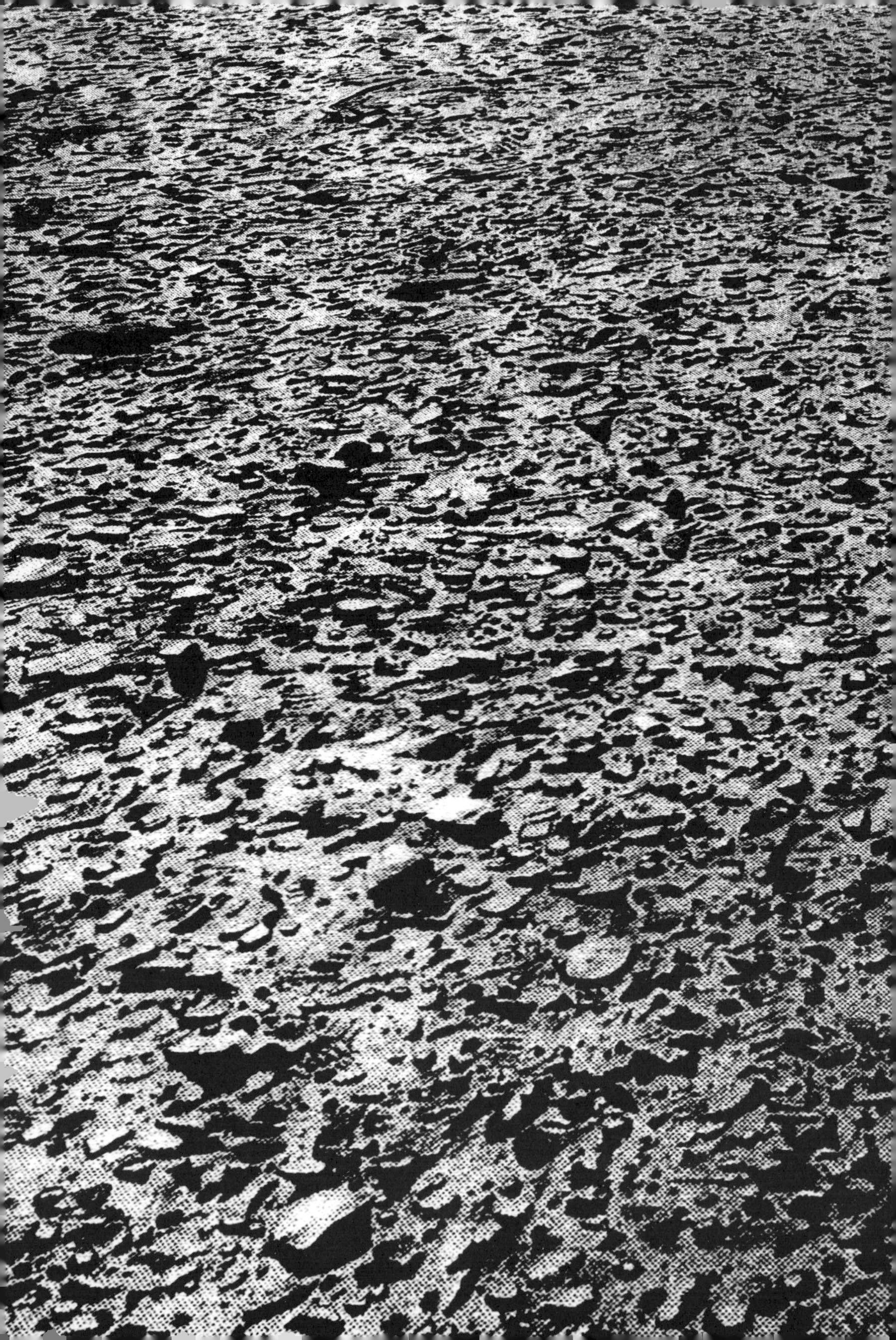

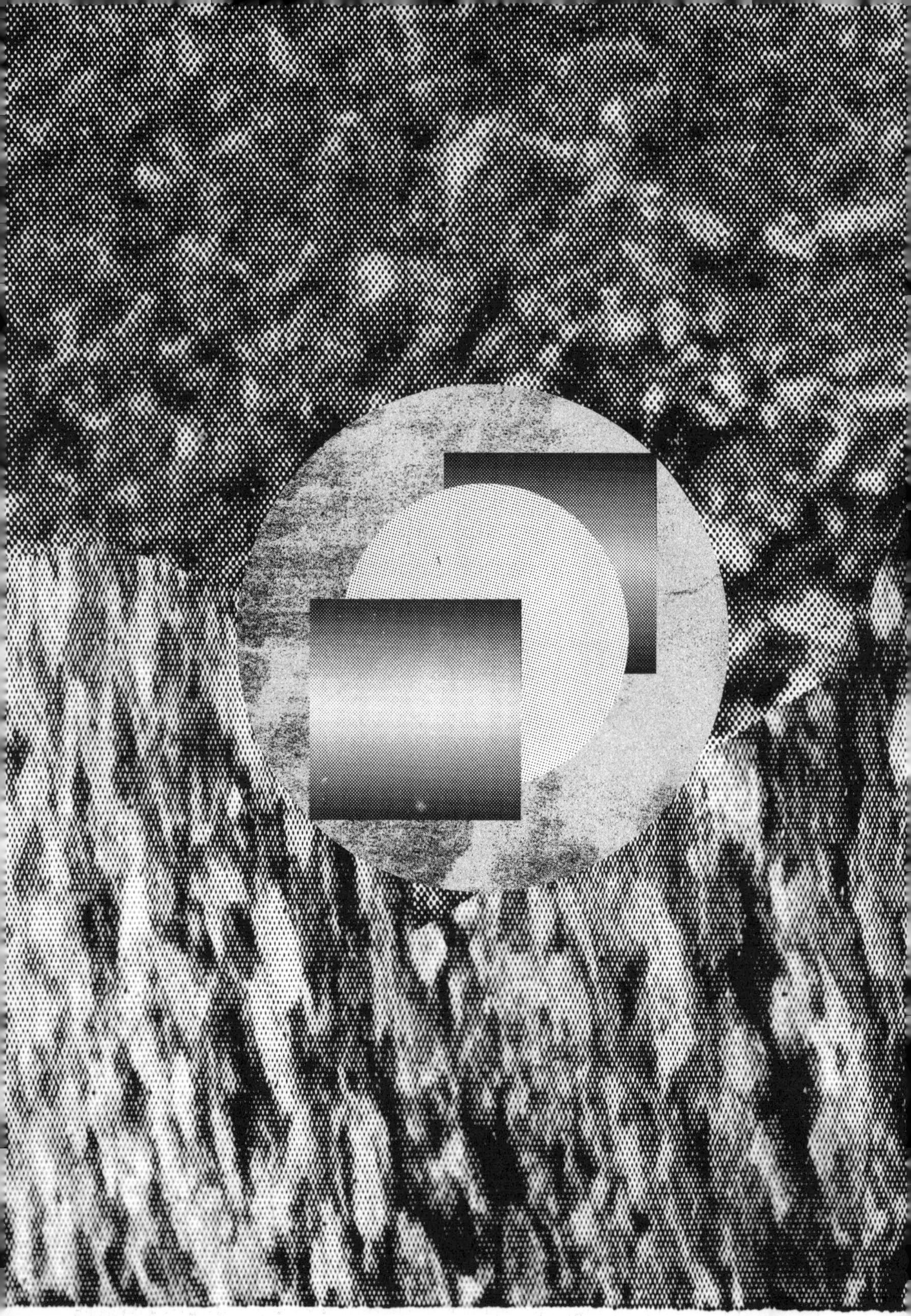